Douglas B. Miller and Loren L. Johns, Editors

BELIEVERS CHURCH BIBLE COMMENTARY

Old Testament
Genesis, by Eugene F. Roop, 1987
Exodus, by Waldemar Janzen, 2000
Deuteronomy, by Gerald E. Gerbrandt, 2015
Joshua, by Gordon H. Matties, 2012
Judges, by Terry L. Brensinger, 1999
Ruth, Jonah, Esther, by Eugene F. Roop, 2002
1-2 Chronicles, by August H. Konkel, 2016
Psalms, by James H. Waltner, 2006
Proverbs, by John W. Miller, 2004
Ecclesiastes, by Douglas B. Miller, 2010
Isaiah, by Ivan D. Friesen, 2009
Jeremiah, by Elmer A. Martens, 1986
Lamentations, Song of Songs, by Wilma Ann Bailey, Christina Bucher, 2015
Ezekiel, by Millard C. Lind, 1996
Daniel, by Paul M. Lederach, 1994
Hosea, Amos, by Allen R. Guenther, 1998

New Testament
Matthew, by Richard B. Gardner, 1991
Mark, by Timothy J. Geddert, 2001
John by Willard M. Swartley, 2013
Acts, by Chalmer E. Faw, 1993
Romans, by John E. Toews, 2004
2 Corinthians, by V. George Shillington, 1998
Galatians, by George R. Brunk III, 2015
Ephesians, by Thomas R. Yoder Neufeld, 2002
Colossians, Philemon, by Ernest D. Martin, 1993
1-2 Thessalonians, by Jacob W. Elias, 1995
1-2 Timothy, Titus, by Paul M. Zehr, 2010
1-2 Peter, Jude, by Erland Waltner, J. Daryl Charles, 1999
1, 2, 3 John, by J. E. McDermond, 2011
Revelation, by John R. Yeatts, 2003

Old Testament Editors
Elmer A. Martens, Mennonite Brethren Biblical Seminary, Fresno, Calif.
Douglas B. Miller, Tabor College, Hillsboro, Kan.

New Testament Editors
Willard M. Swartley, Anabaptist Mennonite Biblical Seminary, Elkhart, Ind.
Loren L. Johns, Anabaptist Mennonite Biblical Seminary, Elkhart, Ind.

Editorial Council
David W. Baker, Brethren Church
W. Derek Suderman, Mennonite Church Canada
Christina Bucher, Church of the Brethren
John R. Yeatts, Brethren in Christ Church
Gordon H. Matties (chair), Mennonite Brethren Church
Jo-Ann A. Brant, Mennonite Church USA

Believers Church
Bible Commentary

1 & 2 Chronicles

August H. Konkel

HERALD PRESS
Harrisonburg, Virginia
Kitchener, Ontario

Library of Congress Cataloging-in-Publication Data
Names: Konkel, August H., author.
Title: 1 & 2 Chronicles / August H. Konkel.
Other titles: First and Second Chronicles
Description: Harrisonburg : Herald Press, 2016. | Series: Believers church Bible commentary ; 30
Identifiers: LCCN 2015044350 | ISBN 9781513800011 (pbk. : alk. paper)
Subjects: LCSH: Bible. Chronicles--Commentaries.
Classification: LCC BS1345.53 .K66 2016 | DDC 222/.6077--dc23 LC record available at http://lccn.loc.gov/2015044350

Scripture quotations, unless otherwise indicated, are from the Holy Bible, *New International Version®, NIV®*. Copyright ©1973, 1978, 1984, 2011 by Biblica, Inc.™ Used by permission of Zondervan. All rights reserved worldwide. www.zondervan.com. The "NIV" and "New International Version" are trademarks registered in the United States Patent and Trademark Office by Biblica, Inc.™ Other versions briefly compared are identified with Abbreviations.

© 2016 by Herald Press, Harrisonburg, Virginia 22802
    Released simultaneously in Canada by Herald Press,
    Kitchener, Ontario N2G 3R1. All rights reserved.
Library of Congress Control Number: 2015044350
International Standard Book Number: 978-1-5138-0001-1
Printed in United States of America
Cover design by Merrill Miller
Interior design by Merrill Miller and Alice Shetler

All rights reserved. This publication may not be reproduced, stored in a retrieval system, or transmitted in whole or in part, in any form, by any means, electronic, mechanical, photocopying, recording, or otherwise without prior permission of the copyright owners.

For orders or information, call 800-245-7894 or visit HeraldPress.com.

20 19 18 17 16   10 9 8 7 6 5 4 3 2 1

To my grandparents, Jacob and Elizabeth Berg,
and my mother, Nettie,
in recognition of all they suffered
in faithfulness to our Mennonite faith and heritage

Abbreviations

*	The Text in Biblical Context
+	The Text in the Life of the Church
AHw	*Akkadisches Handwörterbuch.* W. von Soden. 3 vols. Wiesbaden: Harrassowitz, 1965–81.
ANET	*Ancient Near Eastern Texts Relating to the Old Testament.* Edited by James B. Pritchard. 3rd ed. with supplement. Princeton, NJ: Princeton University Press, 1969.
ANEP	*The Ancient Near East in Pictures Relating to the Old Testament.* Edited by James B. Pritchard. Princeton, NJ: Princeton University Press, 1954.
Ant.	*Jewish Antiquities.* By Josephus.
AP	*Aramaic Papyri of the Fifth Century B.C.* Edited by A. Cowley. Oxford: Clarendon, 1923.
app.	apparatus
ARAB	*Ancient Records of Assyria and Babylonia.* By Daniel David Luckenbill. 2 vols. Chicago: University of Chicago Press, 1926–27.
ARM	Archives royales de Mari
AT	author's translation
b.	Babylonian Talmud
BCE	before the Common Era (= BC, before Christ)
BHS	*Biblia Hebraica Stuttgartensia.* Edited by Karl Elliger and Wilhelm Rudolph. Stuttgart: Deutsche Bibelgesellschaft, 1983.
ca.	*circa*, approximately
CD	Cairo Genizah copy of the Damascus Document
CE	Common Era (= AD, after Christ's birth)
cf.	*confer*, compare
ch./chs.	chapter/chapters
EA	*The Tell El-Amarna Tablets.* Edited by Samuel A. B. Mercer. 2 vols. Toronto: Macmillan, 1939.
ed(s).	edition, editor(s)
COS	*The Context of Scripture.* Edited by W. W. Hallo. 3 vols. Leiden: Brill, 1997–2002.
d.	died
DJD	Discoveries in the Judaean Desert
e.g.	*exempli gratia*, for example
emph.	emphasis
Eng.	versification in most English translations
esp.	especially
et al.	*et alia*, and others
etc.	*et cetera*, and the rest
GKC	*Gesenius' Hebrew Grammar.* Edited by E. Kautzsch. Translated by A. E. Cowley. 2nd ed. Oxford: Clarendon, 1910.

HAL	*Hebräisches und aramäisches Lexikon zum Alten Testament*. L. Koehler, W. Baumgartner, and J. J. Stamm. 5 vols. Leiden: Brill, 1967–95.
i.e.	*id est*, that is
JPS	Jewish Publication Society translation of the Tanakh, 1917
KAI	*Kanaanäische und aramäische Inschriften*. H. Donner and W. Rölig. 2nd ed. Wiesbaden: Harrassowitz, 1966–69.
KBo	*Keilschrifttexte aus Boghazköi*. Leipzig: Hinrichs, 1916–23; Berlin: Mann, 1954–.
KJV	King James Version, 1611
KTU	*Die keilalphabetischen Texte aus Ugarit*. Edited by M. Dietrich, O. Loretz, and J. Sanmartin. AOAT 24/1. Neukirchen-Vluyn, 1976. 3rd enlarged ed. of KTU: The Cuneiform Alphabetic Texts from Ugarit, Ras Ibn Hani, and Other Places. Edited by M. Dietrich, O. Loretz, and J. Sanmartin. Münster: Ugarit-Verlag, 1995.
L&N	*Greek-English Lexicon of the New Testament: Based on Semantic Domains*. Edited by J. P. Louw and E. A. Nida. 2nd ed. New York: United Bible Societies, 1989.
lit.	literally
LXX	Septuagint, the Greek Old Testament
mg.	marginal note or footnote
MT	versification/readings in the Masoretic Text, the standard Hebrew version of the OT, preserved by Masoretes, a group of early medieval Jewish scribes
n.	note
NEB	New English Bible, 1970
NIV	New International Version, 2011
NJPS	New Jewish Publication Society translation of the Tanakh, 1999
NLT	New Living Translation, 2013
NRSV	New Revised Standard Version, 1989
OT	Old Testament
rev.	revised
RSV	Revised Standard Version, 1952
trans.	translated by
v./vv.	verse/verses

Pronunciation Guide for Certain Transliterated Hebrew Consonants

ʾ	(not pronounced)
ʿ	(not pronounced)
ḥ	ch (Scottish *loch*)
ṣ	ts
ś	s
š	sh
ṭ	t

Contents

Abbreviations...7
Pronunciation Guide 8
Series Foreword 15
Author's Preface 17

Introduction to 1 & 2 Chronicles 21
Chronicles and History Writing...............................23
The Community of Yehud.......................................25
The Composition of Chronicles 27
    Authorship and Date 27
    Sources of the Chronicler................................28
    Methods of the Chronicler 29
Chronicles and Ezra-Nehemiah.................................30
Goals of the Chronicler 32
The Message of Chronicles....................................34
Chronicles and the New Testament 37
The Relevance of Chronicles 39
The Methodology of This Commentary...........................42
Translations Used in This Commentary 44

Part 1: Nation of Promise, 1 Chronicles 1:1–9:34 45
Founding Ancestors, 1:1–2:2..................................48
    *God for the World......................................55
    *Israel among the Nations 57
    *Israel and Ethnic Relations............................58
    +The Church among the Nations...........................60
    +The Church and Related Faiths 62

Royal Family, 2:3–4:23 66
    *Chronicles and the Genesis Narrative..................... 82
    *Complex Family Relations................................ 83
    *Prayer of Jabez... 85
    +Peace in Racial and Religious Relationships 86
    +Pursuit of Blessing 87
The Tribes of Israel, 4:24–9:1a 89
    *Blessing of Joseph..................................... 118
    *Preeminence of Judah 119
    *Centrality of Levi 120
    *Inclusion of Lost Tribes 121
    *Distinction of Benjamin................................ 122
    +Church Universal 123
    +Waiting for the Kingdom.............................. 124
    +Citizens of the Kingdom 126
The Inheritance of All Israel, 9:1b–34............................. 128
    *The City of Jerusalem................................. 135
    +The Church in Times of Transition 137

Part 2: Founding the Kingdom, 1 Chronicles 9:35–20:8.... 141

Removal of Saul as King, 9:35–10:14 144
    *Kinship and Status 147
    *Transition.. 148
    +Unfaithfulness.. 149
    +Transitions 149
David Confirmed as King, 11:1–12:40 151
    *David's Rise to Power................................. 160
    +A United Community 161
Establishment of Worship in Jerusalem, 13:1–17:27 163
    *Significance of the Ark 177
    *Covenant Promise to David............................ 178
    +Theology of Kingdom................................. 180
    +Theology of Temple 182
David's Wars, 18:1–20:8 184
    *Lands of the Kingdom 194
    +The Church in the World.............................. 195

Part 3: Preparations for the Temple,
1 Chronicles 21:1–29:30.......................................199

Designation of the Temple Site, 21:1–22:1...................... 202
    *Mount Moriah 208

  +Worship in the Church Community 209
Charge to Build the Temple, 22:2-19. 212
  *The Rest of Redemption 216
  +Christian Confession of Redemptive Rest 217
Organization of Levitical Officials, 23:1-26:32 220
  *Origins of Twenty-Four Priestly Divisions. 232
  +Orders of Service in the Church. 234
Organization of National Officials, 27:1-34 236
  *Davidic Ordering of the Kingdom 241
  +Paying Taxes Cheerfully 242
Accession of Solomon, 28:1-29:30. 244
  *An Eschatological History 251
  +Eschatology in the Worship of the Church 253

Part 4: The Reign of Solomon, 2 Chronicles 1:1-9:31 257

Confirmation of Solomon, 1:1-17 260
  *Wisdom, Wealth, and Power. 263
  +Wisdom for Christian Use of Wealth. 264
Building the Temple, 2:1-8:16 266
  *The Presence of the Holy in the World of the Common. . . . 287
  +The Temple Built by the Spirit. 288
Grandeur of Solomon's Kingdom, 8:17-9:31 291
  *The Kingdom as a Divine Blessing. 295
  +World at War, Church at Peace. 296

Part 5: Israel until the Exile of the North,
2 Chronicles 10:1-28:27. 299

Reign of Rehoboam, 10:1-12:16. 303
  *Rehoboam and Hezekiah. 308
  +The Root of All Sin 309
Reign of Abijah, 13:1-14:1a. 312
  *The Prophet King 316
  +The Gates of Hell Will Not Prevail. 317
Reign of Asa, 14:1b-16:14 319
  *Worship in Jerusalem. 326
  *The Life of Asa. 327
  +Spirituality in the Church 328
Reign of Jehoshaphat, 17:1-21:1a 331
  *When God Fights for Us. 338
  +Learning to Live with War. 340
  +Working for Peace. 341

Reigns of Terror, 21:1b–22:9 343
    *Divine Faithfulness 348
    +Divine Justice 349
Reign of Joash, 22:10–24:27 350
    *Holy War against Israel 356
    +Teaching Moral Values 357
Reign of Amaziah, 25:1–26:2 359
    *Divine Judgment on Amaziah 364
    +The Blindness of the Enlightenment 364
Uzziah and Jotham, 26:3–27:9 367
    *Uzziah, Isaiah, and Amos 372
    +Sanctity of the Sacraments 372
Reign of Ahaz, 28:1-27 374
    *Isaiah, Ahaz, and Hezekiah 377
    +Trusting in Riches 378

Part 6: Healing under Hezekiah, 2 Chronicles 29:1–32:33 . . . 379

Restoration of the Temple, 29:1–36 382
    *Covenant Confession through Temple Restoration 387
    +The Living Temple 389
Celebration of the Passover, 30:1–31:1 391
    *Faithfulness in Passover Observance 397
    +The Challenge of Renewal 398
Provisions for Temple Worship, 31:2-21 400
    *Managing Temple Resources 404
    +Church Offices and Church Service 405
Deliverance and Healing in the Land, 32:1-33 408
    *Tradition of Hezekiah 413
    *Siege of Sennacherib 414
    *Hezekiah as a Man of Faith 415
    +The Value of Renewal 416

Part 7: Humiliation and Hope, 2 Chronicles 33:1–36:23 . . . 419

Manasseh and Amon, 33:1-25 422
    *The Restoration of Manasseh 425
    +Good and Bad within People 427
Renewal under Josiah, 34:1–35:27 429
    *Josiah in Kings and Chronicles 436
    +Standing on Scripture 437
Exile and Return, 36:1-23 439
    *Sin against God 444
    *Chronicles and the Canon 445
    +Life after Death 446

Outline of 1 & 2 Chronicles 449
Essays 457
    Chronicles and the Ezra Compositions 457
    Chronology in Chronicles 460
    Genealogy 461
    Genealogies in Chronicles 462
    Glossary 464
        Achaemenid 464
        Amarna Tablets 464
        Babylonian Chronicles 464
        Chiasm 465
        Chronological Synchronism 465
        Deuteronomistic History 465
        Elephantine Papyri 466
        Eponym 466
        Ethnographic 466
        Etiology 466
        Hebrew Canon 467
        Inclusio 467
        Negev 467
        Resumptive Summary 467
        Shephelah 467
        Ugarit 467
        Vorlage 468
    Greek Text of Chronicles 469
    History Writing 469
    Masoretic Text 470
    Priests and Levites in Chronicles 471
    Sources for Chronicles 472
    Tendenz in Chronicles 476
    Theology of Chronicles 476
        David and the Temple 476
        God, Justice, and Faithfulness 478
        Blessing and Hope 479
    Torah 481
    War in Chronicles 481

Map of Palestine for Chronicles 486
Map of the Ancient Near East for Chronicles 487
Bibliography 489
Selected Resources 501
Index of Ancient Sources 505
The Author 517

Series Foreword

The Believers Church Bible Commentary series makes available a new tool for basic Bible study. It is published for all who seek more fully to understand the original message of Scripture and its meaning for today—Sunday school teachers, members of Bible study groups, students, pastors, and others. The series is based on the conviction that God is still speaking to all who will listen, and that the Holy Spirit makes the Word a living and authoritative guide for all who want to know and do God's will.

The desire to help as wide a range of readers as possible has determined the approach of the writers. Since no blocks of biblical text are provided, readers may continue to use the translation with which they are most familiar. The writers of the series use the New Revised Standard Version and the New International Version on a comparative basis. They indicate which text they follow most closely and where they make their own translations. The writers have not worked alone, but in consultation with select counselors, the series' editors, and the Editorial Council.

Every volume illuminates the Scriptures; provides necessary theological, sociological, and ethical meanings; and in general makes "the rough places plain." Critical issues are not avoided, but neither are they moved into the foreground as debates among scholars. Each section offers "Explanatory Notes," followed by focused articles, "The Text in Biblical Context" and "The Text in the Life of the Church." This commentary aids the interpretive process but does not try to supersede the authority of the Word and Spirit as discerned in the gathered church.

The term *believers church* emerged in the mid-twentieth century to define Christian groups with direct or indirect connections to the

Radical Reformation, a distinctive faith expression that arose in Europe during the sixteenth century. These believers were concerned that the church be voluntary and not be aligned with political government. *Believers church* has come to represent an identifiable tradition of beliefs and practices that includes believers (adult) baptism, a voluntary fellowship that practices church discipline, mutual aid, and service, belief in the power of love in all relationships, and a willingness to follow Christ by embracing his cross as a way of life. In recent decades the term has sometimes been applied to church communities informed by Anabaptism, evangelicalism, or pietism, such as Brethren Church, Brethren in Christ, Church of the Brethren, Mennonite Brethren, and Mennonites, as well as similar groups. The writers chosen for the series speak from within this tradition.

Believers church people have always been known for their emphasis on obedience to the simple meaning of Scripture. Because of this, they do not have a long history of deep historical-critical biblical scholarship. This series attempts to be faithful to the Scriptures while also taking archaeology and current biblical studies seriously. Doing this means that at many points the writers will not differ greatly from interpretations that can be found in many other good commentaries. Yet these writers share basic convictions about Christ, the church and its mission, God and history, human nature, the Christian life, and other doctrines. These presuppositions do shape a writer's interpretation of Scripture. Thus this series, like all other commentaries, stands within a specific historical church tradition.

Many in this stream of the church have expressed a need for help in Bible study. This is justification enough to produce the Believers Church Bible Commentary. Nevertheless, the Holy Spirit is not bound to any tradition. May this series be an instrument in breaking down walls between Christians in North America and around the world, bringing new joy in obedience through a fuller understanding of the Word.

—*The Editorial Council*

Author's Preface

It is a great privilege to have a contribution in this unique series of commentaries. My maternal grandparents, Jacob and Elizabeth Berg, were among the Mennonite migrants from Ukraine to Canada as Stalinism tightened its grip. My mother was three years old when they eventually made their way to Saskatchewan in 1926. As most Mennonite migrants to Canada at that time, they arrived with nothing more than a few personal belongings. Canada did not prove to be the home they had anticipated. One of my mother's siblings died on the journey and two more passed away in the years that followed. Ten years later, in spite of the trials of the Dirty Thirties, my grandparents had almost completed payments on their farm in Rhein, Saskatchewan. The Bergs then discovered that their trust had been betrayed: they had been defrauded by the agent receiving their payments. The lumber company that had sold them the farm repossessed it. Once again they were destitute and homeless. I learned two things from my grandparents, mostly through my mother, which influenced me profoundly. The first was that talent and hard work did not spare them a life of extreme hardship and severe poverty. The second was that their faith in God gave them strength to persevere and raise three wonderful children. I especially remember my grandmother as a thankful person who could trust God at all times. This faith came to my grandparents through the Mennonite Brethren Church. There were no Mennonite churches of any kind in the area of Yorkton, Saskatchewan, at that time, so they attended a Baptist church. But my grandparents were thoroughly Mennonite in culture and in their understanding of Christian faith. It is my desire that a commentary for the believers church will be a tribute to them for the way they exemplified simple faith.

Chronicles is a history of suffering and loss, faith and hope. I have often thought of the experience of my mother's family in the study of the Chronicler's story as a survivor of exile. The hope expressed in this book helps me understand the profound importance of faith in God, especially for those who have nothing in this world. Chronicles is a captivating book when probed for its information and message. Knowledge of the Bible is not complete without knowing Chronicles, but knowledge of Chronicles demands a thorough knowledge of the Scriptures that the Chronicler used for his story of faith (given the prominent role of men in Israel's history, the Chronicler was most likely male). It has been a challenge to identify the names of the genealogies and lists in Chronicles and determine their significance. But the effort is richly rewarded. The Chronicler has left a legacy of information and history of Israel that is unparalleled. The Chronicler developed a message of hope from the tragic history of his people. My desire is that readers may find this commentary as enriching a study of faith as it has been for me.

Self-authenticating metanarratives of Modernism should generate suspicion, according to Jean-François Lyotard in his work *The Postmodern Condition*. Christian faith, instead, is a confession of how God is at work in his world. History and theology are two aspects of the same truth in which Christians place their confidence for knowledge of God. The study of Chronicles is an exercise in understanding history writing in the present as well as the past. It is an example of why it is not only rational but also reasonable to place faith in this interpretation of the past as the work of God.

I am indebted to many people who have been a part of making this work what it is. I thank the Editorial Council of the series for providing this opportunity. The series editor has exercised great patience as the work has progressed and has contributed significantly to bring it to the high standards expected. His capacity for detail is especially necessary in a work with so many obscure details. Special appreciation is due to Mark Boda, McMaster Divinity College, and Steven Schweitzer, Bethel Theological Seminary, for their willingness to review the manuscript. I have incorporated as much of their helpful contributions as possible and, I hope, all of their corrections. The copyediting of David Garber made a substantial contribution in removing inadvertent errors and providing clarifications. I have also engaged my graduate assistants, Tim Konkel and Meghan

Musy, at different stages in reviewing and correcting the manuscript. The errors and shortcomings that remain in spite of all their efforts are fully my responsibility.

Soli Deo Gloria.

—August H. Konkel
Hamilton, Ontario

Introduction to
1 & 2 Chronicles

Chronicles was written to inspire hope. It is said that if you lose all your wealth, you lose a lot; if you lose all your friends, you lose a lot more; if you lose hope, you have lost everything. Exile had robbed the people of Israel of their wealth; their return to the land of Judah had created much resentment with the surrounding peoples. Despondency and apathy threatened to completely destroy this struggling people.

Hope for the author (or authors) of Chronicles (referred to as the Chronicler in this commentary) lay in the promises of the past. World empires had all but obliterated the visible presence of the people of Israel and Judah. The Persians, beginning with Cyrus, had made possible a return (2 Chron 36:22-23), but its beginnings were disappointing, to the point of disillusionment. It was almost twenty years before the preaching of Haggai and the night visions of Zechariah were successful in generating an effort to lay the foundation for a new temple (Hag 1:1-2; 2:18-19; Zech 1:7-6:15) *[Chronology in Chronicles, p. 460]*. The results of all the effort left some in sorrowful tears (Ezra 3:12-13). The rebuilding of the temple (ca. 515 BCE) did not portend the promise of the kingdom proclaimed in their confessions (e.g., Ps 2:7-12), or in the assurances of the prophets (e.g., Isa 54:1-13).

If this struggling community of the Persian period (ca. 539–330 BCE) were to face the future, it first needed to look to the past. Nothing in the present could inspire hope for the future. The past, however, held lessons for how they might live for the future. The Chronicler intended to inspire hope for the community by his understanding of the past. In the Hebrew text, Chronicles is called "the words (or events) of the days (or times)," that is, a history. In the prologue of the Latin translation, Jerome called it *chronikon*, defined as a universal history beginning with creation. Chronicles is a register of events, an account of ancient times going back to the beginning of humanity. Like the Hebrew title, it correctly defines the genre of the work.

The most condensed way in which a history can be written is simply to list names of people and places. This is the method of the Chronicler for the first nine chapters, which cover the history of Israel from Adam to the province of Yehud established in the Persian Empire (roughly equal to the Judea of Jesus' day). Commentary on the names and places is minimal, mostly achieved by the way in which material is organized. Such a history carries significance only if readers can contextualize the names. Readers must have some familiarity with the narrative from which they are drawn and to which they relate. The names and places of the first nine chapters, for the most part, are identified in Scripture. These must have been well understood by those for whom the Chronicler wrote. There is a tendency to ignore these chapters; it takes a lot of work to coax from them a history meaningful and coherent to a contemporary reader. However, the reward for the work invested is enormous. These chapters yield many details of the history of Israel that are otherwise completely unknown. The Chronicler provides us with the history of a people and a nation, but not the history of a political state or country. The history of such a nation can be much more constructive than the political events of statehood. The method of the Chronicler has the potential to be most instructive to citizens of the kingdom of God.

The Greek translation labels this history *paraleipomena*, "the things/events omitted." This title considers Chronicles to be a secondary complement to Kings, an attitude that often is still prevalent. In Christian Bibles, Chronicles follows Kings and is usually read as a kind of supplement. The Hebrew codices (books rather than scrolls) place Chronicles in the third (concluding) section called the Writings, usually as the very last book of their Scriptures [Hebrew Canon, p. 467]. In the Leningrad Codex, however, which is used as the base text for most translations, Chronicles is the first book of the third section. Chronicles follows what is called the Latter Prophets (Isaiah to Malachi) and precedes Psalms. As the first book of the third section, it introduces the people of Israel's history that revered this collection of psalms, wisdom, and other writings. It defines Israel and their fundamental hope.

Chronicles describes the history of Israel from the beginning to a new beginning: from the inception of human existence with Adam, through the destruction of the first commonwealth during the reign of Zedekiah (587 BCE), to the commencement of a new community with the directive of Cyrus (539 BCE) to restore the temple in Jerusalem (Japhet 1993: 8). Chronicles reviews the whole of the past so the way to the future may be understood. It is uniquely created from many different sources. Chronicles explains why a people with no influence or status should consider their presence and faith to have a profound influence for the future.

Chronicles and History Writing

History writing is one kind of historiography [*History Writing, p. 469*]. History writing is not primarily an accurate reporting of past events (Van Seters: 4). It considers the reasons for recalling the past and the significance given to those events; it examines the causes of present circumstances. In ancient history writing, such as that of the Bible, such causes are primarily moral; since God controls history, faithfulness to the covenant is a primary evaluation. Lessons for the present are to be learned from actions done in the past. History writing is also corporate in nature: it is the accounting of the deeds of the people. Because history is a search for the causes of present circumstances, histories must always continue to be written.

The Chronicler employed a number of techniques in his history: he creates new meaning from texts through what may be called midrash, interprets his sources with careful exegetical work, and has his own theological perspective through which he interprets past events. Each of these are literary methods employed, but the work as a whole cannot be characterized by one of these techniques. Through the use of all of these methods, the Chronicler creates a history from his sources (Kalimi 2005b: 39); he expresses his theology and philosophy of the past. The Chronicler found it necessary to compose a history subsequent to that in the corpus of Genesis to Kings, whatever form that may have had in his day. He provides a distinct identity of Israel, as relevant from its origins, and a defense for the continuance of Yehud. The Chronicler appears to be fully conscious of his methods in writing his history to provide hope for the future. He evidently is convinced that all of his interpretations are the reality of what God was doing in the world and that they speak to the truth of what God will do in the world [*Tendenz in Chronicles, p. 476*].

While the Chronicler has great respect for his spiritual heritage, often quoting his sources virtually verbatim at considerable length, he does not hesitate to present a picture that is a remarkable contrast to the earlier version. Two notable examples are his depictions of the monarchs Solomon and Manasseh. In Kings, Solomon's reign ends in disaster, dividing the nation into two states. In Chronicles, Solomon is ordained and commissioned by David as the one who brings into fruition all the promises vested in David, particularly his desire to build the temple. There is no mention of the contentious issue of succession that dominates in Kings, or the fact that only a minority of Israel would ever worship at the temple that Solomon built. Kings portrays Manasseh as a king so sinful that even a good king like Josiah could never reverse the damage done: the exile from Manasseh's time onward was inevitable. The Chronicler, on the other hand, portrays Manasseh as a repentant king, who did much to empower the state of Judah. The Chronicler never contests the valuation of events found in his sources when he differs from them. Given that knowledge of his sources was essential to understanding much of his history, it is obvious he did not try to obscure or deny that history. However, his times required a reassessment of the story of the past. For him, the questions to be answered were of a completely different nature.

The Chronicler had to establish and validate living relationships in his time. He lived in a small ethnic community in Jerusalem and its immediate vicinity during the later days of the mighty Persian Empire (ca. 420–350 BCE), perhaps just before the advent of the Hellenistic period (associated with Alexander the Great's conquests). This community often suffered the scorn and humiliation of resentful surrounding peoples. It also struggled to maintain its own identity of faith and way of life as surrounding social pressures threatened to absorb it completely. The struggles of Ezra and Nehemiah are testimony to the troublesome problem of intermarriage with wives involved in religions of the surrounding peoples (Ezra 9:1-3). The leadership of the community engaged in intermarriage to the point that the very continuity of the priesthood was threatened. Drastic and painful measures were taken, even to the point of separating marriages with children.

The Chronicler believed his community was critically significant in realizing the kingdom promised to David; it needed to discern its function in order to fulfill its purpose. His genealogies, which are not family trees, were very important to him because they answered two essential questions of history: Whose story needs to be told? Where do these people live? The Chronicler believed his community was the presence of the kingdom of Yahweh as it is described by David (1 Chron 28:5); it needed to understand its own identity in order to appreciate its importance in covenant fulfillment *[Genealogy, p. 461]*.

The Community of Yehud

The Babylonians conquered Judah in the days of Ezekiel and Jeremiah. Ezekiel the priest was among the exiles of the first raid of Nebuchadnezzar in 597 BCE *[Chronology in Chronicles, p. 460]*. Jeremiah lived through the desolation of Jerusalem and the deportation of its leaders in 586 BCE. Within a generation, Babylonian power eroded through its own internal decay. To the east, Cyrus the Great established a new empire, uniting the Medes and the Persians. Babylon fell without resistance, and the Persian Empire extended westward in 539 BCE. In keeping with imperial policy, Cyrus made provisions for the exiles to return to Judah, to rebuild the temple, and to establish a province around the city of Jerusalem.

In Chronicles, it is particularly important to know that Cyrus did not restore Judah. Judah as a political territory never existed again after the time of the exile. Persian seal impressions and coins call this community *Yehud* (Aharoni et al.: 129). In both his genealogies and his language, the Chronicler adamantly maintains that all Israel resides in the province of Yehud *[Genealogy, p. 461]*. This province extended from the northern tip of the Dead Sea to the north of Bethel, west as far as Gezer, south to Azekah and Adullam, and east to En Gedi, on the west shore of the Dead Sea.

In all the late portions of the Bible, the province established by the Persians is consistently designated by the term *Yehud* (e.g., Dan 2:25; 5:13; 6:14; Esther 9:15; Ezra 5:1, 8; 7:14). Most of the references to Yehud are in the Aramaic portions of Scripture. Aramaic was the international language of this period; the above portions of Scripture are all in foreign contexts or correspondence.

The people who lived in Yehud came to be called (individually) *Yehudi* in Hebrew (e.g., 1 Chron 4:18; Neh 5:1, 8), *Yehuday* in Aramaic (Ezra 6:7), and *Ioudaios* in Greek. Transliteration of the Greek term in French and Latin led to the word *Jew* in English. People of Israel before the time of the New Testament were hesitant to use the term *Yehudi* (Gasque). The Dead Sea Scrolls, the apocryphal books written in Hebrew, the Mishnah, the Hebrew part of the Talmud, and the coins minted during the rebellions against Rome—all tend to use the designation "Israel" for the people as well as the land. A New Testament example is "king of Israel" in Mark 15:32. The term *Jew* (*Ioudaios*) has distinct uses in the Synoptics, John, Acts, and Paul. In this commentary, *Israel* rather than *Jew* will be used for the people of God, and *Yehud* will be used when referring to the postexilic Persian province.

As told in Haggai, Zechariah, and Ezra-Nehemiah, there were many struggles in trying to establish the new community of Yehud. The people seem to have suffered from a certain amount of disillusionment. Economic struggles delayed the building of the temple for over twenty years (Hag 1:1-2; Ezra 3:1-13). There was antagonism about rebuilding the city, especially from the Ammonites in Transjordan (Neh 4:1-8). In the middle of the fifth century, the walls of Jerusalem were eventually rebuilt under the leadership of Nehemiah, more than one hundred years after the initial return. This provided some protection and a measure of economic independence. Yet there was no hope of political autonomy; the besieged community did not even resemble the limited independence of the last days of the Judean kings. The people needed to be instilled with a sense of security and hope.

Little information is available about the situation in Yehud after Nehemiah. The difficulties of the community are somewhat known from contemporary writings. The painful trials of mixed marriages were still present in the days of Malachi (ca. 450-400 BCE; cf. Mal 2:14-16). The temptation to marry outside of Israel, rejecting the wife of one's youth, was often irresistible. Foreign marriages gave access to land and wealth that was not available within the confines of Yehud. Adherence to the temple as the social and economic center of the community, as prescribed in the law, continued to arouse resentment and hostility among the surrounding peoples.

The community in Yehud faced profound spiritual questions during the time of the Achaemenid kings [*Achaemenid, p. 464*]. How could they be true to their ancestral faith as a subordinate people, permanently under the control of an imperial power? How can a subject people be the people of God? What did the promise of the eternal throne of David mean under these circumstances? One answer, which found expression in Greek and Roman times, was a nationalist pressure to rebel, to establish political independence. Those who followed the perspective of Chronicles recognized a reality unrelated to political independence. Israel existed whether or not Yehud was an independent state. The people of Israel were concerned with the problems of conflict between political demand and faithfulness to God's promises. Faithfulness demanded a continuous sensitivity to carry out God's will for his people regardless of political status.

The Composition of Chronicles

Authorship and Date

In Hebrew codices, Chronicles is written as a single composition, as are Samuel, Kings, and Ezra-Nehemiah. These likely were divided, at least in the case of Samuel and Kings, due to the difficulty of holding all their contents on one scroll. Current divisions of chapters and books as found in translations first began in the late medieval period. Chronicles contains no direct information about the time and authorship of its composition. Other great histories were more forthcoming. Herodotus, the Greek historian of the classical period (440 BCE), begins his history as follows:

> Herodotus, from Halicarnassus, here displays his enquiries, that human achievement may be spared the ravages of time, and that everything great and astounding, and all the glory of those exploits which served to display Greeks and barbarians alike to such effect, be kept alive—and additionally, and most importantly, to give the reason they went to war. (Holland: 3)

In the late Hellenistic period, Dionysius of Halicarnassus prefaced his *Roman Antiquities* with remarks concerning himself, mentioned records and narratives used as sources, described the periods and subjects of his history, and identified the form he would give to his work. His preface concludes with his name, his father's name, and his place of birth (1 1.1–8.4; Cary: 3–27). If the book of Kings is something of an analogy in composition, it is likely that more than one person was involved in writing Chronicles—and the composition probably expanded over time. Great effort has been given to identifying times and stages of development in Chronicles, but the goal remains elusive. Equally obscure is the identity of the composer(s) and the occasion that inspired this great work. The question is further complicated by the relationship of Chronicles to the Ezra compositions *[Chronicles and the Ezra Compositions, p. 457]*. Some argue that 1 Esdras is a stage of the process before Chronicles and Ezra-Nehemiah came to be two separate compositions as we know them.

Clues to the occasion for writing Chronicles must by sought from its contents. On this basis, the earliest possible date of its completion as it now stands (terminus a quo) is during the latter part of the Persian Empire, probably in the first half of the fourth century (400–350 BCE) *[Chronology in Chronicles, p. 460]*. The genealogy of Jehoiachin (1 Chron 3:17-24) requires a date at least six generations later than Zerubbabel and possibly more (Kalimi 2005b: 57–58). Zerubbabel was ruler during the restoration of the temple in the days of Darius king of Persia (Zech 4:9). The second year of Darius (Zech 1:1) was 520 BCE. Biologically, a generation is about twenty years long (when the first child is born), making the earliest possible date for this genealogy about 400 BCE. Chronicles does not show evidence of Hellenistic influence linguistically or ideologically. The latest possible date of its completion (terminus ad quem) is probably before the first half of the fourth century BCE, but this cannot be established absolutely.

The Chronicler likely lived in or near Jerusalem and appears to have been an ardent supporter of the temple and its services. His work gives prominence to the Levites, a hint that he was among their number. Being a Levite would adequately explain his access to the material he used to compose his history. Temple archives could have been the source of some of his information, such as census reports, building records, and old prophetic materials. The Chronicler has been described as part of the ruling and priestly classes in Jerusalem, who used the imminent or actual demise of the Persians to think big (J. Dyck: 162-64). The ethnic elements included in the genealogical lists suggest that the leadership elite of the fourth century were much more inclusive in their thinking than the returnees of a century earlier [Genealogy, p. 461].

Sources of the Chronicler

Every historian begins with sources that are selected, sorted, and evaluated. The sources available to the historian are therefore of critical importance, but selection and interpretation of these sources are determinative for the impact of the history. The Chronicler uses what came to be canonical Scripture as a substantial source. Significant portions of the Pentateuch, Joshua, Samuel and Kings, Ezra-Nehemiah, Ruth, and some psalms are quoted, and parallel texts appear in Isaiah and Jeremiah. When the Chronicler uses these sources, they seem to have been compiled already as we have them. Arguments that the author of Chronicles did not use Samuel-Kings as a major source in his composition have not proved convincing [Sources for Chronicles, p. 472].

From the evidence of the scrolls of Qumran and the Greek text of Chronicles, as the commentary shows (e.g., 1 Chron 21), it is certain that the text form used by the Chronicler is not the same as the standard Hebrew text [Greek Text of Chronicles, p. 468; Masoretic Text, p. 470]. Caution must be exercised when proposing changes the Chronicler might have made to his text. As any historian, the Chronicler interpreted his texts for the purposes of his work, but

Methods of the Chronicler

There are various aspects to the way the Chronicler did his work. The Chronicler has been called a midrashist in the sense of one *creating new meaning* by commenting on ancient texts. Julius Wellhausen was most influential in his depiction of Chronicles as midrash (Kalimi 2005b: 20–23). Wellhausen regarded midrash as a corruption of sources, an artificial reconstruction of ancient records like ivy growing over the dead trunk of a tree. He regarded midrash as twisted and perverted, bringing foreign accretions to texts in an arbitrary manner. This dismissive attitude toward midrash was specifically motivated. The goal of Wellhausen was to destroy the credibility of Chronicles as a source for Israelite history because it contradicted his theories of pentateuchal sources. He was convinced that all priestly material, much of which is found in Genesis to Numbers, first came to be written in the postexilic period. Since Chronicles contradicted this material, but was also from the postexilic time period, Wellhausen needed to discredit it. He construed the Chronicler as creating his own fantasy of history by rewriting the biblical sources. Wellhausen also had an anti-Jewish orientation and regarded Chronicles as representative of all Jewish work: an artificial midrash created on ancient texts. It is ironic that Wellhausen should have viewed Chronicles so negatively as a midrash when the only two occurrences of this term in the Old Testament are found in Chronicles (2 Chron 13:22; 24:27). In both cases midrash is a term for a historical source of the Chronicler. Midrash is better defined as the study of a text to make it relevant to the needs of a community, an attempt to make a biblical text contemporary and relevant. In the postexilic period, Ezekiel may be considered to be a type of midrash as it is a modification of pentateuchal law. While various modern authors have spoken about Chronicles as midrash, that is not its main literary characteristic. The Bible does not comment on itself in the same manner as nonbiblical texts, such as midrash at Qumran or rabbinic writings.

The Chronicler has been described as *an exegete of earlier Scripture*. Willi regarded the historical writing of the Chronicler as "exegesis in the best sense of the word," having the goal of leading to an understanding of his sources (Willi: 66). Once the Chronicler determined to write a history, he had only one option: to provide an interpretation of the Deuteronomistic History as his principal source [Deuteronomistic History, p. 465]. Texts that had no parallel in Samuel and Kings, such as the genealogies (1 Chron 1–9) or the administrative material of 1 Chronicles 23:2b–27:34, have been regarded as later additions to the work. There are instances in which the Chronicler served as an exegete, interpreting texts for his time, but often he adopts large portions of material just as he finds them, without alteration. At other times he omits material or arranges it in a different order, which is hardly the function of an exegete or commentator. His interpretations are more than just exegesis.

The Chronicler has also been regarded *as a theologian*. His aim was to provide a unifying concept of the Jewish community and to explain the significance of its rich and varied traditions. Chronicles is concerned with the universal relationship between God and humanity, and the vocation of Israel within this relationship. History and theology are not separable: each influences the other, as is evidently true for the Chronicler [History Writing, p. 469]. His understanding of events could never be restricted to human initiative; all human activity was necessarily interpreted as a manifestation of God at work in his world. The world and everything in it belongs to God (1 Chron 29:11; 2 Chron 20:6; 25:9). God is the motivating force behind the actions of the nations; they are instruments, doing the work of his bidding. His interpretation of events converges with his theological convictions, but this does not make his work a theology.

In sum, the Chronicler is best described as a historian, interpreting the past for the present in accordance with his own views of God, human events, and the function of the community in which he lived. He has his own sources, his own perspective, and his own integrity.

Chronicles and Ezra-Nehemiah

Chronicles is part of a complex of other writings. Strikingly, the last verses of Chronicles are identical to the first verses of Ezra. In Catholic and Orthodox Scriptures, 1 Esdras, a Greek writing that begins with 2 Chronicles 35–36, continues through the book of Ezra and concludes with a portion of Nehemiah 8. It is evident that Ezra and Nehemiah can be read as a continuous story with Chronicles. But the question is whether Chronicles should be read as a continuous story with the postexilic accounts of Ezra and Nehemiah, rather than as an independent work with its own purpose and message. Should 1 Esdras be viewed as a stage within the composition of one lengthy work, or is it a separate composition created separately for purposes of its own? These are important questions that must be considered carefully.

Consideration of the relationship of these writings must deal with two fundamental issues: (1) the literary factors of content, vocabulary, and style; and (2) the theological conceptions expressed in the selection and arrangement of material. At the literary level, an obvious point of consideration is the closing of Chronicles. Why should this work conclude with a fragment from the decree of Cyrus reported in the introduction of Ezra, ending with the phrase *Let him go up* (2 Chron 36:23 NRSV), an imperative verb cut off from the rest of its clause? A second question relates to the beginning of Ezra; why does this composition begin with a Hebrew phrase "Now in the first year" (Ezra 1:1 NASB, KJV)? Books that begin this way usually resume a previous narrative (Exodus, Leviticus, Joshua, Judges, Samuel, and Kings), though there are exceptions (Ezekiel, Esther). The conclusion of Chronicles provides links to the prophecies of Jeremiah (2 Chron 36:12, 21-22), making the decree of Cyrus an event-fulfilling prophecy. It serves as a fitting conclusion to Chronicles, and it could logically have been adopted from Ezra for that very purpose. At the same time, it is possible the narrative of Ezra was created as continuous with Chronicles (Knoppers 2004a: 77). It is impossible to reconstruct for certain how these literary features came about in the compositional history of these books *[Chronicles and the Ezra Compositions, p. 457]*. But the doublet of the edict of Cyrus is not in itself evidence for the unity of these two books.

At the end of the nineteenth century, there was a scholarly consensus that Chronicles and Ezra-Nehemiah once formed a continuous work. The linguistic similarity of vocabulary, syntactical phenomena, and stylistic peculiarities were deemed to be decisive in this conclusion. However, a factor to be considered is that the linguistic similarities of these books are common to all postexilic literature. On the other hand, though the data is slim, differences of vocabulary usage within postexilic Hebrew can be detected between these compositions. More significant are matters of ideology. David receives much more prominence in Chronicles, and matters relating to Torah are more dominant in Ezra-Nehemiah *[Torah, p. 481]*. Some counter these differences by observing that these compositions focus on entirely different periods in Israelite and Judean history, and they argue that the different emphases may be more apparent than real.

Yet there is no doubt about the contrast in the conception of Israel and the nature of the community. Chronicles has a much broader and more inclusive concept of Israel as a faith community than does Ezra-Nehemiah, which is focused on the realities of the struggles of Jerusalem and the province of Yehud in the days of Darius and Artaxerxes [Chronology in Chronicles, p. 460]. The Chronicler is consistently inclusive of all those seeking the covenant outside of these boundaries, particularly those who lived in the north, where tribes of Israel once thrived. He also evinces an inclusiveness of foreigners in marriage and community relations, while Ezra-Nehemiah appears consistently more defensive in this regard. These distinctions between Chronicles and Ezra-Nehemiah are obscured if these two books are read consecutively as one composition. Chronicles and Ezra-Nehemiah understandably have much in common, but in their present form they are not a continuous work. Other sources are identified as forming the substance of Ezra and Nehemiah, especially the personal accounts found in these books (memoirs). There is no consensus on how these sources have been integrated in composition.

Goals of the Chronicler

The prominence of the promise to David makes it central to the Chronicler's message. In three speeches David commissions Solomon with the responsibility of fulfilling the task that he had begun (1 Chron 22:7-11; 28:2-10; 29:1-2). When David determined to build a house for the ark of God, Nathan the prophet, through a vision, informed him that his priorities were in reverse order: David would not build a house for God; instead, God would build a house for David (2 Sam 7:11-14). The house that God would build for David was a dynasty; the eternal kingdom of God would come about through the lineage of David. The importance of this promise is expressed in the second psalm: God holds the nations in derision because they have rejected his kingdom and think they can establish their own rule. They ignored the fact that God had already anointed his king on Mount Zion, a king who would shatter the nations and receive the earth (God's world) as his inheritance (Ps 2:1-9). The Chronicler took this promise very seriously. The kingdom of God would come through the promised son of David; the community around Jerusalem represented that promised kingdom and the hope of the future.

The Chronicler had a double task in accomplishing his goal. His first task was to explain why the kingdom of David had failed; the second task was to explain how the small, struggling state in the mighty Persian Empire could hope to become the kingdom that was promised to David. The explanation for the failure of David's kingdom begins with the demise of Saul. Saul was rejected as king over

Introduction to Chronicles

Israel because he was unfaithful: he did not obey God, and in his violation of covenant, he went so far as to consult a medium (1 Chron 10:13). Unfaithfulness (*maʿal*) will become a key word for the Chronicler; he will use it repeatedly to describe the reason for judgment against kings of Judah. The reason for hope is given in the words of God responding to the prayer of Solomon at the dedication of the temple: *If my people, who are called by my name, will humble themselves and pray and seek my face and turn from their wicked ways, then I will hear from heaven, and I will forgive their sin and will heal their land* (2 Chron 7:14). This verse contains the vocabulary characteristic of the Chronicler in demonstrating the conditions necessary for restoration: humility, prayer, repentance, and healing.

Chronicles first establishes the necessary premises for this formula of restoration. The promise to David was not lost with the exile; the nation of Israel was to be found in the people who lived in Jerusalem. For the Chronicler, all the tribes were present in the restoration, including those of the Northern Kingdom (1 Chron 9:3). The division of the kingdom after Solomon did not put any of the tribes outside the nation of Israel. The Chronicler understands Israel to be the people of covenant, not a political entity. His objective was to show that the unity established by David and Solomon was eternal, and therefore the promise made to David was their hope for the future. David and Solomon take up the greatest portion of the Chronicler's history (1 Chron 11:1–2 Chron 9:31); this constitutes almost half his composition (twenty-eight chapters). Much of this is about the temple, which was essential for the function of the faith community. The period of David and Solomon is presented as an ideal, when all Israel was united in worship at the temple (e.g., 2 Chron 7:8). Concern for the correct worship of God dominates the whole of David's reign. The restoration of the ark to Jerusalem and the victories of David provide for the future temple. David made all the necessary arrangements for the officials as worship shifted from Gibeon to Jerusalem. David's reign is a paradigm for the Chronicler's readers; the change of king from Saul to David was an example of how to move out of a state of exile to live as a covenant people. The reign of Solomon brings to fruition David's plans for the temple and its worship (2 Chron 3:1; 5:1; 7:1); Solomon's reign is regarded as equal to that of David.

With the reign of Hezekiah, the Chronicler offers a solution to the problem of the division of the monarchy. Under Ahaz, Judah had come to the same level of disobedience as Israel (2 Chron 28:2, 6). Israel itself is presented in a more favorable light, with representative leaders confessing both their present and former sins (v. 13), indicating that the northerners were prepared for restoration. The Chronicler introduces Hezekiah with his distinct characterization as a second Solomon (see commentary). Emphasis is placed on his invitation to the north to join in the first Passover of his reign, and a good number responded (30:11); there was a celebration more wonderful than any since the time of Solomon.

The Chronicler wrote his history to present his readers with a vision of how they ought to regulate their communal and individual lives in the circumstances of their own day. Their lives would not be determined by what had happened in the past. The Chronicler is not explicit about his hopes for the Davidic house, but he maintains a hope for the realization of the promise to David in historical terms. However remote such a possibility may have seemed in his time, the Chronicler makes evident that the kingdom was not a human institution subject to the whims of political expediency.

The Message of Chronicles

As is the case with the Gospels, Chronicles is history and theology, but more important is the theology (Stinespring: 209). There is a Jesus of history and a Christ of faith. Though the two are inseparable, they must be distinguished. The Christ of faith is more than what the historian can observe. In history, Jesus the man died on a cross at a certain place and time. In theology, the cross is transformational for the whole of humanity. In the book of Romans, the apostle develops the power of the cross for Gentiles and Jews (Rom 1:16-17). The crucifixion of Jesus brought the whole Gentile world into the promises made to Abraham. In the vision of the apostle, the death of Jesus would be the means of bringing his own people Israel back into the promises that they had abdicated in their ignorance and misunderstanding. There is a David of history and a David of faith, which are one. The David of history in Chronicles is also a David of faith, one who receives the promises of the kingdom of Yahweh to be confirmed in his son Solomon (1 Chron 28:5). The Chronicler writes a history to portray this kingdom, not only for what he believes it to have been in the past, but also to develop a theology of the presence and power of this kingdom of God for the future. Chronicles must not be reduced to history. The historian will poke fun at Jehoshaphat for sending a temple choir to meet an imposing army and will find it yet more incredible when the choir conquers the opposing foe with well-chosen praises. Historians cannot reconstruct such events, much less find significance in them.

Introduction to Chronicles

The Chronicler is teaching his people about God and the way they may find God at work in their lives.

The purpose of the Chronicler is to establish, through his narrative of the reigns of David and Solomon, the proper and legitimate pattern of institutions and their personnel for the people of God. These institutions and personnel are the monarchy represented by David and his house, the priesthood by Zadok and his descendants, the city and the temple in the Promised Land. City and ruler, temple and priest—these appear to be the fixed points around which the Chronicler constructs his history and his theology (Freedman: 437-38). The Chronicler's hope for fulfillment of the promise to David was the special concern of the early postexilic community, as indicated by the roles of Zerubbabel and Joshua in establishing the second temple. The genealogy of Zerubbabel at the end of the descendants of David is remarkable (1 Chron 3:19-24), both in the number of individuals named and the length of time reviewed. Zerubbabel is of enduring significance for the Chronicler. The Chronicler's descriptions have something of an eschatological flavor. Support for David at Ziklag was so great that *his camp became immense, like the camp of God* (1 Chron 12:22 AT). Historically, Achish, king of Gath, granted Ziklag as a place of residence (fiefdom) to David and his band of warriors. The Chronicler is more interested in what this group, rallying around David, represented in God's plan and purpose.

History is a treatment of the past, objectively researched, factually presented, and applied to present experience (Goldingay: 109). The Chronicler is not interested in inventing the past; he frequently makes references to sources and gives much evidence of limiting his narrative to their information. But he goes back to the past knowing what he is looking for in order to present his theology of God and his people. Bernard Lonergan provides a helpful definition of a premodern history:

> It is artistic: it selects, orders, describes; it would awaken the reader's interest and sustain it; it would persuade and convince. Again, it is ethical: it not only narrates but also apportions praise and blame. It is explanatory: it accounts for existing institutions by telling of their origins and development and by contrasting them with alternative institutions found in other lands. It is apologetic, correcting false or tendentious accounts of the people's past, and refuting the calumnies of neighboring peoples. Finally, it is prophetic: to hindsight about the past there is joined foresight on the future and there are added the recommendations of a man of wide reading and modest wisdom. (Lonergan: 185)

The Chronicler does not narrate events of the past for their own sake. The past is not only the source for lessons in the present, but also the basis on which the present may be lived. His history is a theology [*Theology of Chronicles*, p. 476].

The Chronicler is concerned with worship. The prophet Isaiah looked forward to the day of fulfillment of "the sure mercies of David" (Isa 55:3-5 KJV) but gave no indication of what that might be. At the dedication of the temple, the Chronicler has incorporated this reference into the prayer of Solomon: *Remember the mercies of David your servant* (2 Chron 6:42 AT). These mercies are to be interpreted as the promises made to David (as in NIV, not as NRSV). The temple is the center of the Lord's kingdom on earth. Its presence, structure, and proper ritual worship are all critical matters. The Chronicler's account of each of the kings is concerned with the practice of worship at the temple. In the theology of the Chronicler, Israel's existence was conditioned by praise, whether it was the time of David or worship at the temple in his own day.

The Chronicler is also concerned about purity. He must safeguard the holiness of the people of God; worship must not be compromised. Jerusalem is the place where the worship of the nation is concentrated from the time when David chose the place where the ark would dwell (1 Chron 22:1). The Northern Kingdom is never acknowledged, let alone given legitimacy as an independent kingdom. Jerusalem and its temple are the sole representatives of the palace of the great king. This does not exclude northerners from participating in worship. All Israel, from south to north, is engaged in bringing up the ark from Kiriath Jearim (1 Chron 13:5). Even when the north separates under Jeroboam, Abijah, the king of Judah, confronts the warriors in a mountain of Ephraim to address all Israel and remind them that the kingdom was given to David over all Israel forever (2 Chron 13:4-5). In resisting the kingdom in Jerusalem, they are turning against the *kingdom of Yahweh* under the Davidide kings (v. 8). They have driven away the priests of Aaron and made priests like those of all the other nations (v. 9). Abijah and his people were resolved to worship God in his temple and under proper priestly order (vv. 10-11). God was at the head of their kingdom; there could be no alternative worship. Place of residence does not exclude anyone from belonging to Israel, but Israel is exclusively loyal to the king in Jerusalem and to worship at the temple there.

The Chronicler has a high priority on obedience. Only the might of God can bring victory, which comes to those who are obedient. Though the armies of Abijah were half those of the Israelites to whom the king gave such stern warning (2 Chron 13:3), the Israelites fell disastrously before the armies of Judah (vv. 13-20), who had chosen God as the head of their army. The word of God must be taken seriously. The Chronicler's heroes are those who teach and obey the word of God (Jehoshaphat, Hezekiah, Josiah). Though obedience is critical, it is only possible through the grace of God (1 Chron 22:12). God draws the minds of his people to himself so they may be loyal to him (1 Chron 29:18). God continuously sent his prophets to his people in his compassion for them, though these prophets were repeatedly spurned (2 Chron 36:15). God is good, and his mercy endures forever (2 Chron 5:13; 7:3). Grace is manifest in God's forgiveness of sin and providing abundant blessing to those who are loyal to his covenant.

Chronicles and the New Testament

Chronicles does not appear to be a book used in the early proclamation of Jesus. There is only one allusion to it in the New Testament, an almost incidental reference, found in the scathing rebuke against the Pharisees in Luke 11:51 (cf. Matt 23:35): they will be held accountable for the shedding of blood from Abel to Zechariah. The blood of Zechariah is a reference to the wickedness of Joash, who ordered the death of the son of the high priest who had saved him as a boy and made him king (2 Chron 22:10-11; 23:20-21). Since Chronicles belonged to the closing section of the canon, if not the final book in at least some circles, these words of Jesus included the murderous activities of the entire period of biblical revelation. This statement is an affirmation of the importance of Chronicles as a part of canonical revelation. It is also an indication that, at the time of Jesus, Chronicles was considered the last book of the Bible, even though it consisted of groups of scrolls. When the Hebrew Bible became a codex (book) centuries later, the order of the biblical books followed an established sequence of individual scrolls. This is an important testimony to Scripture, but it has no relevance to the theology of Chronicles.

Chronicles is important for understanding the eschatology of the New Testament. This might seem surprising since the New Testament is highly apocalyptic in its outlook, both in the Gospels (e.g., Matt 24:4-44) and the book of Revelation. The confession of communion includes the anticipation of the coming of the kingdom as an apocalyptic event (Luke 22:14-18). The watchword of the New Testament is that Christ (the anointed one) will interrupt the present age to establish his kingdom. But there is another eschatology in the New

Testament that says the kingdom is present in the coming of Jesus and in the preaching of his disciples. Healing the sick and casting out demons were signs of the presence of the kingdom (Luke 10:9; 11:20). The preaching of Jesus began in the area of Galilee, to fulfill the prophecy of Isaiah concerning the coming of the kingdom (Matt 4:13-17; Isa 8:21–9:1). This is sometimes called inaugurating eschatology: the kingdom has come, and the kingdom is coming. The followers of Jesus have entered into the kingdom of God. As citizens of the kingdom, they must be faithful in times of upheaval, war, famine, and great tribulation; all these are signs that the end is not yet (Luke 21:9). There will be much deception and tribulation for those of the kingdom. As in Chronicles, there is the hope of a kingdom to come, but a necessity to live as citizens of this kingdom in the present time. The kingdom is manifest in the worshiping community. This aspect of the kingdom is also present in the apocalyptic book of Revelation. John writes to the seven churches, exhorting them to be faithful, reminding them that they have the crown of life, and promising that their names are in the book of life. The church is the temple built on the foundation of the apostles and prophets (Eph 2:19-22), the equivalent of the temple in the days of Chronicles.

A second aspect of eschatology in the New Testament is the concept of Israel and its future. The idea of Israel in Chronicles is most instructive to understanding Paul's teaching concerning the future of Israel. The name Israel is multivalent; it has numerous referents because of its associations in ethnic, political, and religious identity. In Romans 9–11, Israel is employed by Paul in at least three ways (Johnson: 141): Israel is all ethnic Israel (9:1-5, 31; 10:1-3; 11:11-36); Israel is the remnant, composed of faithful Jews, of whom the apostle is an example (11:1-6); and Israel is also the nation of promise (9:8, 24; cf. 4:16-17), Abraham's spiritual descendants, including people of Jewish and Gentile heritage. Israel for Paul is a single reality created by God's mercy of election and cannot be limited by ethnicity. None of these three perspectives of Israel in Romans 9–11 is exclusive; each is used without excluding the distinction of the others. Though Paul never refers to Chronicles, his concept of Israel in his epistles is that of the Chronicler. Israel is a nation, has an ethnic identity, yet is inclusive of all those who join the covenant. All Israel is included in the promises to David.

In Paul's understanding of God's program of salvation, there is an Israel that is not identified with the church. This Israel is part of God's elective purposes to bring about salvation, an election that is as yet unfulfilled. Its fulfillment depends on the full accomplishment of the Gentile mission, which will bring about the completion of the elective purposes of Israel. In the mind of Paul, the salvation of all Israel is the redemption of the nation collectively, though not including unrepentant members. Redemption comes to the repentant ones of Jacob. This restoration of the nation as a whole to God comes at the end; it is an eschatological event in the strict sense. According to Paul, the salvation of Israel dashes any hopes of his contemporaries, as well as those of our own contemporary time, for the reestablishment of a national state in independence and political power. The completion of the salvation of Israel is to receive the mercy of God in forgiveness of sins. It is associated with the second coming of Christ, the time when Israel will receive mercy by the mercy that has been shown to the Gentiles. This is the great mystery. If the transgression, by the grace of God, came to be the salvation of the Gentiles—and the defeat of Israel to be riches for the Gentiles—then "how much greater riches will their full inclusion bring!" (Rom 11:11-12). If their rejection brings the reconciliation of the world, what can their acceptance mean "but life from the dead?" (Rom 11:15). The salvation of Israel will mean their being grafted in again to their own cultivated olive tree. Salvation is complete when Jews and Gentiles are united in Christ. The mystery of redemption will be realized in the coming of Christ. The teaching of Paul concerning Israel is the Christian eschatology that completes what the Chronicler envisioned concerning the fulfillment of the promise to David.

The Relevance of Chronicles

The significance of Chronicles to New Testament hope in itself makes it important to the church. This relevance is intensified with the formation of the modern State of Israel. There are times when it is obvious that Israel in Scripture is not to be equated with Israel as a state. "Israel" as a historical referent to Jacob is clear in Genesis. "Israel" refers to the covenant people in Exodus, in distinction from the term "Hebrew," which is only used in a context of foreigners. Israel is the name of the Northern Kingdom after it had separated from Judah in the book of Kings. For only the briefest period, during part of the reign of David and the reign of Solomon, Israel was the name of one united state consisting of all the tribes. This Israel of the north is of no interest to the Chronicler. The Chronicler manifests an open attitude to the people of promise, distinct from the institution of the monarchy. As the commentary will explain, Hezekiah is portrayed as a second Solomon. With the fall of the Northern Kingdom, Israel was once again united as a people in the worship that Hezekiah initiated with the restoration of the temple (Williamson 1977b: 125). Further evidence of the inclusive sense of Israel for the Chronicler is his use of the term "remnant" to describe those in the north who survived the exile, or for the remnant in both north and south (2 Chron 30:6; 34:9). His narrative specifically qualifies and defines the remnant spoken of by the prophets. The name of the prophet's son anticipates such a repentant remnant (Isa 7:3), which will be realized (10:21). It is inclusive of all the people of promise; the presence of a state is deliberately excluded in the Chronicler's concept of Israel. This description of eschatological Israel is particularly important when the modern State of Israel is thought to be the fulfilment of the promises to Israel.

There are other ways in which the theology of the Chronicler may appear to be problematic but when examined will prove to be instructive. His concept of reward and punishment may seem to support what is colloquially referred to as the prosperity gospel *["God, Justice, and Faithfulness" in Theology of Chronicles, p. 478]*. The prayer of Jabez has been used to teach the doctrine that God desires to "enlarge our boundaries" (1 Chron 4:9-10). The many examples in the book of Chronicles in which individual sin is responsible for illness or loss, or in turn when there is blessing for obedience, may be understood as support for the claims of controlling blessing and avoiding pain. A careful study of Chronicles can provide a valuable corrective. The Chronicler desires to show the mercy of God, but his concept of the sovereignty of God never allows this to become a claim for wealth. His point is that the mercy of God assures blessing to those who humble themselves and seek his face. Humility is an important part of receiving blessing; this is not the kind of attitude that claims rights, and it is not one that is generally heard in prosperity gospel theology. Humility is an acknowledgment of divine sovereignty and a prerequisite to blessing. Such humility is a trusting faith rather than an assertion of the right to receive blessing. The Chronicler is also clear on the point of justice. In his theology, wrongdoing does not go unpunished. The church is often reluctant to speak of God in judgment, but it must not be omitted. Chronicles is unequivocal in declaring the reality of judgment as well as blessing.

One of the most troublesome problems in the world is the presence of war. Wars of aggression are part of the human condition and result in the need for protection and wars of defense. The Chronicler's attitude to war is certain on one point: God wins wars, and the outcome is not determined by military strength *[War in Chronicles, p. 481]*. The Chronicler has his own version of the story of Jehoshaphat responding to the attack by the coalition of the kings from the east. In his version there is complete victory, with the mighty enemy army falling to the praises of a Levitical choir. This version of war is close to that of Revelation, in which the rider on the white horse extinguishes the power of all nations with the sword emerging from his mouth (Rev 19:11-15). Jehoshaphat relies on the promise to seek God and seems to have no plans for the actual engagement of his army. This is exemplary of the Chronicler's attitude to war. War may not be avoidable, but military strength is not the means of victory.

Yet the Chronicler can fully affirm human engagement in war and even wars of aggression. His description of the rise of David is to show how warriors came to support David while he was in the wilderness. The victories of David over the Arameans are wars of aggression, to enlarge the kingdom to its proper boundaries. It is one of the ways that God's choice of David as king of Israel is demonstrated. The Chronicler narrates all of this as part of the preparation for the kingdom. Yet David the warrior is prevented from building the temple: he is a man who has shed much blood.

There is a New Testament parallel, in that the coming of the kingdom of God is not apart from war against the nations who are in pursuit of their own wealth and power. But the New Testament prohibits the citizens of the kingdom of heaven from active combat in such a divine victory. Citizens of the kingdom of heaven are also citizens of earthly kingdoms whose mandate is to serve and protect them in many ways. Can the citizens of God's kingdom serve God in defense of the temporal kingdom to which they belong? Chronicles does not answer that question unequivocally. Modern times are not the times of the Chronicler in discerning how God moves among human kingdoms. But the fundamental theology of the Chronicler is most important on the question of war. God rules among the nations in the redemption of his people. The narrative of Chronicles is a warning against the presumption of military might as a force for good, as well as the claim that it has the power to end wars of human aggression.

Chronicles is filled with theological potential for the church today, often described as a post-Christendom era, in which the church has been marginalized from centers of power (Boda 2010: 19). The contemporary church resonates with a community vulnerable to the temporal powers of its day. The Chronicler speaks to those seeking their identity as God's people when the surrounding culture profoundly dominates. Chronicles provides a model for the rhythms of individual and community living. It may be a call to repentance and renewal, or to the establishment of a robust worship of highest priority. It is a vision for a minority people to live in faithfulness because they represent the kingdom of God in the world.

The Methodology of This Commentary

Chronicles is a challenging book to understand, in part because it is an interpretation of earlier Scripture and frequently assumes familiarity with Scripture. This is noticeably true in its presentation and selection of genealogies, but it is also true in much of its narrative. The significance of what is said often depends on an awareness of what has been omitted or altered from the sources used by the Chronicler. Sometimes this is readily evident, such as the uncontested succession of Solomon as compared to the version in Kings. But there are often subtle differences between the versions that require careful textual analysis. Textual variations are particularly difficult with names, not only due to the occasional scribal error, but also because names are notorious for having variations in spelling. Further, during the period in which the Chronicler wrote, there was considerable fluidity of the biblical text, as is especially evident in the texts found near the Dead Sea. Because the Chronicler's text sometimes appears to omit or change a word, it becomes particularly important to know when he is doing so and why. The impact of his work is significantly reduced if his interpretation of sources is not recognized.

The method of this commentary is to use the MT of the Old Testament as a base text for the sources of the Chronicler. Since the Reformation, this has been the basic text of almost all translations of the Old Testament. However, the MT is used with the recognition that it is not necessarily the oldest text or the best text of the Chronicler's sources, and certainly is not the text the Chronicler used in composition. The Chronicler's text is not available to us, but texts other than MT are often closer to the *Vorlage* he employed and are helpful in understanding his work [*Vorlage*, p. 468]. For this reason there is frequent reference to a Greek textual tradition in the commentary. The Greek also represents various original texts and revisions of earlier translations. Care has been taken to be clear about interpretation based on texts other than MT, since textual criticism is somewhat subjective. It is nevertheless necessary and often informative in dealing with problems of understanding Chronicles. There are times when the original text the Chronicler used cannot be recovered, and best sense must be made from the

Introduction to Chronicles

traditions preserved for us. References to other texts, such as the Samuel scrolls from Qumran, are also given where they are available and relevant to the narrative. This is particularly true in the narratives of the choice of the temple location (1 Chron 21) and the wars against Amon (1 Chron 19).

The most challenging aspect of Chronicles is the genealogical section *[Genealogy, p. 461]*. Introducing a history with such extensive genealogies is unique to Chronicles, not only in the Bible, but in all known historical writing. The genealogies are difficult because of the text itself: textual variation and ambiguity are most prevalent when there is very little narrative. The genealogies are also difficult because they are dense. Knowing the reasons for the inclusion and arrangement of names requires a great deal of knowledge about those names. The genealogies are to be taken seriously: they are the foundational portion of the history and therefore the theology of the Chronicler. The goal of a commentary is to provide understanding of the text. If genealogies are to be understood, they will require more explanation than other narrative. This commentary has tried to explain some of the key issues of the text and the resulting interpretation; thereby the reader may appreciate what the Chronicler was attempting with his selection and organization of names of both people and places. The commentary points out what translators have added and why they disagree more often than in other parts of the text. For this reason the commentary has proportionately dedicated more explanation to the genealogies. The only alternative is to be so generic as to miss much of what the genealogies are about. It may seem tedious to be reading about genealogical information, but much of Israel's history is found only in this section.

Chronicles presents a unique situation in discussing the commentary sections called Text in Biblical Context and Text in the Life of the Church. Because so much of Chronicles relies on the Bible, much of the Text in Biblical Context is by necessity part of the exposition. But much of its relevance requires understanding more inclusively how it is distinct to its time in the use and application of Scripture. To facilitate a better understanding of the Old Testament, the sections on the Text in Biblical Context often deal with the unique message that Chronicles has in relation to the two earlier parts of the Hebrew canon, the Pentateuch and the Prophets (including both Joshua to Kings and Isaiah to Malachi) *[Hebrew Canon, p. 467]*. The relevance of Chronicles for the church frequently must begin with the New Testament. Therefore the New Testament is regularly quoted in application to the life of the church. In many cases, the way in which Chronicles relates to the church of the New Testament is not fundamentally different from the way it relates to the church in the present time.

Chronicles is a book of history, so often the most logical application to the church—and the Anabaptist church specifically—is to show how the present church may benefit from a study of its own history, just as the Chronicler did from his history. The sections on the Text in the Life of the Church will make reference to certain historical situations in the life of the church that are analogous to those of the Chronicler. Yet Chronicles does not readily yield to making direct application to contemporary life. Though this is possible at times, in other instances such a method is at the expense of the theology of the narrative. The promise to David, the temple preparations, and the building of the temple are all mediated to the church through their application to Jesus. The commentary seeks to point the way to using the message of Chronicles in the church's life by careful attention to the theological traditions that emerge from it, which become fundamental to the faith of the church.

Translations Used in This Commentary

This commentary has been written from the Hebrew and Greek texts, with continuous attention to the choices of the NIV (2011) and its interpretation of these texts. The author has tried to have all names correspond to the transliterations in the NIV. Quotations of the biblical text are from the NIV when not otherwise indicated. Biblical quotations outside of Chronicles are put in quotation marks; all quotations from Chronicles are italicized. Other translations are referred to in order to show the reader different textual or interpretive choices. The premise of the commentary is that the reader will refer to the NIV as the base text; however, unique readings of the NIV are pointed out in the commentary, so the choice of translation for the reader is not critical. Scripture is quoted because of a distinct nuance or significance relevant to that text. For example, spelling of names in English translations is much more consistent than the many variants of the original texts, which are sometimes significant. These variants are rarely reflected in translation. When it is necessary to quote the biblical text, it is usually because the NIV translation obscures a particular point through paraphrase necessary for fluent English. In such cases the author has made his own translation and has so indicated (AT).

: 1

Nation of Promise

1 Chronicles 1:1-9:34

OVERVIEW

First Chronicles divides into two distinct sections: (1) the portrayal of Israel in the genealogies (1:1-9:34); and (2) the work of David in preparing Jerusalem for the temple and the rule of Solomon (9:35-29:30). In the second section, the monarchy is introduced with the rejection of Saul (9:35-10:14) and the establishment of David as the anointed king (chs. 11-12). The chapters on David's reign explain his organization of officials and preparations for the temple (chs. 13-27). The reign of David closes with a great public assembly in which Solomon is commissioned as the heir of peace who will build the temple (chs. 28-29) *[Genealogy, p. 461]*.

The first chapter of genealogies moves along the line of God's election from Adam to Israel. Chapters 2-8 deal in much greater detail with the Israelites in the preexilic period. Chapter 9 narrows the spectrum to list the chief representatives of the postexilic community. Chapters 2-4 describe the tribe of Judah, with the house of David in the central section (ch. 3). Chapters 5-7 review Israel, including the Transjordan tribes. The central focus of the genealogical lists is Levi (ch. 6), the most significant tribe for the Chronicler. The transition to the Chronicler's time begins with a return to the tribe of Benjamin and the family of Saul (8:1-9:1a), leading to the restoration of Jerusalem (9:1b-38).

Oral genealogies have three formal characteristics: segmentation, lineage, and fluidity *[Genealogy, p. 461]*. While the Chronicler's genealogies resemble oral genealogies, they are a literary composition. They are not homogeneous in form but contain a mixture of personal, clan, and geographic names, using varying terminology to express relationships. Often different parts seem to overlap and even contradict each other. They appear much more like oral genealogies, with a large degree of segmentation, varying degrees (or generations) of lineage, and a remarkable degree of fluidity [*Genealogies in Chronicles, p. 462*].

The disparities in length are notable; the Judahite list is over one hundred verses, with a long and detailed genealogy on the house of David. Transjordanian Manasseh is represented by a territorial description but with no real genealogical data. Levi includes a mix of forms, with much detail and a list of towns that resembles Joshua 21. Issachar is included as a military census in the days of David (1 Chron 7:1-2); in the MT, Zebulun is not represented at all. Manasseh and Ephraim are segmented and full of geographical information. The genealogies conclude with a second genealogy of Benjamin, which includes a list of inhabitants of Jerusalem.

For all this diversity, there is an order based on status that gives Judah priority and makes Levi central. Geography is a complementary ordering principle, but the prominence of Judah and Jerusalem is dominant. This is explained in the introduction to the genealogies of Israel in 1 Chronicles 5:1-2. The birthright of the firstborn was lost to Reuben as a punishment for his sin. The Chronicler parenthetically states that the birthright was given to the sons of Joseph. They received an honorable inheritance within the nation. But political priority came to Judah because Judah emerged as the leader of his brothers, according to the Genesis narrative (e.g., Gen 37:18-36; 43:1-14). Levi is central as the tribe ordained to maintain the order of the tabernacle.

1 Chronicles 1:1–2:2

Founding Ancestors

PREVIEW

Where do you come from? Who are your parents? These are common questions in any culture, but are prevalent in Mennonite cultures. In some circles, there is something called "the Mennonite game," which consists of individuals with Mennonite names finding out how they may be related. This is not idle talk, which is why it cannot be quenched, no matter how arcane it may seem to be. Identity and social location are important to every individual; they establish how people relate to each other and what responsibilities they may have to each other. At a more comprehensive level, every nation needs to establish its own self-justification *[History Writing, p. 469]*. For instance, the believers church needs to differentiate itself within the larger culture. All of these realities make the writing of history necessary. The book of Chronicles is a national history in the sense that Israel conceived of itself as a nation even though it was not an independent state. For the Chronicler, it continued to have a national history and identity.

History is a narrative of the activities of people. The briefest possible way to summarize a long history is to simply name the people. Such a history can have no significance unless the people named are known. The Chronicler knows his readers are familiar with the names he provides in his introduction, so he can list them without comment. All the names leading up to the sons of Israel (Jacob) are drawn from the book of Genesis. The narrative of Genesis and its people was a sacred text to the exiles of Judah and fundamental to their self-identity. The Chronicler could come to the point of his own history by appropriately selecting names from their Scriptures.

1 Chronicles 1:1–2:2

To position Israel among the nations of the world, Chronicles begins with the generations from Adam to Israel. Those nations begin with descendants of Japheth, the ones farthest away from Israel (1 Chron 1:5-7), then proceed to those of Ham (vv. 8-16) and Shem (vv. 17-23), which are nearer to Israel. This chapter is a condensed version of the genealogies found in Genesis 5, 11, 25, 35, and 36. Within the descendants of Abraham, the Chronicler first deals with Ishmael (1 Chron 1:28-33) and Esau (vv. 34-54), then proceeds to the focal point of his interest, the descendants of Israel. The genealogy is segmented, indicating the status of other nations at the point when Israel emerged as a nation. Israel is portrayed as a constituent member of a world order established by God at creation.

OUTLINE

Adam to Abraham, 1:1-27
Abraham to Israel, 1:28–2:2

EXPLANATORY NOTES

The genealogies found in Genesis 5 begin a third account of creation. Beginning with the origins of the human race, the Chronicler develops the significance of his community. Before the flood, humans had attempted to be gods (Gen 3:5); in grasping for the tree of knowledge, they made it their own prerogative to determine good and evil. Rebellion against the Creator, whom humans were to represent, led ultimately to the declaration of Lamech about what is good: revenge in full measure (Gen 4:23-24). The earth came to be filled with violence, leading to complete corruption of the human race (6:11). The flood was a reversal of creation: the waters burst up from below and came down from above (7:11). Theologically, this is to say that the waters separated at creation merged once again. Noah became a new beginning for the human race. Once again the human race was given the mandate of filling the earth in order that they might properly exercise dominion (9:1, 7). With the ten names of Genesis 5, the Chronicler takes us directly to the genealogy of Noah in Genesis 10; his goal is to lead his people to their place among the nations. His history begins with the names of Adam to Noah without explanation. Their significance depends on a knowledge of Genesis. His *chronikon* (universal history beginning with creation) presents an identity of Israel for their role and place in human order according to Scripture known to them.

Adam to Abraham 1:1-27

The introduction of ten prominent figures of antiquity leads to the three sons of Noah. The descendants of the sons of Noah are presented in segmented genealogies (vv. 5-23), listing approximately seventy nations for three sons (textual variants make an exact count impossible). The enumeration of approximately seventy nations is followed by another linear genealogy, again composed of ten members, beginning with Shem and culminating in Abram (vv. 24-27). The arrangement gives a portrait of the world after the flood, framed by an inclusio of the descendants of Adam and the descendants of Shem *[Inclusio, p. 467]*. The names of the introduction appear to function somewhat like other ancient king lists, which have a close relationship to genealogies. They connect contemporary generations to their ancient counterparts, a connection that has great significance. The Egyptian, Sumerian, and Babylonian king lists are the closest parallel to the genealogies of Genesis 5 and 11 (K. Sparks: 345-47; COS 1.37; 1.134, 1.135). The Sumerian version lists about ten antediluvian rulers (the number varies between copies) who are linked to known historical rulers after the flood. Both biblical and Sumerian lists are linear in form, begin with creation, and are interrupted by the flood. In Chronicles the ten names drawn from Genesis 5 provide a comprehensive history of the world before the flood. The Chronicler draws his conclusion with names found in Genesis 11:10-26, in the genealogy following the flood. These individuals, most never mentioned again, form the background for developing the main genealogical lines that contextualize Israel.

The general division of the nations among the three sons of Noah is clear: three spheres of peoples and lands converge in the region of Israel. The world is described from an Israelite point of view, looking in the three directions of inhabited lands. A number of the names used by the Chronicler, such as *Magog* and *Tiras* in 1 Chronicles 1:5, are not geographically identified in other ancient Near Eastern texts, but the intended locales in the north are evident (e.g., Ezek 38:15). The territory of Japheth lies to the north and west of Israel. These nations occupied territories in ancient Ararat (*Urartu*) to the north and east, the most distant region being the Medes (*Madai*) south of the Caspian Sea. This territory also extended west through Asia Minor as far west as Greece (*Javan*). The descendants of Ham are located south of the Mediterranean in North Africa and in the Arabian Peninsula, including Palestine and Syria. Ham stands for Egypt in several biblical texts (Pss 78:51; 105:23, 27;

106:22). Canaan was one of three Egyptian provinces east of the Mediterranean. The descendants of Shem begin in the east in Mesopotamia, spread westward along the Euphrates River, and south into Arabia.

Nimrod was legendary in the region of Mesopotamia, in the areas of Babylon and Akkad rather than the southern territories of Cush (Gen 10:8-12). He has been identified with such legendary heroes as Gilgamesh or mighty kings like Sargon of Akkad. Since the Chronicler omitted the verses of Nimrod's identification in Genesis, the geographical disparity is not noticed. There evidently was a territorial overlap between the descendants of Ham and Shem in Mesopotamia (Sarna 1989: 72). It has been observed that Nimrod and Nebuchadnezzar are the first and last Babylonian rulers of Chronicles (cf. 2 Chron 36:6-13) *[Chronology in Chronicles, p. 460]*.

Shem is of particular interest to the history of Israel (1 Chron 1:17-22). He is the great-grandfather of Eber (vv. 18-19), the eponymous ancestor of the Hebrews *[Eponym, p. 466]*. Though the Israelites lived in Canaan, their ethnic identity and language was with the Semitic peoples. The lists are geographic as well as ethnographic *[Ethnographic, p. 466]*. Elam is located east of ancient Babylon and just north of the Persian Gulf (in modern southwestern Iran). Elamite was not directly related to either Semitic or Indo-European languages. Canaan fell outside the geographic area, as it belonged to Ham, but it was the homeland of the Israelites, whose origins went back to Mesopotamia, as the Chronicler will explain (vv. 24-27).

Eber had two sons, Peleg and Joktan (v. 19). The verbal root of Peleg (*plg*) means to "split or divide," a significance that is observed in the Chronicler's source (cf. Gen 10:25). The Akkadian *palgu* means "canal," which refers to a river. In Hellenistic times (the fourth to second centuries BCE) the region where the Upper Euphrates and Balih Rivers join (south of ancient Haran) was called Phalga. Peleg might be the ancestor of the northern Semites (in the area of Syria). The division of the earth, however, is more likely a reference to the division of languages at the tower of Babel, which is followed by the ethnic designation of the Semites, to which Abraham belonged (Gen 11:10, 27). As Semites, Israelites specifically identified their origins with the Arameans (cf. Deut 26:5). Abraham and his family lived with the Arameans in the northern area of Haran, near the Euphrates (Gen 11:31-32). In the latter part of his life, Abraham left the Arameans to travel south to Canaan (12:4-6). Both the language divisions and the territory of the Arameans were significant in the history of the Israelites.

The Chronicler's sketch of the entire world of nations has taken up the names of the three sons of Noah in reverse order, concluding with Shem (v. 17), who then comes first in the linear genealogy of ten names leading to Abraham. The Chronicler turns his attention to the ancestral line that will lead to Israel and the other nations descended from Abraham (1 Chron 1:24-27). This highly condensed lineage again does not indicate relationships between the names; they can only be understood with reference to their source in Genesis 11:10-26.

Abraham to Israel 1:28-2:2

The heading to this section names Abraham's descendants in the order found in his burial account (Gen 25:9), but the family genealogy of the two sons begins with Ishmael, as in the Genesis narrative (Gen 25:12, 19). The descendants of Ishmael are all located to the south and east of Palestine (northwestern Arabia). A third line of descent from Abraham through Keturah is incorporated without introduction (1 Chron 1:32). The Chronicler goes back to Genesis 25:1-4, before the death of Abraham, to include the children through his second wife (in Chronicles referred to as a concubine, or auxiliary wife). The descendants through Keturah range far afield to the south and southeast of Israel. This portion of the genealogy concludes with the announcement of Isaac's birth.

The children descended through Abraham and Sarah are found in two separate narrative sections in Genesis (25:19-26; 36:10-13). The Chronicler creates an introduction for them in 1 Chronicles 1:34b. He follows an almost exclusive practice of referring to Jacob as Israel. The only two exceptions are in the citation of a psalm (1 Chron 16:13, 17; cf. Ps 105:6). The introduction to Abraham's descendants is followed by a long section enumerating individuals directly or indirectly associated with Esau (1 Chron 1:35-54) and a listing of the twelve sons of Israel (2:1-2).

The descendants of Esau are significantly abridged and adapted from their source in Genesis 36:2-14. The Chronicler moves directly from the descendants of Esau to Seir (1 Chron 1:38-42; cf. Gen 36:20-30). No genealogical link from Esau to Seir is provided in Genesis or Chronicles. An etymological link is made at the birth of Esau (Gen 25:25); the firstborn of Rebekah was both red (Edom) and hairy (Seir). The geographical location of Seir is uncertain. Edom is generally east of the southern Arabah (the rift valley through the Jordan and the Dead Sea and extending southward); a traditional site for Mount Seir is located there (Jebel esh-Shera'), southeast of the Dead

Sea. Seir often appears as a synonym for Edom (Gen 32:3; Num 24:18). Seir was the home of the Horites until they were displaced by the Edomites (Deut 2:12; cf. Gen 36:20). The designation of Seir probably changed over time.

Teman is a descendant of Eliphaz (1 Chron 1:36). The author of the book of Job consistently identifies Job's friend Eliphaz as a Temanite (Job 2:11; 4:1; 15:1; 22:1; 42:7, 9). The land of Uz in Job 1:1 was located in the territory of Seir (1 Chron 1:42; cf. Gen 36:28). The appendix to the Greek translation of the book of Job places Uz on the borders of Edom and Arabia and makes Job one of the kings of Edom. The Chronicler also makes Teman a territory in the land of Edom (1 Chron 1:45); Teman can be a synonym for Edom (cf. Jer 49:20).

In the Chronicler's genealogy as given in the MT, Timna and Amalek are children of Eliphaz and grandchildren of Esau (1 Chron 1:35-36). In Genesis, Timna is a female concubine of Eliphaz, and together they are the parents of Amalek (Gen 36:12). Timna is also said to be a daughter of Seir and sister of Lotan in both Genesis and Chronicles (Gen 36:20-22; 1 Chron 1:38-39). The Greek translations of 1 Chronicles 1:36 agree with Genesis: Amalek is a son of Timna, who is the concubine of Eliphaz. The MT of 1 Chronicles 1:36 may be a misreading of the Genesis text (Curtis and Madsen: 76). But the textual problem may have been in the source of the Chronicler's genealogy, resulting in Timna being made a daughter of Eliphaz, according to the MT. The Hebrew text of the Chronicler's source may have been abbreviated, with the exact relationship between Timna and Amalek not stated, as is the practice elsewhere in the Chronicler's genealogies. Most likely, Amalek is a son of Timna (as reflected when the NIV follows LXX Vaticanus in v. 36). Territorially, Timna may have been the mining region just to the north of Elath, on the Gulf of Aqaba. The Amalekites were traditional enemies of Israel (Exod 17:8-16; 1 Sam 15:2-3), dwelling in the southern desert area known as the Negev. The Negev is a triangular area with corners at the tip of the Gulf of Aqaba, to the southern point of the Dead Sea, and west to the Mediterranean *[Negev, p. 467]*.

The Chronicler introduces the early kings of Edom with a direct citation from his source (1 Chron 1:43; cf. Gen 36:31). The eight kings listed hail from different cities and do not form a dynastic succession. The writer presents Edom's past up to the time of the inception of the Israelite monarchy, which is the beginning of his own narrative history (1 Chron 10:1). Hadad, of the royal house of Edom, is remembered as one of the kings that was an adversary of Solomon (1 Kings 11:14-15). Two kings named Hadad (meaning *thunder*) are enumerated in the king list (1 Chron 1:46, 50). Previous to Solomon, David conquered an Edomite king in the expansion of his empire (2 Sam 8:13-14), a feat that is remembered in the superscription to Psalm 60. The Edomite king Saul (the same spelling as the Israelite king) is said to be from Rehoboth on the river (1 Chron 1:48). The unqualified term "the river" refers to the Euphrates in other contexts (e.g., Gen 31:21), but in an Edomite milieu such a remote location would hardly be indicated. Monarchies at such an early period in Edomite history are unknown in any other sources, and there is no archaeological evidence for a state in Edom before the eighth century. For this reason, some historians have proposed that this king list for Edom has been confused with Aram. The two names are almost identical in Hebrew; the names were sometimes confused, as is indicated in conflicting traditions (e.g., 2 Kings 16:6; cf. 2 Chron 28:17). The Chronicler, however, describes a series of regional dominions in Edom before the beginning of a unified kingdom in Israel.

A list of Edomite chiefs succeeds the king list (1 Chron 1:51-54). Chiefs such as Timna and Oholibamah are not to be identified with the individuals named previously (Klein 2006: 79). The source in Genesis provides the names of a series of chiefs without chronological relationship (Gen 36:40), but the Chronicler presents these as succeeding the previous list of kings. Genesis states that these were chiefs of local areas (v. 43b), a phrase omitted in Chronicles, perhaps suggesting that they were national rather than regional leaders. The ancient poem in Exodus, praising God for his redemption, uses three parallel terms to describe the rulers of Edom, Moab, and Canaan (Exod 15:15), all being equal in rank and distinction. Many of the names of chieftains in Edom are place names, which may indicate a regional jurisdiction.

Leaders of Teman and Kenaz have previously been listed among the descendants of Esau (1 Chron 1:36; cf. Gen 36:11, 15). Teman is a region in northern Edom. Caleb, who along with Joshua entered the Promised Land, belonged to the Kenizzites and inherited the territory around Hebron (Josh 14:13-15; Judg 1:12-13; cf. 1 Chron 4:13-16). Othniel, also a Kenizzite, became the first judge in Israel (Judg 3:7-11). Oholibamah is named as the wife of Esau (Gen 36:2, 5, 14, 18, 25), but she is not to be confused with the chief named in 1 Chronicles 1:52. The latter may be a man (Klein 2006: 79). The passages naming Esau's wife are not included in Chronicles.

The order of the sons of Israel in 1 Chronicles 2:1-2 is unique. No mention is made of the mothers of the descendants, though the Chronicler's source is organized according to the wives and concubines of Israel (cf. Gen 35:23-26; 46:8-27). The Chronicler begins with the six sons of Leah and ends with the sons of Zilpah (Gad and Asher). The two sons of Bilhah (Dan and Naphtali) are not mentioned in sequence; Joseph and Benjamin, the two sons of Rachel, are preceded and succeeded by the sons of a female servant. The names of the descendants of Israel are always given as twelve but are found in various combinations. Where the sons of Jacob are named, the names include Joseph and Levi (Gen 35:22b-26). If the tribal territories are named, Joseph and Levi are omitted, but Joseph's sons, Ephraim and Manasseh, are named (Josh 14:1-5). The Chronicler follows the first pattern in 1 Chronicles 2:1-2, but the genealogies are inclusive. Manasseh and Ephraim have genealogies as territories in Israel (7:14-29). Levi receives an extensive genealogy (ch. 6), which is obviously the most important for the Chronicler. The Chronicler assumes the variables in the number twelve as applied to Jacob's sons.

THE TEXT IN BIBLICAL CONTEXT

God for the World

The Chronicler provides an understanding of humanity from texts he considered to have divine authority. He begins his history with Adam, providing continuity between the very origins of humanity and his own time. In his thinking, the role of Israel is unique and divinely ordained. His objective is to portray Israel within the circle of nations and to bring his introduction to a climax with Israel. His genealogies are unlike those of Genesis; in Genesis, genealogies are inserted into the historical narrative, providing a thematic and chronological framework *[Genealogies in Chronicles, p. 462]*. Their literary purpose is historiographical, somewhat akin to the Mesopotamian lists (Levin 2003: 234-37). The genealogies in Chronicles are schematic, having gone through a purposeful process of editing and arranging. Jerome, in his famous "Helmeted Preface" (Prologus galeatus) to his translation of Kings, gives a brief review of the twenty-two books of the canon. He refers to "Words of the Days" (Chronicles) as a "chronicle of the entire divine history" (Jerome: 1893, trans. Fremantle).

The Chronicler understands the world as both a unity and diversity and believes that Israel has a role within the family of nations as a witness to all nations. His world extends (in contemporary terms) from southern Russia in the north to Ethiopia in the south, from Spain in the west to India in the east. He is true to his own history as he found it in Genesis; his own people have come to occupy a land that was once the home of others. His ancestry is to be found among the descendants of Shem, although Canaan, the ancestor of the land that bears his name, is among the descendants of Ham. The descendants of Shem can only occupy the land of Ham as outsiders, those who have come to it from elsewhere (Knoppers 2004a: 293). Their story in time and place is one of divine ordination, called from among the nations to bring divine blessing to the nations.

The Chronicler continues the theological tradition of the prophets. Israel in the exile had been a blind and deaf nation. The prophet looked for a day of renewal, a time when Israel would come to understand the name of God, that all nations might know the work of God.

> Bring forth a blind people, though they have eyes,
>   A deaf people, though they have ears.
> Let all the nations come together,
>   Let all the peoples be gathered.
> Who among them has declared this?
>   Who could tell us of the former things?
> Let them produce their witnesses, that they may be right,
>   Let them hear and say, "It is true."
> "You are my witnesses," says the LORD,
>   "My servant, whom I have chosen,
> That you may know and believe me,
>   That you may understand, I AM HE,
> Before me, no God was formed,
>   After me, none will come,
> I, I am the LORD,
>   No one saves apart from me." (Isa 43:8-11 AT)

The Chronicler does not use the terms of election, as found in Isaiah, but he means the same thing. Isaiah does not mean selection from among the nations when he speaks of election. The prophet repeatedly speaks of God's creative work in the formation of Israel; creation is the poetic parallel to the term "election."

> Now, hear, Jacob my servant,
>   Israel, whom I have chosen.
> Thus says the LORD who made you,
>   The one who formed you from the womb, he will help you.
> Do not fear, my servant Jacob,
>   Jeshurun, whom I have chosen. (Isa 44:1-2 AT)

God's choice was an act of will to carry out a plan. God's purpose was the creation of a people so that the majesty of his name might be known in the world. In his genealogy the Chronicler is making just this point. God created all the nations, but his interest is the nation Israel, created by God for a particular calling. That calling is not less urgent in his day than at the time of the prophet's proclamation.

Israelites can be traced through time as descendants of Adam, Noah, Abraham, and Isaac; yet they must be located geographically among a great diversity of peoples. Though the nations are linguistically, geographically, and ethnically dispersed, they share a common origin. At the same time, this diversity of nations exists in specific places and regions. Many names have geographical associations: Cush (Ethiopia or Sudan), Egypt, and Canaan (1 Chron 1:8). The Chronicler himself was situated within the Persian state of Yehud. His closest ethnographic connections were with the peoples situated to the south and southeast of Judah *[Ethnographic, p. 466]*. With this specific geographical interest, he develops material about Ishmael, Keturah, Esau, Seir, and the Edomite kings. His genealogies of Judah and Simeon will develop many of these connections (1 Chron 2:3–4:43). By situating the emergence of Israel among peoples in other lands, the Chronicler develops a view of the world in which the experience of Israel has a universal significance.

Israel among the Nations

The most significant aspects of the Chronicler's use of Genesis are his distinct additions. In his transition from the world after the flood to the ancestors of Israel (1 Chron 1:24-27), the Chronicler brings us to *Abram* and then adds, *that is, Abraham* (v. 27). This explanation is based on his reading of God making a covenant with Abram and giving him the sign of circumcision (Gen 17:1-14). This clarification bridges the genealogy of Abram to the descendants of Israel in the next section. The change of name calls attention to the creation of the chosen people. Among the descendants of Noah, the Chronicler has drawn special attention to Shem. Among the descendants of Shem, special privilege is given to the descendants of Abraham and Isaac. While the genealogy in Genesis 10:1-32 gives very little attention to the ancestors of Israel, inserting this genealogy in 1 Chronicles 1:5-23 links Adam and Abraham to narrow the focus of the descendants of Noah to the descendants of Isaac. The Chronicler never directly makes reference to the creation of Israel as the means by which all nations may be blessed (cf. Gen 12:1-3), but that is the effect of his presentation.

A second change made by the Chronicler to his source is the way he introduces Keturah (1 Chron 1:32). The Chronicler makes no mention of Abraham marrying again following the death of Sarah (cf. Gen 25:1). The lineage of Keturah is inserted to include all of Abraham's descendants, even though no mention of her was made in the introduction to the genealogy (1 Chron 1:28). Keturah is introduced as Abraham's concubine rather than his wife (v. 32). The Chronicler has not included the explanation that Abraham gave gifts to all the children of his concubines, and gave all his possessions to Isaac (Gen 25:5-6). The point in Genesis is that Isaac is the only true heir of Abraham. Isaac, the miracle child, is the only eligible successor to Abraham and the promise; he is the means of God creating a nation for himself. In order to make clear that Isaac is exclusively God's chosen for the creation of the nation, the Chronicler includes Keturah as one of the concubines (Assis: 293). The Chronicler recognizes the importance of the peoples to the south and southeast of Israel, but they range far afield and are more distant from Abraham's children through Sarah and Hagar. Isaac is given preeminence, consistent with the introduction to Abraham's descendants (1 Chron 1:28), where he is named first even though he is the second child to be born. The birth of Isaac is repeated (v. 34a) with the introduction to his sons (v. 34b).

Israel and Ethnic Relations

The treatment of Esau in Chronicles is notable for its length and the selection of material included. The Chronicler includes a genealogy of Esau, a king list, and a list of chiefs. Isaac is named first as the chosen son, but the sequence for the sons of Isaac is Esau and Israel. The situation between Esau and Jacob in Genesis is quite distinct from that of Isaac and Ishmael. There is never any question about Isaac being the chosen son, as Ishmael is the son of a concubine. God announces to Abraham that a son of Sarah will be his heir (Gen 17:15-21), a child born at the appointed time, exactly as God had said (21:1-7). Ishmael shall be a great nation as Abraham's child, but Abraham's descendants shall be known through Isaac alone (21:12). With Isaac's sons, a struggle for primacy between Esau and Jacob begins at birth and continues throughout their lives. It was divinely announced that the struggle of the twins in Rebekah's womb would end with the elder serving the younger (25:22-23), and the younger is born grasping the heel of his brother (vv. 24-26). In respect of this, the second son is named Jacob; the name "deceiver" etymogyically anticipates the impending struggle between the sons of Isaac. The struggle was made manifest with the sale of the birthright and intensified with the deception that led to Isaac blessing the younger son (Gen 27:28-29, 39-40). On the advice of his parents (27:41–28:5), Jacob fled for his life: even on his return from Haran, he had to resolve relations with his brother (33:1-4). Twin brothers were a very different situation than the son of a concubine. Unlike the situation with Isaac, the reason for the choice of Jacob as God's elect is not explained in Genesis. The Chronicler seems to be following Genesis when he names Esau first and reports at length about the inhabitants of Edom (Assis: 296). Though the Chronicler's goal is to demonstrate the election of Israel, he is true to his authoritative sources in acknowledging Esau as the firstborn.

The list of kings and the list of chiefs in Chronicles are presented as two separate entities, each with their own introduction. The list of early kings of Edom acknowledges the initial primacy of Edom, recognizing the claim of Esau as the elect son (Assis: 302). This claim, however, was nullified with the end of kingship, pronounced summarily in the announcement that Hadad, the last king of Edom, died (1 Chron 1:51a). A list of chiefs in Edom follows. The superiority of Esau over Israel ended; the rejection of Edom is the Chronicler's way of establishing the election of the sons of Israel.

The choice of Edom was a very live issue in the days of the Chronicler. The destruction of the temple had left Judah in great despair, with a sense that they were rejected as the chosen people. For this reason the prophet Isaiah could describe them as blind and deaf (Isa 42:18-19). The people of Edom took full advantage of this despair. The gloating of Edom at the fall of Jerusalem would not be forgotten (Obad 10-15). Judah would repossess its land from the Edomites, a reversal of the dominance of Edom over Israel (vv. 17-19). The prophet Malachi began his message with a polemic against fearing the election of Edom (Mal 1:2-5). "I have loved you" is the phrase used for the ratification of a covenant; Jacob is the brother chosen by God. "Esau I have hated" is the phrase used to describe the one not chosen. The mountain of Esau will become desolate. The prophet Joel looked for the day of the Lord in the restoration of Israel; Edom along with Egypt is named as responsible for the crushing of Jerusalem (Joel 3:19-21). The Chronicler was fully aware of this sense of losing national identity. It was important for him to acknowledge both the claims of Edom as present in his sources and also the promise to Israel in God's plan for the nations.

THE TEXT IN THE LIFE OF THE CHURCH
The Church among the Nations

In the days of the Chronicler, the people of Yehud were not a significant political, social, or spiritual force. They appear to have lacked cohesion, making it necessary for the Chronicler to place much emphasis on their common ancestry. They needed to understand the inclusive nature of Israel. No matter how events may have scattered these people, their distinction and calling came as a collective whole. In this chapter the Chronicler has reviewed all the nations in such a way as to make the twelve sons of Israel the center of history. The unity and totality conceived by the Chronicler was not visibly evident to the small group of people that returned from Babylon. The exile of the state of Israel and Samaria, its capital, had taken place in the eighth century (e.g., 2 Kings 17:9-11), making the identity of the northern tribes obscure. But for the Chronicler, unity continued to the present, and the people needed to know that.

As in Yehud, the church generally is weak in its social and political influence; for all the vitality it still manifests, Christianity in North America and the West more generally is a weak culture. James Davidson Hunter says:

> [It is] weak insofar as it is fragmented in its core beliefs and organization, without a collective coherent identity and mission, and often divided within itself, often with unabated hostility. Thus, for all the talk of world-changing and all the good intentions that motivate it, the Christian community is not, on the whole, remotely close to a position where it could actually change the world in any significant way. (Hunter: 274)

Christians do have important influence in interpersonal settings or in particular locales. But the church as a whole is politically marginalized and has no realistic strategies or positions capable of changing societies and civilizations. The church has no significance whatever among the power of nations.

Political power and influence were not the goal of the Chronicler, nor should they be for the church. Power has tendencies toward conquest and domination. Christian activism, as influential in the political sphere at various times, has embraced a means to power that breeds resentment, anger, and bitterness for the injuries perceived to have been suffered. Christians need to have a faithful presence, knowing that this presence is their calling. The goal of the church is not to change the world, but to be present among all nations, faithful to the values and truths that are to represent the presence of God in the world. The church should be visible among the nations in a way that is not just religious. Recognizable rituals, such as church attendance and participation in the covenant confessions of baptism and communion, are important, not only to the believers but also as a confession to the surrounding world. A faithful presence calls Christians to enact the shalom of God in the circumstances in which God has placed them and to actively seek it on behalf of others.

Such a concept is not new. An apologetic of the early Christian era is found in a famous Epistle to Diognetus, written by an unknown "disciple of the apostles," in all likelihood the tutor of Marcus Aurelius. Though romanticized, it is worth quoting:

> Christians are distinguished from other men neither by country, nor language, nor the customs which they observe. For they neither inhabit cities of their own, nor employ a peculiar form of speech, nor lead a life which is marked out by any singularity. The course of conduct which they follow has not been devised by any speculation or deliberation of inquisitive men; nor do they, like some, proclaim themselves the advocates of any merely human doctrines. But, inhabiting Greek as well as barbarian cities . . . and following the customs of the natives in respect to clothing, food, and the rest of their ordinary conduct, they display to us their wonderful and confessedly striking method of life. They dwell in their own countries, but simply as sojourners. As citizens, they share in all things with others, and yet endure all things as if foreigners. Every foreign land is to them as their native country, and every land of their birth as a land of strangers. They marry, as do all [others]; they beget children, but they do not destroy their offspring. They have a common table, but not a common bed. They are in the flesh, but they do not live after the flesh. They pass their days on earth, but they are the citizens of heaven. They obey the prescribed laws, and at the same time surpass the laws by their lives. They love all men, and are persecuted by all. They are unknown and condemned; they are put to death, and restored to life. They are poor, yet make many rich; they are in lack of all things, and yet abound in all; they are dishonored, and yet in their very dishonor are glorified. They are evil spoken of, and yet are justified; they are reviled, and bless; they are insulted, and repay the insult with honor; they do good, yet are punished as evildoers. (Hunter: 284)

This description has parallels with the Chronicler that should be observed. While the province of Yehud was ethnic, with a very specific culture, Israel remains the focus of history. In the structure of the genealogy, Israel is divinely called but has become widely scattered. The Chronicler is concerned to identify Israel; not all of Israel shared the same nationality or language. They were all to share the same manner of covenant life. Likewise, the church is to be visible through the physical presence of its assemblies.

This description also has parallels with the ideals of Anabaptism. The movement began with a group of young intellectuals who were followers of Huldrych Zwingli. They rebelled against Zwingli's apparent subservience to the magistrates. The church, which to them was the redeemed community, was to be separated from the state, which for them was to punish wrongdoers. Most rejected the use of the sword by Christians for maintaining social order, and they refused to swear civil oaths. At the time of the Reformation, these were very radical statements by believers seeking to be faithful to the Christian calling. Their desire was to be a faithful presence, in contrast to a church that resisted reform. The revolutionary implications of their teaching led to their expulsion from one city after another. Many outstanding leaders were executed or died in prison. Hans Hut died in prison in Augsburg; Balthasar Hubmaier was executed in Vienna; Melchior Hofmann was imprisoned and died in Strassburg (Strasbourg).

Each generation of Christians must discern the ways in which they may be a faithful presence. This comprehensive genealogy of the Chronicler is a call to that ideal. The Christian calling goes back to God's purposes, which began with Adam and came to be focused in Israel, then in Christ. For the Christian, the ideals of the calling of Israel find their physical presence in the worshiping church.

The Church and Related Faiths

The Chronicler goes to considerable length to develop the ancient kingdom of Edom, which was part of their ancestral heritage. The nation southeast of the Dead Sea and thus east of the deep rift valley (the Arabah) was part of their ancestral heritage. The Edomites were brothers as well as neighbors and could become Israelites (Deut 23:7-8). Israel was never to disparage an Edomite. Yet as is evident in prophetic works such as Obadiah, there was much hostility between Edom and Israel. The satisfaction of Edom at the exile of Israel had left a legacy that carried into the days of the Chronicler. Irrespective of this pleasure at the misfortunes of Israel, the Chronicler does not revise history. The preeminence of Edom is acknowledged in the early kingship of that nation and its later sequence of chiefs. But the promise of the kingdom of Yahweh, as David calls it (1 Chron 28:5), was through Israel. The Chronicler is very clear about the children of Isaac; they are Esau and Israel (1 Chron 1:34b). He names the children of Israel (2:1), not the sons of Jacob. The election of God is found in the change of two distinguished names: Abram to Abraham and Jacob to Israel. By this means the Chronicler distinguishes the role of Israel in the purposes of God. Edom receives its due recognition as descendants of Isaac, but the primacy of Israel is prominent.

The church has a conviction analogous to that of the Chronicler in its relationship to Jews and Muslims. Jews, Christians, and Muslims all worship the God of Abraham, Isaac, and Israel. The inescapable divide comes over their understanding of God and salvation. For Christians, Christ is the very representative of God the Father; Isaiah saw the glory of Christ in his vision of the exalted king (John 12:39-42). Christ alone is the way, the truth, and the life as John says it: "No one comes to the Father except through me" (John 14:6).

The confession that Jesus is God revealed in human form, the one who is to be called by "the name that is above every name" (Phil 2:6-11), is not acceptable in Jewish or Muslim faith. While all three faiths share in a common heritage, their theology of God and salvation cannot be reconciled. It is not possible for Jews and Christians to have a common theology of the Hebrew Bible, because Christians are committed to following New Testament interpretations of the older covenant. Luke tells of an Egyptian official reading Isaiah 53:7-8 and pondering the question that biblical scholars into modern times have discussed: "Who is the prophet talking about, himself or someone else?" (Acts 8:34). Whatever may have been the referent of the servant in the time of the prophet, a point on which Jews and Christians might agree, there is no question about the identity of the servant in Christian theology. Philip began at that very Scripture and taught about Jesus. In discussing how not to conduct Jewish-Christian dialogue, Jonathan D. Levenson sums up by saying, "Participants in Jewish-Christian dialogue often speak as if Jews and Christians agreed about God but disagreed about Jesus. They have forgotten that in a very real sense orthodox Christians believe Jesus is God" (Levenson: 37).

The confession of the Nicene Creed, the definition of orthodox Christianity, is just as unacceptable to Muslims, for whom Jesus is not more than a prophet. This is understandable in the origins of Islam. Though the early influences on Muhammad are obscure, he was influenced by both Christians and Jews through merchant caravans passing through Mecca (Noss and Grangaard: 548). At commercial fairs, representatives of both these faiths would address the crowds. Some of Muhammad's acquaintances in Mecca were versed in the traditions of both Jews and Christians. In particular, his employer Khadija had a cousin by name of Waraqa who was well versed in the traditions of Jews and Christians, as well as the poet Umaiya (born Abi'l-Salt). Muhammad was influenced by Nestorian conceptions and popular traditions that denied the affirmations of the Nicene Creed.

The form of Christianity that influenced Muhammad was a grave compromise of the orthodox doctrines of Christ established at the first council of Nicaea (325). There were important reasons why Athanasius so opposed Arianism, the doctrine holding that God is too remote to come into direct contact with humans. Arianism held that Christ was neither God nor man, but something between the two. Such a compromise did not definitively make Christ the final revelation of God as his incarnation in human flesh. The Nicene Creed was adopted as the official expression of Christianity by all of Christendom at that time. Later, Nestorian Christianity, which claimed that there were two separate persons in the incarnate Christ, was condemned at the council of Ephesus (431), though in the following centuries Nestorian Christians carried out vast missionary enterprises in central Asia. The views of Nestorian Christianity, however, could not be regarded by orthodox Christians as an acceptable understanding of the Son of God.

In spite of irreconcilable differences, the common heritage of Jews, Christians, and Muslims needs to be acknowledged and its potential impact must be affirmed. Lamin Sanneh was appointed D. Willis James Professor of Missions and World Christianity and professor of history at Yale Divinity School. Gambian-born, Sanneh is a descendant from the Nyanchos, an ancient African royal line (Bonk: 112–16). He was raised in an orthodox Muslim family; emphasis was placed on the community, tradition, fidelity to past models, respect for parents and elders, and rote memorization of knowledge. Sanneh had no access to the Bible or to a church; the Qur'an was his only source for knowledge of Jesus. He kept his interest to himself because his teachers would react unpredictably and his Muslim friends would be scandalized. Sanneh embraced Jesus as the one who brings salvation. Because of suspicion and skepticism in his community, his most difficult step was his resolve to join a Christian church. The Methodist church he approached put off his desire to be baptized and asked him to go to the Catholic church. He did that for a year, but with the same result. It took over two years until he was finally baptized in the Methodist church, as a result of an ultimatum he gave them.

Sanneh's efforts to study theology were equally difficult. He was denied permission to study at the mission school and was told the decision was final, with no appeals to the mission headquarters in

London. Sanneh explains that he was so profoundly affected by the message of Jesus, so inexplicably transformed at the roots of faith and trust, that he felt himself in the grips of an undeniable impetus to give himself to God, whatever his ultimate career path. He never had cause to fret about the work to which God might call him, so steadfast are God's promises.

It should not be surprising that there are those such as Sanneh who might find their way to Christian faith from the traditions of Islam. The danger is that hostilities breed suspicion and fear that impede the inquiries of an honest seeker. Hostilities and differences cannot be denied, but neither can the reality of a common heritage. Like the Chronicler, Christians need to find ways to acknowledge and affirm their history in Judaism and be aware of its influence in Islam. Realities and experiences of the present must not blind us to the possibilities of reconciliation and redemption.

1 Chronicles 2:3–4:23
Royal Family

PREVIEW

Family rivalry is one of the most painful and most ironic experiences of human life. From the beginning, humans were created male and female, to provide for unity and harmony between siblings. Instead, the curse on Eve was that the bearing of children would be a pain. In the very next chapter, one of her sons kills his brother. Such is the history of human families: the most painful of conflicts are those within families. All of us know children who do not speak with their parents or with each other, a pain aggravated by the intimacy they once shared. At the end of his life, Jacob would say to Pharaoh, "Few and troublesome have been the years of my life" (Gen 47:9 AT). Though Jacob shared in the responsibility of the conflict and violence among his sons, the pain he experienced in their conniving and treachery cannot be imagined. There was nothing orderly in the relationships of the twelve sons of Israel. But for the Chronicler, all this was part of divine providence in working everything together for good, as Joseph would say to his fearful brothers (Gen 50:20). The genealogies of the Chronicler indicate how he understood divine providence to be at work.

The genealogy of Judah is the longest and most complex genealogical unit in the Bible *[Genealogy, p. 461]*. It provides the history of the royal family of Judah down to the Chronicler's day. The promise to David, the anointed descendant of Judah (1 Sam 16:1-14), was of paramount importance to the Chronicler, since this promise pointed the way to the future for his community. Judah was also the most important tribe in the postexilic community. The tribal history of

Judah is arranged to put the family history of David at the center. It is arranged in the form of a chiasm *[Chiasm, p. 465]*. The royal genealogy in Chronicles is introduced with the Judahite ancestors of David in chapter 2. David's descendants are recorded in chapter 3. The tribal history is resumed and concluded in chapter 4. The final section of the Judahite history appears to be a collection of various sources about the tribe. These genealogical records often cannot be connected directly with Judah or with each other.

Judah is the first to be considered in the tribes of Israel, though Judah was not the firstborn, and he was not entitled to the birthright. The Chronicler provides a justification for Judah being the first in the genealogies of the tribes when he introduces the sons of Reuben:

> *The sons of Reuben, the firstborn of Israel—he was the firstborn, but when he defiled his father's marriage bed, his rights as firstborn were given to the sons of Joseph son of Israel, so he was not registered as the firstborn. Although Judah prevailed among his brothers and a ruler came from him, the birthright belonged to Joseph—the sons of Reuben the firstborn of Israel.* (1 Chron 5:1-3a AT)

In this lengthy explanation, the Chronicler makes two points for his presentation of the kingdom of Israel. Reuben lost the birthright through indiscretion (cf. Gen 35:22; 49:3-4). Judah became the leader of Israel. The reference to Joseph is not directly relevant to these two points (Williamson 1977a: 89-95). There is no justification for the birthright passing to the sons of Joseph. In explaining that Reuben is not first in the genealogy, the Chronicler goes out of his way to establish the distinction of the sons of Joseph among the tribes. Jacob had claimed the sons of Joseph as his own in Genesis 48:5-6; Joseph would be the father of other sons born to him. The consequence is that Ephraim and Manasseh have the full status of sons in the tribal league. For the Chronicler, the Northern Kingdom had a distinguished place in the family of Israel. Judah received primacy in succession because he surpassed his brothers and became the father of a great ruler. The Chronicler therefore placed Judah first in reckoning the history of Israel.

The goal of the Chronicler was to link the families of his own day with those who preceded the exile to Babylon. In the central section, the descendants of David are given in segmented and linear genealogies, providing clear lines of succession for all periods. Linear genealogies were sufficient during the period of the monarchy. Segmented genealogies were used to relate status and relationships within the Davidic family. These include the relationship between

David's sons in the early period, and relationships between Davidic families living in the exilic and postexilic times.

OUTLINE
Records of Judah, 2:3-55
Davidic Family, 3:1-24
More Records of Judah, 4:1-23

EXPLANATORY NOTES
The Chronicler begins and ends with the descendants of Shelah, the surviving son of Judah (1 Chron 2:3-8; 4:21-23). The sons of Perez (2:4) are expanded in greater detail (4:1-20), further complementing the initial introduction of the sons of Judah. The middle section of this chiasm begins and ends with the family of David *[Chiasm, p. 465]*. The Davidic clans are introduced with their eponymous ancestor Ram, son of Hezron (2:9-17) *[Eponym, p. 466]*. The family of Caleb, brother of Ram, is introduced (2:18-24), then the family of the oldest brother, Jerahmeel (vv. 25-33). The genealogy continues with further descendants of Jerahmeel (vv. 34-41), then returns to the descendants of Caleb (vv. 42-55). The detailed account of the Davidic family follows. Extended relations of the Davidic family through their ancestor Hezron are provided within this inclusio *[Inclusio, p. 467]*. The Chronicler has arranged his history of Judah to call attention to the central importance of the Davidic clans within the territory of Judah:

A^1 Davidic family descended from Ram (2:9-17)
   B^1 Calebite families in Judah (2:18-24)
      C^1 Jerahmeelite families in Judah (2:25-33)
      C^2 Expansion of Jerahmeelite families (2:34-41)
   B^2 Calebite settlements in Judah (2:42-55)
A^2 Davidic descendants to Persian period (3:1-24)

Records of Judah 2:3-55

2:3-9 Sons of Judah
Judah had five sons, three born to a Canaanite woman, and two to Tamar, his daughter-in-law. Perez, the oldest son of Tamar, was the son to carry on the royal line. Er died without descendants, as did Onan (Gen 38:10). Zerah, second son of Tamar, was father of Zimri (1 Chron 2:6), known in Joshua as Zabdi (Josh 7:1), a phonetic variant

of the same name. Achar (also spelled Achan), son of Zimri, violated the covenant through procuring that which belonged solely to God at Jericho. The "troubler [ʿoker] of Israel" brought trouble on himself (Josh 7:24-25); he was put to death and his possessions burned. Other descendants of Zerah (1 Chron 2:6) are known in the time of Solomon as outstanding sages (1 Kings 4:31), but not part of the royal family.

Perez had two sons, Hezron and Hamul (1 Chron 2:5). Hamul is known in biblical genealogies (Gen 46:12; Num 26:21). The lineage of Perez is provided in the story of Ruth (Ruth 4:18-22). This was a source of information enabling the Chronicler to trace the lineage of David through Hezron and Ram (1 Chron 2:9-15). It is only in Chronicles that Caleb (here vocalized as *kelubay*) and Jerahmeel are called brothers, both being the sons of Hezron (v. 9), along with Ram, the ancestor of the Davidic line. This information was apparently known to the Chronicler through sources outside of Scripture. These sources can still be identified in the Chronicler's presentation (Williamson 1979: 352–56). The sons of Jerahmeel are marked as a unit by a distinct beginning and ending (vv. 25a, 33b), and the sons of Caleb by an identical formula (vv. 42a, 50a). The formulas introducing and concluding each of these units are a sign of units belonging to one document employed by the Chronicler for his history.

This Caleb is not to be identified with the hero of the conquest stories (Num 13:30; 14:24; Josh 14:6-15; 15:13-17), who is consistently said to be the son of Jephunneh (Num 13:6; 14:6, 30, 38; 26:65; Deut 1:36; 1 Chron 4:15; 6:56). Both families belong to Judah, but they are presented as distinct genealogical entities in Chronicles. These sources of the Chronicler are distinct from those of the Pentateuch traditions. The Chronicler makes the Calebite descendants of Hezron a central group within Judah (1 Chron 2:18-20, 42-50a). Caleb, son of Jephunneh, and his relative Othniel (Josh 15:17; Judg 3:9) are recorded separately (1 Chron 4:13-15). The genealogical links of these latter Caleb and Kenizzite groups to Judah are not clearly established. The two traditions are an indication of social and ethnic developments in distinct historical circumstances. The sources of the Chronicler record an earlier stage in the formation of the Calebite clans in Judah.

A second source of information for the Chronicler is a history of Ephrathah and Bethlehem, the place of David's birth. Hur is the firstborn of Ephrathah (1 Chron 2:50b); Ephrathah is also described as the father of Bethlehem (4:4). The genealogy of the sons of Hur leads up to Haroeh (2:50b-52). Following the genealogy of David (3:1-24), the genealogy of Hur is resumed in a very deliberate manner

(4:1-4). This resumptive summary takes the reader back to Hur in the first verse *[Resumptive Summary, p. 467]*. The descendants of Judah through Shobal, son of Hur, are traced in a linear genealogy, bringing the reader back to Reaiah (4:2). Haroeh (2:52) is to be identified with Reaiah; Haroeh may be the form of the name Reaiah that associates him with his tribe (GKC 125d, n. 1). The Chronicler has situated the Davidic genealogy within the ancestry of Ram. This allows him to begin and end with the oldest ancestors of Judah (2:3-8; 4:1-23. All the families of Hezron, the dominant clans in Judah, form the center of this Judahite history (2:9-3:24).

2:10-17 Jesse, Descendant of Ram

Having established Ram as central in the families of Judah, the Chronicler provides a linear genealogical link to Jesse, father of David (1 Chron 2:10-12). The list provides ten generations from Judah to Jesse. Aside from the note about Nahshon being a chief in Judah (v. 10), and several variations in spelling of names, this is the same genealogy found in Ruth (4:19b-22). The Chronicler varies the ending in a segmented genealogy of Jesse, which makes David his seventh son.

Jesse is rooted in the most ancient and venerated families of Judah. Nahshon was chosen from the tribe of Judah to assist Moses and Aaron in taking the census of the people; he and the other assistants are called princes of their ancestral tribe (Num 1:7, 16-17; cf. 2:3), a note included by the Chronicler (1 Chron 2:10). According to the records accessible to the Chronicler, Salma, son of Nahshon (v. 11), was the founder of Bethlehem (1 Chron 2:51, 54). It may be assumed that records of the king's family were kept in the royal archives.

The Chronicler preserves an independent record of the children of Jesse. The first three sons are named in the account of Samuel anointing one of the sons of Jesse to be king (1 Sam 16:6, 8, 9; cf. 17:13); the other three brothers are not named elsewhere. The Chronicler has followed his own records in making David the seventh son of Jesse. In the story of the anointing, David is an eighth son (1 Sam 16:10). Abigail, named as the sister of David (1 Chron 2:16), is the daughter of Nahash in the story of Absalom in 2 Samuel 17:24-25. This appears to be an error in the text tradition. Several Greek manuscripts of Samuel make her the daughter of Jesse and sister to Zeruiah; they seem to be a correction of the earlier texts *[Greek Text of Chronicles, p. 468]*. If the texts are not in error, Nahash must be regarded as an earlier deceased husband of Jesse's wife

(McCarter 1984: 392). Zeruiah had three sons: Abishai, Joab, and Asahel (cf. 2 Sam 2:18). Abigail was mother to Amasa, making him a cousin of the other three warriors. Absalom made Amasa head of the army, in the place of Joab, at the time of his revolt (17:25). Jether, the father of Amasa, was an Ishmaelite (1 Chron 2:17). There were various affiliations between Judahites and the neighboring peoples. After the revolt was crushed, David appears to have been speaking literally in telling Amasa, while making him commander in the place of Joab, "Are you not my own flesh and blood?" (2 Sam 19:13). These relationships indicate how much David relied on family to establish his military strength and administer his kingdom.

2:18-24 *Calebite Families in Ephrath*

The Chronicler returns to the descendants of Hezron to show the integration of different families in the region of Bethlehem, the home of Jesse, the father of David (1 Chron 2:18; cf. v. 9). These include the descendants of Caleb in the regions of Ephrath and Hebron to the south (vv. 19, 42). The introduction of Hur brings in another tribal relationship (v. 20). Hur is the grandfather of Bezalel, the chosen craftsman in the building of the tabernacle (Exod 31:2; 35:30). In the time of the exodus, Hur is the fourth generation from Judah. This is consistent with the genealogies found in the books of Exodus through Joshua, all of which are three to six generations from Jacob's sons (Rendsburg: 186-89). The relationship of Judah to the sons of Aaron is found in his marriage to Elisheba, daughter of Amminadab (Exod 6:23). Amminadab is a leader of the tribe of Judah (1 Chron 2:10; cf. Ruth 4:19-20).

The marriage of Hezron to the daughter of Makir further links the tribe of Judah to Joseph (1 Chron 2:21). Makir is the son of Manasseh (Gen 50:23; Num 26:29; 27:1), whose territory was in Gilead. Chronicles also affirms the relationship of Makir to Manasseh (1 Chron 7:14-17). Chronicles describes the settlements of Jair (Havvoth Jair) as founded by the descendants of Judah, but in the exodus account they are said to be taken by conquest from the Amorites (Num 32:39-42). A further tradition in Judges makes Jair a judge of thirty cities in this territory in Gilead (Judg 10:3-5). His territory of thirty towns was situated south of Argob (Num 32:41). This area was just south of the Yarmuk River (Milgrom 1990: 276). Kenath is the modern Qanawat, at the foot of Mount Hauran (Jebel Druze). It is the most northeasterly point of the land of Israel. Makir as the founder of Gilead introduces a collection of personal, ethnic, and place names (1 Chron 2:21). The genealogies convey a variety of social, ethnic, and geographical connections among individuals, peoples, and places.

This territory in Gilead was conquered by Geshur and Aram (1 Chron 2:23), which probably took place during the reign of Baasha, shortly after the division of the kingdom. During the reign of Solomon this area was part of the district of Ramoth Gilead (1 Kings 4:13). When the monarchy divided, there was continuous war among Israel, Judah, and Aram. After the demise of all three of these nations, during the Greek period the territory became a federation of cities known as the Decapolis.

The Chronicler concludes this section on Caleb with the information that Caleb was married to Ephrathah after the death of Hezron (1 Chron 2:18-24). It is best to follow the Greek version (cf. RSV), which informs us that at this time Caleb became married to Ephrathah (cf. v. 19), rather than creating a place name of Caleb Ephrathah (NIV, NRSV). The difference in the MT is the omission of one letter (*aleph*), which causes the loss of the verb. Hezron had married Abijah and through her became the father of Ashhur (2:24), father of Tekoa (cf. 4:5). The people of Tekoa, south of Bethlehem, were also related to the descendants of Hezron. Tekoa was part of the Judahite tribal inheritance. It was the home of the prophet Amos (Amos 1:1) and famous for its wise people (2 Sam 14:2). Through these genealogical links, the Chronicler explains the various tribal relationships of Judah and also provides a history for the region of Bethlehem, the home of David.

2:25-41 Jerahmeelite Families in Judah

Having dealt with the sons of Ram and Caleb (1 Chron 2:10-17, 18-24), the Chronicler turns his attention to Jerahmeel, the firstborn of Hezron (vv. 25-33). Because Jerahmeel was the oldest descendant of Hezron, his descendants may be regarded as among the most established of Judah's families. They divide into two groups. The first is a total of eight families, but only the eldest son, Ram, extends to a second generation in the genealogy. A second wife, whose name means "crown" (*Atarah*, v. 26), provided him only one son (v. 26), but the genealogy extends as far as six generations through Appaim (v. 31). In the latter group, two families became extinct: Seled and Jether died without descendants.

None of the names are associated with towns; this may be an indication that this group of Judahites was somewhat nomadic. In the books of Samuel, the Jerahmeelites reside in various settlements rather than named towns (1 Sam 30:29). They lived in the deep south of Judah, in the arid hill country, where Edomites mingled with the people of Judah (1 Sam 27:10). Some of the names among the Jerahmeelites are close to those found in Edomite genealogies: Oren (1 Chron 2:25) and Aran (1:42); Onam (2:26; cf. 1:40); Shammai (2:28) and Shammah (1:37). Relationships between Judah and Edom were often hostile (Joel 3:19; Obad 18; Ps 137:7), but there were close social and economic ties between the two.

The clan of Sheshan is distinguished by a genealogy extending to the twentieth generation from their ancestor Jerahmeel (cf. 1 Chron 2:26, 28, 30, 31, 35-40). Only the linear genealogies of David, Saul, and the priestly line are longer. Sheshan is also unique in that he had no sons, but he did have descendants (cf. v. 31, where *son* apparently is used to indicate tribal relationships). Sheshan extended his family legacy through an Egyptian married to his daughter (vv. 34-35). Israelites expanded through the children of their servants, who then became heirs (Exod 21:4-6) and members of the covenant (12:44, 49). Egyptians and Edomites could be full members of the community in the third generation (Deut 23:7-8). The genealogy of Sheshan ends with Eleasah (v. 40), the same name as the grandfather of the man who killed Gedaliah (2 Kings 25:25; Jer 41:1), the leader in Jerusalem after the exile. In midrashic tradition, these two references to Eleasah were regarded as the same person. Though this may be based on nothing more than the identity of the names, a grandson of Eleasah in the sixteenth generation from Sheshan could have been alive at that time.

2:42-55 Calebite Settlements at Hebron

The sources of the Chronicler provided him with specific information concerning settlements in the area of Hebron closely identified with the family of Caleb (1 Chron 2:42-50a). Many of the names given may be found in the Judahite settlements listed in Joshua (15:21-62). None of the names in this list are found in the other Calebite genealogies (1 Chron 2:18-20, 50b-55). Mesha, the first listed, is found in Moab and area (2 Kings 3:4; 1 Chron 8:8-9). Ziph is to the south of Hebron (2:42; cf. Josh 15:55). Mareshah is in the Shephelah to the northeast of the major fortification of Lachish (Josh 15:44; Mic 1:15) [Shephelah, p. 467]. Hebron was also central to Caleb and Kenaz as a city of conquest (1 Chron 2:43; Josh 15:13-19; Judg 1:12-15); the reference here is to later inhabitants of the city. Of the families associated with Hebron (1 Chron 2:43-44), Tappuah is a town located northwest of Hebron (Josh 15:34). Maon and Beth Zur are listed in the tribal inheritance (1 Chron 2:45; Josh 15:55, 58). Maon, frequented by David (1 Sam 23:24-25), is south of Ziph; Beth Zur is north of Hebron.

Other groups were less directly related to the Calebite families. Ephah and Maakah are listed as concubines (1 Chron 2:46, 48). This may have involved immigration, merger, or expansion of families. Not all the affiliations are made specific. Jahdai appears without any genealogy (v. 47); ancient lists did not always provide direct links for family relationships but simply indicated membership within a group (Knoppers 2004a: 313). The Chronicler also notes that Aksah was the daughter of Caleb (v. 49). In the settlement of Debir, Aksah is the daughter of Caleb son of Jephunneh (Josh 15:16-17; Judg 1:12-13). The Chronicler is fully aware of this latter Caleb but does not introduce him until after the David genealogy (1 Chron 4:15). It seems unlikely that the Chronicler would mean Caleb son of Jephunneh in the context of Caleb son of Hezron. Aksah as the daughter of the Caleb who was brother of Ram must be the relationship intended by the Chronicler (2:9).

The Chronicler returns to the descendants of Hur, son of Caleb through Ephrathah (2:50b), introduced earlier with the families of Caleb (cf. v. 19). This genealogy (vv. 50b-52a), from another source, will be resumed following the account of the descendants of David in chapter 3 (cf. 4:1-2). In this section three descendants of Hur are named with the towns they founded. Shobal belongs to Mount Seir (cf. 1:38) but was also founder of Kiriath Jearim, to the northwest of Jerusalem, on the border of Benjamin and Judah (Josh 18:14). Salma is noted twice as the father of Bethlehem (1 Chron 2:51, 54). Beth Gader is not known.

The Calebite genealogy concludes with various territorial and family associations (1 Chron 2:52-55). In founding Kiriath Jearim, Shobal became the progenitor of *half of the Manahathites* (v. 52); half of this same group is also said to be sons of Salma (v. 54). Such descriptions of ethnic development are far removed from direct biological descent. The same is true in listing various people groups as offspring: Ithrites, Puthites, Shumathites, and Mishraites. Further divisions were found in Zorathites and Eshtaolites. Settlements grew through mixed populations and geographic expansions of the various groups. Other descendants of Salma, the founder of Bethlehem (cf. v. 51), were found in the town of Atroth-beth-joab, and consisted of three groups: Netophathites, Manahathites, and Zorites (v. 54).

The families of the scribes were very important to the state's functions and were of special interest to the Chronicler (v. 55). It has been suggested that scribes should be understood to mean citizens of Kiriath Sepher (cf. Josh 15:15-16; Judg 1:11-12), interpreted to mean *cities of the scribes*. As it stands, however, the text refers to scribes located in the city of Jabez. Scribes were extremely important for the functioning of state and society. They are always associated with palace and temple, but their activity was not limited to those spheres as households became sources of employment for skilled workers. Their activity in Egypt and Mesopotamia has its parallel in Israel and in the creation of Hebrew writings (van der Toorn). Scribes were active in Israel from early times, though the evidence for their activity in earlier periods is scarce and the extent of their practice uncertain (Demsky; Hess). The gathering of specialists within a particular town or geographical area is known elsewhere.

The location of Jabez is not known, nor has it been mentioned previously in the genealogies. The Kenites came to be absorbed into the tribe of Judah, though without genealogical descent from a patriarch. The Chronicler lists various groups of Kenites as localized scribes well before the monarchy. Kenites are known as Canaanite artisans (Gen 15:19; Num 24:21-22), whose cultural skills go back to their eponymous ancestor Cain (Gen 4:17-23) *[Eponym, p. 466]*. The Kenites had friendly relations with Israel and were related to Israel through the marriage of Moses in Midian (Judg 1:16; 4:11). Shimeathites might be part of the tribal inheritance in Shema (Josh 15:26). Chronicles also names two other groups of Kenites integrated into the inheritance of Judah. They originated in Hammath, a location known in Naphtali (Josh 19:35), but otherwise unknown in Judah.

3:1-24 Davidic Family

The Davidic genealogy documents an unbroken succession of Davidides for approximately seven centuries. The genealogy names these descendants without distinction. There is no reference as to which were monarchs, nor to the tumultuous events that divided Israel and finally ended the monarchy of Judah. A pedigree of seven centuries is in itself a testimony to the divine preservation of the house of David. The survival of the Davidic house testifies to God accomplishing his divine purpose through David. All the other lineages of Judah merged in various ways to form new entities, as indicated in the records of Judah. The return from exile did not bring about a restoration of Davidic rule within the community of Israel. The absence of political authority made it all the more important to demonstrate the continuation of a particular line of succession within the Davidic house. The capital had been conquered, the temple burned, and members of the dynasty humiliated, exiled, or executed, but the concept of an eternal Davidic kingdom survived (1 Chron 28:4). Though history might seem to have refuted the promise to David, it was the Chronicler's conviction that God had elected Judah, and within Judah had chosen David to bring about his eternal kingdom.

3:1-9 Sons of David

The description of the house of David begins with a segmented genealogy naming the sons of David's wives (3:1-9). The family of David continues with a linear genealogy of the kings of Judah from Solomon to Josiah (vv. 10-14). The killing of Josiah brought a succession of Josiah's sons to the throne, as appointments were made by foreign monarchs. The Chronicler gives distinct attention to the various sons of Josiah (vv. 15-19a), without any mention of which were monarchs. The members of the Davidic family are concluded in the postexilic period (vv. 19b-24), providing segmented genealogies beginning with Zerubbabel, the prominent leader of restoration (Hag 1:1; Zech 4:6-7).

The list of David's sons follows naturally within the distinguished family of Ram and their centrality within the other families of Judah (1 Chron 2:10-17). The list of sons born to David in Hebron follows the version in Samuel (3:1-4; 2 Sam 3:2-5). Daniel, the second son, is Chileab in Samuel; the various spellings of the name in other versions indicate that some transformation of the name took place. This son is otherwise unmentioned. Only the firstborn sons of the wives are named. A second list of sons born to David in Jerusalem follows the record of Samuel (1 Chron 3:5-8; 2 Sam 5:14-16). The Chronicler says Solomon was the fourth son born to Bathshua (a phonetic variation of Bathsheba), a surprising notation not made in Samuel (1 Chron 3:5; cf. 2 Sam 5:14). The three older brothers are disqualified; the fourth accordingly is chosen to be king and build the temple (Kalimi 2002: 557). The information on David's sons is repeated in the account of David's reign (1 Chron 14:4-7). Note is also made of their sister Tamar (3:9; cf. 2 Sam 13:1). Jerusalem seems to be depicted as the central and almost continuous residence of the Davidic family.

3:10-24 Descendants of David

A list of fifteen generations following Solomon extends over the whole period of the monarchy in Jerusalem, ending with Josiah

(1 Chron 3:10-14). This information is listed as found in Kings, with no mention of the fact that all these were monarchs. With the death of Josiah, the kings in Jerusalem were under the control of foreign powers, preempting the usual lines of succession.

A segmented genealogy of Josiah's sons, modeled on the pattern of Jesse's sons and David's sons born in Hebron, follows in verses 15-19a (cf. 2:13-15; 3:1-3). According to 2 Chronicles 36:1 (cf. 2 Kings 23:30), the first son to succeed Josiah as king is Jehoahaz, called Shallum in the genealogy, as in Jeremiah (cf. Jer 22:10-12). Shallum is the fourth son of Josiah in the genealogy (1 Chron 3:15). The Chronicler records an older son of Josiah named Johanan (who may have died prematurely); the second son is Jehoiakim, who is the second to rule after Josiah. The third son of Josiah is Zedekiah. According to the genealogy, Jehoiakim, second son of Josiah, is father of Jeconiah and grandfather of Zedekiah (v. 16). Jeconiah is called Jehoiachin in 2 Chronicles 36:8-10 (cf. 2 Kings 24:6), but Jeconiah in Jeremiah (NRSV: Jer 24:1; 28:4; 22:24, "Coniah"). In the account of the exile, 2 Chronicles 36:10 in MT makes Zedekiah the brother of Jehoiachin (Jeconiah in the genealogy), the last king of Judah (NRSV). In Kings, the last king of Judah is Zedekiah, the uncle of Jehoiachin (2 Kings 24:17). He is a son of Josiah named Mattaniah, whose name was changed by Nebuchadnezzar. The names of the last kings of Judah show the following correlation [*Chronology in Chronicles*, p. 460]:

Jehoahaz (Shallum)	2 Chron 36:1	2 Kings 23:31	fourth son of Josiah
Jehoiakim (Eliakim)	2 Chron 36:4	2 Kings 23:34	second son of Josiah
Jehoiachin (Jeconiah)	2 Chron 36:9	2 Kings 24:8	son of Jehoiakim
Zedekiah (Mattaniah)	2 Chron 36:10	2 Kings 24:17	son of Josiah

The last king of Judah was a son of Josiah, not a son of Jeconiah (Jehoiachin). Zedekiah also is not the brother of Jehoiachin (both sons of Jehoiakim), as suggested by the NRSV, ESV, and other translations. The problem is a textual error by MT in 2 Chronicles 36:10; MT should say *brother of his father* (as in the Greek), because Zedekiah is Jehoiachin's uncle (so NIV). Instead MT says simply *brother* (NRSV, etc.; cf. NIV footnote, 2 Kings 24:17). In 1 Chronicles 3:16-17, the genealogy continues through Jeconiah (NIV, Jehoiachin) rather than the sons of Zedekiah. The sons of Zedekiah were all put to death (2 Kings 25:7); the line of Josiah continues through Jehoiakim, Jeconiah (Jehoiachin), and his sons.

The MT continues the genealogy with *'assir* as a son of Jeconiah (1 Chron 3:17), but the name seems to be a corruption of *ha'assir* (the prisoner). Most translations interpret as *Jeconiah the prisoner* (cf. NIV). Interest in the status of Jeconiah is found in Kings, which speaks of his later release (2 Kings 25:27-30). It may be that his son Shenazzar in verse 18 is to be identified with Sheshbazzar, who led in the return (Ezra 1:8). Both names are deemed to be variant transliterations of the Babylonian name Šîn-ab-uṣur (Knoppers 2004a: 328). Jeconiah's grandson Zerubbabel is son of Shealtiel in the account of the return (Ezra 3:2, 8). The genealogy of Chronicles makes him son of Padiah (1 Chron 3:19). Zerubbabel may have been the son of a levirate marriage, the case of a brother marrying the widow of a deceased brother (Rudolph: 29). This assumes that Shealtiel, son of Jeconiah (1 Chron 3:17), died without children, so Padiah, the younger brother, married his widow. It is also possible that two variant lineages for Zerubbabel have been preserved.

The concluding section of Zerubbabel's descendants has several textual and interpretive problems. Zerubbabel's descendants conclude with a sister (v. 19), which normally indicates the end of a list. This leaves the five sons of the following list outside the succession (v. 20). Either these must be included as sons of Zerubbabel, or they are actually sons of Meshullam, oldest son of Zerubbabel. The New Jerusalem Bible adds *sons of Meshullam* at the beginning of verse 20. This textual restoration provides a link to the preceding verse (Knoppers 2004a: 321). The sons of his second son, Hananiah, follow as a natural sequel (v. 21). His first son is Pelatiah, but the following sequence of names beginning with Jeshaiah has two textual traditions. In the Greek version these are a linear genealogy in a succession of father to son (*his son* in each case rather than *sons of*), as in the sequence of the descendants of Solomon (vv. 10-19a). The difference in the Hebrew is simply a longer stroke of the letter following the word "son" (*bnw* rather than *bny*) in the *Vorlage* of the translator *[Vorlage, p. 468]*. The Greek version is preferred in some translations (e.g., NRSV, RSV), which adds five generations to the lineage of Zerubbabel. Other translations follow the MT (e.g., NIV), regarding Pelatiah and Jeshaiah as brothers, both sons of Hananiah; and the sons of Rephaiah, Arnan, Obadiah, and Shecaniah are various Davidide families among the clans of Hananiah. Yet another interpretation assumes an ellipsis and counts Rephaiah, Arnan, Obadiah, and Shecaniah as sons of Jeshaiah, making it only four generations shorter than the Greek version (NJPS). The Greek version is the most defensible. An error between the letters concerned (*yod* and *waw*) is common. One would expect the MT to have used a more standard method of introducing various clans of Davidides if that were intended.

The sons of Shemaiah only number five (v. 22), though there are said to be six. It seems that Shemaiah is to be counted as one of the six, and that all six are actually sons of Shecaniah. The list provides eleven generations following Zerubbabel, if there are five generations from Pelataiah to Shecaniah. If the average actual age for a generation is about twenty years, and Zerubbabel was born about 575 BCE, the chronological time period from Zerubbabel extends to about 335 BCE. The shorter genealogy would be about one hundred years earlier.

4:1-23 More Records of Judah

The records of Judah begin again with a linear genealogy from Judah to Reaiah (4:1-2). These names are a resumptive summary of the descendants of Judah in chapter 2 *[Resumptive Summary, p. 467]*. Reaiah is last mentioned at the end of the genealogy of Hur (2:50b-52a); *Haroeh* (NIV, NRSV) is likely a variant form of Reaiah (*BHS* app.). A list of related ethnic groups follows in 1 Chronicles 2:52b-55. The records of Judah that resume in chapter 4 do not have connecting links. The first section deals with the sons of Hur, the firstborn of Caleb through Ephrathah (1 Chron 4:2-4; cf. 2:19). A miscellany of genealogies follows (4:5-23) that are not integrated with each other, nor are they linked to the previous Judahite genealogies (2:3-55). The descendants of Caleb and Hezron compose the main body of Judah, while other groups were part of the tribe but remained somewhat independent.

Shobal, son of Hur, was the father of Kiriath Jearim (2:52). His genealogy is continued through Reaiah (4:2) to name families known as the Zorathites. The Zorathites and the Eshtaolites were previously named as two family groups of the various peoples of Kiriath Jearim (2:53; cf. Josh 15:33). The Zorathites were also associated with the tribe of Dan (Josh 19:41; Judg 13:2). Migrations to the area in the north may account for the association.

The sons of Etam lack an explicit link to Hur, though they are fully identified with him. The Hebrew text of the verse is in disarray; it says *these were the father of* (KJV). Modern translations follow the Greek text, which says *these were the sons of* (NIV, NRSV) *[Greek Text of Chronicles, p. 468]*. Since genealogical information has been given for the first two sons of Hur, Shobal and Salma (2:52-55), one might suppose that these are the sons of Hareph, the third son of Hur and the father of Beth Gader (2:50-51). If this reconstruction is accepted, the Harephite element would be the largest among the Hurites, comprising four localities (Beth Gader, Etam, Gedor, and Hushah) and six ethnic groups (the peoples of Etam, Jezreel, Ishma, Idbash, Penuel, and Ezer), with an additional branch of their sister, the Hazzelelponi (4:3; Japhet 1993: 107). Penuel, north of the Jabbok, was one of the chief cities of Jeroboam I when he established the separate state of Israel (1 Kings 12:25).

The Hezronite lineage continues with Ashhur, father of Tekoa (1 Chron 4:5-8; cf. 2:24). The localities extend from the area near Bethlehem to farther south (Teman and Ethnan; cf. Josh 15:23). The names that follow the descendants of Ashhur in verse 8 are phrased as a continuation but have no actual antecedent. The text of this verse is in disarray. Verse 8 states that *Koz begat . . . the families of Aharhel, who are descended from Harum* (AT). This makes Koz the father of a group of families whose actual patronym is Harum. Based on the Greek, it may be that *the families of Aharhel the son of Harum* is a corruption of *the families of the brothers of Rechab and the sons of Harum* (Knoppers 2004a: 338). The note about Jabez has no connection to the other genealogies (vv. 9-10). It is unique in rendering a lesson based on the etiology of a name *[Etiology, p. 466]*. The lesson conforms to the Chronicler's theology of divine blessing.

The Chronicler provides additional important historical information on the relationship of the various Calebite and Kenizzite peoples in Judah (vv. 11-15). Kelub is a variation of the name Caleb (v. 11; cf. 2:9). The genealogical relationship of this Calebite group is not connected to the descendants of Hezron (2:18-19, 42-50a). There appears to be a relationship between this Calebite group and the Kenizzites (4:11-13). The Greek text expands verse 12 to say Tehinnah, the *father of the city of Nahash* (bronze), is *brother of Eselon the Kenizzite [Greek Text of Chronicles, p. 468]*. If *Ir Nahash* (*City of Bronze*) is a place engaged in the production of bronze (*neḥošet*), it could be connected to the people in verse 14 (Williamson 1982: 60). In this case the name *Ge Harashim* should be translated to reflect its meaning as *Valley of Skilled Workers* (cf. NIV mg.). Craftsmen of metal and pottery were an essential and valued group. Caleb the son of Jephunneh is called a Kenizzite in the historical narratives (v. 15; Num 32:12; Josh 14:6, 14). Othniel, son of Kenaz, brother of Caleb, captured Debir (or Kiriath Sepher: Josh 15:16-17; Judg 1:12-13). Chronicles might seem to make certain Kenizzites descendants of Caleb (v. 15). These may have been another group of Kenizzites. Another possibility is that *son of Elah* (v. 15b) should be emended. *Elah* is also a Hebrew pronoun; verse 15b may be a summary saying *these were the sons of Kenaz,* including Caleb as a Kenizzite (Japhet 1993: 11). Kenaz is also Esau's grandson by Eliphaz (Gen 36:11; 1 Chron 1:36). Kenizzite peoples settled in the southern parts of Israel and were absorbed into both Edom and Judah. These groups were not as centrally connected to Judah as the descendants of Hur (1 Chron 2:18-19).

The genealogies following the Calebite families are not connected to any of the sons of Judah (1 Chron 4:16-18). It may be that a lost heading identified the fathers of Jehallelel and Ezrah (vv. 16-17). If Ezrah is to be identified with Ezer in the family of Hur (v. 4), this is a continuation of the peoples south of Bethlehem. Ziph, located south of Hebron, is well known from the stories of David's flight from Saul (e.g., 1 Sam 23:14). Two localities go by this name (Josh 15:24, 55). Asarel is also known as a family in Manasseh (Josh 17:2; Num 26:31), another link to Gilead (cf. 1 Chron 2:21). The problems of 1 Chronicles 4:17b are observed in a comparison of translations (e.g., KJV, NIV, NRSV). The mother of Miriam is not introduced in the preserved texts. The Greek text says that Jether was the father of Miriam; this is probably the original, corrupted in MT *[Greek Text of Chronicles, p. 468].* One may resolve the MT by transposing verse 18b to follow Jalon, making Miriam the daughter of Bithiah (NRSV), herself a daughter of Pharaoh married to Mered, who was son of Ezrah (v. 17). Egyptians were also included within the families of Judah in Gedor, Soco, and Zanoah.

The genealogy of Hodiah in verse 19 may be a corruption associated with the previous verse (Knoppers 2004a: 341). Following the Greek text in verse 17, which says Jether is the father of Miriam, Knoppers transposes the text of verse 18b to precede 18a: Bithiah thus was the Egyptian wife of Mered, whose sons were Jered, Heber, and Jekuthiel. Knoppers then makes Hodiah a corruption of Judahite. Verse 19 then names the sons of the Judahite wife of Mered. The village of Keilah, located northwest of Hebron, southwest of Bethlehem, was in Philistine territory. Under divine direction, it was once delivered by David during his desert wanderings (1 Sam 23:1-13). The Maakathites appear as a non-Israelite group; they are located within Manasseh (Deut 3:14; Josh 13:11), as a kingdom among the Arameans (Josh 12:5; 2 Sam 10:6). Some of these peoples became part of Judah and were present at the time of the exile (2 Kings 25:23). Here a Maakathite is related to a family in southern Judah.

The brief genealogy of Shimon in verse 20 is not directly connected to the Judahite genealogy and is fragmentary. The preserved texts end abruptly in verse 20 with *the son of Zoheth,* but no son is given. Most modern translations paraphrase the text and make this a place name (Ben-Zoheth), treated as a second son of Ishi (NIV).

The Chronicler's history of Judah concludes with a return to Shelah son of Judah (1 Chron 4:21-23; cf. 2:3), whose mother was a Canaanite from Adullam (Gen 38:1-2). He lists the main families of Shelah but provides very little genealogical information. Mareshah (cf. Josh 15:33, 44) is a well-known town in the lowlands, the western edge of the hill country of Judah *[Shephelah, p. 467]*. These people were also associated with Perez through Hezron as sons of Caleb (1 Chron 2:4-5, 42). The *house of Ashbea* (*Beth Ashbea*, NIV) might be a town or an ethnic affiliation with a guild of linen workers. Three individuals and a group associated with Kozeba are enigmatically described as lords (or at least married) in Moab, as known from ancient records (4:22). The name Jashubi Lehem (NIV) should say that they *returned to Lehem* (NRSV). Lehem is short for Bethlehem. The story of Ruth is another example of relationships between Judah and Moab. Kozeba may be identified with Chezib, where Shelah was born (Gen 38:5). This may also be Achzib, mentioned with Mareshah (Josh 15:44). At a later time these families became potters enlisted in royal service.

THE TEXT IN BIBLICAL CONTEXT

Chronicles and the Genesis Narrative

In making Judah superior and the leader of the sons of Jacob (1 Chron 5:2), the Chronicler has judicially interpreted the Genesis narrative according to the story of the people. Judah suggested the sale of Joseph to an Ishmaelite caravan (Gen 37:26-27) and then became the spokesperson for his brothers to their father (43:3-5, 8-10). Judah assumes a position of leadership when the delegation comes into trouble in Egypt (44:14-16) and negotiates on behalf of the family for release of the youngest brother (44:18-34). Finally, Jacob selected Judah to spearhead the migration to Egypt (46:28). The narrative of Genesis tells of the rise of Joseph, but it also includes the supremacy of Judah. In the history of the people, Judah became the name of the Southern Kingdom while the Northern Kingdom was known as Joseph (cf. Zech 10:6). The Chronicler will deal extensively with the military power of Benjamin and its distinguished role among the people of Israel, but the promise to Abraham would be realized through Judah. Political power would come to be centered in David as the descendant of Judah. Before the formation of the nation, Judah had prevailed among his brothers.

Complex Family Relations

The genealogy of Judah begins with the tribal patriarch and his five sons (1 Chron 2:3-4), including some of the details found in the account of Judah marrying a Canaanite (Gen 38:1-11). Contrary to Ezra-Nehemiah, the Chronicler has as his goal to be inclusive of all ethnic groups in all Israel. These are regarded as positive rather than negative. Judah had three sons through Shua's daughter, who was a Canaanite woman (Gen 38:2-5); this is the Bathshua of Chronicles (NRSV, NLT). Er, the eldest, lost the birthright through sin and died. The Chronicler did not consider as relevant the judgment of Onan, who died because of his refusal to accept responsibility to provide a family for the widow of his brother (Gen 38:9-10). Judah sinned unwittingly in his relationship with Tamar, his daughter-in-law, but is exonerated in the narrative (Gen 38:26). The Chronicler continues the genealogical line in the descendants of Judah through Tamar (1 Chron 2:4). She left two sons, Zerah and Perez. According to Scripture, Perez had two sons, Hezron and Hamul (Gen 46:12; cf. Num 26:21). Hezron, father of Ram (1 Chron 2:9), is of primary interest for tracing the central families of Judah.

Before dealing with Perez, the Chronicler must first explain how the line of Zerah came to be disqualified as leaders in Judah (2:5-8). Joshua informs us that the Zerah line produced Achan son of Karmi, a son of Zabdi (Josh 7:1, 17-18 NRSV). In Chronicles this Zabdi has become Zimri (apparently a variation of similar Hebrew letters), father of Karmi (1 Chron 2:6-7), whose infamous son Achan came to exclude himself from the covenant by procuring for himself property that belonged exclusively to God. In the Greek translations, Achan is consistently Achar in Joshua (7:1, 18, 19, 20, 24), as he is in the Chronicles genealogy. The alteration of the name provides assimilation to the Hebrew word for *troubler* (ʿoker), as the Chronicler explains. The execution of Achan in the valley of trouble ended the line of Zerah through Karmi.

The Chronicler lists four other sons of Zerah (1 Chron 2:6), named in Kings as sages whose legendary wisdom was exceeded by Solomon (1 Kings 4:31). Kings refers to Ethan as an Ezrahite, an alternate form of the ethnic designation Zerahite. In Kings, Ethan, Heman, Kalkol, and Darda are described as sons of Mahol, which probably identifies them with a musical guild. Ethan and Heman are known for their poetry and music (titles of Pss 88 and 89), a tradition known to the Chronicler (1 Chron 15:17-19; 25:1-7; 2 Chron 5:12). The leaders of the musical guilds are Levites, but the Chronicler also lists them as brothers of Zimri and thus within the tribe of Judah. Azariah son of Ethan (1 Chron 2:8) is otherwise unknown.

As is often the case in genealogies, these individuals had ancestral claims with both Levi and Judah. The genealogy of Moses and Aaron in Exodus indicates a relationship between Levi and Judah. Aaron was married to Elisheba, the sister of Nahshon, who belonged to the tribe of Judah (Exod 6:23; cf. 1 Chron 2:11). The Chronicler establishes their lineage in Judah, though their distinction was as musicians in the tribe of Levi. The historical relationship between these representative wise men during the age of Solomon and the ancient descendants of Judah from the wilderness period is not explained. In his genealogical history, it was the Chronicler's intention to include individuals appearing in his narrative sources in order to develop the tribal relationships of the ancient past.

After explaining the destinies of the earliest descendants of Judah, the Chronicler turns his attention to the clan of Ram, the ancestor of David (1 Chron 2:10; cf. Ruth 4:18-22). Ram was a son of Hezron, one of the two sons of Perez. Hezron is also listed by the Chronicler as a son of Reuben (1 Chron 5:3), as he is in all the parallel genealogies of Reuben (Gen 46:9; Exod 6:14; Num 26:6). This is another case of multiple relationships. The territory of Hezron is found in the southern part of Judah, between Kadesh Barnea and Karka (Num 34:4; Josh 15:3, 25). In the sources of the Chronicler, both Caleb and Jerahmeel were brothers of Ram and sons of Hezron (1 Chron 2:9). This relationship is not found elsewhere in Scripture.

Outside of Chronicles, Jerahmeel is found mainly in Samuel. His was an independent clan within a district of the Negev south of Aroer (1 Sam 27:8-10; 30:26-30) *[Negev, p. 467]*. Though Jerahmeelites have the appearance of a fringe group, they are incorporated among the towns of Judah. The Chronicler knows Jerahmeel to be the firstborn of Hezron (1 Chron 2:25). What must not be overlooked among the families of Jerahmeel is the application of regulations concerning land. Sheshan did not have any sons (2:34); one of his daughters was married to Jarha, his Egyptian slave (v. 35). Attai, the son of that union, inherited the ancestral land. The land became the inheritance of the grandson as progeny of a daughter and a slave. The regulation is first found in Numbers 27:1-11, a decision concerning the daughters of Zelophehad. It is one of the cases not covered in earlier legislation that needed to be settled by divine oracle.

A second association found only in Chronicles is that of Celubai (1 Chron 2:9), the same name as Caleb (cf. 2:18, 42). It is doubtful that this Caleb is to be identified with the hero of the conquest stories (Num 13:30; 14:24; Josh 14:6-15; 15:13-17), who is consistently said to be the son of Jephunneh (Num 13:6; 14:6, 30, 38; 26:65; Deut 1:36;

1 Chron 4:15; 6:56). The two Calebs both belong to Judah but are presented as distinct genealogical entities in Chronicles. This information is drawn from sources additional to those of the Pentateuch. The Chronicler makes Calebite descendants of Hezron a central group within Judah (1 Chron 2:18-20, 42-50). Caleb the son of Jephunneh and his relative Othniel (Josh 15:17; Judg 3:9) are recorded separately (1 Chron 4:15). The two traditions are an indication of social and ethnic developments in distinct historical circumstances.

Prayer of Jabez

Within his history of Judah, the Chronicler introduces a nongenealogical story that demonstrates his central theological concern. Whatever may be the disasters of history, prayer and humility have the power to access the grace and deliverance of God. Although Jabez has no connection within the genealogical history (1 Chron 4:9-10), the story of this one individual is profound. Jabez (Yaʿbeṣ) was famous for his name: it was a play on the word "pain" (ʿeṣeb). The name his mother gives him includes an interchange of the last two letters in that word.

The story of Jabez alludes to the curse against Eve (Gen 3:16). The claim of knowledge—the ability to determine what is good and evil (vv. 5-6)—had resulted in conflict. The first curse was conflict due to being the image of God; humans representing God would continually be in conflict with the snake (v. 15). The second conflict was within the family, the closest of human relationships (v. 16). The third conflict was with the earth (vv. 17-18), created for humans as their home. The ground would be cursed on their account: instead of humans living in harmony with the earth, its plants would function as thorns. All three alienations are closely related; struggle within families affects both spiritual and material matters. God had made humans as male and female to be fruitful and multiply (1:22). What had been good now became a pain. At times children are a pain, but apparently Jabez received a specially designated moniker from his mother because of the pain she felt.

For the Chronicler, Jabez is an example of the possibility of receiving blessing from God through prayer. Jabez prays that he might be free of pain (NIV), but the genitive is ambiguous; it may equally refer to the pain he might cause. Penitence would seem to be implicit in the prayer as well, which would follow the theology of the Chronicler. His name now must be explained because his life became so prosperous. Jabez was more honorable than his brothers because of his prayer (1 Chron 4:10a). The prayer is the longest element in the Jabez story and is somewhat complex. It begins with either an abbreviated vow (GKC 167a) or a wish (GKC 151e). The plea for blessing, or the condition of the vow, involves three requests: expansion of territory, prosperity, and protection (4:10b). The honor of this request made a special point to those struggling in the harsh conditions of Judah during the Chronicler's day. The prayer of humility can overcome all adversity, deserved or otherwise.

THE TEXT IN THE LIFE OF THE CHURCH

Peace in Racial and Religious Relationships

The history of Judah was remarkable for the way in which it incorporated the surrounding peoples into its community. Judah married a Canaanite woman (1 Chron 2:3); Jether was an Ishmaelite (2:17); Jarha was an Egyptian slave (2:34); the descendants of Shelah were related to families in Moab (4:22). Race was not an issue for the Chronicler; covenant fidelity was important.

Intermarriage with those of other races who did not adhere to the Israelite covenant was always a problem, but intermarriage for those who would be Israelites was the history of the people. The many warnings against intermarriage with the Canaanites were always conditioned by the danger of infidelity to the covenant (e.g., Deut 7:1-6). Syncretism with Canaanite religious faith was always intolerable, because the God of Israel is holy. His holiness sets him apart from all that is common, but particularly any comparison or identity with other gods that are identified with elements such as sun and storm. This is what sets the Israelites apart as a treasured people from all other nations (v. 6). It is only Israel that recognizes such a God; it is therefore intolerable that the worship of Yahweh be compromised.

Race and religion are two of the greatest tensions of modern times, including in Europe and North America, where large populations of immigrants have transformed some of the largest cities. In this respect there are lessons to learn from the Chronicler, who tried to encourage a very small state of people within the vast Persian Empire. His attitude seems to be one of not compromising community identity, but a willingness to be inclusive of all peoples that desired to be incorporated within it.

The attitude of the Persians themselves must be recognized. In the famous Cyrus Cylinder, the great king declares that he "returned the (images of) the gods to the sacred centers [on the other side of] the Tigris whose sanctuaries had been abandoned for a long time, and I let them dwell in eternal abodes. I gathered all their inhabitants and returned (to them) their dwellings" (COS 2.124). This imperial policy made possible the Chronicler's vision; his community was encouraged to express its faith and pursue its ideals. This is a striking contrast with certain contemporary attempts to use state coercion to suppress all religious symbols or expression of faith in public. The province of Quebec, for example, proposed a charter of Quebec values in which the government would ban from public buildings symbols such as hijabs, crucifixes, kippas, and turbans (Fulford). A state should allow religions to flourish because no one religion holds power. Fear of certain cultural customs seems to be shifting that attitude to one in which the state seeks to enforce limitations to expressions of faith.

Pursuit of Blessing

In the prayer of Jabez (1 Chron 4:9-10), the Chronicler is anxious to have all his readers know there is no circumstance or calamity in life that precludes the possibility of receiving the blessing of God. This is true even when as individuals we are liable for the circumstances that we cannot escape.

These two verses in Chronicles are best known through a little book by Bruce Wilkinson titled *The Prayer of Jabez*, published in 2000. It was at the top of *Publishers Weekly* and the *New York Times* bestseller lists for many months. The book not only sold millions but also generated ancillary markets such as Jabez bracelets, posters, videos, and shirts. It is most unusual that any book should generate such sales, let alone one on two verses in Chronicles. The book, however, is not about the Chronicler's view of divine justice and mercy *["God, Justice, and Faithfulness" in Theology of Chronicles, p. 478]*. It is an example of what has been popularly called "prosperity gospel," a belief that the prayer of faith and a life of faithfulness (esp. generosity) will bring wealth and abundance. This teaching has been advocated in various forms in countries all over the world. It has often flourished among people trapped in poverty and desiring a better life.

Poverty is a curse, but it has many causes. The biblical solution is not wealth through divine intervention. Human efforts to alleviate poverty and pain frequently fail. The complexity of poverty is illustrated in one of Bruce Wilkinson's very noble attempts to house, educate, and feed children whose parents had died of AIDS in Swaziland. This small country, between Mozambique and South Africa, was afflicted with one of the world's highest AIDS rates. The

African Dream Center was to house 10,000 children on a 32,500-acre complex. But the proposal was not approved by King Mswati III, and Wilkinson eventually resigned from the whole project. As reported by Timothy Morgan, the failure was disillusioning to supporters. Zakes Nxumalo, a Swazi pastor, was reported as saying, "I don't know how to handle this. People won't understand—to them Bruce is everything" (Morgan 76). Morgan further quotes a close associate of Wilkinson to say, "Bruce was quite broken at this time. [Dream for Africa] had physically, emotionally, spiritually, and financially taken a serious toll on Bruce." Before the failure, the organization had been sending hundreds of volunteers per month to assist in the struggle against AIDS. Reversals of good projects can happen without notice, even to people who have experienced the greatest of God's blessings.

God is more concerned about our character than our comfort. As with the apostle Paul, God may allow those he loves to live with a "thorn in the flesh" that repeated prayer does not alleviate, perhaps to keep them humble (2 Cor 12:7-8). But the story of Jabez illustrates that it is not always that way. As an etymology on the name, "its core is contradictory rather than causal: how did it happen that a man by the name of 'Jabez' was, nevertheless, prosperous!" (Japhet 1993: 109). The prayer of Jabez is to encourage us to "be more honorable" in our prayers and by that means experience God's blessing in our lives.

1 Chronicles 4:24–9:1a
The Tribes of Israel

PREVIEW

Every person needs an identity, a family identity, a community identity, and a national identity. If necessary, identity is pursued at considerable cost. Identity can be lost for various reasons. Sometimes a person may not know their biological parents; one such case discussed on national radio in Canada was a woman who discovered that her father had been a sperm donor. She was compelled to try to find her biological father, to the point of personally writing over six hundred letters to men who might have been the candidate, but to no avail. In Canada, identity can also be worth money; First Nations peoples can potentially get significant benefits if they can identify as such. They are rightly concerned about preserving their culture and their language. Each people group of Aboriginals constitutes a nation but not a country; to most of them, their identity as a nation is personally more significant than their citizenship, though obviously they need the rights of Canadian citizens. The Chronicler composes his national genealogy to establish the identity of his nation, wherever they may reside. It was not only important to him, but also to his nation spread throughout the Persian Empire. It was valuable because the Chronicler's claims were greater than money: foremost were the promises of the Yahweh's kingdom.

The Chronicler elaborates his identity of Israel (1 Chron 2:1-2) with a genealogical and territorial history of each of the tribes, beginning with Judah. A summary conclusion brings the history of the sons of Israel to a close. *So all Israel was genealogically registered, and their records were written in the book of the kings of Israel* (9:1a AT). This is *not* merely a list (NIV). It was common for ancient histories to establish their connection with the past through genealogies. Ancient scribes in Greece, Mesopotamia, and Egypt had formulated genealogical registers for centuries. Noble families of Greece established lineages to heroes and gods in the mythological past. The Greek historian Herodotus traces various royal families to the ancient past. Hecataeus of Miletus goes back sixteen generations to a god. Sumer and Assyria left ancient king lists going back to times before the flood. The famous Turin Canon of Egypt connects a dynastic succession of monarchs of Upper and Lower Egypt to a lineage of dynastic succession of gods and spirits. The methods of the Chronicler were familiar to his cultural world.

A geographical principle governs the order of the tribes. The Chronicler begins with Judah (1 Chron 2:3-4:23) and returns to the center of Israel with the genealogy of Benjamin (8:1-40) *[Genealogy, p. 461]*. In the biblical sources, Jerusalem is located on the border between Judah and Benjamin. Joshua tells us that Judah was unable to dislodge the Jebusites from Jerusalem (Josh 15:63), but in Judges we read that the people of Benjamin could not drive out the Jebusites (Judg 1:21). The two verses are identical except for the name of the tribe responsible for conquering Jerusalem. Jerusalem was the center of the Chronicler's interests. In the prophetic teaching of Israel, Jerusalem was the one central location where worship and confession of God's divine rule were to take place, with pilgrimage festivals three times annually. Jerusalem always represented the hope of the divinely instituted kingdom.

Simeon is second in the order of Israel's sons, and Judah is the fourth: Reuben, Simeon, Levi, Judah (Gen 35:23-26). In Chronicles, the history of Reuben follows Simeon: Judah, Simeon, Reuben. As the other tribes east of the Jordan, Gad and the half-tribe of Manasseh are associated with Reuben. They are treated as one group, possessing one territory (1 Chron 5:18), a viewpoint that follows an earlier tradition (Num 32:33-42; Josh 1:12-18). When enumerating support for David, the Chronicler counts these tribes as one (1 Chron 12:38). The tribe of Levi is next to Judah in rank among the tribes; its identity and function are placed centrally among the tribes (6:1-81). No events of the tribe's life are recorded, and the registration of the house of the fathers is given in the organization of the temple officials (1 Chron 23-26). The record of Levi in the tribal list details the cities of the Levites (derived from Josh 21). Genealogically, the record of Levi describes the registration of the three singers: Heman, Asaph, and Ethan. The account gives their registration; precise affiliation to the main Levitical families of Kohath, Gershon, and Merari; and the circumstances of their establishment as singers.

The genealogy of 1 Chronicles 7 lists more of the Israelite tribes and sketches their tribal identities: Issachar, Benjamin, Dan, Naphtali, Manasseh, Ephraim, and Asher; Zebulun is absent from this listing of tribal genealogies. The omission seems to be a loss that occurred in the transmission of the text. The registration of the tribes according to the official records is completed with a return to the tribe of Benjamin (8:1-40). It is a sequel to the earlier treatment of Benjamin (7:6-11). The material of the sequel is substantially different and probably derives from other sources. This brings the history back to the center of Israel, where it began with Judah.

OUTLINE

Simeon, 4:24-43
Transjordan Tribes, 5:1-26
Levi, 6:1-81
Northern Tribes, 7:1-40
Military Record of Israel, 8:1-9:1a

EXPLANATORY NOTES

Simeon was partner with Judah when the settlement in Canaan began (Judg 1:1-3). The settlements of Simeon were located within territory of Judah (cf. Josh 19:1), in the southern regions. Simeon did not proliferate as did the other tribes (1 Chron 4:27). The history of Simeon was necessarily included with that of Judah, but the people of Simeon were distinguished from the divinely chosen tribe of royalty. Simeon therefore is first in the numeration of the tribes following the history of the royal family.

Simeon 4:24-43

The genealogy of Simeon leads to Shimei (vv. 24-27), son of Shaul, who was Canaanite (cf. Exod 6:15; Gen 46:10). The Chronicler gives only five sons of Simeon, as found in the tribes of Israel in Numbers 26:12-14. The Chronicler's list contains the same names as Numbers, except for Jarib; this is Jachin in the other three lists. The Genesis and Exodus lists have Ohad as a third son, and they have Zohar instead of Zerah (a reversal of two letters in Hebrew). The Chronicler gives no genealogical information concerning the other sons of Simeon.

Three sons are listed for Shaul, whether brothers or three generations is not distinguished (v. 25). The same is true for the sons of Mishma (v. 26). The pattern is like that of the kings of Israel and Judah (3:10-14), which may indicate that Shimei is six generations from Shaul. Mibsam and Mishma appear in the same order as sons of Ishmael (Gen 25:13-14; 1 Chron 1:29-30). The first name suggests association with the spice trade. Arabian names are found in Assyrian inscriptions in the areas of Ammon, Moab, and Edom. Ishmaelite families may have entered the family of Simeon, or conversely, Simeonite families may have settled in southern Palestine among Ishmaelite groups.

The Chronicler has a distinct concept of the settlements of Simeon (vv. 28-33). His information is drawn from Joshua, with some variations of names from the MT (cf. Josh 19:1-9) *[Masoretic Text, p. 470]*. In Joshua these cities are presented as an inheritance (vv. 1, 9), but in Chronicles they are described as native dwellings of the Levites. The Chronicler presents an alternate perspective of settlement, unrelated to the conquest, which appears to have been present in his sources (Japhet 1979). This was God's design for his people to accomplish his purpose. The Chronicler interrupts the Joshua source to point out that this was the situation when David came to reign (1 Chron 4:31). This chronological notation is critical to the purpose of his history. The reign of David and Solomon becomes the ideal of the kingdom of God. Historically, the nation has had opportunity to return to this dominion of God. This is the essence of what the nation of Israel was meant to be. In the viewpoint of the Chronicler, Israel may yet be what it is.

The history of Simeon continues with a list of thirteen princes (4:33b-38a). They are not directly linked by genealogy to the sons of Simeon. The princes are distinguished by being recorded in the genealogical record. The verse division appears to interrupt the introduction of these princes. *And they kept a genealogical record* serves as an introduction to these chieftains (v. 33b), which is then brought to a conclusion with an inclusio: *These were the princes recorded by name with their families* (v. 38a AT) *[Inclusio, p. 467]*. Enrollment in a genealogical record is an indication of notable rank: families are remembered by their leading representatives. A "chieftain" may be the leader of a tribe or a military leader (cf. Num 1:4, 16), but the term is used as the title of a respected and exalted individual (Gen 23:6; 34:2).

These thirteen princes are otherwise unknown. Their number may be related to the thirteen cities and surrounding settlements in the area of Bethlehem that composed the initial tribal inheritance

(Josh 19:2-6). It is also possible that Shemaiah is to be identified with Shemei of the sons of Simeon (1 Chron 4:27, 37b). Such formal changes are common among name lists. The list itself has all the signs of belonging to an ancient record. Of the thirteen, Amaziah alone has a patronymic (father's name), Asiel has a genealogy of three generations, and Shemaiah has a genealogy of five generations.

An expansion of the Simeonite territory took place during the days of Hezekiah (4: 38b-41). The settlers were clans of the princes that were registered as Simeonites (4:41a; cf. v. 38). Hezekiah ruled in the late eighth century, almost three hundred years after the time of David. The Simeonite numbers had significantly increased in the intervening period. They found suitable pastureland in the Valley of Gerar (following the Greek text; the MT has Gedor, but this appears to be a confusion of a similarly written letter) *[Greek Text of Chronicles, p. 468]*. The Valley of Gerar had served as a refuge to Isaac in time of drought during patriarchal days (Gen 26:17). Gerar was to the northwest of Beersheba, in formerly Philistine territory (Gen 26:1, 6, 26). Hezekiah had invaded Philistine territory as far as Gaza (2 Kings 18:7-8). Gerar was in the western Negev, west of Ziklag, and outside the historical territory of Israel *[Negev, p. 467]*. The inhabitants were the descendants of Ham (1 Chron 4:40; cf. 1:4), the second son of Noah, whose descendants settled in southern Canaan and in Egypt. The Philistines who lived there formerly were also regarded as descendants of Ham (1:8, 12). The Meunites may be identified with Maon in the hill country of Judah (2:45; cf. Josh 15:55; 2 Chron 26:7), or a site by the same name south of Gaza. The territory was taken by conquest (1 Chron 4:41). The Chronicler uses the term of warfare described in Deuteronomy for taking possession of Canaan (Deut 20:16-18; cf. 1 Chron 2:7 and the reference to Jericho). All such properties of conquest were regarded as belonging to God and were not to be taken as military plunder *[War in Chronicles, p. 481]*.

The Chronicler also knows of a later expansion to the east into the territory of Edom (1 Chron 4:42-43). The traditional Mount Seir is located to the southeast of the Dead Sea. A military force of five hundred Simeonites was involved in the raid; David's soldiers numbered four hundred (1 Sam 22:2) or six hundred (23:13). The Amalekites were decimated in wars with Saul (1 Sam 14:48; 15:2-3) and David (1 Sam 30:1; 2 Sam 8:12). The Simeonites attacked at a time when the Amalekites were weakened after a military disaster. While other tribes expanded peacefully, the Simeonites were legendary for their violent ways (Gen 34:25-29; 49:5-7). The Chronicler reports the Simeonites as living in these areas *until this day*. It is possible that this is not just the time in which the record was written, but to the time of the Chronicler himself. The Babylonian exile never deported all of the Israelite peoples.

Transjordan Tribes 5:1-26

The Chronicler distinguishes three levels of status for Reuben, Joseph, and Judah. At the death of Rachel, Reuben tried to prevent Bilhah from assuming his mother's position as the chief wife of his father (Gen 35:22; cf. 49:3-4). His attempt to prematurely lay claim to his inheritance and become successor to his father resulted in disgrace and loss of leadership (Sarna 1989: 244–45). The birthright was given to Joseph, who achieved a special distinction from his father. Joseph's two sons became sons to Jacob (Gen 48:5). Each of them received an inheritance, so that Joseph was given a double portion (48:22), the right of the firstborn (Deut 21:17). The Chronicler uses this interpretation of the Genesis record to say that Reuben could not be registered as having the birthright (1 Chron 5:1), though he was the firstborn.

This interpretation is consistent with the tradition of Israel. Reuben is first in naming the tribal representatives (Num 1:5-15), but Judah occupies the primary position in the encampment of the tribes (2:3-31) and in the order of presenting daily offerings (7:12-83). According to the blessing of Jacob, the scepter belonged to Judah and would not be taken from him (Gen 49:8-12). Judah was the lion among his brothers, and they would bow before him.

5:1-10 Reuben

Having explained the status of the leading sons of Jacob (1 Chron 5:1-2), the Chronicler resumes with the descendants of Reuben, the firstborn of Israel (v. 3). According to the record, Reuben had four sons (Exod 6:14; Num 26:5-6). The names Hezron and Carmi are also found in the genealogy of Judah (cf. 2:5, 7). This may indicate some affiliation between the tribes. Bohan son of Reuben lived on the western side of the river (Josh 15:6; 18:17), indicating that some Reubenites lived within Judah. The Chronicler then lists seven generations of Reuben to the time of Tiglath-Pileser in the mid-eighth century (1 Chron 5:4-6). The list is not connected to the four sons of Reuben, but it represents Reubenites as a distinct tribe to the time of the captivity of northern Israel (cf. 2 Kings 15:29). It is only in Chronicles that Baal occurs as a personal name (1 Chron 5:5; cf. 8:30;

9:36); this might be an indication of an early source and a northern tradition. The role of Beerah as a chief would explain his genealogy being remembered for seven generations. The relationship of Jeiel the chief and his brothers to the ancestor Joel is ambiguous (vv. 7-8a). Shema son of Joel (v. 8) may be identified with the previous Shemiah (cf. v. 4), with the name being abbreviated. If this identity is assumed, Bela must have been several generations previous to Beerah, in the days of Tiglath-Pileser.

The Chronicler's concern is the documentation of authority and genealogical relationships. He discusses registration of the families of Beerah (v. 7a) according to the subdivisions of each tribe. Unlike Joshua, where individual families are not identified (cf. Josh 13:15, 24, 29), the Chronicler supplies some of the tribal subdivisions. There is no indication when this registration occurred; it could have been any time from Saul to the Assyrian period.

The Chronicler goes on to describe the Reubenite residences (1 Chron 5:8b-10), either those of the tribe of Reuben (v. 6) or the families of Bela. Aroer was just north of the Arnon, which flows into the middle of the Dead Sea from the east. It was a city built by Gad (Num 32:34) and formed the border between Reuben and Gad (Josh 13:16, 25). Nebo and Baal Meon formed the northern border of the territory. Nebo was taken from the Amorite king Sihon (Num 32:3, 37-38); it is located west and south of Heshbon, the city of Sihon, near the northeastern rim of the Dead Sea. The Mesha Stela celebrates the capture of Nebo and other Moabite territory from Israel after the days of Omri; King Mesha claims to have built the cities of Baal Meon and Aroer. During the days of Jeremiah, these cities belonged to Moab (Jer 48:1, 6, 19, 22). The eastern boundary of the Reubenites extended to the wilderness, which constituted the limits of settlement all the way to the Euphrates. The watered plateaus of the southern Transjordan blend into desert about twenty-five to thirty miles from the Jordan rift.

The growth of the tribe of Reuben led to the expansion of their territory to its eastern limits. During the days of Saul, the three tribes east of the Jordan went to war against the Hagrites (vv. 10, 19-22). The Hagrites are listed with Edom, Moab, and Ishmaelites as traditional enemies of Israel, as reflected in Psalm 83:6. Judging by the date of the psalm, which is postexilic and characterized by prose-like features, hostilities with the Hagrites continued into the time of the Chronicler. It is not possible to establish an etymological relationship between Hagrites and Hagar (Gen 16:15-16), the ancestor of the Ishmaelites.

5:11-17 Gad

The tribe of Gad settled next to Reuben in the territory of Bashan (v. 11). Bashan is the fertile basaltic tableland mainly north of the Yarmuk, the river that flows into the Jordan just south of the Sea of Galilee. The area was proverbial for its cattle ranges (Amos 4:1). Mount Hauran (Jebel Druze) rises east of Bashan, protecting it from the desert; its snow-capped peaks have significant rainfall in spite of its eastern location. Salekah is the traditional eastern province of Bashan (Deut 3:10; Josh 12:5; 13:11), often associated with a spur of Mount Hauran. This is far north of the original settlement of Gad and the Arnon in Dibon, Ataroth, and Aroer (Num 32:34). The Gadites migrated northward, making Ramoth Gilead one of their cities (Deut 4:43). The Chronicler describes the Gadites as occupying Bashan alongside the half-tribe of Manasseh.

The Gadite record begins with one clan distinguished by four notable leaders and a total of eleven family heads (1 Chron 5:12-13). These are not connected to other known genealogies (Gen 46:16; Num 26:15-17). The relationship of the sons of Abihail (1 Chron 5:14) to the previous families is ambiguous. The name Ahi is textually uncertain (v. 15). Abihail may be regarded as the father of the preceding eleven family heads, having a pedigree of seven generations. Ahi is then identified as a chief among these Gadite clans, though his relationship to Joel, the first chief mentioned (v. 12), is left unexplained. If the name Ahi is omitted, Abihail is an earlier chief with a genealogy of nine more generations.

Gilead is a rugged mountain region that reaches altitudes of over three thousand feet on the north and south sides of the Jabbok. The actual tableland is fairly narrow, as the western slopes dominate the area, and the eastern desert draws nearer than Bashan, which has the protection of the Hauran Mountains. Gilead sometimes is a general reference to Transjordan; in the genealogy Gilead is a descendant of Gad (v. 14). The depiction of Gilead and the *outlying villages* of Bashan is unusual (v. 16); normally the expression is used of villages surrounding a major city, such as Jabesh in the mountainous area of northern Gilead. It may be that "Jabesh" was the original reading (Knoppers 2004a: 379); the loss of an initial letter *yod* resulted in the reading Bashan. In the Mesha Inscription of Moab, Sharon is a region or city in the area of Medeba, the northern area of Moab. "Pasturelands" is a term used for a designated grazing area about one thousand yards outside of town limits (Num 35:1-5). If this identification of Sharon is correct, the Chronicler names the northern and southern regions of Gad.

The registration of Gad took place in the days of Jotham, whose reign overlapped with that of King Uzziah. According to the Chronicler, the reigns of Jotham and Jeroboam of Israel briefly overlapped; this may be dated to 750 BCE. It is difficult to conceive of the rival kings initiating a joint census. There may have been some broader historical significance to the two kings in the sources. This was the time the Northern Kingdom began to disintegrate.

5:18-22 War with the Hagrites

The war against the Hagrites took place as the tribe of Reuben expanded to the east. The report is given in the typical style of the Chronicler. It describes the military expertise of the warriors, the enemies, the spoil, and the victory as a divine provision in response to their cry. The report appears before the genealogy for the tribe of Manasseh (vv. 23-24) and therefore is sometimes considered to be out of place. The structure, however, follows the pattern of God keeping his promise in granting land, the tribes dwelling in the land (vv. 23-24), and the exile as a result of disobedience (vv. 25-26). It also avoids the juxtaposition of divine victory with the punishment of exile. The whole becomes a history of the Transjordanian tribes parallel to that of Israel and Judah.

The Hagrites were allied with three other Arabic tribes. Jetur and Naphish are found elsewhere in the genealogies, among the descendants of Ishmael (Gen 25:15; 1 Chron 1:31). The battle description makes God the warrior on behalf of the three tribes, as in Pharaoh's defeat as Israel crossed the Red Sea or the fall of Jericho. The victory was not a result of military strategy or the massive number of warriors present. Land is a gift of God to his people; it is consistent with the Chronicler's theology that trust in God is rewarded with his provision.

The sources of the Chronicler provided the numbers of soldiers mustered for war. Though the number may seem large (1 Chron 5:18), it is smaller than those recorded elsewhere for these tribes (Num 1:21, 25, 35; 26:7, 18, 34; cf. 1 Chron 12:37). The method of a military census, as may be discerned from Numbers, was to set a minimum age for eligibility. As far as the numbers are concerned, there is no provision for exemption or retirement from military service. The numbers as typically found in ancient Near Eastern documents are only partially understood, but there is an identifiable relationship between human hosts and heavenly hosts. Tribal figures correspond to celestial movements, identifying human armies with configurations of the stars.

The booty taken is consistent with depictions of seminomadic tribes. The numbers of animals and captives are very large and not specific (v. 21). They are not representative of actual calculations, but are meant to be indicative of the great scope of the divine victory.

5:23-26 Exile of Transjordan

The record concludes with the exile of Transjordan. The inhabitants of Transjordan included the half-tribe of Manasseh. Their territory extended to the northern limits of Israel. Mount Hermon is the highest southern peak of the Anti-Lebanon range, which is situated between Lebanon and Damascus. It is known as the Mountain of Snow. Baal Hermon is also referred to as Baal Gad (Josh 11:17; 13:5; cf. Judg 3:3), possibly referring to the southern peak of Hermon, above the region of Dan. Mount Hermon was called Sirion by the Sidonians and Senir by the Amorites (Deut 3:9). The Chronicler provides no names from the descendants of Manasseh (cf. Num 26:29-34); his interests at this point are territorial.

The exile of the Transjordanian tribes was because of their unfaithfulness to the covenant, described as an adulterous relationship with other gods (v. 25). The campaigns of Tiglath-Pileser were primarily directed against Damascus, but his campaigns included northern Israel (2 Kings 15:29). A summary inscription in Tiglath-Pileser's annals recounts the overthrow of Pekah, whose base of operations began in Transjordan (COS 2.291, Summary Inscription 9-10). The location of the deportation is known from 2 Kings 17:6. Gozan was a location on the Habur River, a tributary to the Euphrates. Halah was a town and district northeast of Nineveh; the name *Hara* describes this area as the mountain. From the viewpoint of the Chronicler, that territory remained in exile in his time.

Levi 6:1-81

The Levites are central among the tribes of Israel. The royal family (Judah) and the leading military family (Benjamin) anchor the historical record of Israel, but the temple, representing the earth as God's domain, is at the center of the Chronicler's history. In each of these three genealogies, identity is critical. Each has a long descending family record: David (1 Chron 3:1-24), Jeiel (8:29-40), and Levi (6:1-53). Residence was also important to the Chronicler; land is essential to human habitation and an evidence of God's faithfulness to the covenant. The Levites did not have a territory of their own; the Levitical genealogy concludes with the identification of their habitations to the time of David (6:54-81). The sons of Levi are introduced twice (6:1, 16); the Levites divide into a lineage of priests (vv. 1-15) and a lineage of nonpriestly families (vv. 16-30). The establishment of the temple under Solomon brought about a change in the Levitical duties. David instituted temple music with the move of the ark to Jerusalem (vv. 31-32). Once Solomon had built the temple, these became a permanent order, and previous duties of the tabernacle were no longer required. The duties of the priests continued as before (v. 49). The lineage of Levi concludes with a summary statement of the priests from Aaron to Zadok (vv. 50-53), the time from the institution of tabernacle duties to the transfer of these duties to the temple in the days of Solomon.

6:1-15 *Priestly Lineage to the Exile*

The priestly genealogy of Levi (the sons of Aaron) provides a continuous lineage from the patriarch to the exile (6:1-15). Though this has often been interpreted as a list of high priests, the Chronicler does not describe them as such. He provides a genealogy from Levi to the exile without distinguishing the role these individuals had in priestly duties. Azariah is notable for his service as priest under Solomon (v. 10; cf. 1 Kings 4:2); his inclusion may be indicative of the function of the genealogy. It anchors the priestly line to the patriarch Levi, irrespective of their role in temple administration. Several high priests known from other texts are not included in this list: Jehoiada, the priest who assisted in preserving King Joash in the time of Athaliah (1 Kings 22:10-11); Azariah, who resisted Uzziah in offering incense (2 Chron 26:16-18); and Uriah, who built an altar for King Ahaz (2 Kings 16:11). The priests of the restored temple have their credentials as descendants of the patriarch Levi. The patriarchal period is more important than the Mosaic period in establishing the authority of the priests. Royal, military, and priestly leaders were all determined through the distinct roles of the sons of Jacob.

The genealogy from Levi to Aaron is found in several sources (Gen 46:11; Exod 6:16-25; Num 3:17-20). The priests descended through Kohath, Amram, Aaron, and Eleazar; the list provides a linear genealogy of twenty-two priests following Aaron until the exile. An important function of this list is to establish the Aaronide ancestry of Jehozadak, the father of Joshua the first high priest when the temple was rebuilt (Hag 1:1-2; 2:1-2; Ezra 3:2). Seraiah, the father of Jehozadak, was put to death following the capture of Jerusalem (2 Kings 25:18-21; Jer 52:24-27). The genealogy connects the priests of the second temple with the priests of the first temple, descended from Aaron and Eleazar.

A comparison of the priestly lists in the Scriptures indicates that all of them are related to common sources (cf. Ezra 7:1-5; Neh 11:10-11; 1 Chron 9:10-11). It is also evident that all of them are abbreviated; in some cases there appear to be accidental omissions, but in other cases there are intentional abbreviations (e.g., 1 Chron 6:50-53; cf. vv. 3-8). The genealogy of Ezra is identical to the genealogy of Jehozadak (Ezra 7:1-5; 1 Chron 6:3-14), with one notable omission. Ezra lacks all the priests between Amariah son of Meraiot and Azariah the father of Amariah (1 Chron 6:7, 11). This gap leaves out all the priests known from the narrative of David and Solomon (2 Sam 8:17; 15:27; 1 Kings 4:2). A comparison of all the priestly lists (including Josephus and 1 Esdras) shows that many of the differences were the result of accidental scribal omissions (haplography). A repetition of names, as is common in the priestly lists, makes it very easy for the eye of a scribe to skip to a second occurrence of the name, omitting all the priests between them.

Repetition of names in priestly lists is partially a consequence of the ancient custom of naming someone after a grandfather (the practice of papponymy). Name sharing can lead to various confusions. Kings tells us that Azariah son of Zadok was priest in Solomon's reign (1 Kings 4:2). In Chronicles the priest in Solomon's time is Azariah son of Johanan (1 Chron 6:10); however, Azariah (grand)son of Zadok is named immediately preceding (vv. 8-9). It may be that the reference in Chronicles has been accidentally misplaced, making the second Azariah the priest of Solomon's time.

If the first Azariah is the correct identification of the priest in Solomon's time, he is the thirteenth priest from the time of Aaron. Kings tells us that there were 480 years between the exodus and the building of the temple (1 Kings 6:1). Forty years is often the length of time expressed symbolically for a generation in biblical history. The forty years in the wilderness is counted as the entire life of a generation, though biologically and therefore chronologically a new generation begins with the first child, when the mother is about age twenty. It is likely the building of the temple was understood to be twelve generations from the time of the exodus. If the Chronicler held this view, he appropriately provided the names of twelve priests for the period from the exodus to Solomon. This was followed by a list of eleven priests until the exile of Jehozadak, indicating that the temple endured for approximately eleven generations. The Chronicler's genealogy of priests is designed as a representative list to establish the lineage of high priests for his time.

6:16-30 Levitical Genealogies

The Chronicler lists the sons of Levi a second time (1 Chron 6:16-19) to provide a genealogy for the three sons of Levi (vv. 20-30). David appointed temple singers from each of the three family lineages (vv. 33-47). Repetition of the segmented family of Levi unites priests and singers in the same genealogical pedigree; both are authentic representatives in the temple service. The differences between them are status and function. Aaron and his sons were officers of the sanctuary and officers of God (1 Chron 24:5). Their task was to perform *the work of the most holy place* and *to make atonement for Israel* (6:49 NRSV). The task of the singers was to give praise at the times of the offerings and the festivals (23:30-32). These genealogies seem to be a lineage to the time of David, when the Levites were reorganized. Asaiah (6:30), the last named descendant of Merari, is twice named when David assembled the Levites (15:6, 11).

The genealogy of the descendants of Levi lists those families not in priestly lineage descended from Amram through Aaron. The sons of Gershom (var. of Gershon), Kohath, and Merari are given as found in the earlier genealogies (Exod 6:17-19; Num 3:18-20). The Kohathites (Num 4:2-15), Gershomites (vv. 21-28), and Merarites (vv. 29-33) were responsible for assembling, maintaining, guarding, dismantling, and moving the tabernacle in the wilderness. This was all part of the work in which the Levites served as assistants to the priests, who were descendants of Kohath through Amran and Aaron.

Having introduced the families of the three sons of Levi, the Chronicler goes on to provide a lineage to the time when they were appointed by David and installed by Solomon for the ministry of song at the temple of the Lord (vv. 20-30). The lineages of Gershom and Merari are each given in a descending list of seven sons. The lineage of Kohath is extended by the inclusion of the genealogy of Samuel. This genealogy is found in the introduction to the story of Samuel. Elkanah is introduced in Samuel as an Ephraimite, the son of Jeroham, son of Elihu, son of Tohu, son of Zuph (1 Sam 1:1). The sons of Samuel were Joel and Abijah (1 Sam 8:2). Despite some spelling differences, Chronicles gives the same genealogy, probably derived from a different source. There is no genealogical link of Elkanah, father of Samuel, to the tribe of Levi in the history of Samuel. The father of Samuel came from the territory of Ephraim (1 Sam 1:1); it is possible he was a Levite living in Ephraim (cf. Judg 17:7-8), or Samuel may have been adopted into the Levitical families because of his role as a priest. The consonantal MT and the Greek texts make Samuel a son of Elkanah who is son of Ahimoth, the reading of most English translations *[Masoretic Text, p. 470; Greek Text of Chronicles, p. 468]*.

The appearance of Amminadab as a son of Kohath is surprising (1 Chron 6:22). The usual listing for the sons of Kohath is Amram, Izhar, Hebron, and Uzziel (cf. vv. 2, 18); Izhar is also the son of Kohath through whom Heman descended (v. 33-38). The son of Amminadab is Korah, according to the Chronicler in this genealogy. Korah is a son of Izhar in the genealogy of Aaron (Exod 6:21), which is found in some versions, but this cannot have been the Chronicler's source. Amminadab is found among the Levites serving David (1 Chron 15:10-11). The appearance of an ancestor by that name might be indicative of family continuity.

In 1 Chronicles 6:25 the MT makes Amasi and Ahimoth sons of Elkanah, the fourth in the line of Kohath. In 6:35-36 Amasi the son of Elkanah is the father of Mahath. Mahath, the son of Amasi, is also a Kohathite attested in the reign of Hezekiah (2 Chron 29:12). Ahimoth appears to be a reversal of letters in the name Mahat. The MT in 6:24-25 should follow the pattern of Shaul his son, Elkanah his son, Amasai his son, Mahath his son, Elkanah his son, Zuph his son (Knoppers 2004a: 417, 421). A comparison of English translations indicates that there is a further error in the MT in omitting Samuel's name in verse 26 and the name of Joel his firstborn son in verse 27. The names are found correctly in verse 33. Heman the Kohathite is the son of Joel, the son of Samuel, the son of Elkanah. According to Chronicles, Samuel son of Elkanah (1 Sam 1:1, 20) belongs to the Kohathites within the tribe of Levi.

6:31-53 Levites as Musicians and Priests

A change in the Levitical duties was instituted with the transfer of the ark to Jerusalem (1 Chron 6:31-32). The duties for transporting the tabernacle were over; the symbol of divine rule over creation would be localized with the king's residence in one place, as was customary in ancient culture. The primary function of the Levites in Chronicles is their leadership in song at the temple. Their work was done *following all the regulations* (v. 32), an indication that the practice of music was begun earlier at the tabernacle in Gibeon, led by Heman and Jeduthun (1 Chron 16:41). The ark found its resting place in Jerusalem, in the tent (house of the Lord) David prepared for it, when it was brought up from Obed-Edom (15:1–16:1). Song and liturgical ritual (service) in Jerusalem were part of the Levitical duty.

Heman the singer (6:33), Asaph (v. 39), and Ethan (v. 44) are the heads of three classes or guilds of singers who received appointments during the time of David (15:17), first provisionally and then permanently. The Chronicler is very specific; until the temple was built, the singers served *before the tabernacle of the tent of meeting* (6:32). During this time certain Levites attended the ark in Jerusalem (16:1-6, 36-37), while others served at the tent of meeting in Gibeon (16:39-42). Heman, Asaph, and Ethan are referred to as the singers (cf. 15:19). Heman is the grandson of Samuel, giving him preeminence. The singing of Heman, Asaph, and Jeduthun is described as a kind of prophecy (25:1). Song is very important in Chronicles; Levitical choirs appear some thirty times in the work.

The Levitical genealogies focus on two periods of Israelite history. The first, beginning with the patriarch Levi, provides a list of descendants going on to the time of David. The second begins with the singers assigned by David, lists their descendants, and traces their ancestors back to the patriarchal age. The time of the united monarchy was the critical period for establishing the credentials of the singers. The authority of the priests was established earlier in the patriarchal and Mosaic periods. The lists should not be expected to be identical, since one is authenticating the Levites as a tribe to the time of David, while the second traces back the lineage of the families of singers during the time of David. The genealogies of the singers are longer, but in all cases share common names with the previous genealogy of Levites. The Kohathite lineage, which provides the ancestry of Heman through Samuel, has the closest parallel to the genealogy of Levi's descendants. The genealogy of Ethan through the Merarites is significantly longer and has more differences than similarities. It is likely that the two genealogical lines of each of the three sons of Levi are drawn from different sources.

The family of Levi is concluded with a priestly genealogy through Aaron (6:50-53). This brings the history of Levi back to the prominent distinction with which it is introduced (vv. 1-15). These two genealogies of priests form an inclusio around the family members of Levi *[Inclusio, p. 467]*. The sons of Kohath are eminent in the tribe of Levi, as the lineage of priests goes back to Amram and Aaron, while the lineage of the chief singer Heman extends through Samuel back to Izhar. The respective genealogies focus on the time period important to their function.

The priests were responsible to officiate within the sanctuary and to make offerings (v. 49). The details of these duties are specified elsewhere (e.g., Exod 29:38-42; 30:1-10). Only priests could officiate at the inner sanctuary. Temple worship was an essential part of the covenant because it included confession of the Israelites' relationship with God, both as individuals and as a community. Confession of sin along with seeking forgiveness was also a daily requirement in maintaining the covenant relationship; it was part of the daily ritual. This ritual included incense offerings, a testimony to the presence of the invisible God, and sacrificial offerings as a testimony to the need for the life-giving power of God received through the covenant.

6:54-81 Levitical Cities of Residence

The history of a people is an account of who they were and where they lived. With each of the tribal records, land is an important topic for the Chronicler. The distinction of the Levites was that their settlements established by lot were diversely located throughout the whole region of Israel. These allotments are described in Joshua 21, which has served as a source for the Chronicler. As is often the case in Chronicles, his source was not the version of Joshua known to us. It appears to be antecedent to the form that came to be finalized as Scripture. The Chronicler begins with a list of the Aaronide (priestly) cities in Judah, Simeon, and Benjamin (1 Chron 6:54-60; cf. Josh 21:10-18). The immediate introduction of the settlements of Kohath's priestly descendants is consistent with the distinction they receive in Chronicles. To establish their priority, the Chronicler has rearranged his source in Joshua, making his starting point after the introductory section in Josh 21:1-9. The Chronicler then uses material from the introduction of Joshua to summarize the allotments to the rest of the Kohathites, Gershonites, and Merarites (1 Chron 6:61-63; cf. Josh 21:5-7). He concludes the whole section in verses 64-65 with an adaption of Joshua 21:8-9 as a summary of those cities assigned to the Levites in Judah, Simeon, and Benjamin.

The Chronicler does not explain the occasion for the assignment of these cities. The book of Joshua tells us that the Levites appealed to the high priest Eleazar, Joshua, and the tribal heads to fulfill the command of Moses for their provision (Josh 21:1-4). Two factors are evident regarding the Chronicler's sources. There are variants of text; for example, the names Ephraim and Dan in Joshua 21:5 do not appear in the assignments of the rest of the Kohathites in 1 Chronicles 6:61. The Chronicler also changes the function of sections of his source material. The introduction in Joshua states that part of the inheritance of the Levites was the allotment of thirteen cities to Kohathite priests from the tribes of Judah, Simeon, and Benjamin (Josh 21:3-4). Joshua 21:5-7 goes on to enumerate cities given to the remainder of the Levitical families from the other tribes. The Chronicler takes up Joshua 21:5-7 following his list of priestly Kohathite cities of Judah and Benjamin in 1 Chronicles 6:54-60, drawn from Joshua 21:10-19. The designated cities of the nonpriestly Kohathites of Ephraim, Dan, and Manasseh in 1 Chronicles 6:61 anticipate the cities that will be named west of the Jordan in 1 Chronicles 6:66-70 (cf. Josh 21:20-26). In Joshua 21:5 the rest of the Kohathites are a sequel to the summary of thirteen cities allotted to the Aaronide portion of Kohath.

Dan is not mentioned when the Chronicler comes to name the cities of the nonpriestly Kohathites (1 Chron 6:66-70). However, cities named in Dan in the source list are included: Aijalon with its fields and Gath Rimmon with its fields (v. 69; cf. Josh 21:24). The omission of Dan can be regarded as accidental, or the Chronicler may be depicting the situation in the time of David, when the singers of the Levites were appointed. The new situation would require adaption of the earlier source material. However, the Chronicler retains much of the form and language of the Scriptures from which he drew his information.

The Chronicler has structured his information on settlements to correspond with that of the genealogies of Levi. The city list of Levi begins with the sons of Aaron (the priests) of the Kohathites (1 Chron 6:54-60), the rest of the Kohathites (v. 61), the Gershonites (v. 62), and the Merarites (v. 63). The cities of the Levitical families are then added as specific information (vv. 66-81; cf. Josh 21:20-42). This is also the sequence of the genealogy of Levi (1 Chron 6:1-47), which begins with the priests (6:4-14), followed by a genealogy of the nonpriestly Levites (vv. 16-30). The families of the Levitical singers appointed by David are then named as descendants of each of the three sons of Levi (vv. 31-47). An abbreviated genealogy of Aaronides (vv. 50-53) anticipates the enumeration of the residences of the Kohathite priests (vv. 57-59). The Chronicler has selected and arranged his material to portray the sons of Levi as ordered around the high priest.

The Levitical cities did not become the domain of the Levites to the exclusion of other Israelites. Levites had the prerogative to live in these towns and may have had certain rights within them. Hebron, for example, belonged to the descendants of Caleb for his faithfulness when the spies were sent from Kadesh Barnea (Josh 14:6-15). Open land outside each of the cities was included with each of the designated locations, since this was the only territory available to Levitical families for their livelihood.

One of the functions of specified Levitical cities was to serve as asylum for involuntary manslaughter until proper investigation could be conducted (Josh 20:1-9). Six cities are so designated among the Levitical cities in Joshua: Hebron in southern Judah (21:13); Shechem in Ephraim (v. 21); Golan in Bashan (v. 27); Kedesh in Naphtali (v. 32); Ramoth Gilead in Gad (v. 38). Bezer in Reuben is also a city of refuge (v. 36) but is not called a Levitical city. The Chronicler's presentation of the cities of asylum is unique. He employs the plural (*cities*) in two general introductory rubrics: 1 Chronicles 6:57 and 67. It may be that he intends all the cities in the respective following sections as cities of refuge: all cites belonging to the descendants of Aaron (vv. 57-60) and cities of the Kohathites in Ephraim (vv. 67-69). Some relationship exists between the cities of refuge and Levitical cities. Perhaps Levites administered the responsibilities for the case of a manslayer as part of their overall duties.

The Levitical settlements spread across the territories of ancient Israel (Aharoni et al.: 108), which would be necessary if they were to serve as cities of refuge and places of covenant instruction. The Kohathites were in the more southern tribes west of the Jordan (Judah, Benjamin, Ephraim, and Manasseh). The Gershonites were in the more northern and eastern territories, including Golan and Ashtaroth in Bashan (Transjordan Manasseh); they were also found in the tribes of Issachar, Asher, and Naphtali to the west and north of Galilee (vv. 71-76). The Merarites were located in Zebulun, Reuben, and Gad, territories in the southern Transjordan, though their territory extended west to Tabor and Rimmono, the area north of Ephraim and Manasseh (vv. 77-81). The Aaronide cities were located in Judah and Benjamin, indicating that they were a southern group. Though not all these locations can be identified, the concentration of the Levitical cities was largely in Judah, Ephraim, and western Galilee, but their distribution extended to the far north in the remote parts of Transjordan.

Northern Tribes 7:1-40

The Chronicler fashions noble if not heroic lineages for the tribes of the north, which would have had very limited prominence in his time. His presentation is a notable contrast with that of other Scripture. Due attention is given to Levi, Judah, and Benjamin, but passages such as Genesis 48–49 devote most of their attention to Reuben, Gad, Asher, Naphtali, Issachar, Zebulun, Dan, and Simeon. Particular attention is given to Joseph and his two Egyptian sons Ephraim and Manasseh. In the Song of Deborah, Judah does not appear at all (Judg 5:1-31). The northern tribes occupy the largest part of the census numbers in Numbers 1 and 26. It might well be asked why the northern tribes should matter to the Chronicler at all, since in his time their presence could have been virtually disregarded. But it is not the present with its attendant special interests that governs the thinking of the Chronicler. He describes the northern tribes as warriors fit for a military campaign. Since all the descendants of Benjamin have a high profile, the selection of names itself accentuates their status. Manasseh and Ephraim do not have the same military status, but they occupy significant territory, including towns not listed as conquered in Joshua.

The Chronicler includes all the tribes of Israel not yet discussed. Dan is not actually named (see on 1 Chron 7:12 below), but a comparison with the Chronicler's sources shows that he included it as one of the sons of Bilhah. The absence of Zebulun seems to be a result of some serious textual disruptions present in this chapter. The chapter breaks down into five sections: Issachar (7:1-5), Benjamin (vv. 6-11), the sons of Bilhah (vv. 12-13), the sons of Joseph (vv. 14-29), and Asher (vv. 30-39). These five sections are quite different from each other. Issachar, Benjamin, and Asher are distinguished by the length that is devoted to one tribe. Each records the father's house (rather than a simple genealogy), and all three have an emphasis on military enumeration. The sons of Bilhah are highly abbreviated; the sons of Joseph lack the military associations but include information on their settlements.

7:1-11 *Issachar and Benjamin*

The descendants of Issachar are given as found in earlier sources (Gen 46:13; Num 26:23-24). The segmented genealogy traces his descendants through his son Tola, his grandson Uzzi, and his great-grandson Izrahiah (1 Chron 7:3). These are distinguished as heads of their ancestral house and as *valiant warriors*. The tribe was strong and prolific; in the census of David they numbered 22,600 (v. 2). In the time of Izrahiah the totals of their military detachments was 36,000 (v. 4). The census totals of their kinsmen are given as an astonishing 87,000 registered warriors. This number exceeds those given earlier: 54,400 (Num 1:29); 64,300 (Num 26:25). The large numbers of these ancient records are not fully understood. The numbers given are not simply totals of a census but are representative calculations. There is a relationship between the census totals in Numbers and the computations of solar and lunar cycles used in calendar computations well known to the ancient Babylonian astronomers

(Barnouin). The tribal figures seem to have been made to correspond to celestial movements presenting Israel as the armies (hosts) of the Lord, like the stars (hosts) of the heavens. Though the term used for "thousand" can have other senses, such as a clan or military unit, its intended meaning as a number in these census counts seems to be consistent. The military muster of Issachar is the largest recorded anywhere, except for that of Judah (2 Sam 24:9; cf. 1 Chron 21:5). The Chronicler portrays Issachar as having very high distinction among the tribes of Israel.

The genealogical record of Benjamin, like that of Issachar, appears to be drawn from a military census (1 Chron 7:6-11). The source of the record may have influenced its repetition of the genealogy in the military record of Israel. It is found again in chapter 8, the history given to explain the appointment of Saul as Israel's first king. The military census list may also explain the inclusion of Benjamin among the northern tribes of Issachar, Naphtali, and Manasseh. The three sons of Benjamin are Bela, Beker, and Jediael. The list follows the record of Genesis 46:21 in naming Beker as the second son of Benjamin but is the only genealogy to have Jediael as a third child. Ashbel is the third child in Genesis, but second elsewhere (cf. Num 26:38; 1 Chron 8:1). Jediael seems to have replaced Ashbel in this genealogy. He is found only in Chronicles (1 Chron 7:10, 11; 11:45; 12:20; 26:2). After the first three sons, each of the genealogies goes its own way.

The three sons of Benjamin are each given segmented genealogies (7:7-11). Jediael is extended to the third generation through Bilhan, his only son (v. 10). The descendants are said to have been registered according their lineages as heads of their ancestral houses. The number of military warriors is not large, but in the case of Bela it is remarkably specific: 22,034. The total number of soldiers from the tribe of Benjamin is 59,434 (vv. 7, 9, 11). This compares to 35,400 (Num 1:37) and 45,600 (Num 26:41). Benjamin grandson of Jediael (v. 10) is also a tribal grouping within the tribe of Benjamin. Anathoth and Alemeth, listed as sons of Beker, are place names, appearing previously in the list of Levitical cities belonging to Benjamin (cf. 1 Chron 6:60). Anathoth was a priestly city several miles northeast of Jerusalem, mentioned as the home of Abiezer and Jehu, two of David's bodyguards (1 Chron 11:28; 12:3; 27:12). It is best known for being the home of Jeremiah, who came from among the priests living there (Jer 1:1). Throughout the genealogies there is an interchange of place and person names. Places may be named after the people living there, and it can be that the people in a locale are sufficiently homogenous that they are thought of as one family. The whole conceptual system presents social and geographical circumstances in genealogical terms.

7:12-19 *Dan, Naphtali, Zebulun, and Manasseh*

Following the very orderly summary of Benjamin, serious textual problems revolve around the genealogies of the northern tribes of Dan, Naphtali, Zebulun, and Manasseh. The complete omission of Zebulun cannot have been the intention of the Chronicler. Attempts to find a genealogy for Zebulun elsewhere in the chapter (as in rewriting the genealogy of Ephraim) are completely conjectural. Verse 12 provides some textual information to indicate that Dan was once listed as a tribal name. Hushim is the name of the only son of Dan in the Genesis genealogy (Gen 46:23). The Greek translation of verse 12b in Chronicles would indicate that the Hebrew originally read *Hushim, his one son*. In the MT, *sons of Aher* orthographically in Hebrew script appears much like *his son, one*. Verse 13 introduces the sons of Naphtali as they are given in their genealogy in Genesis 46:24-25a, concluding with *sons of Bilhah*, as does Genesis. Dan and Naphtali are the only two sons of Bilhah. The ending of verse 13 is a convincing indication that verse 12 once read *descendants of Dan, Hushim, his one son*. Aher is not a Hebrew name, though it could be regarded as a corruption of a Benjamite name as Aharah (1 Chron 8:1). Shuppim and Huppim are variants of Shupham and Hupham, named as sons of Benjamin in Numbers 26:39. Verse 12a appears to be the remnant of a Benjamite genealogy. The vestige of these Benjamite names appears to have caused the name Dan to become corrupted to Ir, similar to Iri found in verse 7 of the Benjamite genealogy.

The inclusion of the sons of Bilhah is important to the concept of Israel as the Chronicler found it in his Scriptures. Zebulun was a part of those same Scriptures (Gen 46:14; Num 26:26-27) but is no longer included. Dan, Naphtali and Zebulun are the most northern tribes, the first to be deported by Tiglath-Pileser (2 Kings 15:29). The census data available for those tribes may well have been minimal as a source. If this was lost, the only information remaining would have been limited to the biblical text; but the omission of the data from the biblical text is a further indication of problems in transmission of Chronicles, perhaps even the loss of a full column of information on these tribes.

The problems of transmission continue in the record of Manasseh (1 Chron 7:14-19). The record begins with Asriel, followed by *whom she bore*, with no name for the subject. Translators have made *his Aramean concubine* the subject, which is the best that can be done with otherwise unintelligible Hebrew. We then read that Makir, son of Asriel, took a wife for Huppim and for Shuppim, sons named in verse 12 in continuation of the genealogy of Benjamin. The ambiguity continues with naming Maakah as sister of someone (v. 15), and the name of the second as Zelophehad, with no indication of the first or how Zelophehad fits into the genealogy. The tribal relation becomes more confused in verse 16, where we read that Maakah is the wife of Makir. Verses 16-17a record the descendants of Makir, summing up with *these were the sons of Gilead*, who has not previously been mentioned. Another sister named Hammoleketh is mentioned in verse 18, apparently intended as a sister to Gilead. Verse 19 concludes with the sons of Shemida, also not previously mentioned here. Numbers 26:32 indicates that Shemida was one of Gilead's sons and originally must have been named with some relationship to Gilead and Makir.

The number of ambiguities and disjunctions in the genealogy of Manasseh make a reconstruction of the original text highly conjectural. The best way forward is to seek help from other genealogies of Manasseh (see esp. Josh 17:1-3 and Num 26:29-34). These texts are of limited assistance to understanding the Chronicles genealogy for two reasons: by their very nature, genealogies are fluid over time, and this is the only segmented genealogy of Manasseh that has been preserved. As different families gain prominence, clan relationships come to reflect the realities current to their time. Making sense of what has been preserved in the genealogy of Manasseh must be tentative, but it does at least provide an indication of the representatives of Manasseh.

Asriel, the first descendant named, is found in all the Manasseh genealogies. There is also good reason to retain the information about an Aramean concubine. The Greek text of Genesis retains the memory of Makir being the son of the Syrian concubine of Manasseh (Gen 46:20), who in turn became the father of Gilead. This seems to be the genealogy known to the Chronicler. Historically the tribe of Manasseh had geographic affinity with the Arameans, but the Genesis genealogy takes Syrian affiliation back to Joseph in Egypt. Genealogies retain social, ethnic, historical, and geographic connections among a variety of individuals, peoples, and places. Makir is the firstborn of Manasseh in the other genealogies (Josh 17:1; Num 26:29; cf. Num 36:1), which must have been the intent of the Chronicler. For reasons of sense, the Benjamite names Huppim and

Shuppim in verse 15 should be omitted, and the sister of Makir should be Hammoleketh rather than Maakah, as is reported in verse 18. Following the information of verses 14, 17, and the other genealogies, Gilead should be the firstborn son of Makir. His name should be supplied in verse 15 before the second son Zelophehad, who had many daughters. On the basis of verse 17, Maakah in verse 16 is the wife of Gilead, and the names of his descendants follow. The fragmentary genealogy of Manasseh then makes Makir the firstborn through an Aramean wife. The sons of Makir were Gilead and Zelophehad. The sons of Gilead are given in verses 16-17. These are followed by the descendants of his sister Hammoleketh, which should include Shemida, whose descendants are given in verse 19.

The Chronicler provides a Transjordan and Aramean influence on the settlements of Manasseh. In Joshua 17:2-3 the majority of the descendants of Makir settle west of the Jordan. Gilead and Bashan are assigned to Manasseh (v. 1), but no clans are designated as settling there. In Chronicles the primary line of Makir is traced in the east through Gilead and his sons. The western affiliations of the tribe are given through the descendants of Hammoleketh, the sister of Makir.

7:20-29 Ephraim

The record of Ephraim bears little relationship to the earlier Ephraimite lineages (Gen 46:20 in Greek; Num 26:35-37). Numbers provides a segmented genealogy where three descendants of Ephraim are Shuthelah, Beker, and Tahan. The Chronicler alternately provides a linear genealogy of eight generations beyond Ephraim (1 Chron 7:20-21a). The genealogy is interrupted by a short narrative concerning a raid in which two brothers were killed. A linear genealogy continues in verses 25-27, leading to Joshua of the conquest. No relationship is established between the two genealogies, though presumably at one time they belonged together. In the history familiar to the Chronicler and his readers, the patriarch Ephraim was born in Egypt centuries before the exodus. Williamson concludes that the resemblance of this genealogy to Numbers is artificial (Williamson 1982: 80). He proposes that this is a linear genealogy of Joshua the son of Nun separately compiled, much like that of Samuel in 1 Chronicles 6:22-27 and 33-38. The Ephraim of 7:22, as the ancestor of Joshua, is therefore to be dated long after the patriarch. The inclusion of the narrative within the genealogy resulted in the interpretation of the Targum and other midrashic literature, which assumed a premature and unsuccessful exodus of the tribe of Ephraim long before the days of Joshua.

The book of Joshua locates Joshua as an Ephraimite within the tribe of his territorial inheritance (Josh 19:49-50; 24:30). The Chronicler has no other interest in Joshua or the conquest. This genealogy of Ephraim was included from his sources. The Chronicler inserts his own observations into the genealogy, much like the story of Jabez (1 Chron 4:9-10). In this case a very negative event, in which two sons were killed by Canaanite natives, resulted in the birth of a son whose name commemorated this tragedy (7:21b-23). The name Beriah in Hebrew designates trouble, based on the Hebrew word *ra'ah* (evil) preceded by the preposition *b*. His daughter Sheerah built the Levitical city of Beth Horon (1 Chron 6:68), which had two locations on the slope on the southern boundary of Ephraim in the Valley of Aijalon. This valley was the most important of all the routes in the hill country from the coastal plain. The location of Uzzen Sheerah is unknown; this is the only reference to this city (7:24). The Chronicler included the narrative of the Canaanite raid to show how the lament of Ephraim and the consolation of his brothers came to distinguish the history of the tribe.

The close relationship of the sons of Joseph is evident in the territorial summary of the tribes (7:28-29). The allocation of the people in the land is of great significance to the Chronicler. This list for Ephraim locates the major cities of their territory: Bethel in the south, Naaran in the east, Gezer in the west, and Shechem in the north. All the sites named for Manasseh (Beth Shan, Taanach, Megiddo, and Dor) are situated along the northern border and are said to be under their control. The lack of emphasis on the southern border for Manasseh may be another indication of its intimate affiliation with Ephraim.

7:30-40 Asher

The military census of Asher begins with the names as found in Genesis 46:17 (1 Chron 7:30-31). The census is highly segmented, tracing the descent of the tribe through the fourth son Beriah and his firstborn Heber (v. 32). It is the sons of Hotham (Helem; cf. v. 32, 35) who receive the most detailed description (v. 35). It is often proposed that the text should be emended at the end of verse 36. Instead of giving Zophah eleven sons, the names *Beri, Imrah* should be read *sons of Imna*, the second son of Hotham/Helem. Imna would then have seven sons, with the sons of Jether extended to the next generation. Ulla is otherwise unknown (v. 39b); if identified with Amal (v. 35), his sons are descendants of Hotham (Helem). All these are described as select valiant warriors, heads of the tribal chiefs.

The total number of their muster is 26,000, considerably reduced from the earlier numbers of 41,500 in Numbers 1:41 and 53,400 in Numbers 26:47.

The geographical region of Heber is not certain (1 Chron 7:32). Beriah, father of Heber, is found in Ephraim as well as Benjamin (7:23; 8:13). Heber is also found in Benjamin (8:17). In the story of Deborah, Heber is a Kenite who has traveled north to the Jezreel Valley (Judg 4:11, 17, 21). Is Beriah the son of Asher to be identified with the head of the ancestral house of the inhabitants of Aijalon who put to flight the inhabitants of Gath (1 Chron 8:13)? Aijalon was originally in the territory of Ephraim but came to be a part of the expanding territory of Benjamin. Japhlet, son of Heber, is given territory on the southern border of Ephraim in Joshua 16:3. The Chronicler may be describing a southern Asher that was much smaller in number, as indicated by the census number. Traditionally Asher is a northern tribe west of Naphtali and northwest of Zebulun.

Military Record of Israel 8:1–9:1a

8:1-3 Family of Benjamin

The geographical principle governing the order of the tribes now comes full circle. The sequence began with Judah and now with Benjamin returns to the center of Israel. The two tribes converge in the capital city, Jerusalem. The family of Benjamin is given in two generations. Five sons of the first generation are enumerated. It is not surprising that these cannot be harmonized with the other lists of Benjamin (cf. 1 Chron 7:6; Num 26:38-41). The differences show the alterations of which clans were prominent at a given period.

The list for the second generation follows with a different formula, using a narrative form. The end of verse 3 should not be translated *Gera and Abihud* (so NIV, NRSV) but *Gera, father of Ehud* (NIV mg., NRSV mg.). The difference is one of letter division, which is not always clear in an ancient text. Ehud the son of Gera was well known for his exploits in the settlement period (cf. Judg 3:15). Gera appears twice in this list (1 Chron 8:3, 5). There has been displacement in the text of these verses. The sons of Ehud are introduced without names in verse 6, then three names appear in verse 7a when the verb requires one. The text should be emended, moving the phrase *these are the sons of Ehud* in verse 6a to introduce the sons of Ehud in verse 4 (Williamson 1982: 83). The militia of Ehud actually begins in verse 4, which places the second Gera in the family of Ehud rather than Bela.

8:4-28 Militia at Jerusalem

In this report the members of the militia are from the clans of Ehud (vv. 4-7) and Shaharaim (vv. 8-28). The Ehud group was moved from Geba to Manahath (v. 6). Geba is a Levitical city of Benjamin on the northern boundary of Judah, six miles northeast of Jerusalem (Josh 18:24). It was fortified by Asa (1 Kings 15:22) and later occupied by Benjamites (Neh 11:31). Manahath is customarily identified with Malah, three miles southwest of Jerusalem. The reason for this internal exile is not explained, but it was probably due to tribal conflict.

The MT is ambiguous about who was responsible for the move of the sons of Ehud (1 Chron 8:6-7 NIV). The sons of Ehud naturally follow *Gera, father of Ehud* (a redivision of the letters of *Abihud* in verse 3). The sons of Ehud are *Abishua, Naaman, Ahoah, Gera, Shephuphan, and Huram* (vv. 4-5). Naaman and Ahijah in verse 7 may be regarded as repetitions from verse 4, caused by the misplaced phrase *sons of Ehud.* The textual error appears to be haplography, the accidental omission of *these are the sons of Ehud* at the beginning of verse 4, since verse 3 ended with *father of Ehud.* The omitted phrase was later entered in the margin and subsequently placed in the text at the wrong location. Moving the *sons of Ehud* to the beginning of verse 4 provides a syntactically intact text. The militia leaders of the Ehud clan are introduced (vv. 4-5), followed by a short report of the deportation of the group by Gera (vv. 6-7). The translation *Gera, that is, Heglam* (NRSV) has mistaken the verb for a personal name.

The second family of the militia is that of Shaharaim (1 Chron 8:8-28). This name is not found in the preceding list, nor is it known elsewhere. It probably is a variation or corruption of one of the sons of Benjamin introduced in this chapter; either Huram (v. 5) or Aharah/Ahiram (v. 1) could be a variation of the name. The family history tells of the fortunes of the tribe (vv. 8-13). Shaharaim was first married to Hushim and Baara. From his wife Hushim he had two sons, Abitub and Elpaal (v. 11). He then divorced his wives and moved to Moab, where he had another seven sons by Hodesh (vv. 8-10). Benjamin was a warrior tribe with a small territory (Gen 49:27; Judg 20:12-16). In the west they mixed with the tribe of Hushim son of Dan (cf. Gen 46:23) and built the areas of Lod and Ono in the territory of Dan (1 Chron 8:12). Other clan leaders lived in the area of Aijalon in Dan and were victorious over the inhabitants of Gath (v. 13). This is most likely a reference to Gath-gittaim, west of Gezer. This brief notation of the tribal history in the Philistine territory is given more fully in Samuel (2 Sam 4:2-3). Whether the Chronicler is referring to movements in the period of the monarchy or the later time of the Persians cannot be established (cf. Neh 11:31-35), but the series of episodes is indicative of the earlier time.

Five militia lists are given for the clan of Shaharaim. The texts do not agree on who belongs to the first list of Beriah. The received Hebrew text interprets Ahio as a name (v. 14). The Greek translators took the letters to mean *their brothers*, making Shashak and Jeremoth brothers of Beriah and Shema of the clan of Elpaal. Since it is these four brothers along with further clans of Elpaal who appear in the militia lists, the Greek interpreters were no doubt correct. The militia lists are Beriah (vv. 15-16), Elpaal (vv. 17-18), Shema (vv. 19-21), Shashak (vv. 22-25), and Jeremoth/Jeroham (vv. 26-27). It is not specified whether all these lived in Jerusalem (v. 28), but the inference would be that this does not include those garrisons in Manahath and Aijalon.

8:29-32 Militia at Gibeon

This list is supplementary to the Benjamites that lived in Jerusalem. The name of the father of the Gibeonites is not in the text; the name Jeiel is found in the parallel passage in Chronicles (cf. 1 Chron 9:35) and in a few Greek manuscripts. The parallel passage includes Ner as a son of Jeiel (9:36), a significant point because the genealogy of Saul begins with Ner (8:33). Reference to his wife Maakah may allude to a non-Israelite element within the Benjamites. Gibeon was at the center of the Hivite population of the area (Josh 9:3-7), a foreign enclave within the Benjamite territory. Descendants of Mikloth *resided opposite their brothers* (8:32 AT) in Jerusalem, another reminder that in the division of Benjamin, Jerusalem was within its territory. Some families from Gibeon relocated to Jerusalem, in proximity to other Benjamites.

In the time of Solomon, Gibeon and Jerusalem were affiliated with each other. Solomon offered sacrifices in Gibeon, where God granted him wisdom in a vision (1 Kings 3:3-14), but returned to Jerusalem to offer sacrifices there after the vision (1 Kings 3:15; cf. 2 Chron 1:3-6). After the temple was built in Jerusalem, Solomon received a second vision like that at Gibeon (1 Kings 9:2). For a time both Gibeon and Jerusalem served as places of worship, as indicated by the associations of the royal family in both places.

Though Gibeon was famous as a shrine site, it is recognized here for being a military garrison. The phrase translated *father of Gibeon* (v. 29) perhaps means "commandant of Gibeon" (i.e., the person in charge of the military garrison there) rather than patriarch. The *sons* associated with him would be his subordinate officers. These functioned in cooperation with the garrison at Jerusalem in defense of the country.

8:33-40 Family of Saul

The Chronicler concludes his expansion of Benjamite history with a genealogy of Saul, beginning two generations before Saul and extending many generations to the families of Azel and Eshek (vv. 38-40). These mighty warriors were the continuation of the distinguished royal family. The list records ten generations from Micah, in the time from Solomon to Ulam (vv. 35, 39), a period near the end of the kingdom of Judah, just before the destruction of Jerusalem. Saul is thus connected with his larger tribal history and with a noble heritage that carried on throughout the kingdom period.

The genealogical information about Saul comes in two versions in the Bible. The Samuel texts inform us that Saul's father, Kish, was the son of Abiel (1 Sam 9:1). In this version, Abner and Saul are cousins, sons (respectively) of Ner and Kish, who have Abiel as their father. This version fits the Samuel texts if 1 Samuel 14:51 is emended from "son of Abiel" to "sons of Abiel" (a difference of adding the letter *yod*), and if the ambiguous term "Saul's uncle" in 1 Samuel 14:50 is understood to refer to Ner rather than to the equally possible Abner. For this set of relationships to align with Chronicles would mean that Jeiel (1 Chron 8:29-30 LXX; 9:35-36) is the same person as Abiel, that Kish has both a father and a brother named Ner (1 Chron 9:35-36, 39), and that Abiel/Jeiel is actually the grandfather of both Kish and Ner (making Saul and Abner second cousins). Ner may have named his son Kish after his brother, a case of neponymy, where a son is named after an uncle (Knoppers 2004a: 485), and likewise Kish could have named a son Ner for *his* brother.

In the second version, the Chronicler tells us that Saul's father Kish is the son of Ner (1 Chron 8:33; 9:35-36, 39), and Ner (who also has a brother Kish) is the son of Jeiel (8:30; 9:35-36; Jeiel is called the *father of Gibeon*, a title perhaps equivalent to "founder"). In this case, Abner is the brother of Kish and the uncle of Saul. Chronicles never states the relationship between Abner and Kish, referring to Abner only once as the *son of Ner* (1 Chron 26:28). For this version to work with the Samuel texts, Abiel and Jeiel must again be considered as the same person who lived in Gibeon in the territory of Benjamin. Also, Ner must be inserted between Abiel and Kish in 1 Samuel 9:1, and Abner must be considered Saul's uncle in 1 Samuel 14:50. As Klein notes, no certain decision between these two versions is possible (Klein 1998: 142).

The list here in 1 Chronicles 8:33 gives the four sons of Saul as Jonathan, Malki-Shua, Abinadab, and Esh-Baal. The fourth son is found in Samuel as Ishvi (1 Sam 14:49) and as Ish-Bosheth (2 Sam 2:8, 10). The differences in the name show the development of the tradition. Esh-Baal, meaning "man of Baal," must be the oldest form of the name, going back to the tribe's origin in a territory where Baal was the god of the land. Ishvi would be a form of the name in which a form of Yahweh, the covenant name of God, replaced the original name (*yo* or *yeho*). Ish-Bosheth is a deliberate corruption of the name to say "man of shame." The same change may be observed in the name of Merib-Baal, the son of Jonathan (1 Chron 8:34), who in Samuel is known as Mephibosheth (2 Sam 9:6, 10-11), the father of Micah (1 Chron 8:34; 2 Sam 9:12-13).

Benjamin had always been the prominent representative of the Northern Kingdom of Israel. The conclusion of the list in 1 Chronicles 8:40b, that all these were Benjamites, is not meant as a quantitative statement but as an indication of character. These were all mighty military warriors. In the theology of the Chronicler, this lengthy addition of the tribe of Benjamin serves to put the kingdom of Israel on an equal basis with the kingdom of Judah, which had been given in a corresponding fashion (1 Chron 2:3-4:23), with considerable detail for the leading royal family. It also shows that the totality of the territory once occupied by Benjamin is included in the state of Yehud in the restoration.

9:1a Registration of All Israel

The phrase *all Israel was registered* (AT) has long been recognized as a crux in understanding the thought of the Chronicler. If *all Israel* is to serve as a conclusion to the records of Israel (chs. 2-8), the notation of the exile of Judah serves to mark a transition to the settlement of Jerusalem in the time of the Chronicler (v. 1b). This viewpoint might be regarded as a consensus since the influential conclusions of Rudolph (83). However, the focus of the Chronicler was not chronology but identity. It was critical to him to establish the continuity of the nation in its existence and the manner of its functioning. Nothing is said about the end of the exile or the intervening years. The genealogy makes it clear that people can survive even if they do not inhabit their land.

The *registration of all Israel* forms an inclusio with *these are the sons of Israel* in 2:1 [*Inclusio, p. 467*]. Acknowledgment of the exile of Judah in 9:1b is an assertion that the identity of the people is bound up with their land. Living in foreign lands is an interlude rather than a normal way of life. The Judean distinctiveness in the age of the Chronicler derived from its settlement in the land and the centrality of Jerusalem within it. The identity of the people in the present is to be found in their continuity with the generations of the past. Not all had returned to the land, but Jerusalem remained central to the identity and hope of those Israelites scattered among the diverse nations.

THE TEXT IN BIBLICAL CONTEXT

Blessing of Joseph

Joseph, who preserved the family of Jacob in Egypt, was given special distinction by his father (Gen 47:25-48:22). Ephraim and Manasseh, the sons born to Joseph in Egypt, were given the status of Reuben and Simeon, the two oldest sons of Jacob (48:5-6); Jacob claimed these as his own sons. These two grandchildren came to be heirs in his family and part of the confederacy of Israel. By this means Joseph was deemed to have received the double portion that is the normal right of the firstborn (Deut 21:17). Jacob also granted to Joseph a portion of land that was one more share than his brothers (Gen 48:22). The Genesis narrative assigns to Joseph the privileges of the firstborn. The Chronicler has interpreted this to mean that the right of the firstborn belonged to Joseph.

The final blessing of Jacob accords Joseph a distinct status. Reuben was the son of distinction and strength, but he was as turbulent waters because of his assertiveness in his claiming his father's concubine (Gen 49:3-4). The Hebrew text has a play on words to emphasize the point. Reuben as firstborn had the benefit (*yeter*) of dignity and strength, but he would not benefit (*yotar*) because of his presumptive actions. Joseph is accorded special blessings from his father (vv. 22-26). He is a fruitful vine, one who has prevailed over grievous adversity. The word "blessing" occurs five times (vv. 25-26), bestowing on Joseph riches from the heights of heaven to the great depths, the abundance of the mountains and everlasting hills. Joseph is an anointed prince among his brothers. The blessings from the heights to the depths and the riches of the everlasting hills are repeated in the song of Moses, as the affirmation that he is a crown prince among his brothers (Deut 33:13-17). Ephraim and Manasseh prevail among the nations. Joseph is the only candidate as the chief heir among Jacob's sons.

Preeminence of Judah

Although the blessing belonged to Joseph, Judah prevailed among his brothers and therefore the prince descended from him (1 Chron 5:2). The rise of Judah's prominence begins with the sale of Joseph to the Ishmaelites (Gen 37:26-27). The import of his question is ambiguous: "What do we gain if we kill our brother?" It may be an expression of sordid hostility against Joseph, or it may be a desperate compromise to save his life. But the narrative shows the shift in power from Reuben to Judah. Reuben's intent to restore Joseph to his father in 37:22 had been preempted by Judah. A further indication of Judah's dominance among his brothers is apparent after Joseph has Simeon bound, demanding that the youngest brother, Benjamin, be brought to Egypt. Jacob rejects the vows of Reuben to safely bring Benjamin back from Egypt in order to free Simeon (42:37-38). Yet later he agrees to the same proposal from Judah that Benjamin must accompany them to Egypt in quest of provisions (43:8-14), accepting the fact that he may be bereaved of Benjamin as well. Judah intervenes when Benjamin is to be made a slave because the goblet was found in his possession (44:18-34). The role of Reuben as leader of the brothers has been fully supplanted. In the last words of Jacob, Judah is a lion who has grown on prey; he is the king of beasts that must not be roused, and the scepter will not depart from him (49:9-12). The meaning of *šiloh* in verse 10 may be taken as *that which belongs to him* (the monarchy), or it may be identified with the territory in Ephraim. Ahijah of Shiloh announced that ten tribes would secede with Jeroboam (1 Kings 11:29-34). If the reference of Genesis 49:10 to Shiloh is a place in Ephraim, then Judah will rule over all Israel until the division of the kingdom, but even then the promise to David remains secure. Not all the kingdom will be taken from Solomon because of the divine promise to David and the preeminence of Judah, as Chronicles puts it. Judah will not be subservient to the tribes of Israel.

The genealogy of the Chronicler is established both biblically and historically. The Genesis narrative of the promise to Abraham declared unequivocally that the scepter belonged to Judah. Historically the prince of Judah returned with the exiles, representing the continuation of the promise made to David. Theologically the Chronicler has established two central points of the Torah in his genealogies *[Torah, p. 481]*. He has shown that through the promise to Abraham, God has positioned Israel as the means of blessing to all nations. He has further shown that the ruler of Israel has been ordained through the tribe of Judah, though Judah did not receive the right of the firstborn. The genealogical foundations provided in the Scriptures establish that the rule of the prince of Judah has its authority in the divine purpose, beginning with Adam. Whatever may be the circumstances of the province of Yehud among the nations, this community must know that they are Israel. Judah receives first place in their story. The Chronicler extends the descendants of the prince of Judah right down to his own time.

Centrality of Levi

In ancient times, temple and dominion were inextricably bound together. Kings ruled by divine power; divine power was represented in a fully functioning temple. For the Chronicler, the God of Israel is the ruler of all nations. Therefore the temple and all its personnel need to have central place in his community. The institution of the temple represents the reason for founding *Yehud Medinata*ʾ, the Aramaic name that the Persians used for area that had been a portion of Judah. In the days of the Chronicler, the descendants of Zerubbabel had very little influence in the affairs of the community. The identity of the community was found in the presence of the temple, which Cyrus had authorized and funded to some measure.

The Chronicler does not directly address the origins, nature, and configuration of worship in the time of the tabernacle and does not rewrite the version of the Sinai narrative. He uses the material of the Pentateuch to explain the transformation of older institutions in the time of David. Singers and musicians play an integral role in the later temple. Ascending genealogies highlight the role of Heman, Asaph, and Ethan, establishing the singers within Israel's classical heritage. The Levitical genealogies do not directly address the eras of temple function after David and Solomon. It is sufficient for the Chronicler to transform the tabernacle from being a sanctuary of sacrifice and silence to one of sacrifice and song. The tabernacle is incorporated within the temple. The transformation of the ancient function of the tabernacle connects the worship of Israel to Aaron and the promises to the patriarchs. The worship and confession of the temple does not lose its connection to the past but subverts past practices by providing a divine blessing for the innovations of the kingdom. The singers and the priests have a pedigree that links back to the ancestral era and therefore are a continuation of it.

Inclusion of Lost Tribes

In contrast to the gradual demise of the Transjordan tribes in the Deuteronomistic History, the Chronicler provides a vibrant tradition for Reuben, Gad, and the half-tribe of Manasseh east of the Jordan, until the campaigns of Tiglath-Pileser III *[Deuteronomistic History, p. 465]*. No explanation is given about when these tribes came to occupy their territories, but they have a continuous presence as tribes throughout the monarchy. The contrast of Reuben is particularly distinct. The demise of Reuben as a segmented society with a fixed territory is suggested by David's census, in which Gad is the only territory mentioned north of the Arnon River (2 Sam 24:5). The system of Solomon's districts includes Gilead (1 Kings 4:19), Mahanaim (v. 14), and Ramoth Gilead (v. 13), but there is no mention of Reuben. In Chronicles, Reuben not only survives intact into the eighth century, but also expands by means of population increase and war (1 Chron 5:1-26). In Chronicles individual tribes retain a significant degree of independence. The Reubenites conduct their own military campaign against the Hagrites (v. 10). Reuben, Gad, and the half-tribe of Manasseh muster and raise an army, then conduct a war against their common enemy (vv. 18-22). No losses are recorded until the Assyrian exile. But this hopeful reconstruction of the past had no continuing reality; these tribes remained exiled *to this day* (v. 26). But in the acceptance of a continuing exile, an optimistic vision of history may be discerned; Transjordan tribes still exist, though as exiles in other lands. Israel is a larger reality. The Transjordan tribes are not made distant by dialect, polity, and religious practice. The present must not be allowed to deny the reality of all Israel. The nation's tribes outlast the monarchy that seemed to displace them.

Two observations may be made about the genealogies of the northern tribes. One is the notable fact that they are included; the second is that their family lineages are fragmented and limited. Both observations are important to understanding the goals and methods of the Chronicler. In developing a vision for the future, the Chronicler worked with his records from the past. His portrait of a larger Israel is developed according to his perceptions and evaluation of its history. Genesis, Numbers, and the Deuteronomistic History devote much more attention to northern Israel than can be found in Chronicles *[Deuteronomistic History, p. 465]*. They present a complicated relationship between all of the tribes. Detailed attention is given to Joseph and his sons Ephraim and Manasseh. In Judges, the tribe of Judah is almost absent. Judges begins with an overlap of Joshua, indicating that Judah did not completely conquer its territory (Judg 1:3-20), but from then on Judah is absent among tribal relations.

The Chronicler develops a much more homogenous picture of the northern tribes. His presentation of Issachar, Ephraim, Manasseh, Dan, Naphtali, and Asher is positive and at times heroic. He draws on older materials to produce a fully independent presentation. The Chronicler fashions noble lineages, depicting heads of ancestral houses and valiant warriors (e.g., 1 Chron 7:2-5, 40). No doubt there were members of the Chronicler's community who identified with the phratries (kinship groups) of these exiled tribes. Though the authors of Kings deplore the record of the northern tribes and sermonize on the exile, these deportations were never comprehensive. Hezekiah could appeal to the northerners to participate in his Passover in Jerusalem (2 Chron 30:1-11). This situation persisted through the time of the Chronicler. When the Jews from Elephantine (in southern Egypt) wished to rebuild their temple, close to the time of the Chronicler, they appealed for assistance to the authorities in both Jerusalem and Samaria (COS 3.51-53) *[Elephantine Papyri, p. 466]*. The Chronicler no doubt knew of those who worshiped the Lord in the areas of Samaria and identified themselves with the people of Jerusalem. The author does not relate all these genealogies to his own time. If there is a true Israel in the genealogies, they must be considered collectively, with inclusion of all the tribes. Judah, Benjamin, and Levi were prominent in his time; the minor genealogies accentuate their dominant role. The differences between the Chronicler's sources and the realities of his time revealed the changes that took place in the passing of the centuries. To meet the needs of his time, the Chronicler restructured and supplemented these past traditions.

Distinction of Benjamin

Benjamin played a leading role in Israel. Along with the relatives of Saul, Benjamin is among those who support David's rise to kingship (1 Chron 12:1-6, 16-19). In Chronicles, Benjamin is more closely associated with Judah than with the northern tribes, unlike his portrayal in the Deuteronomistic History *[Deuteronomistic History, p. 465]*. Benjamin, Judah, and Levi remain loyal to Jerusalem and the temple during the crisis of Jeroboam and the separation of the northern tribes (2 Chron 11:1-4, 13-17; 13:4-12). For the Chronicler, the ideals established during the time of David and Solomon continued throughout this turbulent time. The Chronicler consistently mentions Benjamin's involvement with Judah. The Benjamite genealogies in Chronicles indicate the important role Benjamin continued to have in the Achaemenid era [*Achaemenid, p. 464*]. Creating a past and tracing the origins of the group into the ancestral age confers a certain prestige on the tribe. The genealogies provide a sense of continuity to Benjamites and a prominence in Yehud.

The Benjamite genealogy appears to be linear and segmented, with genealogies tied to different towns and to different social and historical circumstances. The town one is from is as important a consideration in determining identity as a directly established lineage. Reference is made to the ancestral heads of Geba's inhabitants and the ancestral heads of Aijalon's inhabitants (1 Chron 8:6, 13). The towns named may have their own major families whose lineages can be traced, but there is no attempt to systematize all the lineages or relate them all to each other. Only in the case of Elpaal is there overlap between the lines (8:11-12, 18). The various family groups (phratries) have few links between them. The importance of the Benjamites as one of the leading tribes of Israel is shown by including all these different groups within a Benjamite identity.

THE TEXT IN THE LIFE OF THE CHURCH

Church Universal

The history of Chronicles is never directly referred to in the New Testament, though it serves an important function as part of the canon. The gospel of Matthew begins with a genealogy of Jesus (Matt 1:1-17), and the gospel of Luke provides a pedigree for Jesus just after his baptism and before he begins his teaching in Galilee (Luke 3:23-38). The past is always essential to understanding the significance of people and events in the present. Genealogies, which relate people to each other, are one of the most effective ways of not only relating the past but also linking it to the present. Matthew found it expedient to begin with Abraham and David in order to identify the person and role of Jesus. Luke uses a different approach, going from the present to the past and extending his genealogy to Adam and to God. Matthew calls attention to the promises fulfilled by Jesus, while Luke further identifies Jesus as a servant to all of humanity.

Genealogies can also be enigmatic; their abbreviated nature can leave many questions unexplained. The genealogies of Matthew and Luke are distinct, Matthew tracing Jesus' line through Solomon and Luke tracking it through Nathan son of David. Jesus' legal grandfather in Matthew is Jacob, but in Luke he is Heli. The differences of the two genealogies cannot be explained, which is not to say that they cannot be reconciled. The royal line in Chronicles has further variations; in the Gospels the father of Zerubbabel is Shealtiel (Matt 1:12; Luke 3:27), in Chronicles it is Pedaiah (1 Chron 3:19). The genealogies share a single goal: the royal line of the anointed king of Israel can be followed to David, Abraham, and Adam. The anointed king of Israel is a universal ruler. In the teaching of the Gospels, Jesus is the royal heir of the kingdom of David, the fulfillment of the hope of Israel in Abraham, and the Savior of all humanity. In Jesus, God has designated affairs so that his Son will fulfill the hope of the Scriptures and the hope of creation.

Waiting for the Kingdom

Though both Matthew and Luke surely knew Chronicles in its present form, nothing suggests that they were influenced by his example. They have followed the same methods as Chronicles because of a similar goal. The good news of the gospel was a hope for all human beings because the lineage of Jesus could be traced to the hope of Israel and the promise that the entire world might receive a blessing through the Israelites. Such a concept could not have succeeded as a novel idea invented by the gospel writers without precedent. The message of Jesus could bear fruit because there was present a people who for generations adhered to such a hope. Luke tells of two such individuals. Simeon and Anna were committed to the hope of Israel and both affirmed the distinct mission of Jesus (Luke 2:25-38). That hope was naturally expressed in terms of the Prophets and the Psalms in the Old Testament, yet the Chronicler shared in a similar vision for his people.

The Chronicler never delineates just what his expectations might have been for the Davidic promise. His conservatism in this regard might have served as an example to many zealots who had all too clear an idea of what the kingdom should be. His concept might be taken seriously as an example of the instruction of Jesus to his disciples concerning the coming of the kingdom. When asked about the coming of the kingdom, Jesus warned his followers about being deceived. "When you hear of wars and disturbances, do not be frightened. All these things must happen first. The end is *not yet*" (Luke 21:9 AT, emph. added). All these things are not a sign of the nearness of the kingdom; rather they are a sign of the present age that God in his mercy has allowed to extend before his apocalyptic judgment falls on the great whore and all her idolatrous ways

(Rev 18). Kingdom will rise against kingdom; great earthquakes will occur in many places; famine, disease, fear, and great signs in heaven are all part of the present age. These things must all take place before the end comes, and his followers must be prepared to live their lives as things intensify. It will not be easy; the followers of Christ will be persecuted, handed over to prejudiced courts, and thrown into prison. It will sometimes be impossible to prepare for these things. When such times come, the followers of Jesus will need to trust their Master to guide them in what their response should be. Fundamentally, Jesus is telling his followers that they must prepare for the coming of the kingdom by learning how to live in the present times, with all of its calamity. They must not try to anticipate when that time will be, for that has not even been disclosed to the Son of Man (Matt 24:36). All too soon Jerusalem would be surrounded by enemies, a catastrophic event that in some way would portend the final apocalypse (Luke 21:20). This would be true even though Jesus' followers could say nothing about the nature of its reality or the time of its coming.

The Chronicler shares a similar vision with his people. His work is eschatological in the proper sense of living for the future. Those who have faith in the promises of God have inherited a tradition of hope centered on the Davidic family, a hope that they must maintain and pass on (Williamson 1977b: 154). The Chronicler's idea of remnant contrasts with that of other Scripture. The remnant is not some rump state of those who survived the ravages of war (Williamson 1977a: 125–26). The remnant of Israel includes all those of faith who have continued in their habitations wherever they might be found; it might be in the south or the north and even in places of exile. All these are counted as among the tribes of Israel. Israel is not conceived as the remnant of a kingdom, nor does the Chronicler suggest that his community should hope for the restoration of such a kingdom. The remnant is not to be limited to those living in Yehud; they are merely representative of the faithful of the tribes of Israel wherever they may be found. The faithful are called to rally around the temple, to join with the priests, the musicians, and all the other Levites responsible for worship in order to give praise to the king of all kings. This is the way to await the coming of the kingdom. It is not to speculate on what kind of kingdom it will be, to prognosticate when it will come, and even less to try to speed its coming by some coercive engagement or political activity. Waiting for the kingdom in the service of the king is to worship the king.

Citizens of the Kingdom

Individualism in the Western world has too often minimized, to its detriment, the necessity of the people of faith to know their history and their larger identity. Faith cannot be lived in isolation; this is particularly significant in a society where individuals are so often isolated. The flourishing of faith can take place only when the individuals of faith grow in their understanding. Anselm of Canterbury (1033–1109 CE) believed that "faith" was a matter of "seeking understanding" (*fides quaerens intellectum*). Anselm was not replacing belief with faith. Belief is essential to faith, but people of faith may hold some wrong beliefs. The errors of belief, especially concerning matters of the kingdom, can only be corrected through growth in understanding.

An understanding of faith must begin with the story of the faithful, with those who have been the instruments of revealing the will of God and the work of God. This begins with the faith community. The faith community of the Christian is inclusive of the past; it must not be isolated from the community of the Chronicler. The apostle Paul was clear on this matter. Those in Christ are a new creation (2 Cor 5:17 NRSV), a shorthand way for the apostle to say that the followers of Christ live in the times and the power of the new covenant (Jer 31:31-34). Those of the new covenant cannot be judged by circumcision or uncircumcision, but are the "Israel of God" (Gal 6:15-16). Paul had come to terms with the error of his former manner of living in Judaism, but in no sense did it sever him from those roots. Conflict with the understanding of the nature of *Israel* was inevitable; followers of Jesus would be persecuted, in particular by the synagogue (Luke 21:12). The apostle grieved and would count himself accursed if he could not by some means lead the synagogue to abandon shortsighted views of Israel and embrace the true promises of Israel (Rom 9:1-5). The apostle understood full well that Christ belonged to the community of the Chronicler: "Of them is Christ according to the flesh, the one who is blessed forever, God over all. Amen" (Rom 9:5 AT). Christians do not have understanding of their faith if they do not understand Israel. Christians do not understand Israel if their idea of the remnant is not that of the Chronicler. Israel is not the remnant of a political kingdom but the nation of tribes that go back to the ancestral fathers. A seriously flawed and skewed concept of Israel underlies so much that is wrong with much of Christian eschatology and understanding of the kingdom of God.

The Chronicler employed a literary genre that would have been familiar to his audience in their lives, that of a segmented tribal genealogy. He transferred what was usually an oral form into a written literary opus on a grand scale, picturing all of humanity as one big tribe, with Israel at its center and Levi as the center of all Israel, leading them in the worship of God (Levin 2004: 636). Lineages depict relationships between the tribe's components. The story moves the reader through time—from the very first humans, through the events that shaped humanity and formulated Israel, through the individual story of each and every tribe, and down to the Chronicler's own time. Each house of the fathers served as the basic social grouping of the postexilic community and was fundamental to its leadership structure (J. Dyck: 198).

These leaders were individually the ruling patriarchs of the community, described in terms of houses of the fathers. The leaders collectively constituted a higher community, which in itself posed certain dangers. The higher community might act in its own interests and advocate a rigid separation from surrounding communities, as implied in Ezra-Nehemiah. Preoccupation with such ideological, social, and economic concerns is in conflict with the interests of the Chronicler. His focus is on the tribes surrounding the Levites and priests making music and worshiping around the temple in praise of the Creator. This is the Israel of the church and for the church, the Israel vital to substantiating the salvation proclaimed by the church.

1 Chronicles 9:1b-34
The Inheritance of All Israel

PREVIEW

Anniversaries are not only about celebrating memorable events or certain achievements. Celebrating anniversaries is a way of putting the present into a life context. For this reason it is important for church congregations to celebrate anniversaries. As they look back to the vision of how a congregation came into being and trace what has happened since then, they may find a focus for decisions affecting the future. Looking back during an anniversary brings about the realization that no one could have predicted the course of events that have taken place, but it shows how they came to be, giving better insight for future potential. The reviewed events may also stir up vision and passion as commitments are renewed. Chronicles has left no information as to what inspired the compilation of genealogy, but the purpose is quite clear. Before Israel can truly be who they are, they must understand who they are. The Chronicler's long look backward on the many centuries of their formation as Israel is to create an understanding and inspire a vision. No one could have predicted Cyrus when Zedekiah met his demise, but the resulting community has a calling and a future. For the people of Jerusalem, this transition initiates the foundation for inspiring the hope of the kingdom of Yahweh.

Beginning with Adam is a strategy for establishing the universal and perpetual significance of Israel as the nation chosen by God to fulfill his purposes in creation. The Chronicler moves to show that the people and institutions of his own generation are a manifestation of that divine election. He classifies the people according to their historic roles in relation to the temple. It might seem unusual that the clerical groups should receive so much prominence in the summary of all Israel, but the Chronicler makes his viewpoint clear. The clerical groups are presented as clans, and their leaders as soldiers (De Vries: 94). The priests are described as *mighty warriors in the performance of the service of the house of God* (1 Chron 9:13 AT), and the four chief guardians of the temple are termed *warriors of the gates* in protecting its premises (v. 26 AT). No doubt the task of the gatekeepers involved a certain amount of police work, but the terminology betrays the Chronicler's view of God's kingdom. In reality, their military battles were spiritual battles, as will be made clear in the battle stories.

The Levites and the priests were at the center of the organization of the nation because they were central to its function and to its success. This was the nature of the nation of which God was king. The Chronicler drew upon the records of ancient times, as far back as Moses and David, to describe the historical possessions of the people and their rank. This description of all Israel not only served to legitimize the situation as the Chronicler knew it in his time, but also to defend it as ideal, a hope for the future.

OUTLINE

Official Records of Israel, 9:1b-2
Jerusalem as the Center of All Israel, 9:3-9
Priestly Families of Israel, 9:10-13
Levites and Their Duties, 9:14-16
Gatekeepers, 9:17-33
Summary of All Israel, 9:34

EXPLANATORY NOTES

Official Records of Israel 9:1b-2

The Chronicler says that the Israelites and their territories were registered in the *book of the kings of Israel*. This is apparently the same book mentioned elsewhere (2 Chron 20:34; 33:18), which is also given the title *the book of the kings of Israel and Judah* (2 Chron 27:7; 35:27; 36:8). The term "book" in biblical Hebrew is not part of the title but a reference to the actual copy of the writing (Haran: 159). Copies of a single work would be referred to in the plural (e.g., 1 Kings 21:8, 9, 11). The singular indicates that the reference is to one single official scroll known to the Chronicler. The information he derived from it must have come from quotations in other sources, since there is no evidence he had access to the official copy, and it is unlikely that the official copy was available long after the destruction of the first temple.

The Chronicler had previously pointed out that Judah went into exile (1 Chron 6:15). A second specific notice of the exile of Judah in his summary statement is important (9:1b). It appears to be significant to the Chronicler's understanding of the exile (Japhet 1993: 206). The Chronicler explains that the tribes on the east side of the Jordan had gone into exile for their disobedience (1 Chron 5:22, 25-26), but in his view the tribes of Israel west of Jordan remained in their territories even after the Assyrian deportations; Hezekiah can appeal to them to come to his Passover (2 Chron 30:1-21). Judah later suffered an exile at the hand of the Babylonians for violations of the Sabbath year (2 Chron 36:20-21). This fact is acknowledged in reporting the registration of all Israel, but in this regard Judah appears to be distinguished from the remainder of Israel. The Chronicler does not mean that Israel and Judah went into exile (implied by NIV); this ignores the Hebrew meaning as punctuated by the Masoretes. Judah was only one territory at the time of the exile and did not represent the remnant of Israel. The Chronicler makes his focus the continuity of the nation as registered in the official records.

For the record of those who lived in Jerusalem, the Chronicler relies on a source like that used by Nehemiah (cf. 1 Chron 9:2-21; Neh 11:3-19). The differences between the two lists are more than can be explained by scribal error (Williamson 1982: 89). The burden of Nehemiah was to establish the chiefs of the province of Judah who lived in Jerusalem and in the towns. The Chronicler makes no reference to the leaders of the community; he limits his subject to the inhabitants of the towns and their properties. The translations generally assume that the reference in 1 Chronicles 9:2 is to those who returned to Jerusalem (NIV, NRSV), but this is a matter of interpretation. The central interest of the Chronicler is in the dwellings or territories of the tribes (Japhet 1993: 208). Rather than identifying the first or principal (*riʾšon*) returnees to Jerusalem, the nuance of the word calls attention to the properties of the ancient inhabitants in their towns, the families established on these properties. This same use of *riʾšon* is found in describing "the prophets of old" (Zech 1:4; 7:7) or "the days of old" (Eccl 7:10). *Those inhabiting family property from ancient times in their towns included the Israelites (the ordinary people), the priests, the Levites, and servants* (1 Chron 9:2 AT).

The servants, literally *the ones given* (*netinim*), appear by this name only in this verse in Chronicles; they are part of the quotation from Nehemiah 11:3. These servants were a part of the community that returned to Jerusalem in the restoration period. In Ezra-Nehemiah they are a distinct group belonging to the temple personnel. They are always placed at the end of the list; their names are unusual and probably foreign (e.g., Ezra 2:43, 58). The Nethinim and the sons of Solomon's servants are mentioned together (v. 58). These two classes of servants were similar to each other, the latter having their origin with Solomon and the former with David (Ezra 8:20). According to tradition, Solomon made the aliens, people not of Israel, a forced levy of slaves (1 Kings 9:20-21). The sons of Solomon's servants never appear in Chronicles. The Chronicler appears to attribute the origin of these levy workers to David. David organized the aliens as laborers for building the temple (1 Chron 22:2). Solomon took a census of these aliens following that of David and assigned them as laborers to quarry in the hill country (2 Chron 2:17-18). These servants are presented in quite a different way in Chronicles (Japhet 2006: 20-22): they are not given a role in temple worship but seem to be mobilized to build the temple and are not mentioned again.

Each group in the registration of Israel inhabited its territories as affirmed by the official records. The nation had suffered deportations because of its disobedience but had never lost its identity with the land of its inheritance. Whatever the scope of the deportation of Judah, it had been reversed by the decree of Cyrus (2 Chron 36:22-23). The people living in Jerusalem in the days of the Chronicler were regarded as continuous with those of the past.

Jerusalem as the Center of All Israel 9:3-9

The Chronicler turns his attention to the inhabitants of Jerusalem because it had always been the center of all Israel, where people from all the tribes lived. To make this point explicit, the Chronicler says that the inhabitants of Jerusalem came from Judah, Benjamin, Ephraim, and Manasseh (v. 3). Ephraim and Manasseh are not named in the parallel list in Nehemiah 11:4. Their mention is an affirmation of the presence of all the tribes, since the Chronicler does not supplement the list found in Nehemiah with family heads from the northern tribes.

The list of the inhabitants of Jerusalem proceeds according to the classifications of the people (v. 4), then the priests (v. 10), the Levites (v. 14), and the other temple servants (v. 17). Israelites are named from the tribes of Judah (vv. 4-6) and Benjamin (vv. 7-9). The Judahites are traditionally from the principal families of Shelah,

Perez, and Zerah. The Nehemiah list is missing the family of Zerah (1 Chron 9:5-6; cf. Neh 11:5-7). The list of Benjamites begins the same way in both accounts, leading with the family of Sallu. The Chronicler provides four heads of families with abbreviated pedigrees (vv. 7-8), while Nehemiah has one family with a long pedigree, and after the conclusion names two officials (Neh 11:8b-9). The differences of family heads indicate that the list of the Chronicler was variant from that used in Nehemiah.

Priestly Families of Israel 9:10-13

The whole priestly passage appears to give the records of three priests: Jedaiah (v. 10), Adaiah (v. 12a), and Maasai (v. 12b). This short priestly list needs to be compared with related lists of priests in Ezra-Nehemiah. Jedaiah belongs to the house of Joshua (Ezra 2:36), Adaiah belongs to the house of Pashhur (1 Chron 9:12a; Ezra 2:38), and Maasai belongs to the house of Immer (1 Chron 9:12b; Ezra 2:37). No mention is made of the family of Harim (Ezra 2:39), which might indicate that it was absorbed by the other groups. The list begins with three unrelated names: Jedaiah, Jehoiarib, Jakin (1 Chron 9:10). Jedaiah, Jehoiarib, and Jakin are otherwise found as part of the priestly divisions during the reign of David (24:7, 17). Azariah son of Hilkiah (9:11) appears as Seraiah in Nehemiah 11:11. Ezra the priest was son of Seraiah, the son of Azariah, the son of Hilkiah (Ezra 7:1).

There were various offices among the priests. Ahitub was the chief officer of the house of God (1 Chron 9:11). Though the high priest could also be the chief officer, as might have been the case with Azariah of the house of Zadok (cf. 2 Chron 31:10, 13), there could be at least three chief officers at the same time (cf. 2 Chron 35:8b). In his conclusion of the priests (v. 13), the Chronicler refers to three separate titles found in Nehemiah: the heads of the father's houses (Neh 11:13a); the mighty men of valor (11:14a); those who did the work for the house of God (11:12a). The total number of priests who were family heads given by the Chronicler is larger than the totals of Nehemiah (1 Chron 9:13; Neh 11:12-14). These differences could be a change of situation in the time of writing, but the reason for the variables cannot be determined.

Levites and Their Duties 9:14-16

The work of the Levites is distributed in the list of Nehemiah. Three Levites (Shemaiah, Shabbethai, Jozabad) were responsible for the tasks outside of the temple itself (Neh 11:15-16); three others

(Mathaniah, Bakbukiah, Abda/Obadiah) were to take the lead in thanksgiving and prayer (Neh 11:17). The Chronicler includes only Shemaiah of the first three (1 Chron 9:14). Though Bakbakkar, Heresh, and Galal might belong to the list of temple servants (v. 15), it appears that there may be a confusion of names with Bakbukiah (seen in the Nehemiah list) and Galal found later in the Chronicler's list (v. 16). The Chronicler has listed Mathaniah, Obadiah, and Berechiah from the villages of the Netophathites as the singers. Berechiah is not named by Nehemiah, but he does refer to the singers from the villages of the Netophathites (Neh 12:28). The Nehemiah list contains two singers related to Asaph and one related to Jeduthun. Chronicles has one singer each for Asaph and Jeduthun, plus an additional family. The family of Berechiah in Chronicles may be an indication of developments in the families of the singers. Elkanah, the grandfather of Berechiah, is prominent in the genealogy of Heman (1 Chron 6:33-36), a dominant group of singers for the Chronicler. The total for the number of Levites found in Nehemiah 11:18 is omitted, possibly due to the changes in the families of singers.

Gatekeepers 9:17-33

The gatekeepers are given a distinct heritage and position in Chronicles. Their introduction in verse 17 is related to the Nehemiah list (cf. Neh 11:19), but the differences are immediately apparent. Shallum does not appear in Nehemiah but is head of the list in Chronicles and declared to be leader as the guardian of the east gate (vv. 17-18). Nehemiah does not provide a Levitical lineage for the gatekeepers, but the Chronicler declares them to be of the camp of Levi and provides a Levitical genealogy (vv. 18-22). In Ezra-Nehemiah the gatekeepers are an independent order among the temple personnel, usually registered between the singers and the other temple servants (e.g., Ezra 2:42). The gatekeepers are always included among the Levites in Chronicles (cf. 1 Chron 23:3-5). The family names of Ezra-Nehemiah disappear, with the exception of Shallum. Shallum becomes Shelemiah or Meshelemiah (cf. 1 Chron 9:21; 26:1-2, 14), whose firstborn was Zechariah and who was placed in charge of the east gate.

The Levitical status of Shallum and his kinsmen is emphasized in every possible way (9:19-22). Their work is described in detail, as well as their legal and historical foundations and precedents. The genealogical record is brief. Shallum, from the family of Kore, is linked directly to his distant ancestor Ebiasaph, son of Korah. This relationship to Levi is found in the ancestral summary of Moses and Aaron (Exod 6:14-27). Korah, father of Abiasaph (Exod 6:24), was son of Izhar (v. 21), son of Kohath (v. 18), son of Levi (v. 16). The gatekeepers, repeatedly called the Korahites (1 Chron 9:19, 31), are connected immediately to the grandson of Kohath, son of Levi.

The work of the gatekeepers was to guard the threshold of the tent just as their fathers had protected the entrance to the camp. In the historical books the priests guard the threshold of the temple (2 Kings 12:9; 23:4; 25:18), but the Chronicler makes this the task of the Levites (2 Chron 23:4; 34:9); the high priest is responsible for their overall supervision. Phinehas, son of Eleazar, son of Aaron, was leader in the earlier period (1 Chron 9:19b-20; Exod 6:25). The function of the gatekeepers was established with the tabernacle in the wilderness, where they were responsible for the camp. Eleazar was responsible for those in charge of protecting the sanctuary (Num 3:32). The Chronicler further specifies that the task was given to the one Levitical branch whose ancient head was Phinehas (1 Chron 9:20). Gatekeepers were appointed by King David and received divine authority through the prophet Samuel. Unlike the institution of temple singers, the gatekeepers previously had specific assigned duties. David merely made their task appropriate to a later time. Zechariah son of Meshelemiah is distinguished from the gatekeepers previously appointed by David and Samuel the seer.

The detailed description of the gatekeepers' responsibility is divided into the arrangement of the guards at the gates (9:23-26a), and their specific responsibilities (vv. 26b-29). Four chief gatekeepers were responsible for the four gates of the temple court. They received help from their colleagues, who lived in the surrounding villages and at an appointed time would lodge in the vicinity of the temple for a week. They were responsible for protecting the rooms and the treasuries, opening the gates each morning, keeping count of the sacred utensils, and providing the supplies for the regular services.

Certain other temple functions were carried out by other members of the clergy (9:30-33). The gatekeepers were responsible for maintaining the flour, wine, oil, incense, and spices (v. 29); the priests prepared the mixture of the spices (v. 30). Other Levites prepared the flat cakes (v. 31) and arranged the table bread every Sabbath (v. 32). The Levitical singers, who also lived in the temple chambers, were free from all such duties (v. 33) because they had responsibility for their own work day and night.

Summary of All Israel 9:34

This conclusion and transition to the next major section of the book refers to the two major sections of the previous passage. The Levites have been the central concern in designating the responsibilities of the community (vv. 14-33). The reference to Jerusalem brings the reader back to the topic of defining all Israel in terms of its representatives living in the city (vv. 3-9). All the tribes were represented in the residents of Jerusalem.

THE TEXT IN BIBLICAL CONTEXT

The City of Jerusalem

The Chronicler says nothing about the situation in Jerusalem that the exiles returned to. Like the other Scripture passages, his history of Israel ends with the destruction of Jerusalem and begins again with those who returned from exile. Jerusalem did not cease to exist in the interim, nor was its previous population entirely removed. The fate of Jerusalem after its destruction is left in obscurity. Nothing is known of the struggles of its inhabitants in the interim or of their conflicts with those who returned about two generations later. Passages like Isaiah 65:1-16 indicate some intense differences between apostates and true servants of the Lord, but they are left completely unidentified historically. Situating these disputes in a time and place with identifiable groups has eluded the most erudite critical analysis. Such passages leave no doubt about the tragic and negative legacy of the exile, but they provide no information as to how this affected the restoration that began with the decree of Cyrus. Nor is there any indication of how the restoration may have brought some measure of healing to families disrupted by death and deportation. The Chronicler is concerned with continuity. For him, this was the best way forward in resolving differences, overcoming apathy, and inspiring commitment to the opportunities of the new era.

The Chronicler implicitly defends the right of the inhabitants of Jerusalem and the area around it to their land claims. His use of *riš'on* to describe the first or principal inhabitants of Jerusalem carries the nuance of an ancient claim (1 Chron 9:2). This is the interpretation of the Greek, which translates this with *proteron: those who previously lived in their possessions* (AT). This meaning is found in passages like Zechariah 1:4; 7:7, 12; and Nehemiah 5:15. The Jubilee provisions of the Torah and the laws of inheritance were provisions for the land to remain perpetually with the families to whom it was allotted *[Torah, p. 481]*. This land was given as their possession (Lev 14:34; 25:24). Shifts over time were inevitable, and there were many disruptions of war, but the principle remained along with the claims. Sixteen times in this section, the claims of repatriated leaders in Yehud are established by recourse to genealogy.

Individual claims are largely subordinated in 1 Chronicles 9:3-33 in comparison with the the Chronicler's source in Nehemiah 11:4-19. Nehemiah focuses largely on the individuals, their pedigree, and their destination. Chronicles supplements information about Judahites, Benjamites, priests, and Levites with information about the functions of priests, Levites, gatekeepers, and singers. Such coverage of the temple parallels the Chronicler's concerns for the centralized practice of religion during the Davidic monarchy. Connections to the late monarchy were insufficient to establish the primacy and importance of the Jerusalem temple. Status was bound up with heritage. The second temple was an innovation two full generations removed from the temple that was destroyed. Further, this new temple was authorized, endowed, and supported by a foreign power. Not everyone viewed this positively. The Jerusalem temple in the Achaemenid era did not claim the exclusive loyalty of all those who were devoted to the Lord *[Achaemenid, p. 464]*. By this time, Judaism was an international religion, with communities from southern Egypt to Babylon. The priority given to Jerusalem and the temple has its parallel in the priority of Jerusalem in the time of the united monarchy.

During the Persian period, worship is described in terms of two critical eras: Moses and Aaron; David and Samuel. The function of the temple in Jerusalem was viewed as a continuation and fulfillment of the tabernacle worship of the earlier period. Shallum was the gatekeeper at the entrance to the tent of meeting (1 Chron 9:19). The gatekeeper work at the King's Gate in the east was done by those who belonged to the *camp* of the Levites (v. 18). Further connection to the time of the wilderness is made in the detail of the sacrificial ingredients: the holy utensils, the choice flour, the wine, the oil, the frankincense, and the spices (v. 29). Continuity with the institutions of antiquity was more important than the more recent past that ended with the exile. Identifying with an ancient heritage reduced the trauma of the more recent events and contextualized the significance of the new era that had begun.

THE TEXT IN THE LIFE OF THE CHURCH
The Church in Times of Transition

What should Israel look like in Yehud? This was the fundamental question for the Chronicler. The answer could not be given by trying to re-create the institutions and people of Israel as they were when they went into exile. This was a different time and set of circumstances; these were different people. The identification of Israel was subject to time and circumstances. There was an Israel of the covenant at Sinai and the wilderness wanderings, an Israel in the chaotic days leading to the establishment of the kingdom, an Israel of the united monarchy, and an Israel that survived the succession of exiles, those to Assyria in the days of Ahaz and Hezekiah, and those to Babylon in the last days of Judah. The history of the Chronicler has depicted Israel in these various periods. Common to them all is the bond of the houses of the fathers among the various tribes, preceding even the covenant at Sinai and going back to the times when Jacob became Israel (Gen 32:28). The actual etymological significance of the name is obscure to us (Sarna 1989: 404–5). If the name Israel is related to "Jeshurun" (Isa 44:2), it would signify the transformation from deviousness (Jacob) to moral uprightness. These were not questions for the Chronicler, who read the event correctly in its main import. Jacob had feared for his posterity. That fear dissolved in the faith derived from his struggle with God. The Chronicler has quite rightly found a single consistency in the identity of Israel, a name he uses exclusively for Jacob.

Similar questions of identity face the church as time and circumstance transform its manifestation within its respective communities. One such critical time was the Reformation in sixteenth-century Europe. The Reformation confronted the church with the question of its relationship to powers of state. This question became the burden of more radical reformers under the influence of Ulrich Zwingli. For George Blaurock, Felix Manz, and Conrad Grebel, the confession of baptism had been eroded as seriously as the confession of repentance in the buying of indulgences. Baptism into the church was a confession of belonging to the state as much as a confession of belonging to the kingdom of God. For this reason they chose the route of rebaptism and came to be known as Anabaptists. The impact of this profound insight would not have its real effect for generations, but that in no sense diminishes the significance and sacrifice of these devout reformers in their time.

The relationship of church and state continues to be a vexing question, but the issue of the Anabaptist reformers is now so remote that it is largely forgotten. Only vestiges remain of the formal structures of church support by the state. The struggle now is to understand the church as the presence of an eternal kingdom within a secular state. Citizens of the eternal kingdom must live as participants within the secularism of temporal kingdoms. They enjoy their benefits, while at times rejecting some of their core values. The Anabaptists have struggled as none other with these questions and in this regard have much to contribute in consideration of what the church should look like in a postmodern world.

The postmodern world is embroiled in conflict, in many ways more widespread, more lethal, and more menacing than at any time in history. Every conflict seems to have the potential of worldwide implications. States must use coercive force to maintain order within their societies and to survive against the aggression of other societies. The mission of the church is quite another order. Its mission is not to enable the state within which they live to survive, but to live for a kingdom that will be present long after all states of this time are forgotten. Individuals within the church are committed to give their life for only one kingdom, the kingdom of God. Churches as institutions have been granted concessions that allow its members to abstain from much of the direct violence that is involved in state relations. But situations are constantly in transition and require innovative responses of faith.

The Chronicler provided a single focus for his people: the confession of the Creator in giving praise and adoration to him in the function of the temple. The church can do no less; it will find its identity solidified if this function remains paramount. For the Chronicler the variables of that confession were much more limited. Worship by the church as the living temple of God has vastly more avenues of expression, which should not be limited if they are genuine confessions of faith and praise. While the church as an institution can profitably engage with institutions of state, such engagement should not compromise the call to praise. The functions of the leaders, their names and titles, may have their roots in New Testament terminology, but they are hardly the same thing in any sense but one: leading God's people to worship and serve him. Congregations are free to define bishop and deacon as they see fit, on analogies with past meanings of these words. But one fundamental continuation must always define the leaders and people of the church: they are the temple of the living God, manifest in the world as the worshiping congregation. Once this is lost, the church has lost its way. The Anabaptist vision for the church made this perspective clear. It is one that finds its defense in the Chronicler's vision for Israel.

Part 2
Founding the Kingdom

1 Chronicles 9:35–20:8

OVERVIEW

The Chronicler moves from the organization of Israel as a nation to the way in which God would fulfill his purposes. The Chronicler must not only show that the nation survived, but also that God would still accomplish his purposes through it. The books of Samuel are extensively occupied with kingship and its succession. There is a lengthy account of the wars between the north and the south, the extended rivalry between the house of Saul and the house of David. For the Chronicler, Saul was a failure because of his unfaithfulness and has no role to play in the kingdom. He introduces Saul only to show that David is the legitimate founder of the kingdom, which would be forever.

The Chronicler begins and ends his narrative on a similar theme (Mosis: 17–43). The death of King Saul and the dispersion of the people brought a situation analogous to the exile of Judah and the end of its monarchy. This connection is essential to the message of the Chronicler. The exile of Judah and the loss of the temple understandably brought disillusionment to the people who had placed their hope in the divine promise. The Chronicler reminds them that the kingdom began in just such a situation. The circumstances of the exile of Judah were not to leave them in despair. If the kingdom of God could begin in such a time, then the return of such times did not mean the kingdom had come to an end. The future for Yehud had the same potential as when the kingdom began with David.

The Chronicler makes his transition to the mission of the kingdom by introducing the house of Saul (1 Chron 9:35–44). The place of the house of Saul in the kingdom had already been established (1 Chron 8:29–40), but the deliberate repetition of that material serves to make the shift from genealogy to narrative. The story of the founding of the kingdom begins with the circumstances in which it took place. For the Chronicler, the establishment of the kingdom with David as its first ruler was a matter of divine appointment. The covenant at Sinai had created a nation but not a political kingdom. Political cohesion between the tribes began with David; before that time the nation was divided by tribes making war with each other. Though Saul had gained the allegiance of the northern tribes, his war with David prevented him from completely bringing the nation together. The struggle of Saul was not only with David but also with the Philistines. Saul not only failed to bring the nation together; he also failed to establish a secure place for the nation in its land.

Three elements were central to the kingdom: the Davidic kingship, the establishment of the temple personnel, and the presence of the temple itself. The establishment of the kingdom focuses on each of these three elements to the neglect of all other matters. David's failures and their consequences (2 Sam 12:11-12), the question of the succession of David (1 Kings 1:18-21), and the fatal compromise of Solomon in doing what was wrong (1 Kings 11:5-6)—these have no part in the Chronicler's account. The Chronicler presents David and Solomon as divinely anointed kings through whom God established the three central elements of the kingdom. David received the kingdom and the eternal promise; David made all the preparations for the temple and installed Solomon as his successor; Solomon completed all the work that David had begun.

1 Chronicles 9:35–10:14
Removal of Saul as King

PREVIEW

"The race is not to the swift, or the battle to the strong" (Eccl 9:11). The preacher was making an observation on the unpredictability of life. Fish are caught in a cruel net and birds are taken in a snare, so people are trapped by unexpected events that fall upon them. But for the Chronicler, events are the result of decisions made. Outcomes may be bad even though motives were good. In this respect the tragic story of Saul is sobering. His distinguished lineage and his personal potential were to be envied. But he ended up as a disgraced soldier whose body was abused by the Philistines. He might be regarded as a victim of circumstances: the battle was not to the strong. But this is not the view of Chronicles. Saul was not a victim: he was guilty of unfaithfulness, the subtle sin that would be the demise of many great leaders in his narrative.

Since Saul forfeited his role in the kingdom, it was not necessary for the Chronicler to recount his struggles and failures. It was sufficient to point out the reason for his rejection, which became the occasion for the kingdom to be established under David. The Chronicler introduces Saul by identifying his place in the nation as part of this distinguished military family. The moment the house of Saul has been introduced, it is removed from the scene with the account of the death of Saul and his entire house. The purpose of the story is to provide the explanation for this terrible end. The failure of Saul is one of the main lessons of the book. The unfaithfulness of Saul and his failure to seek the Lord will be illustrated in each case where the kingdom falters.

OUTLINE
Family of Saul, 9:35-44
Death of Saul, 10:1-14

EXPLANATORY NOTES
Family of Saul 9:35-44

The genealogy of Saul is identical to the concluding section on the military record of Benjamin (cf. 1 Chron 8:29-40) *[Genealogy, p. 461]*. It differs in providing the names of Jeiel (9:35), Ner (v. 36), and Mikloth (v. 37), all of which are omissions in the first passage. Ahaz is missing from the royal family at 1 Chronicles 9:41 (MT; cf. 8:35). The duplicated material includes the list of the militia at Gibeon of Jeiel (9:35-38; cf. 8:29-32) and the members of the royal family from Gibeah of Saul (9:39-44; cf. 8:33-38). By introducing the narrative of Saul with a genealogy, the Chronicler is following a literary tradition of history writers of ancient times. Biblical examples include Noah (Gen 5:28-32) and Abraham (Gen 11:27-32): each is introduced by providing a historical setting through a family record. This is a most useful method of situating a particular story in the larger picture of the human story. (See discussion of Saul's genealogy at 1 Chron 8:33-40.)

In the record of Saul, the introduction of the military at Gibeon continues the theme of residence. The introductory phrase *those who lived in Gibeon* (1 Chron 9:34 AT) forms a literary parallel with *those who lived in Jerusalem* (9:3 AT). Gibeonites also lived in Jerusalem (v. 38). The Chronicler provided the abrupt genealogy of Saul (Ner was father of Kish) with an introduction (v. 39). It is generally recognized that the Chronicler was responsible for joining together the militia list of Gibeon with the genealogy of the royal family of Saul. There were logical reasons for such a union: both had to do with the military, both were very significant components in the social order of Benjamin, and though distinguished by genealogy, both came from the same area and were closely related to each other. The Chronicler regarded both as essential to his portrayal of Benjamin. As he embarks on the story of the nation, he begins with the aspects that best represented its roots.

Death of Saul 10:1-14

The account of the death of Saul has been adapted from 1 Samuel 31:1-13. The similarity should not suggest that the story carries the same message. Not only is the narrative given a completely different context, the Chronicler has also made several special contributions of his own to establish a distinct significance for the event. The purpose of the Chronicler was to point out the effect of the death of Saul. The first point concerns the house of Saul. In 1 Samuel 31:6 we are told that Saul died, his three sons, his armor-bearer, and the contingent that was with him. The Chronicler says that Saul died, his three sons, *and all his house* (1 Chron 10:6). Though these might seem equivalent, the difference is in their function. In Samuel, the death of Saul brings to a conclusion the story of a long war between Saul and the Philistines. In Chronicles, the death of Saul brings a definitive end to his claim to royalty, which never did include all Israel. The Chronicler makes no mention of the defeat of the army; his point is that the overthrow of the house of Saul was complete. The death of Saul was a divine action, which terminated the claim of Benjamin to rule the nation. This divine action was not capricious; though the details are not given, a summary distinct to the Chronicler makes the point clear (10:13-14). Saul sought a medium instead of God, a violation of the covenant that disqualified him entirely as a representative of the divine kingdom.

The account is composed of three main parts: the war with the Philistines (1 Chron 10:1-7), the fate of Saul and his sons (vv. 8-12), and the summary conclusion (vv. 13-14). The description of the battle has the quality of a moving picture that comes to focus in on the central figure. The Israelite contingent was routed, the Philistines overtook Saul and his sons, and the three sons were killed in battle. Saul was left wounded on the battlefield and determined that death was the only way to avoid disgrace at the hands of the Philistines. Saul took his own life, a very rare act in the Bible (cf. 1 Sam 31:5; 2 Sam 17:23; 1 Kings 16:18); it was a final desperate act required because his armor-bearer refused his orders. The Philistines had to be content with abusing Saul's body. The Chronicler has a slightly different account of the fate of the body. The Samuel account does not inform us about the eventual fate of Saul's head, but reports that his headless body was hung on a wall in Beth Shan. Chronicles makes no reference to the body but does tell of the head being hung on a wall in the temple of Dagon. The Chronicler makes no reference to the heroic acts of the men of Jabesh Gilead in recovering the bodies of Saul and his sons (cf. 1 Sam 31:12). In his account it seems that they were simply recovered from the battlefield (10:12). Finally, there is no indication in Chronicles that Beth Shan was occupied by the Philistines. The head of Saul was hung in an unspecified temple of the grain god of the Philistines. The whole effect is to minimize the effect of the Philistine victory and the defilement of the land. The focus is on the judgment of Saul. The conclusion provided by the Chronicler gives the story a theological and historical context.

The account of the end of Saul in Chronicles is somewhat incongruous. The Chronicler tells us that the whole house of Saul was destroyed, but he has just given a genealogy that extends well beyond Saul *[Genealogy, p. 461]*. Though he has isolated his account from the reign of Ish-Bosheth (2 Sam 2:8-9) and from the continuation of Mephibosheth as a member of the royal household of David (9:1-13), he and his readers were well aware of these traditions. In his view neither Ish-Bosheth, who was finally slain (2 Sam 4:5-12), nor Mephibosheth, who was crippled in the chaos that followed the death of Saul (4:4; 21:7), had any real claim to the throne of Saul. Abner, who made Ish-Bosheth king, never granted him independent authority (3:6-11); eventually Abner deserted Ish-Bosheth in favor of David. Though the line of Saul continued through Mephibosheth, there never was opportunity for him to even claim succession to Saul. Instead, David effectively preempted it by making him a part of his own household. In the view of the Chronicler, the dynasty of Saul ended conclusively on Mount Gilboa.

THE TEXT IN BIBLICAL CONTEXT

Kinship and Status

The genealogy of Benjamin takes the reader from the tribe's origins through some of the most important events in its history to the times of the Chronicler (Levin 2004: 623-24) *[Genealogy, p. 461]*. The tribal patriarch and the eponyms of the ancient clans of the tribe are traced in the Geba branch through the premonarchic period to later settlements *[Eponym, p. 466]*. A branch of Benjamites is traced to their origins at Gibeon (1 Chron 8:3-28). Jeiel, the "father" of Gibeon, is probably to be understood in the sense of "founder" (Knoppers 2004a: 485). The Saulide line is traced from its origins in Gibeon through known historical individuals to the later generations, which are mostly place names: Alemeth, Azmaveth, Moza, Eleasah, and Azel (8:36-37). These places are well known in the postexilic period. The Geba branch is traced through Ehud son of Gera (1 Chron 8:4-6), the well-known warrior of the judges (Judg 3:15). They are traced to their later settlements at Ono, Lod, and Aijalon (1 Chron 8:12-13). These are connected to the episode of Beriah and the men of Gath, mentioned in the Ephraim and Asher pericopes (7:21-24, 30). Inhabitants of the areas of Geba and Gibeon in the Persian period could trace their heritage back to Benjamin. Gibeon stamp impressions from jars storing oil and wine show that it thrived as an important industrial center in royal service until the exile (Vaughn: 37-38). The Saulide family resided in the area for many generations into the postexilic period.

The inclusion of the long Jeielite genealogy points to the importance of Saul's ancestral house (1 Chron 8:29-40; 9:35-44). With the inclusion of Esek, the genealogy of Jeiel extends to seventeen generations (8:39-40), one of the longest in both linear and segmented forms. The Chronicler lived in an age when kinship relations and lineage were of great consequence for determining status and identity. The stories in Samuel about the demise of Saul the Benjamite and the rise of David the Judahite were no doubt sensitive issues in postexilic time. Tension between families was one aspect of the stress of the times, as may be seen in Ezra and Nehemiah. Benjamites were traditionally a leading family in Israel, but royalty belonged to Judah. Rivalry would be unavoidable, aggravated by close relationships and proximity of the two tribes.

Saul and David were first related through the marriage of Saul's daughter Michal to David. With the death of Saul's sons, David was in line for a substantial inheritance of the former king. The Chronicler settles such questions by showing that the Jeielite lineage continued long past the united monarchy. The Chronicler freely acknowledges that the tribe of Benjamin provided Israel with its first king and stresses the contributions the Benjamites made to the establishment of David's kingdom (1 Chron 11:31; 12:2, 16-18, 29; 27:12, 21). The lineage and tribe of Israel's first king are given their due.

Transition

The Chronicler's presentation of Saul presents his death as the fulfillment of Samuel's prophecies (1 Sam 13:13-15; 15:26-28; 28:16-19). The oracles of Samuel not only justified Saul's demise but also authorized the rise of David. The Chronicler describes the transgression of Saul in his typical vocabulary as a disobedience (*maʿal*) and a failure to seek (*daraš*) the Lord (1 Chron 10:13-14). In omitting the Samuel material on the conflict between Saul and David, and generalizing the judgment of Saul in his own idioms, the Chronicler provides a sense of continuity with the institution of the monarchy.

The death of a king might portend the demise of the institution and the nation, but the presentation of the Chronicler emphasizes instead the continuity of the kingdom in the transfer of the royal house from one tribe to another. By focusing on the death of Saul without mention of Jonathan's achievements, the failure of the first king is limited to one member of the Benjamite tribe. The narrative of Samuel shows that David's ascent to power was a long and protracted affair and that negative relations continued throughout much of David's reign. The Chronicler brings closure to the reign of the first king. His transgression ends the legitimacy of his royal claims, but it does not end the Israelite kingdom or the distinction of the Benjamite tribe.

THE TEXT IN THE LIFE OF THE CHURCH

Unfaithfulness

Unfaithfulness is a personal matter, but its effects are never limited to one person. The tragic story of Saul was the consequence of the low priority he placed on obedience to God. His personal potential as a representative of a leading family in the tribe of Benjamin was eroded. He became increasingly insecure and desperate, even to the point of seeking help from a medium. Saul did not determine to be unfaithful; his intentions were not to turn away from God, who had called him and anointed him (1 Sam 10:1). His unfaithfulness manifested itself in a lack of trust that then led to a succession of wrong choices.

The subtleties of unfaithfulness have not changed. They have been the constant threat of the church collectively down through history as well as the most dangerous threat to the church locally. Faithfulness produces a continuing influence for good in spite of the most severe adversity. Failure of faithfulness need not be irreversible, as it was for Saul. Yet the faithfulness of God cannot be undermined by human failures of faith.

The story of the Chronicler and the story of the church is that God is faithful to people of faith. The Chronicler moves on from the failure of Saul to explain how God continued to bring about his kingdom, which would be an eternal kingdom. It is a reminder of what Jesus said about his kingdom: "I will build my church, and the gates of Hades will not overcome it" (Matt 16:18). Pride and power in the church have threatened it repeatedly, but through the faithfulness of God the church continues to be built.

Transitions

The church that began under the most adverse conditions, threatened constantly by the powers of the Roman Empire, came to be one of the most powerful influences within the empire. That also became its greatest danger. Rivalries for power threatened the faithfulness of church leaders, which in turn came to threaten the very mission of the church. The church came to have two seats of power: Rome in the West and Constantinople in the East. In Roman Catholic tradition, the institution of the papacy became the authorized authority. The Eastern Orthodox Church, mainly in the Balkans, the Middle East, and Russia, rejected the papacy but retained the authority of their traditions. The schism of 1054 CE was a major transition in the long and troubled relationship between the Roman and Byzantine churches, leading to agreed divisions of territorial power. But this was not a transition of the church becoming more faithful to its mission.

The failures of the Roman Church came to crisis with the protest of one its own priests against the selling of indulgences to raise money for building projects in Rome. Martin Luther had struggled mightily to find peace with God. His peace came through his own study of the book of Romans, not through the assistance of the church. His efforts to bring the church back to its mission ended with his trial at the Diet of Worms in 1521. His very life threatened by the church he sought to serve, he took his stand upon Scripture as the authority through which he could challenge the power of the church. A new era for the church began with the translation and dissemination of Scripture for the people.

1 Chronicles 11:1–12:40
David Confirmed as King

PREVIEW

How can we be successful in our endeavors? The way to success is never self-evident. For modern Westerns, the path to success is often perceived to be the achievement of a good education that leads to a chosen profession. But there is never certainty about outcomes of the goals pursued. In Canada, highly trained specialists in medicine have entered their field with impeccable credentials but have been unable to find work. This is the case even while there are long waiting lists of people seeking medical assistance. On the other hand, there are many stories of very successful people who had inauspicious beginnings, lacking education, and with no evidence of opportunity. King David in the Bible has such a story. He was the youngest in his family, a mere shepherd lad, whose brothers had the attention of the king. This shepherd lad comes to be the king who unites the nation.

According to Samuel, David was directed by God to go up to Hebron, where he was anointed king by the tribe of Judah (2 Sam 2:1-4). After a long struggle with the forces of Benjamin (3:1), David was eventually able to gain supremacy over the northern forces and win their allegiance. Chronicles begins with the conclusion of that story and makes all Israel responsible for establishing David as king (1 Chron 11:1-9; cf. 2 Sam 5:1-10). David was not responsible for uniting the tribes into all Israel, but all Israel came together to make David their king. Hebron becomes the place where all Israel gathers to declare their uncompromising allegiance to David as their king. This purpose is declared repeatedly: 1 Chronicles 11:1-3, 10; 12:23,

31, 38. The account begins and ends with those who came to Hebron to make David king: 11:1-3; 12:38-40. The military success of David is not presented as a personal achievement but as a saving event in the history of the nation.

The coronation was according to what the Lord God of Israel had said (1 Chron 11:2b, 10b; 12:23). Samuel is named as agent in making a covenant with David in 1 Chronicles 11:3b, an additional phrase not found in his source (cf. 2 Sam 5:3). The covenant was made according to divine mandate: *The LORD your God said to you, "You shall shepherd my people Israel; you shall be a leader over my people Israel"* (1 Chron 11:2b; 2 Sam 5:2b AT). This affirmation is used to structure the presentation. The Chronicler joined this anointing with a roster of David's men found in 2 Samuel 23:8-39. He creates an introduction to this roster, affirming that these soldiers supported David as their king *according to the word of the LORD for Israel* (1 Chron 11:10b AT). The account then moves back to the earlier time, with a list of soldiers that joined David at Ziklag (12:1-7). It proceeds back in time to give a roster of the men who had joined David at the fortress (12:8-18). From this earliest chronological point, the account returns to a report of the troops that joined David at Ziklag (12:19-22). The narrative concludes with an enumeration of the men that joined David at Hebron (12:23-37). They gathered there *according to the word of the LORD* (12:23 NRSV). The Chronicler begins and ends with the affirmation that all Israel came to Hebron at the command of the Lord. His description lists armed troops from all the tribes who had joined David from the time he fled to the fortress in Judea to protect himself from Saul. The coronation account is set in a chiastic structure (Williamson 1981: 169) *[Chiasm, p. 465]*:

A^1 Coronation of David at Hebron (11:1-9)
   B^1 Support for David at Hebron (11:10-47)
      C^1 Support for David at Ziklag (12:1-7)
         D^1 Support for David at the Fortress (12:8-15)
         D^2 Support for David at the Fortress (12:16-18)
      C^2 Support for David at Ziklag (12:19-22)
   B^2 Support for David at Hebron (12:23-37)
A^2 Coronation of David at Hebron (12:38-40)

The Chronicler has ordered his material by theme. He does not follow the chronological sequence known to his readers from the books of Samuel.

OUTLINE

David Made King in Hebron, 11:1-9
Support for David at Hebron, 11:10-47
Support When David Was a Fugitive, 12:1-22
Transfer of the Kingdom to David in Hebron, 12:23-40

EXPLANATORY NOTES

David Made King in Hebron 11:1-9

The first section on the enthronement of David at Hebron is composed of three parts: the enthronement of David (1 Chron 11:1-3); the conquest of Jerusalem and its rebuilding (vv. 4-8); conclusion (v. 9). Striking in this regard is the inclusion of the conquest and rebuilding of Jerusalem within an extensive account that has its focus on the coronation of the king in Hebron. The conquest of Jerusalem follows the crowning of the king in Samuel (cf. 2 Sam 5:6-10), but that is not sufficient reason for it to be included in these two chapters in Chronicles, where the topic is limited to David becoming king. The Chronicler omitted the summary of the rule of David (2 Sam 5:4-5), which in Samuel provides the transition to David establishing Jerusalem as his capital city. In Samuel, the conquest of Jerusalem was one of a number of events that followed David's accession to the throne in Hebron. The Chronicler makes theological concerns a priority over chronology. Though David was made king at Hebron and ruled there seven years and six months (1 Chron 3:4; cf. 2 Sam 5:5), it was never his capital city. The capture of Jerusalem and making it the capital was the first act of the new king, but in Chronicles this is integrated with the celebrations of the coronation at Hebron. The main point is to show the support of *all Israel* for David as king. The Chronicler develops this point by associating the heroic acts of David's mighty men with the coronation at Hebron. This serves to illustrate the strong support for David as king. Support for David is the theme of the following chapter, as indicated by the introduction to each of its main paragraphs (12:1, 8, 16, 19). Support grew until his army was immense, *like the army of God* (12:22). The Chronicler's purpose was to develop an ideal portrayal of Israel united around David as king at Jerusalem (Williamson 1981: 168). Though the coronation was at Hebron, for the Chronicler the kingdom began with Jerusalem as its capital. Chronology is subordinated to the more comprehensive theme of the succession of David as king over all Israel in Jerusalem. The Chronicler has made the bond between David and Jerusalem inalienable.

The Chronicler does not acknowledge a partial kingdom of David over Judah. He makes no reference to the tribes of Israel (2 Sam 5:1) but begins with *all Israel* coming to Hebron to make David king (1 Chron 11:1). Then King David and all Israel captured Jerusalem (v. 4). The details of the capture are omitted (cf. 2 Sam 5:6-8), but more important, it was not just a contingent of warriors (the men of David, 5:6) that was responsible for the capture of Jerusalem. In Chronicles, the conquest of Jerusalem is not a limited foray of a few soldiers but involves the people as a whole. The fortress of Zion came to be known as the city of David (v. 5). The origin of the name "Zion" is unknown, but etymology based on Arabic suggests that it referred to a range of hills serving as a base of security. Geographically it was the southern end of the eastern slopes of Jerusalem. These were built up with a fill to establish an inaccessible fortification. Zion came to refer to a political center, either as a synonym for Jerusalem, or as a reference to the capital of Judah. Perhaps even more important, the location of the temple on Zion made the name representative of divine presence. Zion as the capital of the kingdom of David and the location of the temple quickly became a synonym for the city of God (Ps 48:1-2). Such theological confessions were familiar to the Chronicler; in his introduction to the kingdom they are given a solid basis in history.

Support for David at Hebron 11:10-47

The Chronicler goes on to establish the extensive support David received as king. Most of this section is drawn from an appendix about "the Thirty" in Samuel (1 Chron 11:11-41a parallels 2 Sam 23:8-39). The Chronicler has provided a supplement to this list of warriors in the remainder of the chapter (1 Chron 11:41b-47), drawn from an ancient source of his own (Japhet 1993: 235-36). All the identifiable locations are east of the Jordan, so the list has a common geographical denominator. David would have had an eastern group of warriors during his reign, though these are not mentioned in Samuel. The roster listing chiefs of David's mighty men names four warriors: Jashobeam (1 Chron 11:11), Eleazar (v. 12), Abishai (v. 20), and Benaiah (v. 22). They are identified by their patronym, their rank, and the exploits that entitled them to be included among *the Three* (Jashobeam, Eleazar; vv. 11-12) or *the Thirty* (Abishai, Benaiah; vv. 20-22, 25). A lengthy anecdote forms the center of this list of names (vv. 15-19). It illustrates the loyalty of the troops to David and David's respect for those who would risk their lives on his behalf. Only two of the three chiefs are named in Chronicles.

There are discrepancies between 1 Chronicles 11:11-14 and our version of his source in the MT of 2 Samuel 23:8-12. Chronicles refers to Jashobeam as chief of *the Thirty* (1 Chron 11:11 MT), while Samuel says that he was head of "the Three" (2 Sam 23:8). Samuel lists the three as Jashobeam (v. 8), Eleazar (v. 9) and Shammah (v. 11). In Samuel it is Shammah who takes his stand in the field, protecting the lentils and routing the Philistines. Samuel tells of a single-handed exploit of Eleazar against the Philistines in which the rest of the army followed merely to strip the booty (2 Sam 23:10-11). Chronicles omits these verses but includes the incident in defending the field as among the exploits of Eleazar (1 Chron 11:12-14). In Chronicles the rescue of the field involved more than one soldier, as indicated by its consistent use of plural verbs (v. 14). Other differences, as to whether the crop was lentils or barley, or whether the number slain by Jashobeam was eight hundred or three hundred, cannot be resolved. The number *three hundred* (in 1 Chron 11:11) is often considered to be confused with the number slain by Abishai (cf. v. 20), assuming that eight hundred is the true number (2 Sam 23:8). The name of the crop in Chronicles may have been a substitution of a more familiar word at a later time. *The Three* are particularly recognized for their loyalty to David (1 Chron 11:15-19). Their heroic feat of penetrating the Philistine camp to provide water for David is given central place in the feats of the warriors.

It may be that two separate events have been brought together in the story of the heroic deeds of the Three (Japhet 1993: 245-46). There are two settings for the armies, in Adullam and at Bethlehem. The account opens with David in the cave of Adullam while the Philistines are in the Valley of Rephaim (southwest of Jerusalem). Three brave men joined David at Adullam, going down by the rock (1 Chron 11:15). Adullam was an ancient fortress city near the Philistines in the Shephelah, south of Beth Shemesh *[Shephelah, p. 467]*. For security, David used a cave in this area for his private army when he was a fugitive. The Philistines were stationed in Bethlehem, deep in Judahite territory, while David was in the fortress with his men. It was here that the three brought water to David from a well within the gate of the occupied city. This event seems to be connected with early conflicts when David was an outlaw leader, before the first years of David's reign. If this is the case, the geographical discrepancies may be explained (McCarter 1984: 495). This was not a case of his army being parched for lack of water, but a daring and strategic infiltration of the Philistine military. David's thirst for the water of Bethlehem may have been more of a nostalgic memory of his former home.

The Chronicler follows the story of the foray into the Philistine camp as it is in Samuel. Though the Chronicler often harmonizes such disparities, in this case he leaves them as they are in his source (Knoppers 2004b: 549). The goal of the Chronicler is to illustrate loyal support for David when he was made king. David in turn had demonstrated what kind of king he would be. Water brought at the risk of the lives of his soldiers was as sacred as their blood; it could not be consumed as an ordinary drink. David poured it out as a sacred oblation to the Lord and to honor of his chief warriors.

Abishai was one of the three sons of Zeruiah, the sister of David (1 Chron 2:16). These three are distinguished for their ruthless tactics in warfare (2 Sam 3:39; 16:9-10). Abishai was distinguished among the Thirty but was not among the Three (2 Sam 23:18; 1 Chron 11:21). Both texts are problematic, but the MT in Chronicles is contradictory. It says that Abishai *was chief of the Three* but *was not of the Three* (vv. 20-21). One harmonization is to add another group of three: *He attainted not to the first three* (JPS). Another harmonization is to make Abishai a commander above the three: *He was doubly honored above the Three and became their commander, even though he was not included among them* (NIV). Though this requires emendation of the Samuel passage, the text there should be interpreted to say that Abishai was among the Thirty. The MT of these verses in Chronicles is problematic; it must be emended in accordance with Samuel (cf. NRSV, NLT).

Benaiah is given pride of place among the chiefs. Three heroic deeds illustrate his achievements as a warrior (1 Chron 11:22-23). He killed two *ʾariʾel* from Moab. The import of the term—literally *lion of God*—is unclear. *Ariel* may refer to sons of a man by that name (cf. Ezra 8:16), or this may be a certain term for *warrior* (HAL 1:80). The meaning "warrior" may be found in a Phoenician inscription (KAI 30), but the context there is not complete. Benaiah also killed a lion on a snowy day, an act not associated with war, but simply a daring deed that showed his courage and valor. Finally, Benaiah killed an Egyptian over seven feet tall, much as David killed Goliath, by snatching the giant man's weighty weapon and then using it to kill him. Benaiah may have been among the later warriors of David. He became commander over the Davidic militia of twenty-four thousand who served during the third month (1 Chron 27:5-6). He was a chief commander instrumental in establishing Solomon as king during the revolt of Adonijah (1 Kings 1-4).

The Chronicler's list of David's mighty men omits their identification as the Thirty (1 Chron 11:26; cf. 2 Sam 23:24). The list begins after Asahel; according to the heading in Samuel, it contains thirty names. In spite of the designation and the listing of thirty names, this was not intended to be an absolute enumeration, for the Samuel account concludes by saying that there were thirty-seven in all (2 Sam 23:39). The Chronicler apparently did not equate the mighty men of David with the Thirty. The names are variously related by family (son or brother), tribe, or place, or some combination of these. The Samuel list ends with Uriah the Hittite (cf. 1 Chron 11:41a), but the Chronicler continues with additional names that were not part of Samuel's list. It is distinguished by its reference to the Reubenite contingents under the leadership of Adina, who was head of an affiliated contingent of thirty (11:42). The addition provided names of warriors from the east side of the Jordan. In addition to Reuben, some names can be definitely identified: Ashtaroth and Aroer (v. 44), as well as Moab (v. 46). Perhaps the Mahavite belongs to Mahanaim (v. 46), and the Mezobaite to Zoba (v. 47), also places east of the Jordan. The support for David is shown to come from both sides of the Jordan.

Support When David Was a Fugitive 12:1-22

Support to make David king did not begin with the demise of Saul's reign. The Chronicler goes back in time to show the support that David received while Saul was king and David was a fugitive. This list is to be distinguished from the preceding in that these warriors are not part of all Israel that made David king in Hebron (11:1). The main point of this list is that warriors kept coming to David until they became a vast camp of various tribes, capable of representing all Israel in support for David as king (12:1, 8, 16, 19-20, 22). Their support for David as his helpers is emphasized repeatedly (vv. 1, 17-18, 21-22). The Chronicler establishes the illegitimacy of Saul's reign with incidental observations that God had already chosen David to be king (12:22; cf. 11:10). In Samuel, God commissions the prophet to anoint David at Bethlehem (1 Sam 16:1-13), but the Chronicler does not include that narrative. The time when David was a fugitive is described as Saul imposing a restraint on David (1 Chron 12:1; the Hebrew word translated *banished* is often used for imprisonment). This was recognized by members of Saul's own household who deserted to David to support him as king (v. 2). David was very prudent about such deserters (vv. 17-18), making sure that they were not traitors who would betray him to Saul. Saul was the obstacle standing in the way of David receiving his legitimate role as king. Well before the actual anointing at Hebron took place, the will of God and the will of the people were that David should be king.

The Chronicler's account of David's days as a fugitive harmonizes remarkably well with the events related in Samuel, but Chronicles provides the perspective of inclusive support from all areas of Israel. Those named who came to David are from four tribes: Benjamin (1 Chron 12:2), Judah (v. 16), Gad (v. 8), and Manasseh (v. 19). The bond between David and those across the Jordan seems to have been established early and lasted to the end. David left his parents with the king of Moab (1 Sam 22:3-4); when Absalom rebelled, David escaped to Gilead (2 Sam 17:24-29). The desperation of Saul in his struggle against the Philistines (1 Sam 28:4-5), with whom David had taken up refuge at Ziklag (27:5-7), led many from Manasseh and Benjamin to side with David. In Samuel these are described as malcontents and debtors (1 Sam 22:1-2) who sided with David until he became a considerable force (23:13). According to the Chronicler, these were mighty military men; some of them were specially trained in archery and slinging (1 Chron 12:2), some were specially equipped with shield and spear (v. 8), some were military officers (v. 14). Some from the east of Jordan crossed the river at flood stage in the spring, defying all the inhabitants of the valley to the east and west (v. 15). The central section of the passage goes back to the earliest times at the fortress to establish the fact that from the beginning the best of the military forces had demonstrated their loyalty to David.

At the center of this enumeration of warriors is a short poem declaring loyalty to David (1 Chron 12:18). In the early days of David's rise, various proverbs were used to claim support for David or rejection of him (Williamson 1981: 172-75). The first is the song of the women at the triumph over Goliath (1 Sam 18:7), declaring that Saul had slain his thousands but David his ten thousands. The rebellion of Sheba is an example of the rejection of David, declaring, "We have no portion in David, no inheritance in the son of Jesse! Each to his tent, Israel!" (2 Sam 20:1-2 AT). Such sayings were long remembered as expressions of intense struggle; they no doubt surfaced again at the time of the kingdom's division. To express recognition of the divine choice of the Davidic house, the Chronicler has created the converse of such a denial of David's right to the throne. The power of the Spirit coming to Amasai gives this saying prophetic force.

Transfer of the Kingdom to David in Hebron 12:23-40

Succession of a king was often a contentious matter, particularly when the new king was of a different family lineage and different tribes were at war with each other. The repetition of all Israel coming to Hebron for the coronation of David shows the total support that David received both before and after the time he became king (1 Chron 12:23, 38). David became king at Hebron; he conquered Jerusalem and established his throne there (11:1-9). Before he took counsel with the elders to bring back the ark (13:1), all the tribes are listed as supporting his coronation at Hebron. Those who were his earliest supporters before he became king were also his latest supporters in the establishment of his reign. The muster of all twelve tribes confirming the rule of David at Hebron shows that the animosity of the long war following the death of Saul had been completely overcome (12:23-37). Those who were of Saul's own family are particularly mentioned as being among the Benjamites who came to Hebron (v. 29). The unity of all the tribes is stressed by repeatedly declaring that all were of one mind in the matter, without any reservation (vv. 33, 38). It was vital to show that all the tribes were aware of God's choice of David as king, the motivating force that led them to come to Hebron for a lengthy festal celebration.

The elaborate detail of the tribal listings is prominent. Both Levi and the two sons of Joseph are enumerated (1 Chron 12:26, 30-31), with the eastern half-tribe of Manasseh receiving separate mention, thus making a total of fourteen tribes (v. 37). Within Levi the two priestly groupings of Aaron and Zadok each receive separate enumeration. The Chronicler seeks to embrace the people of Israel in their fullest sense. A great variety of terms are used to describe their military association and preparedness for battle. The numbers associated with each of the tribes are large, though it is possible that in this case we should understand the term $'elep$ (thousand) to refer to military units. Notable in the list are the northern tribes of Issachar and Zebulun (vv. 32-33). Issachar is enumerated by its military leaders, who had particular knowledge of military procedure, and Zebulun is credited with the largest and best-equipped military force. The military capability of all the tribes is remarkable, since in the days of Saul there was no ironworking in Israel (1 Sam 13:19-22), and farmers were dependant on the Philistines for maintenance of agricultural tools.

In Chronicles, the depiction of the events at Hebron contrasts with that of 2 Samuel 5:1-3, where the leaders of Israel come to Hebron to make a covenant with David and put an end to the war that has been destroying both kingdoms. The Chronicler has gone to some length, perhaps through the use of a military census list, to portray an ideal enthronement for David as God's anointed king.

Though no ceremony is mentioned in Samuel, Chronicles has a fitting festival, including the northern tribes assisting in making provisions for a three-day feast. The unfaithfulness of Saul had led to the near dissolution of the nation, but God had intervened. By the time David was made king, a vast and well-equipped army was present to support the new ruler with singular resolve.

THE TEXT IN BIBLICAL CONTEXT
David's Rise to Power

The Chronicler has somewhat reversed the presentation of Samuel in describing David's rise to power. The Chronicler does not speak of a union formed under the influence of David but of a union of Israel that made David king. These are not in contradiction to each other. The Chronicler does not deny that the union of Israel came about through David gathering popular support during a protracted conflict with Saul. There is a story for each of the groups that came to support David, but Chronicles does not provide details of David's sojourns among the Philistines, battles with the Philistines, tenures at the stronghold and at Ziklag, and period of rule at Hebron. By beginning and ending with David's reign at Hebron, the author recognizes a long rise to power without representing it as violent or divisive. The picture that emerges is that of an orderly and continually expanding intertribal consensus.

The rise of David is also depicted as divinely ordained. The account begins with a word from the Lord: *You will shepherd my people Israel, and it is you who will be leader over my people Israel* (1 Chron 11:2 AT). The decision of the gathered army to turn the kingdom over to David was at the word of the Lord (12:23). Popular election simultaneously acknowledges and implements divine election. Royal rule requires both the popular support of the people and the expressed will of their God.

David draws some of his greatest support from the tribes that are most distant from his own (Knoppers 2004b: 577–78). Of the total of approximately 340,800 troops drawn from the various Israelite tribes, only 9,800 come from Judah and Benjamin (12:24, 29). Levi with about 8,300 warriors (vv. 26-27) and Benjamin with 3,000 (v. 29) do not equal Dan, which numbers 28,600 soldiers (v. 35). Logically the people of Judah would be the greatest in number because a native monarch would serve their interests the most. The Chronicler goes to great lengths to promote David as king for all Israel. The support he receives from outside his immediate base of power consolidates his kingship as a further sign of the divine initiative in his anointing. David does not make Israel, but God and Israel establish the throne of David.

This symmetry of the divine and human initiatives culminates in a joyful banquet as one of the high points in Israel's history (1 Chron 12:38b-40). The long-protracted conflict related in 2 Samuel 2:1–4:12, in which David's army subdued the warriors of Saul, is not included in the Chronicler's version of David's rise to power in Hebron. The growing consensus ends in the solidarity of a great celebration at Hebron.

THE TEXT IN THE LIFE OF THE CHURCH

A United Community

Unity is a matter of perception and of function; the two are interdependent. Every church and every congregation has its conflicts and its divisions, as did the Israelite tribes in coming together to unite with David as king. Unless a unity can be created and perceived that enables a bonding between the various factions of every group, it becomes impossible for that group to function together. In the church this can be at the level of the congregation or a gathering of congregations that function together as a denomination. The history of the group is an important factor in creating a perception of unity and reconciling the various factions that might cause division. This happens through the distinction and inclusion of all groups, not by trying to eliminate or deny the differences of various groups.

The Chronicler needed to provide another dimension to the story of how Israel came to be a kingdom united under David. Human jealousies and conflicts are a part of the process by which God sovereignly accomplishes his purposes. It is important that these not be exacerbated and perpetuated, as they so frequently are at all levels of community. But it is inevitable that these will sometimes be present. Benjamin and Judah were tribal neighbors whose past included intense rivalry and warfare. The history of those rivalries had potential to extend to the time of the Chronicler, as prominent families in each tribe were acutely aware of their history. But within the stories known to them through the Deuteronomistic History was an important theme: God was continuously at work in bringing them together as a united kingdom *[Deuteronomistic History, p. 465]*. The Chronicler is not seeking to repeat the past, but to relate the past so it may foster a similar unity and opportunity in the community of his time.

One of the conflicts in the Mennonite past that has divided families is the question of baptism. Mennonite Brethren practice baptism by immersion, and most other Mennonite groups practice pouring. Longer ago, this was frequently a problem in transfer of church membership between the denominations since it required one group to accept the practice of the other. For many congregations or members, such an acceptance was a compromise of their own group. I once asked the adult Sunday school class of a Mennonite Brethren church to consider what was essential to congregational membership as opposed to what might not be essential. I discovered that some decades previous they had determined that baptism by immersion was not essential to membership. While this was a past distinctive that had caused strife at times, this congregation had resolved to see their past differently. Baptism was a confession of the faith of adults in Mennonite theology, but the mode by which that confession was made should be subordinated to the significance of the act itself. Mennonite Brethren had their own history that specified how baptism should be practiced. But that history had to be brought into perspective for what it represented rather than the specifics that were a part of the original context. A reconsideration of the past was necessary for unity in the present.

Illustrations of this type can be readily multiplied. They can revolve around church practices, structures of church leadership, particulars of doctrine and theology, the practice of peace in a violent secular society, and so forth. But the whole of the past is much greater than the sum of the particular events. The Chronicler resolves those issues that had once been a matter of intense conflict. This is a lesson in construing the past with integrity for the purpose of order and harmony in the present. Such construals can be done if past events are observed as the way in which God was at work in his world, bringing about his purposes for his people.

1 Chronicles 13:1–17:27
Establishment of Worship in Jerusalem

PREVIEW

Failure is a frightening prospect. Failure is worst when a matter is important, and it is more distressing when it is a public event viewed by all. The question is not whether failure will come; the only question concerns the response to failure. This section begins with a tragic and culpable failure. The conquest of Jerusalem provided an ideal location for a capital that could unite Benjamin and Judah, north and south. This development required a provision for worship at both Jerusalem and Gibeon (13:1–16:43). Provision for worship required that the most sacred object, the ark of the covenant, needed to be recovered from its place of exile. To that end, the Chronicler's narrative begins with David's first attempt to bring the ark to Jerusalem (ch. 13). The attempt results in a death and the aborting of a national celebration.

In the chronology of Samuel, David's first attempt to return the ark is the sequel to the Philistine attack. It follows the coronation of David at Hebron, his capture of Zion, and establishing himself as king (2 Sam 5:17–6:12). The Chronicler reverses this sequence; the rule of David and the consequent Philistine attack follow David's failed attempt to restore the ark. David makes proper preparation for the restoration of the ark, accompanied by national celebration. Failure concludes with the promise of an eternal kingdom.

OUTLINE

Failed Transfer of the Ark, 13:1-14
David Established in Jerusalem, 14:1-17
Installation of the Ark, 15:1-16:3
Establishment of Worship, 16:4-43
Promise of an Eternal Kingdom, 17:1-27

EXPLANATORY NOTES

Failed Transfer of the Ark 13:1-14

The transfer of the ark is not a new topic in the narrative, as the chapter division might suggest. The attempt to return the ark is a continuation of the celebration that began at Hebron. All the remnant of Israel that made David king at Hebron is now urged to participate in the return of the ark (1 Chron 12:38; 13:2-3). In Hebrew syntax this is a direct sequence. Though readers are well aware of a significant gap in time between the seven-year rule of David at Hebron and his conquest of Jerusalem (11:4-9), the Chronicler invites them to view events from the perspective of the divine plan for David and Jerusalem. David immediately takes initiative for the restoration of the ark. His initiative is an evident contrast to the days of Saul, when the ark had been neglected for about twenty years (13:3). The presence of the ark was essential to the confession of divine rule. The Chronicler's history presents the anointing of David and his initiation of worship in Jerusalem as the visible commencement of the kingdom of Yahweh (28:5-6). His history explains the events known from Samuel as the work of God in moving all Israel to inaugurate divine rule from Jerusalem.

The Chronicler creates his own introduction to the story of the restoration of the ark (13:1-5). It stresses the involvement of all Israel, irrespective of the massive presence of elite troops. David consults these leaders with a proposition: *If it seems good to you and if it is the will of the LORD our God, let us send word far and wide to the rest of our people throughout the territories of Israel* (13:2). This (NIV) translation obscures an important word in the exhortation to the leaders (Mosis: 60–61). The Chronicler uses one of his strategic words to lend a particular nuance to the command: *Let us burst out [paraṣ], let us send a message to the remnant of our brothers in all the regions of Israel* (AT). There were times when God *burst out* against them, as when the ark was mishandled (13:11; 15:13). Such judgment was more than offset by God bursting out on their behalf in the defeat of the Philistines (14:11). Bursting out with a message to the faithful remnant is a literary technique to signify inclusion of all Israel in establishing worship at Jerusalem (Williamson 1982: 114). God was bursting out on their behalf, as he had promised Jacob in the vision of the ladder that stretched to the heavens (Gen 28:14). There God renewed the promise to Abraham that all nations of the earth would come to be blessed through Abraham. Events at the restoration of the ark were an example of Jacob's people bursting out to the west, east, north, and south.

The ark did not possess powers of magic, but under no circumstance could the power of its symbolism be denied. Its importance in affirming the presence of God in fighting on behalf of his people was one of the most ancient confessions in Israel (Num 10:35-36). But the assumption that its mere presence would assist in military victory was met with the disaster of it being captured by the Philistines, amid a massive loss to the Israelites (1 Sam 4:1-11). The presence of the ark proved to be a catastrophe to the Philistines, who made several attempts to rid themselves of it before it came to rest in Kiriath Jearim (1 Sam 5:1-7:1). Neglect of the ark was part of the curse of the days of Saul (1 Chron 13:3), and violation of the regulations for handling it correctly resulted in the Lord bursting out against Uzzah (vv. 9-11). Though the ark could never be used to manipulate the power of God, under no circumstances did the ark lose its representative power as the throne of God (v. 6). Divine petition was by the name *Yahweh enthroned upon the cherubim* (AT). The ark itself was deemed to be the footstool of the throne of God (e.g., Ps 132:5-8). Its attendant cherubim apparently served as the sides of the throne, as depicted in ancient iconography (Keel: figures 233, 235). The throne in the Jerusalem temple had no seat, though God could be metaphorically described as sitting on his throne. The ark and its attached winged cherubim unmistakably identified it as the throne of God.

Violation of the sacred was a specific offense designated by the Hebrew term *maʿal* (Milgrom 1976: 17; e.g., Num 5:6). These offenses fell into the category of violating objects that represented God or the breaking of an oath, which is against the very person of God. The reparation (compensation for damages) for such inadvertent offenses is a specific sacrifice called *ʾašam* in Hebrew (e.g., Lev 5). However, there were cases in the realm of the most sacred where no provision was possible for inadvertent sin, as was the case with the *ʾašam* restitution. The ark was such a case. When the ark was in the captivity of the Philistines, the people of Beth Shemesh died for simply looking into the ark (1 Sam 6:19-20), certainly not a premeditated violation. The case of Uzzah in 1 Chronicles 13:10 is a similar violation of a most sacred object (Milgrom 1976: 43). The ark was to be carried by poles, not loaded on a wagon. Later David would come to understand the violation (15:13-15); the priests and Levites were not carrying the ark on poles as prescribed, to protect its sanctity [*Priests and Levites in Chronicles, p. 471*].

When Uzzah died, David's immediate response was anger at the outburst (*pereṣ*) of God against him (13:11). The great celebration with all manner of musical instruments (vv. 7-8) had instantly turned to tragedy. Uzzah died at the hands of the Lord he worshiped and whose sacred throne he had attempted to protect. The Lord *bursting out* against Uzzah resulted in a breach (*pereṣ*) of his family lineage; the place came to be known as Perez Uzzah from that time onward. At that moment it seemed to David that it was impossible to please God. The ark did not make its way to the citadel of Mount Zion that David had prepared for it; it was redirected to the house of Obed-Edom the Gittite.

The ark came to rest at the home of a man from Gath, the Philistine city where David had lived during the time that he was a fugitive (1 Sam 27:2). His non-Israelite name means "servant of [the god of] Edom," but his city of origin suggests that he was a Philistine (McCarter 1984: 170). In those early days he may well have been a leader among David's troops, someone whom David could trust. His name, however, is found in the lineage of the Levites (1 Chron 15:21; 16:5), and it is likely that the ark would find a temporary station in the care of a Levite whose house served as a kind of sanctuary. David resigned himself to God's will. All Israel—from Shihor, usually identified with an area of the Nile, to Lebo Hamath (Lebweh), north of Damascus and at the source of the Orontes (13:5), the whole extent of the Promised Land—had been summoned to an event that ended in tragedy. Instead of a triumph, founding worship in the new capital, the ark ended up in the residence of a Gittite. But none of this disappointment is commented on by the Chronicler. He endorses the initiative of David in the critical task of restoring the ark. The Chronicler concludes with God's providence in blessing the house of Obed-Edom, a purposeful sign to show David that moving the ark from the house of Abinadab met with divine approval.

David Established in Jerusalem 14:1-17

The narrative continues with the record of David consolidating his rule in Jerusalem. The statement that the ark was left for three months at the house of Obed-Edom serves as a transition to David making Jerusalem his capital city. Second Samuel 5:11-25 is the primary source for this material. In the Samuel narrative, David captures Jerusalem from the Jebusites (2 Sam 5:6-10) and, with the help of Hiram of Tyre, builds a palace confirming his kingdom (vv. 11-12). With the move to Jerusalem, David adds to his royal retinue and significantly enlarges his family (vv. 13-16). The attack of the Philistines comes as a result of this new threat. David goes down to the fortress to determine how to deal with the Philistines who are encamped in the Valley of Rephaim just southwest of Jerusalem. In this event, the fortress is not named or even mentioned in Chronicles (cf. 1 Chron 14:8). The occasion of this battle does not seem to have been when David had made Jerusalem his fortress (McCarter 1984: 153, 157-58). In the stories of David's conflicts, "the fortress/stronghold" refers to David's defenses at Adullam (1 Sam 22:1, 4; 24:22; 2 Sam 23:13-14). The Philistines are not said to have encamped in Rephaim for war but are in search of David; they spread out in the valley, perhaps looking for an opportunity to plunder. The battle the Chronicler describes may have been while David was ruling at Hebron. The sequence in Samuel made this victory an example of the Lord enabling David to make Jerusalem his fortress. The Lord broke out against David's enemies (*paraṣ*). This reverses the way judgment broke out against Uzzah. David is blessed, along with Obed-Edom.

The rule of David in Jerusalem received international recognition from the king of Tyre, who allied with him to assist in building a royal residence. This was the beginning of a long and profitable relationship with Hiram, which continued into the time of Solomon (2 Chron 2:3-16). Tyre was dependent on Israel for food, and the Tyrian king provided materials and skilled workers for major construction projects. Tyrian expansion began in the days of Hiram; Phoenician colonization extended as far as Carthage (Katzenstein: 84-86). David and Hiram had a common enemy in the Philistines. Philistia battled with Israel on land and the Phoenicians at sea.

The cedar logs supplied by Hiram (1 Chron 14:1) were from the *Cedrus libani*, trees renowned for their beauty and height, reaching as high as thirty meters. Kings of Mesopotamia, Phoenicia, Persia, and Greece all used cedar for building temples and palaces. The legendary cedar forests of Lebanon go back to the beginnings of written script (Daoud: 49-51). Cedar was particularly desirable for its fragrance.

The royal family of Jerusalem (1 Chron 14:3-7) is recorded here as it was given in the genealogy of David (3:5-9) *[Genealogy, p. 461]*.

The list of David's sons is substantially the same as in Samuel (2 Sam 5:14-16). The list of nine sons after Solomon is likely not intended to indicate that they were all born of Bathsheba but indicates those born in Jerusalem rather than Hebron. The construction of a palace, the recognition of the new state by a powerful neighboring kingdom, and the growth of a harem are all features of an established king. *David knew that the LORD had established him as king over Israel and that his kingdom had been highly exalted for the sake of his people Israel* (1 Chron 14:2). This kingdom belongs to God. To further demonstrate the point, the new king seeks divine guidance in military decisions (v. 10), which assures his victory in battle.

The Philistines raided the Valley of Rephaim, the northern end of the Sorek Valley that led south and west into Philistine territory. The northern end of the Rephaim Valley was the Valley of Hinnom, which joined the Kidron Valley on the east. The Hinnom Valley lay just below the fortress of David in Jerusalem and formed the boundary between Israel and Judah. David's strategy in dealing with the Philistines was to seek divine instruction directly.

The method specified for such inquiry was consulting the Urim and the Thummim (Num 27:21; cf. 1 Sam 23:9-12). These two stones were part of the very ornate priestly vestments, placed in the shoulder straps of a full apron called an ephod. The two stones were next to the breastplate, which had twelve stones representing each of the tribes. The function of the stones can only be inferred from the meaning of their names: ʾ*urim* is the word for light and *tummim* the word for perfection. The divine response seems to have been associated with a revelation of light in which complex answers could be received, as in the events narrated here. In the first episode, the Lord burst through the enemy like a flood of water (1 Chron 14:11). The victory gave the place its name: "Lord of the Bursting Out" (*Baal Perazim*). In contrast to the failed attempt of bringing up the ark, when God burst out against Uzzah, David followed divine direction precisely. With these affirmations, the way was prepared to give attention to bringing the ark to the city of David.

Installation of the Ark   15:1-16:3

In Samuel, bringing the ark up to Jerusalem is the immediate sequel to the failed attempt to restore the ark (2 Sam 6:12b-19). The motivation for David to return to the ark is the blessing that comes to the house of Obed-Edom because of the presence of the ark there (2 Sam 6:12a). The Chronicler omits this half verse; blessing to David is shown in the description of the rise of his kingdom. The three-month interval when the ark was with Obed-Edom provides time to make the proper preparations for the ark as well as for the ordering and purifying of those who would carry it. First Chronicles 15:25–16:3 draws on this record of Samuel to feature the inauguration of worship in Jerusalem, including the function of the Levites in relation to the ark.

The Chronicler reports extensive preparations in making Jerusalem the capital city and the home of the ark. In addition to the fill to provide level building areas and Joab's restoration of the city (1 Chron 11:8), Hiram constructed the palace (14:1), and various other dwellings associated with the palace were built (15:1). David provided a temporary dwelling for the ark in Jerusalem. While worship continued at the tabernacle at Gibeon (1 Chron 16:39-40), an important place of worship where Solomon received his visions (1 Kings 3:4), a new order of worship began at a sacred site in Jerusalem. David's preparation for moving the ark was carried out with due attention to scriptural injunction: "The LORD separated the tribe of Levi to carry the ark of the covenant of the LORD to stand before the LORD to serve him and to bless his name until this day" (Deut 10:8 AT). All Israel united with David in his efforts (cf. 1 Chron 11:1; 12:39). After detailing the particular duties of the Levitical participants in the celebration, the Chronicler again emphasizes that this event was done with the support of all Israel (15:28; 16:3). The assembly of such a widely scattered group so soon after the first attempt is a further indication of the profound significance of proper location of the ark and the eventual building of the temple in Jerusalem.

The officials are the sons of Aaron and Levites. The Levites are held in the highest esteem, affirming the blessing of Moses, where the tribe is described as "faithful," the ones assigned to instruct Israel in all matters (Deut 33:8-10). Priests, the sons of Aaron, are a subset of honored Levites. Nonpriestly Levites are assigned distinct roles for service. Order was critical in the movement of the ark. In the wilderness, dismantling the most holy place of the tabernacle and covering the most sacred objects was the exclusive jurisdiction of the priests (Num 4:4-14). The Kohathites were made solely responsible for carrying the ark (vv. 15, 49). These provisions were to be followed rigorously because death would result if those carrying the ark should touch any of the artifacts associated with the most holy place. The division of labor among the Levites was specifically assigned (Milgrom 1990: 343-44). The portage (carrying) of the ark was the jurisdiction of the Kohathites; the Gershonite and Merarite families of the Levites were responsible for transportation of all the other materials. The tabernacle structure was transported by oxcart (Num 7:6-8); the Kohathites were not given carts because they carried the most sacred objects on their shoulders (v. 9). In assembling the Levites, David was meticulous to ensure that the previous disaster would not be repeated.

In the assembly of the Levites, the Kohathites were most prominently represented. Elizaphan, a son of Uzziel, is a chief of the Kohathites (1 Chron 15:8; Num 3:30). Hebron and Uzziel are also Kohathites (Exod 6:18). Eliel, officer of the Hebron group, is also one of the singers (1 Chron 6:34). The six officers of the leading families of the Levites named are to sanctify themselves along with the priests in preparation for the transfer of the ark to the place prepared in the fortress of David. The requirement is similar to Israel at the foot of Mount Sinai (Exod 19:22), where priests need to remain sanctified lest the Lord "break out" against them. These directives were followed specifically as the processional began to make its way. In the first attempt they had not sought the Lord (or the ark) correctly, reminiscent of how they had failed to seek it in the days of Saul (1 Chron 15:12-15; cf. 13:3). As at the first time, the processional was accompanied by triumphant music, to make the occasion a great celebration of all Israel. The Levitical officers each appointed members of their group for their part in the festivity. Official appointment of singers and musicians is unique to Chronicles. Singers and musicians play an integral role in the national administration established by David. Harps, lyres, and cymbals are frequently associated and seem to be an ensemble that accompanied Levitical singing.

Heman, Asaph, and Ethan are appointed as leaders of the musical guilds (15:17). They are named again as the singers sounding the bronze cymbals in verse 19. The three led three sections of the accompanying musicians, each assigned with particular responsibilities. Musicians of second rank listed in 15:18 appear again in the list of singers in verses 20 and 21, which includes the additional name of Azaziah. These fourteen were also gatekeepers. The multiple functions of gatekeepers result in the complicated presentation of three lists (vv. 18, 23, 24). Musicians with harps set to the *alamoth* refers to the role of female musicians (from ʿ*almah*, meaning "young woman"), either as singers or women trained to play stringed instruments. Female musicians are found as important participants throughout the world of the Bible. Another group of musicians led with lyres set to the *sheminith* (v. 21). This term means "eighth," though it is entirely ambiguous as to whether this indicates "octave" (in the lower register) or "an instrument with eight strings." The term appears in the titles of certain psalms (e.g., Pss 6; 12), which might indicate a term for musical directions.

The role of Kenaniah (1 Chron 15:22), an officer of the Levites, is unclear due to the ambiguity of the word used to describe his expertise (*maśśaʾ*). The Greek translators have taken this as some aspect of music, perhaps the raising of the voice. Music is only one of the functions of the Levites appointed in this circumstance. The occasion is the transfer of the ark, which must be carried, an action that would be conveyed by the word *maśśaʾ*. The following verses have to do with the protection and movement of the ark, making it likely that Kenaniah was responsible for porterage. Seven trumpeters led the way, with the ark and the Levites charged with security right behind them.

As the ark proceeded, sacrifices were offered. Samuel specifies that a fatted ox was offered after the first six paces (2 Sam 6:13). Chronicles says that seven bulls and seven rams were sacrificed (1 Chron 15:26). It may be that the Samuel text should read that a sacrifice was made after every six paces (McCarter 1984: 171). As was typical in such a procession, multiple sacrifices would be expected, as is stated in Chronicles. David and the Levites carrying the ark as well as the singers were clothed with a distinguished outer garment worn by people of rank. As part of the sacred occasion, David was clothed in a linen ephod. An ephod was customarily a simple linen garment worn by priests (cf. 1 Sam 2:18, 28; 22:18). The celebration was most dignified, sacred, and joyful, led by seven priests blowing trumpets, with David and the chief officers following the ark to resounding music of strings, horns, cymbals, and singing punctuated by the guttural blasts of the shophar.

As the ark approached the citadel, Michal the daughter of Saul disdained the whole event (1 Chron 15:29). In Samuel, her response is that of an offended aristocrat who feels that she has been compromised. Samuel has no mention of the garments worn by David; Michal charges him with being exposed in his leaping and dancing (2 Sam 6:20). Michal has a tragic history. She was caught in the conflict between Saul and David. Her marriage to David was encouraged by her father in a sinister scheme to end David's life (1 Sam 18:20-27). She rescued David when her father plotted to kill him (19:11-14), was forcibly separated from David by her father (25:44), and then was victimized in being separated from her second husband in order to be restored to David (2 Sam 3:14-16). The Chronicler makes no mention of any of these details. Michal is portrayed as a member of the house of Saul, which neglected the ark. This is the first and only comment the Chronicler makes about her. In Chronicles, David is the divinely appointed king, acting in a fully appropriate manner with proper dedication, so that he deserves to receive nothing but uncompromised affirmation.

No celebration is complete without food. David dismisses the people with a festal sacrifice that includes offerings to God burned completely on the altar and the peace offerings of well-being for the people (1 Chron 16:1-3). The main function of this latter offering was to provide meat for the table (Milgrom 1991: 221). Meat was too costly for the typical family; it was reserved for times of clan celebration. These times provided the occasion for such sacrifices. David also apportioned to each individual *a loaf of bread, a cake of dates and a cake of raisins*. The actual food meant by *cake of raisins* is not certain.

Establishment of Worship 16:4-43

The transfer of the ark to Jerusalem required that worship be established in two locations, since the tabernacle remained at Gibeon. The various locations of the tabernacle are somewhat obscure in the biblical narrative (Friedman: 293-94). Following the conquest, the tabernacle was located at Shiloh (Josh 18:1; 19:51), which was the designated place of sacrifice (22:19, 29). Jeremiah tells us that Shiloh was destroyed (7:12, 14; 26:6, 9); there is no information on the fate of the tabernacle. The Chronicler tells us that it was at Gibeon when David established worship at Jerusalem (1 Chron 16:39). The Chronicler's source of information may have been the account in Kings (Knoppers 1993: 77-82). Solomon received his visions at Gibeon, where there was an altar sufficient for a thousand offerings (1 Kings 3:4). The worship of Israel at the high place in Gibeon would be the location of the tabernacle at that time, though the record is silent as to its journey after the destruction of Shiloh.

In Jerusalem, David appointed certain Levites to serve in the tent of the ark, to commemorate the return of the ark, make confession of God's work, and give praise (1 Chron 16:4). A number of them were named as part of the return of the ark. Asaph was put in charge of praise and confession (vv. 5, 7), a role he had previously (15:17, 19). Zechariah was second in rank, the position he had held earlier (15:18). Benaiah, one of the seven priests blowing the trumpet in front of the ark (15:24), is now appointed to lead musical services regularly at the ark, along with Jahaziel (15:6). Asaph led with cymbals (16:5). At Gibeon, Zadok was appointed as the high priest to offer the daily sacrifices each morning and evening as required (vv. 39-40). Heman, from the Levitical families of Gershon and related to Asaph (15:7, 17), and others designated by name were appointed to the musical guilds at Gibeon (16:41). Security at Jerusalem was provided by Obed-Edom son of Jeduthun (v. 38). The family of Jeduthun is otherwise named among the singers at Gibeon (v. 41) along with Heman.

Obed-Edom is named as one of sixty-eight members of the singers of Asaph remaining at Jerusalem to direct worship there (v. 38). He is one of the musicians previously mentioned in verse 5. Obed-Edom, son of Jeduthun, and Hosah provided security as gatekeepers, making a total of seventy Levites serving in Jerusalem (v. 38). This is the only case where Obed-Edom is said to be a son of Jeduthun. This is surprising, because Jeduthun is prominent as a singer (1 Chron 25:1, 3, 6; 16:41). Obed-Edom appears consistently elsewhere as a gatekeeper (1 Chron 15:18, 24; 26:4). Thus, 1 Chronicles 16:38 appears to distinguish between Obed-Edom as part of a guild of singers and another Obed-Edom as a son of Jeduthum (Knoppers 2004b: 624). Verse 42 makes clear that the sons of Jeduthun are gatekeepers. If the Chronicler distinguishes two individuals with the name Obed-Edom, the son of Jeduthun refers to the gatekeeper. Of course, the Chronicler's gatekeepers could have more than one function. They are a class of Levites whose responsibilities may encompass more than guard duty.

The song of worship is drawn from three psalms: 1 Chronicles 16:8-22 from Psalm 105:1-15; verses 23-33 from Psalm 96; and verses 34-36 from Psalm 106:1, 47-48. These represent, respectively, a historical psalm, a psalm about kingship, and a concluding doxology. The Chronicler's version of these psalms is somewhat variant from the MT and Greek Psalters, mostly in the omission of lines from the final stanza of Psalm 96 (cf. 1 Chron 16:30-33; Ps 96:9-13). Perhaps the Chronicler had this psalm in a shorter version or had the freedom to create his own version. The formation of the Psalter was a long process. Forty manuscripts found at Qumran are Psalms scrolls or contain psalms. Two conclusions can be drawn from the evidence of these Psalms scrolls: (1) the Psalter came to have its present shape in two distinct stages; and (2) up until the time of Qumran, two distinct versions of the Psalter were present (Flint: 471). The second stage was the formation of books 4-5 of the Psalter (Pss 90-150), which exists in different forms. The longest preserved Psalms scroll represents an alternate Psalter (11QPs^a = 11Q5; Sanders). The alternate Psalter is different both in content (which songs are included) and arrangement (the order in which they are found). The alternate psalms often use earlier biblical material, much as the Chronicler has done here.

The Chronicler has arranged and to some extent modified these psalms to make confession of the promise to Israel and the rule of God as king. One significant change reflects the ideology of the Chronicler. He substitutes Israel for Abraham in Psalm 105:6-7: *Seed of Israel, his servant, sons of Jacob, his chosen ones, he is the LORD our God; his judgments are throughout the land* (1 Chron 16:13-14 AT). There is a marked emphasis on Jacob because he is the immediate father of the children of Israel. The Chronicler consistently uses the name Israel when the name Jacob would be expected (e.g., 1 Chron 1:34, 2:1; 5:1 [twice], 5:3). It is in the citation of this psalm that the only two occurrences of Jacob are found (1 Chron 16:13, 17), in both cases parallel to Israel. This is the only occasion where the Chronicler refers to Israel as those chosen, parallel with the name Jacob. *Children of Jacob* (16:13) reinforces the presentation of Jacob as the father of the people Israel in the genealogies [*Genealogy, p. 461*].

The Chronicler has used these psalms to create a particular message in a specific circumstance. The election of Israel and David as Israel's king had an impact on all nations: *David's fame spread throughout every land, and the LORD made all nations fear him* (14:17). The theological basis for this assertion and the proper response to it is expressed in this confession. This is the time to seek the Lord and to remember the promise of the land of Canaan. The God of Israel chastised kings on behalf of the patriarchs (e.g., Gen 12:10-20; 20:1-18; 26:6-11). The quotation of Psalm 105 ends with the warning not to touch God's anointed or to harm his prophets (1 Chron 16:22). The Lord reigns in all the earth (v. 31); this is the central theme of Psalm 96, which is mirrored in Psalm 98. The Lord is savior, judge, and ruler; the abbreviated version of the Chronicler does not compromise any of these elements. In the circumstances of the Chronicler, the fulfillment of the prayer to gather the nation and save them had begun to be fulfilled (1 Chron 16:35). Their circumstance was viewed as parallel to David. Following the disastrous division of Saul, the nation had come together and the dominion of God was felt among the nations. This was a time to celebrate.

Promise of an Eternal Kingdom 17:1-27

17:1-15 *Oracle of Nathan*

The Chronicler's vision for the future of the people of faith was established on the fulfillment of the promise to David. There were two aspects to this promise: land and dynasty. The promise of land was expressed in terms of rest (Deut 3:20; 12:10; 25:19; Josh 21:44; 1 Kings 5:4). The promise of rest in the land was grounded in God's words to the patriarchs (Exod 6:2-8; Deut 1:8). Fulfillment of rest came with the conquests of David (2 Sam 7:1, 11). This is the occasion for David's decision to build a temple. David regards his conquests as a divine provision; in return he seeks to affirm his loyalty and devotion to God. His proposal meets with prophetic approval from Nathan. God's instructions from the time of the covenant with Moses were to cross the Jordan, enter the rest in possessing the land (Deut 12:9-10), and there establish one central place where all Israel would worship (vv. 5, 11, 14). The conquest of Jerusalem, a central location uniting north and south, was regarded as divine provision, according to the ideal of Deuteronomy.

In the interpretation of the Chronicler, the intent of David to build the temple was premature because David had not yet secured the rest required for building the temple. David was a man of war (1 Chron 22:7-8). Rest would come in the time of his son Solomon, who would benefit from the achievements of David (vv. 9-10). The Chronicler omits the reference to rest found in 2 Samuel 7:1. The omission of the word "rest" in 1 Chronicles 17:1 is consistent with the Chronicler's theology. The Chronicler views the conquests of David as a subjugation of the enemies of Israel rather than a provision of rest for David. In 1 Chronicles 17:10 he changes the word "rest" in his source (2 Sam 7:11) to *subdue*. Half of the thirty-six occurrences of "subdue" in the Hebrew Bible are found in Chronicles. It is the Chronicler's word to call for submission before God. All of the occurrences of "rest" in Chronicles are in texts of his own composition (Japhet 1987: 36). The Chronicler does not consider the achievements of David to be a provision of rest but a demonstration of God bringing about submission of his enemies.

It is natural that a victorious king would build a temple, but David is not just another king, nor is Yahweh in need of a temple, as are other gods. The divine kingdom is of another order. David cannot build a house for the kingdom of God (1 Chron 17:4); it is God who must build David a house (v. 10). The palace for the kingdom of God is for a kingdom that will endure; it is not just a place of worship. In the book of Psalms, the building of a house for David becomes the standard confession for God's eternal promise (89:2-4). This assurance of the kingdom, represented by dynasty and city (127:1-2), provides assurance for the blessedness of all families (vv. 3-5; 128:1-6). David's significance is not in the building of a temple, but in being a man of God's own choosing (1 Sam 13:14). A man after the heart of God does not speak of David's love for God or God's love for David. The metaphor of "heart" in Hebrew most often is a reference to the mind. David is the man of God's choice (e.g., Ps 20:1-4), the one through whom God will fulfill his promises.

The promise of a dynasty to the house of David is unconditional (1 Chron 17:10). It will not be compromised by future disobedience. The possibility of future sin is another omission of the Chronicler (v. 13; cf. 2 Sam 7:14). In the presentation of the Chronicler, Solomon is elect of God and fulfills his divinely ordained calling without failure (1 Chron 28:5-6). Neglecting to mention the possibility of sin does not constitute an alteration of the promise itself. In the future, if descendants commit sins, they will be chastised, but it will not alter the surety of the promise. Unique to the Chronicler is the focus on Solomon as the immediate successor of David, the one who will confirm the hope of an eternal kingdom (Knoppers 2004b: 670). This can be seen in the structure of the promise (1 Chron 17:12-14 AT):

A^1 *I will establish his throne forever.*
  B^1 *I will be a father to him, and he will be a son to me.*
    C *I will not remove my loyalty from him as I did from the one before him.*
  B^2 *I will appoint him in my house and in my kingdom forever.*
A^2 *His throne will be established forever.*

On four separate occasions the Chronicler associates the kingdom of David with the kingdom of God (1 Chron 17:14; 28:5; 29:11; 2 Chron 13:8). On three occasions he associates the throne of God with the throne of David and Solomon (1 Chron 28:5; 29:23; 2 Chron 9:8). In the view of the Chronicler, the Israelite monarchy is the rule of God over Israel and over his kingdom.

The Chronicler also has a distinct concept of the responsibility of the king toward the temple. The promise in Samuel establishes the security of the temple and kingdom forever (2 Sam 7:16). The Chronicler states that the son of David will be appointed over God's house and kingdom forever (1 Chron 17:14). Caution must be exercised in making too much of this difference. Use of the word "appoint" is much expanded in later biblical Hebrew and is used to replace a number of other verbs in Chronicles (Japhet 1987: 31). But in Chronicles the successor of David will have official responsibilities for the temple. In ancient Egypt the king was responsible to build the temple as a kind of filial obligation (Keel: 277). As the builder of the temple, the king was responsible for its maintenance,

17:16-27 Prayer of David

The prayer of David focuses on the redemptive acts of God on behalf of his people (1 Chron 17:20-21), recalling the unique status of Israel among all other nations, who do not have a God such as this (cf. Deut 4:7-8). God has acted freely in creating Israel as his people, and in the same way he has now chosen to create a dynasty (house) for David (1 Chron 17:17-19); God has acknowledged and recognized David in a manner incomparable to any other king. David can only pray that these words be confirmed and that the name of God may be magnified in Israel. This does not absolve David of accountability before God, as is fully shown in the narrative in Samuel. David expresses the desire that the purposes of God may be fulfilled in his dynasty and in God's people Israel (vv. 26-28). The doxology of David's prayer affirms that all of this is so that God may be blessed forever. The marvel expressed in the prayer is that God could be so honored in his action of not only bringing David to his current position but also declaring to him his purpose for the future.

THE TEXT IN BIBLICAL CONTEXT

Significance of the Ark

The importance of the ark in representing the rule of God is made most prominent when it was installed in the temple (1 Kings 8:1-66). When Solomon assembled the people to put the ark in its place, the glory of the Lord overwhelmed those present (vv. 1-11). Solomon triumphantly declared that though the heavens could not contain the presence of God, nevertheless this magnificent palace with its ark-throne set in thick darkness would represent his rule (vv. 12-13). God was in no sense part of the world but was in every sense present in the world. Solomon's prayer engages seven supplications in a literary setting of concentric patterns (Knoppers 1995: 235-36). The central petition (vv. 37-40) implores the Lord to turn to hear the petition of any person for any need (vv. 37b-38). The Chronicler held the symbolic significance of the ark in no less regard. This temple receives its significance from the tabernacle, which derived its meaning from Mount Sinai. In bringing the ark to the temple, David joined the authority of Moses to his new capital. The restored temple in the days of the Chronicler had all the power of Mount Sinai in the days of Moses.

The ark represented the rule of God as the source of life itself. Life is not self-contained within creation, as an endarkened world is prone to conceive it. Reducing the earth to natural law is not enlightenment. All law is God's law, the creative power of God constantly at work on earth (Ps 104:24-30). Apart from continuous life-giving power of God, life ceases to exist. The rule of God is not a matter of power; it is a matter of dependence on God and therefore submission. Human hubris resists the idea of dependence but even more vehemently the thought of submission. The sacred symbolism of the ark as the footstool of God's throne is a continual testimony to human dependence on God for life itself. The ark is most appropriately the place of worship. In worship, humans do not merely acknowledge the rule of God: in worship they acknowledge their very existence as dependent on God.

The ark is most holy. Holiness is not about morality; it is about life and existence. Application to morality derives from the concept "holy" as it pertains to God. The ark represents the bond between the holy and the common. Holiness is the divine power of life outside of creation and the source of life for the common elements of creation. Objects within creation may be holy only if they represent the holy God outside of creation. If they are to represent the holiness of God, their symbolism must be guarded without compromise. This is why the ark is to be carried and never touched; it is outside the limits of those within creation to have contact with the holy that is outside of creation. Only such representation of the holy can truly confess that creation is continuously dependent. Should God hide his presence, life expires (Ps 104:29). The ark is not only holy, but its presence as a confession is also necessary in a temple context. Nothing can take its place. The story of David's resolve to restore the ark and the death of Uzzah in touching the ark testify to this concept of the significance of the ark.

Covenant Promise to David

The promise to David is elsewhere referred to as a covenant (Pss 89:3-4; 132:11-12). Covenant is a relationship established by oaths that involve agreements in several ways. Covenants between nations, such as the Hittite treaties, are understood to be primarily an obligation of the vassal (servant) kingdom to the suzerain (master) kingdom. In parity covenants, both parties (whether individuals or kingdoms) commit obligations to one another. A grant or promissory covenant obligates the master to the servant (Weinfeld: 185). In a grant, the covenant curse is directed against anyone who violates the rights of the servant. In a treaty, the curse is directed against the servant (nation) who might violate the terms of obligation to the master. Applying such covenants by analogy to the relationship between Israel and God, the covenants with Abraham and David are most similar to the grant covenant, while the Mosaic covenant, in which the people pledge loyalty to God, is more like the suzerain-vassal type. Scholars have often interpreted the divine promises to David along the lines of land grants that a king might make to a favored subject.

Care must be taken when using analogy with the practices of ancient cultures. Further, biblical authors draw on a great variety of genres in declaring the provision for David's descendants. The structure, form, and content of royal grants are complicated and diverse, just as the promises dealing with David are presented in a variety of writing forms (genres) and vary according their contexts. It is doubtful that any of the three primary covenant forms described above form a perfect analogy to the Davidic promise (Knoppers 1996: 673-74). For example, while land grants are typically conditional in nature and function, there are clear exceptions. A papyrus of the fifth century is unequivocal in the unconditional bequest of property:

> This house and land I give you for my lifetime and after my death; you have full rights over it from this day forever, and your children after you. To whom you wish you may give it. There is no other son or daughter of mine, brother or sister, or other woman or man who has rights over this land, except you and your children forever. (*AP* 8.8-11)

The unconditional promise to maintain a dynasty, even though its members might sin, is similar to that of an ancient king of Hatti: "If your son or grandson should commit an offense, let the king of Hatti investigate; . . . if he is worthy of death let him die. But his house and country will not be taken and given to (one) from another's issue" (*KBo* 4.10 obverse 9-13). Unconditional language is found in a great variety of forms and treaties. The biblical statements must be interpreted in this more general milieu.

The promise to David in Psalm 89 makes no reference to the Jerusalem temple. Both Samuel and Chronicles play on the various connotations of "house" to make the temple a confession of the eternal dynasty. In Psalm 132 the divine pledge is associated with the procession of the ark (vv. 6-8) and the election of Zion (vv. 13-16). Such an element is found in neither the vassal treaty nor the royal grant. In addition, Psalm 132 makes the dynastic promise conditional (v. 12), distinguishing it from the unconditional promise.

To understand the Davidic promises, we must consider the whole of the biblical witness. The divine pledge to David in Psalm 132 is associated with the elevation of the ark and the election of Zion. In Psalm 89 the sure provision of David is associated with God's handiwork in the heavens. The narrative in Chronicles reinterprets the dynastic oracle of Nathan in Samuel, making the Davidic promise dependent on Solomon's success. The Davidic promise cannot simply be a covenant defined as an oath of divine obligation.

Covenant is a formal relationship established by oath involving at least two parties. Because covenants involve at least two parties, all parties are affected in the making of a covenant. Such covenants may not affect all parties equally. Some may emphasize the promise made by the dominant party; others may stress the commitments made by the lesser party. But in all cases there is some sense of mutual obligation. A covenant ensures that the relationship will be continued into the future, but the dynamic of the relationship may be altered. One or both parties may accept obligations, but these may not be imposed in all cases. There may be unconditional language, but this does not mean that the covenant is one-sided or that there is no further accountability on behalf of one of the parties. Continuing future loyalty can be assumed or stipulated even though the fundamental promise is not affected by disloyalty. Even in the most one-sided covenants, there may be an element of reciprocity. All biblical covenants and the promise to David must be understood in this more comprehensive manner.

The divine choice of David as king and the covenant are the most prominent ways in which the church of the New Testament understood itself to be the fulfillment of Scripture. The New Testament begins with Jesus Christ, son of David, son of Abraham. A genealogy follows to substantiate this claim. The writer to Hebrews joins Psalm 2 with the narrative promise to David to declare that the Son of God cannot be compared to angels, since he represents a much greater heritage (Heb 1:4-5). The new covenant is central to the writer to the Hebrews; twice he quotes at length from the prophet Jeremiah (Heb 8:8-12; 10:15-18). The two themes of a divinely appointed king and a covenant relationship define the foundation of the New Testament church.

THE TEXT IN THE LIFE OF THE CHURCH

Theology of Kingdom

Jesus came preaching the message of the kingdom (Matt 4:17; Mark 1:14-15; Luke 4:42-44). His hearers understood this well; Scripture was about the coming of the kingdom. If the gospel is to be understood, it must begin with the message Jesus brought to Galilee. Unless gospel preaching begins as the Gospels present it, the Gospels and the gospel will not be truly understood. Chronicles is perhaps the best place to understand the preaching of the kingdom.

The message of the kingdom is comprehensive. The metaphor of "kingdom" in application to the gospel may seem to connote political power, but the kingdom of God is not about political power as a type of temporal control as typically understood. Those belonging to the kingdom of God may rightly engage in political and judicial process; they may be obligated to do so. The comparison of the kingdom metaphor is to the way in which the rule of the Creator manifests itself in the world. This is the Chronicler's concern. His teaching of kingdom has no relevance to seeking independence from the Persian Empire. The kingdom of David is to live faithfully for God in the service of the temple and the observance of the covenant.

"Kingdom" as a metaphor for the rule of God is inseparably bound with the concept of covenant. The rule of God is through covenant relationship. The ark is the footstool for the throne of God. The Chronicler refers to it consistently as *the ark of the covenant* (1 Chron 15:25, 26, 28, 29; 16:6, 37; 17:1). Its significance in representing the covenant is indicated by the fact that the ark was lost by the time of the Chronicler. The covenant rule of God comes through his chosen king. The promise to David of an eternal kingdom is a covenant promise (Pss 89:3-4; 132:11-12). The rule of God becomes a reality in the lives of people through the king of the covenant promise. Jesus taught his disciples to make their confession of following him as their king by taking the cup of the Passover wine and saying, "This cup is the new covenant in my blood, which is poured out for you" (Luke 22:20). Here is a confession of the truth that God's rule in the world comes through the death of the anointed king. In death, the king comes to rule through the redemption that he brings to all creation. The covenant of the king is to give his life for those who will be part of his kingdom. The Scripture of the kingdom is therefore called *hē kainē diathēkē*, "the new covenant."

"New covenant" was the prophetic term for renewal after the exile. Hope in time of such crisis was possible because of God's covenant with his people and the promise of an eternal kingdom. The end of the presence of the ark in Jerusalem and the dissolution of all independent governance in Judah required a rethinking of king, temple, and covenant. The prophet Jeremiah confronted these questions directly. He encountered enormous conflict in proclaiming judgment that included the destruction of the temple. His exasperation is heard in his protest against the deception that his opponents propagated. "Do not trust in deceptive words and say, 'This is the temple of the LORD, the temple of the LORD, the temple of the LORD!'" (Jer 7:4). Just as the ark had been taken captive by the Philistines, the temple could be destroyed by the Babylonians. But the destruction of the temple was not the end of God's rule or the relationship of the covenant. Jeremiah stood on the hope of the covenant.

Jeremiah described the renewed relationship with God as a new covenant because this relationship would come to be of another kind. It would be a relationship in which the very minds of the people would be transformed (Jer 31:31-34). The promise of the prophet is fulfilled in the words of Jesus when he says, "This cup is the new covenant in my blood" (Luke 22:20). Participating in communion is a confession of following the king, the king whose dominion comes through his death, a death that transforms the minds of those who follow him.

Theology of Temple

It took time to understand that the person and presence of Jesus replaced the ark and the temple. The apostle John reports a confrontation with the Pharisees in which Jesus said "Destroy this temple, and I will raise it again in three days" (John 2:19). This authentication of Jesus' authority utterly mystified his disciples. It was not until after the resurrection that the disciples began to understand that Jesus was speaking of his body. John says, "Then they believed the scripture" (v. 22). John is referring to a theology of the temple as it applied to Jesus; this theology came to be essential to Christian teaching.

The Chronicler understood the temple. He records at length the power of the symbolism of the ark, the footstool of God's throne. Uzzah died because they failed to follow the instruction as to how the ark was to be handled so that its distinction and sanctity were evident at all times. Solomon would move the ark into thick darkness to represent the absolute distinction between the Creator and creation (1 Kings 8:12), the life-giving power of the holy and the complete dependence of the common. The God of Israel could never be represented by images drawn from creation, because the Creator was not part of creation. Jesus declared himself to be the very presence of this holy God. John the apostle identifies Jesus with Yahweh of the temple, as seen in the vision of Isaiah 6:1-4. John quotes Isaiah 6:10 to describe the incorrigible unbelief of the people, saying that Isaiah said this because "he [Isaiah] saw Jesus' glory and spoke [these things] about him [Jesus]" (John 12:41). Seeing Jesus and not believing in the Word was the equivalent of Isaiah seeing Yahweh and preaching to those who would not understand. For followers of Jesus, there was no more place for the physical temple once they realized that he now was the divine presence in their midst.

Christian orthodoxy determined that Jesus is the presence of God as defined by the Nicene Creed: "We believe in one Lord Jesus Christ, the Son of God, begotten of the Father, only-begotten, that is of the substance of the Father." The word "substance" translates the original Greek word *homoousion*, meaning that Jesus shares a personal common essence with the Father. He is *ek tēs ousias tou patros*, "from the inmost being of the Father." For the orthodox Christian, denial of the Nicene Creed might have an analogy in Uzzah touching the ark. It is a failure to understand the full presence of God in the person of Jesus Christ. We confess that Jesus Christ is utterly separate from all that is in the world, yet in the mystery of the incarnation, God is fully present in the person of Jesus Christ. The practice of reciting the Nicene Creed in worship is a profound confession of the truth of the new covenant.

1 Chronicles 18:1-20:8
David's Wars

PREVIEW

If there is an argument for war that can be respected, it is that war may provide for peace. Annually in North America there is a tribute to fallen soldiers in the context of being grateful for the peace these countries have endured. The justification for armaments is to provide protection so a nation may enjoy peace. The next section of Chronicles explains how David achieved rest in preparation for the rule of Solomon. But this did not make war good. The wars of David are the reason that God did not permit David to build the temple (1 Chron 22:8; 28:3).

David would establish the capital, build his own palace, and develop his military forces. It was not until sometime after the oracle in which David received the promise of an eternal dynasty that he undertook the task of taking control of the surrounding territories. The ambiguous chronological phrase *in the course of time* completes the promise made in the oracle to David (17:10): *I will also subdue all your enemies.* Between the dynastic oracle in chapter 17 and David's purchase of the threshing floor of Araunah the Jebusite (Ornan, NRSV) as the location of the future temple (ch. 21), the Chronicler has provided a summary of the wars of David that provided the circumstance in which Solomon had peace to build the temple.

Each of the summaries in this section begins with the same very general chronological notation that serves as a literary marker to the separate units (18:1; 19:1; 20:4). Each of these sections is drawn from 2 Samuel: 1 Chronicles 18:1-17 from 2 Samuel 8:1-18; then 1 Chronicles 19:1–20:3 from 2 Samuel 10:1–11:1; 12:26, 30-31; and

1 Chronicles 20:4-8 from 2 Samuel 21:18-22. The whole is framed by reference to David's subjugation of the nemesis of Saul: *He took Gath and its surrounding villages from the control of the Philistines* (18:1); *they fell at the hands of David and his men* (20:8). This summary by the Chronicler omits large sections from Samuel. The omissions include several famous stories, such as the Bathsheba affair, Amnon's rape of Tamar, Absalom's murder of Amnon, the death of Absalom, the revolt of Sheba, and the execution of the house of Saul. The precision with which the Chronicler refers to the wars of David is evident in the choice of particular verses. The Chronicler is particularly interested in the military and political activities of David that describe the securing of Jerusalem and the ending of Philistine power. He includes episodes of David's warriors selected from the final summaries at the end of the Samuel narrative (2 Sam 21 and 23). The Chronicler does not add to these descriptions. His selected passages stand in the same sequence they have in Samuel, but the new composition has a coherence of its own.

David's victories are extensive: the Philistine territory along the Mediterranean (1 Chron 18:1), Moab across the Jordan (v. 2), Hadadezer and the Arameans of Damascus in the north and northeast (vv. 3-8), Edom in the southeast (vv. 12-13). He is known as far north as Tou of Hamath, who receives relief from his own wars with Hadadezer (vv. 9-11). Booty is garnered from Edom, Moab, the Philistines, Ammonites, and Amalekites (18:11), though no battles are mentioned for the last two. These military gains reach the ideal limits of the Promised Land, from Shihor in Egypt to Lebo Hamath (cf. 1 Chron 13:5). The war stories of 1 Chronicles 19:1-20:3 show how David is rewarded for faithfulness, especially in bringing the ark up to Jerusalem.

As indicated by the indefinite temporal notices that begin each section, this material is not presented in historical order. There is no precise antecedent to the expression *in the course of time*. While there is chronological progression as the Chronicler deals with each of his topics (David established as anointed king, David establishing worship in Jerusalem, David extending the boundaries of his dominion), the arrangement of materials is to establish the veracity of David's conquests. The Chronicler does not provide a biography of David's life. In part, this has already been dictated by the sequence in Samuel, but in large measure he has further selected material to focus on the record he seeks to establish.

OUTLINE

Expansion of the Kingdom, 18:1-13
Administration of the State, 18:14-17
Victories over Ammonites and Arameans, 19:1–20:3
Victories over Philistines, 20:4-8

EXPLANATORY NOTES

Expansion of the Kingdom 18:1-13

David's earlier wars with the Philistines in 1 Chronicles 14:8-17 were defensive battles to preserve Israelite territory. The wars described here are to subjugate enemies, as Nathan the prophet had promised (17:10), to eliminate threat and fear, to provide security and rest. The conquest of Gath and all its settlements may be a more general reference to the southern territory of the Philistines (Aharoni et al.: 77). Gath is one of the five major cities of the Philistine pentapolis (cf. Amos 6:2), just to the south of Ekron. If this is Gath Rimmon, to the northwest of Gezer, north of Ekron, David secured a route that protected access to this important territory, leaving the indigenous peoples unmolested north to the seaport at Joppa.

Moab was an occasional enemy of Israel, located on the east of the Dead Sea, mostly along the Arnon, and occupying the area south to Edom. Occasionally it expanded north into the territory of Gad and Reuben. The genealogy of Judah mentions intermarriage with Moab (1 Chron 4:22), and Ruth is well known in the ancestry of David. David subjugated Moab so that they became a tribute-bearing vassal to Israel and could not ally with other nations as a military threat.

The wars against the Ammonites and the Arameans granted David control of the territory east of the Jordan as far north as the kingdom of Tou at Hamath, on the Orontes River (1 Chron 18:9-11). Though the wars against the Ammonites are related in the following chapter, a reconstruction of the historical sequence from all the information provided suggests that in historical order the Ammonite wars preceded those against the Arameans (Aharoni et al.: 78). Initially the Ammonites would have resented and feared the Israelite presence east of the Jordan in the area of Medeba, with the subjugation and control of Moab (v. 2). This hostility broke into open warfare with the change of leaders in Moab, which also drew in the Arameans north and south of Damascus (1 Chron 19:6-7). The Israelite defeat of the coalition at Rabbah led to a second Aramean attack, with support from allies as far as the Euphrates (19:16-19), which also failed. This brought Israelite forces into Aramean territory as far as the Euphrates, enabling them to become the nominal leader of the Aramean league. David set up garrisons in Damascus to control and protect his significantly expanded territory.

The encounter with Hadadezer king of Zobah, a territory north of Damascus toward Hamath, is introduced immediately following the subjugation of Philistia and Moab (18:3). It was the result of an intervention in setting up a monument at the Euphrates River. Kings would set up monuments outside their own territory to represent their presence in territory they controlled. The Euphrates was a natural boundary for such a monument because it separated the northwest from the east. It is not certain whether David or Hadadezer was engaged in setting up the monument, which was north of both of their territories. The inference of the Chronicler, made from 2 Samuel 8:3, is that David was setting up the monument as a testament to his expanded conquests when Hadadezer resisted him. The result was an expanded war with the Arameans (2 Sam 8:4-6), which brought about a very significant dominion to the young state. The territory of David now extended to the boundaries of Tou, king of Hamath, and its territories on the Orontes River (1 Chron 18:9-11). The king of Hamath was eager to form an alliance with David since the Israelites effectively ended his conflict with the Arameans to the south. Tou had no desire to engage the military might of David, but he was content to have a secure southern border to his territories. Summary statements are given in verses 6 and 13: *The LORD gave David victory wherever he went.* These episodes demonstrate the fulfillment of the prophetic promise in 17:8-10a.

The record of the spoils of war in the battles with Hadadezer in 1 Chronicles 18:4-5 is at variance with the same report in 2 Samuel 8:4. Samuel reports the capture of seventeen hundred cavalry and makes no separate mention of chariots. Numbers are the most difficult to reconcile. Discrepancies often appear in parallel texts, such as the number of Solomon's chariots and horses (2 Chron 1:14; 9:25; 1 Kings 5:6; 10:26). Mistakes happen very easily when numbers are given by ciphers. This is the case in earlier texts, as is seen regularly in the Aramaic papyri. Sometimes numbers are unreasonably large, but at other times very reasonable. Wenham regards the Chronicler as having the more coherent and original account (Wenham: 45). These were very demanding wars, resulting in a large number of losses. The Chronicler's numbers follow those of the Greek text in Samuel, which seems to be the more original (McCarter 1984: 244) *[Greek Text of Chronicles, p. 468].* In military contexts, the word "thousand" (*'elep*) often represents the number of troops contributed by a family unit (as is certainly the case in Judg 6:15), so it may be that the actual count of soldiers and weapons was much smaller.

David also engaged in destroying the weaponry of the Arameans. The Chronicler tells us that David *hamstrung all but a hundred of the chariot horses* (1 Chron 18:4b). This practice follows the analogy of Joshua 11:6-9, where God requires that the horses be disabled and the chariots burned. In both cases this was to cripple the military of mercenary forces. It may have been a precaution against them being hired again in a military attack, but it also may have been regarded as a stipulation of what is termed holy war. All booty of those battles won by direct divine intervention belonged to God and could not be used as plunder *[War in Chronicles, p. 481]*. In Joshua 11:6 the spoils of war at Hazor were regarded as profane (*halalim*) for Israel, a categorization that always carries moral implications.

The Chronicler also gives an account of booty taken from the Arameans; he names the cities of Tebah (Tibhath) and Kun (1 Chron 18:8). Tebah is a city in the Beqaʿ Valley named in the letters of the Amarna tablets (*EA* 179.15, 24, 26) *[Amarna Tablets, p. 464]*. Kun is in the Lebanon Valley, found in execration texts of Rameses III (Albright 1941: 33). The *gold shields* are probably to be identified as bow cases, based on Akkadian parallels (1 Chron 18:7; *AHw* 1151). In this case they were probably made of wood and gold plated. According to the Chronicler, the bronze that David captured in these wars became part of the preparations David made for Solomon in providing for materials for the temple (v. 8); he make the same point regarding the silver and gold gained from Tou and other nations (vv. 10-11), including Edom, Moab, Ammon, the Philistines, and Amalek.

The subjugation of all the north and east side of Jordan provided David with the opportunity to subdue Edom and establish garrisons there. This not only granted Israel a strategic seaport to the south; it also secured the southern border. By this description, David had created a small empire. He had enlarged the size of his territory in the conquest of Philistia, and had secured subordination and contribution of tribute from all the surrounding nations.

Administration of the State 18:14-17

The state of David described by the Chronicler has parallels with those of other suzerains that had treaty agreements with client states that retained significant autonomy. The territories and residents of Moab, Aram Damascus, Edom, and Hamath were not absorbed into Israel, nor did they become Israelite provinces. Israel itself was a confederation of disparate tribes, genealogically related, but they retained their separate identities. David was able to reduce the hostile states to agreements of taxation and thereby provided domestic security. This could be described in a brief eulogy as *governing with justice and equity* (18:14 AT), much as could be said of King Solomon (1 Kings 4:21). If such a kingdom were to survive, it would require very judicious administration.

Joab, Abishai, and Asahel are the infamous sons of Zeruiah, the sister of David (1 Chron 2:16), engaged in leadership of the military. Joab survived as the chief of the military until the time of Solomon, but his support of Adonijah as the successor of David resulted in his execution by Solomon (1 Kings 2:28-35). Both Abiathar, the priest of David's time (1 Chron 18:16), and Joab as the old guard came into conflict with the success of Solomon as the designated heir of David (Konkel 2006: 59). Abiathar was banished to Anathoth and forbidden to receive support from the sanctuary. Though he had been David's faithful priest from the years before David achieved power, he was displaced by Zadok.

The situation of the priesthood appears conflicted between Chronicles and the other texts. The Chronicler is unequivocal in stating that Abiathar was succeeded during David's time by his son Ahimelek (v. 16). But in other references Abiathar is priest throughout the time of David; his father is Ahimelek (1 Sam 22:20; 23:6; 30:7). In other texts in Chronicles, Ahimelek is the son of Abiathar (1 Chron 24:3, 6, 31). Accepting the information of Chronicles, it may be suggested that he has assumed the practice of papponymy, naming a grandson after his grandfather (Knoppers 2004b: 705). All of these may have been priests in David's time. The position of high priest does not seem to be officially designated, as it was in later times.

One of the positions in the king's administration was that of recorder. It is not possible to determine his precise function, but it may have included the oversight of public records, necessary in a royal court, as well as reporting to the king and transmitting royal decrees, as was true in Egyptian courts. Kings were reliant on scribes, who no doubt had to function in several languages for international correspondence. Shavsha is not a Hebrew name (v. 16); it is possibly Egyptian.

The royal bodyguard, consisting of Cherethites and Pelethites, was under the direction of Benaiah (1 Chron 18:17; cf. 11:22; 2 Sam 20:23). The king's immediate circle quite naturally consisted of his sons and their wives. These would be trained for positions of leadership in the kingdom and observed for their particular abilities. The parallel text in 2 Samuel 8:18 says the sons of David were priests, but that text has suffered some kind of corruption. The Greek translation describes them as princes of the royal court (*aularchai*). Chronicles and ancient versions of Samuel appear to be interpretations from an earlier unambiguous Hebrew text that made them priests.

Victories over Ammonites and Arameans 19:1–20:3

Hostility with Ammon went back to the days of Saul. Saul had rescued Jabesh of Gilead, a city near the Jordan River, from the Ammonite king Nahash (1 Sam 11:1-11). An important text, preserved only in the fragments of Qumran, provides background to this hostility (Cross, Parry, and Ulrich: 65–66, plate X [DJD 17]):

> Nahash king of the Ammonites had oppressed Gad and Reuben severely. He gouged out the right eye of each person, and did not allow any help for Israel. There were no Israelites left east of the Jordan whose right eye had not been gouged out by Nahash the Ammonite. But seven thousand had escaped the Ammonites and came to Jabesh Gilead. The next month Nahash went up and camped against Jabesh Gilead; all the people of Jabesh said to Nahash, king of the Ammonites, "Make a treaty with us and we will serve you." Nahash the Ammonite said to them, "On this condition I will make . . ." (cf. 1 Sam 10:27–11:2a NRSV, NLT)

When David came to power, he negotiated terms of agreement with Nahash that were successful in maintaining peace. As was the case with treaties, this probably included taxation revenues from the Ammonites. Nahash was succeeded by his son Hanun (2 Sam 10:1; 1 Chron 19:2). The death of a king could trigger instability, as treaties were made between individuals. Even though an heir was appointed before the king's death, the previous agreement could be challenged. David hoped to renew a covenantal agreement (*ḥesed*) with the ascension of the new king. The overture of David was spurned, not surprising under the circumstances. The messengers were disgraced, with half their beard shaved and half their garment cut off up to the hip. They were treated somewhat as prisoners of war. This humiliation outraged David. The Ammonites then hired mercenary soldiers of the Arameans to help them in hope of relief from Israelite control. This is a classic scenario of how wars begin.

Jericho was a logical place for soldiers engaged east of Jordan to be stationed until their dignity was restored, with their beards grown back (19:5). The Ammonites marshaled their forces at Medeba, on the northern plains of Moab, the southern territory of Ammon. There is uncertainty about this location, which is about twenty miles south from the apparent scene of the conflict (vv. 9-15), in which the forces of Joab and Abishai could support each other. It is often suggested that this should be *the waters of Rabbah* (*my rbh*) rather than Medeba (*mydbʾ*). Others would locate Medeba as an unidentified city nearer to the Israelite border (Japhet 1993: 359). The term *waters of Rabbah* might designate the city of Rabbah (cf. 2 Sam 12:27), but it would seem unlikely the Ammonites would choose their capital as the place of battle. Perhaps the Chronicler is implying that the Moabites were also involved in the coalition.

The mercenaries of the Ammonites came from an extensive area. Aram of the two rivers referred to the territory northeast of the Euphrates and west of the Tigris River. Maakah was a small Aramean state in the area of Golan, south of Damascus and east of the Sea of Galilee. Aram Zoba, in the Beqaʿ Valley, was to the north and west of Damascus, east of Beth Rehob; both of these territories bordered on Maakah. The Chronicler describes thirty-two thousand chariots plus foot soldiers and cavalry opposing David. Samuel tells us there were twenty thousand foot soldiers from the further territories of Beth Rehob and Aram Zoba, one thousand from Maakah, and twelve thousand from the land of Tob, north of the Jabbok River (2 Sam 10:6). The Chronicler apparently includes the soldiers of Maakah with those of Tob in his summary. But on all counts these are huge numbers, signifying the significance of the battle. Comparable are only the thirty thousand chariots of the Philistines in 1 Samuel 13:5 MT.

The stakes of this battle were very high. The forces involved included all the areas to the east and north of Israel, making it potentially vulnerable to attacks on all sides, or to their being subject to Aramean and Ammonite powers. In summary form the Chronicler has identified the forces involved so he can focus on the strategic victory that God granted David in giving him rest from his enemies all round (1 Chron 19:9). This battle was on behalf of *the cities of our God* (v. 13). All the territories, including the Arnon and Jabbok Rivers to the south and north respectively, were regarded as Israelite.

The Ammonites used the fortress of their city as a base of operations. *Rabbat bene ʿammon* (*Rabbah of the sons of Ammon*; MT of Deut 3:11; 2 Sam 12:26; cf. 1 Chron 20:1), the modern-day Amman, was located on the upper course of Wadi Zeqa, where powerful springs serve as the sources of the Jabbok. The city is elsewhere referred to as "the city of the waters" (2 Sam 12:26-27 ESV). The other forces were marshaled outside the city, creating a battle on two fronts. A selection of elite forces was assigned to attack the Arameans. The rest of the army was assigned to Abishai, to attack the Ammonites. Depending on the fortunes of the battle, either could come to the assistance of the other. The battle and its outcome are described in terms of divine warfare. The outcome of the battle depended on God's purposes for his people.

The strategy of the allied forces of Aram and Ammon worked against them. Panic on the part of mercenary Arameans led to the further disintegration of the Ammonite forces. Royal inscriptions are replete with descriptions of terror overcoming opposing armies, resulting in their dissolution. The Ammonites retreated to their own fortification, and Joab returned to Jerusalem. The situation, however, was not acceptable for the Arameans, who now further marshaled their forces (1 Chron 19:16-17). Samuel tells us that this was at Helam (2 Sam 10:16-17), an area somewhere in the northern Transjordan. The second attempt to defeat Israel again worked against the Arameans. David was able to secure treaties with them that extended his influence of control to the area of Hamath and removed any possibility of future alliances with the Ammonites.

The Chronicler creates a final summary of the Ammonite wars by mining his material for specific verses dealing with the Ammonites (20:1-3). The first is drawn from 2 Samuel 11:1; the war against Ammon resumed at the turn of the year. The interpretation found in the Targums and Josephus is to make this the year-end in spring (the month of Nisan before Passover). Their assumption is that David's war against the Arameans was at the turn of the year in fall (the autumn rains), and that Joab took up the cause against Ammon the following spring. The elite soldiers are to be distinguished from the entire army. The Chronicler understands the victories of Joab to be a part of the achievements of David. Strong leaders attract good leaders, who carry out their goals on their behalf. For the Chronicler, there was nothing negative about David remaining in Jerusalem. As he will show in the next section, David always relied on his elite soldiers to wage his battles.

The information on the crown of Milkom (1 Chron 20:1b-3), the god of Ammon (Molek; see NIV mg.), is drawn from 2 Samuel 12:26, 30-31. The Hebrew (*mlkm*) should be read as the name of their god Milkom, rather than *their king* (cf. 1 Kings 11:5, 7, 33). As the crown of the deity, its weight is reasonable. A talent was about the weight that a man could carry, around seventy pounds. The crown was taken from the head of the idol, but the narrator relates it as if it were from the head of the god himself. The biblical writers delight in satire on the religions of idols.

The booty report is introduced very abruptly: the information from 2 Samuel 12:27-29, which explains how David came to the battlefield, is omitted. The omission may be accidental, as it is included in some Greek manuscripts. Others would regard this as the literary method of the Chronicler (Japhet 1993: 363), adhering strictly to the text of his sources while at the same time focusing without distraction on his objective, which is to show the Davidic accomplishments. Much booty for the Chronicler was the sign of divine blessing and support.

Victories over Philistines 20:4-8

The Chronicler's closure of the military achievements of David brings him back to the Philistines. His source is 2 Samuel 21:18, which begins with his chronological refrain: *In the course of time* (1 Chron 20:4). This brings him to three encounters with the Philistines: battle at Gezer (v. 4), defeat of the brother of Goliath (v. 5), and defeat of the six-fingered giant at Gath (v. 6). In choosing this starting point, the Chronicler omits an episode in which David became exhausted and had to be rescued from a mighty Philistine warrior by Abishai (2 Sam 21:15-17). The episode is often regarded as being omitted out of respect for David, but there may have been other considerations. The Chronicler does not rearrange any of this material; the refrain clearly marked for him the concluding section. In his selection the Chronicler has left out all the material of divine judgment against the household of David because of his sin with Bathsheba and its aftermath (2 Sam 11:1-21:14). The Chronicler has used the promise to David as his guide for depicting David's dominion.

All three of the episodes against the Philistines engage *descendants of Rapha in Gath* (1 Chron 20:4, 8). This has traditionally been interpreted to be descendants of legendary giants of the past (Gen 14:5; Deut 2:10-11, 20-21; etc.). Their habitat was Bashan, the most northern part of the area east of Jordan (Deut 3:13). *Descendants of the Rephaites* (1 Chron 20:4) and *descendants of Rapha* (v. 8), literally *those descended (nulledu) from Rapha*, is a metaphorical use of the verb *yld* (to bear a child). In this case it refers to a group bound by another loyalty, such as a servant giving military service (cf. Gen 14:14; *yalid*, Schreiner and Botterweck: 81). Inclusion in the group was by adoption, initiation, or consecration. At Ugarit the term "Rapha" is the name of a deity who functions as a patron of elite warriors. It may be that these warriors were devoted to the god Rapha, a divine epithet meaning "one who is in a healthy condition" (L'Heureux: 84-85). These may have been warriors who constituted a choice group of soldiers *[Ugarit, p. 467]*.

The first battle was at Gezer, located at the entrance to the Aijalon Valley in the Shephelah, to the west of Gibeon [*Shephelah*, p. 467]. This may have served as the Philistine boundary. Sibbekai the Hushathite was one of the valiant warriors who came to be in charge of one of the military divisions (1 Chron 11:29; 27:11). Elhanan is also one of David's valiant warriors (11:26), who killed the brother of Goliath (1 Chron 20:5). The parallel MT in Samuel says that he killed *Goliath* (2 Sam 21:19) and also, previously, that David killed Goliath (1 Sam 17:50-51). It is often assumed that the Chronicler harmonized the tradition to resolve the contradiction in Samuel; but there is reason to conclude that the Samuel text used by the Chronicler was itself corrupted (Williamson 1982: 142). The word "weaver" (*'oregim*) appears twice in 2 Samuel 21:19 (AT): "Elhanan son of Jair-Oregim the Bethlehemite killed Goliath the Gittite, who had a spear with a shaft like a weaver's rod [*'oregim*]." The Chronicler omitted the first *'oregim* and determined the *bet hallaḥmi* of the Samuel text (lit. *of the house of bread*, i.e., *the Bethlehemite*) to be the personal name *Laḥmi*. The Chronicler is clear in his interpretation of his text of Samuel: Elhanan killed the brother of Goliath. Textual corruption makes it impossible to know the actual relationship of David, Elhanan, and Goliath.

The list of heroes found in 2 Samuel 21:15-22 appears to derive from an ancient archive (McCarter 1984: 451). As the Chronicler interpreted it, there may well have been two giants. The description of their armor was based on this record. The giant David slew may have come to be called Goliath, a name known from this record. The final duel was at Gath (1 Chron 20:6), one of the five principal cities of the Philistines to the south of Gezer and Ekron. David had previously resided there, rendering mercenary service to Achish.

THE TEXT IN BIBLICAL CONTEXT

Lands of the Kingdom

The Chronicler presents a highly complimentary view of David's accomplishments and the support of Israel. In Samuel, David's conflicted personal affairs become affairs of state. David is driven into exile while Absalom and the Israelites take control in Jerusalem. Much more than the personal life of David is at stake. The Israel of Samuel is divided, with factions between tribes and within tribes. The struggles in the succession of the kingdom are not only the failures of David but are also the result of deep divisions within the nation. The Chronicler's summary of David's administration describes him as governing with *justice and equity* over a united Israel (1 Chron 18:14 NRSV).

The questions of David's reputation and the unity of Israel are closely related. To appreciate the force of David's campaigns, it is helpful to contextualize them within the Chronicler's larger presentation (Knoppers 2004b: 740). The Chronicler uses the dynastic oracle of Nathan as a charter to organize David's reign. Nathan's promises have both dynastic and national implications. David is forbidden to build the temple but receives a series of divine commitments. Most important is victory over foreign enemies (1 Chron 17:8, 10).

These victories earn David a formidable reputation among his contemporaries. These victories extend to David's power in international affairs, making his a kingdom that extends deep into Aramean territory. The battles against the Philistines are no longer appendixes to long narratives about David's domestic troubles, but continue the theme of David's power as king and the unification of the nation. His many and repeated victories secure a place for Israel where they will not be disturbed any more. The humbling of the nations is seen in immediate conquests of the Philistines; it is not projected as a promise for the distant future.

The ordering of the kingdom enables David to prepare for building the temple and organizing all its personnel. He secures the endorsement of all Israel for his projects. The wars of David create an image of David's reign as the normative experience of Israel. The exodus and the wilderness wanderings provide instruction for the life of the covenant people, but the time of David and Solomon are the classical age in which prosperity and unity are possible. This is the time when the monarchy, the city, and the temple define the Israelite kingdom. It is the standard by which other times are measured.

THE TEXT IN THE LIFE OF THE CHURCH

The Church in the World

Western history following the first centuries of the Common Era is largely the story of the church. Unhappily, most of Western history is also a story of war and conflict. Though somewhat misleading, the name Thirty Years' War (1618–48 CE) is used to describe part of the fifty years of struggle (1610–60) for a balance of power between the states of Europe following the Protestant Reformation. Germany was deeply divided by Catholicism, Lutheranism, and Calvinism. Conflicts continued between the monarchical tendencies of the

Holy Roman emperor and the aspirations of the German princes. Politically, the wars of this period were centered in the struggles of France against encirclement by the Hapsburg powers of Austria and Spain, and the efforts of provinces of the Netherlands to preserve independence from Spain. But these wars could not be separated from the powerful interests of ecclesiastical bodies that had a great deal of influence in the fortunes of the state. Much of the violence in England and Ireland following the sixteenth century was the result of conflict between Catholicism and the Church of England. Conflicts that were part of the process in founding the kingdom of Israel have a parallel with conflicts in which the church was embroiled with state relationships. Just as the Chronicler writes a history showing the ideals of his faith, so the church needs to see its own history as the pursuit of its hope for the kingdom of God in a conflicted world.

In the end, Israel came to have no political influence at all. The Chronicler could only look back on a time that to him was God's work in the turmoil of human history. The days of David inspired hope for a future in which the divine purposes for life on earth might be realized. Similarly, the political influence of the church has come to be completely marginalized in the present time. The concept of the separation of church and state was to separate political interests from all other influences. Efforts to implement this doctrine have removed the church from direct involvement in much of the conflicting politics of state. But cultural and religious matters invariably influence politics if they are important to a significant proportion of a population. Attempts to rigidly exclude religious values are to the detriment of the state. No member of state governance can divorce personal religious convictions, whether atheistic or theistic, from their work as a state official, whether in elected office or as a state employee. Christian faith convictions have had a powerful influence for good. William Wilberforce, by the sheer power of his personal faith convictions, was able to stimulate political change that gradually brought an end to the horrible practices of human slavery in his era. The example of Wilberforce shows how the church can be a force for good within human society. It is also possible for the church as an institution to be a positive influence. Western history must include that perspective in recounting the past.

The Chronicler's hope in depicting David's kingdom was not to suggest that such an era could or should be repeated. It was rather to show that God is at work in the world and that God's purposes can be accomplished in spite of the most conflicted circumstances. The Chronicler remains open to the way God will bring about the promised kingdom. The same is true of the church. The conflicts of the past must not be construed in such a way as to think that religion poisons everything, as claimed by Christopher Hitchens (*God Is Not Great*). The conflicts of the past are a testimony to human propensity for conflict rather than for any particular faith or institution. These conflicts must not be allowed to obscure the mission for peace that is the promise proclaimed in the Christian faith.

The church often serves the kingdom of God best when it lacks political power. Christians need to understand their past without denying the negative, yet also not allow past conflicts to obscure the church's mission and achievements. The church's influence in Western history is a positive legacy. Christian values were the impetus for founding educational institutions essential to the well-being of every individual. The most stable and supportive governments in the world are found in countries where the church has been present. However marginalized the church may seem to be in the present, it must not lose its vision for the future of God's kingdom.

Part 3

Preparations for the Temple

1 Chronicles 21:1–29:30

OVERVIEW

With chapter 21 the Chronicler begins the narrative of the construction of the temple. Preparation for building the temple and its future operation become the entire focus of the remainder of the Davidic narrative. The Chronicler moves to the very last chapter of Samuel to continue his story of David, which he develops as an introduction to temple building. In 1 Chronicles 11:11-41 much of the intervening material of 2 Samuel 23:8-39 was used to show support for David in becoming king. The story of David taking a census in 2 Samuel 24 is the last section he will use in his narrative of David.

When Chronicles next returns to the Deuteronomistic History, it will be to introduce Solomon in 2 Chronicles 1:1-13 *[Deuteronomistic History, p. 465]*. The story of Solomon begins with the vision at Gibeon in 1 Kings 3:4-15. Chronicles has its own version of David anointing Solomon to become king. Solomon is the designated heir to the promise of an eternal kingdom. He is the man of rest, as can be observed in his name *šelomoh*, which means *šalom*, peace, prosperity, wholeness (1 Chron 22:9). Solomon is designated by David as the dynastic successor and therefore temple builder. In Solomon, the Chronicler continues the two main themes that are central to David's reign: the legitimacy of the king, as affirmed by all Israel, and concern for the temple. The eternal kingdom was centered exclusively on Solomon as the temple builder. For Solomon, faithfulness would be measured by his diligence in completing the task of temple building. The future of the dynasty is made dependent on Solomon bringing to completion the work of his father, David.

The remainder of David's reign is dominated by preparations for temple building: site, materials, plans, personnel, and political conditions. David prepares for everything that can be anticipated. In Chronicles, the temple becomes the focus of unity for the people of Israel. The Chronicler has gone back in history to the common heritage of all the various groups that diverged over time. His concern is to provide continuity in temple institutions from the time of their origins, long before the decline and failure of the monarchy. These become models to address the Chronicler's own situation, in which diversity and conflict have taken on new dimensions.

1 Chronicles 21:1-22:1
Designation of the Temple Site

PREVIEW

Where should the church's meetinghouse be built? Virtually every congregation has a history of debating this question for many hours. The first church for which this author was pastor had its building in a village where all else that remained was a well and a grain elevator. Half the services were held in a town about fifteen miles away. When a new church building was constructed, it was determined that it must be in the original village, where no one lived. Locations have their own logic. In Israel the tabernacle was mobile: it had various residences. The location of the temple was forever.

The account of David's census, the consequent plague, and David's purchase of the threshing floor of Araunah the Jebusite are all developed to explain the choice of the site for building the temple. The story in Samuel is an appropriate transition to the succession of Solomon in Kings. David is portrayed in a positive light as the contrite and submissive king, who accepts responsibility, has great compassion for his people, and acts immediately on the instructions to bring an end to the plague. The Chronicler has his own closing for this passage in 1 Chronicles 21:26b-22:1. In conclusion he gives his interpretation of the significance of the preceding narrative. His aim is to establish the divinely willed continuity between the Mosaic sanctuary (the tabernacle) and the future Jerusalem temple. Fire from heaven confirmed this as the chosen place for the altar, as happened with the initiation of the tabernacle altar (cf. Lev 9:24). This anticipates the dedication of the altar in the temple in 2 Chronicles 7:1. There is an implied transfer from the tabernacle at Gibeon to the house of the Lord in Jerusalem.

The purpose of David's census is conscription for war. In Numbers, the Israelites are enumerated from the age of twenty and upward according to their family leaders (Num 1:2-3). A census is taken by divine command in Numbers and is taken regularly before military campaigns (Josh 8:10; 1 Sam 11:8; 13:15; 15:4; etc.). The narrative in 2 Samuel 24:1 tells us that the Lord was angry with "Israel" and that he enticed David to conduct a census. The conjunction in Samuel (angry "again") links this episode to the earlier famine (21:1) in which David discovered that Israel was suffering judgment because of Saul's attempt to liquidate the Gibeonites. In this case David was fully aware of this guilt. There is no indication how this guilt is related to the census, which David undertook at the divine initiative (2 Sam 24:1). A good thing can of course become sin; motives and pride are intangibles that are the most dangerous sorts of sins. The anger of the Lord is not explained, though there is no doubt that it is the result of David's guilt. But penitence has a positive outcome. The census accentuates the king's responsibility for the plague and affirms the king in bringing about divine blessing.

OUTLINE

Census of David, 21:1-7
Judgment and Confession, 21:8-17
Purchase of Threshing Site, 21:18-25
Divine Response and Choice of Temple Site, 21:26–22:1

EXPLANATORY NOTES

Census of David 21:1-7

The Chronicler says that śaṭan stood up against Israel. In the time of the Chronicler, this term could not have been understood to be the devil with the name "Satan." There is no linguistic evidence for such a concept in the Hebrew language of this period. The term could refer to an adversary, such as the one resisting the anointing of Joshua as priest in Zechariah 3:1-2. In the visions of Zechariah, it is uncertain as to how this adversary was conceived. The visions include an intermediary who appears as a human and interprets the message of the vision. Thus, the usual meaning of śaṭan is a human adversary.

David was regarded as just such a potential śaṭan in the days when he was allied with Achish, king of Gath, during the Philistine wars with Israel ("adversary," 1 Sam 29:4 NRSV). The Philistine generals forced Achish to send David back lest his greater allegiance prove to be with Saul. David would then become a śaṭan to them. In Chronicles this adversary remains completely anonymous. In 2 Samuel 24:1 the impetus for the census comes from the Lord. The situation may be analogous to Job, where the śaṭan is part of the divine court, acting under divine authority (Job 1:6-12). But the term as used by the Chronicler is ambiguous. The Lord could also have acted through one of the advisers of David's army. The Chronicler is not contradicting his sources, which say that this test was from the Lord.

The Chronicler has significantly reworked the account of the census. He omits 1 Samuel 24:5-7, which gives details of the enumerating progress through the various regions. The Chronicler summarizes this by simply saying they went through all Israel (1 Chron 21:4). The census totals are given in verse 5, where a separate total is given for Judah. Vaticanus, the most complete and best manuscript of the Greek translation [Greek Text of Chronicles, p. 468], does not include a separate total for Judah. It is unlikely that this was an omission on the part of the translator. Leslie Allen asks, "Did a copyist's eye slip two lines of sixteen letters?" (Allen: 135). It appears that this is a gloss (addition) drawn from the text of Samuel. The Chronicler adds a note saying that the census was never completed because it was so abhorrent to Joab. Levi and Benjamin were never counted. The reasons for leaving out these two tribes are not given. Levi is excluded from military census and so is not enumerated (Num 1:49; 2:33). The tabernacle was then located at Gibeon in Benjamin, which may have been a consideration in the omission of that tribe. Chronicles further has Joab sharply point out to David that this census is going to bring guilt on Israel (1 Chron 21:3). In Chronicles the conflict between David and his chief general is bitter. All this makes David fully responsible for the judgment that follows.

The Chronicler's reworking of the census has also required a recalculation of the numbers of the census. His methods in this regard are not transparent, but the simplest solution proposed is that he took the numbers of Samuel as representing 100,000 arms-bearing men for each tribe. There are in total thirteen tribes, including Levi. The numbers in Samuel provide a total of 1,300,000 (800,000 plus 500,000). Because Levi and Benjamin were not counted, this number would be reduced by 200,000, yielding the number 1,100,000 (1 Chron 21:5). The numbers regarding Judah are an addition in the

MT, as noted above, and are incongruous with the Chronicler's emphasis on *all Israel*. The later addition of 470,000 might be a calculated reduction from 500,000 in Samuel, based on the omission of Benjamin in Chronicles. The number of textual variables make any solution conjectural.

Whatever the literary process in Chronicles, the numbers in both texts are impossibly large. The Song of Deborah relates that six tribes in Israel were able to muster 40,000 soldiers (Judg 5:8). This compares with those of other rosters. The city-state of Mari, located on the Euphrates River, cites armies of 6,000 and 10,000 men (ARM 1.23.42; 6.33.65; Milgrom 1990: 339). At times texts use hyperbole; King Kirtu at Ugarit claims that "his host was a numerous force, three hundred myriads" (*KTU* 1.14 iv 16.17), that is, three million fighting men [*Ugarit*, p. 467]. But as Barnouin observes, it would be illogical to fabricate numbers used in the report of a census (Barnouin: 286–87). The numbers must have had a functional significance. In Numbers there is a correlation with the calendar; the armies of Israel are numbered in analogy with the hosts of the heavens. The Hebrew word *ṣaba*ʾ (hosts) refers to both military men and stars. Armies are depicted in consort with constellations.

Wenham takes an entirely different approach with this census (Wenham: 33–34). He takes ʾ*elep* (thousand) to mean either an officer of a clan or a specially trained soldier (*HAL* 1:58; Num 10:4; Judg 6:15). He further assumes that errors of digit placement have created extraordinarily large numbers. By his proposal, the original number in 1 Chronicles 21:5 would have been eighty thousand soldiers for Israel with thirty officers (ʾ*alapim*); this came to be distorted to three hundred officers (ʾ*alapim*), and the term ʾ*elep* came to be misunderstood as the numeral "thousand"; the total then became 1,100,000 armed soldiers. Such a progression is purely conjectural. No calculations are able to account for the obscurity of data in the various texts. There has been textual confusion with numbers, but it is less certain that terms such as ʾ*elep* have been misunderstood in representing numbers.

Judgment and Confession 21:8–17

The Chronicler has his own interpretation of the confession of David. In 2 Samuel 24:10, David is smitten when he receives the enumeration and asks for forgiveness. The prophet Gad is then commissioned to confront David with the consequences of his sin. This census is for military purposes; David is relying on strength in numbers rather than on God. In Chronicles, divine punishment is immediate, as might be expected, given the stern warnings of Joab. The nature of the manifestation of judgment is not specified, but David immediately recognizes it as punishment for his sin. It is then that he asks for forgiveness and is given the choice of the consequences.

All three of the choices involve all the people of Israel, indicating the national significance of David's role. Sin is never an individual matter; one person's sin invariably negatively affects all the persons impacted by the offense. This is especially true in war. In his military ambitions, David violated the covenant, with devastating results for the entire nation. This is characteristic of all decisions regarding warfare, but usually those responsible for victimizing the citizens of their country feel no guilt and suffer no consequences. David models a good leader in accepting full responsibility for his sin.

In making the choice of punishment, David makes confession of the central truth of the covenant God: he is gracious (1 Chron 21:13). This is the essence of the covenant name "Yahweh"; the God of the covenant "will be gracious to whom [he] will be gracious" (cf. Exod 33:19 NRSV; 34:6). His graciousness to Israel is the remembered deliverance of the exodus (Ps 103:7-8). But the choice brings David great anguish; the judgment is a severe mercy. The Chronicler gives a much more graphic description of the divine agent sent for destruction (1 Chron 21:14-16), but this is not due to a more developed concept of angels. The Chronicler's version of Samuel is not like that of the MT; he is following a text similar to a Samuel scroll found at Qumran (1QSam[a]; Cross, Parry, and Ulrich: 192-95 [DJD 17]). In Chronicles, the location of Jerusalem has become more directive: *And God sent an angel to destroy Jerusalem* (1 Chron 21:15). In 2 Samuel 24:16 the messenger extends his arm over Jerusalem to destroy it. As the plague begins, the Lord relents and orders the destruction to cease. It is then that David and the elders, covered in sackcloth, plead for mercy (1 Chron 21:16). At the threshing floor of Araunah, David prays for mercy, naming the sin of taking the census as the offense. He and the elders are prostrate in repentance, seeking the mercy of the Lord.

Purchase of Threshing Site 21:18-25

The command to build an altar comes as an explicit divine instruction through the prophet Gad. David is meticulous in following these instructions. He approaches Araunah (known in Chron as Ornan, so NRSV) to acquire the site so the altar can be built. The text in Samuel is in considerable disarray at this point (Cross, Parry, and

Ulrich: 194–95). Two phrases seem to have been variants that came to be jumbled in the transmission of the texts: (1) four of his sons with him hid themselves with sackcloth; and (2) the king and his servants were coming toward him covered with sackcloth. Confusion of similar texts and accidental omissions have resulted in variations in all extant texts of Chronicles and Samuel. Notable in Chronicles is that Araunah turns and sees the divine agent rather than King David (1 Chron 21:20). This is a difference of only one letter (*mlk* = king; *ml'k* = messenger), but it seems that *messenger* (God's agent) is intended. This extraordinary appearance may be why Araunah's sons hid themselves in his version of events.

The negotiations with Araunah play on the word "give." David asks Araunah to give him the place of the threshing floor and insists that he should give it at full price. Araunah counters with the offer that David should take the place, and he in turn will give the oxen, the wood, and the grain for the offering. The king counters with the insistence that he will pay for it at full price and would not offer to the Lord anything that he did not purchase. David then gives Araunah six hundred shekels of gold for the place. There is an emphasis on *the place* (AT), which echoes "the place that the LORD your God will choose" for all the people to worship (Deut 12:5-7). The price that David pays is multiple times that in Samuel, both in the amount (six hundred shekels as opposed to fifty) and the metal (gold instead of silver). The purchase described in Chronicles is the entire area, not just the threshing floor itself. Six hundred shekels amounts to fifty shekels per tribe, which may be an indication that this is on behalf of all Israel.

Divine Response and Choice of Temple Site 21:26–22:1

The Chronicler's conclusion to the choice of the temple site establishes the theological points of critical importance. God answers David's prayer for mercy in two ways. First, fire from heaven consumes the offerings upon the altar. Second, God commands the divine agent to restore his sword to its sheath. There is more to these events than just ending the plague (cf. 2 Sam 24:25), which is decisively terminated following the earlier suspension (1 Chron 21:15-16). The function of the altar is divinely approved in the same way as the altar of the tabernacle in the wilderness (Lev 9:24). For the Chronicler, this sign from heaven provides continuity between the Mosaic tabernacle and the future temple. The consumption of the sacrifices by *fire from heaven* is the divine approval of this altar for the temple that is to be built (1 Chron 21:26).

A somewhat parenthetical explanation justifies the offering of the sacrifices on this altar at Jerusalem rather than at the altar in the court of the tabernacle at Gibeon. *At that time, when David saw that the LORD had answered him* refers the specific events just narrated (1 Chron 21:28). David feared the dreadful plague, so he could not go up to Gibeon to seek the Lord and make offerings on the altar there (v. 30). It is an indication that the function of the tabernacle will be transferred to the temple to be built. It was when David made the offerings consumed by the fire from heaven that David declared, *The house of the LORD God is to be here, and also the altar of burnt offering for Israel* (1 Chron 22:1). David's announcement takes on prophetic force, a description found only in Chronicles. The worship of all Israel will be unified. With the transfer of the ark to Jerusalem, in the tent David had made for it, there were two official sanctuaries, each with its own officials. Further, it was evident that the ark and the tabernacle belonged together. These events, which established a divinely sanctioned altar at Jerusalem, settled the question of where the ark should be and provided for the worship at the place that the Lord had chosen.

THE TEXT IN BIBLICAL CONTEXT

Mount Moriah

The inclusion of the census might seem to tarnish the image of David as an ideal king. But this acknowledged culpability does not disqualify him from serving as a paradigmatic figure. In the story, David becomes a model of accepting responsibility for wrongdoing. David's confession, intercession, renewed obedience, and the resultant divine blessing all contribute to portray David as exhibiting the proper response to failure. The positive outcome in the choice of the temple site becomes an example of how actions with disastrous consequences may become positive in the legacy of a life. The first part of the narrative accentuates the king's responsibility for the plague, but the latter part emphasizes the divine approval of intercession and obedience. The choice of the temple site is narrated to establish the divinely willed continuity between the Mosaic sanctuary and the future temple (Williamson 1991: 20-25). At the same time, there is a conscious contrast between the tabernacle and its altar of burnt offering, and the house of the Lord God and the altar of burnt offering. The divine will had prevented David from seeking the Lord at Gibeon and directed him toward Jerusalem.

The Chronicler provides verbal allusions that connect the choice of the temple site with other events. The description of Araunah at the threshing floor is a deliberate comparison with Gideon in Judges 6. The theme is the encounter of an angel with someone threshing wheat. The appearance of the Lord to Gideon also led to the establishment of a permanent holy place (6:24). The Chronicler further patterns the purchase of the threshing site in 1 Chronicles 21:22-25 on Abraham's purchase of the cave of Machpelah from Ephron in Genesis 23. A site for sacred purposes is purchased from a member of the indigenous population. Verbal parallels such as the purchase *at full price* help to make the analogy evident.

The purchase of the field at Machpelah was the only piece of property the patriarchs secured in the Promised Land. The Chronicler was no doubt aware of this fact and made use of it in his valuation of the temple site. It represented firstfruits of the future promise and formed a bond with the promise to the patriarch. This point is made more explicit in 2 Chronicles 3:1. Solomon began to build the temple on Mount Moriah, at the place David had chosen, on the threshing floor of Araunah the Jebusite. Mount Moriah is referred to elsewhere only in Genesis 22 as the site where Abraham was commanded to offer up Isaac. Reference to the mount of the Lord is the vocabulary used of the Temple Mount (Gen 22:14; Ps 24:3; Isa 2:3; 30:29). Abraham was told to sacrifice Isaac "on a mountain I will show you" (Gen 22:2). The answer to David's prayer at the threshing floor of Araunah was to him the divine designation of the mountain for the house of the Lord (1 Chron 22:1), similar to the choice of Mount Moriah for Abraham.

The association between the mountain of Abraham and the Temple Mount is explicit. The Lord had appeared to David as he had to Abraham. Continuity of worship is established at this site; temple worship is linked to the promises of the past. While David initiates worship at a new location with unprecedented features, it stands in continuity with not only the tabernacle but also the worship of the patriarchs before that.

THE TEXT IN THE LIFE OF THE CHURCH

Worship in the Church Community

Understanding common origins is critical to establishing congregational relationships. History provides the foundation for cultivating a shared experience of unity in worship. The Chronicler begins with the divine choice of a central place of worship to bring cohesion to the diverse community of Israel. His goal was to provide an unbroken continuity between the establishment of the temple in Jerusalem and the circumstances of Israel in his time.

There were many places of worship among the Diaspora of the Jews. Some places of worship were syncretistic (a mixture of religions), such as the Jewish temple at Elephantine in Egypt *[Elephantine Papyri, p. 466]*. This temple was established by a Jewish colony in the sixth century BCE. Though it was destroyed around the time of the Chronicler, it is representative of the disparity in Israel's worship. Their affinity for the Jerusalem temple can still be seen in an official letter, sent in the time of Darius II (ca. 420 BCE), seeking clarification on Passover observance from the officials at Jerusalem. The Chronicler's task was to bring continuity to the worship of Israel. The temple at Jerusalem was always central to the worship of the God of the covenant.

Origin is a critical common point in establishing acceptable continuity in worship. In the Mennonite experience, the church was instrumental in immigration to Canada from the Ukraine. In 1774 Catherine II appointed Prince Potemkin, a general of the Turkish wars, as governor of South Russia. He implemented a vigorous colonization policy. Through Georg von Trappe, a colonization agent, the oppressed Mennonites of Prussia were invited to come to this promising Russian location. They would be exempted from military service, have their own schools, and be tax-exempt for ten years. They would have free transportation to Russia and would receive some start-up money. Over time, large settlements were established along the Dnieper River. The largest two settlements were the Chortiza and the Molotschna. Changing times in Russia brought about further migrations, beginning in the last half of the nineteenth century. These migrants formed churches that came to be very diverse in character as they conformed to new cultures or retained very traditional ways of worship.

Though these churches became diverse, they had common origins and a continuing relationship. These were evident in the names of congregants, in the Low German language familiar to them, and in the interrelatedness of their families. Like the community of the Chronicler, their members had endured much oppression and experienced difficult migrations. These Mennonites had common roots in faith and worship through their geographical origins. With great emotion I remember a visit to Zaporozhye in Ukraine, where so much of my grandparents' story and their spiritual life is embedded in the buildings, the graveyard, the landscape, and farmland.

Though I do not share in the kind of worship where there are no musical instruments and where men and women are segregated on separate sides of the church, I identify with them and their faith because of our common origins.

The temple the Chronicler was seeking to support could not be compared to the one that Solomon had built. Though the Chronicler traces the lineages of temple personnel back to the time of David, he was well aware of differences. To some extent he created the institution of David's time on the basis of temple practice as he knew it. But for all the differences, this was still the same worship and the same institution. When congregations have tensions over their differences of worship, it is important to retain the fundamentals of their common origins.

1 Chronicles 22:2-19
Charge to Build the Temple

PREVIEW

Life goals may not be achieved in one lifetime. Success may be making provision for goals to be achieved. Sometimes this is convenient. Politicians set goals to reduce climate change that extend to the lives of their grandchildren. Failure to achieve a goal is disappointing, but it need not be failure in all ways. Moses did not enter the Promised Land, a failure that grieved him deeply (Deut 3:23-29), but this was not a failure of his life. His goal would find success in Joshua.

The transition of the kingdom from David to Solomon in Chronicles is modeled on that of the transfer of leadership from Moses to Joshua. In Chronicles, David immediately declares that Solomon is the successor who will build the temple (1 Chron 22:6). The Chronicler goes to Deuteronomy 31 and Joshua 1 for material by which he presents the last words of David to Solomon. He brings together the reigns of David and Solomon so they become one single event (Williamson 1976: 356–57). The parallel drawn with Moses and Joshua enables the Chronicler to show that the role of Solomon is to complete the work begun by David.

In several ways the roles of David and Solomon are parallel to those of Moses and Joshua. Moses, because of the sins of the people, is never able to enter the Promised Land (Deut 3:23-29). David will never be able to build the temple because of his many wars (1 Chron 22:7-8). Moses exhorts Joshua to be "strong and courageous" in continuing the task of entering the land (Deut 31:6-7; Josh 1:1-9). Solomon must remain faithful to the words of Moses as David taught him: remain *strong and courageous*, without fear and discouragement (1 Chron 22:13). The charge of Moses to Joshua is given personally and directly, just as that of David to Solomon. It is immediately embraced by all the people as the transition to another phase of the promise being fulfilled.

OUTLINE

Provision of the Temple Materials, 22:2-5
Charge to Solomon, 22:6-16
Charge to Leaders of Israel, 22:17-19

EXPLANATORY NOTES

Provision of the Temple Materials 22:2-5

An alliance with Tyre and Sidon to supply building materials for David and Solomon in their building projects is well established in the records (1 Chron 22:4; 1 Kings 5:1-12). Agreements David made with Hiram king of Tyre were continued under Solomon at the initiative of the king of Tyre. By the time of David, Tyre had become a maritime power. During the days of Israel, it colonized territory as far as Carthage (Katzenstein: 84-86). Hiram provided David with wood, carpenters, and stone masons (2 Sam 5:11; 1 Chron 14:1). The attitude of the kings of Tyre appears to have changed with David's victory over the Philistines. Philistines competed with Phoenicia in maritime power. Abibaal, father of Hiram, founded a dynasty and may have initiated a change of policy with David. Their political loyalty was based on a mutual need. Israel lacked technical skills for advancing its material culture, and Phoenicia lacked adequate agricultural production.

Conscription was the usual means for undertaking public works projects. Chronicles is clear on the point that labor procured was from resident aliens (1 Chron 22:2). The sojourner is distinguished from the foreigner in that he has settled in the land for some time and is recognized as having a special status (Konkel 1997: 836-39). The sojourner is generally in the service of an Israelite who is his master and protector. The resident alien could participate in public festivals, though this would assume his acceptance of circumcision. In Kings, the Phoenicians serve as skilled tradesmen for Israel (1 Kings 5:6), which may be what the Chronicler implies in saying that David assembled the resident aliens as stone masons.

Abundance is the key concept in the Chronicler's account of David making preparation for the temple materials (1 Chron 22:3-4). These include sculpted stone, iron to secure fasteners for the doors of the gates, material for the joins (it is not certain if these *fittings* were wood or metal), and bronze and wood in large quantities. The bronze would be used for the columns, the altar, and the great molten sea. The cedars of Lebanon (*Cedrus libani*) were renowned for their impressive size, reaching to nearly one hundred feet; by the mid-nineteenth century CE this vast resource was depleted (Konkel 2006: 123). These trees were legendary for building palaces in Egypt, Mesopotamia, Assyria, Babylon, Persia, and Greece.

David makes such meticulous preparation because of his recognition that Solomon is young and inexperienced. The temple is to be an edifice so distinguished that it will be famous for its splendor throughout the nations. The God of Israel is the God of all nations, so the temple that represents him must have international significance. The word for "young" is apparently a Canaanite loanword that has a range of meanings (1 Chron 22:5). In many instances it distinguishes an official position such as officer. It may define a servant of any age. The narrative, however, makes Solomon relatively young when commissioned by David. He was born in Jerusalem (14:4), and David only reigned in Jerusalem for thirty-three years (29:27). Solomon was born during the Syrian and Ammonite wars nearer to the beginning of David's reign (1 Chron 19; cf. 2 Sam 12:24-25), yet he would necessarily be working with administrators who had much more experience in David's complex empire.

Charge to Solomon 22:6-16

David selected Solomon to be his successor and charged him with sacred responsibilities. This is the first of a series of steps to succession. A public announcement will follow and in due course lead to the actual installation and anointing of the king. Solomon is the man of rest, enjoying the proper conditions for temple building. His very name signals the fact that peace would characterize his reign (1 Chron 22:9). Rest is the circumstance of possessing the land that makes salvation possible (Ps 95:7-11).

The Chronicler has transferred the fulfillment of rest to the dynastic promise, so that Solomon shares with David the establishment of the kingdom. This has an analogy with Moses and Joshua; Joshua, as the successor of Moses, brings the people to rest (Josh 1:13, 15; 21:44; 22:4; 23:1). As will be true for Solomon, Joshua brought peace to the people of Israel (Josh 11:23; 14:15). In the

Chronicler's version, the dynastic promise to David is confirmed in Solomon. The clauses have been rearranged to make Solomon the immediate subject of the Lord's declaration: *He . . . will build a house for my Name. He will be my son* (1 Chron 22:10). The final clause is supplemented: *I will establish the throne of his kingdom over Israel forever*. The added mention of *Israel* coheres with the Chronicler's emphasis. The dynastic promise pertains to all the tribes of Israel and is not limited in any sense to Judah.

The speech of David is emphatic that he has been disqualified from building the temple. God tells David that he is a man of war who has shed much blood (1 Chron 22:8). Shedding of blood is an expression of culpability incurred for the death of another human. This is normally not the way a soldier is viewed. However, in this verse David's many wars are given as the basis for the complaint that he has shed much blood. It is not explained why this should be the case. This is not a case of ritual impurity, as would occur when touching a corpse (Num 31:19-24). Impurity is not a problem when David participates in sacrifices in dedicating a place for the temple (1 Chron 21:28-29). In Kings it is stated that David was prevented from temple building because peace had not been achieved (1 Kings 5:3-5); with Solomon there is rest and no opposing adversary.

The Chronicler states things quite differently: David is a man of blood. There is no suggestion that David has incurred bloodguilt (e.g., Num 35:33-34), which would pollute the land. David was guilty of murder in the case of Uriah and responsible for the death of seventy thousand Israelites because of a census (1 Chron 21:14), but neither of these transgressions appears to be part of the Chronicler's rationale in the prohibition. Though the Chronicler does not condemn war, the inference cannot be avoided that for the Chronicler, the shedding of blood in war is a moral problem. War did not make soldiers individually guilty of murder, but at the same time it involved the taking of human life. David had not only engaged in war; he had also waged much war. The *holy temple* to be built (1 Chron 29:3) would represent the power and gift of life within the kingdom. For the Chronicler, David was far too closely associated with death to be the one who should build a house representing a kingdom of life and peace.

As with Joshua succeeding Moses, success in fulfilling the mission requires rigorous observance of the terms of the covenant (Deut 31:10-13; Josh 1:7-8; 1 Chron 22:12-13). Such a task requires courage and resolve that overcomes all discouragement. David had made significant sacrifice of his own treasury as he prepared for the building of the temple. His humility may recall the testimony of his personal sacrifices when he determined to bring the ark to Jerusalem (Ps 132:1-5). The stupendous figures for gold and silver dwarf the tribute of Hiram (1 Kings 9:14) or the gifts of the queen of Sheba (10:2, 10). These are not reasonable estimates but hyperbole given to emphasize the extravagance of the temple. The gifts and all the preparations are made to be excessive. Solomon, however, cannot be passive; he must add to these preparations. Materials are only one aspect of temple requirements; skilled labor is also required. To ensure that the temple is not delayed, David has made provisions for these as well.

Charge to Leaders of Israel 22:17-19

Though the successor to the king is already designated, this can be contested, as well as the plans that may have been made. So David takes preemptive action by addressing all the leaders of Israel. This is the opportunity to fulfill the ideal of Deuteronomy, that all Israel worship at "the place" that "God will choose" (Deut 12:1-7). In its immediate context, this may have been a prohibition against worshiping at pagan altars; yet the ideal of all Israel worshiping at one location is unmistakable. This is the time of rest anticipated by the conquest of Joshua; the Promised Land is subdued before the people, and they have rest on every side. All this could be compromised by lack of resolve on their part to seek the express mandate of the covenant. Worship at the place God has chosen, confirmed by the sign of *fire from heaven* (1 Chron 21:26), requires a sanctuary for the altar that has been brought to Jerusalem, along with all of the sacred artifacts that belong with it.

THE TEXT IN BIBLICAL CONTEXT

The Rest of Redemption

Rest is a central theological motif in the redemption story. It carries through in its application to the church. "Rest" is the term that is used to describe the significance of the Sabbath confession (Deut 5:14): your servants must also rest; you remember that the Lord gave you rest from your oppression in Egypt and redeemed you. This theme is developed in a psalm of praise:

> Know, this day, if you would hear his voice;
> > do not let your mind be stubborn,
> > as in the day of testing in the wilderness,

when your fathers tested me;
> they tried me though they had seen my work.
Forty years I loathed this generation;
> I said, "A people whose minds wander,
> and they do not know my ways."
Of them I swore in my wrath,
> "They will never enter my rest." (Ps 95:7b-11 AT)

The rest highlighted in this psalm is the land of promise. The referent of rest is the same as in the Deuteronomistic History and in Chronicles [*Deuteronomistic History, p. 465*]. The judgment of Kadesh Barnea was that the rebellious generation would die in the wilderness. Forty is a representative number for a generation. Except for Joshua and Caleb, those entering rest in the days of Joshua had not seen the revelation of God at Mount Sinai.

The Chronicler identifies Solomon as the focus of this rest and makes this rest the equivalent of peace and quiet for a man whose very name (*šelomoh*) signifies peace. The fulfillment of rest for the Chronicler is the people of Israel worshiping around the temple. David had provided security from the threat of surrounding enemies, thus providing for the people's rest.

Such rest could not be experienced apart from the covenant. The generation entering the land would be required to renew the covenant and take the vow of loyalty to God (Josh 8:30-35; 24:1-29). The stones under the oak at Shechem stood as testimony to the oath that was taken. Peace and rest for Solomon and his people require the same commitment (1 Chron 22:13). Rest can be present only when commitment is made to relationships that provide for peace. The responsibilities of relationships with God and others are summarized in the Ten Words of the covenant. The application of these to specific situations is provided in decrees and judgments that Solomon and his people must observe.

THE TEXT IN THE LIFE OF THE CHURCH

Christian Confession of Redemptive Rest

One of the most contentious issues in the church has been the practice of observing Sunday as a day of rest. If it is not contentious, it is usually because Sunday has become neglected and irrelevant. The Christian church has too often viewed Sunday more legalistically than theologically; if Sabbath is anything, it is one of God's rules. But in biblical theology, Sabbath was never a rule. As part of the Ten Commandments, which really are covenant words of instruction rather than commandments, it was part of the confession of God's holiness, along with not having idols and not taking the name of God in vain. Sabbath, in biblical theology, is a testimony of the rest of redemption, as emphasized in David's words to Solomon.

The writer to the Hebrews interprets the new covenant to be the fulfillment of the rest of redemption. He quotes Jeremiah 31:31-34 in their entirety (Heb 8:7-12) and again in summary (10:16-17). The rest provided by God cannot be found outside of this covenant. The author fears that some, having endured great suffering, are becoming weary and are in danger of abandoning the covenant they committed to observe. He begins the first of his warning passages with a full quotation of Psalm 95:7-11 (Heb 3:7-11). His point is that those who had received the promise of rest and experienced the redemption of Egypt died in the wilderness because of their disobedience. This failure to enter rest has direct application to those in the church. "Let us therefore fear, lest having been left a promise to enter into rest, some of you appear to fail to attain" (Heb 4:1 AT). The term translated "fail to attain" indicates a failure in some measure to accomplish a particular state or condition (*hystereō*, L&N 13.21). The author urges his readers to remain faithful so that they may enjoy the rest found in Christ.

The writer to the Hebrews applies this lesson to Christian Sabbath observance (Heb 4:4-7). He is exercising good biblical theology in associating the rest of Joshua with the rest of the seventh day, for that is the association of terms he has observed in Deuteronomy 5:14. Those in the church, those who belong to Christ, have entered into the rest of the Sabbath. This is the Sabbath that remains for the people of God (Heb 4:9). Those entering into the rest of Christ (the church) rest in the same way as God rested from all his work (v. 10). No effort should be spared in being faithful to the new covenant; there is no other place where rest may be found.

Sabbath rest was never a prohibition from all physical activity. Sabbath rest was always a confession of redemption by exemplifying a cessation from conflict. In ancient creation stories, creative activity was overcoming conflict; this motif is found in such creation accounts as Psalm 74:12-17, where God crushes the heads of Leviathan. The Genesis account removes all mythological language; Leviathan is the "formless and empty" of Genesis 1:2. In a process of three separations (light, water, and land) and three orders for the function of each separation (time, marine and bird life, plus land life), God brings complete order to precreation disorder. He can rest. If this order is broken, he must rise up, as in the call of Isaiah 51:9-10. On the seventh day, God did not cease to be active; his activity was the sustenance of order achieved in the creative process (Ps 104:24-30).

The Sabbath rest of the seventh day was a world without conflict, a world we do not know. Everything was at peace, including people. Redemption is the restoration of that Sabbath, where the conflict of toil and suffering is ended. Such redemption is found in Christ. It is found for those who are members of the church. The rest of which the Chronicler speaks is a redemption rest under the former covenant. In the new covenant it is found by trusting in Christ. But the exhortation to the faithful is the same. As David exhorted Solomon, the achievement of this rest is found in faithfulness to the covenant (1 Chron 22:13). The writer to the Hebrews exhorts believing Christians in the very same way.

Sabbath, which is to be a confession of peace, has come to be instead the source of much conflict. In the church there has been conflict over which day is the Sabbath and conflict over what the practices on that day should be. In the Old Testament this day was the seventh because it was directly related to the gift of life, as taught in the creation narrative (Gen 2:1-2). The New Testament is never specific about the day. The first day of the week is theologically natural, for that is the day of the resurrection, the day to commemorate the peace that Jesus gives to us (John 14:27; 20:19; Acts 20:7; 1 Cor 16:2). Sunday as the day to remember the rest of redemption is almost universal in Christian practice.

In each culture, Christians need to determine how they will make confession of Sabbath rest. In a Christian context, the question is not so much what one refrains from doing; it is rather that which one chooses to do. The choice to gather for worship in praise of God and thanksgiving for his salvation is a necessary way to express Sabbath rest; it should be a highest priority for every Christian. Christians in a culture devoted to self-indulgence find this priority particularly difficult. But worship on Sunday in most Christian cultures is the way to experience the rest that is present in the kingdom (1 Chron 22:9-10). There is a present reality to the peace of the kingdom as well as an eschatological fulfillment.

1 Chronicles 23:1–26:32
Organization of Levitical Officials

PREVIEW

"Administration" does not sound positive to most people. It is too closely affiliated with concepts of bureaucracy, thought of as a cumbersome interference in getting things done. But worse than bloated bureaucracy is a lack of organization. Organizations have the name because they involve an administration capable of accomplishing desirable tasks. The Chronicler spends much of his work in laying out good administration. This unique section on administration concludes the reign of David.

The remainder of 1 Chronicles is directed to assemblies of people. Chapters 23 through 27 address smaller groups of officials with specific duties. Chapters 28 to 29 address all Israel concerning their responsibility for the temple.

Chapters 23–27 are unique within Chronicles, set apart by introductory headings and also by their distinct material. The greatest portion of these chapters takes up concerns of the temple and involves those responsible as priests, singers, custodians, treasurers, and other officers. The first verse of this section introduces the remainder of the reign of David: *When David had grown old and reached the limit of his days, he made his son Solomon king over all Israel* (23:1 AT). The sequel to this chronological reference is found in 2 Chronicles 1:1: *Solomon, son of David, took full command of his kingdom; Yahweh his God was with him and made him exceedingly great* (AT). The second verse in this section (23:2) describes the gathering of the leaders and religious officials. These are assembled to be assigned their divisions and their duties within each division. Chapter 27 deals with the political organization that David provided for the new kingdom, including military organization, domestic structure, and the king's own officials. Solomon received a meticulously ordered kingdom.

David's administrative assignments conclude with the introduction of a much larger assembly (28:1), which includes all the military and administrative leaders, every distinguished person in Jerusalem. David gives his final charge to this group, making all of them responsible for the successful completion of the temple.

The structure of the headings and the unique arrangement of material have led to intense analysis of the process of composition. This material likely was assembled over a period of time by various individuals, leaving it with a number of layers of composition. Chapter 27 may be the final level of composition. Some argue that this material actually disrupts the concerns of the Chronicler, which are found in the speeches of David that the Chronicler has composed. As a result, these speeches have become somewhat repetitive and redundant.

Various conclusions are drawn from these observations. Some regard the whole of chapters 23:2 to 27:34 to be a secondary development. Others believe the Chronicler himself inserted some of these lists later, from sources of his own. It may be that complementary supplements have been made to the Chronicler's composition. The material is consciously integrated. Solomon does not come to reign until after the death notice of David (1 Chron 29:28-30).

OUTLINE

Levitical Families, 23:1-24:31
Musicians, 25:1-31
Gatekeepers, 26:1-19
Officers and Judges, 26:20-32

EXPLANATORY NOTES

Levitical Families 23:1-24:31

The census of Levites follows the pattern of including them only in connection with their assigned tasks, not in a general census (1 Chron 23:3-4; cf. Num 1:3, 49-50). The census classifies Levites according to their clerical function (those supervising the work of the temple, officers and judges, guards, and musicians). The enumeration and registration of the Levites are not in the traditional system of father's houses or families. The organization of the Levites is according to smaller administrative units that the Chronicler calls divisions (1 Chron 23:6-23). The anticipation of centralized worship at a national sanctuary required a system of divisions of alternating services. Chronicles introduces a system of organization unlike those of earlier tribal divisions (cf. Josh 11:23; 12:7; 18:10). In earlier lists, such as those found in Ezra-Nehemiah, the organization of the temple personnel or the people in this way does not exist (Japhet 2006: 14-17). There are designations of the chiefs of priests, as in Nehemiah 11:10-14. Priests are enumerated according to their families (12:12-21). The Chronicler describes the work of the Levites as complementary to that of the priests (1 Chron 23:24-32), a feature that is also unique to him.

The divisions of the priests follow the description of the divisions of the Levites (1 Chron 24:1-19). Divisions of the priests would be necessary since their numbers far exceeded the requirements for a single temple. Priests necessarily shared in the privileges of service; divisions were a time-sharing mechanism. The priests are of the highest order, described as *officials of the sanctuary and officials of God* (v. 5). The divisions of the Levites are discussed first because of the way the Chronicler conceives of Levites. The sons of Amram are one component of Levites, set apart for a specific role in cultic service (23:13-14). Priestly divisions are not a part of Levitical divisions. According to genealogical heritage, priests are a group within the Levites. Divisions of remaining Levites conclude this section (1 Chron 24:20-31). These appear to be analogous to those of the priests. The whole concerns the organization of the Levites, with an inclusion of the particular status and work of priests.

23:1-23 Divisions of Levites

According to Numbers, Levites involved in the transport of the sanctuary were enumerated between the ages of thirty and fifty (Num 4:3, 23, 30, 35, 39, 43). Only the entrance age is part of this enumeration in Chronicles. The head count of Levites indicates that they are ample in number. The overseers responsible for the construction of the temple constitute the largest number (24,000; v. 4). Levites customarily have a leading role in construction and restoration (Ezra 3:8-9; 2 Chron 34:8-13). The Levites are further divided into officials and judges (6,000), guards (4,000), and musicians (4,000). Officials and judges are a category not usually found in the divisions of Levites. The order is expressed in terms of decreasing numbers.

The count of Levites is according to the three traditional families: Gershon, Kohath, and Merari (cf. 1 Chron 6:1, 16). Fundamental to the enumeration is to name heads for a total of twenty-four ancestral houses of Levites: ten of Gershon, nine of Kohath, and five of Merari. There is a textual problem with the sons of Shimei in verse 9. Shimei is one of the sons of Gershon (v. 7) but appears in the list of sons of Ladan. The reference must be to Jehiel or one of the sons of Ladan (*BHS*). The Chronicler enumerates the Levitical heads of the houses of Ladan, Jehiel, and Shimei, the three sons of Gershon (vv. 8-10). The Levitical heads of the various ancestral houses of the Kohath clan were Shubael, Rehabiah, Shelomith, Jeriah, Amariah, Jahaziel, Jekameam, Micah, and Ishiah (vv. 16-20). Merari has two sons, Mahli and Mushi. Two sons of Mahli and three sons of Mushi are heads of these ancestral houses (vv. 22-23). These divisions of Levites correspond with those of the priests in the next chapter, but they are not listed by ordinal number, leaving the parallel with the priests ambiguous.

There are two notable developments within these divisions of Levitical families. The first is that two of the families of Shimei became too small to support a division of Levites (1 Chron 23:11). They came to be enumerated as one ancestral house. Presumably another of the father's houses that was more prolific divided and came to fill the void. The replacement is not named since this was a development that took place after the time the divisions were established. A second development was that Eleazar, one of the sons of Mahli, son of Merari, did not have any sons (v. 22). This did not eliminate that ancestral house from having a share in the Levitical divisions. Here is a case of implementing the provisions of Numbers 27:1-7 and 36:1-12, made for instances of property inheritance when there were no sons. The daughters through their husbands would retain the property within the family. The daughters of Eleazar married their relatives of the house of Qish, but their family retained its identity. As in the regulations of Numbers, the women do not actually assume the role of the male but bridge the generational gap.

23:24-32 Levitical Duties

The head count of Levites doing duty in the temple includes those aged 20 and older, as opposed to 30 and older in the enumeration of the heads of ancestral houses (cf. 1 Chron 23:3). The final section of rules regarding the Levites in the book of Numbers gives the starting age as 25 (Num 8:23-26), which conflicts with the earlier age of 30, as it is in Chronicles. The starting age changed with time and changing conditions. Milgrom suggests that the key to the change was the removal of the upper age limit (Milgrom 1990: 65). By the time of David there was no longer any need to transport the sanctuary. Levites became responsible for the maintenance of the temple, the preparation of sacrificial ingredients, guarding the temple, and the musical liturgy.

These additional duties of Levites did not entail excessive labor but made necessary the extension of the employ of Levites from age 20 until death. In later rabbinic tradition, Levites could not be disqualified by age, only by an impaired singing voice (*Sifre Num* 63; *Sifre Zut* on Num 8:26). The entrance age of 25 remains in the earlier tradition. The rabbis harmonized the age in Numbers by suggesting that the earlier age may have represented service as a type of apprentice. The sect at Qumran had the same tradition, but they applied these ages to their entire community, as given in the appendix to the Community Rule and the War Scroll (1QSa 1.12-19; 1QM 7.3). It is not certain that the age differences are anything other than variant traditions.

With the establishment of the temple at Jerusalem, the Chronicler describes the transformed work of the Levites. The Levites serve alongside the priests (1 Chron 23:28); it does not mean that *their office was to wait on the sons of Aaron for the service of the house of the* LORD (KJV). The appointment of the Levites is to serve with the sons of Aaron and not in subordination to them. Levites are not assistants to the priests. The service of the Levites is in every aspect of temple function. This is a complete evolution from their service to the tabernacle. Before the temple, Levitical service pertained to the physical labor in moving the tabernacle and providing security (Num 8:25-26). The tabernacle, the outer altar, and their respective utensils are forbidden to Levites on the pain of death (Num 18:3). As Milgrom has unequivocally established, this situation pertained so long as the tabernacle functioned (Milgrom 1983: 18-28, 30-38). In Chronicles this situation changes with the building of the temple (1 Chron 23:25-26). The work of the Levites becomes cult service and is described in considerable detail. This shift of meaning shows conclusively that priestly writings must be dated long before Chronicles, contrary to the source criticism of Wellhausen.

Chronicles gives no details on how Levitical duties complemented the work of the priests. Several tasks are without parallel in the priestly texts. These include care for the storerooms, ensuring the purity of all the sacred objects, assisting with the rows of sacred bread, and providing music during the daily offerings. Other descriptions of ritual are unique, such as the choice flour for grain offerings, the unleavened wafers, the griddle, well-mixed cakes, and all measures of capacity and length (1 Chron 23:29). The regular duty of protecting the sanctuary from encroachment of unauthorized persons is now applied equally to all the families of the Levites.

24:1-19 Divisions of Priests

The priestly divisions of David's time have their authentication in the ancestral houses of Eleazar and Ithamar. They were the two surviving sons of Aaron, as related in Numbers 3:2-4. Zadok, of the house of Eleazar, and Abiathar, of the house of Ithamar, served as the leading priests when David restored the ark to Jerusalem (1 Chron 15:11). Ahimelek comes to replace his father, Abiathar, in the list of officials when David expanded his kingdom (1 Chron 18:16). David had the assistance of Zadok and Ahimelek in assigning the duties of the priestly divisions (24:3). The house of Eleazar was the more numerous. They were assigned 16 divisions of the 24. The procedure honored both the traditional genealogy and the organization of the priesthood. Though the house of Eleazar was numerically superior, they received no special prerogatives in the casting of lots. The casting of lots was a way of determining that the divisions were divinely directed and fair to all. Honor must be shown to the priests as officials of the sanctuary and officials of God. The priests are selected from the Levites, but they are distinguished as leaders. The Chronicler seeks to portray a complementary relationship between priests and Levites [Priests and Levites in Chronicles, p. 471].

The Chronicler has a special interest in scribes (cf. 1 Chron 2:55), who have a most critical and influential role in any organized society. This is particularly true in maintaining records of fulfilling responsibility. The registration of the officials was done so that order could be firmly established and preserved in the performance of duty. This order followed the procedure of alternating the ancestral houses of Eleazar and Ithamar for the first sixteen divisions. The Levitical list of Nehemiah 12 shows ten of the names given in these divisions; some appear later, in Maccabean times, and five of the names are otherwise unknown. In most instances there is not enough information to determine what relationship may exist between names. The assignment of twenty-four courses indicates that each division served for two weeks each year. Though the divisions are assigned to David, this order of priesthood is not documented until the time of the Chronicler. Calendar and assignments of priestly duties are elaborate and contentious in the times leading to the

New Testament. In the sophisticated calendrical documents found in the Qumran scrolls, festivals and Sabbaths are all aligned with detailed enumeration of successive priestly divisions.

24:20-31 Further Divisions of Levites

The introduction designating *the rest of the descendants of Levi* in verse 20 is a sequel to the preceding list of Levites in 1 Chronicles 23:3-23. The singers and the gatekeepers of the following chapters are also Levites, so this list must be a supplement to the divisions of the Levites already given. It is modeled on the list of priests. The closing verse parallels the introduction of the priests (1 Chron 24:6, 31), the only omission being the king's officers. For reasons not evident, it does not include the families of Gershon. Moses and Aaron are not given as descendants of Amram, but Shubael and his son Jehdeiah are in that lineage. Rehabiah is a new descendant in the house of Kohath, with Ishiah his one descendant. In three cases the descendants of Kohath are extended by a generation (Jahath, Shamir, and Zechariah). A new branch of four Levitical families is added to the Merarites from the descendants of Jaaziah. These Levites were also divided by lot. It may be inferred that courses of duty were associated with these divisions, as were those in the previous list of Levites. The list has every indication of being a subsequent addition, bringing the divisions of the Levites up-to-date. It seems likely that when it was composed, the authors had access to the earlier material. The authors do not explain whether the courses were reorganized in this list of Levites.

Two textual emendations of the MT are required to clarify the supplementary Levitical divisions. The first is the addition of the name *Hebron* in 24:23, accidentally omitted (cf. 23:19). It is supplied in most translations (NIV). The second is to clarify the descendants of Jaaziah. In 24:26-27 the MT reads, *The sons of Merari are Mahli and Mushi, sons of Jaaziah, his son; sons of Merari, belonging to Jaaziah his son, Shoham, Zakkur, and Ibri* (1 Chron 24:26-27 AT). *His son* in verses 26 and 27 (*Beno*, NIV) should be *bani,* a short form of Baniah (*bny* instead of *bnw*). The repetition of *the sons of Merari* in verse 27 may be accidental duplication (dittography) or it may be a secondary reading that includes Bani (short for Baniah) as a son of Jaaziah. The Greek text of Vaticanus might be evidence for an alternate reading since it has no reference to *his son* (Bani) in verse 26. But the omission in the Vaticanus manuscript appears to be accidental: most other Greek versions include Bani in verse 26 (Allen: 52). The best conclusion, followed by most translations (e.g., NIV), is to make Jaaziah an additional house of Merarites, with Bani as one of the family heads [*Greek Text of Chronicles*, p. 468].

Musicians 25:1-31

David and his military officials designated singers from the families of Asaph, Heman, and Jeduthun. The earlier assignments of Levitical musicians for worship at the ark were Heman, Asaph, and Ethan (1 Chron 15:17, 19; cf. 6:33, 39, 44). Asaph is appointed to serve in Jerusalem (16:5, 7, 37), and Heman and Jeduthun at the tabernacle in Gibeon (vv. 41-42). Several psalm titles list Jeduthun as a leader in music (Pss 39:1; 62:1; 77:1). The family of Jeduthun is also found as gatekeepers at Gibeon (1 Chron 16:42). The history of Levitical divisions no doubt developed over time. The Chronicler reflects these realities without providing the details. As indicated by the ancestral heads, divisions of responsibility between music, worship, and security overlapped. The temple was a sacred place of enormous treasure. It needed to be protected from intrusion by unqualified individuals and from those with nefarious intentions. In time of war or political instability, the temple was a primary object of attack. Those leading in music and worship shared in security matters. This was not just a matter of musical capabilities, but also of character and loyalty. Officials responsible for state security were actively engaged to watch over all individuals employed by the state. Ancient governments did not have sharp distinctions of civil and military departments.

Music is described as prophecy (1 Chron 25:1-3). Heman is also described as a seer (v. 5). Prophets and seers were important personnel in royal courts, frequently consulted in times of war and distress. It is only in Chronicles that prophets are immediately associated with music of the temple, but prophets are elsewhere a part of the court of the king, to advise him (such as Nathan and Isaiah), and prophets also made use of music (1 Sam 10:5; 2 Kings 3:15). Prophecy included a broad range of activities that were carried out in a great diversity of ways. In the view of the Chronicler, an important function of prophecy was to make confession and give praise, which involved music. This conforms to fundamental concepts of prophecy, to lead people in knowing the work of God in his world. Certain psalms are exhortation, drawing lessons from the past (e.g., Ps 77); others are confessions about the character of God as the Creator (e.g., Pss 103; 104). Psalms were one of the most important aspects of prophets doing the work of admonishment, correction, and confession.

The head count of the working men, those employed as servants by the king, was according to their service. The census was probably taken by the heads of the singers, Heman, Asaph, and Jeduthun. In bringing the ark to Zion, the Levitical officials were to appoint their kinsmen as singers (1 Chron 15:16-24). The goal of the enumeration was twenty-four heads of families drawn from the families of Levites: four from Asaph, six from Jeduthun, and fourteen from Heman. Large families are regarded as a blessing; the three daughters of Heman are not named, but all are engaged in temple music (25:6). All twenty-four families were under the command of their father for temple duty, and all were under command of the king. Their total number is relatively small, providing for twelve singers for each of the twenty-four divisions.

The casting of lots for the priests was to assign the rotation of duties without prejudice (1 Chron 24:3, 31). The divisions rotated every week, each serving for a total of two weeks of the year, irrespective of the festival times. The casting of lots for the musicians is not specific to the rotations of service, as in the case of the priests. Equality is emphasized in casting lots for the duties of the singers (25:8), so there could be no discrimination in the assignment of less significant responsibilities or in the skill level of the performer. Both apprentice and skilled performer are assigned their duties by lot. These assignments appear to be the designation of performers and their duties within the divisions. The singers seem to be in general groupings to fulfill the requirements of duty, which may have helped facilitate considerable responsibility for a relatively small number of people.

The orders of the musicians listed in 25:9-31 are not in the arbitrary manner of being cast by lot, a further indication that the casting of lots was not to establish the rotation of service for each division. It has long been observed that the last nine names of the sons of Heman are unusual (v. 4). These same names are all grouped as the last nine in the order of divisions (vv. 23-31). The order of these names in verse 4 can be constructed to form a poem, but there is no question that these function as names in the family orders of the musicians. The best explanation for this unique phenomenon is that these names are incipits (Williamson 1982: 167): parts of the first line of five different psalms that served as title for each group. Five families or divisions of the guilds came to be known by the openings of psalms they customarily sang.

Gatekeepers 26:1-19

David's administrative reorganization included the integration and assignments of security personnel. The rotation of sanctuary guards provided continuous protection for the temple complex. Korah is a descendant of the Levites through Levi's second son, Kohath. The other line of gatekeepers is from Merari (v. 10). No gatekeepers are named from Gershon. Meshelemiah, the first ancestor of the gatekeepers, is known in Ezra-Nehemiah as Shallum (Ezra 2:42), Meshullam (Neh 12:25), or Shelemiah (1 Chron 26:14). He is a descendant of Abiasaph (1 Chron 26:1 NLT); Asaph (NIV, NRSV) is a faulty reading of the MT. This group is not to be associated with the familiar family of singers (cf. Exod 6:24). Obed-Edom is a Levite and a gatekeeper in Chronicles (cf. 1 Chron 15:18, 24), though he is given no ancestry; in this context he appears to be associated with Korah. He is blessed with sixty-two sons, a reference to his being blessed for protecting the ark of the covenant when its return to Jerusalem failed (13:13-14). The gatekeepers are also under twenty-four ancestral heads: seven to the family of Meshelemiah, thirteen to Obed-Edom, and four to the family of Hosah. The family of Obed-Edom is divided between the eight sons of Meshelemiah and the six sons of Shemaiah, his firstborn. Shemaiah is not counted in the total, as his family unit is further divided (ramified). The total number of gatekeepers is 93 (26:8-9, 11), described as head warriors (26:12). These are not merely their *chief men* (NIV), but are the heads (leaders) of elite soldiers (*ra'še haggebarim*). The main obligation of gatekeepers was to guard the sanctuary; the function of a gatekeeper was military duty (Wright 1990: 69-81). Numbers in other lists of gatekeepers appear to be more comprehensive: 212 in 1 Chronicles 9:22; 139 in Ezra 2:42; 138 in Nehemiah 7:45; and 172 in Nehemiah 11:19. Their duties are described as corresponding to those of their brothers, namely, those of the priests and musicians who are also a part of the state service.

There are several references to the capabilities of the security personnel, whose task was very demanding and often dangerous. The sons of Shemaiah became dominant because they were all valiant warriors. Zechariah, the son of Shelemiah, is described as an insightful counselor and as a consequence receives his own lot in the assignment of duties. Equality is again emphasized in the assignment of the duties (1 Chron 26:16), each watch being equal to another.

As in the case of the musicians, lots were cast to determine which family would serve at each gate. This served to treat all equally (v. 13), irrespective of the size of the family concerned. The description of the assignments requires some clarification. The term *šuppim* is a textual error (v. 16). Some translations take this as a name (NRSV; NIV paraphrases: *The lots . . . to Shuppim and Hosah*), but it appears to be a repetition of the similar word for "storehouses" in the previous verse (*haʾasuppîm*). The function of the storehouses in not known. The cognate term in Akkadian describes a structural feature of the building, such as an annex, an upper level, or exit (*AHw* 77). Roddy Braun thinks they are to be identified with the treasury (Braun: 252; cf. 1 Chron 26:20). The descendants of Hosah were assigned to the west gate and to the chamber gate at the top of an ascent (*šalleket bamsillah haʿolah*; 26:16). Some translations transliterate the term as *Shallecheth* and make it the name of a gate on an ascending road. However, the context here is Jerusalem, not a road between towns. The structure must be in relation to the temple complex. The Akkadian parallel is a temple or palace door leading to an outside stair (*AHw* 684). Some similar feature is described here and has been understood along these lines by the Greek translator. It may have been a gate at the top of an ascent that led to the temple.

There were twenty-four gatekeepers on duty at any one time (1 Chron 26:17-18): six at the east, four at the north, four at the south, two at the storehouse, four at the west, two at the gate above the ascent, and two at the colonnade (*parbar*; NIV, *court*). The word *parbar* is of uncertain derivation. The translation *colonnade* is derived from its use in the Temple Scroll found at Qumran (*prwr*, 11QT 5.13; 35.10). Some of the text in the description of gate assignments has become confused. The west is introduced by *at the colonnade* (1 Chron 26:18), duplicated from its occurrence at the end of the verse. The number two has been duplicated at the end of verse 17 in relation to the storehouse and is missing at the end of verse 18. The MT is a jumble: *two and two at the storehouse, for the colonnade on the west there were four at the road (ascent) two at the colonnade*. The text should read: *at the storehouse two; at the west gate four; at the ascent (stair) two; at the colonnade two* (cf. NIV, NRSV). The Greek has a somewhat better preservation of the allocations.

Officers and Judges 26:20-32

This closing section deals with two main topics: responsibility for the treasuries and duties of administration in the northern areas west and east of the Jordan. The treasuries are said to be those of the temple and the dedicated offerings. There is frequent reference to temple and palace treasuries. The dedicated offerings are not likely a third treasury, but are a part of the temple treasury, to provide for its maintenance. Those responsible for supervision are the brothers of the Levites. In 26:20, the MT incorrectly reads *Ahijah* for *ʾaḥehem* (their brothers); the Greek texts testify to the correct reading. The gatekeepers and the other officials were all drawn from the ranks of the Levites *[Greek Text of Chronicles, p. 468]*.

Temple treasuries are the responsibility Ladan, a Gershonite (cf. 1 Chron 23:7), his son Jehiel, and his two sons Zetham and Joel. The Amramites, sons of Kohath, the brother of Gershon (cf. Exod 6:18; 1 Chron 23:12), were responsible for the dedicated offerings. Shebuel, a Kohathite through his father, Gershom, son of Moses, son of Amram (1 Chron 23:12-16), is the commander over all the treasuries (26:24). It might seem that he should have been first named, but the register follows the genealogical order (Gershon, Kohath). Shelomoth, one of the descendants of Kohath through Eliezer, brother of Gershom (23:15), is put in charge of the dedicated offerings (26:25-26). Shebuel's authority over all the treasuries is the reason for the assignment of Shelomoth to the dedicated offerings.

The dedicated offerings are an accumulation of booty from many wars, going all the way back to Samuel and Saul. These were dedicated to repair of the temple (26:27), the usual meaning of the word (*leḥazzeq*). These dedications were gathered in anticipation of the temple that would be built. Treasure left for repair of the temple is a most noble legacy. Israel's military and civil leadership are credited with the foresight of not only building the temple but also of maintaining it for later generations.

Order in the outlying regions is carried out by the appointed officers and judges. In the enumeration of Levites, these were listed as six thousand (1 Chron 23:4). Deuteronomic legislation required that judges and officials be appointed in every city to maintain order (Deut 16:18-20). These were to include temple officials (17:8-13); the king was not to have the primary role in these matters (vv. 14-20). The role of the officials (*šōṭerim*) is not described (1 Chron 26:29); in Akkadian the *šaṭāru* is a scribe responsible for records and registrations (*AHw* 1203). Their office is often associated with the judiciary; though they are first named, they seem to be subordinate to the judge.

Hashabiah, a Hebronite of the Levitical family of Kohath (1 Chron 23:12), and 1,700 valiant warriors of his family are responsible for the area from beyond the Jordan to the west (an unusual designation; 26:30). Jeriah, a Hebronite, had responsibility for all the area east of the Jordan (Reuben, Gad, and the half-tribe of Manasseh). He found warriors in Jazer of Gilead, a Levitical city of the family of Hebron (Josh 21:39; cf. 1 Chron 6:81). The relationship between the Levitical family of Hebron and the Judahite family of that name is not specified, but there are genealogical bonds between Hezron of Judah and Gilead (1 Chron 2:21-22). Hezron father of Caleb is the ancestor of the Hebronites of Judah (2:9, 42). The inference is that families from David's city of Hebron had links to those living in Gilead and became the core for David maintaining security there. These provisions were made in the fortieth year of David; they are envisioned as the last stage of David preparing to install Solomon as king.

THE TEXT IN BIBLICAL CONTEXT

Origins of Twenty-Four Priestly Divisions

It has often been maintained that 1 Chronicles 23-27 disrupts the narrative of Chronicles. Some ascribe these five chapters to later editors; others interpret them as an insertion marked by resumption in 1 Chronicles 28:1, which repeats the substance of 23:2 (Williamson 1982: 179) *[Resumptive Summary, p. 467]*. There is much to be said in favor of viewing 1 Chronicles 28:1 as a repetitive resumption. Such insertions into a narrative provide important information to understanding the narrative. One very notable insertion of this type is the genealogy of Moses and Aaron inserted into the narrative in Exodus 6:14-25 *[Genealogy, p. 461]*. The resumption after the insertion explains its purpose clearly: "It is that Aaron and Moses to whom the LORD said, 'Bring the Israelites from the land of Egypt with all their hosts'" (Exod 6:26 AT). This section in the Chronicler's narrative is analogous, though it is much longer. David has given Solomon charge to build the temple and provide for its daily functions. Between the private charge to Solomon and the public installation of Solomon as king is a list of the plans that David handed over to Solomon to help him fulfill the mandate he had been given.

In this section the sources of the Chronicler are of quite a different order than the biblical sources that have served as a resource for much of his history. They are also quite different from the sources of the prophetic narrative that he will refer to repeatedly as he narrates the history of the kings following Solomon. These records must have been used in temple functions in his own time, though the Chronicler has given them great antiquity, placing them in the time of David. It is impossible to know what correlation there may have been between worship in the time of David and that of the Chronicler, but these records were used to explain how David prepared for the order of temple worship. The record of the Levites is supplemented by a later record of additional Levites (1 Chron 23:3-23; 24:20-31). It is one of the most evident uses of complementary sources, indicating that the material of Chronicles was intended for active use in his time.

The Chronicler's organization of priests into twenty-four orders is very significant (24:1-19). This is the only such description in the Old Testament; it may be indicative of the origin of such an order of priestly rotation. Williamson has subjected 1 Chronicles 24:7-18 to detailed analysis, within the context of chapters 23-27, with the objective of determining the origin of such a priestly division (Williamson 1979). His main conclusions concern two literary levels detected in these chapters. The first much shorter composition was the original. It concerned the three categories introduced in 23:3-6a: officials and judges, gatekeepers, and musicians. The second literary level consistently introduces the concept of twenty-four courses. It was added about a generation later, by a pro-priestly reviser under the impact of the system of twenty-four priestly orders. Williamson dates the institution of such orders at the end of the Persian period. The actual reasons for the development of these orders cannot be known, but they were an innovation as calendrical rituals became much more elaborate.

The calendars of the Qumran scrolls provide elaborate detail on the function of priestly orders. Priestly rotations of the Sabbath are the subject of 4Q329 (Mishmerot F^b). The first several lines of this writing tabulate the name of the priestly family that is serving when each new quarter of the year begins. They provide a priestly taxonomy for a six-year rotation, with each family serving for three months: Gamul, Eliashib, Maaziah, and Huppah in the first year; Jedaiah, Bilgah, Seorim, and Hezir in the second year; Mijamin, Pethahiah, Abijah, and Jachin in the third year; Shecaniah, Delaiah, Jakim, and Jehoiarib in the fourth year; Jeshebeab, Harim, Immer, and Malchijah in the fifth year; Happizzez, Hakkoz, Jehezkel, and Jeshua in the sixth year. The list then breaks down the orders to the lists of families that serve in each month. The concern was for order; such classifications created a reality that also provided for power. Many of the calendrical works of the scrolls are a record of struggle for authority among Jews of the time.

By the late period of the second temple, calendars were very elaborate and highly conflicted. Sabbaths and festivals for one complete year, without corresponding priestly divisions, are plotted in 4Q327 and 4Q394 section A (Mishmerot E^b). This is one of the few calendars that designate the Festival of Oil, which fell on the twenty-second day of the sixth month. The Temple Scroll also supports the Wine Festival and the Festival of Wood Offering. These calendars are the work of a particular school, not a single small sect. But the times of Sabbath and even more so the festivals were highly conflicted: there was no consensus on calendar calculations.

This section of Chronicles is the only biblical material that indicates how such orders began to develop. But their purpose in Chronicles is quite well integrated and has a function different from that of the later scrolls. The Chronicler's succession narrative is designed to show how David prepared for Solomon's kingdom (Wright 1991). It serves to describe how the order of temple personnel was established and legitimates the rule of David. Temple preparations are the chief legacy of David within the Chronicler's history. These chapters function as a central narrative within the Chronicler's account of David's reign.

THE TEXT IN THE LIFE OF THE CHURCH
Orders of Service in the Church

The church has a parallel to this kind of material in the development of its own systems of clergy and its own liturgical calendars. An example is the Book of Common Prayer, first authorized for the Church of England in 1549 and radically revised in 1552, with subsequent more minor revisions. This prayer book continues to be used as a standard liturgy in the Anglican Communion. It can be a valuable resource for all manner of celebrations and for following a yearly liturgy irrespective of church denominations. Each daily and weekly reading includes all parts of Scripture: Old Testament, Psalms, Gospels, and Epistles. These are chosen in a manner that provides a connecting motif grounded in biblical theological concepts. Churches also have orders for personnel, at times with very clear requirements for various levels of ordination. Other traditions, particularly among independent churches, require no particular qualification for levels of service, though there usually is a defined procedure. Personnel and procedures have grown to vastly different levels of diversity and complexity in church traditions.

The tendency to increase complexity is evident when reading Chronicles. Chronicles is the beginning of a trajectory that becomes increasingly complex by the time of Jesus. Most of the harsh criticisms the Gospels make against traditions have to do with moral transgression of the Torah *[Torah, p. 481]*. For the sects at the time of Jesus, all injunctions were a moral matter. Violation of cultic rule was a moral culpability, sometimes regarded as worse than violations of personal relationships. The same phenomena are also present in the church. Failure to abide by a church liturgy or custom can become more offensive than sins such as fraud or dishonesty.

Liturgy and ritual is inescapable. It is important to understand the reasons why practices are maintained, and sometimes it is necessary to change them. The role of women in leadership is an example of such a question in modern times. These are not moral questions, but questions of practice and order. The greatest spiritual hazard to the church is a hardening of the categories. The Chronicler is an example of dealing with change and establishing a stable order, key goals that must always be pursued. Christians, as much as the community of the Chronicler, must have order of duties and persons sufficient to enable them to function, but sufficiently flexible so they can deal with change.

1 Chronicles 27:1-34
Organization of National Officials

PREVIEW

Governments today take a census in order to plan for future provisions, whether it be infrastructure, healthcare, education, or any of the other functions that are their responsibility. In ancient times the primary purpose of a census was for military purposes, as illustrated in the book of Numbers. A census could also make provision for administration of royal properties. The organization of David's kingdom concludes with a list of Israelites by their census. The chapter begins with its own heading for military leadership. It does not deal with David's final arrangements for the transition of the kingdom, but instead describes his reign in general.

The chapter appears to be a secondary supplement to the earliest material of chapters 23–26 since it does not deal with Levites or Davidic arrangements (Williamson 1979: 261). This section is made up of several units: the commanders of the monthly relays (1 Chron 27:2-15); the register of tribal chiefs after the census of David (vv. 16-24); a register of stewards of royal properties (vv. 25-31); and the royal advisers, other royal assistants, and the king's inner council (vv. 32-34). The supplement complements the whole presentation of chapters 23–27, which describes the Davidic era as one in which the nation was arranged in order around the temple and its service. This supports reforms in the Chronicler's own time, yet it was intended to provide a model for a future kingdom that was anticipated on the basis of prophetic vision, such as that of Ezekiel 40–48.

1 Chronicles 27:1-34

OUTLINE

Military Commanders, 27:1-15
Tribal Officers, 27:16-24
Civil Administrators, 27:25-31
Royal Council, 27:32-34

EXPLANATORY NOTES

Military Commanders 27:1-15

The heading of verse 1 introduces only the first section dealing with military rotations. A heading and summary pertain to commanders over the tribes (vv. 16, 22b), and a final summary refers to the managers of royal properties (v. 31b). The final section describes the immediate council of the king, including mention of the special status of *friend of the king* (v. 33 AT). The conclusion does not follow the order of the first verse, which is limited to ancestral heads and military leaders.

The rotation of military units each month ensured continuous protection for the major institutions of Jerusalem. This arrangement anticipates the expanded administrative system of Solomon, in which there were twelve districts, each headed by an officer, to provide regular revenues from all parts of the country (1 Kings 4–5). The Chronicler makes no reference to areas outside of Jerusalem, nor do these duties appear to involve any responsibility for administrating and collecting revenues. This list of commanders shows continuity with the previous descriptions of officers in 1 Chronicles 11, but there is deliberate indication of this being a later time. Asahel, commander of the fourth division (1 Chron 27:7), brother of Joab, died before David became king in Jerusalem (2 Sam 2:18-23) and thus could not have been the individual appointed commander. It was his son Zebadiah who served in the position of the division that went back to when David was king in Hebron.

There are divergences of family associations between this list and the officers supporting David in 1 Chronicles 11. Jashobeam, in charge of the first division, is of the family of Perez, a family of Judah to which David belonged (1 Chron 2:4-15). He is a Hakmonite in the register of those who came to make David king (11:11). These differences are not contradictory, but it is not possible to know the reason for them. This register is independent of the previous one, but there is continuity of tradition between them.

The MT has suffered some disruption at the beginning of this section. Verse 2 appears to conclude the information of the first division with *his division of 24,000*, but this has been displaced from its proper position at the end of verse 3 (*BHS*). The number should conclude the genealogical information of Jashobeam, son of Zabdiel, belonging to the family of Perez. The second division in verse 4 names Dodai the Ahohite over a division, with Mikloth the commander over his division of 24,000 (NRSV, ESV mg.). The Greek text makes no reference to Mikloth the commander. It is omitted in most English translations (contra NIV; cf. NRSV) *[Greek Text of Chronicles, p. 468]*. Mikloth might have arisen from the Aramaic word meaning corruption (*qlql*) in a marginal note (Allen: 144–45; cf. Rudolph: 178). In 1 Chronicles 11:12 Eleazar son of Dodai is a warrior among the three. A corrupted form of the marginal note entered the text as the name of a general.

The third division records that Jehoiada, father of Baniah, was a priest. There was no reason for priests to be excluded from the military. In 1 Chronicles 12:27 there is a Jehoiada serving as a leader for Aaron. The two are not known to be related, but it is possible that this is the same person. Two leaders are said to be from Ephraim (1 Chron 27:10, 14), but most of the warriors listed hail from Benjamin and Judah. This shows continuity with David's previous warriors, who were awarded positions of leadership in the new administration. Unlike Levitical divisions, rotation of military leaders does not correspond to a tribal sequence. Administration of the kingdom is distinct from that of the temple.

Distinctions of jurisdiction between temple and state are not mutually exclusive. The military could include a priest. Duties of gatekeepers providing security for the temple were by necessity carried out by warriors.

Tribal Officers 27:16-24

The list of officers is closely related to the registry of tribal names, an indication that these leaders had responsibility in gathering the census data. The census of David was not entirely misguided; the fault lay with David's personal motives. Reference to that census in verses 23-24 indicates that it was the basis for establishing tribal officers, unless the enumeration of 27:1 is regarded as a separate census. Tribal information has evident parallels with the divinely mandated census in Numbers 1:1-19. As in that census, those under age twenty are not counted. The Chronicler indicates that to do so would cast doubt on the promise to Abraham (1 Chron 27:23). The tribal order is substantially followed. Naphtali is out of place in comparison with any other list, as it usually comes near the end (cf. Gen

35:23-26). Differences with Numbers arise out of the circumstances current with David establishing his kingdom. Levi is omitted in Numbers, as the Levites there had a dedicated task of caring for the tabernacle. Levi is necessarily included in Chronicles as one of the tribes receiving royal protection (1 Chron 27:17). Zadok is listed separately as head of the priests. This administrative registry is to maintain order in the respective territories as well as make provision for the temple.

The list of officers for tribal administration is unique. The tribes of Gad and Asher are not named. Apparently they did not have independent administrative status at this time. In their place is a separate official for each of the two territories of Manasseh. Levi is included since administration includes the temple. Zadok is named as the chief official for the priests. The result is a total of thirteen officials responsible to assist David in the rule of the kingdom. This registry is not alien to history but retains its independence as a document representing a short specific period in the organization of the kingdom.

The officer for the tribe of Judah in the MT is Elihu the brother of David (1 Chron 27:18). The Greek text may be followed in this case, which says it is Eliab, known as the eldest brother of David (1 Sam 16:6; 17:13, 28; 1 Chron 2:13). Elihu is not otherwise known as a brother of David. The word *brother* could be taken in the more inclusive sense of relative, or this could be a ninth son of Jesse (cf. 1 Sam 17:12), as has been suggested (Rudolph: 180). The reason for a textual corruption in the MT does not have an obvious explanation, which might indicate that the Greek texts are a correction *[Greek Text of Chronicles, p. 468]*.

The Chronicler points out that the census taken by Joab was not entered into official records (1 Chron 27:24). In the closing summary of David's reign, the Chronicler names records of *Samuel the seer, Nathan the prophet,* and *Gad the seer* (29:29). Anson Rainey has compiled all such references summarizing the reign of a monarch in Chronicles and compared them to those in Kings (Rainey 1997: 38). He draws the conclusion that the Chronicler had access to a composition of prophetic historical essays written from reign to reign for the kings of Judah, corresponding to the chronicles of the kings of Israel. These were not official royal records because they are frequently critical of the kings concerned. The census of Joab may have belonged to such records. The registry of administrative officials was drawn from other official records of the Davidic kingdom.

Civil Administrators 27:25-31

Royalty typically owns vast property holdings, generating significant industry. Twelve administrative officials are listed, following the pattern of the two previous enumerations of officials. The administration of royal affairs includes storehouses in Jerusalem and the outlying provinces, as well as property for various types of agriculture and livestock. Included in the list of names are an Ishmaelite (v. 30) and a Hagrite (v. 31), which is quite natural in the time of David.

Wine and oil were two staples of a Palestinian economy. An example of this is the archaeological retrieval of more than a thousand fragments of storage jars, representing but a fraction of the total, used to move massive quantities of oil and wine during the reign of Hezekiah (Lance: 184-85). These seem to be part of the preparations made by Hezekiah in anticipation of the Assyrian attack against Judah (2 Kings 18-19; 2 Chron 32). An industrial wine complex, functioning during the time of David, has been excavated at Gibeon (Pritchard: 19-21). Grapes were pressed by foot in a shallow vat, connected by a channel to a fermentation tank. After fermentation, the wine was dipped out and passed through two cylindrical settling basins. From the second of the basins, the wine was dipped into large storage jars that were lowered into wine cellars, where they were maintained at a constant temperature of about sixty-five degrees Fahrenheit. More than sixty-three such cellars were excavated.

Camels and donkeys were not related to agriculture but to trade routes (Aharoni 1979: 15-16). The main arteries of commerce passed through Palestine, making trade an important branch of the economy. Control over this commerce was a virtual monopoly of kings and rulers.

Royal Council 27:32-34

Jonathan, uncle of David, and Jehiel were employed in David's court to train his sons (De Vries: 214). Comments on the qualifications of Jonathan may indicate that he was otherwise unknown. Hushai, at the head of the council, had earned the title *friend of the king* (AT) because of his loyalty during Absalom's rebellion (2 Sam 15:37). Absalom recognized that loyalty, but the subterfuge of Hushai led him to think Hushai had joined in the attempted coup (16:15-19). There is no small irony when he asks Hushai, "Is this your loyalty to your friend?" (v. 17 NRSV). *Friend of the king* is an official title for Hushai as chief executive. Ahithophel, Jehoiada, and Abiathar were immediate advisers with Hushai. Joab is listed last, possibly an indication of his having power next to that of the king as the head of the military.

The list of royal advisers and supporters comes from an early time in David's reign, before the revolt of Absalom. Ahithophel was a highly valued adviser whose wisdom was like that of God (2 Sam 16:23), but he sided with Absalom in the rebellion. When he realized his cause was lost, he committed suicide (17:23). Joab fell out of favor with David at the end of his reign and was executed by Baniah (1 Kings 2:28-35). Baniah is the son of Jehoiada in 1 Chronicles 27:5. In verse 34 Jehoiada is son of Baniah. Some manuscripts reverse the names as given in verse 34, conforming to the earlier reference (cf. *BHS*). Baniah was the head of the Cherethites and Pelethites (1 Chron 18:17), responsible for the protection of the king. The practice of papponymy, naming a child after his grandfather, makes it entirely possible that Jehoiada succeeded his father in protecting the king and served as his adviser.

Abiathar the priest had a long association with David, going back to the time when he fled Saul (1 Sam 22:20-23), but then Abiathar sided with Adonijah in the attempt to displace Solomon (1 Kings 1:7). Solomon spared his life but banished him to Anathoth (2:26-27). This conforms to Solomon's coronation as described in 1 Chronicles 29:22. In Chronicles, Abiathar is priest along with Zadok (e.g., 1 Chron 15:11), but the leading role for priests consistently belongs to Zadok (cf. 24:3; 27:17). If these officials represent the royal council at an earlier point in David's reign, this may be Abiathar the priest. This is the only text in Chronicles where Abiathar is named without corresponding reference to Zadok.

THE TEXT IN BIBLICAL CONTEXT

Davidic Ordering of the Kingdom

This section shows the active role of the king in the economic life of Israel. He controls extensive holdings and operates storehouses in urban and rural areas. This is true for most of Israel's kings. One era best documented archaeologically concerns the reign of Hezekiah. Hundreds of pottery handles have been discovered in a range of cities that show Hezekiah was very engaged in managing agricultural activity. King David has his own advisers and officials in all his territories, which serve as an example for the kind of administrative order other kings maintained. The Deuteronomistic History says nothing about this aspect of David's administration of his kingdom, so this material is particularly instructive *[Deuteronomistic History, p. 465]*. A territorial division of the administration of Solomon is found in 1 Kings 4, but David's kingdom is never so described.

This section of Chronicles describes a way of life far removed from that of the Torah. The regulations of the Torah are based on a rural tribal society, not an empire engaged in international relations, with a complex internal economy and a highly structured national order *[Torah, p. 481]*. This does not make the Torah irrelevant to the new circumstance, but it demands that the values of individual enablement for livelihood must be applied in very different ways. Chronicles gives no indication as to whether this was consciously done or how such applications might have been made. It does assume that this is an administration that is fair to all of its citizens.

THE TEXT IN THE LIFE OF THE CHURCH

Paying Taxes Cheerfully

According to John Longhurst, reporting in the *Winnipeg Free Press*, "Religions should 'rejoice' at the chance to pay taxes" (Longhurst: E-9). He was commenting on a forty-page document of the Roman Catholic Church titled "Taxation for the Common Good." It was written to spark discussion about taxation and public services in the United Kingdom. Bishop Howard Tripp opined, "Taxes are very much based on the principle of solidarity, which is based on the commandment to love your neighbor." Christians should desire to contribute toward the sort of society that they want. "This document is suggesting taxes are a way to play our part, and it is something we should be pleased to do," according to Tripp. The Most Reverend Peter Smith, the Archbishop of Cardiff who headed the committee that created the report, said, "Taxation is a sign of social health, a moral good. Our willingness to pay it is a sign of our solidarity with one another, and of our humanity."

Members of the church are also members of the state and its taxation system. The church must instruct its members how to live in the world as citizens of the kingdom of God. The reflective document produced by the Roman Catholic Church may be a way of helping Christians live as good citizens. Christians must also live according to the values of their faith, which may be compromised by the taxation system. Citizens are coerced to pay taxes to causes that contradict their personal values. State taxation may be influenced positively by Christians, but it is not controlled by them. Refusal to

1 Chronicles 27:1-34

pay taxes is a civil disobedience. Christians must decide as congregations or individuals if their testimony to the values of the kingdom of God is advanced by such disobedience. Taxation may be a moral good, but not all things taxes support are morally good.

1 Chronicles 28:1–29:30
Accession of Solomon

PREVIEW

Transfer of government is not usually a matter of taking over a program that has been fully prepared for implementation. Good governments do not simply reverse benefits of a previous government in order to implement their ideology or please their supporters, but invariably they promise change. The Chronicler envisages a completely different situation in the establishment of the new regime. Solomon, the chosen successor, is given charge for everything he will do.

The enthronement of Solomon is presented as a gathering of all of the leaders and officials of David's kingdom, including the administrators of the various divisions, whether Levitical or civil, all of the military officers, and all those engaged in state employment. The gathering is representative of all Israel (Willi: 161–62); they must accept responsibility for enabling the new king to carry out his charge for the divine kingdom. A great festivity accompanies the installation of the new king, and a summary statement provides assurance that all Israel supported their new king, who was increasingly successful in his rule. The section concludes with a summary statement of David's reign typical of that found for other kings.

The Chronicler has composed his own account of the investiture of Solomon. It bears no relationship to the narrative in Kings, where David in his last days is weak and aged, scarcely aware of the mayhem swirling around him. The turmoil in his house continued, with Adonijah seeking to take the throne. There Nathan the prophet—realizing that his own life is in danger after being excluded from the retinue of Adonijah, as well as the lives of Zadok, Banaiah, and Solomon—hastily arranges for the anointing of Solomon. Solomon, with the power of the military at his disposal, quickly assumes control and dispatches his detractors (Konkel 2006: 51-60). David affirms the divine promise to Solomon (1 Kings 2:2-4), with closing instructions concerning matters needing to be settled (vv. 5-9). Solomon consolidates his rule (v. 12), confirming his succession.

The Chronicler's version is what von Rad has described as a "Levitical sermon" (von Rad 1966: 278-79). These compositions make use of authoritative ancient texts employed to advance the interests and viewpoint of the speaker. The quotations are used without any introductory rubrics and are not employed in the prophetic sense of an immediate word from God. Three such motifs are prominent in this exhortation by David. (1) Solomon is the one who will bring rest (28:20). (2) Solomon is a successor of David as Joshua was of Moses. He must be resolute and courageous (28:7, 10, 20; cf. Josh 1:6-7, 9, 18); he must observe and protect God's commandments (1 Chron 28:7-8; 29:19; cf. Josh 1:7-8), which will ensure his success (Josh 1:8; 1 Chron 29:23). (3) Finally, there is strong emphasis on Solomon as the one whom God has chosen (28:6, 10; 29:1), a distinction that never applies to Levites or kings other than David.

OUTLINE

Charge to the Assembly, 28:1-10
Transfer of the Temple Plan, 28:11-21
Contributions for the Temple, 29:1-9
Blessing of David, 29:10-20
Installation of Solomon, 29:21-25
Conclusion of David's Reign, 29:26-30

EXPLANATORY NOTES

Charge to the Assembly 28:1-10

David's speech to the dignitaries of all Israel divides into two parts. The first deals with plans for succession to the throne and Solomon's mission to build the promised sanctuary (28:2-8). The second part is addressed directly to Solomon (vv. 9-10), instructing the heir in piety and exhorting him to build the sanctuary. Both parts of the speech are infused with language previously used in narrative and speech. The first part emphasizes the promise to David as articulated in 1 Chronicles 17; the second incorporates 1 Chronicles 22:7-16, where David has privately instructed Solomon concerning his plans and intentions. Here nothing is added to the concepts already expressed. This is the next stage as David publicly declares his aspirations for the future to the luminaries of all Israel.

As is Moses, David is depicted as active and vigorous right until the end of his life. The vision of Moses was filled with intense desire for a future in the Promised Land (Deut 3:23-29). Yet Moses would not experience this future; he would not even be permitted to step over the river. The divine mandate to Moses was to commission Joshua to this task. The Chronicler sees this as the divine pattern to be repeated in David. This example of Scripture is authoritative for him in interpreting history. David is depicted as Moses whose "eye was not dimmed and his vigor unabated" right until the time of his death (Deut 34:7 AT). David would never see the temple, but his energy and vigor in preparing for it were present to the end of his life.

David desired a resting place for the ark of God (1 Chron 28:2); in his speech he recalls Psalm 132, words surely familiar to all those who had knowledge of temple worship. Psalm 132 belongs to the Psalms of Ascent, the only classification in which all psalms of that type are found in one place. The Psalms of Ascent give testimony to making the pilgrimage from distant regions to worship at the temple (Pss 120–122). Psalm 132 depicts David's refusal to rest until he has found a resting place for the ark, the artifact that symbolizes the footstool of God's throne and contains the covenant words that give testimony to the relationship in which Yahweh would be their God and they would be his people.

In Chronicles, Solomon is the uncontested son of God's choice. Out of David's many sons, he is the one designated to carry the promise forward. This election is equally applicable to dynastic rule and temple building. The charges to observe and seek out God's commands are in the plural, indicating that this exhortation is to all those present and hearing this address. There is a responsibility for all the people collectively as well as for Solomon individually. In the words of Joshua, they are to inherit this good land (1 Chron 28:8; cf. Josh 1:11, 15). These words are relevant not only to the conquest, but also to all future generations. This is fully in keeping with the Chronicler's theology, which promises the reward of blessing for obedience. All these elements are typical of the "Levitical sermons" composed by the Chronicler to teach and exhort.

Transfer of the Temple Plan 28:11-21

This whole section has emphasized the divine plan for the construction of the temple (28:11-12, 18-19). The plan was a written document rather than a blueprint or drawing, thus comparable to the divine instructions that Moses received on Mount Sinai for building the tabernacle (Exod 25:9, 40). The plan provided much more than architectural designs or the shapes and sizes of utensils and furnishings. It included weights of metals, their quality, and even the organization of personnel to carry on the rituals of the new temple. The plan presented everything David had in mind (v. 12), though it may be that this is a reference to the mind of God that came to David via God's spirit (*ruah*). In any case, none of this was of David's own initiative. Every detail given by God was put in writing (v. 19); God granted David insight over every aspect of the plan.

The description of the written plans that David gave to Solomon is inclusive of everything to do with the temple. First listed are aspects of the building itself: the entrance area, the building with its storerooms, the upper levels (perhaps some architectural feature of the temple roof), the inner rooms, and the most holy place, where the ark was located. The temple was surrounded by courts, and there were store chambers around the sides. Some of these served as treasuries for the temple revenues and for the offerings dedicated to temple maintenance (cf. 26:20). The weight of gold was calculated for the lampstands; usually there were ten, with seven lamps on each one. The other basic furnishings were the table for the rows of bread, and silver tables, unknown in other contexts. The altar furnishings included the long-tined forks for turning roasting meat, bowls for collecting blood (28:17), jars of pure gold for libations, and basins, both gold and silver. These basins are only mentioned in late sources and are not found in Exodus. The articles most closely associated with the most holy place were the altar of incense and the cherubim. The Chronicler describes the base for the cherubim as a chariot (1 Chron 28:18). This description is unique and intriguing in the light of Scripture and ancient practice. The throne of a king could be placed on a chariot styled as a cherub (Keel: figures 231-36). In the visions of Ezekiel, the throne of God is above the cherubim and is swiftly mobile, with imagery like that of a chariot (Ezek 1:4-24; 10:1-22). In the case of the temple, the giant wings of the cherubim, which served as the throne of God, were a protection to the sacred covenant ark.

Contributions for the Temple 29:1-9

This address of David has several distinct emphases: Solomon is the one whom God has chosen; generous provision has been made for all the materials of the temple; the leaders are enthusiastically dedicated to completing the work. David himself has been exemplary in his personal generosity for building the temple. The palace was more than a human project. The term "palace" is only found in late writings; it seems to include all the fortifications on the citadel of Jerusalem. It may have included the Tower of Hananel and the Tower of the Hundred (Neh 3:1). However, the main point is that this palace represented the kingdom of God; it was not for humans. The whole cluster of buildings associated with the royal complex therefore gained a certain sanctity. This task could not be accomplished by one person; it required the complete dedication of all the leaders. Further, Solomon was young and inexperienced. If Solomon was born shortly after the time David conquered Jerusalem, he would have been about thirty years old. Very few can be prepared for the highest levels of executive leadership at that age. It was necessary that Solomon receive complete support, without detraction of competing interests.

The generosity of the people and the materials of the temple are modeled after the pattern of the tabernacle (Exod 25:1-7; 35:4-9, 20-29). Many of the materials are the same as those found in Exodus. *Onyx* is a semiprecious stone with alternating bands of color (1 Chron 29:2). The stones of the priestly ephod were onyx (Exod 25:7) and are also described as stones "to be mounted," the term used by the Chronicler (*for the settings*, v. 2). Stones *for the settings* might be their setting in the priestly garments but could also refer to a consecration, often associated with the term (Snijders: 307). *Antimony* (NIV, *turquoise*) is a decorative, metallic mineral, generally used in combination with other elements. *Marble* (*šayiš*) is found only here but probably refers to alabaster (*šeš*), a white translucent gypsum used for carvings and ornamental purposes. Of his own free will, David gave generously from his private treasury to this *holy house* (v. 3 AT; NIV, *holy temple*), a term for the temple that became common in later use.

David's example is a challenge to the leaders to give equally generously, *filling their hands* for the work of the temple (v. 5). This expression is typically used for the dedication of priests. David has given according to his ability; the people accordingly should have an undivided desire to complete this task. Thus David is asking for a consecration similar to that of priestly dedication to finish this task

(Snijders: 305). The officials responded accordingly with vast amounts of wealth. Five thousand talents of gold may be compared with the thirty talents of gold that Hezekiah paid to Sennacherib (2 Kings 18:14), a tribute from the country.

The whole description of temple contributions is in terms familiar to the time of the Chronicler. *Darics* (v. 7) were not minted until Darius I, in the postexilic period (cf. Ezra 2:69), long after King David. But the Chronicler is understood to be using terms contemporary to his writing, presenting the equivalent of what David said in his speech.

Blessing of David 29:10-20

The blessing of David is the climax of his history as told in Chronicles. The leaders and officials are united with Solomon for the task of temple building. The proper response is a prayer of joyful faith, expressing humility and submission before God. The prayer draws on a rich liturgy of worship. Much of what is expressed here can be found in other biblical texts, but this prayer more likely draws on a common heritage of praise. Several themes are prominent: (1) the people of Israel are sojourners, even within the secure boundaries of the kingdom; (2) the kingdom belongs to God alone; and (3) the people have freely given of themselves to God. If Israel now enjoys an unprecedented prosperity, it is testimony to the truth that all things come from God (1 Chron 29:14). David prays for their minds to remain so devoted that the impulse of every thought may forever be directed toward God. David's closing petition is that the heart of Solomon may never be compromised in his commitment to this great work.

When the ark was brought to Jerusalem, praise was expressed by using the first fifteen verses of Psalm 105, Psalm 96, and the opening and closing lines of praise from Psalm 106. This blessing is a counterpart, an inclusion around the theme of the divine provision for temple's construction, through the efforts of David. The same themes are predominant in this blessing, as David recalls how the landless patriarchs, few in number, received promise of the land. Though this promise has in one sense been realized with David's kingdom, all remain utterly dependent on God. The attitude of David remains the same; verse 14 of the benediction recalls his words in response to the declaration of the promise from Nathan the prophet: *Who am I, LORD God, and what is my family, that you have brought me this far?* (1 Chron 17:16).

Installation of Solomon 29:21-25

The investiture is necessarily accompanied by a great festival described in these verses. The detail that Solomon was made king a second time is likely in reference to the earlier statements of Solomon being made king (cf. 23:1; 28:1-10). This is an explanatory note that has found its way into the text; it is absent in Vaticanus [Greek Text of Chronicles, p. 468]. The whole section following the announcement of Nathan in chapter 17 has dealt with the preparation and process of Solomon being made king. This is the climax of the event, which began with all of David's preparations in ordering the leaders and officials.

A second detail is that Zadok was anointed as priest. Earlier Zadok had been appointed as a leader of the priests among the tribal officers (27:17) and had functioned as a key leader in forming the priestly divisions (24:3). Earlier in David's reign, Zadok and Abiathar are found together (15:11), and later Zadok is priest with Ahimelek when David begins to consolidate his expanded kingdom (18:16 mg.). The anointing of Zadok at the time of Solomon might be related to Zadok receiving a new office when Solomon began to reign. The role of king and priest were central to the preaching of Zechariah; Joshua the high priest and Zerubbabel the Davidic descendant were the leaders in resurrecting the temple in Jerusalem (Zech 3:1-4:14). They were the "sons of oil" (4:14 MT; divinely anointed) to stand before the Lord of all the earth. In the Damascus Document of Qumran times, reference is repeatedly made to the anointed of Aaron and Israel (CD 12.23; 14.19; 19.10). The documents of the community anticipate two messiahs or anointed leaders, one from the priestly order and another of the royal order. The Chronicler may have had a similar concept in mind.

Conclusion of David's Reign 29:26-30

In Kings and Chronicles it is typical to have a closing notice of the reign of a king (Rainey 1997: 32-38). The source notations of the Chronicler are distinct from those of kings, usually making reference to the work of a prophet. This conclusion of David's reign is found only in Chronicles. In the parallel references it is obvious that the same material derived by the Deuteronomists from "the book of the annals of the kings of Judah" (e.g., 1 Kings 14:29) was found by the Chronicler in the works ascribed to the various prophets, in this case Samuel and Nathan. The Chronicler appears to have access to a series of works written from reign to reign by prophets contemporary with the respective kings. These are prophetic writings, not history in the modern sense. They are one kind of historiography *[History Writing, p. 469]*. In the references for Jehoshaphat (2 Chron 20:34) and Hezekiah (32:32), the Chronicler refers to *the book of the kings of Israel*, which is the equivalent of "the book of the annals of the kings of Judah" credited in Kings. The records of the kings used in Scripture were interpretations of the king's reign (2 Chron 24:27), that is, a prophetic history, rather than official royal records, which would have quite different information. This is part of the reason why Joshua through 2 Kings are counted as prophets in the Hebrew Scriptures. They drew on prophetic material to describe the reigns of the kings.

THE TEXT IN BIBLICAL CONTEXT

An Eschatological History

Solomon reigned on the throne of the Lord (1 Chron 29:23). David had made the same declaration in the doxology of his prayer: *Yours, O LORD, is greatness, might, wonder, fame, and splendor; everything in heaven and on earth is yours. Yours, O LORD, is the kingdom, and you are exalted above all things, the head over all* (v. 11 AT). The wars of David were a necessary preparation for God in achieving his plan; they were the means of bringing rest to the land; they made possible a resting place for the ark (28:2); they also provided the resources to build the temple. These wars caused a prohibition that kept David from building the temple yet at the same time were a necessary preparation for it. This paradox would have been particularly pertinent in the time of the Chronicler. His hope for a Davidic ruler in fulfillment of the promise required political changes like those of the time of David.

For the Chronicler, God is not only *in* history, the classic prophetic view, but he also is *above* history (De Vries: 229). For this reason it is imperative for the Chronicler to write another history. Israel already had a history that told of the work of God in history; in that history the promise ended in exile, but the promise did not end. The Chronicler takes in hand to write a history *as it should have happened*, the history that God intended for his people. It is that history of succession that the Chronicler describes. The reality of that history had not been subverted by the exile of Judah. The throne belongs to God, and therefore God's purpose in giving the promise remains as a present reality.

History cannot be defined by a set of scientific criteria, because no such set of criteria can ever prove adequate for the diversity of historical tasks that are undertaken. It is better to define history as the intellectual form in which a civilization renders account to itself of its past (Huizinga: 9). History is a sequence, a chronology of events directly related to each other. However, history in Scripture is not limited to cause and effect as observed and evaluated in human affairs. Isaiah would say, "Woe to the Assyrian, the rod of my anger" (Isa 10:5). The Assyrian attack against Jerusalem in 701 BCE should not be understood merely in terms of the geopolitics of its time, though that could be one way to describe that sequence of events. But the Deuteronomistic evaluation of past events was made in terms of the critical reality of the covenant requirements. These were the revealed will of God; this reality explained what happened when Judah was ravaged in 701 BCE.

The same perspective held true for the succession of David. The consequences of David's failures could not be ignored; nor could these be ascribed to the usual conflicts of succession that destroyed many royal households. The Deuteronomists described the succession of David in all its ugly realities; all of these are a part of the story that determined the destiny of the nation as an independent political entity, which ended with the exile.

The Chronicler writes an eschatological history, one that represents God's purposes for these events. This purpose included a future for the promise to David, though it is not in the purview of the Chronicler to specify more precisely what that might be. There is no hint of a redeemer figure that would restore the kingdom of Israel, as was generally present in the movements leading to the times of the New Testament (Collins: 237). Though such views were significantly diverse, with some of the most important documents expressing a messiah of Aaron and a messiah of David, there was generally the expectation of a final eschatological war, which would end the rule of the nations and inaugurate the kingdom of God. The Chronicler had no concept of an apocalyptic solution that would bring an end to the present order. It is doubtful that such eschatological concepts were even present during his time, though there may have been the beginnings of such symbols (e.g., Isa 26:16–27:1). But the Chronicler's doctrine of retribution espoused a firm belief that God was directly involved in history. In his view, the future of his people in part rested on their faithfulness and loyalty to God. In writing the history *that should have been*, he was not only calling attention to that responsibility, but also continuing a hope that rested on the promises of God. The presence of God would be experienced in the worship of the temple. The continuous fulfillment of the covenant in supporting the temple and its festivals was in itself reason for joy, which brought hope for the future and anticipation of life as God meant it to be.

The urgency of this eschatological vision is one that grows out of the latter prophets equally as much as the Chronicler's reading of history. Haggai and Zechariah 1–6 are urgent messages to accept the self-denial necessary to build the temple. It was an enormous demand to ask a poor and struggling community to give of their limited resources and time to build a high-maintenance edifice that would produce no immediate economic benefits. They had plenty to deal with in trying to get their own households in order as fourth-generation exiles, those who returned to a homeland that was completely foreign. It took twenty years from the time that Cyrus enabled the first pilgrims to return until the foundation of this second temple could be laid (Ezra 6:13-15). The struggle for survival in the small province of Yehud had changed little in the intervening years to the time of Chronicler. The temple was a reality, but it seemed to be but a shadow of its former glory. There was no prospect that anything would change. But for the Chronicler the future mattered. It needed to be a future that would give testimony to the *real Israel*, the one that *should have been* and the one that now *should be*. Such a future is the kingdom of God.

THE TEXT IN THE LIFE OF THE CHURCH

Eschatology in the Worship of the Church

The New Testament is decidedly apocalyptic in its hope for the future. Jesus is the Redeemer whose kingdom is not of this world. He is the Redeemer who is coming on the clouds of heaven. In the vision of the Apocalypse, the age will end in a new world in which there is no more sea (Rev 21:1-2). In apocalyptic terminology, "sea" refers to the forces that cause the disruption of the present order. It grows from terminology like that of Psalm 74:12-17, in which Sea, Sea Monster, Leviathan, and the Ever-Flowing River are forces defeated in order to bring about the beauty of day and night, summer and winter. The powers of Sea that threaten God's creation may be death (Leviathan in Isa 27:1) or the violence of human government (Isa 51:9-11). In the apocalyptic vision, all these will be removed, because there is a new heaven and a new earth, in which there is nothing that can bring about tears or death. Instead, there will be a restoration like that of the garden of Eden, where the river of life, clear as crystal, flows from the throne of God, and on either side of it, trees of life grow in all seasons, providing fruit for all twelve months of the year (Rev 22:1-2). There will be no more curse; there will be the presence of the throne and the Lamb and the continuous light of the divine presence.

Apocalyptic eschatology has a tendency to neglect the importance of treasuring the opportunities of the present time and the promises that are fulfilled in them. The present world is important to God, or else the end of the Apocalypse would have already arrived. One response of apocalyptic eschatology is (1) urgency: the message of the kingdom must get out because the end is near. It is important to urge people to commit to Christian faith. Another response can be (2) resignation: hope for the present is over; the present is to be endured until a better world arrives. Sometimes the response is (3) activism: our duty is to be salt and light in this world; therefore we must be that light while there is opportunity, because the night is quickly coming, when the present will be lost. A popular response in contemporary Christianity, ironically enough, comes from Chronicles in (4) the prayer of Jabez (1 Chron 4:9-10): a life of faith will result in the enlargement of the goodness of life in the present; God provides wealth and health for the faithful until such time as life in this world is complete.

The eschatology of the Chronicler calls us back to God's purposes for the present, which began with creation and which can be realized by those faithful to God's will and those trusting in the promise of his kingdom. The promises of God are not those of the kingdoms of this world. There is a kingdom of God in the present that transcends the self-serving powers of this world. This kingdom is a call to the purposes of creation. The garden of Eden is described as a temple in which the presence of a transcendent God is a life-giving power to all of the world of the common (Ps 104). In the garden is a living image, one that belongs to the world of the common, and yet transcends that world to represent the will and the rule of the Creator within it. The symbolism that made confession of such an invisible reality in the present world was the temple. The words and actions of temple confessions were a presence of the glory and majesty of the transcendent, the purpose for which this world was made (Ps 8). This eschatological vision is one that is most relevant to the church of the present.

In the world of the common, the temple as a building no longer has the power to confess the majesty of the transcendent. The temple is the people of God, making the sacrifice of praise. Those living by faith in God do not have here an abiding city; they seek the one that is about to be. But in Christ these faithful offer the sacrifice of praise through all things to God; "the fruit of lips" makes confession in God's name. Therefore God's people must not neglect doing good and fellowship, for such sacrifices are well pleasing to God (Heb 13:14-16). The church is to grow as a holy temple in the Lord, a tabernacle structure for God in Christ, built together in the Spirit (Eph 2:21-22). There remains a sacrifice and worship for the people of God. This temple is not a growth in numbers; it is a growth in its offering sacrifices of praise in lives lived to the glory of God.

This eschatology of the present time is realized in the confession of meeting together (Heb 10:24-25), in urging others to join in this worship, and so much more as we see the apocalyptic end approaching. It is no shame to exercise such sacrifice of praise in buildings designed to reflect that confession, perhaps even buildings with stained-glass windows and steeples. There is more to the present than waiting for the apocalyptic end. The eschatology of Chronicles, and the eschatology of the present, calls upon us to treasure this opportunity of worship, to engage in it faithfully. This is the kingdom of God and the work of God. It is recognition of the fulfillment of the divine promise as a visible presence in the present, a presence that began in a particular way with the promise to David brought to realization in the kingdom of Solomon. This is the present that *should be*, analogous to the history of the Chronicler *that should have been*.

Part 4
The Reign of Solomon

2 Chronicles 1:1-9:31

OVERVIEW

The organization of this section makes temple building the focus of Solomon's reign. Wisdom, piety, and riches were necessary to accomplishing the task of erecting this holy house. Temple building is introduced and concluded by attributes that make temple building possible. These qualities introduce and conclude the account (De Vries: 233). This account follows a chiastic pattern, in which the material emphasized is placed at the center *[Chiasm, p. 465]*. The impact of the main point is created by a series of premises that are recapitulated. In a literary structure, chiasm leads the reader to the themes of the narrative. The reign of Solomon manifests the following structure in 2 Chronicles:

A^1 Seeking the Lord (1:2-6)
   B^1 Gift of wisdom (1:7-13)
      C^1 Power, wealth, and influence (1:14-18)
         D Building of the temple (2:1-8:16)
      C^2 International trade and great wealth (8:17-18; 9:13-21)
   B^2 Queen of Sheba seeks Solomon's wisdom (9:1-12)
A^2 God grants Solomon wisdom and wealth (9:22-28)

The Chronicler has drawn substantial material from the narrative in Kings (1 Kings 3-11): Solomon seeking the Lord at Gibeon, the installation of the ark, the prayer of dedication, and the visit of the queen of Sheba. But to create the chiastic effect, he has introduced summary material on the wealth and influence of Solomon as part of the qualifications for temple building. This material is then repeated in his conclusion of Solomon's reign.

The Chronicler has been selective in the use of the narrative in 1 Kings. The positive assessment of Solomon's administration is not mentioned (1 Kings 4). The Chronicler has already given his own version of the organization and administration of the kingdom under David. None of the information concerning the demise of the kingdom at the end of Solomon's reign in 1 Kings 11 is included, nor any other notices that might suggest something negative about Solomon's reign (e.g., 1 Kings 3:1-3). Other sections that the Chronicler does include are significantly abbreviated. The Chronicler has provided much of his own composition in the narrative of Solomon alongside the material that he has restructured.

The Chronicler has adopted a number of models in his portrayal of Solomon (Dillard 1980: 292-98). Solomon is a second David. He is king by divine choice and immediately enjoys the complete support of all the people. As David, Solomon's central concerns are the temple and its personnel. Solomon is the successor of David just as Joshua was the successor of Moses. Just as Moses did not enter the Promised Land, so also David did not build the temple. Solomon and Huram-Abi are the new Bezalel and Oholiab. Huram-Abi's services are offered in the very first exchange with Hiram of Tyre. Further, the skills inventory of Huram-Abi is expanded to coincide with that of Oholiab.

Temple building and dedication have parallels with Kings, but Chronicles has more focus on the inauguration of temple worship. The construction of the temple and the engagement of non-Israelite labor constitute the beginning and end of the temple account (2 Chron 2-4; 8:1-9:12), forming an inclusio *[Inclusio, p. 467]*. Two central sections deal with the inauguration of worship: 5:2-6:11; 7:1-22. Each includes references to the assembly, the glory cloud, sacrifice, and song. The dedication prayer stands at the center of the description (6:12-42). The Kings narrative gives a sense of progression, with Solomon establishing his administration, building the temple, and encountering conflict with the surrounding kingdoms at the end of his reign. The Chronicler makes temple building the sole focus of the reign of Solomon.

2 Chronicles 1:1-17
Confirmation of Solomon

PREVIEW
Wealth and wisdom seem to be a rare combination, as much as they are universally regarded as desirable. Not many in contemporary time would be generally acclaimed as having both qualities. Solomon is legendary in both respects. The Chronicler shows how the legend is true.

The main point in the consolidation of the kingdom is that God increasingly exalted Solomon. Translations that say *Solomon son of David established himself in his kingdom* are misleading (NIV, NRSV). The form of the verb translated *established himself* is often treated as reflexive but should not be so understood in this case. The *declarative reflexive* presents someone as existing in a certain state (Waltke and O'Connor: 26.2f). A better translation would be *Solomon son of David was secure over his kingdom. Yahweh his God was with him. He increasingly esteemed him* (v. 1 AT). God alone was responsible for securing the kingdom.

Solomon is introduced as wise and wealthy, a result of God's gifts to him. Wisdom in Chronicles is precisely for building the temple. Solomon is modeled after Bezalel (Dillard 1980: 296); it is only after seeking God at the altar built by Bezalel that Solomon is endowed with wisdom. In 2 Chronicles 1:12, God promises to grant Solomon riches, wealth, and honor; these are declared in verses 14-17 and again after the account of temple building in 9:25 and 27-28. The wealth of Solomon frames the narrative to highlight Solomon's wisdom as temple builder. The word *ḥokmah* (wisdom) is used for technical skill and life skills. The wisdom of technical skill is given to

Bezalel to build the tabernacle (Exod 31:1-3; 35:30-35). This is the wisdom the Chronicler attributes to Solomon at Gibeon.

OUTLINE

Worship at Gibeon, 1:1-6
Revelation to Solomon, 1:7-13
Wealth of Solomon, 1:14-17

EXPLANATORY NOTES

Worship at Gibeon 1:1-6

Solomon's first action is to assemble all the elite of Israel, the group David brought together for the investiture of Solomon. They gather at the high place (*bamah*) in Gibeon. In physical description, a high place was not an altar, though it could be used as an altar for sacrifices and offerings (1 Kings 3:3; 12:31-32). A *bamah* refers to sculpted stone in the center of a paved courtyard (Zevit: 262-63; cf. Lev 26:1). In 2 Chronicles 7:7 Solomon made offerings on such a courtyard. It seems to have been a publicly accessible place, with standing stones (pillars) called *maṣṣebot*. In a cultic context these pillars represented the continuous presence of the Deity. The house of the high place excavated at Dan had an almost square ashlar (large square-cut stone) *bamah* measuring about sixty feet (twenty meters) on each side. It had a small altar and apparently once had a large altar for animal sacrifices, judging by the presence of a large basalt horn (Biran: 40). Steps led up to the high place, and two long chambers were associated with it.

The high place at Dan had standing pillars (*maṣṣebot*) on three cult corners, with flagstone pavements (an open area of flat level slabs of stone). It is possible that these served the many different merchants and travelers that came that way. Syncretistic high places were condemned in Israel (e.g., 1 Kings 3:2-3). However, it was possible for Israel to have a standing stone erected to represent Yahweh, as in Isaiah 19:19, and a place of sacrifice associated with it. The Chronicler is fully supportive of the high place at Gibeon. This high place is part of the process by which a single location for centralized worship can be established. David had already moved the ark with its cherubim to Jerusalem, at the location he had designated. The bronze altar and worship at the tent of meeting were still accommodated at Gibeon. Solomon went there to worship, offer sacrifices, and seek divine guidance. The action and the location are both laudatory.

Revelation to Solomon 1:7-13

The revelation to Solomon at Gibeon is reported much as it is in Kings. No reference is made to a dream, as is the case in 1 Kings 3:5 and 15, but no particular significance can be drawn from the omission. Solomon asks for wisdom on the basis of God's loyalty, as has been seen in his faithfulness to David and the promise. In Chronicles the emphasis is significantly different than in Kings. The people of Israel are described as like the dust of the earth in multitude, recalling the divine promise to Abraham (Gen 15:5-6). In Kings they are described as difficult (1 Kings 3:9), and though the word carries the nuance of numerous, it also implies that a great number of people will bring great difficulties. This circumstance is illustrated when Solomon is called on to settle a dispute between two prostitutes, who both claim a living child as their own when the other child died. Wisdom can be the ability to exercise judgment in difficult cases or the exercise of leadership. Governors are also referred to as judges. In Chronicles the request for wisdom is the latter (2 Chron 1:10-11). Solomon needs to know how to be a good leader since he has been made responsible for this vast people.

God grants Solomon wisdom and knowledge. Wisdom is further qualified by knowledge because the request is for a range of skills in exercising governance. The granting of this wisdom is stated with an impersonal verb, the equivalent of a passive. In the narrative such wisdom and knowledge have already been granted. The divine response to Solomon has a symmetrical structure and unique emphasis: *You did not ask for riches, properties, and honor; the life of your enemies and a long life you did not ask for* (v. 11b-c AT). The items Solomon did not ask for are in a group of three and a group of two. God grants the first set of three things that Solomon does not ask for (v. 12 b-c), in a measure that is unequaled for any other king. Nothing is said about the second set of two items for which Solomon did not ask. In Chronicles no mention is made of the enemies named in Kings (1 Kings 11:14, 23), neither those whom Solomon dispatched nor those who later threatened his kingdom. Here the emphasis is limited to the mission of the temple, the wealth that supported it, and the honor that it brought.

Wealth of Solomon 1:14-17

The statement about Solomon's wealth and international influence involves the trade of horses. These verses have been adopted from 1 Kings 10:26-29; they are repeated at the conclusion of Solomon's reign in 2 Chronicles 9:25-28. The wealth of Solomon provided for a strong military, which for the first time included chariotry. The opulence of his wealth was evident in the spectacular luxury found in the capital city.

Solomon's kingdom straddled the land bridge between the continents of Africa, Europe, and Asia. He was the middleman in the arms trade, particularly between Syria and Egypt. Solomon obtained his horses from Kue (Kizzuwatna in the Hittite period, Cilicia in the Greco-Roman period), on the southeastern seacoast of Asia Minor, near the Taurus Mountains. The text is somewhat uncertain as to whether Solomon also obtained horses from Egypt. It is possible the area of *muṣri* in Anatolia just north of the Taurus has been confused with *miṣrayim* (Egypt). The area was rich in wood for chariots and was known as the home of horse breeders. But Assyrian records from a couple of centuries later do show that Nubian horses were one of the most valuable aspects of trade with Egypt. In any case, Solomon's merchants traded in chariots and horses with Hittite and Aramean kings. Egypt may have been a recipient in the trade of horses and chariots as well as an exporter. The engagement of Egypt is a natural explanation for why Solomon would have been involved in military trade with Kue (Cilicia).

Archaeological excavations at Megiddo indicate that Solomon was deeply involved in chariotry, approximating the numbers indicated by the Chronicler. Excavations of the tenth century have uncovered five units of stabling built in a row in the southern complex of buildings (Ussishkin 1992: 677). Each unit contained about 30 horses, and the entire complex about 150 horses. The stables opened into a large courtyard, leveled on a large artificial fill. This indicates that a unit of chariot horses was maintained and trained there. There is also evidence of stables for riding horses in several units that would have housed over 300 horses. Megiddo is on the route that Solomon would have used in trade between Cilicia and Egypt, as well as for his own military units at Jerusalem.

THE TEXT IN BIBLICAL CONTEXT

Wisdom, Wealth, and Power

Two points are made about Solomon in Kings: Solomon became richer and wiser than any king on earth (1 Kings 10:23), and Solomon did what was wrong in the sight of the Lord (11:6). The queen of Sheba could not tell of half the glory of Solomon (10:7). The condemnation of Solomon was based on his support of the high places and even constructing shrines for other gods in Jerusalem (3:2; 11:7-8). The sins of Solomon result in the attacks of enemies and divisions in his own ranks.

In the Hebrew language, wisdom is not just an understanding of life to make good decisions possible. In Kings, the vision at Gibeon is primarily to enable Solomon to exercise judgment over a difficult people (1 Kings 3:9). This may be translated as a *great people* (NIV, NRSV, et al.), but the sequel suggests the word *kabed* (heavy) should be understood in terms of the demanding responsibility of governing this people. Solomon is the very wise judge between two prostitutes who lay claim to the same living child (1 Kings 3:16-28). This is not the function of Solomon's wisdom in Chronicles. Wisdom in Chronicles is a highly prized virtue. Success in economic matters is a sign of wisdom, the wisdom of seeking divine favor.

THE TEXT IN THE LIFE OF THE CHURCH
Wisdom for Christian Use of Wealth

The apostle Paul provides two perspectives on wealth. The first is summarized in the statement, "I can do all things through the One who gives me strength" (Phil 4:13 AT). This statement is in the context of having received a generous gift. It is evident that the apostle was in need, and the gift from the Philippian church was a timely answer to that need. However, the apostle was determined that physical needs would not be the controlling force of his life. He worked to provide for his own needs, but he labored so that he could engage in the ministry of bringing the good news. Christians should help those who have served them in spiritual matters of life, such as church instruction. But this was not the criterion by which the apostle did his work; he did not require support from those he served.

The apostle feels positively about those who are rich but has a great concern for them. They are in a precarious situation, perhaps cherishing a false sense of superiority and security and trusting in their wealth (1 Tim 6:17). Such attitudes are anathema to the Christian life. The rich have a particular opportunity to be rich in good works, but too often this opportunity is subverted by the dangers of riches. In Chronicles, Solomon is in this latter category of the apostle Paul. His wealth is indicative of status; the Chronicler considers this to be a noble tribute. Yet the Chronicler does not think Solomon is the model that everyone can pursue. He is seeking to show that God ordains such positions as an enablement for a much greater kingdom.

The Bridgeway Foundation of Ontario grants millions of dollars annually to support education and family life and to alleviate poverty. At one time the founder, Reg Petersen, needed to assist his parents financially. His father had to retire as a pastor due to a throat ailment and asked his son for help in a nursing home business. Through very hard work, the business prospered. In his late thirties, Reg assessed his financial situation and determined that he and his family were adequately cared for. He then established the foundation and for the next forty years worked harder than ever to grow investments for the purpose of giving away the profits.

Similarly, the apostle Paul urges the Ephesians to have a Christian mind, one created according to God's image in righteousness and true holiness (Eph 4:20-24). This mind affects every area of life, including work and wealth. "Anyone who has been stealing must steal no longer, but must work, doing something useful with their own hands, that they may have something to share with those in need" (v. 28). Few Christians work to have a surplus to give away, but according to the apostle Paul this is the mind of Christ.

Solomon is renowned for wealth and wisdom. The Chronicler is correct in affirming these virtues. Sadly, Solomon's end was not as the beginning. Solomon's life ended in disaster, and his kingdom divided at his death. Nevertheless, the kingdom promised to David endured. Many Christian fortunes have been lost, but the work represented need not be lost to the kingdom of God. In ways that often cannot be anticipated, God is able to turn such reversals into the work of his kingdom.

2 Chronicles 2:1–8:16
Building the Temple

PREVIEW

Governments like to leave a legacy of great building projects. Constructions like the Egyptian pyramids and the Taj Mahal are monuments that are frequented with admiration to this very day. Ancient temples were often a legacy to the king that constructed them. The biblical temple in this regard was to be of a completely different order. It was not a large building, yet it was very significant.

The beginning and the end of temple construction are clearly marked: the intent of Solomon to build is declared (2 Chron 2:1); the conclusion is marked by establishing the regular rituals of each day, week, and regular festivals (8:12-16). The closing verses include the Chronicler's central themes, the institution of all the priestly divisions as established by David, including the security of temple guards, and Solomon's adherence to all the instructions. Closure to the section is marked with the precise words found in Kings: the house of the Lord was completed (1 Kings 9:25; 2 Chron 8:16). A number of rubrics indicate progression in temple building: Solomon began to build (3:1); all the work Solomon did for the house of the Lord was completed (5:1a); Solomon was successful in everything he intended to do for the house of the Lord and his own house (7:11b). These are adapted from Kings (cf. 1 Kings 6:1; 7:51; 9:1, respectively) and are further evidence of how the Chronicler has been very conscious of his sources as well as a particular portrayal of temple building.

The chiastic structure of the temple-building account may be outlined as follows [Chiasm, p. 465]:

A¹ Foreign provision of labor and materials (2:1-18)
  B¹ Temple structure and furnishings as ordained by God (3:1–5:1)
    C¹ Dedication of the temple (5:2–6:2)
    C² Dedication of the people (6:3-42)
  B² God consecrates the temple and its function (7:1-22)
A² Foreign labor and material provisions (8:1-16)

At the center of this account are two complementary and critical concepts: the function of the holy place as God's presence amid his people, and the prayer that the people will know their utter dependence on the presence manifest in the temple. This is the way the promises of the Lord may be realized. Obedience to the instructions of David is met with tangible divine approval as fire from heaven consumes the sacrifices (7:1). With the completion of the temple, God gives Solomon the formula that constitutes the criteria for blessing (7:14): *If my people, who are called by my name, will humble themselves and pray and seek my face and turn from their wicked ways, then I will hear from heaven, and I will forgive their sin and heal their land.* The Chronicler will repeatedly use this vocabulary to show that the possibility of God's people being blessed around the temple is always open.

OUTLINE

Preparations for Temple Building, 2:1-18
Temple Structure and Furnishings, 3:1–5:1
Installation of the Ark, 5:2–6:11
Dedication Prayer, 6:12-42
Consecration of the Temple, 7:1-22
Military and Labor Provisions, 8:1-16

EXPLANATORY NOTES

Preparations for Temple Building 2:1-18

Building the temple required a lot of stone and timber, much labor to supply that, and skilled workers to construct it. Solomon needed to access resources outside those of Israel to facilitate these needs. The statement enumerating Solomon's labor force begins and ends this section. The whole has a structure typical to the Chronicler in his composition of Solomon's reign:

A^1 Conscription of labor force (2:2)
  B^1 Solomon's letter to Hiram (2:3-10)
  B^2 Hiram's response to Solomon (2:11-16)
A^2 Conscription of labor force (2:17-18)

Ancient building projects were accomplished by a conscripted labor force. The main point of this passage is that the laborers and the materials were not native Israelites.

The levy required for the work of the temple was a total of 153,600 men; apparently conscription of labor was part of the reason for the census of David. This labor was apportioned to 70,000 porters (men carrying loads) and 80,000 quarrymen bringing rocks from the mountains. The commissioners are likely to be broken down to 3,000 supervisors over labor and 600 officers in the higher echelons of government. Each supervisor would be responsible for about 50 men. The levy is recruited from the alien population, non-Israelites living within Israelite society. Apparently the census was in part necessary because of Israelite hegemony expanded over the new areas that David had brought under his control (Rainey 1970: 201-2). These non-Israelites would now be participants within Israelite society, but they would not have had the same status as those from native Israelite families. The Chronicler will return to the question of conscripted labor when he concludes the account of Solomon (2 Chron 8:7-10). A second kind of forced labor is introduced there, which apparently was also conscripted from nonnative peoples living among Israel.

Solomon turns to the Phoenicians for assistance in resources and skilled labor. Tyre was famous for its skilled labor and building techniques. David had already established a relationship with them; they may well have been his allies in wars with the Philistines. In Kings, Hiram takes the initiative in the relationship, congratulating Solomon on his accession to power (1 Kings 5:1). In Chronicles, Solomon takes the initiative in asking that Hiram continue the relationship that began with David by supporting his building projects.

The letter of Solomon comprises two sections. The first describes the grandeur of the temple. Without apology, Solomon declares this to be a temple for God, who is above all other gods, who has no real earthly dwelling, since even the heavens are insufficient for his presence (2 Chron 2:4-5). However, the temple is a representative place where incense can be burned, representing his divine presence. The second section is an appeal for craftsmen and materials. These skilled workers will join those David has already prepared. From Egypt to Mesopotamia, Lebanon was renowned for its huge cedar trees, which could reach a height of 100 feet (30 meters). The pine tree may be a collective name for several types of fir. Algumwood is not precisely identified; it was used to make supports for the temple (possibly pillars or balustrades) and musical instruments. This was imported by the Phoenicians and perhaps further processed there. Solomon in turn promises foodstuffs for the Phoenicians. A *cor* was a Babylonian measure; the homer of Canaan was an approximately equal dry measure, the amount of grain a donkey could carry. In preexilic times each was equal to about 100 liters or 3 bushels (a U.S. bushel is about 35 liters). If *cor* represents the preexilic homer, Solomon was providing about 60,000 bushels of wheat and barley. In later times, *cor* was about double that amount. A bath was about 22 liters (almost 6 U.S. gallons, or 5 imperial gallons). Solomon was providing about 100,000 imperial gallons of wine and oil. It is impossible to know how the Chronicler calculated the equivalents for his time. He would have faced all the same challenges of the modern reader if he were trying to be precise about quantities. In Chronicles, the foodstuffs are specified to be for the workers, while in Kings they are for Hiram's household.

Hiram in turn gives great praise to Solomon as the man who is worthy to succeed David and capable of carrying out all the plans that David had made for building a temple and palace. Hiram promises to send David some men skilled at every level of working with metals, wood, and cloth. In Kings, the leading skilled artisan is simply Hiram (1 Kings 7:13-14); in Chronicles, he is Huram-abi, which may include a title such as *my craftsman* (2 Chron 2:13-14). He was a Phoenician from Tyre, but his mother was an Israelite. The Chronicler says she was from Dan, while Kings says she was from Naphtali. This may be reconciled by separating her place of residence from her place of birth, or her lineage may be given through parents of two different tribes. Without doubt an important point for the Chronicler was that the skilled worker Oholiab was from Dan (Exod 31:6; 35:34). Hiram promised wood sufficient for all building requirements. The logs would be bundled in rafts, floated by sea to Joppa, and from there transported to Jerusalem. This would mean that Solomon had full control of the routes through Gezer.

Temple Structure and Furnishings 3:1–5:1

3:1-2 Founding of the Temple

The Chronicler has created his own introduction of the temple construction, which establishes a history of worship for the place on which the temple will be built. It is the place David had designated for the temple site when the plague was stopped (1 Chron 22:1), though the text does not quite say that. A strict translation would say *which he (Solomon) prepared on the site of David at the threshing floor of Araunah the Jebusite* (2 Chron 3:1 AT). But the *site of David* is not the customary designation of the temple site, nor does Solomon establish it. The usual expression is *the site that David established*, the way it reads in the Greek, which seems to be the intent of the verse.

Two designations are brought together: the threshing floor of Araunah, where the plague was stopped, and Mount Moriah, where Abraham offered Isaac to God (Gen 22:2). This is the only verse where this association is explicitly made, though it is unlikely it was created by the Chronicler. It is impossible to geographically establish the place meant in Genesis 22, but there is no doubt about the tradition of it being a sacred place of worship. The name Moriah (vision of *Yah*) is derived from verse 8 of the Genesis narrative, where Abraham responds to Isaac, saying God would see for himself a lamb for the offering. Abraham then names the place "The LORD will see" (v. 14 AT), which comes to be known as "the mountain where the LORD appeared." The mountain of the Lord as the place of the temple is found in Psalm 24:3 and Isaiah 2:3; the temple is where the Israelites appear before the Lord (Deut 16:16). David had further designated the land he purchased from Araunah (a Hittite word meaning "lord") the Jebusite king (2 Sam 24:23)—known in Chronicles as Ornan—as the temple site because there the angel of the Lord appeared when the plague was stopped. For the Chronicler this is the equivalent of a divine theophany (2 Chron 3:1): the Lord appeared to David. The place where God appeared to Abraham and to David, already in Genesis called the "mountain of the LORD" (Gen 22:14), was the place where Solomon would build the temple.

The building of the temple began in the second month, the month following the Passover celebration, in the fourth year of Solomon's reign, that is, almost immediately after Solomon had the affairs of the kingdom in order. The Chronicler makes no reference to this being 480 years after the exodus (1 Kings 6:1), an important date for the significance of the temple. For Israel, the temple represents the rule of God over all the earth (Ps 24:1), and the exodus was the time of redemption. The rule of God over Israel began in Egypt, where they became a nation. The Chronicler is particularly concerned with the sacred place and the fulfillment of the promise through David and Solomon.

3:3-7 *Structure of the Temple*

The Chronicler's description of the temple provides the dimensions of the building and a general depiction of its splendor, but it entirely lacks the detail of the structure in 1 Kings 6:4-18. A comparison of translations or their attendant notes indicates immediately that there are difficulties with the text in Chronicles. The dimensions should correspond with those found in 1 Kings 6:2-3. The temple structure was long and narrow, 60 cubits in length, 20 cubits in width, and 30 cubits high (a cubit is the length of a forearm, about half a yard/meter). The building consisted of the holy place, 20 cubits in width and 40 cubits in length. The most holy place behind the veil, which housed the cherubim, was a cube of 20 cubits. It may have been elevated, or there may have been a space above it. The temple dimensions given are twice those of the tabernacle in the wilderness. This is the structure typical of Phoenician, Canaanite, and Aramean temples, comparable with that excavated at ʿAin Dara in northern Syria (Monson). Some features of that temple help explain the somewhat opaque descriptions in Kings.

The Chronicler seems to say, as does Kings, that the porch in front of the temple spread across the entire width of the building itself. Kings adds that it was 10 cubits deep. It is possible that the original Chronicles text read this way as well. If the entrance was like that of the temple at ʿAin Dara, then the porch was integrated with the courtyard and served as a transitional passageway leading into the building. It is unlikely that the porch was 120 cubits high (2 Chron 3:4 NRSV, NIV mg.), which would have constituted a tower. This seems to be an error that came about through simple metathesis (reversal of letters), so that instead of saying "cubit," the text read the number "one hundred." The Chronicler notes that this was the standard of the old cubit; a cubit one handbreadth longer was known to Ezekiel (40:5; 43:13). In the Chronicler's time this distinction would be significant.

Chronicles refers to fine gold and gold from Parvaim (2 Chron 3:6). Not enough is known about ancient metallurgy to distinguish the different grades of gold. Parvaim seems to have been a place in Yemen from which gold was imported, but it came to mean nothing more than a special quality of gold. The particulars in Chronicles are sketchy. Kings says that pine (Cyprus tree) was only used for the floor (1 Kings 6:15), while the walls were paneled with cedar. The building was ornate: the beams, doorposts, walls, and doors were overlaid or inlaid with gold and precious stones, depending on the feature intended (Dillard 1987: 28). The carefully carved figures of cherubim, palm trees, and chain festoons (curved lattices as if suspended from two points) were probably enhanced by gold and stone gems. The reliefs were possibly covered or embellished with gold, distinguishing them on the flat surface of the surrounding walls. The quality of materials increased in proximity to the most sacred spaces. Foundries and metallurgists were often associated with temples.

3:8–5:1 Furnishings of the Temple

The central feature of the temple was the most holy place, which signified the throne room of the King of the universe. It was covered with the most precious gold, with a total weight of more than 22 tons (a talent is about 75 pounds or 30 kilograms). This is not a large number in comparison with what David amassed (1 Chron 22:14). The standard unit of measure is the shekel. In the period of the first temple, a talent was 3,000 shekels. A shekel was about 10 grams, or less than half an ounce, so 50 shekels for nails would be a very small amount to fasten the total amount of gold. But it is hardly possible to use gold for nails since it is a soft metal. It may be that the gold of the nails was used to guild the heads of the nails that held the sheets of gold in place, which were fastened to the walls. The Greek translation interprets the gold proportionately: a shekel of nails would hold in place 50 shekels of gold. It is not specified what upper room was gilded with gold, but the Chronicler had earlier referred to the upper room, inner chambers, and room of the mercy seat (1 Chron 28:11). Second Chronicles 3:8 affirms that all the chambers of the temple were gilded with gold.

The cherubim are enormous in size, filling the entire twenty cubits of the most holy space, five cubits to each wing, so one wing of the cherub touched the wall and the other touched the wing of the other cherub. Kings says these were made of wood and covered with gold (1 Kings 6:23, 28). The Chronicler uses a unique word with the meaning "form" or "shape" in Arabic, meaning they were fashioned by an overlay of gold (2 Chron 3:10). The cherubim were behind the curtain. Kings describes the doors that separated the most holy place (1 Kings 6:31-32) but makes no mention of the curtain. There was a curtain in the tabernacle as well as in the temple of the

Chronicler's day; likewise the curtain of Herod's temple was torn at the death of Jesus (Matt 27:51). If there was not a curtain in the temple Solomon built, it would be anomalous.

The two pillars naturally generate a great deal of interest, partly because they remain somewhat mysterious. They seem to be freestanding pillars in front of the porch, but what they represent is never explained. In a vision Zechariah sees chariots burst out from between two bronze mountains (Zech 6:1), which is the closest biblical reference that might be an analogy to the significance of the pillars. The prophet depicts a scene at the entrance to God's divine council. The meaning of the pillars was probably not one simple analogy, but a way of representing the rule of the Creator over the earth. The cosmos can be described as resting on pillars (Job 26:11), and in the garden of Eden, life and knowledge of God were represented by trees (Gen 2–3). All of these concepts are related. The names of the pillars are equally ambiguous: *Jakin* (it is firm) might refer to the security of the divine promise; *Boaz* (with strength) might be testimony to the strength of God for his kingdom.

The pillars are giant structures, each standing 18 cubits tall, with a large capital on the top (1 Kings 7:15; 2 Kings 25:17). The Chronicler gives a length of 35 cubits for each pillar, apparently not a reference to their height (2 Chron 3:15; NIV is incorrect to consider 35 cubits their combined length). The number is a sum of the dimensions of the pillars: 18 cubits high, 12 cubits in circumference, and 5 cubits for the height of each capital. The capitals were very elaborate. Kings describes them as having the shape of a lily, with seven sets of latticed festoons around each one, each having one hundred pomegranates suspended in two rows around the pillars (1 Kings 7:16-20). The description in Chronicles is not inconsistent, but neither explains precisely how the encircling chains are to be envisaged in relation to the capitals.

The bronze altar (2 Chron 4:1) is not described in the temple account in Kings. This is not evidence that the Chronicler has created this verse. As Rudolph observes, the author of Kings says that Solomon built the altar (1 Kings 9:25), and it is referred to several times (1 Kings 8:22, 64; 2 Kings 16:14; Rudolph: 207). The measurements are not in the Chronicler's style, indicating that this has been drawn from an available source (Williamson 1982: 210). The dimensions show that this is the base of the altar; steps would enable the priest to reach the altar itself.

The giant water container called *Sea* follows the description in Kings quite closely (2 Chron 4:2; 1 Kings 7:23-26). It was over 4 meters in diameter (15 feet) and over two meters in height (7½ feet), cast with two rows of decorative engravings beneath the rim. There are two anomalies in this description. Kings says these engravings were a gourd; Chronicles says they were like a bull. Some translations consequently read gourds in Chronicles, but this is unwarranted. The Chronicler is interpreting his text, which does not seem to have been clear to him (Willi: 139), and describes the engraving ambiguously. The Chronicler also follows the Kings text in describing the ornamentation around the circumference *for ten cubits*, which seems anomalous. Some translations correct to *thirty cubits*, the full length of the circumference (NRSV); others say there were ten to a cubit (NIV), which would make them very small on such a large structure. This is also a doubtful translation; if ten to a cubit were meant, the number should be masculine (Cogan 2001: 264). It may be that in Kings the number for the diameter of Sea in the previous verse was inadvertently repeated (cf. 1 Kings 7:23-24) and has been followed in Chronicles. The capacity of Sea is also ambiguous; Kings says it was 2,000 baths, Chronicles says it was 3,000. It is not known whether these figures were measurements or calculations. If they were calculations, the amount would have been dependent on how the shape of Sea was conceived, whether cylindrical or as a hemisphere. There is enough ambiguity within the texts themselves and the various sizes of measurements in use that all attempts at reconciliation can be successful and therefore none convincing. From the general descriptions, Sea would have contained between 11,000 and 15,000 gallons of water (a bath is about 22 liters, or between 5 and 6 gallons). It stood on top of 12 bulls facing outward, 3 in each direction, making the total height of Sea about 4 meters (12 feet) at minimum.

The water was used for washing, which was facilitated by ten smaller basins, five on the south and five on the north. These on their bases are given a much more elaborate description in Kings. Sea itself is said by the Chronicler to be for the priests, a detail not given in Kings. Kings gives no reason for the presence of Sea, suggesting that it had a confessional function as part of the entire temple structure. The earth was created from the sea (Ps 74:12-14), an association suggested by the name given to Sea. The size of Sea would not make it very practical for cleansing purposes. It is possible that the meaning and function of Sea changed over time. Its significance as a creation symbol would have been well understood within Canaanite terminology of cosmology. Psalm 74:13-14 is exemplary of such creation imagery: "You shattered Sea in your strength;

you broke the heads of the Sea Monster upon the waters; you crushed the heads of Leviathan" (AT). Such vivid creation imagery was natural when the Baal Epic held sway. The Baal Epic would have been unknown in the days of the Chronicler, however. Such imagery in his time would convey more the mystery of creation than an active polemic against Canaanite culture.

Inside the temple structure were ten menorahs. They were arranged five to each side of the holy place (south and north), made according to regulation (2 Chron 4:7). Each menorah had seven branches, three on each side of a central stem, with a lamp on top of each. There were ten tables also arranged five to a side. The function of these tables is not specified; their arrangement might suggest that the lamps stood on them. The construction of the table for the bread is not separately mentioned, so it may be that the ten tables of bread correspond to the ten lampstands. There were two courts, an inner court for the priests and a large outer court. Chronicles speaks of the bronze doors, a much less precious metal, which served as entrance to the large court. The great Sea stood on the south side of this court, in front of the temple itself, which faced east.

The summary of the artifacts made by Hiram for Solomon follows the account in Kings very closely (2 Chron 4:11–5:1; cf. 1 Kings 7:40-51). The terminology for the artifacts is that of Kings, particularly the description of the pillars and capitals. Kings describes the pillars as having bowl-shaped capitals (1 Kings 7:41). Chronicles separates these as the *bowls and the capitals* (2 Chron 4:12a MT), a hendiadys (two nouns joined by "and" rather than a noun and adjective), to be translated *bowl-shaped capitals* (NIV). This is the only description of a bowl shape (*gullah*) as part of the pillar; in Akkadian, a *gullu(m)* forms the base of a column (*AHw* 297). It may be the *gullah* is not a bowl but a bulge, the base that supports the pillar and capital. The bronze used is said to be beyond measure, smelted in the Jordan Valley just north of the Jabbok, where the thick clay was most suitable for molds. Items inside the temple are all gold to signify the sacred area. Items inside the temple included tools to service the golden altar of incense and the lamps. Tongs and wick trimmers were necessary for the oil lamps; the bowls, ladles, and fire pans were for the service of the altar, to spread fragrant aroma designating the divine presence. Not part of the artifacts were the doors that led into the most sacred space and the gold associated with them. Chronicles makes no mention of the enigmatic gold hinges or sockets in 1 Kings 7:50. It cannot be determined what architectural feature may have been meant. The reference in Kings has led to a rabbinic tradition of golden keys or perhaps some sort of latching device that formed part of a ritual entrance ceremony (Cogan 2001: 270). The Chronicler only makes reference to the entrance of sacred space. Some consider the doors to be in conflict with the violet curtain that separated the sacred space (cf. 2 Chron 3:14); they then count this as part of the reason for regarding this entire section to be a late insertion taken over from Kings.

Installation of the Ark 5:2-6:11

The elite leaders of Israel assembled for the ark processional. The description of such occasions as involving an assembly of leaders is typical of the Chronicler. The temple dedication took place in the seventh month, the most sacred month of the year, which celebrated the Feast of Tabernacles (Booths). The seventh month was the culmination of the harvest and, in the cultural world of the Bible, a celebration of creation itself. In Jewish tradition, Rabbi Eliezer and Rabbi Joshua (120-80 BCE) debated whether creation was during the fall festival (Feast of Tabernacles) or the spring festival (Passover). Both the seeds of spring and the fruits of harvest were associated with God's creative acts. The temple itself stood as a symbol of God's presence within his creation.

The Chronicler specifically makes the point that it was the *Levites*, not the priests, who brought up the ark (2 Chron 5:4), changing this one word in a passage that is otherwise copied directly from Kings (cf. 1 Kings 8:3). This follows the specific directives of David in bringing up the ark from the house of Obed-Edom (1 Chron 15:2), correcting the fatal error of mishandling the ark when he tried to bring it up from Kiriath Jearim on a cart pulled by oxen. The requirement that the Levites carry the ark is the directive found in Numbers (see esp. 4:1-15). Remarkable is his further statement that the other sacred artifacts and the tent of meeting (meaning the tabernacle, not the tent set up for the ark) were brought up by *the Levitical priests* (2 Chron 5:5). This information has been taken over from 1 Kings 8:4, though there the phrase is found as "the priests and Levites," and modern English versions often translate it that way in 2 Chronicles 5:5 (so NRSV). The phrase "priests and Levites" makes sense in Kings, where the priests carry up the ark. *Levitical priest* is a designation for priests found consistently in Deuteronomy, as may be seen in the instructions for priests in Deuteronomy 18:1-8. Deuteronomy has the distinct view that any descendant of Levi may qualify to be a priest, while elsewhere this prerogative is limited exclusively to descendants of Aaron (Tigay: 169-70). Deuteronomy 18:1 specifies that the provision for priests apply to the whole tribe of Levi. As part of the Deuteronomistic History, it makes sense for Kings to assign work of the Levites to priests, but this is a contradiction in Chronicles *[Deuteronomistic History, p. 465]*. The Chronicler, as is also true in later tradition, assumes that the distinction in Deuteronomy is more apparent than real. All priests must be Levites, but it can be assumed that Levitical priests are descendants of Aaron, without needing to specify that to be the case. The Chronicler and his readers similarly assume a consistent distinction between priests who are descendants of Aaron and all other Levites. Levitical priests may be understood in Chronicles as a secondary clergy; they are not sons of Aaron and do not function as priests that are sons of Aaron *[Priests and Levites in Chronicles, p. 471]*. Traditional interpretation, including that of Chronicles, does not regard Deuteronomy as unique. Moses is addressing how the public are to treat Levites. While all Levites are to be remunerated as priests, it is to be assumed that priests are sons of Aaron, and Levitical priests may not perform their duties. However, Deuteronomy 31:9 is specific; according to the instruction of Moses, the priests, the sons of Levi were to carry the ark. Explicit biblical statements indicate different practices. Chronicles is just one period in a long priestly history.

The actual placement of the ark in the most holy place is carried out by the priests (2 Chron 5:7), since they are the only ones allowed to entered the sacred space of the temple. The wings of the cherubim stretch over the ark, signifying an invisible firmament that supports the throne of God above it. Their wings protect the ark. An important feature is the permanence of the poles used to carry the ark, which were left in place and were visible as a priest approached the most holy place. In Kings these poles are said to be in place "until this day," a phrase retained in Chronicles. This is a characteristic phrase of the preexilic source of these materials, composed when the temple still stood and the poles protruded from the holy space (Geoghegan: 224). In the ark was nothing but the two tablets of stone representing the terms of the covenant with God, whose feet rested on the pedestal. In pentateuchal tradition the manna and Aaron's rod that budded were placed in front of the ark (Exod 16:32-34; Num 17:10-11), but not inside as is said in later traditions (Heb 9:4).

At the installation of the ark, the great celebration with all the temple musicians is a contribution of the Chronicler not found in Kings (2 Chron 5:11-13). It has all the distinctive marks of the earlier celebration of moving the ark, including the line from Psalm 106:1 (*for his mercy endures forever* [AT]), which is part of the earlier anthology (1 Chron 16:34). All the priests were sanctified, regardless of their division, since there would not have been an assignment such as this within their rotations. The 120 trumpeters are also an assembly brought together for this occasion. The unison of the voices and instruments as the ark was put in its place was attended by the descent of the glory cloud (2 Chron 5:13-14), as when the tabernacle was completed, signifying the place where God's name would be known.

The ceremony concludes with a confessional statement made by Solomon, which follows very closely its source in Kings. The words of Solomon in Kings reiterate the main themes of the Chronicler concerning the covenant with Israel and the election of David as king. This central theme from Scripture is the basis of the Chronicler's history. The temple, which David had intended to build, is now the place where the name of God dwells. Name indicates possession; in the Amarna letters it is an idiom for ownership *[Amarna Tablets, p. 464]*. Just as the Pharaoh owned Jerusalem by placing his name there, so the Lord now owns the temple and all that it represents. The repeated reference to name in this promise is to establish a memorial to perpetuate a reputation. It was customary for kings to establish the legitimacy of their rule by building or refurbishing a temple as an affirmation of the god that enabled their rule. David was denied this assurance, but in its place he received a divine promise now fulfilled. Solomon utilized the name to make the temple the ultimate symbol of the faith of the Israelites: it fulfills the promise, is the place of covenant preservation, and embodies the land promised to Israel and owned by God. The temple signifies the election of David and the choice of Jerusalem as the central place of worship.

The confession is introduced with a poem (2 Chron 6:1-2; cf. format in NJPS), like others found in Scripture (e.g., Num 21:17; Josh 10:12). The first line of this poem has been lost in the Masoretic Text. The full poem is found in the Greek text of Kings, where it is placed at the end of the prayer *[Masoretic Text, p. 470; Greek Text of Chronicles, p. 468]*.

> The Lord made manifest his sun in the heavens.
>   He has chosen to dwell in deep darkness, saying,
> "Build my house!"
>   a house fitting for you yourself,
>   that you may abide in a new way.
>   (3 Reigns 8:53 AT; cf. 1 Kings 8:12-13)

The first line provides the parallel contrast: the Lord made known his sun in the heavens, but he chose deep darkness as his dwelling, in the temple prepared for him by Solomon. As at Sinai, the presence of God is symbolized by the darkness of a cloud. The tabernacle and the temple represent a continuity with the revelation and the covenant made there. It is not possible to directly encounter the divine presence (e.g., Exod 33:17-23), because the holy and the common have no basis for comparison.

Dedication Prayer 6:12-42

The confession of Solomon concludes the ceremony of the ark installation, but it does not introduce the prayer. This is made explicit in Chronicles with the inclusion of a section describing the dais on which Solomon prayed. Solomon takes his place before the great altar to petition that the temple may serve the purpose for which it was built, to keep God's covenant central in the lives of the people. The dais was necessary for Solomon to kneel as he prayed (1 Kings 8:54), spreading his hands toward the heavens. This dais was in the great court of the people, indicated by the word used for that court, as would be expected, since this was the area of the temple that was accessible to all people.

The prayer of Solomon has a different emphasis from that in Kings. This is achieved by the alternate closing with its use of Psalm 132. The Deuteronomistic History repeatedly emphasizes the exodus as the basis for God keeping his promises *[Deuteronomistic History, p. 465]*. While this is not omitted in Chronicles, its significance is diminished by the emphasis on the fulfillment of the Davidic promise. This becomes the confirmation on which God will act.

The petitions of the prayer are appropriate for any period in the history of Israel. They are given in the language of covenant, requiring obedience and seeking forgiveness. This was the fundamental message of the Deuteronomistic History, which recounted the story of Israel by evaluating their covenant faithfulness. The circumstances anticipated in Solomon's prayer are inevitable in human life and relationships. The first concerns oaths to determine guilt and innocence, a fundamental challenge of governing with justice. The second addresses attacks from an enemy, one of the curses that comes because of covenant failure. Drought was also one of the curses that might fall when the people were unfaithful. Famine is frequently associated with drought, though it may also be the consequence of war. Grasshoppers regularly accompany drought; at least ten terms are used to describe the various species and molting stages of the locust, indicating the indelible impression they made. All these conditions are the occasion of personal suffering and victimization. In keeping with the universal nature of God's rule and his care for all people, prayer is also made for the foreigners, those who see that the divine teaching of Israel is the wisdom of all nations (Deut 4:1-8). Exile is the ultimate consequence of covenant disobedience; it is anticipated in the Pentateuch and is part of Solomon's prayer. The words "take captive" (*šbh*) and "repent" or "return" (*šwb*) are homonyms in certain forms and become a matter of wordplay for the Chronicler in appealing for repentance (2 Chron 6:36-39). If enemies take them captive (*šabum šobehem*) because of their sin, for everyone sins, but in that land they wholeheartedly turn in their minds (*hešibu*), and turn toward the city God has chosen (*šabu*), then may God hear and forgive. The captivity motif was painfully relevant on many occasions in the history of Israel.

The prayer closes with a quotation of Psalm 132:8-10, calling attention to David's deep passion for the restoration of the ark to its proper function. "Arise, O LORD" is a military cry given in Numbers 10:35-36 (NRSV). God arises to scatter the enemies when the people move, and returns as the Lord of Israel's myriads of thousands when they rest. The ark is the ultimate symbol of God's rest, his claim to the land that carries his name. David seeks a resting place for the ark, the place where the throne of God rises and he is worshiped by the hosts of Israel. The impact of Psalm 132 is increased by two changes in this citation. In 2 Chronicles 6:42 the lines from verse 10 of the psalm are reversed, placing an emphasis on the faithfulness of God. Second, part of the last line is drawn from Isaiah 55:3, which makes reference to the mercies of David. This phrase can be taken in two ways: (1) it may be the mercies David receives, or (2) it may be the mercies that God gives through David—which is meant in both Isaiah and Chronicles (NIV). The mercies of David express loyalty to a commitment made. Loyalty to promises is the best way of showing mercy. God's loyalty through his promises to David has just been demonstrated, providing assurance that these mercies are available for Israel.

Consecration of the Temple 7:1-22

7:1-11 Affirmation and Celebration

This passage is divided into three parts by the double occurrence of the refrain *He is good, his mercy endures forever* (2 Chron 7:3, 6). This refrain is found previously with the praises that accompanied the installation of the ark (2 Chron 5:13). It is taken from Psalm 106:1, one of the hymns sung when David brought the ark up to Jerusalem (1 Chron 16:34). The first section describes divine affirmation of the ark's installation; fire from heaven consumes the sacrifices made to celebrate the event (cf. 2 Chron 5:6; 7:3). Fire from heaven was the sign of divine approval when David determined that this was the site on which the temple would be built (1 Chron 21:26; 22:1). The cloud and fire are reminiscent of Mount Sinai, which was covered with the black cloud and blazed with fire when the divine words of the covenant were given (Exod 19:18). Displays of fire from heaven unite all these events in expressing God's presence. As at Mount Sinai, all the people worship in humility, bowing to the ground. The second division enumerates the sacrifices of the festivities and describes the proceedings of the celebration of worship. Blowing trumpets, the priests stood at their stations, opposite the Levites, who were making music with Davidic instruments. All the people stood at attention in reverence. The third section provides details of the whole festal period (2 Chron 7:7-11). The two events of dedicating the altar and celebrating the Feast of Booths lasted for fifteen days (7:9), double the usual length of the fall festival.

The Festival of Booths began on the fifteenth day of the month and concluded on the twenty-second day (Lev 23:34-36). An eighth day, called (like the first day) a *solemn assembly*, concluded the celebration. The people were dismissed on the twenty-third day (2 Chron 7:10), after the conclusion of the eighth day. In the Chronicler's version of events, the dedication of the altar had begun seven days before the commencement of the festival. The Chronicler never makes mention of the Day of Atonement, which occurs on the tenth day of the seventh month (Lev 16:29-31) and would have been during the first week of festivities. This was not a usual circumstance. It would not have been possible to observe a customary Day of Atonement since the ark itself was being dedicated in its new location.

The sacrifices served for the entire fifteen days of the two festivities. The large numbers correspond to the size of the assembly. Pilgrims to the festival came from the farthest reaches of the Davidic kingdom. It extended from the town Lebweh (NIV, *Lebo Hamath*, v. 8), at the source of the Orontes River in Aramea (Aram Zoba of David's conquests), to the Brook of Egypt, identified as Wadi el-ʿArish, which marks the southern extent of Judah. These are the ideal boundaries of Israel, as already anticipated in the covenant with Abraham (Gen 15:18). The number of sacrifices would have required twenty sacrifices a minute for ten hours a day for twelve days (Wenham: 49). The numbers may be hyperbole, an emphasis of the grandeur of the event. To accommodate the large number of offerings, Solomon used the fitted stones of the court floor because the huge altar (about 30 feet or 10 meters square) was too small (cf. 2 Chron 4:1). The center of the court served as the equivalent of a high place, which was constructed with a fitted stone platform and an altar. Communal peace offerings introduce the other sacrifices and appear to be the central aspect of the dedication. The main function of these offerings was to provide food for the table. These sacrifices were meant to be joyous occasions of celebration (Milgrom 1991: 220-21). Worshipers and priests share the peace offerings, providing a bonding of the community and a celebration of the covenant (Lev 7:11-15, 30-36). The blood, fat, and entrails of the peace offering are all devoted to God.

The Chronicler concludes this unit on the dedication festivities with a note on building completion that has been adapted from Kings (2 Chron 7:11). In 1 Kings 9:1 this is a subordinate clause introducing the account of the Lord's appearance at Gibeon. The Chronicler has altered it to be an independent sentence, enabling him to begin an entirely new unit with the divine message of the vision. Chronicles is really about dedication rather than the building, but the verse still serves as closure to this passage. The Chronicler will provide his own conclusion to the building project at 2 Chronicles 8:16.

7:12-22 Instruction and Exhortation

The second night vision at Gibeon occurs after Solomon completed all his building projects (2 Chron 7:11), which was twenty years after the previous assembly at Gibeon (1:3). The first vision was before the seven years of temple building (1 Kings 6:37) and another thirteen years of building projects (7:1; 9:10). If these building projects were in sequence, as seems to be the case in the Deuteronomistic presentation (cf. 9:10), and if the ark installation took place immediately when the temple was completed, this vision is thirteen years after the festivities celebrating the ark. The Chronicler makes no reference to Gibeon on this occasion of the night vision. He has fashioned God's response to correspond to the prayer at the altar dedication, naming several of the future conditions that may pertain because of sin: drought, grasshoppers, and pestilence (2 Chron 7:13). Human responsibility in response to these situations is fashioned entirely in the theology and terminology of the Chronicler (v. 14). Essentially the Chronicler thinks in terms of immediate retribution; these calamities are the signs of a need for repentance. The vocabulary of humbling, praying, turning, seeking, and healing will appear repeatedly in the accounts of the following kings as this formula for restoration is shown to be at work.

One of the most prominent examples is Hezekiah. In the very first month of his reign, he began to restore the temple (2 Chron 29:3). He extended an invitation to all Israel, especially those in the north, to come to a Passover at Jerusalem (30:1). Those from the north were not ritually ready to observe the Passover. The messengers of Hezekiah urged them to turn to the Lord (v. 6); many humbled themselves and came to Jerusalem (v. 11). So many arrived that there was insufficient preparation to accommodate them all. Hezekiah prayed for all the people because he saw they were resolved to seek the Lord (vv. 18-19). In spite of the irregularities, the Lord healed them (v. 20), so the festival had to be extended another seven days (v. 23). Hezekiah followed the principles stated here and became a primary example of the power of receiving forgiveness and healing.

The remainder of the vision's message has some notable differences from the account in Kings. The Chronicler repeats the assurance that this is the place God has chosen (2 Chron 7:16); he refers to the Davidic promise as a covenant that God has made (v. 18), rather than just a word spoken. He also makes a change to say there will always be a successor to *rule over* Israel, as opposed to a successor *on the throne* of Israel (1 Kings 2:4; 8:25). This change brings his words into conformity with the promise of Micah 5:2, which is a prophetic affirmation of the promise to David. This indicates the Chronicler's hope for a transformed kingdom, as prophesied by Micah. Finally, the exhortation to faithfulness is not limited to Solomon and his descendants, but is in the plural, to include all the leaders present (2 Chron 7:18-22). Previously the conditions for blessing king and leaders were kept separate, but now after the dangers have been spelled out, they are brought together. Although the full horrors of loss of national sovereignty and exile are listed, there is no suggestion that this will threaten the dynastic promise.

Military and Labor Provisions 8:1-16

In this section the material of Kings is modified to serve the centrality of the temple in Chronicles. The details of Solomon's kingdom serve as a support to the function of his building projects, much as the notes about Hiram in chapter 2 were part of the preparations for temple building. The note in Kings about the annual pilgrimages to the temple in 1 Kings 9:25 is significantly expanded in 2 Chronicles

8:13-16 to name the pilgrimage festivals, to affirm the work of the Levitical divisions in music and security, and their assistance to the priests as David prescribed in every matter, with special mention of the treasuries. The whole is then concluded with a closing statement on all the building activities.

8:1-6 Economic and Military Activities

At the end of twenty years of building, the economic alliance with Hiram of Tyre continued with exchanges of property and money. The Chronicler says that *Solomon rebuilt the villages that Hiram had given him*, an account about which we have no other record. It is possible that this alludes to the twenty cities Solomon gave Hiram in response to cedar, juniper, and gold received and about which Hiram was not pleased (1 Kings 9:11-13). The circumstances regarding this record cannot be recovered. Willi observes a number of variants in this passage between the various versions, including the unique reference to Tadmor (see below on 2 Chron 8:3-4), and concludes that the *Vorlage* of the Chronicler did say that Hiram gave Solomon cities (Willi: 75-78) *[Vorlage, p. 468]*. The Greek translator of Kings complemented the text with reference to Pharaoh's daughter, but otherwise it reads as the MT. It is scarcely credible that the Chronicler simply altered the record to enhance the image of Solomon. The scriptural records of Solomon were well known and could not simply be contradicted. The historical circumstance has been abbreviated, but there will have been various economic exchanges. The cities given as payment were unsatisfactory to Hiram. He may have given them back to Solomon for payment, or Solomon may have temporarily given them to Hiram as collateral until his debts were liquidated, at which time they were returned.

This passage (2 Chron 8:3-6) is the only record in Chronicles of the military activities of Solomon, the man of peace (1 Chron 22:9). The kingdoms of David and Solomon extended to Hamath, far north of Damascus, on the Orontes River. Tou, the ruler of Hamath, sought the support of David against Hadadezer the king of Zobah (18:9-10). Hadadezer is also referred to as the king of Zobah-Hamath (18:3). Solomon was obliged to conduct an expedition in this territory to maintain the security of his northern border. There is no report of any military engagement. Tadmor is the later Palmyra, an oasis city in Syria, 120 miles northeast of Damascus and along the desert trade route connecting with Mesopotamia. This city is not mentioned anywhere else in the Bible. At some point it came to be identified with the list of fortified cities of Solomon's kingdom given in 1 Kings

9:18, where it is the vocalized reading of the MT. It is also found in a number of versions. Tadmor is geographically incongruous in the context of Kings. The consonantal text of Kings names Tamar as a significant point in the southern part of the kingdom, the last of a series of fortifications beginning with Hazor in the north and moving southward. The Chronicler has compiled his own account of Solomon's kingdom. He describes the northern reaches of Solomon's kingdom, in the territory of Aram. Control over Hamath and Tadmor would assure sovereignty over the main trade routes to Mesopotamia.

Upper Beth Horon and Lower Beth Horon sit astride a ridge, which rises from the Valley of Aijalon and extends to the plateau north of Jerusalem. Fortifications were important to protect the route that connected Jerusalem to the major coastal trade route. Certain cities served for storage and for military cavalry. Large building complexes at Hazor, Beth Shemesh, and Megiddo consist of a long room, with two rows of pillars dividing it into three sections. They may have been used as stables and storehouses, or may have been barracks for a professional army. Baalath, originally assigned to the tribe of Dan (Josh 15:9), is probably the city also known as Kiriath Jearim, on the western boundary of Judah.

8:7-10 Labor Provisions

The Chronicler is clear in his statements that native Israelites were not a part of conscripted labor. Two categories of labor must be distinguished. There were those under a levy for transporting materials in building projects, discussed earlier, in the preparations for temple building (2 Chron 2:1, 17). Others were part of the corvée who served the state as a compulsory labor force. Solomon's conscripted labor force consisted of 10,000 men who served in rotations of one month out of every three months (1 Kings 5:13-14); separate from this forced labor were 70,000 porters and 80,000 quarrymen in the mountains (v. 15). In this passage the Chronicler refers to regular labor rotations of the corvée that serve *until this day* (2 Chron 8:8), meaning that these were under perpetual royal obligation. From an early time, corvée is well attested across the whole Mesopotamian region. These men were given wages of some type, like other personnel in royal service, and did their work outside that capital, sometimes outside the country (Rainey 1970: 192–93). The Chronicler states unequivocally that corvée labor was not derived from native Israelites, but from the subjugated population that chose not to become Israelite. The expansion of the kingdom brought in whole new categories of aliens who were absorbed into the people of Israel.

Laborers under the levy were possibly drawn from the aliens who had become Israelite and hence may not have been native-born Israelites. Other groups did not attain this status and were subjected to the corvée.

Those serving in the corvée were under commissioned officers (2 Chron 8:10). Corvée labor included military service in some texts. Some of the corvée might have been under military leaders listed over the soldiers, commissioners over military officers, and commanders over chariotry and cavalry. The numbers given are disparate: 250 in Chronicles and 550 in Kings. A similar disparity is found in the commissioners over the levy: 3,600 in 2 Chronicles 2:16; 3,300 in 1 Kings 5:30. Such textual differences of numbers are impossible to reconcile.

8:11-16 Temple Worship

The Chronicler has not included earlier references to Solomon's alliance with Egypt through marrying Pharaoh's daughter. These occur repeatedly in Kings (1 Kings 3:1; 9:16, 24; 11:1). Such an alliance signifies the greatness of his kingdom and his international influence, though it is difficult to be sure that the Chronicler was so impressed. The daughter of Pharaoh is mentioned only in the context of the function of the temple, the Chronicler's primary concern. Solomon's action in moving Pharaoh's daughter to her own residence is in the context of the completion of his building activity. The installation of the ark has created a new situation. Solomon knew well the dangers of inappropriate contact with the holy and takes all possible precaution.

The temporal particle in 2 Chronicles 8:12 (*Then* in ESV, NRSV) expresses the new situation: the temple is now functioning in a normalized manner. The Chronicler first clarifies the statement in 1 Kings 9:25 that Solomon burned incense, which could be taken to refer to the altar inside the temple itself. It may be that the text should say that Solomon offered incense with his fire offering (Cogan 2001: 305). The Chronicler makes clear that Solomon's offerings were outside the temple itself. The Chronicler further affirms that Solomon instituted temple worship precisely as David had prescribed, with all the officials performing their duties in the orders assigned. The closing statement on the work of the temple from start to finish provides closure to the statement in 2 Chronicles 2:1 that it was Solomon's intent to build a temple.

THE TEXT IN BIBLICAL CONTEXT

The Presence of the Holy in the World of the Common

The temple is a confession of the presence of a holy God within creation. The absolute holiness of God is represented by the separation of his throne room from the holy place. The table of the bread, the menorah, and the etchings of the tree of life on the walls are all designed to represent the created order, over which God is king. The temple is an image of the cosmos. Its lights are those of the starry heavens, an image used to describe God's creation of the heavens in Genesis 1:14-16. The luminaries function to mark time, God's ongoing care for the universe, and his rule in the midst of the starry host. The temple is regarded as a fountain of life for its people:

> They feast on the abundance of your house;
>   you give them drink from your river of delights.
> For with you is the fountain of life;
>   in your light we see light. (Ps 36:8-9)

The last of the Ascent Psalms suggests that the creation of heaven and earth is represented in the temple in Zion. Those going on or off night watch are invited to bless the God of the temple:

> Lift up your hands in the sanctuary,
>   and bless Yahweh.
> May Yahweh bless you from Zion,
>   Maker of heaven and earth. (Ps 134:2-3 AT)

The metaphor of the poetry is that Zion (the temple) represents the cosmos, the true temple created as the residence of the great king.

The metaphorical depiction of Psalm 134 is made explicit in the prophets:

> Heaven is my throne,
>   and the earth is my footstool.
> Where is the house you will build for me?
>   Where will my resting place be?
> Has not my hand made all these things,
>   and so they came into being? (Isa 66:1-2)

Creation serves as the palace of the divine King. Those who would build a temple in the world bring him no glory if they neglect the ethical implications of his cosmic rule. The temple as a confession of God's universal rule makes natural the expression "the fear of the LORD" as the metaphor for faith (e.g., Deut 10:12-16). The God of the temple is the Judge of the whole earth. Failure to understand the absolute rule of the Creator and the uncompromising nature of his judgment is to forfeit a right to life itself. The prophet Habakkuk understood this clearly (Hab 2:7-20). He warns the Chaldean who thinks he can build his net secure and plunder the lives of all the nations around so their inhabitants are caught like a fish in a massive net (1:14-17). A series of woes express the judgment that is to come against such a tyrant, concluding with a doxology: "The LORD is in his holy temple; let all the earth be silent before him" (Hab 2:20). The temple is the cosmos; there is no escape from his judgment. God rules his hosts on earth when they remain in relationship with him, just as he rules the hosts of his palatial abode.

This concept of the temple adds force to the lengthy prayers of Solomon. The petition of Solomon for Israel and all peoples makes the temple the place of prayer from which they call to the Creator of the universe. The dedication prayer expresses the condition under which prayer may be made efficacious. In seeking the face of God, it is necessary to be humble; earthly citizens are in every way subservient to the Creator. But petitions made with such an attitude of trust have an unfailing response: God will hear from heaven and will heal (2 Chron 7:14). The eyes of the Lord are ever open to the place that makes confession of his dominion in all the earth.

THE TEXT IN THE LIFE OF THE CHURCH

The Temple Built by the Spirit

In postexilic times the temple was of great controversy because it came to represent temporal power more than a place of prayer or confession of God as King of creation. Those alienated from the physical temple developed an alternate concept of temple. The equivalent of a constitution of the Qumran Sectarians (Community Rule, 1QS; 4Q255–264a; 5Q11) describes their *Yahad* as twelve laymen and three priests (1QS 8.1). When such men as these come to be in Israel,

> then shall the party of the *Yahad* truly be established, an "eternal planting," a temple for Israel, and—mystery!—a Holy of Holies for Aaron; true witnesses to justice, chosen by God's will to atone for the land and to recompense the wicked their due. They will be "the tested wall, the precious cornerstone" [Isa 28:16] whose foundations shall neither be shaken

nor swayed, a fortress, a Holy of Holies for Aaron, all of them knowing the Covenant of Justice and thereby offering a sweet savor. (1QS 8.5-9; Wise, Abegg, and Cook: 129)

The concept of the people being the temple is the way the church is described, but it has a precedent. It is a novel idea within Scripture, but it was not created by the apostles. It was simply applied by the apostles to those who are the followers of Jesus.

The concept of worship around a temple may seem distant and foreign to many contemporary Christians, but it was not so for the writers of the New Testament. Christians are citizens of the household of God, established "on the foundation of the apostles and prophets," Jesus Christ being the "chief cornerstone," in whom the whole edifice is bonded together, growing into "a holy temple in the Lord," in whom they are constructed together to be the dwelling place of God by the Spirit (Eph 2:19b-22). Paul moves irresistibly into describing the church as a temple. The temple of the Chronicler could no longer have a function once the Word had come to tabernacle in the world (John 1:14), incarnating the glory of God in the midst of humanity. The presence of that Word abides in the function of the church. In the mind of the apostle, the church is not an abstract concept; it is concretely visible in the congregations of Christians. These congregations individually and collectively are the temple in the description of Paul. The faithful come to the Lord as living stones, erected as a spiritual temple, "a holy priesthood, offering spiritual sacrifices acceptable to God through Jesus Christ" (1 Pet 2:4-5). Christians are both the temple and the priests; they are the musicians offering the sacrifice of praise. Alternately, they are "the elect, a kingdom of priests, a holy nation, a treasured people, declaring the praises of the one who called them out of darkness into his marvelous light" (cf. v. 9).

The concept of all Israel as a nation of priests was familiar to the Chronicler (Exod 19:9). He would have agreed that the Israel of his day could be so conceived. But his concern was the function of Israel, being what they were created to be. They are a community of worship, not primarily defined by economic and social solidarity. Levites and priests are at its center, leading in worship. But their function is kept in perspective by the presence of the other tribes, their individual relationships established by the preeminence of Judah, and the promise it embodied as the tribe of the one divinely anointed (Ps 2:6). Christian faith will advance in understanding as believers come to embrace the vision of Chronicles for the kingdom of God.

The gathering of the church as a congregation is essential in biblical theology. The church is never an abstraction of individual people. The church is a community bonded in covenant to one another, to support each other and to give glory to God. Individuals are to glorify God in every word spoken and every deed done. The church is to glorify God, not only in the love members show to each other, but also in their collective sacrifice of praise. There is a tradition that this be done in a building suitable to the glory of God. Historically, stained-glass windows and steeples are an aspect of enhancing worship. This has a role in identifying the congregation as the temple, the presence of God in his creation as all creation awaits its redemption (Rom 8:19-21). The times and the manner in which the church is visibly present as the temple are not specified. Christianity is truly cross-cultural in that respect. But just as baptism and communion are the universal confession of faith, so the giving of praise in congregational worship is the manifestation of God ruling his world. The church of the new covenant becomes the temple of the older covenant.

2 Chronicles 8:17-9:31
Grandeur of Solomon's Kingdom

PREVIEW

Presidents work to have a strong finish. When a president knows that this is a final term, particular effort is made to leave achievements that will be a final legacy. Ideally, leaders leave a contribution that is perpetually associated with their name. Winnipeg, the home city of the author, was perpetually plagued with flooding. A premier by the name of Duff Roblin had the foresight, in spite of considerable opposition, to build a bypass for the Red River. In his honor, it will forever be Duff's Ditch. The Chronicler depicts a kingdom of grandeur that had international fame.

This concluding section on Solomon has its counterpart in the introduction in 2 Chronicles 1. In the vision at Gibeon, Solomon asked for wisdom and knowledge to bring justice as he led the people. Solomon used his wisdom and wealth for building the temple. He is now rewarded with an ever-greater abundance of these gifts, with an accompanying esteem in the sight of all the surrounding nations. Correct priorities brought about national reward for David. The converse was true for Saul. This lesson is of great significance for the Chronicler and is repeatedly illustrated.

The close association between the first and last sections may be observed through the substantial repetition of the account of military trade with Kue and Egypt (9:25-28; cf. 1:14-17). This entire section follows 1 Kings 9:26–10:29 without any substantial omissions or additions. The incorporation of the last portion of this section in the introductory chapter is a concrete literary marker providing an inclusio for the reign of Solomon *[Inclusio, p. 467]*. The Chronicler omits 1 Kings 11 entirely, except for the summary of Solomon's reign (1 Kings 11:41-43; 2 Chron 9:29-31). The remainder of 1 Kings 11 narrates the dissension and conflict that came at the end of Solomon's reign. For the Chronicler, none of this compromised the wisdom and wealth of Solomon exemplified in his completing all the plans that David had made.

OUTLINE
Maritime Activities, 8:17-18
Exchange with the Queen of Sheba, 9:1-12
Royal Pageantry, 9:13-20
Commercial and Military Trade, 9:21-28
Epitaph, 9:29-31

EXPLANATORY NOTES
Maritime Activities 8:17-18
Two of Solomon's international contacts are described in great detail: Hiram to the north and the queen of Sheba to the south. Hiram had a treaty with Solomon that provided for long-term economic and political security. The Chronicler shows the extent of Solomon's empire by discussing his activities in the most northern and southern borders.

Solomon had control of ports to the Red Sea, which provided for international trade to the south. Ophir is traditionally thought to be southwest Arabia. It is associated with the queen of Sheba (cf. 1 Kings 10:10-12), and is located there in the table of nations (Gen 10:28-29). The Phoenicians had extensive trade networks, were expert mariners, and so were a very valuable alliance to Solomon. The Chronicler says that Hiram provided the ships for Solomon, making Hiram a subordinate partner supplying everything. This change from Kings has practical ramifications; how did Hiram get ships to Elath? Such questions do not concern the Chronicler, whose motive is to portray the relationship between the two states.

Exchange with the Queen of Sheba 9:1-12
The visit of the queen of Sheba was a onetime event with personal and direct interaction. Ancient Saba (roughly modern Yemen) was

noted for important female rulers and also for a wealthy economy based on trade in frankincense and myrrh. Trade in these aromatic resins would have been worthy of the queen's attention.

The unusual grandeur of Solomon's court was not merely a demonstration of his wealth but especially of his wisdom. The Hebrew text does not refer to his sacrifices (as in Kings), but to his *upper room* (2 Chron 9:4), which does not fit the context (see NIV mg.). The word may have its later sense of his procession going up to the temple.

The queen presented Solomon with an amount of gold equal to that received from Hiram (cf. 1 Kings 9:14). Frankincense and myrrh were in high demand for use in cosmetics and embalming, as well as in religious offerings. High demand and repeated taxation in the long route made them as valuable as gold in gifts for a king (cf. Matt 2:11). Solomon's wealth is indicated by the enormous gift the queen needed to give to be appropriate for the occasion.

The ships of Hiram also brought algumwood, used to make supports for the temple (possibly pillars or balustrades) and musical instruments. Algum is well known in ancient writings (Ugaritic and Akkadian); its exact identity is uncertain, but it was a hard reddish-brown wood.

Royal Pageantry 9:13-20

The gold Solomon received in one year may have been the income in one particular year rather than an annual income. Solomon also collected taxes from foreign traders and local merchants (2 Chron 9:14). Kings of Arabia were probably merchant princes who used the routes from Edom to Damascus, and governors of the land were district officials.

Ornamental and ceremonial shields are well attested in ancient Syria and Assyria. Large shields were body length, possibly three sided; small shields were a light protection worn on the arm. Guards displayed the shields as the king went up to the temple.

The throne of Solomon was a work of grandeur. The six steps may indicate that the throne was situated on a platform, which constituted the seventh step. Babylonian temple towers were built in seven stages to represent the entire cosmos. Ascent to the throne may have represented sovereign order in the world. Lion figures stood at the sides of each step and beside each of the armrests. The throne had ivory inlays and was covered with gold.

Commercial and Military Trade 9:21-28

"Tarshish ships" (NIV, *trading ships*) describe the kind of ship used to transport cargo. These vessels were distinguished by their strength, large size, and peculiar shape, which allowed them to sail long distances in the open sea. Tarshish is also a place, though it cannot be certainly identified; in certain references it seems to be simply generic of distant places. The Chronicler was probably aware of Tarshish ships, but speaks of ships going to Tarshish from Ezion Geber (the only place where he locates ships for Solomon; 2 Chron 8:17-18; cf. 20:36-37). Perhaps the Chronicler used the term to simply indicate the farthest reaches of shipping. The identity of the imports is uncertain. *Ivory* translates a rare term, which is associated with a Sanskrit word meaning "elephant." This identification is suspicious in a language that has a common word for ivory. The reference may be to ebony, a black wood highly valued for carving that comes from trees in southern India and Sri Lanka. The word customarily translated *apes* appears in late Akkadian but may ultimately be derived from Egyptian. *Peacocks* (NRSV; NIV, *baboons*) may be a loanword of Indian origin; the Syriac, Arabic, and Targums translate this as *peacocks*.

Solomon's trade in horses is discussed in 2 Chronicles 1:14-17. The numbers involved cannot be reconciled or restored. They are a "thicket of textual difficulties" (Dillard 1987: 74). The 40,000 stalls for chariot horses of 1 Kings 4:26 is completely out of proportion with the other numbers. Four thousand stalls for chariot horses in 2 Chronicles 9:25 is a number complementary to 1,400 chariots in 1:14 (cf. 1 Kings 10:26). Assuming one horse to a stall and teams of two, the ratio of 4,000 horses to 1,400 chariots would allow for spare animals and may be representative of the chariotry and cavalry involved.

Epitaph 9:29-31

Among his sources, the Chronicler appears to have used collections of prophetic materials. These collections seem to have been incorporated into anthologies or annalistic sources. The names of individual prophets may have been portions of the larger collection (Rainey 1997: 38). All these materials are too critical of the monarchy for them to have been the official archives of kings. On the other hand, it is likely that prophets compiling these records would have had access to official records. Gad, David's seer (1 Chron 21:9), would have been one such prophet. Heman, head of one of the music guilds, is also called *the king's seer* (25:5). Nathan and Ahijah were active in the days of David and Solomon. Iddo the seer is also cited as an authority for the reigns of Rehoboam (2 Chron 12:15), and Abhijah (13:22). Nothing is known of his personal activities, but his vision concerning Jeroboam son of Nebat has led to his identity as the prophet who spoke against the altar in 1 Kings 13, an identification already made by Josephus who refers to him as Jadon (*Ant.* 8.231).

THE TEXT IN BIBLICAL CONTEXT
The Kingdom as a Divine Blessing

The Chronicler wanted to highlight the glory of Solomon's kingdom under God's grace in Israel. His goal was to present this era as the realization of an ideal in fulfillment of the promise to David. He has recast the narrative of Solomon as found in Kings to end with the splendor of Solomon's kingdom, a testimony to his divinely ordained wisdom and blessing. Three elements compromise Solomon's rule and result in disaster for his reign: (1) the importation of Egyptian horses and chariots, (2) intermarriage with Pharaoh's daughter (and other wives), and (3) the influence of Egyptian rule. The Chronicler does take account of all three elements (Jeon: 241–69). The Chronicler mentions Pharaoh's daughter in 2 Chronicles 8:11 in the context of not compromising the sanctity of the temple and palace. The Chronicler's inclusion of this note is an indication that he and his readers are well aware of this compromise. The importation of horses and chariots is described in 2 Chronicles 1:16-17 as part of the description of Solomon's economic activities. Two important distinctions must be observed in the Chronicler's approach. The first is that Solomon's engagement with Egypt is made prominent immediately in the introduction of his reign. The second is the disclosure that intermarriage with Pharaoh's daughter was a problem for Solomon. Both of these items negatively qualify his reign.

The Deuteronomistic History presents these elements as affecting Solomon at the end of his reign *[Deuteronomistic History, p. 465]*. This must be regarded as a schematic presentation. The objective of the prior history was to show how covenant failure resulted in the disasters that followed. Events are construed so that the failure of the covenant is made evident to the reader. The reality is that Solomon's rule was compromised from the beginning. Intermarriage with Pharaoh's daughter and provision of a separate residence for her is already indicated in 1 Kings 3:1-3, but it is glossed as not being a problem. Solomon loved the Lord, following in all the regulations of David his father. The negative notation in the early part of Solomon's reign is that he allowed the high places to flourish, a constant concern in the Deuteronomistic History. But the high places do not figure in the description of the demise of Solomon's rule. Solomon is in conflict from the invasion of foreign powers and revolt within his own reign, led by Jeroboam. In Kings, these elements are presented at the end of Solomon's reign, depicting his failure to keep the covenant.

The Chronicler does not present a contrasting view of Solomon so much as he shapes the story to emphasize the divine blessing. Both he and his readers are well aware of the compromises and failures in the rule of Solomon, which are included within the Chronicler's account. But they are included as a part of the description of Solomon's achievements. The message would seem to be that God may bless in spite of these compromises, though it will become clear that there are consequences. But the Chronicler does show one aspect of the rule of Solomon that is not to be forgotten: God is faithful to his word, and the blessing of David has its effect.

THE TEXT IN THE LIFE OF THE CHURCH

World at War, Church at Peace

The description of Solomon's kingdom is not recalling fond memories from an idealized past. They represent an eschatological program and give expression to the hope of many in the restoration community, a day when the nations would once again make their pilgrimage to Jerusalem (Dillard 1987: 72–73). The prophet Zechariah provides quite a different description of the ideal king. He comes on a donkey, removes all chariots and horses for war, proclaims peace to the nations, and rules from sea to sea (Zech 9:9-10). The connection with Solomon is not to be missed. Zechariah adopts a line from a prayer for the king in Psalm 72:8: "His dominion will be from sea to sea, and from the river to the ends of the earth" (AT). Solomon does represent the kingdom of God. This prayer for the king is that he may be endowed with justice, that the mountains will bring prosperity to the people (Ps 72:1-3). This is the kind of king the Chronicler has portrayed. The realities of history make evident that the ideals of Psalm 72 are to be anticipated in the future, but they are exemplified in the past.

The followers of Jesus were considerably challenged by the orientation required to understand his message of the kingdom. The depiction of an ideal kingdom in Chronicles led naturally to the expectation of temporal rule with the coming of Messiah. But the Chronicler is far removed from the kind of messianic domination over all other nations depicted in the Targums (the Aramaic translations of the Torah and prophets). The Chronicler's vision is much closer to that of Isaiah 2:2-4, where all nations are drawn to the mountain of the Lord, to learn from his ways. Then they beat their swords into plowshares. Peace between the nations is the way to prosperity, not military power to conquer nations. According to the Chronicler, Solomon is a peacemaker: he qualifies to build the temple.

Jesus came to show how the church as the kingdom of God in this world could engage in the kind of peacemaking that is to represent the rule of God. But Jesus fulfills the promise to David in ways the Chronicler could not anticipate. The disciples of Jesus serving in the kingdom of God would not seek to create a kingdom of temporal power. Their peacemaking would be within the conflicted arena of human society, where they would frequently be victims of political change. This has repeatedly happened in the history of the church and still is happening in countries around the world today.

The plight of Christians in the Middle East is a painful example of the church suffering in conflict and war. Revolutions in Libya, Egypt, Syria, and Iraq in the second decade of the twenty-first century have been devastating to the Christian church. Christians have been driven from country to country, their churches plundered, their lives and families constantly under threat, as they often suffer death. The same is true in many African countries such as Nigeria and Sudan. But this should not be surprising; Christians living in comfort should be warned. No follower of Jesus is immune from the threat of temporal powers. Faithfulness to Jesus will bring about the peace of God's kingdom, the kind of peace the Chronicler sought to depict in his description of Solomon's reign. This is not a lost hope, but one that all followers of Jesus are taught to embrace. It will be the kind of transformation that leads the apostle John to describe it as a new heaven and earth (Rev 21:1-2). Whatever that may mean in the metaphors of apocalyptic vision, it includes the kind of kingdom the Chronicler envisaged for his people.

Part 5

Israel until the Exile of the North

2 Chronicles 10:1–28:27

OVERVIEW

With the accession of Rehoboam, *all Israel* responded to the prospect of being subjected to the rule of Solomon's son:

> What heritage have we in David?
>   What inheritance in the son of Jesse?
> Each to your home, O Israel.
>   Now look to your house, O David! (2 Chron 10:16b AT)

It has been assumed that for the Chronicler *all Israel* after this point is constituted solely by Judah and Benjamin (von Rad 1930: 24, 30–32; see vv. 1, 3, 16a). It would seem that the Chronicler affirms the loss of the other tribes.

Two verses in the account of Rehoboam are important to this argument. Immediately upon the secession of ten tribes to Jeroboam, the prophet Shemaiah is mandated to speak to Rehoboam and *all Israel in Judah and Benjamin*. The alteration from "all the house of Judah and Benjamin" in 1 Kings 12:23 to *all Israel in Judah and Benjamin* in 2 Chronicles 11:3 is a conscious alteration from the source of the Chronicler. A second pivotal reference is found in 2 Chronicles 12:1b, where it is said that Rehoboam *abandoned the Torah of Yahweh and all Israel with him* (AT). This verse is unique to the Chronicler. It equates the kingdom of Rehoboam with Israel. Von Rad believed this to be unequivocal evidence that for the Chronicler, after the Babylonian exile, those living in Judah and Benjamin constituted all Israel. Other verses can be adduced to support this concept. In 2 Chronicles 28:19, Ahaz, king of Judah, is said to be *king of Israel*. Idolatry becomes the downfall of Ahaz and all Israel in verse 23. In some sense Judah does constitute Israel, even before the exile of the northern tribes. Von Rad uses as his strongest argument the lack of reference to the northern tribes in Chronicles.

Unlike Kings, Chronicles does not engage in political distinctions. Chronicles is a religious history; nationalistic considerations are not under consideration. The prophetic speech of Abijah in 2 Chronicles 13:4-12 substantiates this view. Abijah, king of Judah, speaks for all the tribes in reminding Jeroboam that the eternal kingdom of David is *all Israel* (vv. 4-5). *All Israel* from the time of David remains unaltered. The exhortation of Abijah to Jeroboam is that the northerners belong to the people of promise represented by the kingdom of David in Jerusalem. Jeroboam has an opportunity to realize the promise of *all Israel*. Israel consists of those faithful to the Davidic promise, including northerners. Judah as a political entity does not constitute Israel in postexilic times. The faithful are *all Israel*. The faithful are found in all the tribes of Israel.

The thesis of von Rad does not represent the Chronicler's view of *all Israel*. All Israel is more than Judah in the narrative of Rehoboam (2 Chron 10:1, 3, 16). All Israel is not a political identity but a reality of the promise of kingdom of Yahweh to David, as Ahijah declared (13:5, 8).

A comprehensive review of the history of Israel until Hezekiah provides a more balanced view of the Chronicler's attitude toward the Northern Kingdom. There were good reasons for the northern tribes to reject the rule of Rehoboam. In this rejection, the Lord was affirming the word of Ahijah the Shilonite to Jeroboam the son of Nebat (2 Chron 10:15): ten tribes would be separated to Jeroboam. The Chronicler presumes his reader's knowledge of 1 Kings 11:29-33. The admonition of Shemaiah in 2 Chronicles 11:4 was a prophetic affirmation justifying actions of the north. The speech of Abijah in 2 Chronicles 13:4-12 is a turning point regarding the tribes of the north (Williamson 1977a: 98).

After the death of Rehoboam, the refusal of the Northern Kingdom to return was unacceptable apostasy. Their sin lay in rebelling against the unity of the nation realized in the Davidic dynasty. The Northern Kingdom fared badly in the battle against Judah in spite of their significantly superior forces. The Chronicler condemned a rival kingdom, but he did not consider them to be lost tribes.

The northern tribes as a state had no share in the promise of David. The Chronicler differs from Kings in the presentation of the two kingdoms. Kings conceives of the division as political and geographical rather than historical and spiritual. The Chronicler has no comment on the political history of the Northern Kingdom. He limits his presentation to the kings of Judah. But the Chronicler is always inclusive and affirmative of the people of the north (Williamson 1977a: 110). *All Israel* is nothing less than the unity of all the tribes within the covenant. This is why the genealogies of all the tribes of Israel are so important *[Genealogy, p. 461]*.

2 Chronicles 10:1–12:16
Reign of Rehoboam

PREVIEW

Tribal or ethnic divisions and hostilities are quite irrational. Humans of the most diverse origins share with all other humans all the characteristics essential to human life. Emotion seems to have no respect for the rational. Hostilities and even genocide are almost always based on ethnic and social differences. Politically, the kingdom brought together by David was always tenuous. Social and economic rivalries proved to make political unity unsustainable.

Under Solomon, Jeroboam had become a very capable leader. He was made supervisor over the compulsory state service, but conflict later forced him to flee to Egypt (1 Kings 11:40). Jeroboam was affirmed by the prophet Ahijah, who declared him to be a true successor of David (v. 38). The promise of dynasty applied to Jeroboam as it had to David, but it was not promised in perpetuity. In Chronicles, Jeroboam appears as a leader of the revolting northern tribes without introduction. When the rebellion broke out, he returned from Egypt as a champion of relief from the hated levy. In response, Rehoboam dispatched Adoniram, the senior officer in charge of the hated corvée, to force the recalcitrant subjects back into line (2 Chron 10:18). The rebels had come to respect Jeroboam as an able administrator. Even if those serving in the levy were resident aliens, their overseers in the lower and higher echelons were Israelites. They were very capable of assessing the labor regulations and operations. Adoniram may have been an excellent civil servant, but he represented a bureau of the government that could hardly have had respect of Israelite citizens. It was as if the new young king was seeking to reduce the entire population to corvée status (Rainey 1970: 202). It is small wonder that the Israelite notables stoned hapless Adoniram to death.

The Chronicler reports all this as he finds it in Kings. He has considerable sympathy with the sentiments of the northern tribes. Theirs was not an enviable situation; it could not be expected that they would accept this tyranny without resistance. There is question about the chronological sequence in the MT of Kings. In 1 Kings 12:1-3 it is reported that Jeroboam was in Egypt when he heard that Rehoboam went to Shechem to be crowned king. He returned to take an active part in the negotiations. Verse 20 seems to say that Jeroboam returned later, when summoned by the Israelite tribes to become their king. It is not necessary to assume that these are two contradictory accounts, as has been frequently asserted in commentaries. In 2 Chronicles 10:2 Jeroboam returns from Egypt to participate actively in the negotiations. The coronation of Jeroboam in 1 Kings 12:20 is not a sequel to these discussions. It is a separate notice of Jeroboam's return from his self-imposed exile to be crowned king (Cogan 2001: 346). The Greek text of Kings has a completely divergent narrative of the return of Jeroboam *[Greek Text of Chronicles, p. 468]*. However, the Chronicler's version of the events of the division is sound.

OUTLINE

Division of the Monarchy, 10:1-11:4
Establishment of Rehoboam's Rule, 11:5-23
Shishak's Invasion, 12:1-12
Conclusion of Rehoboam's Rule, 12:13-16

EXPLANATORY NOTES

Division of the Monarchy 10:1-11:4

Rehoboam was required to go to Shechem for negotiation or confirmation, a telling sign of the weakness of national unity. Shechem was located between Mount Gerizim and Mount Ebal, with an ample water supply and fertile plain. It was a military, political, and religious center from the time of the patriarchs. Shechem was the location of covenant renewal when the Israelites entered the Promised Land (cf. Josh 24:1). Rehoboam did not have the power to enforce taxation over the northern tribes. They were in a position to demand concessions. Though conscripted labor may not have been directly enforced on native-born Israelites (2 Chron 2:17-18; 8:7-10), it was a burden to the leaders of Israel incommensurate with its benefits for them.

Elders traditionally exercised considerable influence in royal decisions. When Ben-Hadad of Damascus, king of Aram, attacked Samaria, the elders were decisive in rejecting his harsh terms of surrender (1 Kings 20:7-9). When Absalom revolted against David, the elders of Israel were an influential force in critical decisions (2 Sam 17:4, 15). These elders were distinguished from officers, nobles, and guardians who had official roles in governance (Judg 8:14; 1 Kings 21:8; 2 Kings 10:5). Rehoboam was forty-one years old when he began to reign (2 Chron 12:13), so the *young men* who had grown up with him had certain expectations (10:8-10). They may have been royal princes, sons of Solomon's other wives. They expected a role in governance, such as Rehoboam's promotion of Abijah (11:22). Referring to these princes as inexperienced is a comment on the worth of their advice, since it was understood that wisdom did not reside with youth (cf. Job 12:12). The words of the younger counselors corresponded to the disposition of Rehoboam. They lacked the experience of the elders and found Rehoboam's inclinations preferable. Their answer came with metaphors and rhetorical acumen appropriate to a royal court. The *scorpion* was a whip tipped with weights and barbs, though there is no actual evidence for the use of such a weapon in Israel (2 Chron 10:11).

The scenario at Shechem is a test of Rehoboam. It became the occasion for the fulfillment of the prophecy of Ahijah. Jeroboam would receive ten tribes, and one would be left to Solomon in continuity of the promise to David (cf. 1 Kings 11:29-39). The Chronicler follows his *Vorlage* in recalling the prophecy of Ahijah in 2 Chronicles 10:15, even though he has entirely omitted the conflict with Jeroboam and the judgment of Solomon from his narrative *[Vorlage, p. 468]*. His goal is to put these events in perspective with a more comprehensive understanding of the kingdom.

The rejection of Rehoboam is expressed as the converse of the poetic saying affirming loyal support for David from all the tribes of Israel. Amasai, head of the chief officers, under the influence of the Spirit, expressed loyalty and support for David:

We are yours, O David,
   We are with you, son of Jesse!
Peace, peace to you.
   Peace to your helpers.
Truly, your God helps you. (1 Chron 12:18 AT)

The rejection of the house of David by ten tribes was not the end of Israel. But there is no Israel apart from the Davidic promise. *All Israel went home, but the sons of Israel lived in the cities of Judah under the rule of Rehoboam* (2 Chron 10:16c-17 AT). The actions of Rehoboam and his advisers were rash, but this turn of events was from God and in fulfillment of prophecy (v. 15). These events were under divine control and did not undermine the Davidic promise.

Internecine (mutually destructive) warfare characterized the first fifty years of the divided kingdom, until the unity achieved under the Omride dynasty. The summary of Rehoboam characterizes his reign as continual warfare with Jeroboam (2 Chron 12:15). Immediate war was averted by the prophetic intervention of Shemaiah. The address of Shemaiah to *all Israel in Judah and Benjamin* suitably expresses the Chronicler's concept of Israel (11:3). The kingdom of Judah was never exclusive to people from Benjamin and Judah (cf. 1 Chron 9:3; 2 Chron 11:16), but neither was Israel limited to the territory of Judah. The separation of the ten tribes persisted because of Rehoboam's folly (2 Chron 10:12-14; 13:7). The prophetic word through Shemaiah and Ahijah affirmed that the purposes of God for Israel were fulfilled.

Establishment of Rehoboam's Rule 11:5-23

The blessing of the Lord on Rehoboam is demonstrated in his building activities. The fortified cities provided defense from east, south, and west. Valleys leading into the Judean hill country and important road junctions all appear to be covered. Fortifications to the north were not as necessary. Rehoboam's first task was to fortify a minimal but more securely defensible position. The northern towns available to Rehoboam did not meet this criterion. The defensive lines make strategic sense for protection against an Egyptian attack and likely began before the invasion of Shishak. The boundaries are conformable to Rehoboam's reign. Lachish formed the pivotal southwestern corner of Rehoboam's fortifications. It was a junction for the road north to the other fortified cities. Lachish guarded the southern road to Egypt, connected with the coastal highway to the west, and the way eastward through Adoraim to Hebron. The watershed toward the east was protected by Bethlehem, Etam, Tekoa, and Ziph. North of Lachish the cities of Mareshah (Moresheth), Gath, Azekah, Zorah, and Aijalon provided security from the west. Socoh and Adoraim monitored internal movement. The Levitical cities and some key centers were previously fortified.

The defection of faithful priests from the north to the south was a second sign of divine blessing. Those in the north who desired to remain faithful came to worship at Jerusalem. The loyalty of the faithful continuously bonded north and south. The three-year limit of support for Rehoboam is explained by his unfaithfulness in the fourth year, which was immediately punished by Shishak's invasion in the fifth year.

The north was condemned for its syncretistic religion introduced by Jeroboam (2 Chron 11:15; cf. 13:8; 1 Kings 12:28; cf. Exod 32; Hos 8:5; 10:5-6). Jeroboam's calves likely were not intended to be idols themselves, but the pedestal for the invisible presence of the Lord. Hadad the storm god is depicted as standing astride a bull, with lightning bolts in his hands (*ANEP* 140). Scholars have conjectured that the goats are demons or satyrs (part human and part goat, noted for lasciviousness), but this may be an unwarranted intrusion of Greco-Roman models into a Palestinian environment. Goats might be identified with Palestinian fertility deities. Egypt routinely portrayed its deities in animal form. Both Solomon and Jeroboam had established strong links with Egypt.

A large family was the third sign of divine blessing. The number of wives and children of Rehoboam are probably the total of his reign rather than those accumulated by his fifth year. The genealogy may explain why the eldest son did not receive the kingdom. It was a violation to transfer the privilege of firstborn because of a greater love for one wife (Deut 21:15-17), but rights of primogeniture were not always followed. The appointment of Abijah may have been as coregent to provide for orderly succession. Rehoboam's dispersal of the royal princes extended control of the royal family into the outlying districts and provided for a smooth transition of power. It made the chance of a revolt or attempted coup less likely.

Shishak's Invasion 12:1-12

War was not the result of sociopolitical power struggles in relation to Israel. The Egyptian attack was because Israel abandoned Torah and was *unfaithful (maʿal)* [*Torah, p. 481*]. Unfaithfulness is the key word that explains disaster. Shishak was king over a reunited Egypt, founder of the twenty-second dynasty (945-924 BCE). His Palestinian campaign was a significant political achievement, recorded on the walls of a temple built to Amun at Karnak in southern Egypt. The names on this registry have been reviewed extensively (Rainey and Notley: 185-89). More than 150 towns are named, but Jerusalem is not mentioned. Of Rehoboam's fortified cities, only Aijalon is named.

The topographical list includes almost 70 place names in the Negev, some in the area of Arad and Beersheba, others farther south (Mazar: 396) *[Negev, p. 467]*. The name Gibeon is evident; Shishak may have extorted heavy tribute from Jerusalem from there. A fragment of a statue of Shishak has been found at Megiddo, indicating that he did occupy that city. Egypt was eager to break the Israelite monopoly over commerce with their control of the land bridge to Mesopotamia. The main objective of his expedition was the kingdom of Israel and the Negev of Judah rather than central Judah and Jerusalem.

Shishak came with a vast coalition of peoples (2 Chron 12:3-4). Sukkites are not mentioned elsewhere in the Bible but are known from Egyptian history. They were Libyan forces from the oases of the western desert. Shishak himself was a Nubian (Cushite in the Bible), the area of southern Egypt.

Looting the royal treasuries and the temple was the punishment meted on Rehoboam for his disobedience. The gold shields served a ritual function. They were carried by the guard accompanying the king when he moved from the palace to the temple. Royal processionals lost much of their splendor with the bronze shields, but these were safely stored in the huge armory Solomon had built.

The speech of Shemaiah expresses the requirement for restoration given in the vision to Solomon at the dedication of the temple (2 Chron 7:14). The leaders of Israel and the king humbled themselves (*knʿ*); the verb is repeated three times in response to the prophet (12:5-8), and again in recalling the good remaining in Jerusalem (v. 12). The good was the repentance of the people, their resolve to seek the Lord, and the preservation of worship.

Conclusion of Rehoboam's Rule 12:13-16

The summary of Rehoboam's reign concludes with the succession of Abijah. He is called Abijam in Kings (e.g., 1 Kings 15:1 mg.). It has been conjectured that Abijam was the Canaanite form of his name, which would mean "My father is *Yam*." Yam was the Canaanite god of the Sea, prominent in the Baal stories. In Israelite faith his name would have been "My father is *Yah*," the usual short form for *Yahweh*, the God of Judah.

THE TEXT IN BIBLICAL CONTEXT
Rehoboam and Hezekiah

The Chronicler created parallels between Rehoboam and Hezekiah, who is shown to be an ideal king. Both these kings display arrogance followed by humility (2 Chron 12:1, 6-7; 32:24-25). Both suffered the loss of treasures, but in each case Jerusalem was spared. The description of the invasion of Sennacherib in 2 Kings 18:13 is adopted for the Chronicler's description of Shishak's invasion. *Shishak conquered Judah's fortified towns and then advanced to attack Jerusalem* (2 Chron 12:4 AT). His description of the invasion of Sennacherib has a tempered version of the same lines: *After all these faithful deeds, Sennacherib king of Assyria came against Judah and encamped against all its fortified cities, intending to invade them and take them for himself* (32:1 AT). The Chronicler has abbreviated the account of Sennacherib's invasion, but his description of the invasion of Shishak uses all the same rubrics. Shemaiah in the time of Rehoboam and Isaiah in the time of Hezekiah both spoke of repentance. In the case of Rehoboam, the Chronicler acknowledges that the Judean cities were captured (12:4), much as is said of the invasion of Sennacherib in Kings (2 Kings 18:13-16). The account of Hezekiah in Chronicles only goes so far as to say this was Sennacherib's intent. The accounts of both Rehoboam and Hezekiah are examples of the Chronicler's view of history, but Hezekiah is presented in a much more positive fashion. Although Rehoboam was an *evil* king (2 Chron 12:14), there were positive lessons to be learned from his reign. His humility mitigated the anger of the Lord so that not all was lost (12:12). In the days of Hezekiah, Jerusalem was spared, and the Assyrian king was killed by his own household.

This story would have had a particular relevance to the Persian audience of the Chronicler. It encouraged repentance, and it explained why Judah could be plundered by a foreign power (Boda 2010: 298). Foreign domination was a temporary condition and had a didactic purpose in divine mercy. As in the days of Rehoboam, they would be encouraged to look for the good things left in Judah.

THE TEXT IN THE LIFE OF THE CHURCH

The Root of All Sin

The Chronicler quite correctly saw pride as the insidious evil that lurked behind so many of the calamities that had befallen his people. Pride and greed are closely related sins, both equally deceptive. They cannot be recognized apart from a correct perspective; daily vigilance is required to maintain an attitude that honors God. But even the vigilant may be deceived by pride.

In the postexilic period, the Psalms of Ascent had particular relevance for the faithful community. They were the ones that longed for Jerusalem and the hopes that it represented. The Chronicler expresses the sentiment of humility found in the psalms:

> We lift our eyes to you,
>   who resides in the heavens.
> As the eyes of the servants
>   at the side of their masters,
> as the eyes of the maidservant,
>   at the side of her mistress,
> thus we look to the LORD our God,
>   until he is gracious to us.
> Be gracious to us, O LORD, be gracious;
>   For we have been filled with much scorn.
> The mocking of the secure,
>   The scorn of the arrogant,
>   Has completely filled our lives. (Ps 123:1-4 AT)

It was not difficult for those in the postexilic period to recognize the sins of the past. They lived in dependence and poverty, humiliated by surrounding people, and scoffed at by powerful neighbors. In all of this the Chronicler recognizes that a right disposition toward God begins with humility.

It has been observed that the great difference between us and God is that he never thinks he is one of us. Pride has been the human problem since the tempter said "You will be like God, knowing good and evil" (Gen 3:5). The Genesis expression leaves open a number of possibilities, but the inference is consistent. If knowledge of good and evil means having all knowledge or if it means knowledge to determine good or evil, the effect is that humans decide what is moral. Ever since Eden, humans have grasped at that tree of knowledge, convinced that they have the power to know what is good. Such hubris finds good by beginning with itself. It is inescapable pride, the nemesis of the human race.

The Chronicler could look back over the prophetic records of the kings and readily detect how pride was the governing issue. All unfaithfulness was a sin against God, a denial of his holy name, a failure to seek him. There is good reason why humbling (kn^c) appears repeatedly in his message. Individual Christians and the church collectively will do well to reflect on their own history that they may better understand the sins of the present. Confession is an essential part of Christian prayer, whether individually or collectively.

There is no need to cite examples of pride and disgrace in the contemporary church. It is so prevalent that anyone with the slightest familiarity with any denomination of the church can readily cite examples. Those having no familiarity with the church are well aware of the moral failings of those who have been prominent in leadership. So long as the church awaits its final redemption, there will be moral failures of some of its best and well-known leaders. Consistent total commitment is rare (2 Chron 12:14); repentance and contrition are required of all (12:12). This is the good that must remain in the church at all times, just as it did in Judah under Rehoboam. The arrogance of Rehoboam in his treatment of the north and his failure to serve God with total commitment did not remove the potential for grace and for good.

2 Chronicles 13:1–14:1a
Reign of Abijah

PREVIEW

Spiritual opportunity is not always self-evident. Sometimes conflict is opportunity in disguise. If conflict cannot be resolved but conflicted parties can come to realize their own failures, there is spiritual progress. The Chronicler's presentation of Abijah contrasts sharply with the censure of 1 Kings 15:1-8, where the Judean king is condemned for following in the idolatry of Rehoboam. In Kings, Abijah's reign of faithlessness serves only to exemplify the mercy of God in preserving the Davidic dynasty. The lamp of Israel continued to shine in Jerusalem (2 Sam 21:17). The Chronicler provides an account of a war with Jeroboam in which Abijah wins a decisive victory. In addition, Abijah gives what has been termed a Levitical sermon (von Rad 1966). Such a speech consists of doctrine, application, and exhortation, with an appeal to earlier biblical texts (2 Chron 13:4-12). The reign of Abijah becomes the critical turning point in the Chronicler's assessment of relationships with the northern tribes.

Victory over Jeroboam's superior forces was a divine judgment against the north and an affirmation of Judah's faithfulness. It provides a spiritual opportunity for the northern tribes. The Chronicler absolves the northern tribes of their apostasy during the time of Rehoboam. They were guilty of driving out the priests and replacing them with others who worshiped at the high places. They set up calves and created satyrs (2 Chron 11:13-15). With the death of Jeroboam, there is a possibility of turning to God in faithfulness. There was no benefit to the northern tribes in associating with

Rehoboam, who forsook the law of the Lord (12:1), but there is renewed opportunity with a new king in Judah. Those who followed Jeroboam should join in the company of those who serve the God of their fathers. Abijah's speech is not a negative polemic but an urgent plea to reconcile the division that has come about.

OUTLINE

Preparations for War, 13:1-3
Speech of Abijah, 13:4-12
Judgment of Jeroboam, 13:13-20
Conclusion of Abijah's Rule, 13:21–14:1a

EXPLANATORY NOTES

Preparations for War 13:1-3

The synchronism with the eighteenth year of Jeroboam is the only instance in which the Chronicler coordinates a king of Judah with the northern king [*Chronological Synchronism, p. 465*]. Given the political separation of the northern tribes, the Chronicler does not include activities of the Northern Kingdom, though he does take into account all contacts between south and north, including some not mentioned in his *Vorlage* (1–2 Kings) [*Vorlage, p. 468*]. This state of affairs continues through the whole period of the Northern Kingdom, until its exile during the reigns of Ahaz and Hezekiah in the south.

According to the MT, Abijah is the son of Rehoboam and Micaiah, daughter of Uriel of Gibeah (2 Chron 13:2 NRSV). The Chronicler also states that the second wife of Rehoboam was Maakah, daughter of Absalom and mother of Abijah (2 Chron 11:20). Some translations take the names Micaiah and Maakah to be interchangeable, following the Greek versions of 2 Chronicles 13:2 (NIV mg.), a sound textual decision followed by the NIV. Maakah was Rehoboam's favorite wife, and for that reason Abijah received preferential treatment (vv. 21-22). Maakah is also said to be "mother" of Asa (2 Chron 15:16; cf. 1 Kings 15:10), though Asa was son (not brother) of Abijah (2 Chron 14:1); thus, she is Asa's grandmother (so NIV in 2 Chron 15:16). Maakah as queen mother was removed by Asa (cf. 1 Kings 15:13). The queen mother was a "daughter" (that is, female descendant) of Absalom, the third son of David who was born to a woman named Maakah, daughter of Talmai king of Geshur (2 Sam 3:3; 1 Chron 3:2). Absalom's only known daughter is Tamar (2 Sam 14:27), probably named after his sister. Uriel, father of Maakah, must therefore be the husband of Tamar; Rehoboam's wife Maakah was named after her great-grandmother, the mother of Absalom. This is the view presented by Josephus in his genealogy (*Ant.* 8.249). Rehoboam had determined that succession should be through Abijah, son of his favorite wife. Maakah as the "mother" of Asa in 2 Chronicles 15:16 must be understood as his grandmother.

Continual conflict between Rehoboam and Jeroboam carried on into the reign of Abijah (cf. 2 Chron 12:15). No immediate cause for the war is given, but it may have been an attempt by Abijah to reunite north and south, as suggested by his speech (2 Chron 13:5, 12). The large numbers of soldiers on each side correspond approximately to the census numbers of David (2 Sam 24:9). The double number of soldiers for Israel magnifies the divine intervention on behalf of the righteous few against the evildoers.

Speech of Abijah 13:4-12

Mount Zemarayim may be identified with the town of that name on the northern border of Benjamin (cf. Josh 18:22), about five miles northeast of Bethel. Benjamin was the buffer and battleground between the Northern and Southern Kingdoms. The *covenant of salt* was eternal and efficacious, though the social and religious background of the metaphor is not known. "Salt of the covenant" was necessary for a sacrifice to be efficacious (Lev 2:13). Salt was the preservative par excellence in antiquity and thus an apt metaphor for a covenant of permanent duration.

Josephus understood the scoundrels in Abijah's speech to be allied with Rehoboam (*Ant.* 8.277). The interpretation depends on who is meant in the phrase *gathered around him* (2 Chron 13:7). If this refers to the immediate antecedent, namely *the master* that Jeroboam rebelled against (v. 6), the *sons of Belial* (MT; *worthless scoundrels*, NIV) must be those who prevailed over Rehoboam rather than those who opposed Rehoboam (Williamson 1977a: 112). The latter is a strained meaning of the preposition; more typical is its use found in 13:18, which says that the Judeans prevailed because they relied on the Lord. The *sons of Belial* that prevailed over Rehoboam can be none other than the rash young advisers who demanded more conscripted labor from the north.

If this is the proper interpretation of the syntax, it provides quite a different understanding of Abijah's speech. The blame for the division of the kingdom falls upon Rehoboam as the inexperienced king unable to act wisely (as depicted in ch. 10). Though Rehoboam shared some responsibility for the schism, the whole speech castigates the northerners for their stubborn refusal to support the kingdom of David. The Chronicler does not make Jeroboam into the renegade who revolted and defied his master with the help of worthless men. Rehoboam was the king responsible, partly because his inexperience made him vulnerable. Solomon is also said to be "young and inexperienced" (cf. 1 Chron 22:5; 29:1), but David provided for smooth transition by securing allegiance of the nation's leadership. The determination of the northerners to separate may have been understandable, but it is no longer excusable.

The speech of Abijah introduces the implications of the division for the Davidic dynasty and the purity of worship at Jerusalem. The northerners now have an opportunity to support a good king. Kings says nothing of such devotion by Abijah and condemns him for following in the idolatry of Rehoboam. His dominion was preserved only because the Lord desired to keep the lamp for David preserved in Jerusalem (1 Kings 15:3-4). The Chronicler in turn sees the positive possibility of turning to God after the weakness of Rehoboam and the rebellion of Jeroboam against him had caused the disruption of the kingdom.

In Chronicles, trumpets are a regular component of music at the temple. Their use in battle is described in the wilderness wanderings (Num 10:9; 31:6). The battles in Chronicles have characteristics of what has been described as "holy war." In these battles the power of God enables the defeat of much larger armies; a speech by a prophet or king provides encouragement; cultic purity is required for entering the battle; and victory follows the blowing of trumpets and the battle cry from the army. The battle against Jericho in Joshua 5-6 is one of the most notable examples of such a battle.

Judgment of Jeroboam 13:13-20

The Lord granted Judah miraculous victory. They had met the critical criterion for receiving such divine provision: they relied on the Lord (2 Chron 13:18), with the result that the Israelites were humbled (kn^c) before Judah. They should rather have humbled themselves before God, an obvious play on the word; they had failed to heed the speech of Abijah and humble themselves before the Lord (cf. 7:14). Superior military might is of no consequence when fighting against the Lord. Abijah was able to take the territories surrounding Ephron, Bethel, and Jeshanah from Israel. These, together with Zemaraim, formed a coherent and logical geographical unit (cf. Josh 18:22-23). All these were in the hill country on the northern border of Judah. The later history of this territorial gain is not known. By the time of Amos, Bethel was a major cult shrine in Israel

(760 BCE). Jeroboam outlived Abijah (cf. 1 Kings 15:9); the report of his death is included with his defeat (2 Chron 13:20b), as is typically the case with vanquished warriors (cf. 2 Kings 19:37). For the Chronicler, associating the death of Jeroboam with the defeat of the north makes it a sign of God's judgment for his apostasy.

Conclusion of Abijah's Rule 13:21–14:1a

Whatever may have been Abijah's shortcomings, as mentioned in Kings, these were of no consequence in the success of Abijah. This is completely in keeping with the theology of the Chronicler. Seeking the Lord is the means of healing, whatever may have been the shortcoming. The Chronicler does not record any failing of Abijah; he is therefore able to report the way Abijah was blessed by the Lord for his faithfulness.

The simple summary is that Abijah became strong (2 Chron 13:21). A large family is once again another sign of divine blessing. His account rejoins his *Vorlage* in verse 22 (cf. 1 Kings 15:7), with the omission in his summary of the phrase that there was continual warfare with Jeroboam (a point already mentioned in both 2 Chron 12:15-16 and 1 Kings 14:30) *[Vorlage, p. 468]*. The Chronicler has summarized the outcome of that warfare in the battle he has recounted. The source of his information is not the book of the chronicles of the kings of Judah, but rather is the story (*midraš*) of the prophet Iddo (2 Chron 13:22 MT). The term *midraš* encompasses a considerable variation in the genre of writing it describes; it is found again in 24:27, where it seems to indicate nothing more than a stylistic variation on the source citation. These are the only two occurrences of this term in the Hebrew canon.

THE TEXT IN BIBLICAL CONTEXT

The Prophet King

The writer of Kings devoted his account to Abijah's sinfulness; in quantity he said more about God's fidelity to David than he actually reported on Abijah. In contrast, the Chronicler has presented a prophet king in Abijah, a preacher of righteousness, enjoying the benefits and blessings of his fidelity. Both are adopted in the canon as true perspectives on the reign of Abijah.

The import of Abijah's sermon was not lost on the postexilic community. The kingdom stood on the twin pillars of the Davidic covenant and the temple, both foci of the Chronicler's condemnation of the north. The community of the Chronicler now enjoyed the institution of temple worship; they looked forward to the fulfillment of the promise of Davidic rule. Though they were under foreign domination, the kingdom of God was secure. The future of that kingdom depended on faithfulness.

In 2 Chronicles 28 the Chronicler will draw on the account of Abijah to show that Judah could sink to the same level of apostasy as did the northern tribes (Dillard 1987: 219). The account of Ahaz is reworked from that of 2 Kings 16 to demonstrate a reversal of the relationship between north and south that is depicted in 2 Chronicles 13. There Abijah had declared Israel to be guilty of idolatries, worshiping *them that are no gods* (2 Chron 13:8-9). Now Ahaz makes such images, shuts the doors of the temple, and neglects its ritual. This demonstrates that the apostasy of Judah had reached the same depths as that of Israel described in Abijah's sermon. The Israelites were able to execute a great plunder in Judah because of the people's disobedience under Ahaz. Such a situation is the equivalent of an exile. The alienation of the north in Abijah's day would become true of Judah in the days of Ahaz. Faithfulness requires constant vigilance.

THE TEXT IN THE LIFE OF THE CHURCH

The Gates of Hell Will Not Prevail

The kingdom of God will not fail. All the forces of Jeroboam presumed that they could readily overthrow Judah, but they had not properly assessed the situation. This was the equivalent of taking over *the kingdom of the* LORD (2 Chron 13:8). The forces of the north could make no claim to represent God. They had completely displaced the worship of the temple with a false religion. They were now willfully defying an opportunity to unite again with the promise to David. The sentiment of Abijah's speech is also found in the address of Gamaliel in Acts 5:38-39. This Pharisee understood the matter clearly: ambitions of human volition will come to nothing; that which is the work of God cannot be stopped. If the message preached by Peter and the apostles concerning the resurrection of Christ is fraudulent, it constitutes no threat at all, and these men should be released. If their message is true, it cannot be stopped. In either case nothing is to be gained by putting them to death.

This same situation confronts contemporary Christians and the church in many ways. It is not always easy to discern the will of God in a conflicted situation. But it should not be assumed that God is on the side of those who claim to represent him. In such circumstances of conflict, a venerable figure is Balthasar Hubmaier (d. 1528). Hubmaier was named doctor of theology after his studies at Freiburg and Ingolstadt. He became leader of the Anabaptists in Switzerland, the most prominent region of the Radical Reformation. The doctrine of rebaptism was especially offensive since it had implications for the power of the state; it was seen to refuse first loyalty to the state, which was certainly Christian in name. Hubmaier was persecuted even by liberal Zwinglians for his beliefs. He was forced out of Switzerland but continued his Anabaptist proselytizing in Augsburg and Moravia. Hubmaier represented the moderate version of Anabaptists as opposed to the millenarian anarchism of Thomas Müntzer and Hans Hut.

But Hubmaier could not escape the forces of church and state. Constantly hunted by imperial authorities, he was eventually captured and burned at the stake in Vienna. The authorities of the church who killed him are remembered in disgrace; the theological principles that Hubmaier taught as the truth of the kingdom live on. Hubmaier could not possibly be a threat to the imperial powers of the time. His work would never be remembered unless he actually represented the truth of the kingdom, in which case his followers could never be stopped. For the church today, Anabaptist history confirms the truth that was spoken by Abijah in 2 Chronicles 13:4-12 and demonstrated in his success.

2 Chronicles 14:1b–16:14
Reign of Asa

PREVIEW

The worst record of leadership is one that begins well, with great opportunity, and ends in disaster. Unfortunately this is not an uncommon scenario. There seems to be a natural propensity for things to become worse or to go wrong. But sometime such outcomes are a matter of perspective. The Chronicler portrays the rule of Asa in this fashion.

The Chronicler's narrative of Asa is particularly illustrative of his *Tendenz* [*Tendenz in Chronicles, p. 476*]. Asa began to rule when the land had peace for ten years (14:1b). The theme of peace (*šalom*) is important in the record of Asa. The kingdom of Solomon was to be characterized by peace (1 Chron 22:9). The Chronicler joins this with the theme of *rest* and applies it to military success. Asa builds up fortifications in the land, *for the LORD gave him rest* and *peace* (2 Chron 14:6-7). In the Deuteronomistic History, *rest* carries the sense of fulfillment of promise [*Deuteronomistic History, p. 465*]. When the Israelites occupied the land, they were at rest (Josh 21:43-45). The Chronicler affirms this concept of rest. In the renewal of the oath of the covenant, initiated by Asa, the Lord gave them rest all around (2 Chron 15:15). Rest is the realization of the goal of redemption. Much of the record of Asa is concerned with military encounters. Asa's success in battle is a reward for his faithfulness and an example of divinely ordained rest.

The narrative of Asa ends with his war against Baasha (1 Kings 15:17-22; 2 Chron 16:1-6). In military strategy, Asa was successful in achieving his goals. He not only halted the encroachment of Baasha at Judah's northern boundaries, but was also able to use the wood and foundation stone that he captured for his own fortifications (2 Chron 16:6). His success in battle came through initiating an Aramean alliance. This brought the condemnation of the prophet Hanani (vv. 7-9). His denunciation offended Asa, who made him a political prisoner. The result was divine judgment. Asa did not seek the Lord; there was no turning and no healing. The failure of Asa to follow the divine directive in 2 Chronicles 7:14 led to death.

The Deuteronomist's assessment of the reign of Asa is positive (1 Kings 15:11). It closes with the innocuous note that in his old age he suffered from a disease in his feet (v. 24). The Chronicler considers illness to be a divine judgment; this is not unique to the Chronicler, but his writings make a direct association *["God, Justice, and Faithfulness" in Theology of Chronicles, p. 478]*. Asa became increasingly ill in his thirty-ninth year and died in his forty-first year (2 Chron 16:12-13). His sins began with seeking an Aramean alliance against Baasha, then imprisoning the prophet, and finally refusing to repent.

OUTLINE

Reform and Security, 14:1b-8
Victory over Zerah, 14:9-15
Azariah's Call to Revival, 15:1-7
Covenant Renewal and Celebration, 15:8-19
War with Baasha, 16:1-6
Hanani's Sermon, 16:7-10
Death and Burial of Asa, 16:11-14

EXPLANATORY NOTES

Reform and Security 14:1b-8

Asa's removal of foreign altars and high places seems to be in direct contradiction with the statement that he did not remove the high places from Israel (2 Chron 15:17). The introduction refers to the beginning of Asa's reign, when Asa began his reforms. Idolatry of indigenous cults plagued Judah's history and may have revived toward the end of his reign, over thirty years later. Failure to remove the altars is specifically said to be in *Israel*, which may refer to the cities in Ephraim that came under Asa's control (15:8), where he had engaged in a purge of idolatry. Asa removed the high places of Judah (14:3-5), but nothing is said of removal of high places in Ephraim.

The theme of seeking the Lord is the Chronicler's assurance that restoration will be experienced. The verb "seek" (*bqš*) is one of the key words of God's formula for restoration, given to Solomon through a vision (2 Chron 7:14). A synonym (*drš*) is found five times in the narrative of Asa, beginning with Asa's initial exhortation to the people (14:4). The subject is almost always people, but there is an ambiguity in verse 7, where this verb occurs twice. It may be translated to say *We have sought the LORD, our God we have sought* (AT), or as the Greek translators took it, *We have sought the LORD our God, he has sought us* (AT). The latter translation is in conformity with the exhortation of Asa: *If you seek him, he will be found by you* (15:2). This verb is found twice more in taking an oath to keep the covenant (15:12-13). The final occurrence is in the failure of Asa to seek the Lord (16:12). The other verb "seek" is found twice (15:4, 15, *bqš* rather than *drš*), with no difference in meaning.

Victory over Zerah 14:9-15

Solomon prayed that the Lord would hear his people at such time as they were led into battle (2 Chron 6:34). The battle with Zerah was an example of God responding to such a prayer. Several elements of divine warfare (holy war) characterize the account: Israel faces a foe with much greater forces; Asa prays; the Lord leads at the head of the battle; and their foe succumbs to the fear of God *[War in Chronicles, p. 481]*. Cush may refer either to southern Egypt (Nubia) or to a Midianite territory northeast of Aqaba (cf. Hab 3:7; Num 12:1). The mention of Libya in 2 Chronicles 16:8 and the size of the battle make this comparable to the attack of Shishak against Rehoboam (2 Chron 12:2-4). Zerah may have been a Nubian general dispatched by Osorkon I, the Libyan Pharaoh who ruled Egypt from the tenth year to the fourteenth year of Asa, 900–897 BCE (Spalinger: 356–57). Another view is that Shishak established a buffer state around Gerar, supported by Nubian mercenaries, who invaded Judah. The account only says that Asa and his forces pursued the enemy armies south to the area of Gerar, taking a great spoil, particularly of the herdsmen living in tents around the cities.

Azariah's Call to Revival 15:1-7

The prophet Azariah is unknown outside of this passage. His speech is typical of the concerns of the Chronicler: the Lord will be with his people, he is found by those who seek him, and he will reward their obedience. The promise to Asa and Judah that God will reward their labor would have particular relevance for Judah in the days of the Chronicler, with their struggles in restoring worship amid the trials of making a living and dealing with unsympathetic neighbors.

The description of Israel's cycles of distress seems to best fit the period of the judges, though no time period is specified. The vague reference to a long time was taken by the Greek translators to refer to the future. The times of anarchy are described in exclusively religious terms as a dearth of the knowledge of God. A parallel to Hosea is frequently noted, though Hosea defines lawlessness in religious and political institutions—no king, sacrifice, or ephod (Hos 3:4). Both mention the priestly function, but in different ways; Chronicles names the teaching function, while Hosea stresses divine mediation.

To lay the foundation for the conclusion, the prophecy reverts to the earlier past. The message includes a series of prophetic expressions. *It was not safe to travel* (2 Chron 15:5) is found in Zechariah 8:10, and *problems troubled the people* (AT; NRSV, *great disturbances*) is an idiom borrowed from Amos 3:9. *Nation fought against nation* (*they were broken in pieces*; 2 Chron 15:6 AT) is also reminiscent of Zechariah 11:6. The allusions to Scripture make this another example of a Levitical sermon (von Rad 1966: 270). Having laid down the general principles, the speech concludes with an imperative relevant to the present situation. The exhortation *Do not let your hands be weak* (2 Chron 15:7 NRSV) is a literal quotation of Zephaniah 3:16.

Covenant Renewal and Celebration 15:8-19

Asa's response is described in precise terms of the prophetic exhortation, but his specific actions go far beyond the general directives of the prophecy. As soon as Asa heard the prophetic words, he acted courageously by initiating a comprehensive reform, beginning with the removal of the abominable idols that again infested the land (cf. 2 Chron 14:5). Full trust in God had won the war against the Cushites, and total renewal of the covenant brought about the *rest* that was to characterize the kingdom of Solomon (15:15). The words of David when he commissioned Solomon to build the temple and establish its worship are proved true (1 Chron 22:9-11).

The name Oded in 2 Chronicles 15:8 is either a misplaced scribal note on the father of Azariah in verse 1 or an accidental omission of Azariah's name (NIV mg.). The MT is in obvious error (*BHS*). The problem was encountered in the Greek and later versions, which correct it in various ways. The mention of Asa's conquest of cities in Ephraim acknowledges the constant warfare between Baasha and Asa (1 Kings 15:16), though no mention of these wars is made until the next chapter. This is another instance where the reader needs to be aware of the Deuteronomistic account. The Chronicler is always concerned to include the northern tribes in spiritual reform (2 Chron 15:9). It is notable that Simeon should be included, since its territory was absorbed into Judah. One conjecture is that Edomite attacks in the south had driven the Simeonites northward. The spiritual renewal of Asa is shown to have a far-reaching influence in territories not under his control.

The ceremony of covenant renewal in the third month was probably during the Feast of Weeks (Pentecost), one of the great pilgrim festivals that brought crowds loyal to the temple from all the surrounding regions. The sacrifices were dedicated offerings from the victory over Zerah (cf. 14:15). Disloyalty to the covenant, which meant adherence to a false religion, was treated as treason (15:13), for which the ultimate penalty was prescribed in the Torah (Deut 17:2-7). Disloyalty and betrayal of a covenant oath exacts the harshest of penalties.

The reforms of Asa involved various purifications of both people and artifacts. This included removal of Maakah, the queen mother, who was the first lady of the realm, taking precedence over all the women of the harem (cf. 1 Kings 2:19; 11:19; 2 Kings 10:13). Normally she held the office as long as she lived, and on her decease the title passed on to the mother of the heir apparent. There is no indication that the queen mother held official duties, but she was a person of considerable influence.

Asherah was a place of worship with trees (Lipinski). It could be a sacred grove or a place under a tree where a forbidden cult was performed and where an idol was eventually located. There is no evidence that Asherah could be a wooden pole. The idol placed in the Asherah in 2 Chronicles 15:16 is called an *image* (*mipleṣet*), but it could be a hewn stone or a molded figurine. The terebinth of Moreh at Shechem (Gen 12:6) and the terebinth of Mamre (Gen 13:18; 18:1) marked such places. In Judges 3:7 and in 1 Kings 18:19, Asherah may mean the goddess or her emblems.

The Chronicler inserts a number of chronological notes into his account of Asa. They are designed to divide his reign into periods that show the consequences of his decisions (cf. 2 Chron 14:1; 15:10; 16:1, 12, 13). The Chronicler discounts the earlier battles with the north as having no consequence for the renewal of 15:8-19, though he makes mention of the cities taken from Ephraim (v. 8). The first years of Asa's reign were characterized by divine favor enjoyed by an obedient king.

War with Baasha 16:1-6

The chronology of the Chronicler for the reign of Asa has discrepancies that are difficult to reconcile consistently. According to Kings, Baasha was succeeded by his son Elah in the twenty-sixth year of Asa's reign (1 Kings 16:8), so he could not have gone to war in the thirty-sixth year of Asa (2 Chron 16:1). It has been supposed that the text in Chronicles has been transmitted with an error in the numerical cipher, which should read the fifteenth and sixteenth years instead of the thirty-fifth and thirty-sixth years of Asa (2 Chron 15:19; 16:1). There is no textual evidence for such an error, but more seriously, such a chronology does not correspond with the historical and theological presentation of the Chronicler. It moves the war with Baasha to the early part of Asa's reign, which is characterized as peaceful. It also places the foot disease twenty years after the offense, quite contrary to the usual theology of the Chronicler.

Though the chronology of the kings of Israel and Judah appears very conflicted, they do correspond to an absolute chronology, which indicates that they were used and understood as a reliable record [*Chronological Synchronism*, p. 465]. The Greek gives evidence of attempting to correct apparent discrepancies, but with disastrous results. The details have been worked out by Thiele; Konkel provides a simplified summary (Konkel 2006: 673-81). Chronology in relation to modern calendars is based on Assyrian annals, in which correlations can be made with astrological data. According to this chronology, the reign of Asa began twenty years after the division of the monarchy. Rehoboam reigned for seventeen years and Abijah for three years. The war that the Chronicler introduces in the thirty-fifth and thirty-sixth years of the kingdom of Asa (2 Chron 15:19-16:1) took place in the fifteenth and sixteenth years of Asa, according to the chronology of Kings. Thiele harmonizes the data by dating the thirty-fifth and thirty-sixth years from the time of the schism, which in his chronology is 931 BCE. Thirty-five years from the schism dates to the fifteenth year of the reign of Asa, the actual date of the war with Baasha. There is no other instance of such a synchronism [*Chronological Synchronism*, p. 465]. Thiele also must remove the reference to the thirty-fifth year *of the kingdom of Asa* in 2 Chronicles 15:19 as a later scribal gloss. Such a solution violates the Chronicler's usual accounting for immediate retribution. The foot disease from which Asa died would be twenty years after the offense (Dillard 1987: 124). The lessons of Asa's reign are characteristic of the Chronicler (Williamson 1982: 258). The seer Azariah (2 Chron 15:1-7) speaks of blessing for Asa's reforms, while the seer Hanani (16:7-9) condemns his failure to rely on God, as exemplified by his league with Ben-Hadad and his reaction to his disease.

Theile's chronology is the best provisional interpretation of the data (Dillard 1987: 125), though his harmonization does not solve the chronological problem, which remains unresolved. His proposals ultimately cannot be harmonized with the theological function of the Chronicler's chronology of Asa. The chronology of the Chronicler is part of the method by which he presents and confirms his theology.

The war with Baasha was a boundary dispute. The city of Ramah was located just five miles to the north of Jerusalem. Baasha executed a major expansion into the territory of Benjamin, separating important territory from the control of the king of Judah, very shortly after the victories of Abijah (2 Chron 13:19). Asa bribed the Arameans and appealed to an earlier treaty that his father, Abijah, had made with the Arameans to obtain relief from the aggression of Baasha. Ben-Hadad broke his treaty with Baasha and attacked northern Israel, capturing all the land of Naphtali (2 Chron 16:4). That included the whole of Galilee, almost all the country north of the Jezreel Valley and west of Lake Kinnereth. Ijon was a large village in the southern Beqaʿ Valley, on the southern border of modern Lebanon. It is usually listed together with Abel Beth Maʿakah (1 Kings 15:20), Dan (Laish), and Hazor in northern Israel. Abel Beth Maʿakah was located near a major waterfall of the Jordan River's tributaries, at the juncture of the Huleh Valley and the Beqaʿ Valley in what now is Lebanon.

Asa conscripted workers to use the materials at Ramah to fortify his northern border. Mizpah (Mizpeh) is to be identified with Tell en-Naṣbeh, about two miles north of Ramah and about four miles south of Bethel. Gebaʿ is likely to be identified with the modern village of Jabaʿ located about five miles northeast of Jerusalem on the brow of a steep hill. It guarded a key road that crossed the valley at the Geba and Micmash pass, protecting a wadi leading down to Jericho and the sanctuary at Gilgal. Control of this area was critical to the protection of Jerusalem.

Hanani's Sermon 16:7-10

The judgment declared by the prophet is an explicit antithesis to Asa's earlier trial. In the war with Zerah, the odds were entirely against Asa, but he prevailed (14:9-15). In this conflict, Asa's reliance on military might destined him to continual warfare (16:7-10). The punishment is in accord with his previous reward. The land enjoyed peace (14:5), but reliance on the Arameans would bring continuous pressure from that quarter (16:9).

The confinement of the prophet and general repression of the people proved that Asa's infidelity was not a momentary weakness but a disposition. This is the first recorded incident of the royal persecution of a prophet.

Death and Burial of Asa 16:11-14

The chronological notice marks another period of God dealing with Asa. In Chronicles, sickness is regarded as a punishment for sin (cf. 2 Chron 21:18-19; 26:20). The speech of Hanani declared that the punishment for the Aramean alliance was continuous war (16:9). The sickness seems to have been punishment for throwing the prophet into prison, but the connection is not made explicitly.

Asa had an honorable burial with a "spice-fire," a custom unknown outside of Chronicles and Jeremiah (16:14; cf. Jer 34:5). Asa apparently made extravagant preparations during his lifetime. The "spice-fire" may have been deemed a tribute to the name Asa, which in Aramaic also denotes "myrtle." Myrtle was an aromatic evergreen shrub celebrated for its scent.

THE TEXT IN BIBLICAL CONTEXT

Worship in Jerusalem

Asa is the first example of efforts to bring about an extensive reform for worship at the temple in Jerusalem, efforts that extended into the territories of Ephraim and Manasseh (2 Chron 15:8-9). Many in Israel became loyal to Asa. Just a few verses later, his engagement in war with Baasha is reported (15:19-16:1). This passage, parallel to 1 Kings 16:17, comes like a bolt from the blue (Rainey 1997: 45). There is no obvious rationale for Baasha to fortify the border to control traffic to Judah. However, Baasha's fortification of Ramah makes a lot of sense alongside the Chronicler's information about the impact of Asa's reform activities in the north. Baasha had usurped the throne in the north, and to secure it he systematically exterminated the remaining members of the house of Jeroboam (1 Kings 15:27-29). This would have created considerable unrest in the Northern Kingdom, which gave Asa opportunity to extend his reforms into that area. Further, military conflict with the Philistines, who were centered at Gibbethon when Baasha came to power (1 Kings 15:27), apparently continued: that territory seems to have remained unsettled until the end of Baasha's reign. Asa's victory over Zerah in Philistine territory and his successes in his border war with Baasha surely earned him a lot of respect with many in the north.

The authors of Kings make no mention of Asa's reforms or his victories in Philistine territory. Likely they were aware of this material in their sources. However, they have structured their history to explain the cause of the exile as a religious failure. To that end they have made Josiah the champion of centralization of worship and covenant reform (2 Kings 22:1–23:27). The wickedness of Manasseh in previously desecrating the temple becomes the reason why the exile was inevitable (2 Kings 24:2-3). A comparison with Chronicles indicates that this is a schematized way of viewing the events in Judah. Josiah relied on precedents for his successes. Historically, these began with Asa as part of a program to strengthen his own kingdom; yet all that was in opposition to the religions of the north that were established to fortify that regime.

The Life of Asa

The Chronicler presents his own chronology in developing his interpretation of Asa's life. It does not conform to his *Vorlage* and is internally inconsistent with his own account *[Vorlage, p. 468]*. The Chronicler says there was *no war* (MT; he does not say *no more war*, contra NIV, NRSV, et al.) until the thirty-fifth year of Asa (2 Chron 15:19), when he has already reported the war with Zerah (14:9-15). Several of the central theological themes of the Chronicler are established with this chronology. The victory over Zerah takes place during a period of peace and is a prime example of how God rewards faithfulness. The covenant celebration of Asa's reform includes opportunity to celebrate with the booty provided by the divine victory (15:11). Asa's life divides into two periods, each addressed by a prophet. In the first period, Asa is faithful and is affirmed by Azariah (15:1-7); in the second period, he is unfaithful and is warned by Hanani (16:7-9). From this point onward, Asa will have war and eventually die from God's judgment.

The wars with Baasha must have taken place before the thirty-fifth and thirty-sixth years of Asa. The confusion may have been caused by the conflicts with the north following Judah's separation in 931 BCE. The wars were in the fifteenth and sixteenth years of the reign of Asa. The Chronicler also says that the defections came from Ephraim, Manasseh, and Simeon (2 Chron 15:9). Here Simeon is not the tribe that settled in southern Judah but the town by that name on the northwestern side of the Jezreel Valley (Rainey 1997: 46). It is possible that in Asa's day, Megiddo still suffered from the destruction inflicted under the invasion of Shishak. A similar renewal occurs in the time of Josiah (2 Chron 34:6), when Megiddo was an Assyrian administrative center. The Chronicler supplies a lot of informative detail about religious reforms in Judah and associated conflicted relations with the north, information not given in Kings due to the special interests of those authors.

THE TEXT IN THE LIFE OF THE CHURCH

Spirituality in the Church

Asa's heart was fully committed to the LORD *all his life* (2 Chron 15:17b). This is a remarkable statement. Yet Asa is the king who threw a prophet into prison for correcting him and brutally crushed his opponents (16:10). How does the Chronicler justify this absolute statement about the spirituality of Asa? Spirituality is best described as commitment, the kind of vow in which Asa had led his people (15:14-15). It is one thing to remove idols and false worship; these are religious acts (yet note 15:17a). It is quite another to have uncompromising commitment to doing the will of God. This Asa had demonstrated to be true for himself, and apparently he meant it to be true all of his life. But no spiritual commitment is without failure. That failure may have some fatal consequences, as it did for Asa: he died of disease. But in the judgment of the Chronicler, such failure should not necessarily be assessed as a loss of spirituality.

This has important implications for the church. Most people engaged in the church are committed wholeheartedly. Church requires commitment of time, money, and sacrifices of various kinds. It needs to take priority over sports or other activities at times. This wholehearted commitment, the kind in which Asa led his people, is made by Christians in baptism, at least in the Anabaptist tradition. Baptism means to be buried with Christ and raised to a new life (Rom 6:4-5). This has eschatological implications for resurrection to new life, yet it also has implications for the present: those who are baptized must consider themselves to be dead to sin and alive to God. It is a total commitment; but it is not a commitment without some failure along the way.

One of the most tragic aspects of failure is when it happens to the congregation. There are those who have worked all their lives for the growth of the church, not necessarily in numbers, but especially in character and the practice of worship. But with the passing of time, both of these can be severely tested. Worship changes; in large part in Western churches, change is generated by technology as well as by other shifts in culture. This can be very distressing. Worship is like a language; one may learn other languages, but learned languages never function as a first language. Changes in worship, such as dress, music, and ritual practice, are most distressing to those with the highest level of commitment. It is not easy to maintain the spirituality of right conduct under such stress.

Many evangelical churches that once were the flagship congregations of their denomination have gradually emptied. In many cases this has simply been a matter of intransigence in matters of worship, most often music. There is much to be said for the great hymns of the past and the elegance of an organ. However, these are worship practices that develop in points of time; culture invariably moves on, it affects everyone, and it affects worship. Drums, electric guitars, and sound systems have become almost universal. Some of these things make spiritually committed people absolutely angry. When they have enough influence, they can keep them out of the service, which has *brutally oppressed some of the people* (2 Chron 16:10). Soon only old people are left; the life of the church ends when there no longer are enough people left to support a budget.

This is spiritual failure among the most highly committed. In essentials we need unity, in nonessentials we need liberty, and in all things we need charity. Manner of worship in terms of ritual and music falls under the categories of liberty and charity. Both must be exercised by all parties. Failure to do so will result in the death of a congregation, unless such failure is acknowledged, forgiveness is granted, and reconciliation is effected. Such a death is not a result of the loss of spirituality, but of the failure to exercise true spirituality, much as the prophet Hanani warned Asa. Asa's ambitions were noble, his commitments were strong, but his actions were wrong. When confronted, Asa simply became angry at those who pointed out his guilt. His great gains suffered loss, including personal loss.

Asa is a lesson in spiritual success. Spiritual achievement can have dangers of its own. The exercise of faith in one situation does not make a second situation any easier for learning to trust God. The appalling aspect of Asa's approach to Ben-Hadad was that it involved a bribe drawn from the royal and temple treasuries. The very things that were a mark of his faithfulness, building up the temple treasuries (2 Chron 15:18), were utterly betrayed in another test of war. Alliances were bad enough, but the use of temple treasuries was a complete contradiction to his arguments that the northerners should join his reform. Asa missed the opportunity to extend his influence even beyond Israel. The Lord is omnipresent, seeking to support those who are faithful, as declared by Hanani the prophet (16:9). Alliances have lasting consequences. Asa's example was followed by his son Jehoshaphat, whose alliance with Ahab and Ahaziah would also corrupt his own son Jehoram (21:6) and grandson Ahaziah (22:3, 5). It nearly resulted in the extinction of the Davidic line under the bloody reign of Athaliah (22:10-12). Faithfulness requires reliance on God even when the political opportunity for alliances may seem to be expedient.

There is never a time when learning to be faithful is complete. Faithfulness is an attitude that must be practiced; it is learned again in each new circumstance. Failures in faithfulness strike without warning. The consequences of such failures are not limited to the individual who sins. Like all sins, unfaithfulness affects all those around, and its effects continue far into the future. Asa is an example of such a disastrous failure, both at the individual level as well on the institutional scene. Leaders of institutions, whether denominations or congregations, therefore carry a particular responsibility to learn to trust God in every situation and to recognize that success at one time does not make future success more likely.

2 Chronicles 17:1–21:1a
Reign of Jehoshaphat

PREVIEW

How does a nation deal with a hostile attack? Usual political strategy requires an armed resistance; the alternative is to be taken over by invading forces. Ideally, aggressive nations would self-destruct, ending the hostility. That sometimes happens in part, but the story of Jehoshaphat is unparalleled in this regard. His primary defense is a Levitical choir. How this should be interpreted historically will depend on the reader's ideology. How such a tactic might be employed in contemporary hostilities is a thought to ponder. Jehoshaphat is an example of spiritual power and influence.

The eventful reign of Jehoshaphat in Chronicles is parallel to that of Asa. The comparison to Asa is made at the beginning of the narrative and again at the end (2 Chron 17:3; 20:32). As in the reign of Asa, peace was a sign of divine blessing. As in the days of Asa, there was peace and rest in the kingdom (20:30; cf. 14:6). The statement that Jehoshaphat did not eliminate all the high places has its parallel in Asa, where some of the high places continued to function (cf. 15:17; 20:33). Both Jehoshaphat and Asa engage in reform, building programs, and have large armies. Jehoshaphat has his own compromises, first with Ahab (18:3) and then also with Ahaziah (20:35). But he does not end in open rebellion, as does Asa, and he does not die under judgment. Jehoshaphat's war with the Moabite coalition has its parallel in Asa's victory over Zerah (20:1-30; 14:9-15), though the war of Jehoshaphat integrates all the elements of a battle fought by God, a true holy war [*War in Chronicles, p. 481*].

The battle against the Moabite coalition has a different outcome than the battle reported in 2 Kings 3. In Kings, the battle ends in great wrath coming upon Israel (2 Kings 3:27). Though this wrath is not explained, in Deuteronomistic theology the fury can only be that of the Lord and a consequence of a failure of faith on Israel's part. This results in the Israelite retreat. The campaign is unsuccessful: none of the territory is regained. In Chronicles, Jehoshaphat acts completely independently of any alliance and in total dependence on the Lord. The result is an outstanding triumph. The many parallels with the event in Kings serve to contrast the different circumstance in this battle. The great booty taken (2 Chron 20:25-26), which left its significance in the etiological name of a valley, is a central feature in accentuating the Chronicler's theology in Jehoshaphat's life *[Etiology, p. 466]*.

OUTLINE

Religious and Political Achievements, 17:1-19
Jehoshaphat and Ahab, 18:1-19:3
Judicial Reform, 19:4-11
Victory over Moab and Ammon, 20:1-30
Conclusion of Jehoshaphat's Reign, 20:31-21:1a

EXPLANATORY NOTES

Religious and Political Achievements 17:1-19

The last years of Asa's reign were characterized by internal uprising and oppression. Jehoshaphat needed to consolidate his power within Judah to restore it to peace and stability. Israel had been an enemy during the days of Asa, but Jehoshaphat soon entered into alliance with Ahab (18:1-2). He established control over Israel (17:2), which included territory in Ephraim that Asa had taken over.

Jehoshaphat is positively compared with the devotion of the first period of his father, Asa. The reference to David appears to be an addition to the text (17:3 MT). The name does not appear in the Greek versions *[Greek Text of Chronicles, p. 468]*. The translation *his father David before him* (NIV) is dubious (cf. NRSV). The first part of the reign of his father is specified, which pertains to Asa and not to David. For the first time the Chronicler compares the practices of Judah with the northern tribes, showing his awareness of the introduction of the Tyrian Baal cult into worship in the north.

All Judah donated to the royal treasury with necessary contributions (2 Chron 17:5). Usually *gifts* means taxes (*tribute*, NRSV), but taxation does not yield the correct sense in this context. The people of Judah voluntarily made Jehoshaphat rich. Riches often result in pride, as in the case of Uzziah (26:16) and Hezekiah (32:25). In this case Jehoshaphat's exalted heart was not in his achievements but in the ways of the Lord. Jehoshaphat had a positive pride that led him to remove idolatrous worship from his kingdom.

Five royal officers, eight Levites, and two priests were commissioned to instruct the people in the book of the covenant. Tob-Adonijah in the MT is not found in the Greek version (2 Chron 17:8) *[Masoretic Text, p. 470]*. The name either is a repetition from the previous two names or was accidentally omitted in the Greek text. Jehoshaphat carried out the requirements of Deuteronomy (cf. Deut 5:1; 17:18-20). Teaching was a Levitical and priestly function, but this group included laypeople. The function of Levites as teachers was common during the Second Temple period (cf. Neh 8:7) *[Greek Text of Chronicles, p. 468]*.

The dread of the Lord on the nations and their bringing tribute is comparable to that of the time of Asa (2 Chron 17:10; 14:14). Tribute of the Arabs came from the desert tribes south of Judah, in territory contiguous with the Philistines. Jehoshaphat succeeded in establishing control within his kingdom and the borders surrounding it as the result of his righteousness and fidelity.

Jehoshaphat's international status, building enterprises, and army characterized the greatness of his rule. Archaeological excavations have revealed extensive fortification in rural Judah. A line of highway forts in the Jordan Valley near the Dead Sea date to the time of Jehoshaphat (Mazar: 416-17; Japhet 1993: 751). It is impossible to say whether the distinctions of the commanders were positions of rank and duty or general description. The numbers, totaling more than a million troops in Jerusalem, are excessive. Since the leaders are based on tribal divisions (2 Chron 17:14), some have suggested that "thousand" (*'elep*) in this instance is a military unit. The totals may have included reserve divisions that served on rotation (cf. 1 Chron 27:1-15). The figure assigned to Jehoshaphat is approximately triple that of Abijah (13:3), Asa (14:8), Amaziah (25:5), and Uzziah (26:11-15). The number is comparable to the warriors at the time of David's census (1 Chron 21:5). Large numbers are a sign of political strength, divine blessing, and royal piety.

Jehoshaphat and Ahab 18:1-19:3

In Kings, the battle at Ramoth Gilead is in the context of the Aramean wars. Jehoshaphat appears in a scene between the king of

Israel and his servants (1 Kings 22:3-8), when the northern king seeks his support in war. In Chronicles, Jehoshaphat pays a visit to Ahab and is given a grand royal reception. The juxtaposition of the wealth of Jehoshaphat with an alliance to Ahab through marriage is one of the ways the Chronicler gives a warning on the danger of wealth (cf. 2 Chron 19:2). The Chronicler says that Ahab lured (*urged* NIV; *induced* NRSV) Jehoshaphat to go up to Ramoth Gilead. There is usually a negative nuance to this word. It may be used to describe leading someone into apostasy (Deut 13:6; 1 Kings 21:25). The intent of Ahab is deceptive, and Jehoshaphat is being used in a cause that does not have God's approval.

Ramoth Gilead was a fortress city in the eastern portion of the tribal territory of Gad (Josh 20:8). This was one of the cities of refuge for inadvertent homicide and an important administrative center in Solomon's kingdom (1 Kings 4:13). It was an important fortress, protecting the eastern trade routes. Following the great battle at Qarqar, where Ahab had allied with the Arameans in successfully stopping the advance of the Assyrians under Shalmanezer III (853 BCE), the Arameans tried to regain control of an important trade route to the south, the King's Highway. Ahab needed an ally against the superior Aramean forces to regain control of a city critical to his kingdom.

The interchange between the two kings acknowledges that the four hundred prophets of Ahab served to promote the interests of the king. Ahab is not surprised that Jehoshaphat should ask for the opinion of a neutral prophet and knows in advance that such a prophet would contradict the prophets serving the state. The actions of the prophets involved some type of ecstatic behavior, similar to the Baal prophets at Mount Carmel (1 Kings 18). The sign actions of Zedekiah were rhetorical nonverbal communication, persuasive in nature and intent. The confession of Ahab shows that he understood full well the will of the Lord (2 Chron 18:15). The text does not indicate anything in the manner of Micaiah to suggest that his answer was sarcastic. Perhaps it was sufficient that his answer was given in precisely the same words as those of his rivals. If Ahab did not understand the prophetic word to be a prophecy of his death (vv. 16-17), he understood full well that his own army would be the proverbial leaderless flock. His defiance is seen in the contempt he held for the prophet, throwing him into prison (vv. 25-26), though he knew full well that his fate was declared by God.

The vision serves to explain the willful self-deception of the false prophets (2 Chron 18:18-24). It legitimates the word of Micaiah.

Micaiah does not claim, as charged by Zedekiah (v. 23), that the spirit of the Lord had left Zedekiah and had gone over to him. Micaiah could only speak the truth he had seen in the vision. The prophets, in their desire to affirm the intent of the king, had carried out the will of God as determined in the heavenly court. The enticement was to guarantee that Ahab would fall in battle: his judgment was decreed. The effective accomplishment of the divine will through the will of the false prophets could take place without their conscious participation.

Ahab's defiance of God is further revealed in his careful preparations for self-protection (2 Chron 18:28-34). His immediate concern was the Aramean army, though he knew he had violated God's will and was therefore subject to the consequences. This is a further indication of his disregard for the God of Israel, believing that he could defy divine judgment against him. His error was fatal for him. The Chronicler here adds his own note to indicate the divine protection of Jehoshaphat (v. 31), which is not found in his *Vorlage [Vorlage, p. 468]*. The Lord helped Jehoshaphat by luring the Aramean soldiers away from the king. This is a reference back to verse 2, where Ahab had lured Jehoshaphat into battle in the first instance. The enticement of Ahab proved to be fatal for him; in turn, the Lord reversed this deception in providing deliverance to Jehoshaphat.

Jehu son of Hanani is the son of the prophet who had rebuked Asa for his reliance on the Arameans. He chastises Jehoshaphat for his alliance with Ahab (19:1-2). "Love" is a technical term for entering into a covenant (v. 2); "hate" is the term for breaking a covenant. Jehoshaphat has entered into a covenant with someone who had broken covenant with God. For the Chronicler, the chief point of the Micaiah story is to show that foreign alliances are a fundamental violation of the covenant. The whole story serves a different purpose than that of Kings, where it is to avenge Ahab for his horrible crimes. The death of Naboth had become the rallying cry against the greed of Ahab (1 Kings 21). In Chronicles, the focus is entirely on Jehoshaphat and the way he has been compromised in this alliance.

Jehoshaphat is said to have removed the Asherah (2 Chron 19:3) and *not* to have removed them (20:33), as was also the case with Asa (cf. 14:5; 15:17). The Asherah are the cultic places of foreign worship. The distinction is geographical; places of foreign worship were removed from Judah, but not from those cities outside of the control of Jehoshaphat. The removal of foreign high places is an affirmation of Jerusalem being the single legitimate place of worship, with the building of the temple (Rainey and Notley: 195). This program not only closed local places of worship, but also established royal centers in those same towns with a public program of fortifications.

Judicial Reform 19:4-11

The description of judicial reform is composed of two symmetrical paragraphs (vv. 5-7 and 8-11), patterned with an action and an admonition. In the second paragraph, some of the reform measures are included in the exhortation, providing balance to the accounts. Local court officials were appointed in the fortified cities, and a central court was established in Jerusalem. The reform is a realization of the law of Deuteronomy (16:18–17:13), but in this context only judges are appointed and only in fortified towns. Every citizen had obligations toward the king and toward God; this dual loyalty was fully consistent with covenant obligation. There may have been a lower and higher court in Jerusalem, one that served as the ordinary jurisdiction for citizens, and an appeals court for all the lower courts. Priests and Levites had some judicial role in the Jerusalem court, but no such role is mentioned for them in the local courts [*Priests and Levites in Chronicles, p. 471*].

Victory over Moab and Ammon 20:1-30

According to the Greek text (followed in the NIV), the coalition allied against Jehoshaphat (2 Chron 20:1) included Meunites (cf. 1 Chron 4:41) [*Greek Text of Chronicles, p. 468*]. Ammon is repeated in the MT, which is likely corrupted (cf. 2 Chron 26:7). The Meunites were a nomadic group on the southern borders of Judah and probably survive in the Arab town of Maʿan, twelve miles southeast of Petra. Edom fits the geographical description of an attack from the southeast. The coalition is later described as Ammonites, Moabites, and inhabitants of Mount Seir (20:22-23). En Gedi was located on the center of the west bank of the Dead Sea. Hazezon Tamar indicates an oasis of palm trees on the route between En Gedi and Bethlehem. The military expedition may have used the shallow ford westward across the Dead Sea, establishing a base camp at En Gedi. Moab gained independence from Israel after the death of Ahab. Jehoshaphat, ally of Ahab, was a natural target.

In this instance, Jehoshaphat followed the petitions of Solomon's prayer (2 Chron 20:3-13; cf. 6:34-35). In time of war, he gathered the people together to seek deliverance from God. The prayer of Jehoshaphat does not appeal to compassion or divine favor; it was a petition that God would keep his promises against the attack of his adversaries. Powerful and treacherous invaders had taken advantage of a powerless and righteous people. The prayer has typical elements of lament; it includes a lengthy invocation, a confession, a statement of assurance, and the petition itself.

Jahaziel's speech functions as an oracle of deliverance following the lament given by Jehoshaphat (20:15-17). It has the form of the prescribed speech from a priest before battle (Deut 20:2-4). A jihad is a war in which men fight for God. The biblical view is that God does not need human help to fight his battles. According to the Scriptures, in holy war God fights for his people. The foe may be superior, but fear is completely inappropriate, except for fear of the Lord [War in Chronicles, p. 481].

It is not normally good military strategy to meet a mighty foe with a choir, yet this is the appropriate method of divine warfare. In this case the prophets were the Levitical musicians, such as Jahaziel; musical praise for the battle march was itself prophetic. Through the millennia music has had a vital role in warfare, but in the context of divine warfare, it was a declaration that God was at the head of the army. As at Jericho, the battle belonged to the Lord; the task of the human army was simply to stand still and wait for the outcome of the battle. The battle cry was replaced by a chorale. The Lord set ambushes against the enemy. The Chronicler is saying that the heavenly army confused the enemy armies so they turned on each other in the rough terrain. The army of Jehoshaphat returned to the temple, confirming the answer to prayer; they ended where they began.

Conclusion of Jehoshaphat's Reign 20:31-21:1a

The comparison with Asa is adopted from 1 Kings 22:43-46 without alteration. This stands in a certain tension with the earlier comparison, where the qualification is given that it was the earlier part of Asa's reign that was exemplary (2 Chron 17:3).

The Chronicler provides a variant version of the alliance of Jehoshaphat with Ahaziah. In 1 Kings 22:48, the ships never set sail but were destroyed in port. Jehoshaphat then turned down an offer from Ahaziah to have a joint undertaking (v. 49). In Chronicles, the breakup of the ships was a consequence of the initial alliance with Ahaziah. The second effort to build a fleet was rejected, perhaps under the influence of the preaching of Eliezer (2 Chron 20:37). This report is not a contradiction to that of Kings. The breakup of the ships shows the divine displeasure with the alliance, an important point for the Chronicler.

THE TEXT IN BIBLICAL CONTEXT

When God Fights for Us

The persistence of holy war themes in a work addressed to the small restoration community after the exile is notable. The community was politically subservient, surviving under the protection of the Persians. These holy war motifs had a message for the people of the Chronicler's time. Military power is not the factor to be considered when it comes to the kingdom of God. The triumph via Persian horses in maintaining order and control in the whole civilized world must have been a cause for dismay. Nothing could suggest that their community had a particular significance in the future of humanity. The story of Jehoshaphat is told to show that in the kingdom of God, such military power does not determine the future.

Holy war is a motif found throughout the Old Testament. From every period of Israel's existence, there are battle reports in poetry and prose that unite the divine and human dimensions. The exodus material is unique in that the Hebrew nation is not called upon to engage in battle in the usual sense. They are to trust the Lord as the sole warrior against the military might of Egypt. The redemption from Egypt is the model of how God will create the nation of Israel apart from any of its own abilities to survive in the world (Lind: 170). In Israel, this created a fundamental tension between the way of the Lord and the way of the nations. The Song of the Sea (Exod 15) exhibits none of these tensions. This tension is evident, however, in the Song of Deborah (Judg 5), which celebrates Israel's participation in warfare. The prophetic personality (Deborah) and the military leader (Barak) are both part of the battle in the narrative (Judg 4). The prophetic presence was essential to victory. The irony of that story is that the victory would be gained by a woman (Jael) rather than the general. There would be no glory for Barak. It is one of the many ways in which the failure of the judges is exemplified. The relationship between God and his people is not synergistic. The victory belongs to God, though in the narrative there is the engagement of the Israelite armies. But the model of exodus warfare is evident in the achievement of victory.

Lind divides the tension of warfare in Israel into two separate institutions. The concept of holy war is applied to the historical situation by prophetic leadership and points to divine victory. There is holy war as applied to the historical situation by a political or kingship type of leadership (Lind: 108). Lind regards the tension in Israel as a result of the tradition grounded in the exodus experience, which set Israel apart from its neighbors, and the tension within itself to become like the neighboring nations. There is much truth in these observations that is evident in stories like that of Jehoshaphat. It is insightful to keep that continual tension in mind.

Kings repeatedly find themselves in conflict with the prophets. In extreme cases the reason is simple: the Lord is the warrior and will avenge himself against his enemy, even as represented by the leaders of Jerusalem (Isa 1:24). Kingship in Israel can be diametrically opposed to the rule of God. But many other situations are much more ambiguous, like that of Jehoshaphat. The victory belongs to God and is the result of the king making his choice to trust God in the situation, but it was not apart from his engagement in battle. The tensions of holy war in Israel result in part from the conflicts of prophetic office and royal office, but also because in part they are inherent to the human situation. God does not fight every battle as he did in the Song of the Sea. There is a role of human military in situations like that of Jehoshaphat, who is the model of a political leader acting in a prophetic role. He gathers all of Judah together, including wives and children, for a long exhortation on relying on God (2 Chron 20:4-13). They are instructed to wait to see the salvation of the Lord (v. 17). He then proceeds to meet the enemy armies with a Levitical choir.

The covenant of Israel required authorized human engagement as a fundamental necessity in violent human society. Before the flood, good was determined by the dictum of Lamech: "If Cain is avenged seven times, then Lamech seventy-seven times" (Gen 4:24). The result is violence among the whole human race, which brings it to a state of total corruption (6:11). With the flood, creation begins again. Following the flood, the mandate of creation to form human society over all the earth is issued again (9:1, 7). Violence in society following the flood is mitigated by human authority, which can be described as human government. "Whoever sheds human blood, by humans shall their blood be shed; for in the image of God has God made mankind" (9:6). Only the context can help us with the implications of being the divine image. On the one hand, it makes intentional capricious manslaughter a capital offense. Though the blood of animals must be respected, killing of animal life is not a capital offense. But a second consequence of being the image is the responsibility to restrain violence so that the conditions leading to the flood do not repeat. Human government therefore is a divinely ordained institution and as such is mandated to restrain violence.

The human situation is one of continual conflict, one in which those who represent the authority bestowed on the image will need to coercively stop the actions of the violent. Into this situation must be added all the obscurity of human motives, particularly of those entrusted with power. So in the Bible, human government is a divinely appointed institution, but it is often a monster that attacks the very people it is supposed to protect. The best of examples are those like Jehoshaphat; there is no doubt that the Chronicler depicted him as a model for his time in the postexilic Persian period. It was his testimony of hope for a better order that could come only by means of direct divine intervention in human affairs.

THE TEXT IN THE LIFE OF THE CHURCH
Learning to Live with War

The Chronicler was far removed from being apocalyptic in theology, but his ideas of holy war have their ultimate resolution in apocalyptic literature (Lind: 174). As the Lord had intervened in the exodus, so he would intervene again in the ultimate fulfillment of the hopes of Israel. Daniel, notable among the wise in a king's court, was a representative of this kingdom. The Zealots of the first century reduced their holy warfare to warriors fighting on behalf of God. The Maccabees were their precedent. In their minds, God would win his victory for a kingdom under their power, through their engagement in war. The War Scroll at Qumran describes the eschatological last battle in gory detail as righteousness is fully victorious and evil is forever destroyed. The scroll introduces a lengthy three-stage battle between "the sons of light" and "the sons of darkness," a Jewish conception of Armageddon at the time of Jesus. The Son of God identified himself with the wisdom of Daniel (Mark 13:26-27). The apostle John, in his message to a suffering church, incorporated the substance of the Song of the Sea as the message of its triumph (Rev 19:1-8). The final "Hallelujah!" is that of the rider on the white horse, destroying forever the corruptions of the great whore with the word of his mouth. The account of the last war of Jehoshaphat is precisely this kind of war. It is the unequivocal view of the Chronicler that the might of human armies has no relevancy for the kingdom of God. This must also be the view of the church.

The church of today is no different from the church of Revelation or the Israel portrayed by the Chronicler. The church represents a "kingdom . . . not of this world" (John 18:36), and therefore it does not engage in the powers of state warfare. In many places of the world, the church today suffers under temporal powers, under a whole array of political ideologies and regimes, as it did during the time of the apostle John. Thus the church today does await the final day of judgment, when all such suffering will be ended. However, in many countries individual Christians have the protection of state and to some measure the support of state power. While all Christians await the rider on the white horse, they do so in very different ways. Christians living under the protection of the state have the opportunity and obligation to engage in powers of government that could never be envisaged in the province of Yehud or the seven churches of Revelation. The question of engagement in warfare in such contexts is very relevant.

Human history is mostly an account of warfare. The greatest evil in all times is that created by humans, who find themselves powerless to stop it. The question for Christians is how to live with it. Some Anabaptists have taken the position that it is the duty of the church to refrain from all involvement in military power by the state. Whatever the merits of such a position theologically, it has no existential possibility. States in the present time, as at all times, survive by defending themselves in one way or another by military force. Christians today do not have opportunity to give speeches like that of Jehoshaphat. Modern methods of warfare are not comparable. However, Christians have a responsibility to represent their participation in a kingdom that is not of this world, even while engaged with kingdoms of this world. This cannot be done without compromise, at least to the level of paying taxes for use as a secular power chooses. Christians must always be engaged in assisting the victims of war and finding ways to make peace possible.

Working for Peace

Much can be learned from this account of Jehoshaphat in working for peace. No effort can be spared in providing education and instruction of the ways of God. War is made by humans; peace begins by instructing humans in the ways of redemption and reconciliation. As in the example of Jehoshaphat (2 Chron 17:7-11), this must be as extensive and inclusive as possible. Christians will still find ways to engage in the conflicts of their world. Jehoshaphat was confronted by Ahab, a king bent on engaging the Judean king in the wars of Israel. Ahab knew perfectly well this was contrary to the will of God; it is undeniably manifested in his dealings with the prophet Micaiah. The Chronicler presents Jehoshaphat as resolved to act under divine guidance and as divinely protected against the wiles of

Ahab in the heat of battle (18:31b). This divine deliverance from death is a specific statement of the Chronicler (cf. 1 Kings 22:32-33), in spite of the fact that Jehoshaphat will be censured by the prophet Jehu for getting involved with Ahab (2 Chron 19:2). It is important to remember mercy, because choices in conflict will not always be right. Jehoshaphat's response is to work for peace by the appointment of judges and providing for justice. There are two critical pursuits for peace: (1) education to know the will of God, and (2) justice for the conflicts of daily life. When the next battle confronts Jehoshaphat, he is able to meet the armies with a Levitical choir. Christians are called upon to teach the ways of Jesus and to pursue justice until that day when the trumpet sounds and the rider on the great white horse defeats evil with the power of his word (Rev 19).

2 Chronicles 21:1b–22:9
Reigns of Terror

PREVIEW

Alliances are both necessary and dangerous. They are necessary in order to provide for peace and stability. Whether at a national or local level, some type of cooperative alliance is necessary if there are to be good relations. But alliances are dangerous because an ally may be compromised or forced into destructive situations.

The alliance of Omri with the Phoenicians made Israel a power of international significance. The second register of the Assyrian Black Obelisk depicts Jehu as a son of Omri, though in Israel he was the usurper that terminated the Omride dynasty. He weakened Israel to the point of humiliation; its king is depicted prostrate with his tribute before Shalmaneser III. From a prophetic point of view, the Phoenician alliance was disastrous for Israel and Judah. In the words of the Deuteronomistic author, Judah survived because the Lord would not allow the lamp for David to be snuffed out (2 Kings 8:19; 2 Chron 21:7). Jehoshaphat had given his son Jehoram to Athaliah, the daughter of Ahab and Jezebel (2 Kings 8:18; 2 Chron 21:6). This brought Judah directly under the influence of the Baal religion.

Baal religion was a fertility cult. It was a form of materialism under the guise of religious piety. Worship of Baal, the rider of the clouds, ostensibly brought rain that made crops grow. The pedestal of Baal was a calf; his stela depicts him with a club in one hand for thunder and a sprig or lightning bolt in the other. In the days of Ahab, through the aggressive efforts of Jezebel, Phoenician religion permeated Israel to the point that Elijah would feel that he was the only prophet left. The Chronicler says nothing of this influence, other than the observation that Judah came directly under Baal influence through Athaliah, daughter of Jezebel, wife of Jehoram and mother of his son Ahaziah. Materialism has been a destructive force in much of human history, well illustrated in the reigns of Jehoram and Ahaziah.

The only reference the Chronicler makes to Elijah is the letter sent to Jehoram (2 Chron 21:12-15). It indicates the depravity that had come to control the house of Jehoshaphat through Athaliah, wife of Jehoram. Both Jehoram, king of Israel, and Ahaziah, king of Judah, were killed in the violent purge of Jehu (2 Kings 9:21-24, 27-29). Athaliah, the mother of Ahaziah, tried to purge all the heirs to the throne of Judah, nearly exterminating all succession to the throne of David. The Chronicler has his own version of the reigns of Jehoram and his son Ahaziah. The events he includes and the manner in which he presents these reigns are in keeping with his ideological *Tendenz [Tendenz in Chronicles, p. 476]*. It is obvious that the Chronicler had information not found in Kings. His views do not focus on political conspiracy but on spiritual depravity and divine judgment.

OUTLINE

Ruthless Rule of Jehoram, 21:1b-11
Terrible Warning of Elijah, 21:12-15
Agonized End of Jehoram, 21:16–22:1
Reign of Ahaziah, 22:2-9

EXPLANATORY NOTES

Ruthless Rule of Jehoram 21:1b-11

Jehoram is the first king of the Davidic line who receives a totally negative evaluation. Four times violence was perpetuated against the royal family, so the dynasty was all but ended (2 Chron 21:4, 17; 22:8-11). David's line was threatened with extinction. The Chronicler lays special emphasis on its preservation through the loyal faithfulness of God. The pogroms that took place during the reigns of Jehoram and Ahaziah reduced succession in Judah to the same kind of mutually destructive violence that virtually eliminated the royal families of the Persian Empire during the times of the Chronicler. The line of David had become reduced to the values and tactics of all the other nations. The Chronicler could only be utterly dismayed at the way the hope of the promise could be so subordinated to immediate temporal ambitions. This was no doubt all the more reason for him to so rigorously defend his own views of God's sovereignty and the necessity of holding those beliefs as the greatest treasure.

During the days of Jehoshaphat, Edom was ruled by a royal deputy (1 Kings 22:47), who may be generically referred to as a king (2 Kings 3:9). During the reign of Solomon the territory of Edom afforded Israel access to the rich trade from Arabia. Edom rebelled before Solomon's death (1 Kings 11:14-22) and likely was not under the control of Rehoboam. The failure of the campaign against Moab (2 Kings 3) may have encouraged the revolt of Edom. Libnah, at the western end of the Valley of Elah and on the border of Philistia, also revolted successfully. The gains of Asa and Jehoshaphat were lost through the disobedience of Jehoram. The course of Jehoram's battle against Edom is unclear (2 Chron 21:9), just as it is in the *Vorlage [Vorlage, p. 468]*. Smiting the Edomites did not defeat them. Jehoram managed to break through Edomite lines when he had been surrounded.

Terrible Warning of Elijah 21:12-15

The reader familiar with Kings may be puzzled to observe that, in Chronicles, Elijah sends a terrible letter to Jehoram. In Kings, Elijah was taken up into heaven while Jehoshaphat, Jehoram's father, was still king (2 Kings 2:12). This is not a chronological problem when the coregencies of kings are understood. The war with Moab, in which Jehoshaphat allied with Joram son of Ahab, follows (2 Kings 3:1-27). As integrated in the Kings narrative, the summary of Jehoshaphat's reign is unusual because it is disrupted by the Elijah and Elisha stories. The death of Jehoshaphat and the accession of his son Jehoram are recorded in 1 Kings 22:50. Jehoram, son of Jehoshaphat, is in his second year as king of Judah at the death of Ahaziah, son of Ahab (2 Kings 1:17). Joram, son of Ahab and brother of Ahaziah, becomes king of Israel because Ahaziah had no sons. A second accession of Jehoram king of Judah is found in 2 Kings 8:16-17, quoted in part in the Jehoram narrative in 2 Chronicles 21:5. The accession of Jehoram of Judah takes place in the fifth year of Joram, king of Israel, at the death of Jehoshaphat. Kings understands Jehoshaphat to have made Jehoram king before he went to war with Moab. Jehoram became sole ruler at his father's death. In summary, then, according to Kings there was a coregency of Jehoram and Jehoshaphat for over five years (2 Kings 8:16; Konkel 2006: 676-77). Moab rebelled while Jehoshaphat was king. Jehoshaphat set his son Jehoram on the throne while he went to war. Jehoram, however, tried to seize the kingdom outright. So Elijah sent him this terrible letter just before he was taken up into heaven.

The prophetic work of Elijah is confined to the north in his confrontation with Ahab and the prophets of Baal. Jehoram was related by marriage to the house of Ahab and walked in the ways of the kings of Israel. For these reasons a letter from Elijah is appropriate. Elijah was witness to the sins of Jehoram though not personally present in Judah. The letter recounts the sins of Jehoram: he walked in the ways of Israel, led Judah into unfaithfulness, and killed his brothers who were better than him. The indictment of the letter follows the theology of the Chronicler. Jehoram will lose his family and possessions and will personally die of a painful disease. The letter recounts the sins of Jehoram in the first part of the narrative and pronounces the judgment that unfolds against Jehoram in the second part of the account.

Agonized End of Jehoram 21:16-22:1

Attacks from the Philistines and the Arabs were from the same locales as those of Edom, southeast of Judah, and Libnah, to the west. Jehoram's inability to successfully resist initial revolt fomented other rebellious attacks. The attacks were on the fortified cities outside of Jerusalem. A call to war brought the family of Jehoram together in an encampment, where Arab raiders were able to kill all but Ahaziah (2 Chron 22:1). The plunder was not the treasury in Jerusalem, but the goods in the camp (21:17). If progeny is the measure of blessing, then the loss of Jehoram's family is another indication of divine judgment. Only his youngest son, Jehoahaz, survived; this is a variant name of Ahaziah (21:17 mg.; the divine element *yh* is placed at the beginning of *'ḥz* rather than at the end). The Greek preserves the form Ahaziah in this verse as well.

Jehoram died after a long and painful disease in his bowels; the Hebrew says that in the end he died in *two days*, which may mean that his bowels prolapsed two days before his death. Jehoram was not given the dignity of an honorary funeral rite (cf. 16:14) and was buried in ignominy outside the royal tombs in Jerusalem. The Chronicler says nothing about the records of Jehoram, which may be an indication of the contempt he had for this self-centered king.

Reign of Ahaziah 22:2-9

The decimation of the royal household of Jehoram left Judah and Jerusalem in the precarious situation of disorderly succession. It left the territory in substantial control of the queen mother. She held the position of sovereign, an exalted ceremonial position with considerable influence on matters of state. Athaliah was the mirror image of Jezebel, wife of Ahab. Athaliah is said to be a daughter of Omri in the MT of 2 Kings 8:26 and 2 Chronicles 22:2, though she is a daughter of Ahab according to 2 Kings 8:18 and 2 Chronicles 21:6. The apparent discrepancy is easily resolved if she was the granddaughter of Omri: the Hebrew term for "daughter" can also mean "granddaughter."

The inhabitants of Jerusalem installed the remaining son of the royal family as king. These may be the equivalent of the *people of the land* who participated in the installation of a king in times of dynastic crisis (2 Chron 23:20-21; 26:21; 33:25; 36:1). They must be associated with landed aristocracy or officials within civil service. Perhaps in the immediate crisis the decision was made by leaders in Jerusalem without further consultation.

Ramoth Gilead had come to be under Aramean control in spite of the continuous efforts of the kings of Israel to regain their city. Jehu was fighting there when the prophet Elisha commissioned his servant to anoint him as king (2 Kings 9:1-10). Jezreel was situated at the foot of Mount Gilboa, about ten miles (fifteen kilometers) east of Megiddo, on a ridge extending along the southern edge of the Valley of Jezreel. It appears to have been established as a fortified military center to serve as the base for a large army (Ussishkin 1997: 352-56, 361-63). This city was built concurrently with Samaria, providing for substantial units of cavalry and chariotry. A central building served as a royal residence.

The Chronicler assumes that his readers are familiar with the details of why Ahaziah would go to see Jehoram in Jezreel, which led to his fate in the purge of Jehu. For the Chronicler, this decision was a divine initiative (2 Chron 22:7). The death of Ahaziah is a punishment for allying with the king of Israel. This was an ironic justice; the king who lived by the counsel of the Omrides shared their fate. He had taken advice from Samaria, but found no refuge there at the time of his death. The Chronicler leaves Ahaziah in exile, as he does with Jehoiakim and the three last kings of Judah (Dillard 1987: 175). The much-longer account of Kings explains that Ahaziah was buried in Jerusalem. The details of Kings cannot be reconciled with the impression left by the Chronicler without a measure of credulity. In Kings, Ahaziah flees south toward Samaria but is overtaken at Beth Haggan; he is shot and wounded at Gur, near Ibleam. Knowing that he cannot count on the speed of his chariot in the hills, he turns west toward Megiddo, seeking refuge. There he dies from his wounds and is brought back to Jerusalem. Apparently the Chronicler gives a rather schematic version of the events that leave Ahaziah in exile. He closes with the note that Ahaziah was given a proper burial as a son of righteous Jehoshaphat.

THE TEXT IN BIBLICAL CONTEXT
Divine Faithfulness

Elijah's prophetic letter reveals that Jehoram, though on the throne of Judah, was acting like a northern king. His paranoid eradication of the royal house came to be true for his own house, in which only one heir was left for the throne. But it is precisely at the low point of religious fidelity that the Chronicler reiterates and elaborates on the promise to David (2 Chron 21:7). This may have been of particular significance to his community. Affirming the promise to David in a circumstance where the very survival of an individual heir was in jeopardy would be a powerful confession of faith in the assurance of the promise.

Irony permeates the account of Jehoram's reign. Rather than enlarging the scope of his power through seizing his brother's cities, he loses control over Libnah and Edom. Rather than the succession of his own children through eliminating his brothers, his own children are slaughtered. Instead of power and renown, his life ends in a painful and agonizing death. Jehoram had no sense that the kingdom belonged to God.

The Deuteronomistic Historians tell of the end of the Omride dynasty with the horrible massacre by Jehu. Again there is an irony; the attack of Jehu was against the followers of Baal, but Jehu did not change the religion of Israel. All that changed was the ending of the family relations with the Phoenicians. The dynasty of Jehu would come to international prominence under the reign of Jeroboam II, which would only repeat all the horrors that had already been experienced. The prophetic denunciations by Amos describe the situation of the last dynasty of Israel. The wealth and opulence of the kingdom was at the expense of extracting the means of livelihood from the poor. The kingdom of Samaria ended a generation after Jeroboam II with the invasion of the almost unknown Assyrian king Shalmaneser V. None of these events are of any interest to the Chronicler. They did not affect the Davidic dynasty nor the destiny of Israel as understood by the Chronicler. Israel was not to be defined by national identity but by the families representing the houses of their fathers in their traditional territories.

THE TEXT IN THE LIFE OF THE CHURCH
Divine Justice

In his depiction of retribution, the theology of the Chronicler seems to be more ideal than real. It may seem right that despicable rulers should die a horrible and painful death, with no hope of their tyranny being carried on by their successors. This is not the reality of experience. Stalin enjoyed popular near deification as he approached the end of his life. One of many examples is an oversized and godlike image of the Soviet leader installed in Moscow's Bolshoi Theater in 1951. Similar examples can be multiplied in contemporary times.

Such realities were a problem in consideration of divine justice. The author of Job was dissatisfied with a view of justice that could be reduced to immediate retribution for good and evil. The book of Job is about wisdom. How do the wise deal with suffering and injustice? In God's speech in Job 40:7-14, justice remains an enigma to human comprehension.

> Cut down the rich and the mighty.
>   Make the proud man grovel.
>   Pluck the wicked from their perch.
> Push them into the grave.
>   Throw them, screaming, to hell.
> Then I will admit
>   that your own strength can save you.
>   (Job 40:12-14, in Mitchell: 85)

Can God be trusted? That becomes the critical question for the wise. The answer in Job will be yes. Job repents of his attitude and surrenders to God as a child of "dust and ashes" (Job 42:6). The man of the wise who composed Job would not have said that the Chronicler was wrong. Retribution does happen in the present time. It is not contrary to God's ways of justice, but it must not be used to define them. This the Chronicler does not do. The Chronicler and the author of Job are agreed on one critical point: it is dangerous to live the life of the violent and corrupt. Whatever the appearances, judgment upon the wicked is to be feared. This is one aspect of what is meant by the fear of the Lord as the beginning of wisdom. Anxiety is contrary to a life of trust in God, but trust in God begins with knowing what to fear. Fear of God is the confidence a person of faith has in divine providence, a confidence that guards against all other fears, pain, and evil.

2 Chronicles 22:10–24:27
Reign of Joash

PREVIEW

Leon Trotsky may be regarded as a tragic figure of history. Born to a Jewish family in what today is Ukraine and then well educated, he became a Marxist revolutionary and theorist in the interests of addressing the social evils of Russia. He joined the Bolsheviks and became one of the seven members of the first legendary Politburo, founded in 1917 to manage the revolution. He was a major figure in the Bolshevik victory in 1923. His resistance to Stalin forced him into exile in Mexico, where he was eventually assassinated on Stalin's orders. The story of Zechariah son of Jehoiada is one of similar political intrigue: the son of the priest who established the child king was assassinated by that king, Joash.

Chronicles makes the installation of Joash a sacred event, though in his *Vorlage* it is fundamentally a political coup *[Vorlage, p. 468]*. Instead of the royal bodyguard of Carites (probably to be associated with the Kerethites, the elite soldiers from the area of Gaza who became the core of the royal guard), the Chronicler emphasizes the priests and the Levites (2 Chron 23:2, 13). Rather than reporting the amassing of soldiers to stage a coup, the Chronicler depicts a large religious assembly making a covenant at the temple to support the new king. He further brings in the emphasis of promise. All take an oath affirming the word of the Lord about the Davidic descendants (2 Chron 23:3). The first episode describes the virtually miraculous recovery of the Davidic dynasty (Rudolph: 273).

The first period of Joash's reign is regarded most favorably by the Chronicler, yet it is qualified by a phrase indicating the influence of the priest (2 Chron 24:2). Joash did what was right all the time that Jehoiada the priest was alive. In Kings, this is all the time that Jehoiada "instructed him" (2 Kings 12:2). This seems to be an affirmation of his entire reign, with the qualification that Joash did not remove the worship of the high places (12:3). In Chronicles, this period has correspondences with David's reign, as it is dominated by a concern for the purity of the nation's worship. Just as David had inherited a situation where the ark had been neglected (1 Chron 13:3), so the Chronicler has his own comment that Athaliah's family had abused the temple (2 Chron 24:7). Its dedicated things were corrupted by Baal worship.

The end of the reign of Joash is both blameworthy and tragic, with parallels to the reign of Asa. Joash reverses his policy of faithfulness and rejects the prophetic warning (24:20-22), delivered in the typical vocabulary of abandoning God and his prescribed way of life. In this case the prophet was stoned for delivering the warning. He was son of the priest Jehoiada, who had installed Joash as king and had done so much to instruct him. The result was political disaster. The much superior army of Joash was crushed by a small Aramean contingent. Joash suffered severe injuries in the Aramean attack, then died at the hand of a band of conspirators because he killed the prophet Zechariah. The end of Joash's life confirms the judgment of God for unfaithfulness, as it had for Asa.

The Chronicler's presentation of Joash illustrates well the ideal role of the priest (Williamson 1982: 314). The role of the priest is to support the dynastic promise and to be a faithful adviser to the king. The glowing report of Jehoiada may serve as a polemic against the tendency of the priests, in later times, to usurp the king's power. In Maccabean times this reached the extent that the legitimate priest was murdered and the priesthood was taken over by those who exercised complete political control. The result was irreconcilable conflict in the priesthood. The Chronicler's vision stands opposed to such a role for priests.

OUTLINE

Elevation of Joash to the Throne, 22:10-23:21
Joash under Blessing, 24:1-16
Joash under Judgment, 24:17-27

EXPLANATORY NOTES

Elevation of Joash to the Throne 22:10–23:21

The infidelity of Ahaziah brought the Davidic succession to the same point as that of Saul, with no one left to assume the power of the throne. With the death of Ahaziah, Athaliah ruled as an absolute monarch for several years, interrupting the rule of a Davidic descendant in Judah. She followed the policies of Omride politics, erecting a temple for Baal (2 Chron 23:17) and granting rites to Baal followers in Judah. Athaliah is never regarded as a legitimate monarch. She is given no regnal formulas of age or length of reign. The destruction of the *whole royal family* probably concentrated on potential male successors (22:10). Jehosheba and presumably others survived the slaughter. Jehosheba was a half sister of Ahaziah, a daughter by a wife other than Athaliah. She also was the wife of the priest Jehoiada, which enabled her to hide the heir to the throne in the temple (22:11-12).

The Levites and the people are given a much more significant role in the coup of Jehoiada than in the parallel account in Kings. Jehoiada made a covenant with key military officers. These officers solicited broad popular support among the Levites and tribal leaders, so the people were essential partners in the coup. The initial agreement was then extended to the entire assembly. The content of that covenant was expressed in Jehoiada's declaration *The king's son shall reign* (2 Chron 23:3). The Levites were required to assist the military officers, who were not permitted to enter the temple where much of the action took place (vv. 6-7). Levites themselves served as armed guards.

The most logical time for the coup was at the changing of the temple guards, which normally required large movements of people. One-third of the guards were coming on duty at the temple. These were stationed in three strategic locations to perform their regular duties and watch for any activity from the direction of the palace. The remainder of the armed force was stationed in the temple court, between the altar and the temple, providing a human wall to protect the king.

The king was anointed, the crown was placed on his head, and he received an emblem of the covenant testimony. The presentation at the coronation may have been an engraved amulet, which served as a reminder of the written covenant testimony, or it may have been an inscription like that on the diadem of the priest, which had the words "Holy to the LORD" (Exod 28:36). With the crowning, the people clapped and shouted, "May the king live!" (23:11 AT). The Chronicler (23:16, 18) and Josephus (*Ant.* 9.153) emphasize the restoration of the Davidic line. The coronation affirms the commitment of the king to lead the people according to the book of the covenant, which was to be kept at his side. This commitment obligates the people be loyal to the new king.

Athaliah was removed from the precincts of the temple without violating the sacred space (2 Chron 23:14-15). *The ranks* (v. 14) may refer to the guards stationed in the temple court or some feature of the temple area. The Horse Gate of the palace must be distinguished from the gate of the same name in the city wall (Jer 31:40). Both may have been oriented in the same direction. The gate in the city wall led to the place where dead bodies were cast, which explains the reason for the place of execution.

The covenant had three aspects: a vow between God and the king, God and the people, and the king with the people. The Chronicler expresses this as a vow between priest, king, and people; together they vow to be the people of the Lord. The first vow included the eradication of Baal worship. The institution of temple worship according to the arrangements made by David is a way of emphasizing the restoration of the Davidic rule. Temple arrangements recur in the Chronicler's history in response to necessity.

Joash under Blessing 24:1-16

The first part of the reign of Joash is conducted under the influence of the priest, including the choice of his wives (2 Chron 24:3). There is no parallel reference to the family of the young king in the Chronicler's *Vorlage*, making this addition significant to him *[Vorlage, p. 468]*. Children are a sign of divine blessing in Chronicles, yet in this case they would also be an indication of the restoration of the Davidic dynasty.

Though this account of the restoration of the temple is substantially that of Kings, the account has been recast according to the interests of the Chronicler (Welch: 78-80). Chronicles presents the need of the temple as a single event, largely necessary because of the damage done by Athaliah (2 Chron 24:4-7). The initiative is mostly a tribute to Joash. Kings reports a more long-term crisis, and the practice of directing donations for temple repair becomes a continuing system of maintenance (e.g., 2 Kings 12:4-12). The account in Kings is much more critical of the priests, who are pressured by Joash to make provision for the temple facilities. Their refusal to comply forced Joash to find an alternate means of temple repair.

A second emphasis of the Chronicler is the continuity of the tabernacle in the temple. The chest is a container for the levy that Moses had laid on the children of Israel in the wilderness (2 Chron 24:9; cf. Exod 30:11-16). This levy was required of every individual to serve as an atonement for their life. The poll tax in Exodus was a single imposition for the building of the temple, not an annual obligation (Sarna 1991: 195). It only became an annual levy in later times to maintain communal offerings and other public projects. The Chronicler presents this in parallel fashion as a single provision for refurbishing the temple following its willful desecration. As a further point, the Chronicler observes that a surplus was spent for temple utensils, to use in performing the sacrifices (2 Chron 24:14); there is no hint of any such surplus in Kings.

There is no indication when Joash first tried to refurbish the temple. After the first failure to raise funds, Joash summoned Jehoiada a second time, in his twenty-third year (2 Kings 12:6). Failure to collect the temple tax might have been the result of the king's intervention in what was regarded as a priestly jurisdiction. Over time disagreement had arisen between crown and priesthood over funding the restoration work; priests looked to the royal treasury, but the king wanted to reallocate temple money. The king censured Jehoiada for his failure to act and proposed a plan of action that put the offering on a more voluntary basis.

Donations in the First Temple period were not made with coins, but would have come in the form of ingots, ores, and amalgams of various grades. Foundries were associated with ancient temples. Kings says the funds were used for wages (2 Kings 12:13-14). The Chronicler explains that the funds were used only for temple artifacts after the repairs were complete. Chronicles emphasizes the abundance of revenue that was collected.

The priest Jehoiada lived to the extraordinary age of 130 years (2 Chron 24:15), longer than great figures such as Moses. Living to such an advanced age was a sign of blessing. This again might be considered as a schematic presentation by the Chronicler, particularly in relation to his wife Jehosheba. If she was about 20 when her father Jehoram died at 40 (21:5), she would have been much younger than her husband. If Jehoiada lived almost as long as the 40-year reign of Joash (24:1), Jehosheba would have only been about half the age of her husband at the time of his death. If he married at about age 80, his wife Jehosheba was then about 15. Yet, such marriages were not unusual in antiquity and also happen in the present time. Jehoiada was a distinguished individual, regarded as a priest-king, and so was given a royal burial.

Joash under Judgment 24:17-27

Materialism is exceedingly deceptive and pervasive. Upon the passing of the priest, it immediately began to assert its ugly influence in Judah. The influence of Athaliah had been subdued, but its impulses were ever present, and at the first opportunity the king was pressured to make changes. The wealth of the Phoenicians and their trading empire was constantly alluring. One of the ways to realize those benefits more readily was with the revival of their religion. The impression given is that the change effected by Jehoiada was more a coercive force than a real change of life and values. Another generation had arisen in the decades following the coronation of Joash, and the dramatic transformation of those events had faded. The king himself succumbed to the demands for change.

The invasion of the Arameans correlates with the activities of the Assyrians and Arameans (2 Chron 24:23). During the reign of Jehu, Hazael king of Aram took control of the entire Transjordan southward to the boundary of Moab at the Arnon River (2 Kings 10:32-33). When Jehu began to reign (841 BCE), Shalmaneser III appeared in southern Syria and decimated Hazael, confining him to Damascus. Jehu submitted to the Assyrians, as evident on the Black Obelisk. For Judah, the Assyrian advance provided temporary respite from Aramean interference. Assyrian expansion declined during the reign of Shamshi-Adad V (824–811 BCE). The reforms of Joash in his twenty-third year correlate to the twenty-eighth year of Jehu (Konkel 2006: 513). The death of Jehu ended the treaty he had with the Assyrians. Hazael may have taken that opportunity to reassert his control over the trade routes in the Transjordan.

Divine judgment, especially in Chronicles, does not come without prophetic warning. Condemning people's actions can come at a high price (2 Chron 24:20-22). There is considerable irony in the fate of Zechariah. The son of the priest who had preserved Joash for the throne was murdered in the very place where the king was protected during the coup. The priest Jehoiada had scrupulously preserved the temple from bloodshed (23:14), but later the king he installed (Joash) had Jehoiada's son murdered *in the courtyard of the LORD's temple* (24:21).

Power, greed, and materialism invariably breed violent conflict. The king, incapacitated by the wounds of war, became particularly vulnerable to conspiracy. The mothers of the conspirators who killed Joash were both foreign women, perhaps a reminder of the danger of turning to foreign worship. Materialism and greed leave a terrible legacy. Jehoiada, the faithful priest, was buried as a king;

Joash, the privileged king, was buried in disgrace. The account of Joash was part of the record (*midraš*) of the kings (24:27). This word, popular in later usage to mean "interpretation," is used only one other time in the Hebrew canon (2 Chron 13:22). It stems from the word "seek" (*daraš*), with the sense of "a written account of one's inquiries" (Rainey 1997: 38). This is the history of Joash, which is part of the prophetic record of the kings. The *qere* of the MT is more negative in its final assessment (24:27). It appears to say, *As for his children, may the prophecies against him increase* [Masoretic Text, p. 470].

THE TEXT IN BIBLICAL CONTEXT

Holy War against Israel

The story of Joash is riddled with irony (Klein 2012: 350). Jehoiada and Jehosheba saved his life and put him on the throne, but Joash was implicated in the murder of their son Zechariah. The people conspired against Zechariah at the command of the king, but Joash's servants conspired against him because of the violence done to the *sons* (24:25 MT) of Jehoiada. Zechariah was murdered in the very spot where Joash had been protected; Athaliah had at least been removed from the temple before being killed. Jehoiada the chief priest was buried with the kings, while Joash the king was not. Athaliah used the votive gifts of the temple for Baal. The people looted the Baal temple and killed Mattan, its priest. But in the end Joash and the people worshiped at the Asherim (places of Canaanite worship) with their idols. Jehosheba hid Joash and his nurse in a bedroom of the temple. Joash's servants killed him in his own bed. Joash did not remember the loyalty of Jehoiada and killed Zechariah. The name Zechariah means "Yahweh has remembered." Joash listened to the officers of Judah and fell into sin, but he would not listen to the warnings of the prophets.

Holy war could be a judgment on Israel just as surely as a provision for their deliverance. God uses foreign nations to punish his people and can fight for their cause just as readily as for Israel. God is not a respecter of nations. According to the prophet Isaiah, God is the Creator and Redeemer of Israel (Isa 43:1-4; 44:1-5). As the prophet Isaiah repeatedly states, Israel was not selected from among other nations; God created Israel by his own choice (Gen 12:1-3). Israel did not enjoy a special status among the nations; God created Israel to accomplish his purpose of bringing redemption to the world. But God rules among all the nations; breaking the covenant relationship with God brings judgment to Israel, as to any other disobedient nation.

The Chronicler has cast the life of Joash into two periods that serve to explain why his life would end in Syrian domination and his own assassination. The whole is linked to the loss of the good counsel of Jehoiada. But the punishment does not come without the warnings of the prophets urging him to repent. The account as a whole serves as an alert to the Chronicler's readers; it reminds them that judgment will not overtake them without warning. Disaster can be avoided by accepting responsibility and turning in repentance.

THE TEXT IN THE LIFE OF THE CHURCH
Teaching Moral Values

It is very important for Christians to be mindful that the essence of moral behavior is internal motivation and not external control or influence. Joash becomes one of the most negative examples of turning opportunity into disaster. Faithfulness comes from an internal disposition; influence can help maintain a commitment, but it can never be a replacement for personal choice. The guidance and instruction of Jehoiada apparently did not transform the young king he tutored. Once the priest was no longer present, the forces of power and greed quickly took control. This is not to suggest that the efforts of Jehoiada proved of no value. They did preserve the dynasty of David and changed the course of political events. However, they did not have the effect that the priest desired; no amount of influence has the power to convert. Faith and choice of life values are a personal matter. Only by the grace of God can instruction and perseverance transform individuals to do what is right and good. Believers need to be faithful in doing and teaching what is right, but one must never presume that these have the power to bring others to do the same.

Christians must remember these limitations in seeking to be a positive influence in their world. There is a tendency to change laws to coerce behavior deemed to be moral. Law does not have the power to create a moral society any more than the priest Jehoiada had in his time. The first priority for Christians is not the creation of law. An example in Canada is the absence of an abortion law. An important value to Christians is the protection of life, especially the most vulnerable of life. No life is more vulnerable than the unborn. The practice in Canada concerning the unborn is among the worst. Under Canadian law, a fetus is not a person until fully born, so partial-birth abortion, the killing of an infant in the process being born, is legal. It is the duty of the state to protect such vulnerable life, but in Canada other values of rights and freedoms are deemed to be more important than the life of a child. However, activism for instituting abortion laws has its limits; such laws will not prevent immoral behavior. Killing of a child being born should not only be illegal but must be unthinkable. The best efforts for protecting human life must be to instill a sense of its sacredness, especially at its most vulnerable stage. Rights are a very noble pursuit, but they cannot be the ultimate measure of morality. Pursuit of rights without regard to other moral questions leads to very reprehensible conduct. The highest priority then must be instruction and a change of thinking. Only with such a change can there be real protection for human life.

Such instruction will often be frustrated, just as that of the priest Jehoiada. But it still must be undertaken, with the knowledge that it will not be without results. The immediate outcome for Jehoiada and his family was tragic; but his story is not the end of the Chronicler's story. In the story of the Chronicler, the work of Jehoiada was the means God provided for the continuity of the dynasty and the kingdom. The same will be true for those who are faithful in the work of God's kingdom. Christians must pursue the work of a kingdom that is not of this world.

2 Chronicles 25:1–26:2
Reign of Amaziah

PREVIEW

Pride is rightly regarded as the most insidious of human sins. Perhaps it seems to be the worst of deadly sins because it is so deceptive as well as destructive. Not all pride is bad; there are things to be proud of, but most often pride has a negative and destructive effect. The story of Amaziah is exemplary in its depiction of a complete blindness to hubris.

The reign of Amaziah is compromised, like that of the reign of Joash, his father. This is immediately signaled by the Chronicler by saying that Amaziah *did what was right* but did not have complete integrity (2 Chron 25:2). As with Joash, there are prophets to affirm, encourage, and give warnings. In a section unique to the Chronicler in Amaziah's records, a man of God appears to warn him against allying with Israel through hiring mercenaries (25:5-10). Amaziah does the right thing in dismissing the Israelite troops; without their help he is successful in his battle with Edom. He suffers the retaliation of the troops raiding border towns for their loss of opportunity to retrieve booty (v. 13). However, the failure of Amaziah was his plunder of Edomite idols. This earns a sharp rebuke from another unnamed prophet.

The king's sarcastic response brings the announcement that divine judgment has already been determined (vv. 15-16). Ahaziah rashly undertook a war with Jehoash of Israel, and his army was routed. The Israelite troops broke down part of the wall of Jerusalem, plundered the temple, and brought the loot to Samaria. For the Chronicler, the cause was a spiritual problem. The victory at Edom had resulted in pride (v. 19); ironically, this damning condemnation comes from the Israelite king. That might seem a less convincing source than the earlier warning of the prophet, but the king of Israel makes his point. Pride and idolatry often come as a pair. The price for Amaziah is like that of his father; he dies in a conspiracy after a futile attempt to escape.

OUTLINE

Consolidation of Power, 25:1-4
War against Edom, 25:5-16
War against Israel, 25:17-24
End of Amaziah's Reign, 25:25–26:2

EXPLANATORY NOTES

Consolidation of Power 25:1-4

The coup carried out against Joash involved individuals of status and influence who threatened the rule of the new king. Court plots of this type usually involve extended family members, resulting in whole families being decimated in order to prevent further revolt. Amaziah avenged the death of his father by executing the assassins and consolidating his own hold on power. But Amaziah did not follow the ways of Athaliah in seeking to exterminate all who might have a claim to the throne. The Chronicler reminds his readers that Amaziah was following legal procedure in his actions. He limited his punishment to the actual executioners of his father. Vicarious punishment and extending punishment to those associated with the offender was contrary to the words of Torah (2 Chron 25:4).

The greater threat to Amaziah was the rising power of the Israelite kingdom following the coup of Jehu. The Chronicler gives little account of development in the Northern Kingdom beyond actual encounters with the king of the Davidic line. The decimation in Samaria resulted in subordination to the Arameans during the greater part of the reign of Jehoahaz, the successor to Jehu. Hazael controlled all the major trade routes, southward to the Arnon on the east (2 Kings 10:32-33) and Gath on the west (12:17).

Matters began to change under the reign of Jehoash, with the death of Hazael and the increased pressure under the campaigns of the Assyrian Adad-Nirari III. Samaria was a vastly superior power to the state of Judah. This is of no consequence in the thinking of the Chronicler, for the single criterion of success is faithfulness to God. However, when God is not fighting the battle, the outcome will depend on the power of the combatants. Amaziah utterly failed to appreciate his own weaknesses in this regard, particularly in the border that he shared with the north (2 Chron 25:13). He suffered the plundering of his border towns after he had paid the mercenaries their due. This is not presented by the Chronicler as a theological judgment. It is more an evidence of Amaziah's failure to recognize his vulnerability in the shadow of his much more powerful neighbor.

War against Edom 25:5-16

Amaziah's interest in Edom was to gain control of the trade routes in Transjordan. Edom had gained its independence in the days of Joash (2 Chron 21:8-10). Amaziah mustered his forces and appointed his commanders according to the ancestral clans, the typical way of gathering an army. The inclusion of Benjamin in the muster indicates that it was part of the territory of Judah at that time. Amaziah's force was smaller than that of Asa (580,000) or Jehoshaphat (1,160,000), which may explain his desire to hire additional troops. The fee for the mercenaries amounted to three shekels for each soldier, slightly more than an ounce of silver (a talent is 3,000 shekels). Hiring mercenaries amounted to a foreign alliance instead of relying on the Lord. The situation is addressed by the prophet after the money has been paid, but this does not deter Amaziah from the right course of action in dismissing the mercenaries.

There were two main centers in Edom. Petra was in the south, and Bozrah (Buseirah) was in the north, between Sela and Punon. The initial conquests were in the north, with the aim of dominating the southern portion of the King's Highway, on the east side of the Arabah, the rift valley of the Jordan, which extends south from the Dead Sea. The entire narrative of the war against Edom (vv. 5-16) is an expansion of 2 Kings 14:7. In Kings, the cliff (*selaʿ*) is a place that is given the name Joktheel. It is often identified with Petra, a prominent fortification of the Edomites. Some have regarded its towering mountain, today called el-Habis, as the peak from which the soldiers were cast. The Valley of Salt (part of the Arabah) was the location of battles David had with the Edomites (2 Sam 8:13; cf. Ps 60), the perennial battlefield south of the Dead Sea. Ahaziah did not capture the port at Elath (2 Chron 26:2); his conquest was limited to northern Edom (Bozrah).

Victory occasionally led a conqueror to worship the gods of the vanquished nation. The gods were sometimes regarded as being on the side of the victor, having abandoned their people—which spared the gods from suffering a humiliating defeat. This is analogous to prophetic statements that attest to the Lord fighting on the side of the enemy as a punishment for Israel or Judah's disobedience (Isa 10:5-6). The visible component of the motif was the transfer of images to the territory of the conqueror (Cogan 1974: 9-21). Though the deities of Edom would have been valuable plunder, bringing them to Judah served to show that they had abandoned their land and come to the aid of Amaziah.

War against Israel 25:17-24

The negotiations with Jehoash and the subsequent battle are almost verbatim from the account in Kings. There are two ways in which the moral of the story is made for the Chronicler. The first is the word from the prophet; Amaziah's rejection of the prophetic word is itself a sign that God has determined the demise of the king (25:16). This is then repeated in verse 20; Amaziah's refusal to heed the scornful rebuke of Jehoash was also divinely determined. Amaziah had pursued the gods of the Edomites, and the war with Israel would be his punishment. The sarcastic fable of Jehoash (v. 18-19) should be compared with Jotham's fable about the thornbush in Judges 9:7-15. A favorite technique of wisdom was to give lessons from plants. The account repeats wordplays on "counsel," beginning with Amaziah's scoffing rebuke to the prophet: *Have we made you a counselor to the king?* (25:16 AT). The prophet replies, *God has counseled that you be destroyed, since you act this way and disregard my counsel* (NJPS). Amaziah in turn *took counsel* (v. 17 NRSV) in his attempt to negotiate terms with Israel.

The attack on Beth Shemesh was not one of the usual border wars with Israel. This small but important town in the northeast of the Shephelah protected the entrance to the Sorek Valley to the east and to points north *[Shephelah, p. 467]*. Jehoash may have been seeking control of the major coastal highway (Via Maris) or the east-west roads through Jerusalem to Transjordan. Conquest of the city gave Jehoash direct access to Jerusalem, where he tore down part of the wall to freely enter the city. The Ephraim Gate was on the north side of the city and the Corner Gate on the north side of the western wall. Jehoash removed two hundred yards of wall, which were not repaired until the reign of Uzziah. The hostages were likely nobility or members of the royal family, kept under guard or held for ransom.

End of Amaziah's Reign 25:25–26:2

Amaziah outlived Jehoash, the king of Israel, by fifteen years. This indicates that Amaziah was held as a political prisoner until the death of Jehoash. Jeroboam II, successor to Jehoash, became king in year fourteen of Amaziah (2 Kings 14:23); Amaziah reigned for a total of twenty-nine years (2 Chron 25:1). This also explains the fifty-two-year reign of Uzziah (2 Chron 26:3). Uzziah came to the throne of Judah at age sixteen in year twenty-seven of Jeroboam (2 Kings 15:1). Jeroboam reigned for a total of forty-one years (14:23). The death of Jeroboam was fourteen years after the death of Amaziah. The death of Jeroboam was year thirty-eight of Uzziah (15:8). Uzziah was placed on the throne by the leaders of Judah twenty-four years before the death of Amaziah, probably when Amaziah was taken prisoner by Jehoash. Amaziah may have been set free at the death of Jehoash, nine years after Uzziah began to rule, but Uzziah would have continued as king with the support of those who installed him. Amaziah may have tried to regain rule, and Uzziah may have been involved in protecting his throne (Cogan and Tadmor: 159). In any case, Amaziah retained the status of king and was buried in the sepulchre of the Davidides.

Eventually Amaziah would fall to a conspiracy that had been plotted many years earlier (2 Chron 25:27). He fled to Lachish, a major fortified city and a seat of district government, in hopes of finding sanctuary there. Amaziah had not only betrayed the covenant at the time when the conspiracy was planned, but also, in rash military action instigated by his own pride, he had brought serious loss to the temple at Jerusalem. The same military and temple alliance that had dethroned Athaliah and installed Joash may have been involved in avenging the military humiliation and spoilation of the temple brought about by Amaziah.

The report that the port of Elath was restored to Judah appears in the form of an official record (2 Chron 26:2), with the statement that the king slept with his fathers. The emphatic pronoun at the start of the sentence leaves the subject ambiguous. The unnamed king who dies must be Amaziah (supplied by the NIV), and the king who builds Elath must be Uzziah. It is unusual that a king's achievements would be listed before the introduction to his reign (26:3). It may be that this record pertained to both kings during the time of their coregency (Thiele: 115). Uzziah was able to complete the task begun by Azariah: regaining control over the trade routes of the King's Highway, and providing a port city on the Gulf of Aqaba. With the death of Jehoash and Amaziah, the royal houses of Samaria and Jerusalem come to a new level of cooperation, providing a temporary advantage over the Edomites.

THE TEXT IN BIBLICAL CONTEXT

Divine Judgment on Amaziah

The Chronicler frequently provides chronology to establish the correlation of faithfulness with success and punishment with sin. The man of God promised success in battle if the mercenaries were dismissed (2 Chron 25:8). In spite of losses with the dismissal of the mercenaries, Amaziah was successful in his war against Edom. This success became Amaziah's worst enemy. It led him into idolatry and pride (vv. 14, 19). His refusal to heed the warning of the king of Israel brought him into a foolish conflict in which Jerusalem was breached and looted. He became a prisoner for nine years. But Amaziah's fate was sealed long before his captivity by Jehoash. Judgment came in the form of a conspiracy to kill him about fourteen years earlier, near the beginning of his reign, when he turned from the Lord (25:20, 27). The Chronicler refers to Amaziah's idolatry and refusal to heed the words of the prophet at the time of his victory over Edom (vv. 14-16). He presents the death of Amaziah as a direct and immediate consequence of his idolatry, because that is when a pact was made to kill him. The prophetic speeches and most of the detail in the battle against Edom are unique to the Chronicler. The account of Amaziah is expanded from sources outside of Kings to demonstrate the necessity of faithfulness to those rebuilding Jerusalem and restoring its walls.

The reign of Amaziah is another example of the requirement of covenant faithfulness. On the whole, the record of Amaziah's reign is negative. Instead of royal building programs, the walls of Jerusalem were destroyed. Instead of wealth from the people and surrounding nations, the king is plundered. Instead of a large family, there are hostages. There is war instead of peace, conspiracy and assassination instead of loyalty from the people and a peaceful life. The message to the community of the restoration was clear: hope depends on faithfulness to God.

THE TEXT IN THE LIFE OF THE CHURCH

The Blindness of the Enlightenment

The story of Amaziah follows patterns that are familiar. A king with potential to do much good rejects the warnings of the prophets and brings loss upon his people and ultimately himself. It is very difficult to accept words of correction. The preaching of Isaiah was met with deafness and blindness (Isa 6:9-10). Jesus would use these very words to describe his own ministry (Matt 13:14-15). The repeating themes of the accounts of the kings of Judah must remind God's children of all times that two things will always be true: they should expect that their message may be rejected, and yet their message must be preached. The preaching itself becomes a judgment on those who refuse to hear, just as Amaziah's refusal to hear the scornful rebuke of Jehoash was an indication of the divine judgment that was already determined (2 Chron 25:20). Pride casts a blinding veil that prevents the perception of the obvious.

Amaziah's demise was caused by his pride, seen in his taunting of the prophet who came to correct him (25:16), and in his scorn for the warnings of the king of Israel (vv. 19-20). It is with good reason that pride is considered to be the original sin and the cause of all other sins. Dante's definition of pride is "love of self perverted to hatred and contempt of one's neighbor" (in *Divine Comedy*, part 2, *Purgatorio*, canto 11). Perhaps the most insidious aspect of pride is its blindness to its own excesses. This phenomenon is exemplified well in the conduct of Amaziah, and expresses well why pride should be regarded as the source of all other sins.

The blindness spoken of by Isaiah and by Jesus is well illustrated in the fruits of what is called the Enlightenment, a nineteenth-century term for a seventeenth-century movement of influential philosophers (Bacon, Descartes, Spinoza, Locke). Their goal was to reform society by using reason to challenge ideas grounded in tradition and faith. In the nineteenth century this transformed into Modernism, which may be defined as belief in the power of human beings to create, improve, and reshape their environment with the aid of practical experimentation, scientific knowledge, and/or technology. Modernist thinking rejects faith in anything but itself. The Modernist mind-set is expressed in the Humanist Manifesto articulated by Raymond Bragg in 1933. The eighth point of this manifesto states: "Religious Humanism considers the complete realization of human personality to be the end [goal or purpose] of man's life and seeks its development and fulfillment in the here and now. This is the explanation of the humanist's social passion." This manifesto was updated in 1973; one of the most frequently quoted lines states, "No deity will save us; we must save ourselves."

Nothing manifests the pride of humanity more than the Modernist mentality. It is the blind pride of persons who, though seeing, will not see, and though hearing, will not hear. The blindness of Modernism in believing that humans will save themselves will lead to disaster, just as the pride of Amaziah led to his death.

This makes all the more urgent the preaching of the gospel, the message of the church. It is also a warning that those who confess faith may themselves be blind to their own pride, which will lead to their own loss.

2 Chronicles 26:3–27:9
Uzziah and Jotham

PREVIEW

Whatever office one may hold, there are limitations to privilege that cannot be violated. The higher the office, the more difficult it can be to know and observe such limitations. The chair of the church board does not necessarily have the privilege of leading in the communion service, even if there is power to do so. There are consequences for such violations, as illustrated in the tragic end of the great king Uzziah.

Uzziah (2 Chron 26:1, etc.) is also known as Azariah. The names seem to be interchangeable. He is called Uzziah in the Prophets (Isa 1:1; Hos 1:1; Amos 1:1; Zech 14:5) and frequently in 2 Kings (15:13, 30, 32, 34). He is called Azariah in 1 Chronicles 3:12 and frequently in 2 Kings (15:1, 6, 7, 8, 17, 23, 27). The difference may not have had significance, because both words from which the names are derived (ʿzr and ʿzz) can mean "victory" or "strength." The short form of Yahweh at the end of his name indicates it is the strength of God. The Chronicler seems to have taken advantage of the synonymity by describing Uzziah as a king whose fame spread far and wide, for he was helped marvelously, though by whom or what the Chronicler does not say (2 Chron 26:15). The name of his mother (Jekoliah) similarly means the Lord (*Yah*) is able (*ykl*).

Uzziah is introduced at the conclusion to the reign of Amaziah (2 Chron 26:1-2; cf. vv. 3-5). The Chronicler derives both introductions from Kings. In Kings, the conclusion to the reign of Amaziah forms a transition to the reign of the northern king Jeroboam II (2 Kings 14:18-22). The primary introduction of Uzziah (Azariah) follows the reign of Jeroboam in 2 Kings 15:1-2, in the regular pattern of alternating northern and southern kings. The omission of the intervening material essentially juxtaposes two introductions in Chronicles. Thus the assessment in 2 Chronicles 26:4 that Uzziah *did what was right* as did his father Amaziah, taken from Kings, is included as part of his introduction.

Though Uzziah has a long and prosperous reign, his achievements are left unrecorded in Kings, except to say he did not remove the high places. The single detail of his life that is remembered is that he was a leper (2 Kings 15:5). The Chronicler records a general but extensive development of Uzziah's economic, military, and technological achievements. But as in the case with Joash and Amaziah, his life divides into two parts. Uzziah's leprosy was caused by a violation of temple rites, motivated by pride, resulting in his being a leper for the rest of his life and entirely barred from the temple precincts. Jotham becomes coregent during the time of Uzziah's isolation and essentially continues the work of restoration that Uzziah had begun.

OUTLINE

Military and Economic Achievements of Uzziah, 26:3-15
Sin and Punishment of Uzziah, 26:16-23
Reign of Jotham, 27:1-9

EXPLANATORY NOTES

Military and Economic Achievements of Uzziah 26:3-15

Like Joash before him, Uzziah had a particular adviser that supported him in the fear of the Lord, meaning that he knew how to trust, always following what was right and fearing the consequences for what was contrary to the teaching of Torah *[Torah, p. 481]*. During the time of his counselor Zechariah, Uzziah sought the Lord and was a prosperous king. Nothing more is known of this Zechariah, unless he is to be identified with one of the witnesses named in Isaiah 8:2.

Uzziah's success is described in terms of the expansion of his kingdom (2 Chron 26:6-8). His conquests were to the west, south, and southeast, a description that fits well with the powerful kingdom of Jeroboam to the north (2 Kings 14:23-29). Jabneh (also Jabneel in Josh 15:11) was at the northern boundary of the tribe of Judah, the area where Jehoash had decimated Amaziah. The Meunites in this reference are best identified with the south

Arabian city-state m'n. These people had control of the Incense Road and established colonies in major cities in west Arabia and Egypt. Gaza became their most important colony city (Knauf: 802). Gur Baal, in association with the Meunites, indicates a location somewhere in Edom. The name is likely a transliteration of "rock" and thus might be a place near Petra, which had a sanctuary. According to the Chronicler, Uzziah occupied and fortified the major cities of the Philistines. His strategy would have been to develop control over the coastal highway and to build towns in conquered territory. The name *Ammonites* in 2 Chronicles 26:8 (MT, NIV, NRSV) is incorrect. The Greek text correctly indicates the *Meunites*, the people of this geographical area *[Greek Text of Chronicles, p. 468]*.

Uzziah's domestic activities were to repair damage done by the northern king Jehoash in his campaign against Amaziah and likely also for destruction by the famous earthquake during his time (Amos 1:1; Zech 14:5). Towers and cisterns from excavations in Qumran, Gibeah, Beersheba, and other sites date to this period. Uzziah was a patron of agriculture, a vital industry for an independent society. Gradually increasing state-owned territories provided supplies for the court, employment, and land that could be allotted as grants.

Uzziah's large and well-equipped army enabled him to expand and defend his territory. The name Uzziah is found on a fragmentary text of Tiglath-Pileser III of Assyria, as head of a coalition. The identification remains very uncertain; another fragment mentioning Judah can no longer be associated with it, so the location of this King Uzziah is not known (*COS* 2.117A). The text's association with Uzziah of Judah is scarcely tenable. The technical devices mounted on the walls served as protection for archers and throwers, confirmed in iconography such as the murals of the siege of Lachish in the late eighth century BCE by Sennacherib (Cogan and Tadmor: plate 9). Torsion-operated devices are not known until the late Persian period. They are not what is referred to here unless one regards the Chronicler as anachronistically describing technology from his own time. Assyrian reliefs of siege attacks show defenders on the walls, holding shields with wooden frames to protect from the weapons below. This fits well the Chronicler's description.

Sin and Punishment of Uzziah 26:16-23

The Chronicler explains the cause of Uzziah's leprosy as a punishment. The problem, as was the case with Amaziah, began with pride. Unlike Amaziah, where pride led him to self-destructive military ventures, the pride of Uzziah led him to usurp functions outside that of royalty, in specific disobedience against the Lord (2 Chron 26:16, 18). Uzziah offered incense within the temple, an activity reserved exclusively for the priests (cf. Exod 30:1-10). Incense was widely used in ancient worship. In the temple, incense symbolized the appeasement of divine wrath; it expressed the presence of the holy within the common and protected the worshiper from the divine presence. Offering incense was one of the daily rituals of temple confession. The judgment for Uzziah's violation was that he was a leper for the rest of his life.

Leprosy forced the king to spend the last of his life in quarantine, referred to as a *free house* (26:21 AT, *bet haḥopšit*). The significance of this term is uncertain. In Job the word *ḥopši* (free) refers to freedom from labor or work after death (Job 3:19); in Exodus it is the freedom to leave after seven years of servitude in order to pay off debt (Exod 21:5). In Ugaritic, *bt ḥptt* refers to the netherworld, just as it does in Job (*KTU* 1.4 viii 7) *[Ugarit, p. 467]*. De Moor thinks that *house of freedom* is an idiom for total confinement (de Moor: 66). The use of *ḥopši* in Psalm 88:6 is enigmatic, but like Job it is associated with death and the grave. These references are not all related. Job, Psalms, and Ugaritic texts all are associated with death; other uses involve labor regulation in relation to servitude, and freedom from taxes. Both Josephus (*Ant.* 9.277) and the Targums refer to Uzziah as living outside the city; displaced residence is part of Uzziah's punishment. Yet it may have reference to labor. When not in reference to death, *ḥopši* relates to labor. It is not confinement but isolation or separation from a previous home, as someone freed after years of belonging to another household. The *free house* of Uzziah placed him in isolation; he was free but restricted. Uzziah was unable to perform his administrative and official duties to *the people of the land* (2 Chron 26:21; cf. 2 Kings 11:14, 18, 20). This privileged group empowered the king and received particular services from the king in judicial matters and ritual duties. Jotham was appointed to carry out the king's responsibilities in place of his father.

Leprosy was a judgment in death as well as in life: Uzziah was buried in the royal graveyard in isolation. An inscribed Aramaic plaque dated to the first century has an inscription that claims the bones of Uzziah were located in a solitary tomb (Cogan and Tadmor: plate 5). Though this might confirm the tradition of Chronicles, it is also possible that the plaque was attached to a solitary grave on the basis of the Chronicles tradition.

Reign of Jotham 27:1-9

The chronology surrounding the reign of Hezekiah can only be tentatively reconstructed (Konkel 1987: 9-29). However, the Masoretic chronology is intact and must be accepted against that of the Greek, which has been altered in an attempt to harmonize data that was not understood. The sixteen-year reign of Jotham must be dated from about 750-735 BCE. An absolute date is the attack of Sennacherib against Jerusalem in 701 BCE, year fifteen of Hezekiah. The sixteen-year reign of Ahaz preceded year fifteen of Hezekiah. The beginning of Hezekiah's reign is during the time of Hosea, before the exile of the north under the Assyrians in 722 BCE. Jotham then is coregent with his father, Uzziah, for about ten years. The Chronicler explains that Uzziah lived in isolation for a long period at the end of his life, which again would account for the necessity of coregency. During this time Jotham no doubt exercised significant independence, much as Uzziah did during the nine years when Amaziah was held as political prisoner.

Jotham's enterprises are a sequel to those of his father. The work of restoration begun by Uzziah was continued in sections that had not been completed. His forts and towers were in the forests, providing a network of lookouts and highway defenses, both on the frontier and within the kingdom. Uzziah had received tribute from the Meunites, stated correctly in the Greek text of 26:8. Jotham continued Judah's domination in Transjordan. The cessation after the third year may have been because of rising Aramean power in the region. The Chronicler makes no mention of the incursions of Pekah and Rezin (Israel and Syria) into the territory of Judah (2 Kings 15:37). He does mention other wars, which include some fought while he was coregent with his father, Uzziah *[Greek Text of Chronicles, p. 468]*.

The reign of Jotham functions as a postscript to that of Uzziah. The reign of Uzziah was summarized in a positive manner (2 Chron 26:4), and the reign of Jotham is similarly appraised (27:2). No punishment or correction is attributed to Jotham; his reign in that respect may be compared to Abijah, the king who exhorted his people to faithfulness and was granted victory and blessing. Jotham reigned during the most prosperous times of Judah. Though the Assyrian storm clouds were gathering on the horizon (Isa 6:1), their incursions would not threaten Judah until the reign of Ahaz (7:1). Jotham's son Ahaz was the hapless king who would seek help from the Assyrians but then have his land subdued by them.

THE TEXT IN BIBLICAL CONTEXT
Uzziah, Isaiah, and Amos

Uzziah was a great king who lived in a prosperous time. Uzziah and Jeroboam of the Jehu dynasty shared governance for the first half of the eighth century BCE. The elite of both kingdoms experienced a time of great wealth and prosperity, advancement in territory, and trade. Uzziah controlled strategic trade routes and received tribute. But his life can hardly be considered a success. The year of his death was the occasion for the call of Isaiah (Isa 6:1). In spite of wealth, success, power, and conquests, Isaiah could see the day when the cities of Judah would be deserted, uninhabited, ruined, and ravaged (Isa 6:11-12). The vision of the king of the heavens and earth became the inspiration that empowered the prophet to speak the words that his countrymen would refuse to hear. Uzziah left a legacy that was a disaster for the Davidic kingdom.

The days of Uzziah should be considered in relation to the Northern Kingdom in Samaria. This was the territory denounced by the prophecy of Amos, delivered in the last days of the Northern Kingdom, just before the Assyrians brought it under their domination (Amos 1:1). The message of Amos is one of unrelenting judgment against the rich for their oppression of the poor. The lion of Judah has already consumed his prey. Amos can declare that the funeral of Israel has taken place (Amos 5:1-17). The times of greatest prosperity in Israel and Judah were also the times of greatest peril. The tragedy is that neither nation was aware of its plight. The citizens of Judah paid no heed to the warnings of Isaiah (Isa 2:6–4:1); although seeing, they could not really see (6:9). The nation of Israel was in even more immediate danger, but it gave no heed to the dire warnings of the prophet. Judah would survive beyond the days of the Assyrians, but Israel did not.

THE TEXT IN THE LIFE OF THE CHURCH
Sanctity of the Sacraments

There must be no trifling in matters of sanctity. The temple with its personnel, rituals, and artifacts represented the presence and the holiness of God. The temple could have this function only if its symbolisms and confessions were not compromised. The presumption of Uzziah was an utter violation of everything he confessed.

Two sacraments are found in the New Testament, two special ways that God's grace is communicated to believers. Baptism is the confession of complete loyalty to Jesus Christ; communion, or the Lord's Supper, is the confession that in the new covenant Jesus, by his death on our behalf, fulfills the redemption of the exodus. These are sacred symbols. Those who reject their practice altogether fail to understand the importance of public confessions made by symbolic acts. It is like marriage without a public ceremony or vows. It may not be a desecration of the institution of marriage, but it certainly denigrates the significance of accountability for the vows taken. Perhaps more serious is the practice of Christian sacraments without understanding their true significance. Sometimes it is said that baptism and communion are just following the commands of Jesus. However, the New Testament does not treat them simply as ordinances to be obeyed. The apostle Paul repeatedly appeals to the baptism of believers to remind them of their confessed unity with Christ and their responsibility to live a moral life (e.g., Rom 6:1-11). Communion is a confession of fellowship with Christ and therefore with one another (1 Cor 11:17-33). Failure to live in a morally responsible manner as a baptized believer, or to have harmony with fellow Christians when partaking of communion—such failure is a desecration that should bring the church to exercise discipline.

The actions of Uzziah may seem to be rather harmless, but that view fails to understand the profundity of the temple confession. Similarly, baptism and communion have sometimes been reduced to church rituals. Such attitudes fail to comprehend how actions and rituals communicate, both in their proper observance and in the failure to take them seriously. The punishment of Uzziah is a sobering reminder that if confessions are to have any meaning at all, there are serious consequences for their abuse and neglect.

2 Chronicles 28:1-27
Reign of Ahaz

PREVIEW

God is all you need, but you do not know that until God is all you have. This is sadly true, but even more tragic is the failure to submit to this reality. Such was the case for Ahaz. His schemes for self-preservation were the very forces that would lead to his destruction.

The reign of Ahaz was a disaster both politically and in regard to covenant faithfulness. The Chronicler essentially shares the views of the other prophets regarding Ahaz. Isaiah, through the names of children, had exhorted Ahaz to be faithful in the fear of the Lord. His warning was unequivocal: "If you do not stand firm in your faith, you will not stand at all" (Isa 7:9b). Isaiah offered the king a sign, but it was refused as if it would be tempting God (7:12). Ahaz had already made his own plans when confronted by Isaiah and his son; he would turn to the Assyrians for help against his enemies (2 Chron 28:16). But Ahaz could not escape God; the promise of the sign was that God would be with him (Immanuel). God was indeed with him. The Assyrians would flood through his land like the overflow of the Euphrates and then he would know that God was with him (Isa 8:7-8). The Chronicler speaks of Ahaz's losses to the Edomites and Philistines (2 Chron 28:17-18). The decimation of Judah had begun.

The Chronicler expresses the failure of faith on the part of Ahaz with the key term used in the failure of Saul: he was *unfaithful* (1 Chron 10:13). The Lord *humbled* the people because they had been *unfaithful* (28:19). Though the land was brought down, King Ahaz became utterly unfaithful (*maʿol maʿal*), allowing the people to live without restraint. When he suffered under the oppression of

Tiglath-Pileser, whose help he had sought, he continued to be *unfaithful* (v. 22). The Chronicler expresses a kind of exasperated resignation at the conclusion of verse 22: *this same king Ahaz* (NRSV; cf. KJV). Many translations omit this phrase (e.g., NIV, NLT).

OUTLINE
Transgressions of Ahaz, 28:1-4
Calamity in Judah, 28:5-15
Foreign Alliance and Idolatry, 28:16-27

EXPLANATORY NOTES
Transgressions of Ahaz 28:1-4
The abominations of Ahaz included a rite of *passing his sons through the fire* (2 Chron 28:3 AT, Greek text) *[Greek Text of Chronicles, p. 468]*. MT says he burned his sons (*bʿr*), but this is likely a metathesis (reversal of letters) for the word ʿ*br*, to pass his sons through the fire, as in the Greek. A careful examination of passing children through the fire indicates that it was not child sacrifice (contra NIV), but rather a ceremony involving fire through which one was dedicated to a deity (Zevit: 469). The practice involved a ceremony involving infants or toddlers who were passive. The prohibition of such rituals in Deuteronomy in 18:9-10 is because it is thought to be Canaanite. Passing sons through the fire is named with various practices of divination. The practice of "burning children in the fire" in Deuteronomy 12:3; Jeremiah 7:31; 19:5 is the Hebrew verb *śrp*. This seems to have been a funeral ritual of cremation for premature, stillborn, or very young children (Zevit: 550). They were buried in a *tophet*. Offering children to Molek was one of the practices of the high places (Jer 32:35). In the case of Ahaz, the ritual appears to have marked dedication to a deity (Zevit: 552), but nothing suggests it was a foreign deity. The MT *burned his sons* in 2 Chronicles 28:3 might indicate scarring that left some permanent feature, like a branding, indicating a dedication. But it is highly doubtful MT is correct. The condemnation of the Chronicler is that of the Deuteronomists, namely, that these rituals belonged to the Canaanites, whom the Lord had disposed before them.

Calamity in Judah 28:5-15
In contrast to other accounts of this war against Pekah and Rezin (2 Kings 16:5-7; Isa 7:1-6), the Chronicler makes the attacks of

Samaria and Damascus separate incursions. He reports large numbers of people taken captive, huge numbers slain, and enormous booty taken. Though the size of ancient populations is not known, taken as thousands the numbers seem to be virtually the entire population of Judah. It may be that here again the word for thousand (*'lp*) is used as a military unit.

Though the Lord was using Israel as an instrument of punishment, the covenant forbade the enslavement of fellow Israelites (2 Chron 28:10; Lev 25:39-55). A positive attitude to the north is expressed in the term *brothers* (2 Chron 28:8 MT). It was during the reign of Ahaz that Israel went into exile, removing another obstacle for reunion with the southern kinfolk. This was the time for repentance and return of the northern citizens. The response of the Israelites to the appeal of Oded the prophet is further evidence of the unity that God intends for his people. It is testimony to the firm belief of the Chronicler that this is one nation. The political realities that have come about must not give a false impression of that underlying reality. It is seen in the way the words of the prophet can subvert political and material ambitions with spiritual victory and community concord. In the darkest time of a virtual exile for Judah, there is at the same time the evidence of the light the darkness cannot overcome.

Foreign Alliance and Idolatry 28:16-27

Edomites and Philistines were natural enemies of Judah. During the reign of Ahaz, Tiglath-Pileser III conducted a campaign that overran the Philistine cities and terminated any assistance from Egypt. The Assyrian monarch also took over Israelite territories (Gilead, Megiddo, and Dor) and turned them into Assyrian provinces (cf. Isa 9:1). He captured and destroyed Damascus, executed Rezin, and turned the Aramean kingdom into four Assyrian provinces. Ahaz may have appealed for help as a vassal of Assyria or may have become a vassal in the process of seeking Assyrian aid (2 Chron 28:16-18). Attacks from the north gave Judah opportunity to regain control of trade routes that Uzziah had taken over (2 Chron 26:7-8). The cities captured were all along the Aijalon, Sorek, and Elah Valleys in the buffer zone of the Shephelah or the Negev [*Shephelah, p. 467; Negev, p. 467*].

The Chronicler does not mention the Aramean altar built by Ahaz (2 Kings 16:10-13), but does stress the worship of *the gods of Damascus* (28:23). Though Ahaz met Tiglath-Pileser in Damascus, he adopted a Canaanite religion. Assyrian imperialism did not include imposition of their religion. Judah reached its lowest point under Ahaz. Being at the same spiritual level of the Northern Kingdom, reunification under Hezekiah became possible. Judah was itself in the spiritual equivalent of an exilic situation.

THE TEXT IN BIBLICAL CONTEXT
Isaiah, Ahaz, and Hezekiah

The reign of Ahaz becomes one of two major paradigms in the prophecy of Isaiah. Ahaz lived in the perilous times of the advancing Assyrian army of Tiglath-Pileser III. Isaiah describes the coalition of Samaria and Damascus against Ahaz in their attempt to motivate him into alliance to resist the Assyrian advance (Isa 7:1-9). These were frightful times for Judah and its king. In this context Ahaz is offered a sign that he refuses (v. 12). Instead, Ahaz trusts the Assyrians, who will in turn reward his trust by plundering his land (vv. 18-25). The second paradigm in Isaiah is Hezekiah. When faced with death, he prayed and sought healing; when given a prophetic promise, he asked for a sign (Isa 38:1-22). Hezekiah the faithful king was delivered after Sennacherib attacked Jerusalem.

The account of Isaiah around the reign of Ahaz concerned the Davidic dynasty. Ahaz's rejection of the sign does not have his anticipated result, namely, that the prophetic word would no longer be relevant. Instead, he is given a different sign: Immanuel (Isa 7:14). For Ahaz, this sign would be realized in a fully negative fashion. When the Assyrian armies completely take over his country, he will know that the prophetic word is true; this is God with him (Isa 8:8). Ahaz is not the king who will fulfill the promise to David. But the promise of the Davidic dynasty will be realized. A son will be born whose counsel will be wonderful, whose dominion will be peace and will endure forever (Isa 9:6-7). Though the sons of Jesse be nothing more than a stump (Isa 11:1), from that stump will come the shoot that will bring a dominion in which the earth will be filled with a knowledge of the Lord as the waters cover the sea (v. 9b). The reign of Ahaz is the time of great prophetic assurances that God will fulfill the promise to David.

For the Chronicler, the reign of Ahaz served quite another purpose. Under Ahaz, the kingdom of Judah reached its lowest point. It is equivalent to the depths of depression in the Northern Kingdom at the schism following Solomon's death. The equivalence of the two kingdoms opens the way for *all Israel* to come to repentance and union under the reign of Hezekiah. For the Chronicler, the reign of

Hezekiah is not so much a great example of deliverance from the forces of the Assyrians, but rather is an actual restoration and union that represent his hope for the future.

THE TEXT IN THE LIFE OF THE CHURCH

Trusting in Riches

Ahaz exemplifies unfaithfulness. In Chronicles, in Kings, and in Isaiah, his reign serves as a negative example, the peril of failing to trust God. His unfaithfulness brings about the darkest days of Judah. There seems to be nothing about his character that is commendable, either in the prophets or in Chronicles. His sin is primarily against God; the term *maʿal* designates only those sins that are against God. In the case of Ahaz, it was complete violation of the temple and making sacrifices to foreign gods. For Ahaz, the God of Israel could never have his exclusive worship or trust. He would trust Assyrians rather than God. The Assyrians were a tangible force that Ahaz preferred.

The example of Ahaz may be uncomfortably close to the practice of faith by affluent Christians. There is a tendency to trust ourselves, our resources, and to be most concerned about whatever is immediate. Modern and postmodern Christians manifest deistic tendencies. It is hard to conceive of God as active and present in maintaining life in his world. Everything can be understood as cause and effect; it can all be brought under human control. It is not a disbelief in God, but rather a belief that does not affirm the presence of God in our daily affairs. There is a tendency to cultural conformity without consideration of the ways in which this may be a sin against God. The greatest dangers are perceived to be tangible ones, observed forces that may threaten our well-being. There is no sense that the greatest danger may be less tangible, an implicit faith in ourselves for the needs of life rather than a genuine knowledge that life is a divine gift.

Exclusive trust in God is very difficult in times of power and affluence. God has given the means of life to use and trust, but they must all be recognized for what they are: gifts from God. In a modern or postmodern society, there is a tendency to feel entitled, to believe that government and investments bring security. These are the sorts of compromises of which Ahaz was guilty. It is always a good practice to give thanks for every meal. Life and everything that sustains it must continually be acknowledged as divine gifts. Failure to make this confession readily leads to the unfaithfulness of which Ahaz was guilty.

Part 6

Healing under Hezekiah

2 Chronicles 29:1-32:33

OVERVIEW

The story of Hezekiah is a turning point in the narrative of Israel in Chronicles. The desecration of the temple and the decimation of Judah created a situation of desolation in Israel that was analogous to the time of Saul. When Hezekiah began to reign, the nation was in complete disarray, and there was no functioning temple. Ahaz had closed the doors of the temple and had brought idolatrous worship to all the cities of Judah (2 Chron 28:24-25). Though the Chronicler does not mention that the kingdom of Samaria went into exile during the days of Ahaz, that reality is assumed in his portrayal of the reign of Hezekiah (30:6, 9). Exile is implicit, as Hezekiah appeals to those that remain (Mosis: 186-92). Hezekiah is challenged by two enormous tasks: restoring temple worship and unifying the nation. The obstacles appear to be insurmountable. The nation needed to begin again, because effectively it had come to an end. Everything that David and Solomon achieved was lost. In recounting the reign of Hezekiah, the Chronicler shows how Israel may emerge from the ashes of the fires of judgment. In such situations, God's grace will overcome if his people humble themselves, pray, and seek the face of God (2 Chron 7:14).

The Chronicler depicts Hezekiah as a second Solomon (Dillard 1987: 228-29). Just as Solomon was the godly temple builder, who carried out the mandate of David, so Hezekiah is a king without blemish, who restores the temple and brings the nation together in worship. In Chronicles, there is little to stain the character of Hezekiah; he humbled himself in his pride, making him exemplary of faithfulness (2 Chron 36:25-26). The Chronicler does not ignore the account of Hezekiah in Kings, but shapes it and supplements it. Ninety-five verses telling the story of Hezekiah in 2 Kings 18-20 are reduced to twenty-eight (2 Chron 32:1-26, 32, 33), but all the elements of the previous account are incorporated in them. The

Chronicler also expands the account of Hezekiah with three chapters that have no other parallel (2 Chron 29–31). The Deuteronomists say nothing about the temple reforms of Hezekiah, which began in the very first month of his reign (29:3). The Chronicler's supplementary material for Hezekiah is significantly more than for any other period of his history after Solomon.

The Chronicler has patterned his version of Hezekiah in much the same way as he has presented the Davidic promise. Under Ahaz, the kingdom was decimated by war, and worship was like that of pagan nations. The dismal situation under Saul was transformed under David and Solomon. Solomon built the temple and brought the promise of the Davidic kingdom to fruition. Hezekiah brought north and south together with such success that Levites and priests were completely unprepared for the numbers of people coming to the Passover celebration. Hezekiah initiated innovations that did not conform to the regulations of temple practice, but his efforts did bring healing (2 Chron 30:20). The Chronicler may have adopted the healing metaphor from the prophet Isaiah (Isa 6:10; 53:5), but he has given it a national significance by using it to describe the transformation of Israel after Ahaz.

The Chronicler creates a number of parallels with Solomon in the matter of temple restoration. He specifically likens the observance of the Passover at the time of Hezekiah to the time of Solomon (2 Chron 30:26). Hezekiah appointed the priests and Levites to their respective divisions and duties, recalling the arrangements made by David and Solomon (1 Chron 15:3-24; chs. 23–26; 2 Chron 8:14-15) *[Priests and Levites in Chronicles, p. 471]*. The Chronicler also emphasizes Hezekiah's great wealth (2 Chron 32:27-29), comparable to the report about Solomon (9:15-16). Hezekiah's intercessory prayer at the Passover observance (30:18-20) has a parallel in the prayer of Solomon at the temple dedication (ch. 6). The lesson for the Chronicler's audience could not be missed. The remnant who survived the defilement of Ahaz and the might of the king of Assyria was renewed under Hezekiah (30:6). They restored the temple and its worship, bringing all Israel into union in a great Passover celebration. Such healing was also possible following the Babylonian exile.

2 Chronicles 29:1-36
Restoration of the Temple

PREVIEW

At the beginning of the eighteenth century, England was in a moral quagmire and a spiritual cesspool. Deism was rampant, and a bland philosophical morality was standard fare in the churches. Drunkenness was pervasive. Newborns were exposed in the streets. There are disturbing parallels to North America in the twenty-first century. Revival in such situations is possible. Whitefield and Wesley transformed England; Hezekiah transformed Israel.

Hezekiah signaled a new era of relationship with the Lord by declaring his intention *to make a covenant* (2 Chron 29:10), with the desire that this would remove the divine anger brought about by Ahaz's desecration. Hezekiah ends his speech by calling on the Levites to fulfill their responsibilities of representing the presence of God, burning incense in service to the Lord. The response of the Levitical leaders from all of their divisions was immediate. In just eight days all the defiling objects were removed from the courts, and in another eight days the temple proper was cleansed (v. 17). Only the priests could enter the temple itself; they brought all the unsanctioned objects outside, where the Levites gathered them and carried them to the Kidron Valley for burning. The same procedure was used in the days of Asa (2 Chron 15:16) and Josiah (2 Kings 23:6). Hezekiah then provided for all the kingdom and the sanctuary through the proper purification sacrifices (2 Chron 29:21). Representing the divine presence requires ritual that distinguishes the function of temple and people from the common. The cleansing of the temple was the occasion of a great celebration. It was the first step in renewing the covenant with God.

OUTLINE

Summary of Hezekiah's Reign, 29:1-2
Exhortation to Restoration, 29:3-11
Restoration of the Sanctuary, 29:12-19
Rededication of the Temple, 29:20-30
Sacrifices of Praise, 29:31-36

EXPLANATORY NOTES

Summary of Hezekiah's Reign 29:1-2

The Chronicler begins his narrative of Hezekiah with the accession notice found in 2 Kings 18:1-3, but he omits the problematic synchronism with the Northern Kingdom [*Chronological Synchronism, p. 465*]. The reign of Hezekiah is the first opportunity for unified worship since the time of the division of the monarchy. The absence of a kingdom in northern Israel furnished the possibility of a social and spiritual unification of Israel like that of the reign of Solomon. The Passover celebration, right at the beginning of Hezekiah's reign, is the first example of this great unification.

Exhortation to Restoration 29:3-11

Hezekiah is shown to be like Solomon in his concern for the temple, even in the first month of his first year (2 Chron 29:3, 17). The first month of the first year must mean Nisan, the month of the Passover, the beginning of the year in spring. The language of the Chronicler conforms to his own time (De Vries: 372). By postexilic times, spring was universally the beginning of the year, and the month of accession of new kings; during the time of historical Hezekiah, official accession would have been in fall. The Chronicler is not preoccupied with the month of official accession, but with the actions of the king as soon as the reign of his wicked father had ended, and with the king's immediate concern to celebrate the Festival of Passover, when all Israel would come to Jerusalem on pilgrimage.

Hezekiah's first act as king was to open and refurbish the doors of the temple (2 Chron 29:3). The verb used for *restoration* (make strong) is a deliberate pun on the name of the king; literally he *Hezekiahed* the doors. This provides an occasion for the speech of the king to the priests and the Levites (vv. 4-11). Though both groups are mentioned and must have been involved (cf. v. 11), it is only the Levites who are directly addressed (vv. 4-5). The address indicates the Chronicler's special interest in the Levites. The speech itself is based on common prophetic motifs and falls into the general category of what has been called "Levitical sermons" (von Rad 1966: 275). The address expresses the idea of the exile in a quotation known more fully in the prophets: Yahweh has made his people an object of cursing, of horror, of hissing, and of reproach (cf. Jer 29:18). Hezekiah urges the leaders of the people to renew the covenant.

The speech of Hezekiah uses the vocabulary of exile to describe the failure of the nation. The people have abandoned the Lord as in the days of the separation under Rehoboam (2 Chron 12:1; cf. 13:10). The wrath of God had come upon Judah and Jerusalem, putting them in the same situation as the people in the north. It is the desire of Hezekiah to reverse this situation, but he is dependent on the religious leaders to make it possible. Renewal of the covenant requires the revitalization of the temple as the central symbol of the divine rule. Only the Levites can care for the temple, and only the priests can enter it to burn incense.

Restoration of the Sanctuary 29:12-19

The Levites figure prominently in the cleansing of the temple. Though they are not permitted to enter the inner part of the temple, they seem to be responsible for the entire task, with the priests serving under their supervision. The list of Levites is somewhat remarkable, divisible into two sections: the representative Levitical families and the families of the singers. There are two representatives from each of three families: Kohath, Merari, and Gershon. A further two representatives are from the large Kohathite family of Elizaphan, which is almost a fourth clan. Finally, there are two representatives from each division of the singers: Asaph, Heman, and Jeduthun. In comparison with the list in the time of David (1 Chron 15:5-10), the Levitical singers have replaced Hebron and Uzziel, possibly an indication of the growing influence of these families (Dillard 1987: 235). The main point appears to be that all the branches of the Levitical family responded with enthusiasm.

The Levitical leaders follow the king's orders with great precision. The king takes the initiative in the effort, acting in accordance with the *words* of the Lord (NIV, *word*; 2 Chron 29:15). The king conforms to the instructions for the proper function of the temple (Deut 12:2-4), but the Chronicler goes further. He presents Hezekiah in the pattern of David and Solomon, who had received their directives from God. The Levites begin with their own sanctification, which means they must have brought offerings (cf. 30:15); then they begin to purify the house. The work was carried out in two stages (29:16-17): the cleansing of the temple and then of the courts. There were two separate aspects to the restoration: purification, the deliverance from pollution (v. 16); and sanctification, the dedication of the temple to its specific purpose (v. 17; Japhet 1993: 922). Sanctification began on the eighth day, when the priests entered the temple itself. The word *sanctify* is used in a general sense (v. 17a NRSV; cf. v. 5), denoting the process as a whole. Sanctification involved both the temple building and the altar; it took a full eight days, a length of time that seems to have become traditional for temple dedication (2 Macc 2:9-12).

The Levites announced to the king that the purification was complete (2 Chron 29:17-19). Specific mention is made of the altar in the court; it was the site of the sacrificial rites and was previously separately noticed in the dedication (2 Chron 7:1-3). It is unclear why specific mention should be made of the table of bread inside the temple. The utensils of the lampstand and the altar of incense are included in the total of those placed before the great altar (v. 19a). This indicates that the rituals of the purification offering included the sanctification of all the temple utensils.

Rededication of the Temple 29:20-30

The dedication ceremonies began with the formal ritual of the temple rededication, which was followed by the spontaneous response of the people offering sacrifices of praise (2 Chron 29:31-36). The account of the formal dedication begins with an outline of the preparations and procedures (vv. 21-26) before describing the actual event (vv. 27-30). The preparations involved procuring and preparing the necessary animals (vv. 21-24) and making arrangements for accompanying music (vv. 25-26), a unique element in this ceremony. Music is not mentioned elsewhere in the procedures for sacrificial rituals.

In the account, Hezekiah begins by gathering the representative leadership (2 Chron 29:20), which does not appear to be a designated group of officials but rather a broad range of dignitaries (cf. 1 Chron 28:1; 2 Chron 1:2). All this company then shares with Hezekiah the responsibilities of the ceremony (vv. 29-30). The animals divide into two groups; the bulls, rams, and sheep are for the burnt offering, and the male goats are for the purification offering. It is a linguistic error to call the latter a "sin offering" (Milgrom 1983: 67-68). Rather, this is *a purification offering for the kingdom, for the sanctuary, and for Judah* (v. 21 NIV mg.; also in vv. 23-24). The purification appears to include temple artifacts, such as the utensils laid before the altar (cf. vv. 18-19). The king is distinguished from the people in the purification offering, a distinction followed consistently by the Chronicler. The king represents the royal house, and *the assembly* represents the people of Judah (v. 23). The temple personnel are a third group purified by the offerings. Later the Chronicler will specify that the purification offering is *for all Israel* (v. 24). *All Israel* cannot be the equivalent of Judah (Williamson 1977a: 126-27). The emphatic repetition of the king's command indicates that a wider group of people must be included than that originally envisioned by the priests (v. 21). The Chronicler is emphasizing the inclusion of the total population, without regard for the former divisions.

The combination of sacrifices follows closely that of the dedication of the altar in the wilderness (Num 7:84, 87-88), with the bulls, rams, and lambs for burnt offering and male goats for a purification offering. The burnt offering was to symbolize atonement for the people (Lev 1:4). The burnt offering was the most frequent sacrifice. It did not remove sin or change the sinful nature, but it made fellowship with God possible. Purification offerings provided for cleansing from inadvertent sin, which might have been committed (Lev 4:2-3, 13-14, etc.). The offerings and the accompanying music are described in separate paragraphs (vv. 20-24, 25-30), though they take place simultaneously. As a result there is a duplication in the narrative (vv. 21, 27), but it has the effect of showing the prominence of the Levitical musicians in leading the entire assembly in worship. The whole arrangement is given an authority derived from David, who is numbered among the prophets in receiving the commandments from the Lord (v. 25). All were involved in the service as the sacrifices were offered: the laity worshiped, the Levites sang, and the priests blew the trumpets (v. 28). The ritual was not complete until the king and his entourage prostrated themselves after the completion of the offerings. Further singing by the Levites, who prostrated themselves to the ground, followed the offerings (vv. 29-30).

Sacrifices of Praise 29:31-36

The dedication applied not only to the priests but also to the whole assembly (2 Chron 29:31). The metaphorical expression *dedicated yourselves* (lit. to "fill your hands") is generally used for consecration to an office. Here it describes the consecration of all the people in the renewal of their vows (cf. 29:10). The celebration centered upon the offering of sacrifices by the people themselves (vv. 31-36). This is the only event in which the Chronicler ascribes to the people active participation in the contribution of sacrifices, but popular participation is a constant feature in the Chronicler's view of history.

This celebration has a character distinct from the prior ritual, as expressed by the different kinds of sacrifices. Instead of burnt offerings and purification offerings, the people are asked to offer sacrifices and praise offerings (v. 31), offerings that are eaten by their owners as part of a thanksgiving meal. These are often qualified as peace offerings or offerings of well-being. The Chronicler goes out of his way to show surprise and delight at the spontaneity of the great number of devoted praise offerings consumed as part of the thanksgiving festivities (v. 33). He further points out that the people and the Levites were more prepared than the priests to participate in the sacred celebration (v. 34). It was an indication of how the Lord *had provided for* the people (v. 36 ESV); the same word is used in verse 35 for the service of the temple being *restored* (NRSV; NIV, *reestablished*). The Chronicler particularly emphasizes the readiness of the people for spiritual renewal.

THE TEXT IN BIBLICAL CONTEXT

Covenant Confession through Temple Restoration

It was Hezekiah's intent to renew the covenant so that the punishing divine wrath might be removed from the people (2 Chron 29:10). Covenant renewal was a requirement from the time when the covenant was first established at Sinai. While the people remained camped at Mount Sinai, it already became necessary to renew the covenant because of the creation of the idolatrous calf (Exod 32:4; 34:1). This was a critical lesson in understanding the name Yahweh; if the God of the covenant is to be with them, as he promised Moses at the burning bush (Exod 3:12), it would be necessary for God to be merciful (33:19; 34:5-6). Hezekiah is following the procedure that had been established from the initiation of the covenant. In his context, that procedure needed to begin with instituting the symbolic confessions of the covenant, involving the temple and all of its associated ritual. The temple was to represent the life-giving power of the Holy One, the Creator, on whom all life depended moment by moment. Ahaz had closed the temple to the worship of the Lord so that it was like that of the other nations. The gods of other nations were not separate from creation, as was the Holy One of Israel. The gods of the other nations originated out of the substance of the same matter that constituted the rest of creation. They were also subordinate to superior powers that they themselves could not control. The temple was a symbolic confession of the rule of God over creation, declaring his holiness. God is holy, separate from the common of creation. His holy throne room was absolutely set apart from other spaces by its heavy veil. Hezekiah immediately determined to restore the temple so it could function to represent the God of the covenant. This was a first essential act in renewing a relationship with the God of redemption. Confession of faith must have a tangible form so that it may be observed by witnesses. Faith is expressed in ritual as well as in word and deed.

It is also possible for ritual to be rigorously maintained but to be completely empty of a genuine faith confession. In the time of Jesus, scrupulous attention was given to the purity of the temple, but not in terms of what the temple was to represent. Immediately upon his triumphal entry into Jerusalem, Jesus went to the temple and evicted those who were selling sacrifices there, accusing them of turning it into a den of thieves (Matt 21:12-13). The temple was in a pristine state of ritual purity, at least in the view of the priesthood that controlled it, but some had polluted it with their self-righteousness and greed. The temple was to be a place of prayer for all peoples, as the prophets had said (Isa 56:7). The temple was not to be exclusive to one nation or group, but available to all those who made confession of the covenant (vv. 4-7), whatever their social status or ethnic background. The keepers of the temple had turned it into the very opposite of what it was meant to be. They had made it ethnically exclusive; they had turned its rituals into an opportunity to make profit. Ritual is important, but it must also be protected so that it truly makes confession of the faith relationship.

The Chronicler manifests this attitude toward the temple. The temple was the eminent confession of the faith of Israel to all nations. No king desiring to observe the covenant could ignore its most central physical expression. The faith of Hezekiah is unequivocally stated in 2 Kings 18:5-6. There it is manifested in his trust in the God of the temple during the siege of Sennacherib, when he goes before the Lord with the threatening letters of the invading king (2 Kings 19:14-15; cf. 2 Chron 32:20). The Chronicler demonstrates the faith of Hezekiah in his purification of the temple, an action no less significant and one that explains the trust of the king in the time of crisis. From the very start Hezekiah was a man of faith; hence he could do nothing other than express it in restoration of the covenant and its celebrations. This he put into action immediately upon coming to the throne.

THE TEXT IN THE LIFE OF THE CHURCH
The Living Temple

The church is to be understood in terms of the temple. In the words of the apostle Peter, "As you come to him, the living Stone—rejected by humans but chosen by God and precious to him—you also, like living stones, are being built into a temple of the Spirit to be a holy priesthood, offering spiritual sacrifices acceptable to God through Jesus Christ" (1 Pet 2:4-5). This temple is inclusive of all peoples, as expressed by the apostle Paul:

> Consequently, you are no longer foreigners and strangers, but fellow citizens with God's people and also members of his household, built on the foundation of the apostles and prophets, with Christ Jesus himself as the chief cornerstone. In him the whole building is joined together and rises to become a holy temple in the Lord. (Eph 2:19-21)

This temple is as public as the one restored by Hezekiah; it is seen in persons that have joined in the new covenant and express it in the rituals of baptism and the Eucharist. These persons form congregations that express the praises of the Holy One, just as people did in the temple restored by Hezekiah.

As with the temple of the former covenant, the temple of the new covenant may become desecrated and dysfunctional. As in the time of the New Testament, their rituals may continue, and the participants may be quite oblivious to the actual state of affairs. There are times when the church needs to engage in covenant renewal, just as Hezekiah did. The difference for the church is that there are no prescribed forms that need to be followed. The forms of renewal are established in each situation, with words and rituals that all can understand.

Yet there is one aspect prominent in Chronicles that should be a part of all covenant renewal: celebration. It is hard to calculate the equivalent of Hezekiah's celebration in contemporary terms, but that is not necessary. It is clear enough that celebration includes food and music. As the closing doxology, believers could appropriately sing, "God be with you till we eat again." Such celebrations will be all the more meaningful if they can specifically express renewal of covenant relationships that are always necessary. There are times when such renewal is a restoration from a condition of broken relationships. Though congregations may endure an exile like that of Israel under Ahaz, they may also experience the renewal of the covenant like that under Hezekiah.

2 Chronicles 30:1–31:1
Celebration of the Passover

PREVIEW

Communion is the means by which Christians make their confession of redemption until the time when God's kingdom arrives in its fullness. Unfortunately, communion has come to be removed from its roots in the redemption celebration of Passover. As Jesus celebrated redemption with his disciples, he transformed the ceremony into a Christian Passover in which confession is made of Jesus as the Redeemer. Communion for the Christian should be as compelling as Passover was to Hezekiah.

Celebration of the Passover—remembering the redemption and covenant of the exodus—was the highest priority to Hezekiah. It needed to take place in the first year, but there were several significant problems. The Passover is a pilgrimage festival, meaning that it had to take place in Jerusalem (Exod 23:15). The purification and dedication of the temple had taken sixteen days. The Passover is instructed to begin on the fourteenth day of the first month (Exod 12:2-6). In this situation the length of the purification process made it impossible to observe Passover at the proper time. A second problem was that the priests were not sanctified, and in addition, people had not made the journey to Jerusalem (2 Chron 30:3). These problems were not about to deter Hezekiah. In consultation with the leaders, he determined that under such circumstances the Passover could be held on the second month (v. 2), for which there was precedent (Num 9:9-11). There was yet a further problem when the time for celebration came: most of those who had come from a distance were not in a proper state of purity, but they ate the Passover anyway (v. 18). Yet because they had sought the Lord with their whole heart, Hezekiah could pray for their forgiveness, and they were healed. In spite of the disparities with Passover custom, this celebration was so successful that it was extended an additional seven days (v. 23). The praise and prayer of the people was not just experienced at the newly dedicated temple. It reached the temple of God in heaven (v. 27). This was not just ritual; it was genuine spiritual renewal. The situation was a complete reversal of the conditions under Ahaz less than two months after the inauguration of the new king.

OUTLINE

Summons to the Passover Pilgrimage, 30:1-12
Observance of the Festival, 30:13-22
Continuation of Celebration, 30:23-31:1

EXPLANATORY NOTES

Summons to the Passover Pilgrimage 30:1-12

The celebration of the Passover demonstrates several of the Chronicler's central concerns: the unity of Israel, the spiritual preparedness of the people, and the success of following the formula for restoration that God gave Solomon through a vision (2 Chron 7:14). All three of these motifs are immediately evident as the account of the summons to the Passover is given. Hezekiah, in consultation with his advisers, dispatches couriers from Dan to Beersheba, the traditional designation for the entire territory of the nation (2 Chron 30:5). The king and his advisers are ready to proceed, in cooperation with the people, even though they needed to celebrate a month late. The priests had not been sanctified, nor was there enough time for people to make the pilgrimage to Jerusalem (vv. 2-3). All these difficulties could be overcome because there was a spirit of submission and repentance. The statement that those in the north *humbled themselves* (v. 11) indicates that they had taken the critical first step in meeting the criteria. The Lord then gave them a unified spirit in their efforts.

The nation's unification in Hezekiah's time is stressed by the use of the term Israel (2 Chron 30:1, 5, 6). The political reality of the Israelites was that only Judah existed in Hezekiah's day, and Judah existed only as a dependent province in the time of the Chronicler. The social and spiritual reality was that Israel was inclusive of all those who shared in the faith of the covenant even though they lived outside the political boundaries. The Chronicler distinguishes Judah as the territory, but it is evident that the term Israel includes Judah. The Chronicler appeals to the sons and daughters of Israel to turn to the Lord God of Abraham, Isaac, and Israel (v. 6). Consistently the Chronicler uses the name Israel in place of Jacob in this formula. The Chronicler even substitutes the name Israel for Abraham in his quotation of Psalm 105:6 (in 1 Chron 16:13), where the parallelism of the psalm indicates that Israel and Jacob are interchangeable (cf. Ps 105:10; 1 Chron 16:17). The content of the letters sent by Hezekiah was equally applicable to Israel and Judah. Judah had been in an exile under Ahaz: the province was given over to desolation (2 Chron 30:7) and came under God's wrath (v. 8). Most significantly, the response of both the north and the south is reported by the Chronicler (vv. 10-12), indicating that the total population was being addressed. North and south were united in their apostasy, and Hezekiah became the means of uniting north and south in renewal in spite of the political situation.

The motif of spiritual preparedness through repentance is a development found in the postexilic prophets, in Zechariah in particular. The Chronicler cites couriers who, at the king's command, give a message throughout Israel and Judah employing the word *šub* (turn) successively, first in an appeal for a *return* to the Lord of the covenant (v. 6a), so that (second) the Lord might *return* to the remnant that had escaped from Assyria (v. 6b). Third, God will then *turn* away the anger of his judgment (v. 8b) if (fourth) they *return* to the Lord (v. 9a), because he is a compassionate God, who (fifth) will allow them to *return* to their land (9b), and (sixth) will not abandon them if they will *return* to him (v. 9c). The Chronicler is deliberately extending the words of Zechariah 1:3: "'Turn to me,' utterance of the LORD of hosts, 'and I will turn to you,' says the LORD of hosts" (AT). Zechariah continues with the exhortation not to be as their ancestors, who balked when the prophets appealed to them to turn (*šub*) from their evil ways (v. 4; cf. 2 Chron 30:7). The fierce anger of God against the former generation was nothing other than the curse of the covenant (Zech 1:5-6; cf. 2 Chron 30:8). They had no other recourse but to repent (*šub*), for God had acted exactly as he said he would (Zech 1:6b). The wordplay on *šub*, as adopted by the Chronicler to point the way toward restoration, continues a significant theological development.

Such an extensive and theologically motivated development of the Passover of Hezekiah has naturally invited questions concerning its historical veracity. No mention is made of such a Passover in the corresponding history of Kings. It has often been assumed that the Chronicler unreservedly serves his own purpose in his reconstruction of the events recorded in Kings, that he does not hesitate to present assumptions as facts. It is further assumed that the observance of a centralized Passover at Jerusalem is unlikely before the great reforms of Josiah. More recent studies call into question the superiority of Kings over Chronicles in terms of historical reliability. Chronicles does make use of Kings as a source, but both compositions seem to have common sources as well (Rainey 1997: 38–41). Kings depicts Josiah as the model king; thus in the interests of heightening the importance, effect, and uniqueness of Josiah's reform, the reformations of earlier kings have been suppressed (Dillard 1987: 241). Deuteronomy contains much material older than the reforms of Josiah (Deut 16:1-8), so it cannot be assumed that the practice of a centralized Passover could not have happened in the time of Hezekiah. We do know that Kings and Chronicles testify to common sources. Both compositions use these sources to theological ends; there is no basis for asserting that their rendition of events is simply a literary creation.

The Passover Festival of Hezekiah is unique as a pilgrimage festival in the second month. There is a provision for the delayed observance of the Passover if one has inadvertently become ceremonially unclean or has been away on a long journey (Num 9:9-11), but the Passover of Hezekiah relates to a delay for everyone. As with every initiative, the response to this Passover celebration was somewhat mixed. The priests were evidently not fully supportive (v. 3), as they were not properly prepared. Though the invitation extended from Dan to Beersheba, only Ephraim, Manasseh, Asher, Issachar, and Zebulun are actually reported as responding (vv. 11, 18). Nevertheless this was a significant advance toward Passover observance that had been long neglected (v. 5). It serves to show how right may be done even when there is much that is wrong.

Observance of the Festival 30:13-22

Among the challenges facing Hezekiah in observing the Passover was the problem of the impurity of the city. The first task of the assembled multitude was to remove all the foreign cult objects, which were properly disposed of in the Kidron Valley, where they could be burned (v. 14). A second problem was the failure of the priestly leaders to be properly prepared for the great number of people who had come (v. 15). The problem may have been the consecration of those officials who had come from outside the city and had not been a part of the earlier purification (29:15, 34). Once again the response of the people had outstripped that of the professional clerics, to the great shame of the latter. The priests and Levites had to offer the appropriate burnt offerings before they could take their place in the ceremony. The biggest problem was the impurity of the large number of pilgrims who had traveled great distances from foreign lands and did not have an opportunity to receive the proper purification ceremonies (30:13, 17). This rendered them unfit to perform the sacrifice that they had come to observe. The normal practice was that each person would slaughter his own sacrifice; manipulation of the blood was handled by the priests (vv. 15-16). The ritually unclean state of the pilgrims rendered them unfit to participate in the ceremony for which they had come, a point made very clear in the Passover provisions. This was a perpetual problem in observing the festivals in the Second Temple period.

Three options were open to Hezekiah in dealing with ceremonial impurity: the pilgrims could be forbidden to participate, they could be allowed to participate fully as those from Judah, or they could be allowed to eat the Passover without participating in the sacrificial ritual. Hezekiah chose the third alternative; he placed the Levites in charge of the sacrifices so they would be pure (v. 17). This still meant that the pilgrims ate the festival in a state of impurity (v. 18). The Chronicler makes clear the results of Hezekiah following the programmatic formula for restoration (vv. 18-19; cf. 2 Chron 7:14). Hezekiah prayed, asking that the Lord would atone for all those who had fully set their hearts to seek him (2 Chron 30:18-19). *Healed* is used in a metaphorical sense, expressing the atoning action that had taken place through Hezekiah's prayer (v. 20).

The result of Hezekiah's prayer was that the festival was observed for a full seven days with great joy and celebration each day. Music is again prominent, as the celebration takes place with *powerful instruments* (v. 21b AT). Music and celebration take precedence over the sacrifices. The Levites, referring to the collective group that played the instruments and sang, are commended for their excellent service (v. 22a). The people in turn made their confession by eating the food of the festival sacrifice (v. 22). Hezekiah himself is presented as taking the initiative in allowing all to celebrate in this fashion (vv. 18-19). In this respect he has taken a very pragmatic approach to symbolism. The symbols of purity had to be respected if they were to have any meaning at all, but at the same time symbols are nothing apart from the correct attitude of heart. Since the spiritual condition of the people was correct, the implementation of the symbolism had to be accommodated accordingly.

Continuation of Celebration 30:23-31:1

Just as the celebration of the temple purification carried on for two full periods of seven days (2 Chron 7:8-9), so also did the celebration of this Passover. There was no precedent for such an extended celebration. It shows that Hezekiah is a kind of a second Solomon in the dedication of the temple. The difference is that the second week of celebration in Solomon's case was the Festival of Booths. The extended celebration under Hezekiah was made possible by the enormous contributions of offerings by the king and his leaders (2 Chron 30:24). As well, the consecration of the priests finally seems to be catching up to the people's support of spiritual renewal. It is notable that no celebration like this had taken place since the time of Solomon (v. 26)—another indication that Hezekiah, in his own limited circumstances, made possible the conditions for covenant faithfulness that were equal to those of the time of David and Solomon. This great time of joy served to reunite the people who had been estranged (v. 25). No one was regarded as a stranger or foreigner. The people were blessed; their prayer was heard in heaven, providing assurance of the fulfillment of the divine promise.

With the purification of the temple and the city, Hezekiah had arrived at the third stage of his reformation, the purification of the entire land (31:1). The activity of tearing down all the cult objects extended not only to Judah but also into the territories of the north. This suggests that Hezekiah did take some initiatives toward centralization in Jerusalem. The Rabshakeh recognizes this in his taunts against Jerusalem during the Assyrians' siege (2 Kings 18:22). Jeremiah the prophet also implies the same when he mentions Hezekiah's reformation under the impact of Micah's preaching (Jer 26:18-19). No doubt it was Hezekiah's ambition to undo the havoc of Jeroboam I in tearing the nation apart (cf. 1 Kings 12:25-30). The Chronicler has a contemporary concern in relating these events. He wants to show a struggling and fragmented people of his own day that unity and joy are possible even under the most unlikely circumstances.

THE TEXT IN BIBLICAL CONTEXT
Faithfulness in Passover Observance

The various descriptions of the Passover in Scripture show that it had a history of development, at first observed as a family festival in the home, and later observed as a pilgrimage festival. Hezekiah chose the unusual time of the second month for the pilgrimage festival. This might seem to compromise the significance of the Passover as celebrated on the first month of the year (Exod 12:1), but the second month may have also served to bring unity and spiritual renewal in the time of Hezekiah. Kings reports that Jeroboam I set the fall pilgrim festivals in the eighth month (1 Kings 12:32-33), a further effort to distinguish the religious practice of the north and to discourage a pilgrimage to Jerusalem. Talmon has shown that this change would have been consistent with climactic conditions and calendar reckoning in ancient Israel (Talmon 1958: 54-57). All the festivals were synchronized with harvest, beginning with Passover during the early harvest at the start of the year. With the disappearance of the Northern Kingdom, Hezekiah would have needed to move toward synchronization of the calendars, thereby assisting the northerners to again accept Jerusalem as the religious center. The response to Hezekiah's invitation in Ephraim and Manasseh was ridicule (2 Chron 30:10), perhaps because the initial invitation was for a month earlier than the Ephraimite reckoning of time. It may be that Hezekiah, in consultation with his advisers, made a concession to the north in order to persuade them to come to Jerusalem (30:2-3). If in part this was a political concession, the change in time might seem to be unjustified. For Hezekiah, the compromise was both necessary and spiritual, supported by the word of the Lord.

Though the Chronicler introduces the festival as the Passover (2 Chron 30:1), he also speaks of it as the Festival of Unleavened Bread (v. 13). It is often assumed that these were two separate festivals that had merged by the time of Chronicles. However, a history of the development of the festivals cannot be reconstructed by analyzing the pentateuchal legislation (Dillard 1987: 242). It is impossible to identify the descriptions by the Chronicler with any of the passages dealing with the Passover and Unleavened Bread.

The ancient feast celebrating redemption from Egypt through the symbols of a lamb and unleavened bread could have various traditions in styles of observance. This did not detract from its sacred significance. Hezekiah demonstrated that flexibility in the time and procedure of observance could help revitalize faith in God.

THE TEXT IN THE LIFE OF THE CHURCH
The Challenge of Renewal

In its early decades, Anabaptism attracted persons from a wide spectrum of society and vocations. The church was more communal than sacramental, more concerned with ethics than theology. Often there was conflict between leaders, such as that between David Joris (1501-56) and Menno Simons (1496-1561). Joris was much more figurative in his use of Scripture and his exhortations to the life of discipleship. He was born to a wealthy mother and actor father. Initially a glass-window artist, he became a spiritualist and Anabaptist prophet. During and following the Münster debacle (1534-35), he worked vigorously to bring peace and order to the group. He was a key leader until Menno Simons joined the Anabaptists in 1536. Joris described the church as the final house, temple, mountain, or city of God that would be erected in honor and would remain glorious. He urged the people as living stones to make their hearts level and square, without flaw, crack, or blemish. A building requires that the stones be cut and prepared so they will fit. "O you stones," he urged, "you believing hearts, allow yourselves to be well-hewn, cleansed, leveled, and made fitting and square by the masons.... If you do not arrange yourselves next to the foundation stone, cornerstone, proofstone, and valuable, elect cornerstone (1 Pet 2:2-8), then you will have no place in the valuable work of God" (C. Dyck: 176-77).

Renewal has many aspects. It involves leaders and people working together, each with a clear understanding of their roles. It requires many different kinds of tasks, none of which may be neglected. It calls for overcoming obstacles and at times even compromise. Hezekiah is presented as a visionary leader who could rally his people with forceful exhortations (2 Chron 29:5-11; 32:6b-8). He would not be discouraged when his leaders were not as prepared as they should have been (29:34; 30:3, 15). Renewal must be daring and innovative, reaching out beyond our usual social and economic circles (30:1). This can cause special problems, like bringing in people who cannot conform to our usual customs of worship (30:17-18a). At times there needs to be a temporary but acceptable compromise of correct practice to accommodate the transition (30:18b-20). Sometimes it may seem that enthusiasm runs ahead of reason. Order must be maintained, but it must also allow for special circumstances. Hezekiah had to be innovative in his celebration of the Passover; he encouraged it at an unusual time and allowed it for those who could not be fully prepared. Renewal also involved money; this was not an option but an obligation that was laid upon everyone (31:4). Money must always be handled with scrupulous care (31:14-19). The designated purposes must be clear, and the proper procedures must be rigorously followed. There will also be threats to renewal (32:1). These may be external to the renewal itself, but they must be faced with a confidence that the one who has begun a good work will perform it until the end.

Representing the presence of God as his people requires a knowledge of what binds us together and cannot be compromised; it also requires an acceptance of the diversities that come with our personal circumstances. In this respect Chronicles is a considerable contrast to Ezra and Nehemiah, though both come from similar time periods. In Ezra and Nehemiah the watchword seems to be "separation," beginning with the building of the temple (Ezra 4:3), and continuing even to the extent of separating families (10:3). The Chronicler, on the other hand, portrays a spirit of invitation to those outside the boundaries, insisting that they also belong to the community of faith. These distinctions can be the most difficult of challenges. Sometimes those most like us and closest to us are in reality farthest from us; yet sometimes those who seem most estranged do belong to us. One of the disappointing things about the church is that we often have our strongest disagreements with those most like us. At other times we end up conforming to those whose values are entirely different from our own. The Chronicler presses through to the central values of the ties that bind and quite deliberately ignores differences that might separate. The critical criterion is a commitment to the people's relationship with God in the covenant.

2 Chronicles 31:2-21
Provisions for Temple Worship

PREVIEW

Taking up an offering is customary in worship services. This is as it should be. Giving of our earnings and possessions is an act of worship. Such giving is not only necessary for the function of worship; it also is a necessary part of the act of worship. Our offerings are a confession that our life is a gift from God, a means by which we give our life and live our life for God. In Israel this public confession was made through the temple. The renewal of Hezekiah required the restoration of temple worship. Such restoration began with giving.

The disruption of the temple service under Ahaz led to the dismantling of the liturgical system (2 Chron 28:24-25). At the completion of the celebration for temple purification, the Chronicler reported that the service of the Lord's house was reestablished (29:35b). Chapter 31 now provides the details of Hezekiah's restoration of the temple ritual. This marks a restoration to the order introduced by Solomon, following the instructions given by David (8:14). The handling of the burnt offerings and the peace offerings was the duty of the priests, while the Levites acted as singers and the gatekeepers. *The camp of the* LORD (31:2 NRSV) is a figurative expression for the temple, based on the language of the tabernacle.

OUTLINE

Contributions to the Temple, 31:2-10
Administration of Contributions, 31:11-19
Summary of Hezekiah's Restoration, 31:20-21

EXPLANATORY NOTES

Contributions to the Temple 31:2-10

The provisions for the temple fall into two categories: those from the king, and those from the people (2 Chron 31:3-4). The *portion of the king* indicates obligatory provisions rather than voluntary contributions. The contribution of the king *from his own possessions* was his responsibility for daily sacrifices and the festival sacrifices in their annual cycle. The people were responsible to give provisions for the clergy. The king's order was given to those *who lived in Jerusalem*, perhaps because they were in the closest proximity to the temple (v. 4). Word of the need for temple provisions spread abroad, and the response came from all Israel (v. 5). This included those who lived outside of Judah in the north. Two points emerge from this observation: Israel was united in its support of the temple, and the response became far more than anticipated or even required. The purpose of the gifts of support was that the clergy might *devote themselves to the Law* (v. 4). This use of the verb "make strong" (hzq) in reference to the law is unusual, perhaps a play on the name Hezekiah. The subject of the verb is the people: the instructions of Hezekiah were to encourage all the people to be resolute in keeping the law.

The Chronicler goes on to mention a tithe of the animals (v. 6). The only mention of an animal tithe in the Pentateuch is in connection with the redemption laws referring to the purchase of that which belongs to the Lord (Lev 27:30-33). The Chronicler may be making reference to the problem of bringing animals from a distance. For those far away, the law permitted the exchange of the yield of the field for money (Deut 14:24-26). It also allowed for animals to be consumed in their location (12:15). The Chronicler is describing gifts in kind. He distinguishes Judah from among the Israelites, specifying those who lived in the cities of Judah as opposed to those outside the province yet were also Israel.

There is an additional tithe of consecrated gifts (2 Chron 31:6b). This is incongruous since all of a consecrated gift belonged to the Lord. The word *tithe* may be an inadvertent dittography and so is omitted by some translations (so RSV). Another possibility is that there was a further reference to the tithe of the field lost through haplography and should be restored (cf. NEB). The medieval rabbi Kimḥi interpreted this to mean "tithes even from the sacred things they had consecrated, even though these are exempt from tithes" (Berger: 265). This would be an extreme expression of goodwill.

The cleansing had taken place in the first month and the Passover in the second month. The provisions are said to begin in the third month and are finally completed in the seventh month (v. 7). Harvest begins in the first month, the time of Passover, and ends in the seventh month, the time of the Feast of Tabernacles. These were the normal occasions when the gifts would be brought. It is not often, in ancient times or the present, that offerings exceed need to the point that they are simply *left over* (v. 10). The Chronicler recalls the revival of the time of Hezekiah with unrestrained optimism.

Administration of Contributions 31:11-19

The description of administering contributions provides for their storage and distribution (vv. 11-13). An administrative list prescribes the assigned responsibilities and the regulations concerning the recipients of the gifts (vv. 14-19). Three types of gifts are mentioned: the *contributions*, the *tithes*, and the items consecrated to sacred use (v. 12). The contributions refer to the firstfruits, and the consecrated items could be anything given in a vow. Different terminology is used in verse 14, which does not mention the tithe; the term *freewill offerings* is peculiar to this verse. It might refer to particular offerings for the priests, the usual designation of things most holy (cf. Num 18:8-11). The administrative hierarchy is very clear; the appointments were made by the king and his chief officer responsible for the temple (v. 13b). Two Levites, brothers, were appointed to be responsible for the distribution (v. 12); they in turn appointed ten other Levites. Twelve is always the operative number in the assignment of responsibilities according to the divisions (cf. 1 Chron 16:4-6; 24:7-19). The special circumstances of abundant gifts resulted in broadening the responsibilities of the gatekeepers to store and supervise the surplus.

Administration is often perceived as tedious and thankless, but its importance and worth must not be minimized. An administrative list of the Levites appointed to the task of distribution describes how the contributions were to be apportioned (vv. 14-19). The system was complex. A great number of people were eligible for service, the majority of them living in provincial towns. Small groups of them came to Jerusalem in a rotation system for short terms of office. The division system was further complicated by the fact that all members of the tribe of Levi were entitled to portions, but there were differences between the priests and other Levites. Since all the contributions were collected in Jerusalem, the logistics of distribution were complicated, and standards of eligibility had to be clear. This required an accurate registration and clear rules of status between those who officiated and those who did not, and between those who lived in the provinces and those in Jerusalem.

The administrative list must be clarified on all these points. It is concerned first of all with overseeing the distribution of the contributions to those serving in the temple (vv. 14-17). The point of active service is specified in verse 16; the distribution was to all those who went to the temple in their turn of duty, to fulfill their responsibilities according to their divisions. The reference in the MT to distribution *in the towns* of the priests (NRSV, *in the cities*) contradicts the specification that this service was for priests entering the temple in Jerusalem (vv. 15-16). The Greek version clarifies the matter: the term translated *in the towns* should rather be *at the hand of* (AT), that is, the distribution was under the care of the priests (a difference of two similar Hebrew letters). The distribution was for all males three years and older, according to the ancient custom of the priests. Three years was the age of weaning; from that time onward, the priest was supported by public resources. Priests were entitled to this support for their entire life. Without warrant, many have emended the text to thirty years, the age at which a priest entered active duty.

The section on the priests concludes with the stipulation of their proper registration according to the house of their fathers (v. 17a). This was because of the rigorous rules pertaining to the purity of descent for the priests. It is in contrast to the registration of the Levites by the offices of their divisions, including their entire households (vv. 17b-18). The Levites were enrolled from twenty years old and upward, beginning with the time of their active service. Their entire household is included in the most comprehensive manner (v. 18). The priests are not the subject of verse 18 (contra NRSV; cf. NIV, NLT). According to the Chronicler, the distribution to the Levites included their entire family, but to the priests it included only the males. The shares were allocated personally to each priest, but the Levites received them as families through the registration of household *[Priests and Levites in Chronicles, p. 471]*. The list then concludes with the distribution to those nonofficiating members of the clergy who lived in the common properties associated with their cities (v. 19). Every male among the priests and the families registered among the Levites received their portions from persons appointed to the task.

Summary of Hezekiah's Restoration 31:20-21

The conclusion of Hezekiah's reforming activity has a parallel in the introduction to Hezekiah in the Deuteronomistic History (cf. 2 Kings 18:5-6) *[Deuteronomistic History, p. 465]*. Each passage bears the marks of the distinctive concerns of the larger composition. The Kings passage characterizes Hezekiah as one who trusted the Lord, the one critical factor that becomes prominent in the ensuing narrative of the deliverance from the Assyrian attack. Chronicles stresses that Hezekiah *sought his God* (2 Chron 31:21b), the critical requirement of success. Chronicles does declare that Hezekiah was *faithful* (v. 20), but this is in relation to his activity in restoring the house of God rather than in trusting God in time of peril. Having already demonstrated the faithful character of Hezekiah, there is no doubt of his continued success and his deliverance in time of adversity. Deliverance is anticipated as divine retribution for the good deeds done.

THE TEXT IN BIBLICAL CONTEXT
Managing Temple Resources

Two principal types of resources were necessary for the function of the temple: people and provisions for their livelihood. Hezekiah's appointment of the priests follows the precedents of David and Solomon. He also provided the animals for the daily offerings and the festal occasions, which could serve as an incentive for the community of Yehud to similarly provide for these occasions in the Chronicler's time. According to the Torah, priests and Levites were to be provided for by the rest of the people (2 Chron 31:4). The generosity of their contributions in Hezekiah's reform was abundant; Azariah, the chief priest, could report that they *had enough to eat and plenty to spare, because the* LORD *has blessed his people, and this great amount is left over* (v. 10). Provisions were made for storage at the temple; two supervising Levites and ten assistants managed the distributions. Priestly assignments had to be orderly, and the provisions for all these families had to be scrupulously managed *[Priests and Levites in Chronicles, p. 471]*.

According to pentateuchal regulation, the most holy offerings were restricted to the male priests (Num 18:9-10). These offerings included every cereal offering, every sin offering, and every guilt offering. All other offerings could be eaten by the members of the priestly families, everyone in the household that was ritually clean, including women and servants (vv. 11-13). The Chronicler includes the gifts assigned to the priests (2 Chron 31:14): the voluntary offerings, contributions, and the most holy offerings. These offerings are for the priests who are registered and serve in the temple (vv. 16-17a). The Chronicler does not stipulate any further provisions for the priests' families. The provision for families in verse 18 applies only to the Levites. The Chronicler further distinguishes between priests and Levites in the provisions for those outside of Jerusalem (v. 19). Individuals designated by name living in the common land associated with the various towns were to distribute portions to every *male* among the priests registered by genealogy, but to every *person* registered among the Levites. The Chronicler uses language similar to the Pentateuch, but in his description of the distributions he includes all registered Levites while limiting portions to the males among the priests (Japhet 1993: 970-71). This incongruity has apparently led some translations to make verse 18 apply to the priests (e.g., NRSV), but that is not the intent of the Chronicler [*Priests and Levites in Chronicles, p. 471*].

In the reform of Hezekiah, the provisions for the temple are gifts in kind. In other contexts the support of the temple was given in silver. The conclusion of Leviticus (ch. 27) appears to be an appendix making provisions for maintaining the temple building and the lives of the clergy. The sources of income in that chapter include pledges in fixed amounts of silver, the consecration of animals sold for the temple, consecrations of property, landholdings and acquired agricultural land, donations of property, and other tithes. The temple did acquire land, and animals suitable for sacrifice could be given directly to the temple. But on the whole, the most efficient support for the temple was silver.

THE TEXT IN THE LIFE OF THE CHURCH

Church Offices and Church Service

In restoring temple worship, Hezekiah appoints all the officers and their duties as designated by their registered family associations. This is a complete contrast to the church of the New Testament, in which there were no regular offices. The generic descriptions of leaders, as in Ephesians 4:11, are not defined offices as they become in the second century (Bruce: 204-9). There were individuals who functioned as leaders in two basic categories: (1) deacons and (2) elders, or overseers. There is nothing in the earliest church to indicate that these were established offices. Paul, in writing to the Christians at Philippi, greets the church with its "bishops and deacons" (Phil 1:1 NRSV) or, to use terms expressing the sense of the Greek, its "superintendents and ministers." Though the apostle Paul provides qualifications for those who fulfill these duties in the pastoral epistles (1 Tim 3:1-13), there is no indication that they are ordained to an office.

By the end of the second century, the church had a threefold order: one bishop, several elders, and several deacons. The first unambiguous witness to the emergence of the single bishop over a geographical area is found in the correspondence of Ignatius while on his way to martyrdom in Rome (Bruce: 203). He insisted that the institution of a single bishop was essential in the church and that his authority was paramount. Ignatius himself was bishop of Antioch in this sense. To Ignatius, the bishop or someone delegated by him was the only church official who could conduct a valid baptism or Eucharist; even a love feast (*agapē* meal; cf. Jude 12) could not take place without him. The church had begun to have prescribed offices; in this respect it was establishing the kind of structure that was always present in the worship related to the temple.

In the New Testament there is no need for church offices. Such offices were not essential for the function of the church in its earliest stages. But there is a progression in the appointment of leaders that establishes a hierarchical function, as can be seen in the pastoral epistles. From there it is a short step to establishing actual offices regulated by particular qualifications and certain assigned duties. This replaced the authority of the apostles in making decisions. The church came to embrace these fully. Someone had to be responsible for decisions on new questions that arose.

In churches today there is a great variety of practice, but most churches have a constitution that prescribes offices of leadership. Responsibility and qualifications for office are the prerogative of the values and corresponding organization of each congregation. Nothing in the Scriptures mandates what these should be.

The temple represented holiness; sanctity was established by family pedigree and by anointing to office. The church represents holiness in a different way. Holiness comes to all members through a relationship with Jesus Christ. Leaders of the church are held to a high standard of moral conduct, but they are not otherwise holy by the act of ordination. This has always been one of the distinctives of the believers church. It is a practice to be maintained. Offices and assigned duties are limited to fulfilling particular functions within congregations. Holiness belongs to the church collectively; there is a priesthood of all believers (1 Pet 2:5, 9).

2 Chronicles 32:1-33
Deliverance and Healing in the Land

PREVIEW

Sometimes it seems that our efforts to serve God are rewarded with trouble and opposition. There can be no bargaining with God, no conditions for the sacrifices made to serve God's kingdom. In the Chronicler's presentation of Hezekiah, the most traumatic event of his kingdom comes *after all that Hezekiah had so faithfully done* (2 Chron 32:1). The attack of Sennacherib results in a blessing due to seeking the Lord. A central point of the story is that Jerusalem was spared due to divine intervention. The survival of Jerusalem tended to overshadow another reality: the captivity of all the other fortified cities of Judah (2 Kings 18:13).

The attack of Sennacherib is expressed uniquely by the Chronicler. He speaks only of the intent of the Assyrian invader to breach the walls of the fortified cities. The Chronicler describes Hezekiah as the strategic king, who made extensive preparations for the attack; for his faithfulness, he was protected by God. The menacing army of the Assyrians was annihilated. The visit of the Babylonian delegation from Marduk-Baladan, which becomes the occasion for the denunciation of Hezekiah by the prophet Isaiah (2 Kings 20:12-19), is acknowledged by the Chronicler (2 Chron 32:31) but regarded only as being a divine test. The Chronicler does allow that Hezekiah had a proud heart, but he humbled himself (32:25-26). Hezekiah is portrayed as a model king, whose epitaph speaks of his great wealth and achievements.

OUTLINE
Divine Protection and Provision, 32:1-23
Tried and Found Faithful, 32:24-31
Summary of a Faithful King, 32:32-33

EXPLANATORY NOTES

Divine Protection and Provision 32:1-23

The account of the invasion begins with a summary introduction (v. 1), a description of Hezekiah's preparation for the attack (vv. 2-8), a summary of the Assyrian king's threats delivered by "the Rabshakeh" (2 Kings 18–19 NRSV; 2 Chron 32:9-19, *officers*), and a report of the deliverance (vv. 20-23). The Chronicler's method has been described as a midrash (Childs: 107), an exposition in which a critical effort is made to understand a text. Midrash recognizes difficulties inherent in a text but employs interpretive assumptions unrelated to the original composition. This is an example of how Christians commonly use the Bible, having a desire to be true to the original meaning of the text, but interested in questions that were not the original concern of the author. The Chronicler is reading the account of the invasion of Sennacherib much as we have it in 2 Kings 18:17-19:37. The Chronicler ignores the record of the destruction of Judah (2 Kings 18:13-16) and has condensed the account of the siege to about fifteen verses. His primary purpose is to show that aggression of the mighty nations is sheer folly against the people who do the will of God on earth as it is in heaven. The Chronicler takes certain creative liberties in accomplishing his purpose, but he includes details even when they are puzzling in the story.

In Kings, the Rabshakeh sends a threatening letter after he has withdrawn his forces from the walls of Jerusalem, in order to fight the Egyptian king at Libnah. How would a letter accomplish surrender when the presence of the military force has failed? The Chronicler circumvents this problem altogether. He inserts the report about the *letters* (2 Chron 32:16-17) between the initial threat of the emissaries of Sennacherib (vv. 10-15) and the shouting to the people on the wall (v. 18). In this way the two events (the siege with its attempt to dissuade the people on the wall, and then the later sending of letters) are presented as one single event. Each element serves to show the utter and futile blasphemy of the Assyrian king (v. 19). The shouting to the people does not dissuade them from trusting Hezekiah (cf. 2 Kings 18:29-36), but it is intended to terrify them and persuade them that they cannot trust God (2 Chron 32:15,

18-19). From the Chronicler's viewpoint, the people have already established their commitment to God under the leadership of their king, so there is no question of their loyalty to the king.

The attack of Sennacherib did not come as a surprise; it was provoked by a broken treaty (2 Kings 18:7b, 20), a point not stated by the Chronicler. Faithfulness demanded careful preparation for the inevitable siege (2 Chron 32:3-5). In siege warfare, water is the most critical commodity; a city cannot last long cut off from a supply of water. Cutting off the enemy's access to the water supply compounds the defensive challenge of the city. The Chronicler assumes that Hezekiah had made provision to ensure a supply of water for the city. He states that Hezekiah took measures to prevent Assyrian access to the water supply.

One of the most famous engineering feats of ancient time was the connection of the fresh waters of the Gihon spring to the pool of Siloam, to make water accessible from within the walls of the city. This famous tunnel is about 530 meters in length and about 2 meters in height. The famous Hezekiah Inscription, originally discovered in the tunnel, describes how the excavators met in joining the two ends (for translation and discussion, see Parker). Though some of the channel may have been natural underground aqueducts, the tunnel still stands as a tremendous achievement to protect the city. Both the tunnel and the inscription continue to be of great interest (an excellent pictorial discussion is provided by Gill). The tunnel may have been a larger and more ambitious project than was previously realized (Ussishkin 1976), a project probably undertaken or extended early in the reign of Hezekiah (2 Chron 32:30). The reference to stopping the waters indicates that Hezekiah took measures to ensure that waters drawn off the spring for irrigation purposes were diverted so they would be inaccessible to the Assyrians since the source of water was concealed.

Hezekiah also undertook fortifications of the city, described in general terms as the repair of the walls, the erection of towers on the walls, and the addition of an outer wall (v. 5). There is archaeological evidence for substantial fortification of various cities in Judah at this time, including Lachish (Rosenbaum: 32-33). The addition of an outer wall may refer to a massive wall on the western hill, built to include it within the city (Broshi). The Millo (lit. *filling*) of the city of David refers to the terrace structure that supported the eastern wall. Hezekiah further prepared defensive weapons and enlisted a standing army (vv. 5b-6a). None of this is in conflict with the divine protection that is the real security of the city (vv. 6b-8).

Hezekiah again draws on typical prophetic terminology to provide assurance that the battle belongs to the Lord. "God is with us" was the assurance that Isaiah the prophet had given to Ahaz in the time of the Assyrian threat (Isa 7:14; 8:8, 10). There was therefore no reason for fear.

The threats of the Assyrians served to make clear the critical issues in this situation (2 Chron 32:10-19). The whole question was one of trust in God (v. 10), but not for a moment was there a question of whether God was on the side of Hezekiah. In Kings, the Rabshakeh suggests that the tearing down of "the high places and altars" was an insult against God, who has been offended and so cannot be trusted (2 Kings 18:22). In Chronicles, the worship reform is used by the enemy to suggest that Hezekiah cannot be trusted (2 Chron 32:11-12), but "for the reader the effect is just the opposite since he has been taught to value the reform as Hezekiah's greatest act of faithfulness" (Childs: 110). The question comes down to whether God can be trusted against the might of the gods of Aššur, that is, Assyria (vv. 11-15), but the very notion that God might be compared with the gods of idols is blasphemous (v. 19).

The Chronicler has revised the portrayal of the king and prophet in reporting the deliverance of the city (v. 20). In Kings, Hezekiah rends his clothes, covers himself in sackcloth, and enters the temple (2 Kings 19:1-2). Here he simply prays, for his faith and confidence have been established, and nothing more need be said about it. The story in Kings gives a central role to the prophet, who gives an extensive reassuring prophecy (2 Kings 19:20-34). In Chronicles, his appearance is almost unexpected, and his role is reduced to praying with Hezekiah. The fate of Sennacherib is reported much as in the earlier account (2 Kings 19:35-37), but the note on the deliverance of Jerusalem and the fame and glory of Hezekiah are the Chronicler's own addition (2 Chron 32:22-23). This provides a fitting end to the story; an Assyrian disaster would result in political calm for Judah and would have had international ramifications.

Tried and Found Faithful 32:24-31

The Chronicler is quite aware of Hezekiah's illness, which for the Chronicler is always a sign of sin, and of the Babylonian embassy, which in Kings was an omen of the eventual exile of the nation. True to his theology, the Chronicler indicates that the illness of Hezekiah was due to his proud heart. His response to the great blessing was ingratitude and perhaps self-sufficiency. The Chronicler gives no indication as to the manner in which Hezekiah's pride was manifested. The suggestion that it was the reception of the Babylonians is contradicted by the context: that story is separately reported, with its own theological observation thereon (v. 31). It seems that the illness itself is meant to be the evidence that Hezekiah was proud. In any case, Hezekiah's response to the illness was according to what was required, which is the main point of reporting it. Hezekiah humbled himself and all Jerusalem with him, so the wrath of the Lord was removed from the nation all the days of the king (v. 26). This last phrase is an oblique reference to the eventual exile of Judah, a fact much more prominent in Kings.

The Chronicler is most interested in Hezekiah's achievements (vv. 27-30). He focuses on two matters: his wealth (vv. 27-29) and his water project (v. 30). The meticulous mention of the various items, with the repeated emphasis on quantity, is intended to suggest that the kingdom of Hezekiah was comparable to that of Solomon. The list of Hezekiah's wealth is constructed as one single sentence (in MT), including the building projects necessary to accommodate his possessions: Hezekiah made treasuries for his wealth (v. 27), storehouses for all his produce (v. 28a), stalls for all his cattle and pens for his flocks (v. 28b), and cities (possibly meaning state-owned lands) for his vast herds of sheep and cattle (v. 29). The whole is rounded off by emphasizing his exceedingly great possessions as a sign of God's blessing (v. 29b). The water project fits in general with other references to diverting the waters through a channel so they run into a pool within the city (cf. 2 Kings 20:20). The Chronicler evaluates these material successes in the same terms as the spiritual achievements. For him the two are inseparably linked.

The visit of the Babylonian envoys is cast in terms of well-known eastern interest in astrology (v. 31). Kings accounts for the visit as an inquiry into Hezekiah's health (2 Kings 20:12). For the Chronicler, they came investigating a sign, no doubt a reference to the return of the shadow (2 Kings 20:8-11). This is presented as a test from God, the real cause for their appearance. God was not testing Hezekiah's actions but needed to know what was in his heart (the expression is derived from Deut 8:2). Though this is not presented as a test in Kings, the story there does show that Hezekiah responded positively to the prophet's warning and resigned himself to the divine will (2 Kings 20:12-19). The story in both versions ends on a positive note, indicating Hezekiah's devotion to the divine purpose whether the final outcome be good or bad.

Summary of a Faithful King 32:32-33

The concluding summary of Hezekiah's rule contains the usual items of his achievements, the sources of the account, a note on his burial, and a reference to his successor. This is the pattern found in the Kings summary (2 Kings 20:20-21), but there are several notable variations. Rather than speaking of the great works of Hezekiah (2 Kings 20:20a), the Chronicler refers to his *acts of devotion* (2 Chron 32:32a); what is significant for him is that Hezekiah was being loyal to the divine mandate. The Chronicler refers to his source as *the vision of the prophet Isaiah*. This might serve as an argument for the account of Hezekiah as a written prophetic source antecedent to its incorporation in either 2 Kings 18–20 or Isaiah 36–39. The Chronicler seems to view the larger compositions as having their basis in earlier prophetic activity (cf. 9:29, where he names three prophets as sources for the account of Solomon). Hezekiah is also distinguished by the honor accorded him by the people at his death (2 Chron 32:33). His burial in the upper level of the royal tombs is not likely a simple designation of location but also one of prestige. Not even David and Solomon are said to be honored by the citizens at their death. No doubt it was a regular practice, but its specific mention for Hezekiah again attributes a special status to him.

The concluding summary is characteristic of the entire presentation of the reign of Hezekiah. He is an extraordinary king, in many ways like David and Solomon. Most significantly, Hezekiah demonstrates the way for Israel's spiritual restoration to a status equal with that of David and Solomon.

THE TEXT IN BIBLICAL CONTEXT

Tradition of Hezekiah

The story of Hezekiah is featured at length in three major biblical compositions. In Kings, Hezekiah is the faithful ruler in spite of his lapse in trusting an alliance. In Isaiah, Hezekiah is the antitype to Ahaz, accepting the sign from God, and the prototype for Jerusalem, in that he lives even though threatened with death. In Chronicles, Hezekiah is a model king who brings restoration and healing so the nation may fulfill its ideals. In postbiblical tradition, Hezekiah is larger than life. The Apocryphal book of Sirach shows not a trace of failure or defeat (Sir 48:17-25); the famous Assyrian attack is averted through opportunely answered prayer. In the Talmud (b. Sanhedrin 94a), Hezekiah is the messiah, and Sennacherib is as Gog and Magog in Ezekiel 38. At his death Rabban Joḥanan ben Zakkai asked that a throne be prepared for Hezekiah the king of Judah who is coming (b. Berakot 28b).

It is possible to trace the development of the Hezekiah traditions in the biblical accounts. Textual alterations indicate that the story of Hezekiah in Isaiah (chs. 36-39) is a development from a form like that now found in Kings (2 Kings 18-20). Though in the MT there is a remarkable verbal similarity of the two accounts, the earliest versions of Kings did not have some of the distinct Isaianic phrases now found in both stories (Konkel 1993). The Proto-Masoretic Text of Kings is preserved in the Theodotion Greek version of this portion of the book *[Masoretic Text, p. 470]*. Isaianic phrases were added when the story was made part of the Isaiah prophecy. The Hezekiah story was adapted for the purposes of Isaiah, where it serves as a transition from the Jerusalem that went into exile to the Jerusalem that would return. The Chronicler was also dependent on Kings for his version of Hezekiah, but his procedure was different. He reduced the account of Kings to about eighteen verses but has added three chapters of his own material to portray Hezekiah as a king like Solomon.

Siege of Sennacherib

No other event in the history of Israel is given as much prominence both within and outside the Old Testament as the Assyrian siege against Jerusalem. The event was important not only for Judah but also for the Assyrians. It occupies a significant space in the annals of the third campaign of Sennacherib, first recorded on the Rassam Cylinder in 700 BCE, immediately after the campaign. This became the standard text for campaigns one to three in all the later annals of Sennacherib. Other inscriptions also include detailed accounts of the third campaign (Konkel 1987: 44-45). The accounts emphasize the destruction of Judah and the capture of a vast amount of booty. They grudgingly allow for the escape of Jerusalem; Hezekiah is described as left in his royal city "like a bird in a cage" (*ANET* 288). The importance of this campaign is further indicated by the extensive wall murals of the siege of Lachish, erected in Sennacherib's "palace without rival." They are on display in the Assyrian section of the British Museum (Mitchell: 60-64). Apparently Sennacherib considered the conquest of Judah's cities to be one of his most significant accomplishments.

The biblical accounts provide quite a different perspective on this profound event. There is no doubt that they record the same substantial facts. The summary of the fourteenth year of Hezekiah (2 Kings 18:13-16) contains the same report as the Assyrian annals.

The critical difference in the two perspectives is the significance of the deliverance of Jerusalem. For the Assyrians, this was a despicable example of "the remnant," those territories or cities that did not come under their domain. For the citizens of Judah, the survival of Jerusalem meant the survival of their nation for more than one hundred years.

Perhaps more important, it became a test case for God's purposes for his people and his city. On the one hand, to prophets like Jeremiah, it served to show that divine deliverance always depended on fidelity to the covenant relationship. On the other hand, to the detractors of Jeremiah, it suggested that the temple could never be destroyed (Jer 7:4). Jerusalem could never again be just a capital city; it came to be a symbol for the kingdom of God and would remain as such even when it was captured and burned.

Hezekiah as a Man of Faith

The person of Hezekiah is inextricably linked to the salvation and destruction of Jerusalem. He is the only king accorded extensive involvement with a prophet, in this case a most prominent prophet whose chief burden was to understand God's purposes for Jerusalem. In historical terms he was the king who reigned during the largest portion of the prophetic ministry of Isaiah. Most notable was that fateful fourteenth year, when Hezekiah became ill, when the Babylonians arrived seeking an alliance, and when the Assyrians began their siege. The prophet Isaiah promised him another fifteen years of life, gave him a sign, and announced his future deliverance from the Assyrians (Isa 38:1-8). For the most part, Hezekiah is regarded as a noble and successful king, but it is never forgotten that he too had feet of clay. In contrast to Ahaz, he restored the worship of God, he asked for and received a sign of divine providence, and in his time the city was delivered. Yet he also was unfaithful: his fateful alliance with the Babylonians was the first step toward that nation accomplishing what the Assyrians could not do. Jerusalem would bear the punishment of faithlessness, and Hezekiah would be partly responsible for that catastrophe.

Hezekiah is a good example of how one person and one experience show many aspects of the profound calling to live by faith. In its whole account, the book of Kings emphasizes that Hezekiah demonstrated how to trust God in a manner that was unequaled (2 Kings 18:5). Yet it was this same king who fell into the trap of trusting in human alliances and dooming his city (20:12-19). Hezekiah was the man whose life was declared to be over in his prime (Isa 38:9-20), yet he became the example of how God can revive the dead. Faith is always a matter of faithfulness. The failure of faith brings consequences that are inescapable, but the presence of faith assures us of hope that nothing can destroy.

We know little about the earliest sources of prophetic writing, but the story of Hezekiah is an example of how prophetic material developed. The form of the story in Kings indicates that there was a composition present for the author of Kings that could be incorporated into his account of the kings of Israel and Judah. The story was so arranged that it concluded with the one notable failure of Hezekiah. Though Hezekiah himself would have success, the nation would not. In the composition of Isaiah, this story serves as the centerpiece concerning the purposes of God for Jerusalem. It provides a transition from the city under judgment in preexilic times to a city of hope in postexilic times, a hope that would finally culminate in a new Jerusalem and "new heavens and a new earth" (Isa 65:17-25). In postexilic times this prophetic tradition was developed in a new and creative fashion by the Chronicler. It served to challenge a sometimes despondent community, showing them that there is always the possibility of living in the divine will.

THE TEXT IN THE LIFE OF THE CHURCH
The Value of Renewal

Renewal is continually a matter of concern for the church. Even a good and faithful church like that at Ephesus could be reprimanded because they had lost their first love (Rev 2:4). Every community arrives at a point where they need to make a commitment to new challenges. Changes bring about a need for renewal.

Renewal happens when proper changes take place. The Hebrew word "turn" was most useful in the appeal for change. It could indicate a turning from wrong (repentance), a turning toward God, God turning toward his people, and God restoring blessings for his people. This word šub for covenant restoration after estrangement is prominent in the preexilic prophets (Jenni and Westermann: 888-89). In the postexilic prophets, Zechariah in particular, the words of the preexilic prophets have begun to take on canonical status through their vindication in the exile (Williamson 1982: 368). The Chronicler advances this process by detaching the use of šub as "repent" from the historical circumstance that led to the exile and applying it to his own situation, a time of rebuilding following the exile. Exile is a recurring typical situation within the life of a community. The original prophetic word that applied to a particular event is now universalized. The inclusion of repentance in the programmatic formula for restoration (2 Chron 7:14) has made it applicable for all times and places. The Chronicler could develop the words of Zechariah to describe the restoration that took place in the much earlier time of Hezekiah and thereby show his readers that the same potential for the renewal of all Israel was now available for his time as well. They lived in just such a time as Hezekiah. At some time all of us do; change will be required.

Renewal begins with individuals. They may have powerful influence in society, as Hezekiah had in his day, or be a somewhat obscure and nameless writer, as was the Chronicler in his day. There are many kinds of circumstances and many possibilities for response. The sixteenth century in Europe was a time of intense religious ferment, a time when change and renewal was urgent. It was a time of renewal among various religious leaders and a time when various movements arose, not all of them good.

One story of renewal is that of Menno Simons (1496-1561), a priest from Friesland, ordained to the priesthood in 1524 at age twenty-eight. In 1554 he relates his pilgrimage toward renewal and change in his *Reply to Gellius Faber* (C. Dyck: 45-49). Menno freely confesses his ignorance of the Scriptures at the time he was ordained; he relates that, with two other ministers, he spent his first years of priesthood in playing cards, drinking, and pursuing idle pastimes, as is the habit of unproductive people. When he did begin to study the Scriptures, he found that they did not teach the doctrines of the mass. The beheading of a God-fearing hero named Siecke Snijder for renewing his baptism led Menno to investigate the doctrine of infant baptism. He soon discovered that the leaders of his time (Luther, Bucer, Bullinger) were not agreed on its significance. Out of a desire for gain and to make a bigger name for himself, Menno transferred to another village. He spoke the word of the Lord, but as all hypocrites do, without spirituality or love. A crisis came with the Münster rebellion (1534-35), a violent attempt to establish the new Jerusalem. The blood of the poor, confused, and erring sheep lay heavy on his heart. Menno prayed that God would grant his gift of grace to a troubled sinner, that God would create a clean heart in him. He began to preach the word of true repentance.

After about nine months, Menno was able to renounce his worldly reputation, name, fame, unchristian lifestyle, masses, infant baptism, and meaningless life. He searched for others who were eager for the teaching of truth and found some, but not many. A small group formed that urged him to put his talents to good use, those that he says he had unworthily received from the Lord. Menno was troubled by his limited ability, lack of learning, and timid spirit. In earnest prayer he asked that God would grant him the spirit of Paul so he could say, "Woe is me if I preach not the gospel." "And so," he concludes, "I, a big, miserable sinner, was enlightened by the Lord, given a new mind, fled out of Babel and moved into Jerusalem, and at the last, though unworthy, came to this high and difficult service" (C. Dyck: 49). Such was the renewal of one who initiated a movement that carries his name to this day.

Part 7

Humiliation and Hope

2 Chronicles 33:1-36:23

OVERVIEW

In Chronicles, a comparison of the last kings of Judah accentuates the highly schematic manner in which the Deuteronomistic History portrays the kings of Judah following the Assyrian conquest of Samaria. Kings says almost nothing about Hezekiah's economic achievements and his success at centralizing worship in Jerusalem. Chronicles has a much more historical presentation of Hezekiah's reign. Hezekiah had treasuries, storehouses, herds, and great properties. A reexamination of pottery shards stamped "to the king" (*lmlk*) has led to the conclusion that these belong to the time of Hezekiah and points to a diverse distribution of goods (Vaughn: 81-165). He had vast stores of wine and oil in many cities. Chronicles presents Hezekiah as a second Solomon in wisdom and wealth, and his account is historically substantiated. Hezekiah's support for the temple and the priesthood is never mentioned in Kings, but it is hardly conceivable that such centralization began only with Josiah *[Deuteronomistic History, p. 465]*.

In the Deuteronomistic History, Manasseh, the successor of Hezekiah, is responsible for making the judgment, pronounced by God on Hezekiah's descendants, an irreversible fate, even after the great reforms of Josiah that followed (2 Kings 23:26-27; though anticipated in 20:16-19). All the good of Josiah could not reverse the damage of Manasseh. In Kings, Josiah is accorded a status for his successes with covenant renewal incomparable to that of any other king. Chronicles affirms the reforms of Josiah, but his status in relation to the other kings is much more balanced. For Manasseh, he adds material to show that, in the latter part of his reign, he continued the reforms begun under Hezekiah and made his own contributions to the fortification of Judah (2 Chron 33:14-17). The record of Josiah is considerably more credible if he was building on the actions of his predecessors, as Chronicles explains. The Chronicler was fully aware of the *Tendenz* of the previous history, since he had access to the same sources *[Tendenz in Chronicles, p. 476; Sources for Chronicles, p. 472]*. A corrective to this *Tendenz* for his time may have been part of the incentive for the composition of a second history.

The Chronicler's goal involves the greatest contrast with the previous history. In the conclusion of Kings, the restoration of the exiled king Jehoiachin leaves the people in a kind of exile and lacks any mention of the promise of restoration found in the prophets (2 Kings 25:27-30). In Chronicles, exile is countered by a new era, introduced as the fulfillment of a prophecy of Jeremiah (2 Chron 36:21) and the actions of Cyrus. In Isaiah 45:1, Cyrus the Great is identified as one whom the Lord anointed. In Hebrew, he is *mašiaḥ*, the same term used for the ruler in Zion in Psalm 2:2, the biblical basis for Jesus being called "the Messiah" (as in Matt 1:1). The conclusion of Chronicles shows that humility and repentance will bring healing from exile. Manasseh is a compelling example of restoration rather than being the villain causing exile. However severe his sins, his legacy is presented as a king of restoration. Manasseh prayed, his prayer was heard, and he returned to Jerusalem. The same hope is extended to all those who feel that they live with the burden of exile.

2 Chronicles 33:1-25

Manasseh and Amon

PREVIEW

There is no escaping the consequences of sin, but the consequences of sin do not need to be determinative for the achievements of a life. Sometimes the consequences of sin may be less prohibitive than could be expected because of God's divine grace. Some of the most painful consequences of failure in contemporary society come with the breakup of families. As final as that may seem to be, it must not be regarded as robbing the future of all potential good. The exile of Manasseh might have seemed to be final, but the end of his life was a significant achievement for Judah.

Manasseh was exiled by the Assyrians as divine punishment for his sins. The claim that the Chronicler created this exile based on prophetic judgment against Hezekiah, dooming his sons to exile, is a very weak argument. The Chronicler makes no reference to the prophetic word in 2 Kings 20:18. Although extrabiblical records lack any reference to an offense of Manasseh or his removal to Assyria, that is no reason to call the event into question (Rudolph: 316-17). The restoration from captivity cannot be regarded as an explanation for the length of Manasseh's reign, since there is no reference to how long he was a prisoner. The purpose of including the captivity of Manasseh is hortatory, to encourage those who have suffered a similar captivity. The reference to Babylon in 2 Chronicles 33:11 makes this association explicit.

In Kings, Manasseh is the irreversible cause of the exile following the good deeds of Josiah (2 Kings 24:3). In spite of the faithfulness of Josiah, whose devotion to following Torah was unequaled (23:25), the fate of the nation was determined (also note 20:16-19) [*Torah, p. 481*]. The purpose of the Deuteronomists was to prove culpability for the exile. According to covenant oath, exile was inevitable (Zech 1:6). In Chronicles this fateful destiny is not an irreversible situation. The day of grace is never over for people who seek God in faith. Manasseh becomes a paradigm of the truth that there is never a time when a living generation can think that the opportunity for grace has passed.

OUTLINE
Reign of Manasseh, 33:1-20
Reign of Amon, 33:21-25

EXPLANATORY NOTES

Reign of Manasseh 33:1-20

33:1-11 Idolatry and Captivity

Manasseh ruled longer than any other king in Judah. During his reign, which began early in the seventh century following Hezekiah, Assyria came to the zenith of its power after the conquest of Egypt (*ARAB* 2:554-56). Not much is known about life in Palestine after the campaigns of Sennacherib, but there was peace until the end of the Assyrian domination (Ahlström: 730-33). Rebellion of the kind carried out by Hezekiah was inconceivable during the reign of Manasseh. Though he had no alternative to being a submissive vassal, this does not account for the religious practices he instituted. No Assyrian vassal treaty contains clauses that relate to the practice of religion. It is not even certain that a loyalty oath, like the one imposed by Esarhaddon on his eastern vassals, was ever imposed on Manasseh. The foreign practices of Manasseh were apparently totally voluntary.

In his practices of foreign worship, Manasseh must have had the support of the leaders of Judah. There may have been a reaction to Hezekiah's reforms by those who worshiped at the various country shrines before that king dismantled them. In a number of ways, Manasseh advanced foreign worship. The *starry hosts* were manifestations of Canaanite worship, carried out in two temple courts and on the roof over the stairway or ascending ramp of the temple (Zevit: 472). This interpretation is based on the reference in 2 Kings 16:18 to the exterior entranceway for the king included in the temple renovations of Ahaz.

The sins of Manasseh included passing his sons through the fire, along with sorcery and consultation of mediums (2 Chron 33:6). If the passing of sons through the fire was a ceremony involving fire through which one was dedicated to a deity, the rituals practiced by Manasseh also included forms of divination (Zevit: 469). Necromancy was practiced at a ritual pit through which mortals communicated with the chthonic (underworld) deities of the place of the dead. Second Kings 21:7 says that Manasseh placed a carved image of Asherah in the sanctuary; the Chronicler speaks only of a carved divine image (*semel*). The goddess Asherah appears as *semel* in Phoenician; *sml b'l* is the consort of Baal. The erection of such an image may have been an expression of an alliance with the Phoenicians.

In Kings, judgment on Manasseh comes in the destruction of Judah and Jerusalem (cf. 2 Kings 21:10-16). In Chronicles, judgment on Manasseh for his sin is within his lifetime. The Assyrian annals of Esarhaddon record that Manasseh, together with twenty-one other kings of Phoenicia, Philistia, Transjordan, and Cyprus, had to contribute building materials and transport them under terrible difficulties to his new palace. A more probable occasion for Manasseh's imprisonment would have been the rebellion of Shamash-shum-ukin against Ashurbanipal. This Babylonian king received support from territories that included Syria and Palestine. It is possible that the king of Judah joined in the rebellion, either voluntarily or by coercion. This would explain why he was taken captive to Babylon rather than to Nineveh. If Manasseh was forced into the coalition, it is all the more likely that he would have later been released as an Assyrian ally. The nose ring was a method of completely humiliating a captive. Assyrian iconography portrays such treatment of their prisoners.

33:12-20 Repentance and Restoration

The restoration of Manasseh following his repentance gave him renewed opportunity to purify the temple and restore its worship. Though worship outside the temple continued, it was no longer to foreign deities (33:17). In addition to temple purification, Manasseh fortified the area around the palace and temple. Perhaps he was repairing damage done to the walls when he was taken captive. For the city of David, he built an outer wall west of Gihon in the Kidron Valley, passing the Ophel (the level area created for the temple), and leading up to the Fish Gate in the north. The wall would have passed the temple area on the east and the north. Manasseh also put officers in all the fortified cities of Judah. The defense system was not directed against Assyria, since Manasseh was under their control. But Ashurbanipal may have returned some of the fortified cities that Sennacherib had allotted to the Philistines. Judah would have been part of his defenses against Egypt in a future conflict. The officials outside of Jerusalem would have had more than just military responsibility. The worship carried on at the high places now was in conformity with Israelite faith, not directed to the gods of other nations.

The death formula in Chronicles is elaborated significantly beyond that found in Kings, but the Chronicler does not include all the information found in Kings. Kings notes that the grave of Manasseh was in the garden of "Uzza" (2 Kings 21:18). The name may have been associated with an astral deity of foreign religion introduced by his foreign wives, but that would not seem to be the reason for its omission in Chronicles where mention is made of Manasseh building high places and making Asherah poles (33:19). The same omission of burial in the garden of Uzza is made regarding Amon (2 Kings 21:26). The Chronicler has omitted names of the mothers as well for the last kings of Judah. There is no discernible significance to these omissions.

Reign of Amon 33:21-25

The reign of Amon is reported much as it is found in Kings, with the omission of some details, such as the name and birthplace of his mother. Unique to the Chronicler is the statement that Amon did not humble himself as Manasseh his father did (v. 23). No details are given concerning the revolt that led to his assassination. It may have been an anti-Assyrian uprising in connection with the disturbances during the last years of Ashurbanipal's reign. In any case, the coup failed, and the conspirators were executed. Responsibility again fell on the civic leaders to install the new king, ensuring the continuity of the dynasty.

THE TEXT IN BIBLICAL CONTEXT

The Restoration of Manasseh

The account of Manasseh in Chronicles might be regarded as theologically constructed to explain why the worst king of Judah should have the longest reign. Conversely, it may be argued that the authors of Kings have deliberately suppressed the information of 2 Chronicles 33:14-16 in order to blame Manasseh for the final downfall of Judah (2 Kings 23:26-27; 24:3-4). The Chronicler actually has cited this information from his source, as elsewhere, to support his own view of God at work in history. He does not make any direct correlation between the length of a king's reign and his piety, nor does he confine the consequences of guilt to one generation. The extraordinary sins of Manasseh were worthy of a severe punishment, such as arrest and exile, but no matter how grievous the transgression, restoration is possible. The best human deeds are not always free from the taint of selfish motive, and conversely the worst deeds are not beyond the redemptive grace of God. The views of Kings and of Chronicles are both coherent depictions of Manasseh. The biblical historians are not reductionistic but, taken together, exhibit the contrasting aspects of the kings of Judah.

Odd as it may seem, in Chronicles, the reigns of Manasseh and Hezekiah exhibit a similar pattern toward the end. Hezekiah is remembered as an exemplary king for being faithful. The tribute to his faithfulness extols this virtue as exceeding that of any king before or after him (2 Kings 18:5-6). This faithfulness prevailed when Judah was confronted by enormous threat during the invasion of Sennacherib in 701 BCE. Yet the account of Hezekiah ends with unfaithfulness, the kind that is irreversible in its consequences. His deceit when entertaining the Babylonian embassy brought down the judgment that his royal house would go into exile (2 Kings 20:16-19). The last two events, concerning Hezekiah's sickness and the visit of the Babylonians, are linked with a generic chronological notation (20:1, 12). They were not a sequel to the Assyrian invasion. The judgment announced by the prophet had taken place before his loyal stand to preserve Jerusalem. The account closes with a curious phrase, "Will there not be peace and security in my lifetime?" (v. 19). The last half of this quote is not original to Kings. It is not found in the Theodotion version of Kings, which represents the Proto-Masoretic Text *[Masoretic Text, p. 470]*. It has been adopted from Isaiah 39:8 in the process of transmission, as the two texts came to conform to each other (Konkel 1993: 476–78). Isaiah's refrain is that there is no peace for the wicked (Isa 48:22; 57:21). In Isaiah, peace for Hezekiah is an affirmation that he is not among the wicked. The later actions of Hezekiah vindicate him in spite of his failure. The Chronicler says Hezekiah humbled himself from his proud heart (2 Chron 32:26). Though the Chronicler does not make reference to peace, he makes the same affirmation as Isaiah. Hezekiah humbled himself, the requirement for those who would find divine healing.

Though completely vilified in Kings, the account of Manasseh in Chronicles follows a pattern similar to that of Hezekiah in both histories. Both monarchs were tested, had failures, then experienced grace. The unique information concerning Manasseh's building projects and his restoration of temple worship in 2 Chronicles 33:14-16 is particularly notable because of the central position of this king in Deuteronomistic theology (Japhet 1993: 1001-4). The exile and return of Manasseh constitute an exceptional event, for which there is no biblical model and scarcely even a contemporary one. His building activity is consistent with his long reign and the restoration begun by his father. The Chronicler's historical data have been integrated into his theological framework, providing a striking contrast with the entirely negative presentation of Manasseh in Kings.

THE TEXT IN THE LIFE OF THE CHURCH

Good and Bad within People

We observe a tendency to divide the world into good and bad people. There is a sense in which this is obvious. It is difficult to think of some, such as Mother Teresa, in any way but good. In 1952 she began her work among the poorest of the poor in the city of Calcutta. Her faithfulness and dedication created such an impact for the poor of that city that she became one of the most deserving recipients of the Nobel Peace Prize in 1979 and was beatified in 2003. Though her life seemed to be one of virtually flawless faithfulness, she confessed to deep inner turmoil and great struggle in her relationship with God. It is a reminder that faithfulness is always a struggle for every person of faith.

A converse example, whose horrors affected and destroyed the lives of many Mennonites, was Joseph Stalin. Johan Sawatzky of Minnesota, relative of the author, has written the story of our family, titled *One in Three: How My Family and I Survived Russian Communism* (1996). The title of the book is deliberate; as he told me, only one in three survived. The book is a moving account of how this family trusted God and remained faithful while facing imminent death countless times.

Robert Gellately has revisited this historical period in his book *Stalin's Curse: Battling for Communism in War and Cold War* (2013). "In this book I trace the origins of this misfortune to its incubation period, which stretched from the first days of the Second World War in 1939 to Stalin's death in 1953" (Gellately: 8). Gellately describes how many millions of people shouldered Stalin's heritage as a curse long after he was gone. He takes a fresh look at the issues, using a wide variety of primary Russian documents and other sources from Eastern Europe, released since the demise of the Soviet Union, as well as German, American, and British materials. Gellately shows how Stalin's Marxist-Leninist ideology informed everything in his life, from his politics to his military strategy and personal values. His book documents how the Soviet Union exported revolution, with a resolve to create a Red Empire that would ride waves of revolutions sweeping over Europe and the rest of the world. Most chilling about the account is the way in which people were reduced to objects to be destroyed and manipulated in Stalin's single-minded ambition to control the world. For example, Stalin was anti-Semitic in a secretive, cold, and calculating manner because he knew that Jewish people would be an impediment to his plans. Yet when Stalin died, the response in the camps of the Gulag was mixed. Some wailed for the deceased, some wanted to donate money for a wreath, others heard the news in tomb-like silence. People from all walks of life flooded the streets of Moscow.

The stories of Hezekiah and Manasseh are a reminder that, most of the time, the line between good and evil is not found between particular individuals but within each individual person. The people we regard as exemplary and good will sometimes disappoint us. Those whom we may find to be vile and destructive will sometimes surprise us. For those seeking to be faithful, the difference is not that life will be without failure. The difference is in how individuals deal with failure. In matters of faithfulness, the Chronicler's condition is invariably true: *If my people . . . will humble themselves and pray and seek my face, . . . then I will . . . heal* (2 Chron 7:14).

2 Chronicles 34:1–35:27
Renewal under Josiah

PREVIEW
Written words are essential to the function of civilization. It is no accident that cities and written documents emerge simultaneously. Cities require commercial transactions, and such transactions require written records. In the same way, written revelation has been foundational to the confession of faith. It is the reason why translation and publication of Scripture is so essential to the spread of the gospel. Lack or loss of written revelation has tragic consequences. This was part of the problem leading to the failure of worship in Israel and the reason why, in the time of Josiah, the discovery of the written Torah in the temple was so transformative [*Torah, p. 481*].

The Chronicler's chronology of events is significant in relation to the discovery of the Torah. Kings begins with the reforms of Josiah in his eighteenth year. In Chronicles, Josiah begins to seek the Lord in his eighth year, while still in his youth. His efforts to cleanse Jerusalem and Judah of idolatrous worship begin in his twelfth year, the earliest age at which he could officially carry out his duties as a king. This chronology leads to an alteration in temple cleansing and the discovery of the book of the law. The removal of carved and molten images of Canaanite gods is reported in 2 Chronicles 34:4-7, before Josiah's eighteenth year, when the Torah is found (vv. 8, 14). These verses are his equivalent to 2 Kings 23:6-20, the purifications of Josiah reported after the finding of the Torah and the renewal of the covenant.

The Chronicler's version is much abbreviated from the details of Kings; their equivalent is in 2 Kings 23:6, 16, 19, 20. Temple cleansing requires much less emphasis in Chronicles, since Josiah continues what has substantially been done. The finding of the Torah in Chronicles is during initiation of the temple repair that begins in the eighteenth year of Josiah. The sequel to discovering the Torah and recognizing the severity of covenant failure is not followed by temple cleansing and centralization of worship, but by the celebration of a Passover unequaled in all the days of the kings (2 Chron 35:18). The Chronicler describes the vital function of the priests and Levites in this Passover in great detail. The Deuteronomistic History only mentions the Passover as being unequaled from the days of the judges [*Deuteronomistic History, p. 465; Priests and Levites in Chronicles, p. 471*].

OUTLINE

Purification of Israel, 34:1-13
Discovery of the Book of the Covenant, 34:14-33
Passover Celebration, 35:1-19
Death of Josiah, 35:20-27

EXPLANATORY NOTES

Purification of Israel 34:1-13

Hezekiah reigned for fifteen years after the invasion of Sennacherib in 701 BCE. If the fifty-five-year reign of Manasseh began in 686 BCE, he was coregent with Josiah in the last years of his reign. Josiah's reign began in 640 BCE when he was eight years old. His year twelve as king, when he began centralizing worship, may also have been year one of his sole reign. Josiah began to seek the Lord when he was sixteen and still under the tutelage of regents. He initiated his own acts of reform at age twenty (Num 1:3; 1 Chron 27:23). The geographical extent of these reforms is significant as a sequel to the work of Hezekiah, as they extend to Ephraim, Manasseh, and Naphtali. The thirty-one-year reign of Josiah ended in 609 BCE after challenging Pharaoh Necho at Megiddo. This date is determined by the Babylonian Chronicles [*Babylonian Chronicles, p. 464*].

The Chronicler implies that Josiah executed the priests of Baal (2 Chron 34:5). The priests who burned sacrifices to Baal have their own bones burned on the same altars. By Josiah's twelfth year (628 BCE), the Assyrian Empire was in an advanced state of disintegration. As that empire was dying, the northern territory of Israel under its control was given only weak governance, allowing Josiah more latitude than the kings before him to carry out a radical reform policy outside of his territory. The *incense altars* (34:4, 7, ḥammanim; also 14:5) are not mentioned in Kings. The actual object has been inferred on the basis of the words *Baal ḥammon* found in Punic inscriptions and in Aramaic; it refers to a type of altar. Linguistic and archaeological evidence indicates that these were small or model shrines (Zevit: 338-40). Shrines and wayside chapels, ranging in size from a telephone booth to a generous walk-in closet, were a characteristic feature of the Syro-Palestinian countryside and were found in Israel and Judah in the Iron Age. They were auspicious places where a deity occasionally resided or a place where the presence of a deity could be summoned. These shrines could also be produced in miniature, providing a convenient though indirect access to the shrine. Such shrines manifest a completely different concept of deity than that of the Jerusalem temple. The term *ḥammanim* is probably used for both the model shrines and their larger counterparts. Josiah cut these down, possibly indicating a type of wooden or clay structure.

Security officials (gatekeepers) were responsible for collecting offerings at the door of the temple (2 Chron 34:9). This responsibility had come to be a regular practice by the time of Josiah. Representatives of both palace and temple were involved in collecting and administering funds in ancient temples. The royal representatives would have been involved in determining expenditures, so there was always potential for conflict. The Chronicler includes *all the land of Israel* in the reforms and the gathering of these offerings (vv. 7-9 NRSV). The offerings did not consist of metal coins but metal ingots. Money was paid by means of weighing silver; merchants could cheat by using a nonstandard weight in a balance scale (e.g., Amos 8:5). This metal could be used as payment for workers or melted down and used for repairs and replacement of a variety of artifacts. The note that the musicians were supervising the construction shows how important it was for the Levites to be in charge of the work (vv. 12-13). Music during construction projects is well attested in ancient texts. The rhythm can set a pace for which work is to be done, which was important, but the Chronicler's emphasis is on the supervisory role of the Levites. The Levitical family of Gershon is not mentioned, but nothing indicates a particular significance to this omission.

Discovery of the Book of the Covenant 34:14-33

The Torah discovered in the process of refurbishing the temple was some form of Deuteronomy *[Torah, p. 481]*. This is evident from the emphasis on the centralization of worship to the one place God has chosen to place his name, an emphasis found in Deuteronomy. It may also be observed from the particular regulations required. For example, the Passover meat is prepared by cooking it (*bšl*) in the fire (2 Chron 35:13); this is a combination of terminology from Deuteronomy 16:7, which says the lamb shall be cooked (*bšl*) and eaten, and Exodus 12:9, which says it must be roasted in the fire and not boiled (*bšl*) in water. In common use, *bšl* means "boil," but the addition of water may be necessary for clarity. The reason for the specific Exodus requirement that the Passover be roasted is not given. It may have been to facilitate haste or to ensure that the blood was extracted. There are developments in the Passover from Exodus to later times. One of those developments was to make it a pilgrimage festival at a central place (Deut 16:5-6); every other place was forbidden. In later times any form of cooking was permissible, as indicated in the Deuteronomy regulation (Tigay: 155). The inclusion of language drawn specifically from Deuteronomy indicates the significance of its regulations for this occasion.

Covenant renewal was central to the message of Deuteronomy. It was required at Shechem when the people entered the land (Deut 11:29-32; 27:1-8), but it was to be repeated every seven years (31:9-13). Renewal of the covenant was the transforming event in the reformation of Josiah (2 Chron 34:29-32). The priests and the Levites had a prophetic role in carrying out the covenant renewal (v. 30). The Chronicler names Levites instead of prophets as assisting in the renewal (2 Kings 23:2), since they were the ones to carry out this prophetic role. There is no indication of resistance to such a commitment, just as in the days of Asa (cf. 2 Chron 15:12-15). Curses are a prominent feature in ancient covenants, and in Deuteronomy (e.g., 27:9-26; 28:15-68), a feature prominent in the warning of the prophet Huldah (2 Chron 34:24). The book of Kings evaluates the conduct of Israel and its kings against Deuteronomy; the Chronicler substantially follows that assessment in his history. This does not constitute evidence that the book of Deuteronomy first began to take shape in Josiah's time, as asserted in certain pentateuchal theories of composition history. Deuteronomy in particular contains instructions for the king (Deut 17:14-20), requiring him to have a copy of the law available to him. This message was central for the Chronicler.

The prophetic word for Josiah is positive about the king (2 Chron 34:26-28). The words to the king of the Deuteronomistic History are very much the vocabulary of the Chronicler: "Your mind is gentle, and you have humbled yourself before God" (2 Kings 22:19 AT; cf.

2 Chron 34:27a) *[Deuteronomistic History, p. 465]*. The Chronicler repeats, *You humbled yourself before me*, adding, *and tore your robes and wept in my presence* (2 Chron 34:27b; cf. 2 Kings 22:19), emphasizing again the formula for healing. The prophetic word was that Josiah would die in peace and not experience the curse of judgment that would come upon Judah (2 Chron 34:28). Josiah himself did not die in peace but was killed by the Egyptian pharaoh. A false prophecy would not have been tolerated by the Chronicler. The second half of the verse must explain the first. *This place* (the city) would be at peace at the death of Josiah as a reward for his faithfulness. His repentant spirit had averted disaster in his time, but the ultimate judgment of the city could not be averted. The discovery of the Torah increased Josiah's zeal for the reform he had initiated (2 Chron 34:33). His demise at the hands of Necho was not a consequence of some failure in his life. This indicates that the Chronicler is not predictable in his assessment of retribution. Josiah dies in faithfulness and in battle, with the mercy that he does not endure the Babylonian siege.

The prophet Huldah is unique among all the prophets of the Chronicler, yet a figure that he has found in his *Vorlage [Vorlage, p. 468]*. Though some have tried to trace her ancestry through her husband, Shallum, to Jeremiah (Jer 32:6-7), her only known association is with the temple orders. Shallum was responsible for priestly vestments, an office that is known to belong to the priests of the Baal temple in Samaria (2 Kings 10:22). She lived in the "second city" of Jerusalem, referred to in Zephaniah 1:10 in association with the hills of the city, possibly the Western Hill of Jerusalem, developed in the late monarchic period (Cogan and Tadmor: 283). Though a woman prophet is unusual in the times of the kings, Isaiah refers to the prophetess (Isa 8:3), and women prophets are known in the royal courts of Mesopotamia, delivering messages for the safety of the king.

Passover Celebration 35:1-19

Josiah was required to make proper preparation for observing the Passover. The Chronicler does this consistently with the directives of David and Solomon, according to their duties and their divisions. It is remarkable that this should have included the installation of the ark. Some commentators reduce this to an instruction of Levitical duties: "Since the holy ark has been brought into the house which Solomon the son of David, king of Israel, built, there is no need for you to carry it on your shoulders" (v. 3; Klein 2012: 519). While it is true that the handling of the ark was critical in the duties of Levites and priests, it seems odd that it should be repeated here just to show conformity to previous directives. The Chronicler must mean that the ark had to be installed as part of the preparations after refurbishing the temple. It may have been removed during the apostasy of Manasseh or Amon, refurbishing could have included the most holy place, or there may have been a special ceremony connected with the rededication of the temple after severe desecration. Since only the priests were to enter the most holy place, the instructions to the Levites referred to bringing the ark to the temple from its temporary abode, such as the tent that David had set up for it. The instructions follow closely the procedures of the ark's installation by Solomon.

The assignments to the divisions of the priests and Levites are parallel to that of Solomon, arranged according to the order of their ancestral heritage. Though the Passover animal was normally slaughtered by the offerer (Deut 16:5-6), Josiah continued the practice begun under Hezekiah (2 Chron 30:13-20). For Hezekiah's great Passover, the offerers did not have time to be purified so the Levites slaughtered the lambs; the practice in Josiah's time may have had to do with the large number of participants. The Passover sacrifice required small animals. The bulls were additional offerings made during the Feast of Unleavened Bread. The totals are nearly double the offerings at the time of Hezekiah (cf. 30:24), but much less than the offerings at the dedication of the temple (cf. 7:5). The logistics of carrying out such a celebration in the city must have been very challenging.

The Passover celebration included burnt offerings as well. The Levites gave those portions to the family representatives, who in turn gave them to the priests for burning. These provisions did not specifically pertain to instructions for the Passover. The element of haste was observed in the quick service of the Levites. This Passover was unequaled, meaning that in some way it was even superior to the great Passover of Hezekiah. This apparently has to do with the proper function of the Levitical orders. Hezekiah made special provisions and prayers for observing his hasty sacrifice in a way that was contrary to regulation. Josiah specifically required that musicians and gatekeepers be prepared for their proper roles (2 Chron 35:15-16). The Chronicler also explains that the Levites in this Passover had their prominent and proper role.

Death of Josiah 35:20-27

The narrative moves from the eighteenth year of Josiah (622 BCE) and the time of the Passover to the year of his death (609). The decline of the Assyrian Empire brought Egypt and Babylon into conflict with each other, the two great powers that had long been held subject to the Assyrians. Necho sought free passage for his army to help Assyria against Babylon. Josiah's interception at Megiddo may have been the result of his coalition with Babylon, or his own attempt to establish independence from Egypt. Necho was an ally of Assyria in resistance to Babylonian expansion.

According to Kings, Josiah died at Megiddo (2 Kings 23:29-30). Second Chronicles 35:24 says Josiah died in Jerusalem of the wounds he received at Megiddo. The Chronicler adds information to show that the death of Josiah was caused by disobedience to a divine oracle, this time delivered by a Gentile king. It is not unusual that the pronouncement of a divine message should take place in a political context; such was a tactic of foreign kings, as indicated by the taunts of Sennacherib through his chief general against King Hezekiah in the siege of Jerusalem (2 Kings 18:22). Pharaoh Necho had no interest in Judah, so his words to encourage Josiah to desist make military sense, spoken in words common to ancient warfare. Necho would try to convince Josiah that his God was acting in the interests of the Egyptians. Yet from the Chronicler's perspective, this was a genuine word from the Lord that Josiah disregarded, and he suffered judgment accordingly.

According to the traditional dating of Jeremiah, the prophet began his work in the thirteenth year of Josiah (Jer 25:3), some five years before the discovery of the Torah in the temple. The work of Josiah must have had a tremendous impact on the prophet, and of course conversely the prophet may have had a significant influence on the king. Jeremiah, in addressing Jehoiakim, says "Your father—did he not eat and drink, and do justice and righteousness?" (Jer 22:15 AT). Josiah was a model to Jeremiah as a king who could live well and be just. Nothing is known about the laments that were sung for the good king (2 Chron 35:25). The ongoing practice is recognized in that the prophet forbids lamentations for this dead king (Jer 22:10). It is understandable that memorials and laments may have been held for Josiah long after his death. The death of the king in his prime in such questionable circumstances, at a time when Judah was at the heights of its power, must have brought overwhelming grief to the nation. The demise of the nation following his death can only have increased disillusionment. His life was remembered as one of loyal conduct, according to the instruction of the Torah (2 Chron 35:26). According to the Chronicler, the custom of lamenting Josiah continued to his time, about two centuries later (v. 25).

THE TEXT IN BIBLICAL CONTEXT
Josiah in Kings and Chronicles

The account of Josiah in Kings describes a great covenant ceremony with a Passover that he celebrated in order to win the allegiance of faithful Israelites in the north. The Chronicler is specific on this point: *He purged Judah and Jerusalem. In the towns of Manasseh, Ephraim and Simeon, as far as Naphtali, . . . he tore down the altars* (2 Chron 34:5b-6a). *Simeon* in this verse does not refer to the tribe but to the town, today called Tel Shimron, on the northwest side of the Jezreel Valley (Rainey 1997: 47). Megiddo had long before become an Assyrian city and could not represent residents in the Jezreel Valley. Whether any military action was required on Josiah's part to have influence in this area is not indicated in either Chronicles or Kings. The waning of Assyrian power provided opportunity for Josiah to extend his centralizing activities far outside the boundaries of Judah.

The reform that began in the eighth year of Josiah's reign is a much more complete version of covenant renewal. In the twelfth year of his reign he began the process of purification (2 Chron 34:3). The eighth year would be 632 BCE, during the time when the first of his sons was born. Jehoiakim was the son of Zebidah, the daughter of Pedaiah from Rumah (2 Kings 23:36). The favorite, Jehoahaz, was born about a year later, the son of Hamutal, the daughter of Jeremiah of Libnah (not the prophet of the Bible). It can hardly be coincidence that the young king Josiah was influenced by his father-in-law from the priestly city of Libnah. The twelfth year of Josiah would be 628 BCE. At this time the purification of Jerusalem and Judah was followed by an extension of reforms into the northern territories that had become Assyrian provinces. It may be that this was the year of the death of the Assyrian king Ashurbanipal (Rainey 1997: 68). The reins of power had been turned over earlier, but it may have taken some time for the effects of this transition to reach faraway states such as Judah. The version of Josiah's reforms in Chronicles makes historical sense in every way.

THE TEXT IN THE LIFE OF THE CHURCH
Standing on Scripture

The famous words of Martin Luther at the Diet of Worms continue to ring down through the ages. "Dark eyes flashing, voice clear and strong, Martin Luther ended with ringing defiance: 'Unless proved wrong by Scripture and plain reason, . . . my conscience is captive to the Word of God. I cannot and will not recant. . . . God help me. Amen'" (Severy: 449). Martin Luther has a precedent in the story of Josiah; it is a lesson on the importance of the written Word as a power for reform. Josiah began the work of purification in Jerusalem some ten years before the discovery of the book of the Torah in the temple (2 Chron 34:3). Tradition and symbol are important to faith, but the written Word provides the foundation that informs and instructs. In the hands of the prophet Huldah, it becomes part of the transformation. The revival of the Torah is the great distinction of the Josiah story [Torah, p. 481].

The Word of God is essential and most influential in every age. There were many forces that brought about the Reformation in the various parts of Europe, but the enduring transformation became effective because of the translation of the Scriptures. Martin Luther carried out this task in the German language during his days at Wartburg Castle. His translation was so influential that in some ways it shaped the German language and is still used by many to this day. In the English language the work of translation was largely carried out by William Tyndale. An Oxford scholar and lecturer at Cambridge, he became convinced that the Bible should determine the practices and doctrines of the church and should be available to all congregants. Church authorities were well aware of the power of the Scriptures in the possession of the faithful and went to great lengths to prevent it from becoming available. Tyndale was driven from England to Germany, where he received support from wealthy London merchants. His New Testament was printed at Cologne in 1525. He began work on the Old Testament but was captured in Antwerp and executed at Vilvoorde (near Brussels) in 1536. His translation has become the basis for most English translations, including the King James Version of 1611.

While the written Word is important, it functions within the larger context of an interpretive community, as it was in the days of Josiah. The scroll discovered in the temple was in the language of the people and essentially of their culture. But even in that context it was necessary to consult a prophetess to ascertain its significance.

Contemporary translations are much further removed in time and culture. A translation is an important means of making the truth of Scripture available to people of faith, but left to individuals it becomes subjected to the interpretation of the reader. Readers not familiar with an original context necessarily reinterpret that text within their own context and, in the process, significantly transform its meaning. A great deal of humility is always necessary in reading an ancient text, and it is always necessary to seek additional help if details are to be understood.

Interpretation of Scripture is conflicted for various reasons. At times the Scriptures themselves do not answer important questions that arise. Most important among these in the early church was the undeniable doctrine in the New Testament that Jesus was to be identified with Yahweh, the name by which God is known in the Old Testament. As the apostle declared, "God ... gave him the name that is above every name, that at the name of Jesus every knee should bow ... and every tongue acknowledge that Jesus Christ is Lord, to the glory of God the Father" (Phil 2:9-11). The question to be resolved was the relationship between the human man Jesus and the God whom no one can see. This was the question of the incarnation, a question not resolved until the Council at Nicaea in 325 CE. The creed came to be the definition of orthodox Christianity, as it was officially agreed to by East and West.

There are many other points on which Christians must agree to disagree. Anabaptists have made their own contribution in this regard, especially regarding how individual Christians, as well as the church, relate with the state. Even within the Anabaptist community it is necessary to have vigorous discussion with a great deal of humility and prayer as the church seeks the will of God through Scripture. While Scripture alone is the Protestant Christian guide to faith and practice, it is not left independently to every individual reader.

2 Chronicles 36:1-23
Exile and Return

PREVIEW

Every society has a propensity to disintegration. Historically, all great civilizations have ended, usually under the weight of their own dysfunction and capitulation to opposing powers. It would be unwise to think that present societies will be the exception to that pattern. For people of faith, it is not only history but also the revelation of Scripture that provides the warning. The nation Israel fell to political forces aided by its own intrigue and corruption. Theologically, it was because of their unfaithfulness to God. But the theology of divine judgment is also the reason for hope since God is a God of mercy.

At the death of Josiah, the civic leaders of the land appointed his son Jehoahaz as king. His rule lasted the length of time it took for the pharaoh to return from his battles seeking to resist the Babylonian advance. Jerusalem lost its independence with the death of Josiah. In their strategy against the Babylonians, the Egyptians sought control over Judah. When Nebuchadnezzar came to the throne of Babylon in 605 BCE, he began conducting campaigns into Syria-Palestine; the first of the exiles and the temple treasures were removed from Jerusalem (Dan 1:1-2). A further attack took the prophet Ezekiel in 597 BCE. Eleven years later the city would fall to the Babylonians (in 586 BCE). Judah went from the high point of religious reform to the virtual extinction of its worship in just over twenty years [*Chronology in Chronicles, p. 460*].

In comparison to Kings and Jeremiah, the Chronicler abbreviates the narrative of Jerusalem going into exile. All the events of its last king, Zedekiah, and descriptions of the siege and destruction of Jerusalem are omitted (2 Kings 24:18-25:30), as well as the more extensive parallel material in Jeremiah 40-41 and 52. Chronicles has a brief account of each of the last kings, much as recorded in the other biblical sources, except for Zedekiah. He provides his own version of the revolt of Zedekiah against Nebuchadnezzar (2 Chron 36:11-14), following his usual themes. King Zedekiah did not humble himself (*knʿ*) at the word of the Lord through the prophet Jeremiah. The leaders of the priests and the people became more unfaithful (*maʿal*) in following the abominations of the nations, defiling the house of the Lord. The Chronicler composes his own closing summary (2 Chron 36:15-19), in which he describes the derision of the prophetic messengers until there was no longer a possibility of healing (*rapaʾ*). The plunder of the temple and slaughter of the people, irrespective of their status, age, or gender, were carried out under the ruthless power of Nebuchadnezzar.

The book of Kings ends with a band of guerrillas murdering Gedaliah and his associated Babylonian officials at Mizpah. This was a disaster for the population, now forced to flee to Egypt for fear of reprisals from the Babylonians. The last note of Kings is the release of Jehoiachin by Awel-Marduk, son and successor of Nebuchadnezzar. At the accession of the new king (562 BCE), political prisoners were released. Jehoiachin received a favored status within the court of the Babylonian king. Jehoiachin had been imprisoned thirty-five years for political crimes, not the least of which was his breaking of a treaty with the Babylonians (2 Kings 24:20b). The Deuteronomistic History leaves the hope of the Davidic promise in 2 Samuel 7, celebrated in worship in Psalm 2 [*Deuteronomistic History, p. 465*].

Chronicles is a sequel to the preaching of Haggai and Zechariah 1-8. With the temple rebuilt, Israel, as understood in Chronicles, may yet be what it is. Israel is a nation, not a state. This nation occupies a small territory allotted by the Persians, but the nation is also widely dispersed. Chronicles concludes with the words of Ezra 1:1-2, coming full circle to the history of Israel concluded in 1 Chronicles 9:2-34. Jerusalem as described at the end of the history of Israel is the Jerusalem that began with the return initiated by the decree of Cyrus. The Chronicler encourages his people to live in this new age with a vision for a united Israel that was destined to be the kingdom of God.

OUTLINE

Exile of Jehoahaz, 36:1-4
Exile of Jehoiakim, 36:5-8
Exile of Jehoiachin, 36:9-10
Destruction of Temple and City, 36:11-21
Return under Cyrus, 36:22-23

EXPLANATORY NOTES

Exile of Jehoahaz 36:1-4

The effort of the civic leaders to assert their independence and continue the policies of Josiah by installing his son Jehoahaz as successor failed. Pharaoh Necho confined the twenty-three-year-old king in Riblah, a formerly Assyrian administrative center on the Orontes River in the north Lebanon Valley (2 Kings 23:33). Jehoahaz, also known as Shallum, was the fourth son of Josiah (1 Chron 3:15; Jer 22:11). The circumstances for his choice are not explained. Though his reign was brief, Jeremiah characterizes it as one of self-aggrandizement and injustice (Jer 22:11-17). The young king was exiled to Egypt, never to return to his homeland again.

Pharaoh Necho levied an indemnity against Judah, making it a vassal of Egypt. The amount of gold levied is obscured in textual transmission. The MT has no number for talents of gold. The Vaticanus manuscript has one hundred talents of gold in 2 Kings 23:33, which cannot be right in proportion to one hundred talents of silver [Greek Text of Chronicles, p. 468]. Old Greek has ten talents of gold, which is closer to the correct proportion (cf. 2 Kings 18:14). This tax would be paid by the civic leaders who made decisions concerning the throne. On his return from Carchemish, Pharaoh Necho made Eliakim king, changing his name in minimal fashion by replacing the divine element 'el with the covenant name yeho. The name change may have been connected to an oath of loyalty.

Exile of Jehoiakim 36:5-8

The reigns of the last kings of Judah are summarized in the themes of exile, with foreign raiders plundering the temple. The Egyptians failed to contain the power of Babylon at Carchemish. Jehoiakim became subservient to Nebuchadnezzar and was either taken into temporary exile in Babylon or confined in preparation for exile (2 Chron 36:6 has a purpose statement). The circumstances of Jehoiakim's death and burial are not reported. Jeremiah declares that he would not receive an honorable burial (Jer 22:18-19; 36:30), suggesting that he died in battle as reported by Josephus (*Ant.* 10.6.3). His account is probably based on Jeremiah. According to the Babylonian Chronicles, Nebuchadnezzar followed up his victory with a campaign to the borders of Egypt *[Babylonian Chronicles, p. 464]*. The Chronicler does not report any details of Judah breaking its treaty with Babylon or the attacks it suffered from Arameans, Moabites, and Ammonites as subordinates to Babylonian power. Jehoiakim died before the surrender of the city (2 Kings 24:6), but the Chronicler ends his account of Jehoiakim with his exile.

Exile of Jehoiachin 36:9-10

Jehoiachin was *eighteen years old* when he began to reign; *eight years old* (NRSV) appears in the MT, which has omitted the numeral ten. There are no details of Nebuchadnezzar taking control of Jerusalem. The story is restricted to the exile of the king to Babylon and payment of tribute from the temple artifacts. The capture of Jehoiachin is described in the Babylonian Chronicles:

> Year 7 [of Nebuchadnezzar]. In the month of Kislev, the king of Babylonia mobilized his troops and marched to Hatti. He encamped against the city of Judah, and on the second of Adar, he captured the city and he seized (its) king. A king of his choice he appointed there; he to[ok] its heavy tribute and carried it off to Babylon. (Cogan and Tadmor: 340)

Jehoiachin was taken captive on March 16, 597 BCE. Ezekiel 1:1-2 dates this as the time when the prophet went into exile.

Destruction of Temple and City 36:11-21

More detail for Zedekiah is provided by Jeremiah (52:1-11; chs. 27–28, 34, 37–38). Though the prophet repeatedly urged the king to submit to the Babylonians rather than look to Egypt for help, Zedekiah broke his treaty with Babylon. The vassal oath imposed on him was probably similar to that known from Assyrian treaties, sworn in the name of his God. But from a theological viewpoint, any oath that is broken is an offense against God (Milgrom 1976: 19–21). The curse is the quintessential element of the covenant, as can be seen in passages where curse (ʾlh) and oath (šbʿ) alternate (e.g., Gen 24:8, 41; Num 5:21). The sin of Zedekiah is articulated by Ezekiel: "He despised the oath by breaking the covenant" (Ezek 17:18; cf. vv. 14, 16, 19). This is the sin that the prophet explicitly labels as "the trespass that he committed against me" (v. 20 AT). The condemnation of

Zedekiah is in the violation of the covenant oath with Nebuchadnezzar in the name of God, but not with God! (2 Chron 36:13). Yet because it involves a solemn oath, it is a trespass (*ma'al*) against God. Further, the leaders of the priests and the people multiplied such trespasses against God according to all the abominations of the nations (v. 14). The violation of an oath is essentially always the equivalent of idolatry because it is always taking the name of the Lord in vain (2 Chron 12:2; 33:19).

The offense of *ma'al*, a favorite word of the Chronicler, is oath violation or a violation of the sacred space of the temple (26:16-18). These violations are equivalent because both are directly offenses against God. Zedekiah's refusal to submit to Babylonian rule led him to oath violation and brought all of the people to increasing their unfaithfulness. Destruction and exile on a national scale follow in the wake of the *ma'al* of oath violation (Lev 26:14-17). On this basis, Ezekiel can pronounce exile for the entire nation (Ezek 17:19-21). The Chronicler's view is that *ma'al* trespasses on the divine realm by breaking the covenant oath. It is a lethal sin that destroys both the offender and his community.

Return under Cyrus 36:22-23

The time of captivity given by Jeremiah (25:11-12; 29:10) is joined with a citation from Leviticus (26:34-35, 43). In Leviticus, the exile is punishment for disobedience; the land is left to lie fallow for all the Sabbaths of which it had been deprived. The chronology of the kingdom was from the time Solomon began to reign, about 970 BCE (according to Masoretic chronology, forty years before the division of the kingdom in 931), until the fall of Jerusalem in 586 BCE *[Chronology in Chronicles, p. 460]*. Seventy years could be calculated from the death of Josiah, the last independent king of Judah, in 609 BCE to the return of the first exiles in 539 BCE, or from the fall of Jerusalem in 586 BCE to the laying of the foundation of the temple in 516 BCE under the impetus of the preaching of Haggai and Zechariah. This is a representative number rather than a chronological calculation. From the viewpoint of Israel's restoration, the land's resting prepared for the time of a new covenant, which would not be like the one of the past (Jer 31:31-34). A continuing concern of the Chronicler was the continuity of his community with the past, as a fulfillment of the promises given to it.

The work concludes with verses drawn from the introduction to Ezra. The Chronicler makes use of the Persian emperor's decree to develop the fulfillment of prophecy that he has introduced from

Jeremiah. The decree of Cyrus to restore Jerusalem is also found in Aramaic in Ezra 6:3-5. The form of the decree found there seems not to have been as conducive for concluding this magnificent work. The quotation of the decree is abbreviated, ending the book of Chronicles with a command cut short: "Let him go up" (2 Chron 36:23 NRSV; cf. Ezra 1:3a). The quotation excludes the words "to Jerusalem that is in Judah" as well as the mandate to build the house of God. The exclusion of Ezra 1:3b in 2 Chronicles 36:23 indicates the author's wish to close his work with the migration of the people rather than with the geographical location. This is already indicated in Cyrus's declaration that he has been appointed to build the temple in Jerusalem (2 Chron 36:23a). There may have been a theological motive for omitting the closing portion of the decree. Identifying the house of the God of Israel with the God who is in Jerusalem might suggest that the God of Israel is a local deity rather than a universal deity (Kalimi 2005b: 152–53). Cyrus has made the claim that the Lord God of heaven has made him ruler over all the kingdoms of the earth (v. 23a). The exclusion of reference to Jerusalem in Ezra 1:3b-4 provides the Chronicler's corrective to the claim of Cyrus. Closing with the exhortation to go up to Jerusalem would be an exhortation to those in Babylon in the Chronicler's time to make their own journey to the homeland.

THE TEXT IN BIBLICAL CONTEXT

Sin against God

The Chronicler consistently uses the term *ma'al* to describe the disobedience that leads to the exile of Judah: *Also, all the leaders of the priests and the people became increasingly unfaithful [hirbu lim'al ma'al], according to all the abominations of the nations; and they contaminated the house of the* LORD *that he had sanctified in Jerusalem* (2 Chron 36:14 AT). Cases of the trespass indicated by *ma'al* against the sacred precincts of the temple are found only in Chronicles: Uzziah for offering incense in the temple (26:16-18); Ahaz for corrupting the temple rituals (28:19, 22-25). But this is not evidence for the late appearance of this usage in Israel (Milgrom 1976: 16–35). Trespasses against temple practice are widely attested in Hittite texts. Every act of *ma'al* that involves a trespass upon the temple or the name of God may cause destruction of the community as well as the offender. Trespass against the name involves oaths. Trespass against the temple property has two biblical criteria: (1) sins against God are not punishable by humans; (2) collective punishment is a divine right that cannot be usurped by humans.

The sin of *maʿal* is always against God; sin against God is involved in all sixty-four occurrences of the term in Scripture. Numbers 5:6-7 is definitive for understanding *maʿal*:

> When a man or a woman commits any wrong toward a fellow man, thus breaking faith with the LORD, and that person realizes his guilt, he shall confess the wrong that he has done. He shall make restitution in the principal amount and add one-fifth to it, giving it to him whom he has wronged. (Milgrom 1990: 34)

The case is that of a person who has defrauded his fellow and then denied it under oath. Oath violation constitutes sin against God. Such sin may be mitigated and payment made for restitution only if confession is made (Milgrom 1990: 34-35, 396-97). God will reduce the crime from a deliberate act, punishable by death, to an inadvertency, expiable by sacrifice for the sake of a repentant sinner. Human involvement, both in conscience and deed, is a sine qua non (necessary condition) for securing divine forgiveness. It is not enough to hope and pray for pardon. Such sinners must humble themselves, acknowledge their wrong, and resolve to depart from sin (e.g., Ps 32:5). Penitence and confession must be integral components for all prayers for forgiveness.

The Chronicler has cast the judgment of the exile and destruction of Jerusalem in legal terms of temple violation. Repeatedly his call is for the people to humble themselves, pray, and seek God's face (2 Chron 7:14). This is what Zedekiah specifically did not do (36:12). Further, he had broken the oath that he had sworn by Nebuchadnezzar (v. 13). The oath would have been similar to vassal oaths known from Assyrian treaties, which were also sworn in the name of the vassal's deities, in this case, with Israel's God (Dillard 1987: 300). Zedekiah hardened his mind (being stubborn), refusing to turn to the God of Israel. For such *maʿal*, the judgment of God was inevitable. For the Chronicler, the judgment of exile was not an arbitrary event. Judgment against Zedekiah was legal punishment for his deliberate sins against God.

Chronicles and the Canon

Jerome, in the early fifth century (d. 420 CE) in *Epistolē* 53.8, made a notable comment on the most underappreciated book of the Christian canon: "The book of Chronicles is condensed to such an extent and so well abridged, that whoever claims to know Scriptures without having knowledge of Chronicles would make himself a laughingstock" (Jerome 1864: 548).

Jerome considered Chronicles to be a little Bible (*micro Biblia*) that encompassed the entire Old Testament and as such is most important to the canon (Kalimi 2005b: 159). Christians largely have ignored Chronicles. The attitude of Spinoza (1632–77) was even more demeaning. In chapter 10 of *Tractatus theologico-politicus*, he expresses astonishment that Chronicles should have been included in the canon, while the books of Wisdom, Tobit, and others were regarded as apocryphal (Elwes: 146). Wellhausen, in his *Prolegomena to the History of Israel*, describes Chronicles as a relic of antiquity, an artificial reawakening of dry bones. Jerome's comment is correct: Chronicles contains more history than any other biblical book on how God worked amid his people through the centuries. It is a *micro Biblia*, yet more than that, it contains much information not found in any other biblical sources.

THE TEXT IN THE LIFE OF THE CHURCH

Life after Death

Life goes on. In whatever manner death takes place, the living must adjust to the new circumstances and move on with their lives. Lamentation is necessary for death that has taken place. The equivalent of a funeral service for the exiles of Israel is found in Lamentations. This sequence of five poems was composed sometime after the destruction of Jerusalem, quite possibly for ceremonies commemorating the event. These poems express sorrow, anger, guilt, hope, despair, fear, self-loathing, revenge, compassion, forgiveness, uncertainty, and disorientation. The function of lament is not to resolve a problem but to be a means of orientation to the new situation. The exile led to customs of fasting (Zech 7:3). In modern Judaism these have evolved in the *Bein Hametzarim* (Between the Straits), a period of mourning that runs from the seventeenth day of Tammuz, the fourth month of the Jewish year, to the ninth day of Av, the fifth month of the year (approximately mid-July to early August). This observance commemorates the days between the first breaching of the walls of Jerusalem to the destruction of the temple. Austerity is practiced during these months; marriages are forbidden, and during the nine days of Av, meat and wine are forbidden except on the Sabbath. Such commemoration is a way of dealing with loss in order that life may go on.

The consequences of death and loss are in one sense never ending, but they must not be determinative of the future. The Chronicler desired to point a way forward so that his people could yet realize the hope for which God had created Israel. The church has faced its share of divisions and tragedies, whether those within a congregation or those within a group of people such as the Anabaptists. Divisions within a congregation or the forming of new denominations are not necessarily bad (1 Cor 11:19); they may actually be necessary as circumstances change and people respond in different ways. But whatever may be the memory of the past, it must serve the well-being of the future and not be an impediment for a renewed prosperity.

When Jesus asked about his own self-identity, Peter responded with the words "You are the Messiah, the Son of the living God" (Matt 16:16). Jesus responded with a play on his name: "You are Peter [*petros*, a stone or boulder], and on this rock [*petra*, a solid cliff] I will build my church, and the gates of Hades will not overcome it." The *petra* was not the person of Peter but the reality of his confession. The church is founded on Jesus Christ, the chief cornerstone. This church will not merely survive: it will thrive until it is the mountain that fills the whole earth, as depicted in Daniel 2.

Violence following army displacement of Mohamed Morsi as Egyptian president shattered the Egyptian province of Minya ("Egypt's Coptic Christians Facing Renewed Attacks Following Crackdown," *National Post*, September 9, 2013). In the province, thirty-five churches were attacked, nineteen completely gutted by fire. At least six Christian schools and five orphanages were destroyed. In the city of Dalga, the ancient chapel of the Virgin Mary and St. Abraam Monastery was looted and burned. The fire burned intermittently for three days. The looting continued for a week. The monastery's sixteen-centuries-old underground chapel was stripped of ancient icons, and the ground was dug up on the belief that treasure was buried there. The remains of ancient and revered saints were thrown around. Some of the Christians have been forced to flee for their lives. Mr. Ishaq employed people in his gold shop; on the night of the takeover, it was broken into and looted. He and his family fled to the Nile Delta, north of Cairo, where he is looking for work. "You ask me what life is like? It is like black tar," he said by telephone.

Violence, destruction, and chaos will continue to be the experience of many in this world. Those of faith are exhorted to be faithful. The Chronicler ends with an exhortation to go up to build the temple as those before them did.

Outline of 1 & 2 Chronicles

Part 1: NATION OF PROMISE   1 Chronicles 1:1–9:34

Founding Ancestors	1:1–2:2
Adam to Abraham	1:1-27
Abraham to Israel	1:28–2:2
Royal Family	2:3–4:23
Records of Judah	2:3-55
Sons of Judah	2:3-9
Jesse, Descendant of Ram	2:10-17
Calebite Families in Ephrath	2:18-24
Jerahmeelite Families in Judah	2:25-41
Calebite Settlements at Hebron	2:42-55
Davidic Family	3:1-24
Sons of David	3:1-9
Descendants of David	3:10-24
More Records of Judah	4:1-23
The Tribes of Israel	4:24–9:1a
Simeon	4:24-43
Transjordan Tribes	5:1-26
Reuben	5:1-10
Gad	5:11-17
War with the Hagrites	5:18-22

Exile of Transjordan	5:23-26
Levi	6:1-81
Priestly Lineage to the Exile	6:1-15
Levitical Genealogies	6:16-30
Levites as Musicians and Priests	6:31-53
Levitical Cities of Residence	6:54-81
Northern Tribes	7:1-40
Issachar and Benjamin	7:1-11
Dan, Naphtali, Zebulun, and Manasseh	7:12-19
Ephraim	7:20-29
Asher	7:30-40
Military Record of Israel	8:1–9:1a
Family of Benjamin	8:1-3
Militia at Jerusalem	8:4-28
Militia at Gibeon	8:29-32
Family of Saul	8:33-40
Registration of All Israel	9:1a

The Inheritance of All Israel	**9:1b-34**
Official Records of Israel	9:1b-2
Jerusalem as the Center of All Israel	9:3-9
Priestly Families of Israel	9:10-13
Levites and Their Duties	9:14-16
Gatekeepers	9:17-33
Summary of All Israel	9:34

Part 2: FOUNDING THE KINGDOM	**1 Chronicles 9:35–20:8**

Removal of Saul as King	**9:35–10:14**
Family of Saul	9:35-44
Death of Saul	10:1-14

David Confirmed as King	**11:1–12:40**
David Made King in Hebron	11:1-9
Support for David at Hebron	11:10-47
Support When David Was a Fugitive	12:1-22
Transfer of the Kingdom to David in Hebron	12:23-40

Establishment of Worship in Jerusalem	**13:1–17:27**
Failed Transfer of the Ark	13:1-14
David Established in Jerusalem	14:1-17
Installation of the Ark	15:1–16:3

Outline of 1 & 2 Chronicles

Establishment of Worship	16:4-43
Promise of an Eternal Kingdom	17:1-27
Oracle of Nathan	17:1-15
Prayer of David	17:16-27
David's Wars	**18:1–20:8**
Expansion of the Kingdom	18:1-13
Administration of the State	18:14-17
Victories over Ammonites and Arameans	19:1–20:3
Victories over Philistines	20:4-8

Part 3: PREPARATIONS FOR THE TEMPLE   **1 Chronicles 21:1–29:30**

Designation of the Temple Site	**21:1–22:1**
Census of David	21:1-7
Judgment and Confession	21:8-17
Purchase of Threshing Site	21:18-25
Divine Response and Choice of Temple Site	21:26–22:1
Charge to Build the Temple	**22:2-19**
Provision of the Temple Materials	22:2-5
Charge to Solomon	22:6-16
Charge to Leaders of Israel	22:17-19
Organization of Levitical Officials	**23:1–26:32**
Levitical Families	23:1–24:31
Divisions of Levites	23:1-23
Levitical Duties	23:24-32
Divisions of Priests	24:1-19
Further Divisions of Levites	24:20-31
Musicians	25:1-31
Gatekeepers	26:1-19
Officers and Judges	26:20-32
Organization of National Officials	**27:1-34**
Military Commanders	27:1-15
Tribal Officers	27:16-24
Civil Administrators	27:25-31
Royal Council	27:32-34
Accession of Solomon	**28:1–29:30**
Charge to the Assembly	28:1-10

Transfer of the Temple Plan	28:11-21
Contributions for the Temple	29:1-9
Blessing of David	29:10-20
Installation of Solomon	29:21-25
Conclusion of David's Reign	29:26-30

Part 4: THE REIGN OF SOLOMON — 2 Chronicles 1:1–9:31

Confirmation of Solomon	**1:1-17**
Worship at Gibeon	1:1-6
Revelation to Solomon	1:7-13
Wealth of Solomon	1:14-17
Building the Temple	**2:1–8:16**
Preparations for Temple Building	2:1-18
Temple Structure and Furnishings	3:1–5:1
Founding of the Temple	3:1-2
Structure of the Temple	3:3-7
Furnishings of the Temple	3:8–5:1
Installation of the Ark	5:2–6:11
Dedication Prayer	6:12-42
Consecration of the Temple	7:1-22
Affirmation and Celebration	7:1-11
Instruction and Exhortation	7:12-22
Military and Labor Provisions	8:1-16
Economic and Military Activities	8:1-6
Labor Provisions	8:7-10
Temple Worship	8:11-16
Grandeur of Solomon's Kingdom	**8:17–9:31**
Maritime Activities	8:17-18
Exchange with the Queen of Sheba	9:1-12
Royal Pageantry	9:13-20
Commercial and Military Trade	9:21-28
Epitaph	9:29-31

Part 5: ISRAEL UNTIL THE EXILE OF THE NORTH — 2 Chronicles 10:1–28:27

Reign of Rehoboam	**10:1–12:16**
Division of the Monarchy	10:1–11:4
Establishment of Rehoboam's Rule	11:5-23

Outline of 1 & 2 Chronicles

Shishak's Invasion	12:1-12
Conclusion of Rehoboam's Rule	12:13-16

Reign of Abijah — 13:1–14:1a
- Preparations for War — 13:1-3
- Speech of Abijah — 13:4-12
- Judgment of Jeroboam — 13:13-20
- Conclusion of Abijah's Rule — 13:21–14:1a

Reign of Asa — 14:1b–16:14
- Reform and Security — 14:1b-8
- Victory over Zerah — 14:9-15
- Azariah's Call to Revival — 15:1-7
- Covenant Renewal and Celebration — 15:8-19
- War with Baasha — 16:1-6
- Hanani's Sermon — 16:7-10
- Death and Burial of Asa — 16:11-14

Reign of Jehoshaphat — 17:1–21:1a
- Religious and Political Achievements — 17:1-19
- Jehoshaphat and Ahab — 18:1–19:3
- Judicial Reform — 19:4-11
- Victory over Moab and Ammon — 20:1-30
- Conclusion of Jehoshaphat's Reign — 20:31–21:1a

Reigns of Terror — 21:1b–22:9
- Ruthless Rule of Jehoram — 21:1b-11
- Terrible Warning of Elijah — 21:12-15
- Agonized End of Jehoram — 21:16–22:1
- Reign of Ahaziah — 22:2-9

Reign of Joash — 22:10–24:27
- Elevation of Joash to the Throne — 22:10–23:21
- Joash under Blessing — 24:1-16
- Joash under Judgment — 24:17-27

Reign of Amaziah — 25:1–26:2
- Consolidation of Power — 25:1-4
- War against Edom — 25:5-16
- War against Israel — 25:17-24
- End of Amaziah's Reign — 25:25–26:2

Uzziah and Jotham — 26:3–27:9
Military and Economic Achievements of Uzziah — 26:3-15
Sin and Punishment of Uzziah — 26:16-23
Reign of Jotham — 27:1-9

Reign of Ahaz — 28:1-27
Transgressions of Ahaz — 28:1-4
Calamity in Judah — 28:5-15
Foreign Alliance and Idolatry — 28:16-27

Part 6: HEALING UNDER HEZEKIAH — 2 Chronicles 29:1–32:23

Restoration of the Temple — 29:1-36
Summary of Hezekiah's Reign — 29:1-2
Exhortation to Restoration — 29:3-11
Restoration of the Sanctuary — 29:12-19
Rededication of the Temple — 29:20-30
Sacrifices of Praise — 29:31-36

Celebration of the Passover — 30:1–31:1
Summons to the Passover Pilgrimage — 30:1-12
Observance of the Festival — 30:13-22
Continuation of Celebration — 30:23–31:1

Provisions for Temple Worship — 31:2-21
Contributions to the Temple — 31:2-10
Administration of Contributions — 31:11-19
Summary of Hezekiah's Restoration — 31:20-21

Deliverance and Healing in the Land — 32:1-33
Divine Protection and Provision — 32:1-23
Tried and Found Faithful — 32:24-31
Summary of a Faithful King — 32:32-33

Part 7: HUMILIATION AND HOPE — 2 Chronicles 33:1–36:23

Manasseh and Amon — 33:1-25
Reign of Manasseh — 33:1-20
    Idolatry and Captivity — 33:1-11
    Repentance and Restoration — 33:12-20
Reign of Amon — 33:21-25

Renewal under Josiah	**34:1–35:27**
Purification of Israel	34:1-13
Discovery of the Book of the Covenant	34:14-33
Passover Celebration	35:1-19
Death of Josiah	35:20-27
Exile and Return	**36:1-23**
Exile of Jehoahaz	36:1-4
Exile of Jehoiakim	36:5-8
Exile of Jehoiachin	36:9-10
Destruction of Temple and City	36:11-21
Return under Cyrus	36:22-23

ESSAYS

CHRONICLES AND THE EZRA COMPOSITIONS Four main pieces of evidence have been employed to support the theory that Chronicles and Ezra-Nehemiah were composed as a single work (Williamson 1977a: 5-6): (1) The presence of the opening sentences of Ezra at the end of 2 Chronicles; (2) the arrangement of 1 Esdras, which starts at 2 Chronicles 35 and continues without interruption into the material found in Ezra; (3) the similarity between the books in style and choice of vocabulary; and (4) the similarity of outlook, interests, and theology between the works.

The first evidence carries very little weight when the canonical history of the books is considered. Chronologically and historically, Ezra and Nehemiah are a sequel to Chronicles, but pairing them in this sequence has never been the canonical order (Talmon 1976). According to the Talmud, Ezra and Nehemiah precede Chronicles (b. Baba Batra 15a; cf. b. Sanhedrin 93b), the order followed in most printed editions of the Hebrew Bible. However, in the Masoretic treatise Adath Deborim (thirteenth century), in some predominantly Spanish manuscripts, and in the famous Aleppo Codex (tenth century, which Maimonides considered most accurate), Chronicles actually opens the third section of the canon known as the writings, while Ezra and Nehemiah are put at its close. This is probably the original arrangement, with Chronicles later moved to the end, since it was considered "the chronicle of the whole sacred history" (Jerome 1893, trans. Fremantle). The repetition of the decree of Cyrus at the close of 2 Chronicles (36:22-23) may represent an attempt to provide an optimistic ending for the Old Testament canon in the Talmudic order, or may have been a signpost to call to the reader's attention the proper chronological order. The repetition cannot be used as evidence that the books belonged together or were written by the same author. This judgment is confirmed by an evaluation of the arguments given for the unity of Chronicles and Ezra-Nehemiah (see below).

The second evidence, the composition of 1 Esdras, consists of the extensive common material from Chronicles and Ezra-Nehemiah. First Esdras begins with 2 Chronicles 35 and continues through Ezra, with a small portion from Nehemiah. It does not include Nehemiah 1:1–7:71 and 8:13b–13:31; it assigns a different place to the Artaxerxes correspondence (1 Esd 2:12-26 [Eng. 2:16-30] = Ezra 4:7-24), placing it earlier in the story. Only 1 Esdras 1:21-22 (Eng. 1:23-24) and the story of the three guardsmen (1 Esd 3:1–5:6) are without parallel in the biblical books. Two scenarios may be proposed: (1) 1 Esdras was separately composed of material from the Chronicler; or (2) 1 Esdras was part of the original work of Chronicles. The second view regards Ezra-Nehemiah as a later rearrangement of the Chronicles composition, with the addition of the Nehemiah traditions. These considerations are important for understanding the Judean restoration and the theology of the compositions [*Chronology in Chronicles*, p. 460].

Textual considerations might support the concept of the growth of a single composition that was later separated (Cross). There are other examples of what appear to be expansions of a composition in the Masoretic Text; the longer version of David and Goliath and the longer version of Jeremiah are prominent examples [*Masoretic Text*, p. 470]. First Esdras is deemed to have a shorter and better text, and the ordering of pericopes is historically superior. Three editions of the Chronicler's work have been proposed by those who believe in the growth of a single composition. Chronicles first began with 1 Chronicles 10 and contained the remainder of Chronicles plus 1 Esdras 1:1–5:65 (cf. Ezra 3:13). In this edition "the parallel between the first building of the temple under the direction of David (and Solomon) and the second building under Zerubbabel is too striking to be accidental, and must have formed part of the original structure of the work" (Freedman: 439–40). The original work was designed to support the program for restoration under Zerubbabel, with anticipation of restoring the ancient institutions. The second edition reflects the old ideology of the Judean kings as reformulated in Ezekiel 40–48 and the oracles of Haggai and Zechariah, where king and high priest jointly share political power (Hag 2:23; Zech 3:8; 4:14). This edition still breathes some monarchist fire, with Zerubbabel as the servant of the Lord. It now includes the full story of the building of the temple with the addition of the Aramaic source (Ezra 5:1–6:19) and the remainder of the Ezra narrative (Cross: 13). Cross points out that in 1 Esdras 6:26 (Eng. 6:27), Zerubbabel is called "the servant of the Lord," while in Ezra 6:7 this title is not included. The final edition added the genealogies but excluded the heroic tale of Zerubbabel's wisdom and piety. One may thus observe developments within royal ideology.

The third evidence, style and choice of vocabulary, does not actually support the thesis of the growth of a single composition. The older word lists, such as that of Curtis and Madsen (1910), do not distinguish differences peculiar to these books. They are a reflection of late biblical Hebrew as a whole. Attention must be given to those expressions used by Chronicles as well as by Ezra-Nehemiah in ways distinct from that of other literature. There are important stylistic and vocabulary distinctives that divide Chronicles and Ezra-Nehemiah as complete works (Japhet 1968). Distinctions between Chronicles and Ezra-Nehemiah include syntactical forms, technical terms, and peculiarities of style. In this regard, Chronicles betrays a later stage in the use of Hebrew terms than Ezra-Nehemiah and thus could not have been written or compiled by the same author (Williamson 1977a: 37–59). Scrutiny of the arguments of language used to support common authorship of the books shows that the evidence points to diversity of authorship.

The fourth evidence, theological outlook and historical perspective, was first identified by von Rad (1930). He called attention to the unique theological emphasis of Chronicles. This generated a considerable amount of research into its relationship with the Ezra writings and the development of this theology within these compositions. The narrative of Chronicles was thought to be composed after the completion of the temple (ca. 515 BCE). The genealogies (1 Chron 1–9) and records of Ezra-Nehemiah were added in the latter half of the fifth century, to bring the earlier work up to date and to adapt the work to the changed circumstances of the later period (Freedman: 441) *[Genealogy, p. 461]*. Von Rad did not observe that while the temple was a central theme in all the writing, other ideologies, such as the attitude to foreign peoples, were not similar.

The theology of Chronicles has a much closer relationship to 1 Esdras than it does to Ezra-Nehemiah (Eskenazi), indicating that it is a composition separate from Ezra *[Theology of Chronicles, p. 476]*. Chronicles has a focus on the centrality of David and his dynasty, a distinct concept of Israel and its relation to others, and a doctrine of immediate retribution. It looks back to ideals and is not immersed in the postexilic issues. It is also notable that both Chronicles and 1 Esdras end abruptly with a fragment of a verse, possibly an indication of a literary technique of an open-ended conclusion pointing toward the future. Chronicles interprets preexilic events, using Samuel–Kings as its primary source. First Esdras interprets postexilic events from the same theological perspective as Chronicles, using Ezra-Nehemiah as its source.

It is likely that 1 Esdras was composed as an independent work, unrelated to Ezra-Nehemiah. Both 1 Esdras and Ezra-Nehemiah are included in Hebrew texts translated into Greek as separate compositions. It is hard to conceive of two separate translations of an originally single composition being made within the same time period. Furthermore, the narrative of 1 Esdras does not flow as a continuation of the book of Chronicles. The summary statement of the Passover of Josiah is somewhat variant in the two accounts. Second Chronicles 35:19-20a says that Josiah prepared the temple; the equivalent in 1 Esdras 1:20-23 delares that these deeds were deemed right in the sight of the Lord. First Esdras then adds a verse contrasting the sins of those in previous times who were impious more than any nation and kingdom, words that were conspicuously grievous, so the words of the Lord rose up against Israel (1 Esd 1:24). This added reference to the grievous rebellion of a previous king would suggest the story of Manasseh in 2 Chronicles 33 was never a part of 1 Esdras. The last chapter

CHRONOLOGY IN CHRONICLES

BCE	Political Developments Influential for Judah	BCE	Judean History and Prophecy
		ca. 1010	Anointing of David
		ca. 970	Accession of Solomon
		931	Division of the kingdom
853–605	Assyrian domination in Syria and Palestine (Qarqar to Carchemish)	715–687	Reign of Hezekiah (prophetic work of Isaiah)
		640–609	Reign of Josiah (initial prophetic work of Jeremiah)
605–562	Nebuchadnezzar, king of Babylon	605	Initial deportation to Babylon (Daniel)
562-560	Awel-Marduk, king of Babylon	597	Second deportation to Babylon (Ezekiel)
559–530	Cyrus II (the Great), king of Persia	586	Destruction of the temple
		539	Return under Cyrus
521–486	Darius I, king of Persia	520–518	Prophetic writings of Haggai and Zechariah 1–8
		515	Dedication of the temple
465–425	Artaxerxes I (Longimanus), king of Persia	458	Ezra arrives in Jerusalem (renewal of covenant vows)
		445	Nehemiah arrives in Jerusalem (rebuilding of walls)
		ca. 430	Prophecy of Malachi
425–336	Darius II, Artaxerxes II, Artaxerxes III, and Arses, kings of Persia	ca. 400	Composition of Chronicles
335–323	Conquests of Alexander the Great		
301–200	Ptolemaic administration of Palestine		
200–164	Seleucid rule in Palestine (Antiochus the Great to Antiochus Epiphanes)		
164–63	Hasmonean rule in Palestine		

of 1 Esdras concludes with the separation of marriages, as found in Ezra 10:6-44 (1 Esd 9:1-36), and continues with the reading and teaching of the law (1 Esd 9:37-55), material found in Nehemiah 7:73–8:12. It then ends very abruptly with a fragment of Nehemiah 8:13.

It is remarkable that 1 Esdras includes Nehemiah 7:73 (1 Esd 9:37) to introduce the reading of the law. In Nehemiah this verse concludes the list of those who returned from Babylon and their contributions to the work (Neh 7:6-73). Nehemiah 7:73a concludes the list of returnees; the narrative then transitions to the reading of the law (7:73b). If 1 Esdras is a version of an earlier composition in which the book of Ezra was continued with the reading of the law in Nehemiah 8:1-12, then the inclusion of Nehemiah 7:73 in 1 Esdras 9:37 is completely out of place. It is not easy to explain the existence of 1 Esdras as a fragment from a composition that included Chronicles and Ezra, including Ezra's reading of the law as found in Nehemiah.

While the literary relationship of these compositions is not fully known, Chronicles is best studied as a historical-theological work in its own right, apart from Ezra-Nehemiah. Whatever may have been the developments in the Judean restoration culturally and theologically, Chronicles has a message of its own. It has come to be fully independent in the Hebrew canon, and it should be so regarded in Christian Scripture as well, even though they do fall in sequence. The identity of Israel and its hope for the future are unique in the vision of the Chronicler.

GENEALOGY Genealogies are ways of describing the history of a group and relationships within it. Anthropological studies indicate that oral genealogies have three formal characteristics: lineage, segmentation, and fluidity. *Lineage* traces a line descent through the males of the family. *Segmentation* draws out the families of one of the fathers in a family lineage. Each family is a segment of the whole group. *Fluidity* means that a family can move into the lineage of another group through affiliations of marriage and property. Each of these aspects of genealogy serve specific functions. Lineage determines rights, especially those of king and priest. Segmenting a family into subfamilies shows the influence and uniqueness of each family clan. Fluidity explains how families are related across time and places. It can explain critical relationships that would not otherwise be known.

Segmentation, dealing with a segment of the whole group, shows a person's status, rights, and obligations as determined by relationships to other members of the community, typically those of the same time period. The house of David begins with a segmented genealogy naming the sons of David's various wives (1 Chron 3:1-9). A segmented genealogy of Josiah is found later in the extended genealogy of David (vv. 15-18). This division of Josiah's son explains the status of the king's family when the nation was going into captivity in Babylonia. One of them was a prisoner (v. 17). These two segmentations show relationships between the sons of the royal family at the beginning and end of rule in Judah.

Between these two segmented genealogies is a second characteristic of genealogies expressed in terms of *lineage*. First Chronicles 3:10-14 names the descendants of David who were kings in Judah from Solomon through Josiah, a period of about four centuries. In ancient societies, right to serve in public office was established by pedigree. David is the divinely ordained king of Judah, so it is his sons who serve as kings. A linear genealogy, which traces biological descent, can extend back to the eponymous ancestor who founded the group *[Eponym, p. 466]*.

David's family is expressed both as segmented groups, at two critical times, as well as the right to rule as a line of kings. This presentation of David's family shows in particular instances who has the right to rule and in very concise fashion who the rulers are over centuries of time.

Finally, such genealogies are also characterized by *fluidity*. Genealogies reflect familial and communal ties between people that shift in their status and in their relationships. Marriages and changes in social status can cause a group to move from one lineage to another. Genealogies are necessarily select in what they retain. Elkanah, father of Samuel, is found in a Levitical genealogy in 1 Chronicles 6:25-27, but in 1 Samuel 1:1 Elkanah is an Ephraimite. Either Elkanah was a Levite living in Ephraim, or he became a member of the Levites when given to the tabernacle. These genealogies function in domestic, political, and religious areas. They determine a person's status and obligations, justify holding a political office or rank, and are used to determine office in religious functions.

GENEALOGIES IN CHRONICLES Genealogies were a part of much of ancient history writing, particularly in ancient Greece in the sixth and fifth centuries BCE (Knoppers 2004a: 245–46) *[Genealogy, p. 461; History Writing, p. 469]*. Writers established lineages for Greek noble families, who claimed descent from heroes and gods in the mythological past. Ancient Mesopotamian royal inscriptions include genealogies of the Sumerians, Assyrians, and Babylonians. Examples from ancient Egypt include king lists and priestly lineages. Ancients took great delight in genealogies of divine heroes and human beings, the settlements of tribes, how ancient cities were founded, and essentially everything concerning antiquarian knowledge. This is quite understandable; human life is about relationships between people, where they live, and how they live with each other. Histories are written for self-understanding; this requires a perception of continuity and differentiation. Continuity explains the present, the responsibility for the current order of human society. Differentiation enables function; each individual and group must know their role and responsibilities, and these derive from the past. Identity is intimately tied to heritage and social status. In ancient times, pedigree was established by the past and in large part determined credentials to serve in public office.

Determination of pedigree to establish qualifications for office is an important function of the Chronicler's genealogies. The extensive genealogies used to introduce the Chronicler's narrative have a further comprehensive purpose. The genealogical survey of all Israel asserts the importance of the continuity of God's people, even through a period of national disruption (Braun: 98). These genealogies provide decisive foundations for citizens, Levitical priests, and temple in the postexilic community. The genealogies must contain historical information, but there are various kinds of associations. Genealogies not only describe family relationships, but also geographical, social, economic, religious, and political realities. Genealogies are fluid; they change from time to time in response to social changes. Two genealogies may differ, yet they can still be correct in expressing relationships under consideration at the time. There are also fixed aspects to the Chronicler's genealogies. Israel is always twelve tribes, though the list may require Joseph to be represented as Ephraim and Manasseh or it may list Simeon as one of the tribes. The genealogies of Chronicles contain history, but they do not provide for a complete linear reconstruction of the nation Israel.

Genealogies in Chronicles manifest a number of peculiarities. There are occasions in which the names of peoples and places seem to be interchangeable; in 1 Chron 2:42-45, among the sons of Caleb, Ziph, Mareshah, Hebron, Taappuah, Shema, Jorkeam, and Maon are known place names. Some genealogies describe occupational groupings and communities (4:19-23). The Chronicler is not concerned with providing a complete line of descendants. Only nine generations span the period from Judah to David, which includes the entire period of 430 years in Egypt and 480 from the exodus to Solomon. There are several doublets; the genealogy of Saul is given twice (8:29-38; 9:35-44), as well as that of Levi (6:1-15, 16-30). There are divergent names for the same person, such as Caleb (2:18-19, 42-50; 4:15) and Chelubai (2:9). Genealogies in Chronicles are sometimes contradictory to other lists: the genealogy of Zerubbabel in Chronicles is not the same as the one in Matthew (1 Chron 3:19; Matt 1:12). Genealogical material is arranged by various literary devices to establish the importance of particular persons or groups within a theological framework. The dynasty of David and the centrality of the Levites in the function of the temple are manifestly important, as is evident in their length and detail. The tribes of Judah and Levi occupy the largest portion of the entire genealogy.

The Chronicler does appear to be bound by his sources; for example, neither Dan nor Zebulun appear in the tribal listings (1 Chron 7:12-13), an omission that cannot be intentional. There is evidence of textual disruption at those verses, which was present already in the Chronicler's sources. The genealogies provide continuity in a topical manner. It is not always certain what historical situation they describe. The lineage of Ephraim is interrupted by the murder of his sons in a property raid (7:20-24). According to the narrative of Genesis, Ephraim died in Egypt long before the exodus. It is uncertain how this episode is to be related to the history recounted in the earlier narratives. Yet in the claims to tribal territory for Ephraim, the Chronicler includes Joshua in the lineage of Ephraim (7:27-29).

The genealogies serve to identify Israel in contrast to the other peoples related to Israel but excluded from the community known as "all Israel" (Schweitzer: 11). This is critical to defining Israel. By this means the genealogies legitimate the order of society in Yehud. Thus, the legitimation of the priestly orders are provided all the way to Levi and to the orders David established when he made preparations for the temple. The genealogies also distinguish different groups through ethnic boundaries and inherited territories. They define internal organization within a group. This is most evident with the Levites, who are separated by families into priestly duties, assignments of security, music, and all the various tasks associated with the temple.

The genealogies present an ideal. This is the ideal of the Davidide king at the head of a nation that worships around the temple. The concept of Israel is somewhat fluid; redefinition is accomplished through the genealogies. Israel is not synonymous with those living in the land. Israel does not always occupy its land. Israel is exclusive to foreign elements living among them in the land, though it is not exclusive to foreigners becoming part of Israel. Ruth is one of the best-known examples, but there are many others included in the genealogies. An ideal Israel did not exist at any time, as the genealogies make evident, but they establish the potential for an ideal Israel. In the settlements of Jerusalem after the exile, all the tribes and officials are present, and all are connected to the ancestral heritage. Israel may yet be what it is (De Vries: 20).The history of the Chronicler depicts the ideal that Israel should be; the genealogies prepare for this narrative by determining that the potential for that ideal is present [Genealogy, p. 461].

GLOSSARY

Achaemenid This was the designation of the royal house of Persia from Cyrus the Great (559–530 BCE) onward. It is from the Persian *Hakhāmanish*, possibly meaning "friendly in nature," the eponymous ancestor of the dynasty [Eponym, p. 466]. Chronicles was written to address the community of Yehud Medintah, the little province of Judah established by Cyrus. The vast and varied resources of the empire made possible renowned Achaemenid art.

Amarna Tablets In 1887 a peasant woman digging for fertilizer along the Nile River discovered cuneiform tablets. Systematic excavations and accidental discoveries eventually yielded 380 clay tablets, originally approximately three inches wide and nine inches long. Almost all are in the Akkadian language, the international language of Mesopotamia at that time. These are letters between Egypt and various rulers and countries of the western Orient during the reigns of Amenophis III and Amenophis IV (ca. 1400–1350 BCE, during the Late Bronze Age). They include Sumerian, Akkadian, Hittite, Egyptian, and Hurrian material. Most of the letters were sent to Egypt, providing information on political relationships between various cities of western Asia and the pharaohs of Egypt.

Babylonian Chronicles A series of cuneiform tablets covers the years of 745 BCE into the late Seleucid period (the second century before Christ). Entries follow a chronological order, introduced by the regnal year of the Babylonian king, though not every year is included. Nabopolassar, perhaps a descendant of Merodach-Baladan, wrested control of Babylon from

Assyria in 626 BCE. Nebuchadnezzar ruled Babylon for forty-three years (605–562 BCE), but only the first eleven years are covered by the surviving tablets, which leaves the exact date of the exile uncertain.

Chiasm Chiasm is a literary structure common to the Old Testament: the first and last units are parallel, with two or more parallel units between them, sometimes also with a central unit. These units are often identified as A, B, B', A'. Each unit may be as short as a poetic line or may be a lengthy topic in a narrative or genealogy. See its extended use in the Preview to 1 Chronicles 11–12.

Chronological Synchronism In ancient times, chronologies are often given in relative years rather than absolute years as determined by a calendar. One event or the reign of a king is given as a certain year in the course of another event or reign. In the Bible this happens in tracing the changes of monarchy in Israel and Judah. The reign of successive kings is given in terms of the reigning monarch in the other kingdom. Various factors are involved in establishing these chronologies. What year is considered the first year of reign? It may be the portion of a year in which a king comes to reign, or perhaps the first full year of a king's reign. How are years counted if there was a transitional period in which two kings reigned simultaneously (as coregnants)? Did the calendars of the respective countries begin at the same time (such as spring seeding), or did they sometimes differ, with one of the two beginning during the fall celebration? The methods of synchronization can only be inferred since they are never stated. Developing inferences from the number of variables makes calendar reckoning an interpretive matter, though a very critical one, because chronology is the structure from which the relationship of various events begins.

Deuteronomistic History This term has come to be applied to what is called the Former Prophets in the Hebrew Bible, namely, Joshua, Judges, Samuel, and Kings *[Hebrew Canon, p. 467]*. It has come to be called *Deuteronomistic* because the book of Deuteronomy is the moral measure by which actions and events are evaluated. In the literary theory of Martin Noth, the book of Deuteronomy was written as a prologue, providing continuity from Deuteronomy through 2 Kings. He conceived of this history as the work of a single author, living in the exilic period. This theory of authorship has not proved to be tenable since versions of this history existed long before the exile, at least as early as Hezekiah. The relationship of Deuteronomy to the Former Prophets is also in question. Deuteronomy has always been grouped with the Pentateuch and was written as a conclusion to the work of Moses. But making Deuteronomy part of the Pentateuch does not compromise the cohesion of the prophetic history that follows. That history carries the language and ideology of Deuteronomy and may quite properly be described as Deuteronomistic without implying that Deuteronomy introduced the composition.

Elephantine Papyri Elephantine is an island in the Nile opposite Aswan (biblical Syene), just north (downstream) of the first cataract. The island became an asylum for Judean refugees after the Babylonian conquest (2 Kings 25:26; Jer 43–44). The Elephantine papyri are a group of documents and fragments written in the fifth century BCE, discovered by chance finds and archaeological excavations during the nineteenth and twentieth centuries. The Aramaic material is of interest for Jewish history and biblical studies. There are thirty-five Aramaic letters on papyrus; many are only fragments. Almost all were written by residents at Elephantine or by such who were away from home. The most significant are ten documents of the Jedaniah archive. Jedaniah ben Gemariah was a community leader and perhaps a chief priest. One of the letters is from a certain Hananiah informing Jedaniah of a directive from Darius II to the Egyptian satrap Arsames, instructing him on the observance of the Passover. The Egyptians destroyed the Elephantine temple in 410 BCE, possibly in an anti-Persian riot. Appeal was made to Johanan the high priest in Jerusalem and Bagoas the Persian governor (Neh 12:22) for support to reconstruct the temple. With the end of Persian influence in Egypt at the beginning of the fourth century, the Jewish garrison at Elephantine was moved and the temple abandoned.

Eponym An eponymous name designates a person, real or created, after whom a place, custom, or family is named. An eponymous ancestor is the individual standing at the head of a family genealogy. In Chronicles the twelve sons of Jacob/Israel are eponymous ancestors of the tribes of Israel (1 Chron 2:1-2; 16:13) *[Genealogy, p. 461]*.

Ethnographic The term refers to writing about a particular race of people or the relationship of various races to each other in their life context. Examples of ethnographic perspectives in Chronicles include an all-Israelite identity, a Canaanite identity, and the centrality of Judah to the other tribes. Important in ethnography is the recognition of fluidity, a change of identity. In ethnic relations, a Moabite such as Ruth may come to be part of an Israelite genealogy. Geographically, a town such as Beersheba may be multiethnic. Its earliest settlements were Philistine (Rainey 1979: 450). It became a southern administrative center for Judah (2 Chron 19:4). In the intertestamental period it came to be absorbed into Idumea as the Edomites cut it off from Jerusalem. Ethnic identity can be very important in the relationship of tribes and functions that may be limited to particular tribes.

Etiology The etiology of a name explains why a person, place, or cultural custom is significant by recounting the causes from which the name arose. The explanation provides a positive connection between the name or custom and the cause. Sometimes a person or place acquires a new name because of significance or distinction achieved. The name then serves to recall that distinction. The name of Abram (exalted father) was changed to Abraham (father of a multitude) to recall the promise of God that his descendants would be as numerous as the stars.

Essays

Hebrew Canon The books that compose the Hebrew Bible are the same as those within the Christian Old Testament though their arrangement is different. There are three sections. The first is called Torah, the five books from Genesis to Deuteronomy. The Prophets are next. The Former Prophets are the books of Joshua, Judges, Samuel, and Kings. These books are also known as the Deuteronomistic History. The Latter Prophets are Isaiah, Jeremiah, Ezekiel, and the Book of the Twelve (often referred to as the Minor Prophets because these are shorter compared to the other prophetic books). The remaining books constitute the Writings where are found Psalms, the wisdom books (Job, Proverbs, and Ecclesiastes), Esther, Ruth, Daniel, Lamentations, Song of Songs, Ezra, Nehemiah, and Chronicles. The books of the Writings are ordered differently in various collections and manuscripts *[Chronicles and the Ezra Compositions, p. 457]*.

Inclusio The term is used for a literary structure in which the ending of a section is indicated by repeating a line or subject from the introduction. It is distinguished from chiasm in that it does not require the topics within the unit to be structured in any particular fashion.

Negev The Hebrew name *negeb* (or *negev*) is given to the geographical area just south of the Judean hills. It is a low-lying desert that becomes unstable after periods of rain. The modern term refers to the southern half of the state of Israel, from Beersheba to the Gulf of Aqaba. Only the northern portion of this region was settled in biblical times. The patriarchs are reported to have sojourned in the area of Beersheba. The wilderness wanderings occur around the oasis of Kadesh Barnea, which lies on the western edge of the Negev highlands. The Israelites fought the Canaanites around Arad and Hormah. In the kingdom period this area became very active as a trade route.

Resumptive Summary A narrative or genealogy may be interrupted with additional material. Following the addition, a brief summary resumes the initial narrative. Such resumptions are well known in Hebrew narrative. An example is the inclusion of the genealogy of Moses and Aaron in the exodus narrative (Exod 6:14-25); summary statements provide narrative continuity (vv. 13, 26). The same phenomenon can occur in genealogies (e.g., 1 Chron 2:50b-52; 4:1-4; cf. 23:2 and 28:1).

Shephelah This Hebrew name is given to a geographical territory to the west of the Judean hills, characterized by its being lower than the Judean hills. It is equivalent to foothills and is famous for its sycamore wood (1 Kings 10:27). The Shephelah is separated from the Judean hills by a north-south valley, which was very significant for defending the cities of Judah. Valleys leading to the east provide access to the Judean plateau.

Ugarit This city, an ancient port near modern-day Latakia, was accidentally discovered in 1929. It was a prominent kingdom in the Late Bronze Age, especially from the fifteenth through the thirteenth centuries BCE.

Its wealth was based on maritime commerce. The royal archives have yielded over 1,500 clay tablets. The language of Ugarit was Northwest Semitic, closely related to Hebrew. Its culture and customs provide very helpful information for understanding what the Bible calls the Baal religion. It is also an important resource for understanding grammatical aspects and vocabulary of the Hebrew language.

Vorlage This German word entered scholarly vocabulary as a technical term to refer to the text from which an author or scribe was working. While the sources of the Chronicler in many cases are available to the modern reader, it is also demonstrable that in many cases the *Vorlage* of the Chronicler, the version he had before him, had variants from the version we possess. His *Vorlage* was not the MT but a version of Samuel and Kings much closer to texts available in Qumran scrolls. First Chronicles 21 is an important example.

GREEK TEXT OF CHRONICLES Following the various exiles of Israelite peoples, and particularly after the advent of Hellenism, it was necessary to make the Old Testament available in the Greek language. After Alexander the Great, Greek replaced Aramaic as the international language of his world. The Letter of Aristeas informs us that the Pentateuch (Torah) was first translated in Alexandria in the third century before Christ. Other portions of the Old Testament were also translated during these centuries until it was complete sometime prior to the Common Era.

The Greek Old Testament is most readily accessible through a compilation of Greek translations known as the *Septuagint* (LXX). As commonly used, this term describes a Greek Old Testament compiled from Christian Greek Scriptures of the fourth century CE. The three oldest and largely complete are Vaticanus, Sinaiticus, and Alexandrinus. At various times the Greek translation was revised from older translations. In the third century a church father named Origen attempted a comprehensive comparison of these Greek versions with the Proto-Masoretic Hebrew text *[Masoretic Text, p. 470]*. His work was influential in the later reproductions of the Greek translation of the Old Testament.

Revisions of the original Greek translation moved in the direction of conforming to the Proto-Masoretic Text and to a greater degree of literalness. However, not all evidence of the older Greek translations was lost, which often preserve a Hebrew reading variant from the later standard Hebrew text. These readings are referred to as Old Greek in distinction from the readings of the Septuagint. Vaticanus is the oldest and most complete witness to the Hebrew text outside of the Proto-Masoretic Text.

The Greek Text of Chronicles has numerous variations from the MT of Chronicles *[Masoretic Text, p. 470]*. Many of these go back to the Hebrew version from which the Greek translation was made. At times they are confirmed and complemented by other Hebrew texts from the Qumran scrolls. The original Greek translations were made from a Hebrew text version that often had important distinctions from the text that became standard after the destruction of the temple in New Testament times.

HISTORY WRITING People write about the past in order to organize it in a way that will provide meaning and value for the present. *History writing* may be defined as "the intellectual form in which a civilization renders account to itself of its past" (Huizinga: 9). It is not primarily about accurate reporting of past events, but provides a people's reason for recalling the past and the significance given to these events.

History writing may be distinguished from *historiography*, an inclusive category for all writings about the past, including those that are not history. Thomas Keneally seeks to be absolutely true to all events and even conversations in his novel *Schindler's List*. He writes these actual events as a novel because "only the novel's techniques seem suited for a character of such ambiguity and magnitude as Oskar" (Keneally: 10). Works such as that of Keneally are historiography but not history; they are writings about the past but are outside of the particular genre of history writing. Historiography also includes the records of particular events or purely factual data recorded for future consultation. Annals, chronicles, and court histories are historiography but not history writing. They are limited to the king, his kingdom, or his dynasty, but they do not encompass the people as a whole.

In contrast, the writing of a national history, a people rendering an account to themselves, has a double purpose. One goal is to assess responsibility and pass judgment on actions and their consequences for the present state of affairs. The other is to establish a corporate identity that expresses what a nation is and what principles it stands for. A national history seeks to present the people's essential character and assess praise or blame for their corporate actions, and thus Chronicles is a classic example of history writing.

Broadly speaking, personal identity and self-justification are at the heart of historiographic documents (Van Seters: 2–5). In the ancient Near East, these concerns involve the person of the king, such as his right to rule or an accounting of his actions. Most such writings are not a history, since the king does not embody the nation or the people. It may be argued that history writing begins when the actions of the king are viewed in the larger context of the people as a whole, so the national history passes judgment on the king. The histories of Israel were preserved as part of a larger literary tradition. Historians used sources within the scribal tradition as well as oral tradition. Not all archival material was used, even though it contained information from the past and was accessible. Selection was made according to the purposes of the historian.

Modern historians seek to present an account of the past that is true to the information of their sources. They also try to be as thorough as possible in assembling all the relevant information. Histories remain subjective in a variety of ways. For example, historians must assess the causal relationship between events. As the one-hundredth anniversary of the First World War approached, the *Economist* (March 29, 2014) ran a feature of book reviews on the causes and consequences of the war. Scores of histories have been published, all in some way at variance with each other. Two detailed scholarly histories (each nearly seven hundred pages long) are exemplary: Margaret MacMillan (an Oxford scholar), *The War That Ended Peace* (2013); Christopher Clark (a Cambridge scholar), *The Sleepwalkers* (2012). MacMillan holds Germany primarily responsible for the war; Clark charges the Balkans for it. Each work is described as a tour de force in history writing. Clark's book has sold 300,000 copies in seventeen languages. The prolific number of studies generated by interest in the First World War should not be surprising. In this case the concern to establish the identity and character of nations, and the desire to assess praise and blame for corporate actions—such needs extend to all the great powers of the world. The fact that a consensus on each of these items cannot be reached ensures that much history writing on this subject will continue.

The first narrative and critical history of the ancient world is that of Herodotus, a Greek historian living in the fifth century BCE, who wrote a history of the Greco-Persian Wars (500–449 BCE). Herodotus made use of what the Greeks called *historiē*. In Greek thought, it was a method of scientific "inquiry" that consisted in asking a question, looking for relevant information, and then drawing a conclusion. In writing about the Persian wars, Herodotus worked up a collection of ethnographic, geographic, and mythological materials into a framework in which all past history leads to a struggle between East and West, culminating with the invasion of Greece by Xerxes in 480 BCE. In the process he makes a clear distinction between history and prehistory. The dividing line for Greece is about 600 BCE. Rules of evidence for legendary figures, such as the heroes of Troy, are different from those of historical individuals, such as Croesus, the last king of Lydia, who conquered the Greeks of Ionia (560–546 BCE). Herodotus set an example of universality that was unequaled in the ancient world. He formulated historical materials into a narrative that expressed his understanding of Greek civilization in a way that can be called history writing.

The earliest analogy to Herodotus in the Old Testament would be the Deuteronomistic Historian, who gathered his own material from oral stories, records, and royal chronicles to compose a history (Van Seters: 17). Since this history evaluates the nation and explains its destiny, it should be classified as true history writing. For the same reasons, Chronicles is likewise a composition that fulfils the definition of history writing and its purposes.

MASORETIC TEXT The MT is the only complete Hebrew text of the Old Testament and serves as the basis on which most modern translations are made. The MT was created in the medieval period (during the ninth and tenth centuries) by families of scribes who included marginal notations called masorah. It was created from one particular text tradition of the Old Testament that became the dominant text form at the end of the Second Temple period (ca. 135 CE).

The MT preserves two interpretations of the text called *qere* and *ketib* (or *kethib* or *ketiv*). The main work of the Masoretes was to add vocalization to the consonantal text (Hebrew was originally written without vowels, though they were always interpreted). This had the intended result of removing many ambiguities. In many cases, this technique enabled the Masoretes to preserve a variant reading of the text in another manuscript, or it enabled them to provide a correction to the text without changing any of the letters, a principle that was very important to them. This was done as part of the vocalization process. Alternate vowels would be provided to indicate a word to be read other than the one that was written. Such a reading is called the *qere*, or what is *read* aloud. The reading of the (consonantal) letters *written*, which the Masoretes would not intentionally change, is called the *ketib*.

The term Proto-Masoretic Text refers to that consonantal form of the text that was used to produce the Masoretic Text. Other Hebrew text examples include Hebrew versions of the Old Testament that were the basis for older translations, such as the Greek Septuagint and the Latin Vulgate, and may be reconstructed by examining them. A great variety of Hebrew text forms have been found in the Judean desert (such as at or near Qumran). At times some New Testament quotations differ from the Old Testament in modern translations. One possibility is that New Testament authors quoted from a different Old Testament version (cf. Acts 7:14 and Exod 1:5). Scholars are interested in these differences because such texts may more accurately reflect the original version of the Old Testament.

PRIESTS AND LEVITES IN CHRONICLES Levitical priests (e.g., 2 Chron 5:5) is a phrase that defines priests in Chronicles. In this matter, the Chronicler follows Deuteronomy, which, in distinction from the rest of the Pentateuch, considers all Levites to be eligible for priesthood. Levites are given tasks and remuneration otherwise limited to the sons of Aaron (Deut 18:1-8). The census summary of Numbers 4:47 is descriptive of the work of the Levites: they were subject to the duties of service and porterage relating to the tent of meeting. The term *serving* (*ʿabodah*) describes only the work of the Levites, never the work of the priests (Milgrom 1989: 344). In the later postexilic books it comes to have the broader meaning of "cultic service." Such service is the prerogative of the priests alone, exclusive of Levites. It is clear the priestly sources of the Pentateuch precede the exile significantly.

Another puzzle regarding priests in Scripture is the relationship between the sons of Abiathar and the sons of Zadok. Both are listed as priests in the genealogies, but in the time of David the succession of priests appears to become limited exclusively to the sons of Zadok. Solomon banished Abiathar to Anathoth (1 Kings 2:26), though this is never stated in Chronicles. The traditions changed over time according to the records, but it is not possible to determine how and why the changes took place. By Qumran times the priesthood was extremely conflicted. The teacher of righteousness at Qumran, no doubt himself a priest, and his followers refer to the officially presiding priest in the temple as wicked. As a consequence, they refuse to participate in the temple and consider themselves as a community (*yaḥad*) to be the true temple.

If the interpretation of the list in 2 Chronicles 31 is correct, the Chronicler has access to distinctions unknown in other texts. Most prominent among these is the distribution of the *most holy dedications* (v. 14b AT) to all priests (v. 16). This particular category of gifts was normally limited to priests within the temple precincts. Various regulations are given for many aspects of the temple service, even for such simple matters as the age of active duty (cf. 1 Chron 23:3). It is impossible to know how much the Chronicler reflects the practices of his own day, but these regulations are given in the style of an administrative document that must have served as a source to guide Hezekiah's activation of temple ritual.

SOURCES FOR CHRONICLES Source criticism has been a significant subdiscipline in biblical studies. Identification of sources can be instructive for understanding composition. Sometimes features of the composition are a result of source content, textual format, or integration. In the case of some compositions, such as the Pentateuch, knowledge of sources can be instructive to the history or process of the composition. Chronicles is one of the most fruitful books when searching for sources. Much of the Chronicler's source material is identifiable in the biblical text, though often not in the MT tradition preserved in the Old Testament. Yet for much of his information, the Chronicler also had access to sources outside of those that have been preserved. This should be expected. More than eight hundred separate scrolls are known from the finds at Qumran. Only about one-fifth of these are biblical texts. The Chronicler, as a resident of Jerusalem, would have had access to a great variety of sources. Further, he was not restricted regarding travel in the Persian Empire and could have searched out sources for buildings, military lists, and fortifications at various sites in Judah. It is not possible to know how complete some of these sources were, how internally consistent, or how credible.

Chronicles has been of great interest for source-critical study. Oddly, this was not to clarify an understanding of Chronicles. The founder of the modern study of Chronicles is Wilhelm de Wette (d. 1849). His interest was primarily in the evidence that Chronicles could offer concerning the authorship of the Pentateuch, the question that engaged all biblical scholars of the time. De Wette believed the Pentateuch was written much later than the time of Moses and tried to prove this from the history of Israel as described in the Bible. Until his time, the Former Prophets and Chronicles were regarded as complementary, each describing the same history from differing points of view *[Hebrew Canon, p. 467]*. This assumed that the life of Israel was determined by the covenant laws of the Pentateuch. De Wette undermined this view by basing Israelite history on the Former Prophets alone. He rejected the use of Chronicles as a historical source, regarding it as completely unreliable, a late tendentious history. The *Tendenz* of the Chronicler is to interpret history as divine action in response to the faithfulness of an individual king *[Tendenz in Chronicles, p. 476]*. For more than a hundred years, de Wette's approach set the direction for the study of Chronicles. Wellhausen regarded himself as a follower of de Wette, and not of Graf, with whom he is often associated; Wellhausen's *Prolegomena to the History of Israel* distinctly downplays the importance of Graf. Charles C. Torrey, at the end of the nineteenth century, categorically declared,

> No fact of Old Testament criticism is more firmly established than this: that the Chronicler as a historian is thoroughly untrustworthy. He distorts facts deliberately and habitually; invents chapter after chapter with the greatest freedom, and what is most dangerous of all, his history is not written for its own sake, but in the interest of an extremely one-sided theory. (Torrey: 52)

An unquestioned axiom of the time was that Chronicles and Ezra-Nehemiah were a single composition. Torrey believed that the Chronicler had only two sources: Nehemiah's Memoirs and a late worthless Aramaic source. All the rest of Chronicles he deemed to be free composition. Torrey assessed the restoration as being a very limited phenomenon. There was no significant restoration, no Ezra, no edict of Cyrus or letter of Artaxerxes, and no bringing of the Torah from Babylon.

A corrective to this extreme judgment of the history of the period was made by Eduard Meyer. In great detail he discussed the Aramaic documents in the book of Ezra (Meyer 1896). Meyer tried to show that they were a reliable source, whatever historical inconsistencies might be attributed to the Chronicler. The work of Meyer, further evidence from Elephantine *[Elephantine Papyri, p. 466]*, and many additional Persian inscriptions from the remotest corners of the Achaemenian Empire *[Achaemenid, p. 464]*—all these convinced William Albright that the Aramaic in Ezra was Achaemenian (Albright 1921). The Persian court did take an active and effective interest in furthering Jewish ecclesiastical polity in Judah. Albright came to affirm that the entire work of Chronicles contained valid historical information. This general shift in attitude toward the historical reliability of Chronicles led to a reevaluation of the literary methods of its author, his sources, and the assumption that Chronicles and Ezra-Nehemiah are a single composition.

More recent theories propose that Chronicles did not use Kings as a source. Kings and Chronicles are regarded as concurrent compositions based on a common source. Graeme Auld returned to the notion of a history of the Judahite monarchy that served as a common source for parallel passages in Chronicles and Kings (Auld). He argues that where either history lacks an account—all those passages not found in both of the compositions—that account was lacking in the common source. Since virtually all the history of the north is lacking in Chronicles, he believes the source was largely a Judahite history that was later supplemented in Kings. The resulting source becomes unusual. A history of Judah that begins with Saul, as in 1 Chronicles 10, would be strange since Saul was never king of Judah. Contrary to Auld's hypothesis, many times the Chronicler introduces material that assumes knowledge of content available in Kings. A striking example is 2 Chronicles 10, which follows 1 Kings

12 with few verbal variations. Jeroboam son of Nebat suddenly appears, though none of the material of 1 Kings 11 is included to identify his activities. This is a case where knowledge of Kings must be available to the reader.

Raymond Person has modified Auld's thesis, arguing that Kings and Chronicles were contemporary competing histories, yet with a similar theological viewpoint. His view is that the authors of Kings returned with Zerubbabel and those of Chronicles returned with Ezra or Nehemiah. Both wrote histories based on the same historical sources they had in Babylon. Person does not explain the dissimilarities found between Kings and Chronicles. The Chronicler, for example, has a significantly greater amount of material on Jehoshaphat. But this presumably does not substantially change the portrayal of the king (Person: 152). How is it possible that the teaching ministry instituted by Jehoshaphat in 2 Chronicles 17:7-9, the oracle of Jehu son of Hanani in 19:1-3, Jehoshaphat's appointment of judges (19:4-11), his prayer preparing for war with the eastern kings (20:6-11), and the role of the musicians leading to divine victory are collectively nothing more than additional material consistent with the portrayal of Jehoshaphat in Kings? This extensive material is not incidental but fundamental, significantly altering the portrayal of Jehoshaphat.

The content of Chronicles most plausibly suggests that it is a composition dependent on Scripture, largely as we know it, which the Chronicler used as sources. For example, the genealogies and their interpretation depend on the pentateuchal narrative substantially as we know it. Information from Joshua, Samuel, Nehemiah, and Ruth is utilized, indicating that they were extant in some written form. The Chronicler selects, rearranges, and supplements his source material, the very essence of the work of a historian. Beginning in 1 Chronicles 10, it is possible to follow the parallel passages in Samuel, Kings, and Psalms as we know them.

The genealogical material in 1 Chronicles 2–8 is derived from genealogical collections or from oral sources [*Genealogy*, p. 461]. This information is diverse in genre and may have come from a wide variety of locations, including military census lists, or administrative lists like the one found in 1 Chronicles 27:25-34. Some information must have been derived from his own time, such as the descendants of Jeconiah (Jehoiachin) in 1 Chronicles 3:17-24. As a historian, the Chronicler no doubt contributed information known to him through the guilds to which he belonged and the communities where he lived.

Kings and Chronicles make recurrent reference to sources. Kings and Chronicles have a total of seventeen references to histories of kings. The differences in source citation are minimal; Kings does not cite a source for David (cf. 1 Chron 29:29), and Chronicles does not cite a source for Joram/Jehoram of Judah (cf. 2 Kings 8:23; 2 Chron 21:20) or for Amon (cf. 2 Kings 21:25; 2 Chron 33:24-25). The Chronicler attributes most of his sources to works of the prophets (e.g., Nathan in 1 Chron 29:29; Nathan and Ahijah in 2 Chron 9:29; Shemaiah in 12:15; etc.). The parallel citation with Kings makes it obvious that the same source was meant in each case. A likely instance of such a prophetic source is the citation for the history of Hezekiah (2 Kings 20:20; 2 Chron 32:32). The records of Judah in Kings are the vision of Isaiah cited in Chronicles. The account of Hezekiah in 2 Kings 18:17–20:19 is substantially parallel to Isaiah 36:2–39:8, indicating that this history was part of the prophetic words of Isaiah, as the Chronicler claims. A series of such works were written by prophets contemporaneous with each respective king. Chronicles twice calls these a midrash (*midraš*, 2 Chron 13:22; 24:27), which should be understood in terms of its etymological derivation from the word *daraš*, meaning "to inquire or investigate."

Such prophetic writings would not be official records of the kings. Official records do not allow for portrayals of kings as seriously flawed individuals. At least in some cases such prophets had access to official records. Gad was *David's seer* (1 Chron 21:9), and Heman was *the king's seer* (25:5). The argument that the Chronicler simply made up prophets for the kings is baseless; if that were so, why would he omit naming authors for some of his sources (2 Chron 35:26–27; 36:8)? Taken comprehensively, it must be concluded that prophetic works were available as sources.

The Deuteronomistic History is a compilation of two main prophetic sources, one from the north and one from the south (Rainey 1997: 41–43). Convincing evidence comes from the two chronological systems that have been incorporated into it, as demonstrated beyond question by Edwin Thiele. The chronicles from the north evidently came to Jerusalem with the fall of Samaria, where they were used by the Deuteronomistic Historians in compiling their account. The chronological systems were incorporated as they were received, with corresponding synchronisms, even though they often left the record with the appearance of contradiction (e.g., Omri, 1 Kings 16:23, 29). Such references betray the complicated nature of chronology. They also show the integrity of the prophetic records. Such prophetic documents seem to be the source for much of the material in Chronicles that was not adopted or modified from the book of Kings. The authors of Kings selected the material they incorporated, as did the Chronicler, each creating their own history.

This prophetic material contained much about the achievements of a king (e.g., 1 Kings 15:23; 22:45; 2 Kings 20:20), along with moral censure or approval. Given the *Tendenz* of the Deuteronomistic History, it is likely that these authors omitted records of earlier efforts to purify covenant worship in Jerusalem in order to achieve a greater sense of honor for Josiah (Rainey 1997: 44–47) *[Tendenz in Chronicles, p. 476]*. It is less likely that these events have been created by the Chronicler apart from historical records. Similar examples can be observed in records of building programs and economic projects. The Chronicler had access to the same prophetic history used by the Deuteronomists and drew a great deal of historical data from it. He understood the geopolitical and geographic realities affecting Judah, and he linked periods of economic and military strength with the religious attitudes and policies of the monarchs concerned. It is reasonable to think that this insight was a part of the prophetic sources he relied on *[Chronology in Chronicles, p. 460]*.

TENDENZ IN CHRONICLES The German word *tendenz* is used to describe the methods of the Chronicler. It is distinct from a motif, which is a theme (topos) integrated in the presentation of a narrative. *Tendenz* refers to a more philosophical view of events that gives rise to what may be perceived as a literary motif. The Chronicler has distinct views on the nature of Israel, divine purpose, and actions in history. He interprets events from the perspective that God rewards faithfulness and punishes unfaithfulness within the lifetime of an individual. All Israel is a continuous entity throughout its history. The Chronicler believes that all races and peoples may be included within the practicing covenant community. These perspectives are important to understand events and perceive the message conveyed in them.

The story of Hezekiah is one the best examples of *tendenz* in Chronicles, a contrast of the portrayal found in Kings. Aside from the accession notice (2 Chron 29:1), the Chronicler makes little reference to the parallel history in Kings until his conclusion. The account in Kings provides a brief notice of the religious reforms of Hezekiah (2 Kings 18:3-7) and the exile of the north (vv. 9-12), then concentrates on the confrontation with the Assyrians (18:8–19:37), concluding with the report of Hezekiah's illness and the disastrous visit of the envoys from Babylon (20:1-19). Kings ends with events that preceded the Babylonian siege in order to show the consequences of unfaithfulness and the reason for the exile.

Chronicles in turn expands the religious reform of Hezekiah into a detailed account (chs. 29–31). The victory over the Assyrians is reproduced as an example of divine warfare on behalf of the kingdom of God (ch. 32; Konkel 1987: 272–79). Jerusalem is delivered by divine action similar to the conquest of the Egyptians at the Red sea (2 Chron 32:20-22). The illness of Hezekiah betrays a problem of pride, but the king follows the formula to deal with this shortcoming (32:24-26). The visit of the Babylonians was not a disaster but an occasion of divine testing (32:31) that was of no further consequence. The Chronicler retains the order of events found in the earlier history, but he uses them to show that destiny is determined by faithfulness to the Lord.

THEOLOGY OF CHRONICLES
David and the Temple
The study of Chronicles was changed by Gerhard von Rad, who recognized that Chronicles deserved to be studied as an independent theological work. His now-classic study *Das Geschichtsbild des chronistischen Werkes* (The historical picture of the work of Chronicles) distinguishes the Chronicler's concepts of the people of Israel, the interpretation of the law, and the historical traditions until Saul, concluding with the significance of the reign of David [*Torah*, p. 481].

> In the opinion of the Chronicler, a whole new era of the history of the people of God begins with David. Here the loosely connected genealogies end, and the Chronicler comes to his main theme: David—David and the cult personnel, David and the temple, David and the cult, David and Israel. (von Rad 1930: 134 AT)

The centrality of David in Chronicles is not just to focus on the proper function of the temple, though this concern is consistently present. The Chronicler's views are clear in David's words to the entire congregation of Israel:

> Yet the LORD, the God of Israel, chose me from my whole family to be king over Israel forever. He chose Judah as leader, and from the tribe of Judah he chose my family, and from my father's sons he was pleased to make me king over all Israel. Of all my sons—and the LORD has given me many—he has chosen my son Solomon to sit on the throne of the kingdom of the LORD over Israel. He said to me: "Solomon your son is the one who will build my house and my courts, for I have chosen him to be my son, and I will be his father. I will establish his kingdom forever if he is unswerving in carrying out my commands and laws, as is being done at this time." (1 Chron 28:4-7)

Two points are made in David's speech: the promise of an eternal kingdom is vested in David and Solomon; and the presence of the temple authenticates their representation of God's rule on earth. This theology drives the need for building the temple, in both the time of David and the time of the Chronicler. It is fully in keeping with the confessions of the Psalter.

> Yahweh reigns;
>   let the peoples tremble.
> He reigns between the cherubim;
>   let the earth shake.
>
> Great is Yahweh in Zion;
>   he is exalted over all peoples.
> Let them praise your great and fearful name.
>   He is holy!
>
> The king is mighty;
>   he loves justice.
> You have established fairness;
>   justice and righteousness is in Jacob.
>   You have done it.
>
> Exalt Yahweh, our God;
>   worship at the footstool of his feet.
>   He is holy! (Ps 99:1-5 AT)

Several points relevant to Chronicles become evident in rendering the Psalm in strophes. The psalm is marked by the repeated refrain of holiness, which grants this phrase a particular emphasis. The second stanza, not quoted above, concludes with a variation of the lines that introduce it in verse 5:

> Exalt Yahweh, our God;
> > worship at the mountain of his holiness.
> > for Yahweh our God is holy! (Ps 99:9 AT)

Holiness sets the sovereignty of God beyond the realm of the created order, but his throne within the temple manifests the presence of his rule within the created order. Particular reference is made to the divine throne room. Cherubim form the sides of the throne, and the ark is the footstool, where worship is to take place. The ark is important to the Chronicler as the central artifact in the temple. The temple is the divine palace, the confession of the rule of Yahweh over all the earth. The confession of worship needs to be clear and consistent. For this reason the activities of David and Solomon have their focus on the preparation and building of the temple, including all of its varied personnel and activities. The importance of the temple is inseparable from that of the king (Newsome: 211). The king must give attention to the symbolic confession of God's reign, for his own reign is a gift from God. The king is completely dependent.

The location of the ark is in Zion. This is God's chosen hill and therefore his holy hill. The Chronicler makes much of the divine choice of Zion made through David. Yet this rule of God is not distant and abstract; it finds its particular manifestation in Jacob. Justice and equity are revealed by God for his people and exercised through their king. These must never be taken for anything less than an act of God: *You have done it* is emphatic as the concluding line of the strophe, just before the refrain calling for worship at the temple. God has created his people as the means by which his rule may be manifest on earth.

God, Justice, and Faithfulness
This exalted nature of the divine rule is a fearful thing; the name *Yahweh* is not merely awesome (Ps 99:3 NIV), it should also evoke fear. Kings exercise judgment, and the same is no less true for God. In the Deuteronomistic History, divine judgment is largely collective. Covenant failure drove the nation into exile. The Chronicler takes a much more individual view. Judgment falls on the individual, usually the king, within his lifetime. This *immediate retribution* provides a dominant compositional technique, particularly formative in the narration of the history of Judah after the schism (Dillard 1984: 165). This is already suggested in the words of David to Solomon before all Israel in 1 Chronicles 28:8-9.

> And you, my son Solomon, acknowledge the God of your father, and serve him with wholehearted devotion and with a willing mind, for the LORD searches every heart and understands every desire and every thought. If you seek him, he will be found by you; but if you forsake him, he will reject you forever. (1 Chron 28:9)

Second Chronicles 7:14 states this programmatically in the divine revelation to Solomon after he has built the temple. Although such judgment never falls on Solomon, a faithful king in Chronicles, it is a recurring theme. Unfaithfulness brings rebuke and punishment.

It is unfortunate that the tag "theology of immediate retribution" has become descriptive of the *Tendenz* of the Chronicler. Retribution connotes punishment *[Tendenz in Chronicles, p. 476]*. While this is not inaccurate—the Chronicler includes many examples of such judgment—the fear of God is intended to inspire faithfulness that brings reward. If the term *retribution* is to be used of Chronicles, the term must be understood to include the opposite of what it usually connotes. Asa and Jehoshaphat are good examples of this concept of divine governance. The reign of Jehoshaphat is modeled on that of Asa (Dillard 1986: 18–20). The reigns of Asa and Jehoshaphat are presented in parallel topical sequences: religious reform, building programs, and large armies (2 Chron 14:2-8; 17:1-19). Then their patterns diverge slightly before ending poorly. Asa goes to battle seeking God's help (14:9-15), conducts religious reform (15:1-19), then seeks foreign alliances for which he is criticized (16:1-9), and he ends poorly and dies (16:10-14). Jehoshaphat goes to battle seeking alliance with an ungodly Israelite king, for which he is criticized (18:1–19:3), conducts religious reforms (19:4-11), then goes to battle seeking God's help (20:1-30), then makes an ungodly alliance and dies (20:31–21:1). In both cases, fidelity and obedience are rewarded with building programs, wealth and honor, peace and victory—but infidelity is greeted with swift rebuke by a prophet (16:7-10; 19:1-3) and punishment (16:11-13; 20:35-37). The Chronicler is consistent in stressing God's justice in his dealing with individual kings. When the fear of God fails, unfaithfulness ensues, with the related loss of blessing and experience of judgment. In the theology of the Chronicler, blessing and judgment pertain to individual kings, but the consequences extend to all those under his rule.

Blessing and Hope
The *Tendenz* of the Chronicler is to demonstrate that there is no state of judgment beyond the reach of mercy and forgiveness. In the account of the Judean kings, Ahaz brings the people to a virtual state of exile. Ahaz is followed by Hezekiah, a second Solomon in bringing together north and south in unity of worship around the temple. The most striking example is Manasseh. In Chronicles, his grievous sin is in subverting the worship of God (2 Chron 33:1-9), but judgment in Chronicles is immediate. The Assyrians made Manasseh a prisoner in Babylon. There the wicked king humbled himself and prayed. God heard his prayer, and the repentant king was restored to his throne, becoming one of the most influential in rebuilding and fortifying Judah (vv. 14-16). There is consistent testimony to the possibility of forgiveness and restoration, a message the people of Yehud needed to put into practice.

The possibility of blessing has implications for the eschatology of the Chronicler, the vision of God's ultimate plan for the people of Israel. Future destiny is never made explicit in Chronicles, but it is present in the impact of the history. Interpretations of the Chronicler's eschatology range from the belief that the people worshiping around the temple constitute their hope, to the belief that the Chronicler anticipated some type of future fulfillment concerning the promise of the Davidic kingdom (Klein 1992: 1000). Wilhelm Rudolph denied that Chronicles has any future eschatology. Chronicles stood on the fringe of the canon, without expectations that a descendant of David might rule. For him, any future promise was realized in the establishment of the second temple (Rudolph: xxiii).

But it is not so certain the Chronicler had abandoned hope in the Davidic promise for a greater future. Various references to the Lord's promise to David point to future fulfillment beyond establishing the second temple. The Chronicler quotes Psalm 132:10 in his version of the ark's installation in 2 Chronicles 6:41-42. The variations may be significant (Williamson 1977b: 143–44). The Chronicler has reversed the last two lines in remembering the steadfast love of David. Psalm 132:10 reads, "For your servant David's sake, do not turn away the face of your anointed one" (AT). Chronicles reads, *O Lord God, do not turn away the face of your anointed one! Remember your sure mercies for your servant David* (2 Chron 6:42 AT). The Chronicler decisively removes an ambiguity present in the Psalm. "For your servant David's sake" in Psalm 132:10 could refer either to David's loyalty to God or God's promise to David. The concluding phrase in Chronicles, in the language of Isaiah 55:3b, removes this ambiguity. Solomon implores God to remember your sure mercies for David. Hope is based the divine promise to David, as is evident in Isaiah, which has its entire focus on the eschatological hope of Israel.

Another example of the Davidic promise may be found in the speech of Abijah in 2 Chronicles 13:5-8. The prophet refers to the kingdom of Yahweh *in the power of the sons of David* (v. 8 AT). Such a phrase at least suggests the expectation that the dynasty of David continues. A similar sentiment may be found in the near extinction of the dynasty during the days Jehoram son of Jehoshaphat: *Nevertheless, because of the covenant the Lord had made with David, the Lord was not willing to destroy the house of David. He had promised to maintain a lamp for him and his descendants forever* (2 Chron 21:7). The Chronicler says *house of David*, replacing "Judah" in 2 Kings 8:19; he also adds the phrase *because of the covenant the Lord had made with David* in place of "for the sake of his servant David." Through these changes the Chronicler heightens the message that the kingdom of Yahweh, as he refers to it, continues in David's descendants (1 Chron 28:5; 2 Chron 13:8). While there is promise of an eternal kingdom in 2 Samuel 7:13-15, the Chronicler articulates this more precisely as the kingdom of Yahweh, a phrase unique to him.

The Chronicler is never explicit about his eschatology. The clues that may be deduced allow for various possibilities, none of them mutually exclusive. The eschatology of the Chronicler may be the continuity of the royal house of David or the community worshiping at the temple. Either of these may be viewed as a continuation of the present or as moving toward an ideal future fulfillment. A fair summary is to say that the Chronicler is firmly planted in his present circumstance but longs for a future when God's people will fully realize the core values of God's kingdom. . . . We see an ideal David embedded within a priestly led community and an expectation of a future ideal that will arise from and for a community that remains faithful to the priorities already established at the temple. (Boda 2013: 245)

Such an eschatology is a firm hope for the faithful at any time in history.

TORAH This Hebrew word has a number of meanings. As a title, *Torah* means the Pentateuch *[Hebrew Canon, p. 467]*. In its most frequent use in Chronicles, it refers to the teachings of Moses, which are critical to the proper practice of covenant, especially in the confessions of temple ritual.

The Greek translators chose *nomos* as equivalent, which in English is generally rendered as "the Law [of Moses]." The word *law* is a good equivalent for *nomos*. In Greek culture, *nomos* has to do with customs or regulations that control society and regulate behavior. However, the Hebrew term *torah* has a whole different nuance. God gives his "instruction" about the world (how we relate to the universe) and how we should relate to each other (the values of ethics) in his Torah. The word *law* generally brings associations of law codes, the specific regulations that enable law enforcers to control behavior. In the covenant, *torah* does not function this way. It is God's teaching about life. These are the values his people must hold and express in daily life. Regulation of behavior belongs to the category of *mišpaṭim* (rules) in Exodus 21:1, in contrast to the *debarim* (words) which are the teachings of the covenant in Exodus 20:1. Rules derive from the word group for exercising judgment (*špṭ*). Every circumstance must be considered in such a way that the values and truths of Torah may direct the actions of those under the covenant.

The Chronicler is most concerned about the theological confessions of Torah, which pertain especially to the temple and its ritual. Kings are responsible to be sure that all this functions as prescribed by Moses. The Chronicler's large expansions of the reigns of David and Solomon deal with this aspect of Torah. This is not correctly represented by the English word *law*, which pertains to civil conduct; this is certainly not the conception of the Chronicler. Torah deals with sacred matters of worship, a way of thinking and living, not a code to be enforced and followed. Its stipulations for human relationships under the covenant were the responsibility of kings, judges, and other officials, but these were not treated as modern law code. All ancient covenants expressed values of authority, life, and property that were used to arbitrate situations of conflict.

For lack of a suitable English equivalent, this commentary uses the word Torah consistently, a transliteration of the Hebrew. It refers to those covenant teachings and values that are to inform the faithful of how they are to think and live in the world.

WAR IN CHRONICLES Chronicles is a history written to inspire hope for a kingdom of peace. The history from which the Chronicler derives his hope abounds in military conflict. War is imbedded in every stage of

Israelite history; in Chronicles, however, war serves a particular pedagogical purpose. "Battle accounts in Chronicles serve primarily to establish, maintain, and legitimate a 'historical' norm of a united Israel at peace in their ancestral land under a Davidic monarch, with the proper priestly and Levitical personnel officiating at the Jerusalem temple" (Wright 1997: 175). This ideal depends on complete faithfulness to the Lord alone. Battle accounts in Chronicles conform to this ideal. Israel emerges in a land of peace. David fights against the enemies of Israel, and his reign ends in peace. But the price for this peace does not go unacknowledged. David is forbidden to build the temple, which represents the rule of God. David is a man of war who has shed much blood (1 Chron 22:8; 28:3). What is forbidden to David is mandated to Solomon, a man of rest/peace (22:9), as is implied in his name (šalom, peace; Šelomoh, Solomon). In Chronicles, war never touches Solomon or his kingdom. In Kings, Solomon is embroiled in war even within his own kingdom. Jeroboam, one of his most capable administrators, is forced to flee to Egypt (1 Kings 11:40), where he finds refuge with Shishak, the Egyptian pharaoh who later attacks Rehoboam (2 Chron 12).

Battle accounts serve a pedagogical purpose in Chronicles. The narrative moves to a kingdom of peace under a Davidic king. This kingdom is never exclusive of conflict, but it is protected from being destroyed by conflict. In Chronicles there is an exile of Transjordan, but no explicit Assyrian exile of the north. Sennacherib's siege of Jerusalem results in Hezekiah's prosperity. Jerusalem suffers one defeat under the Babylonians because of the people's unfaithfulness. In this final defeat, not only Zedekiah but also the Jerusalem priesthood is implicated in being unfaithful (2 Chron 36:14). The defeat of Jerusalem is the converse of the kingdom envisaged by the Chronicler in every aspect: king, priesthood, temple, and people.

Warfare is divine judgment that destroys the kingdom. This is true for every military loss in Chronicles. The temple was destroyed; king and people were taken captive to Babylon. But the book does not end without hope for a kingdom of peace. Cyrus the Persian grants permission for Israel to return to Jerusalem, with a mandate to build the temple, much as David went up to Jerusalem to make provisions for temple building (2 Chron 36:22-23). The land has rest without the presence of a Davidic king, a temple, or priests and Levites.

The Chronicler's account of history does not treat battles as individual and isolated events, but as general historical portrayals of different periods. Battle accounts in the genealogies portray a distinct and revolutionary concept of Israel as aboriginals in the land (Japhet 1989: 374-79). There is no conquest; the exile is limited to the Transjordanian tribes. The Chronicler's narrative and a critically reconstructed history may at points converge, but the Chronicler has no interest in the impact of particular wars. The Chronicler seems to have had access to other traditions of the emergence of Israel. He uses them to portray Israel as having a divinely ordained redemptive role among the nations. According to Chronicles, David is a man of war, never fights a losing battle, never fights against fellow Israelites, and never engages in cruel military conduct. Saul's demise comes at the hands of the Philistines because he was unfaithful. There are no wars between south and north in conflict with Saul as the northern king. David does fight offensive battles (1 Chron 18:1–20:8), expanding Israel's realm, collecting tribute, and maintaining honor. Tribute received does not aggrandize David but supplies materials for Solomon's construction of the temple. These wars are a preparation for the future kingdom. As David's reign enters its final phase, warfare ceases completely. Most of all, there is no question about dynastic succession. Solomon has unqualified support, without any necessity of dealing with rivals such as are found in 1 Kings 1–2. The life of a man of war ends with Israel at peace, having every provision for worshiping God in his splendid temple, with proper priestly and Levitical personnel already appointed.

There are many battles subsequent to Solomon, at times involving Judah against the northern tribes. But there are occasions where prophetic intervention mitigates or prevents conflict. The speech of Abijah to the armies of Jeroboam is a prominent example (2 Chron 13:1-12). All of these are wars of defense. All are either punishment because of unfaithfulness or wars of divine victory for the faithful. None is more distinguished than the attack of Sennacherib against Hezekiah: *After all that Hezekiah had so faithfully done, Sennacherib king of Assyria came and invaded Judah* (2 Chron 32:1). Hezekiah makes all the proper military preparations, but the victory came about through the prayers of Hezekiah and Isaiah (v. 20). The divine agent liquidated the mighty Assyrian armies in a single stroke, with no human intervention.

The Chronicler never suggests that there is no need for an army or that soldiers may not be engaged in battle. But these are never relevant to the outcome; frequently the vastly superior army is defeated and disgraced, as with Sennacherib. Large military forces are a sign of God's blessing for a faithful king, but they never have anything to do with military success. Military is engaged in every aspect of the divine kingdom. The registry of the priests in Jerusalem after the return summarizes by saying they were *one thousand seven hundred and sixty mighty warriors (gibbore ḥel), doing the work of serving in the house of God* (1 Chron 9:13 AT). John Wright shows that the Chronicler uses the term ḥyl exclusively with a military sense (Wright 1990: 70–71). Even when the military context is not explicit, as in this reference, the sense is not exclusive of military. While these are described as capable priests, the description chosen by the Chronicler aligns them with his concept that these are warriors in service of the temple. Although the names are largely drawn from Nehemiah 11:10-14, the description of the priests as warriors doing the work of the temple is unique to Chronicles. Such metaphors are natural to his work. Thus in the days of Jehoshaphat, a Levite rallies the troops against the Moabite coalition (2 Chron 20:14); and a Levitical musician adorned in sacred garments leads the soldiers into battle (v. 21). Military is as integral to the work and praise of God as any other aspect of the kingdom.

Israel is not conceived as a state, with various functions of government. It is a nation gathered to be the kingdom that God has ordained. They function in a temporal world, but they do not function as the temporal world. There are no military lessons to be learned from the Chronicler, nor is there a military history. There is no point in trying to reconstruct the influence of the military in the fortunes of the nation. Military is part of divine activity. Susan Niditch suggests that Chronicles provides an "extended critique of human participation in the violence of war and a potential for an ideology of nonparticipation" (Niditch: 139). But the Chronicler does not shrink from human engagement in war as part of God bringing about the kingdom. Nor can war be reinterpreted as part of liturgical acts, as holy war has sometimes been defined. In Chronicles, war is a part of history and endemic to human society. But in his view, humans do not determine the destiny of society, and therefore human warfare does not determine the fortunes of God's kingdom, as it does for all other kingdoms.

The Chronicler's view of war is not comparable to other biblical literature. In the Deuteronomistic History, warfare has much more of the usual aspect of human conflict, amid political opportunism and struggle. In apocalyptic writings, warfare belongs to God, with the primary focus on a cataclysmic final battle that ends all wars. In the New Testament, control by coercive force for the sake of maintaining peace and order is to be recognized as the responsibility of government (Rom 13:1-7; 1 Pet 2:13-17). Christians are exhorted to submit to these powers, to show them respect, and not to revolt against them. Revolt was the tendency of many Jewish sects in New Testament times, resulting in Jews being expelled entirely from the very city they considered sacred. Followers of "the [Jesus] Way" were not to have any part of that kind of attitude toward war. In the view of the Chronicler, rest and wealth will come to Jerusalem once the proper institutions are established, as a result of international fame when the Lord delivers Jerusalem from all its foes. This is predicated on exclusive fidelity to God, in part by supporting the whole temple structure. This never happened in the Chronicler's day, and it is not clear how his thinking may have influenced later understandings of war, such as the Hasmonean battles, the Qumran ideology, or apocalyptic thinking. The Chronicler's view of the role of war in God's program is open to the future, much like the rest of his eschatology [*Chronology in Chronicles*, p. 460].

Several points are clear for the Christian. Life must be lived for the kingdom of God. Each individual has only one life to give; such an ultimate sacrifice must be worthy of serving the kingdom of God. If the Chronicler has a theology to be followed, it is that human warfare does not determine the destiny of human society. Reliance on the power of military has been the way of power in this world, but the kingdom of the Christian is not of this world. A third point is that it is the responsibility of human government to protect its citizens from violence (Gen 9:6). Though government is faulty, often being the beast that tramples its own people, it still is the temporal means of restraining society from anarchy like that of Lamech (4:23-24), which leads to universal destruction like that of the flood (6:5). Unlike the times of the Chronicler, the nature and mission of the church is such that it has no direct engagement in temporal rule. Historically, when such powers have been possible, the result has been nothing short of complete disaster.

But the church does have a role in instructing individual citizens of the kingdom on the complicated ethical decisions they face in particular places and circumstances. In modern times, these issues have changed extremely rapidly. Technology has made engagement in warfare a matter of machines destroying people in an increasingly remote manner. Chronicles has little to contribute directly to such ethical deliberations. The contribution of Chronicles is more philosophical and theological. Citizens of the kingdom must make fidelity to God and service in praise to his name their fundamental priority at all times. God wins wars on behalf of those faithful in service to him. God will end all human wars in the fullness of his King and kingdom.

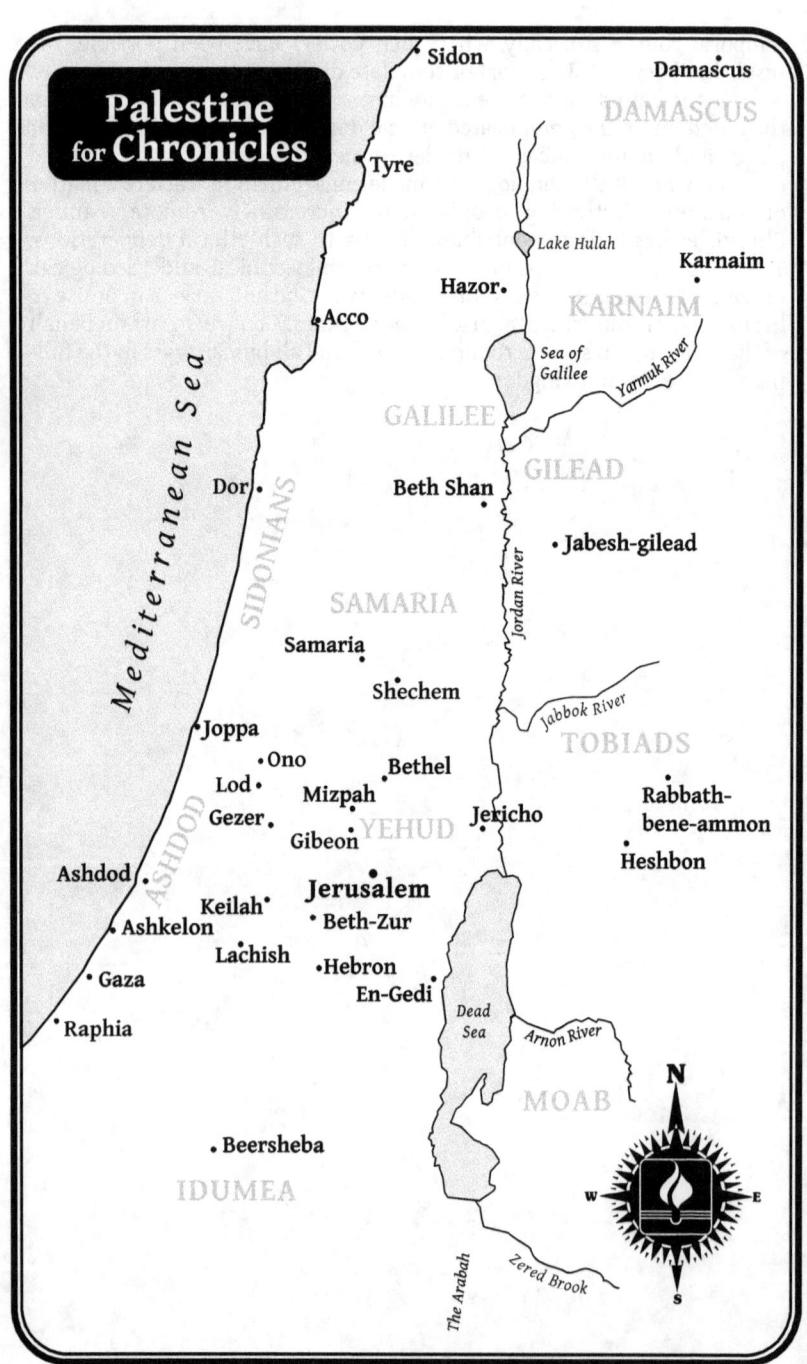

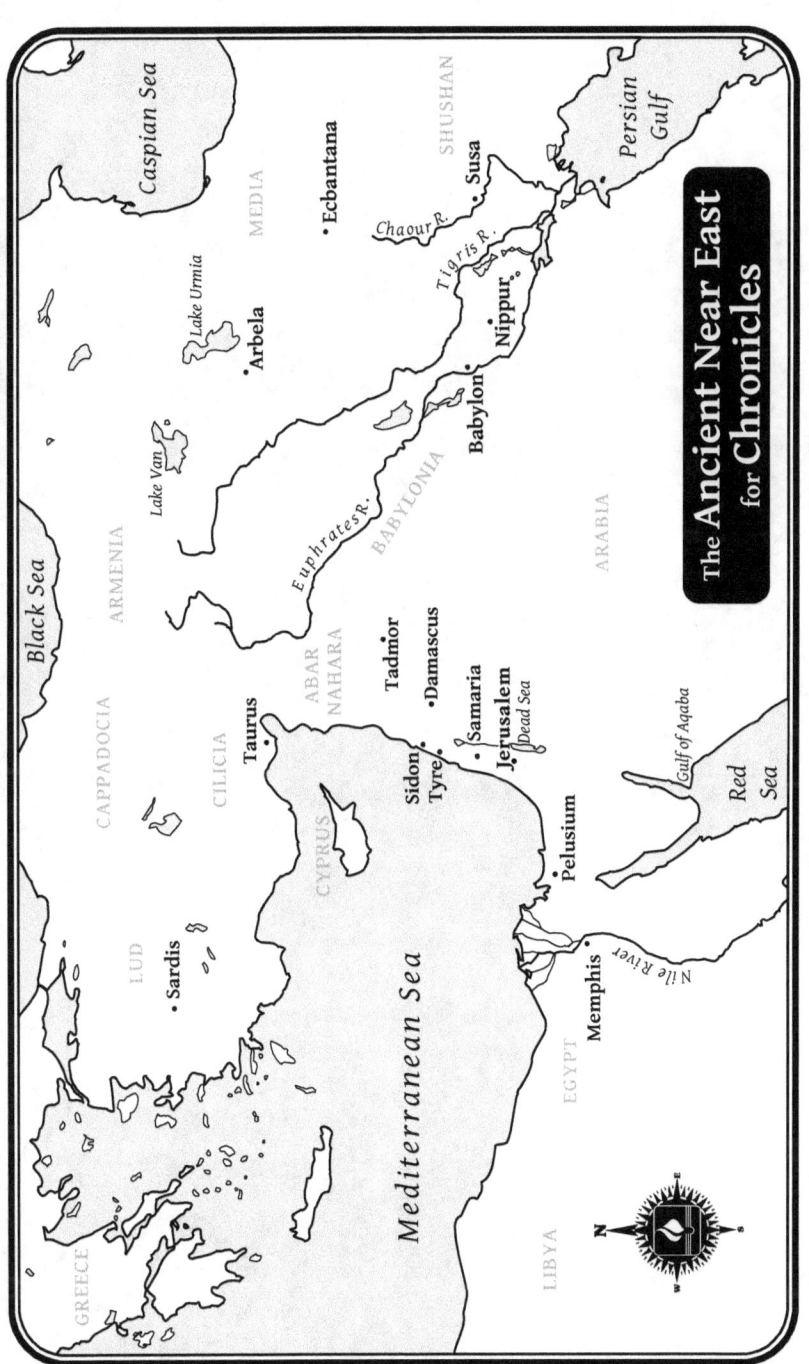

Bibliography

Aharoni, Yohanan
1979 *The Land of the Bible: A Historical Geography*. Rev. ed. Philadelphia: Westminster.
Aharoni, Yohanan, Anson Rainey, Michael Avi-Yonah, and Ze'ev Safrai
2002 *The Carta Bible Atlas*. 4th ed. Jerusalem: Carta.
Ahlström, Gösta W.
1993 *The History of Ancient Palestine*. Minneapolis: Fortress.
Albright, William F.
1921 "The Date and Personality of the Chronicler." *Journal of Biblical Literature* 40:104-24.
1941 "The Land of Damascus between 1850 and 1750 B.C." *Bulletin of the American Schools of Oriental Research* 83:30-36.
Allen, Leslie C.
1974 *The Greek Chronicles: The Relation of the Septuagint of I and II Chronicles to the Masoretic Text*. Leiden: Brill.
Assis, Elie
2006 "From Adam to Esau and Israel: An Anti-Edomite Ideology in 1 Chronicles." *Vetus Testamentum* 56:287-302.
Auld, A. Graeme
1994 *Kings without Privilege: David and Moses in the Story of the Bible's Kings*. Edinburgh: T&T Clark.
Barnouin, Michel
1977 "Les recensements du livre des nombres et l'astronomie Babylonienne." *Vetus Testamentum* 27:280-303.
Berger, Yitzhak
2007 *The Commentary of Rabbi David Kimḥi to Chronicles: A Translation with Introduction and Supercommentary*. Brown Judaic Studies 345. Providence, RI: Brown University Press.
Biran, Avraham
1998 "Sacred Spaces: Of Standing Stones, High Places and Cult Objects at Tel Dan. *Biblical Archaeology Review* 24/5:38-45, 70.

Boda, Mark J.
    2010   *1-2 Chronicles*. Edited by Philip Wesley Comfort. Cornerstone Biblical Commentary 5A. Carol Stream, IL: Tyndale House.
    2013   "Gazing through the Cloud of Incense: Davidic Dynasty and Temple Community in the Chronicler's Perspective." In *Chronicling the Chronicler: The Book of Chronicles and Early Second Temple Historiography*, edited by Paul S. Evans and Tyler F. Williams, 215-45. Winona Lake, IN: Eisenbrauns.

Bonk, Jonathan
    2003   "Defender of the Good News." *Christianity Today* 47/10:112-16.

Braun, Roddy L.
    1986   *1 Chronicles*. Word Biblical Commentary 14. Waco: Word.
    1997   "1 Chronicles 1-9 and the Reconstruction of the History of Israel: Thoughts on the Use of Genealogical Data in Chronicles in the Reconstruction of the History of Israel." In *The Chronicler as Theologian*, edited by M. Patrick Graham, Steven L. McKenzie, and Gary N. Knoppers, 92-105. Journal for the Study of the Old Testament Supplement Series 238. Sheffield: Sheffield Academic Press.

Broshi, Magen
    1974   "The Expansion of Jerusalem in the Reigns of Hezekiah and Manasseh." *Israel Exploration Journal* 24:21-26.

Brown, Francis, S. R. Driver, and Charles A. Briggs
    1951   *A Hebrew and English Lexicon of the Old Testament with an Appendix Containing the Biblical Aramaic*. Oxford: Clarendon Press.

Bruce, F. F.
    1958   *The Spreading Flame: The Rise and Progress of Christianity from Its First Beginnings to the Conversion of the English*. Grand Rapids: Eerdmans.

Cary, Earnest
    1937   *Roman Antiquities of Dionysius of Halicarnassus*. Loeb Classical Library 319. Cambridge, MA: Harvard University Press.

Childs, Brevard S.
    1967   *Isaiah and the Assyrian Crisis*. Studies in Biblical Theology 2/3. London: SCM.

Clark, Christopher M.
    2012   *The Sleepwalkers: How Europe Went to War in 1914*. New York: Harper.

Cogan, Mordechai
    1974   *Imperialism and Religion: Assyria, Judah, and Israel in the Eighth and Seventh Centuries B.C.* Society of Biblical Literature Monograph Series 19. Missoula, MT: Scholars Press.
    2001   *1 Kings*. Anchor Bible 10. New York: Doubleday.

Cogan, Mordechai, and Hayim Tadmor
    1988   *2 Kings*. Anchor Bible 11. New York: Doubleday.

Collins, John J.
    2010   *The Scepter and the Star: Messianism in Light of the Dead Sea Scrolls*. 2nd ed. Grand Rapids: Eerdmans.

Cross, Frank Moore
    1975   "A Reconstruction of the Judean Restoration." *Journal of Biblical Literature* 94:4-18.

Cross, Frank Moore, Donald Parry, and E. Ulrich
    2005   *Qumran Cave 4.XII: 1-2 Samuel*. Discoveries in the Judaean Desert 17. Oxford: Clarendon.

Bibliography

Curtis, Edward Lewis, and Albert Alonzo Madsen
    1910   *A Critical and Exegetical Commentary on the Books of Chronicles.* International Critical Commentary. New York: Scribner.

Daoud, Ali
    2003   "Tree Formations around Places of Worship in the Near East." *Unasylva* 54/213:47-52. ftp://ftp.fao.org/docrep/fao/005/y9882e/y9882e09.pdf.

Demsky, Aaron
    1988   "Writing in Ancient Israel: The Biblical Period." In *Mikra: Text, Translation, Reading and Interpretation of the Hebrew Bible in Ancient Judaism and Early Christianity*, edited by Martin Jan Mulder, 2-20. Compendia Rerum Iudaicarum ad Novum Testamentum 2/1. Philadelphia: Fortress.

De Vries, Simon
    1989   *1 and 2 Chronicles.* Forms of the Old Testament Literature 11. Grand Rapids: Eerdmans.

Dillard, Raymond B.
    1980   "The Chronicler's Solomon." *Westminster Theological Journal* 43/2:289-300.
    1984   "Reward and Punishment in Chronicles: The Theology of Immediate Retribution." *Westminster Theological Journal* 46/1:164-72.
    1986   "The Chronicler's Jehoshaphat." *Trinity Journal* 7/1:17-22.
    1987   *2 Chronicles.* Word Biblical Commentary 15. Waco: Word.

Dyck, Cornelius J.
    1995   *Spiritual Life in Anabaptism.* Scottdale, PA: Herald Press.

Dyck, Jonathan E.
    1998   *The Theocratic Ideology of the Chronicler.* Leiden: Brill.

Elwes, R. H. M.
    1951   *The Chief Works of Benedict de Spinoza.* Vol. 1. New York: Dover.

Eskenazi, Tamara C.
    1986   "The Chronicler and the Composition of 1 Esdras." *Catholic Biblical Quarterly* 48:39-61.

Flint, Peter W.
    1998   "The Book of Psalms in the Light of the Dead Sea Scrolls." *Vetus Testamentum* 48:453-72.

Freedman, David Noel
    1961   "The Chronicler's Purpose." *Catholic Biblical Quarterly* 23:436-42.

Friedman, Richard Elliot
    1992   "Tabernacle." In *Anchor Bible Dictionary*, edited by David Noel Freedman, 6:292-300. New York: Doubleday.

Fulford, Robert
    2013   "Pauline Marois' Monocultural Dream." *National Post*, August 24. http://news.nationalpost.com/full-comment/robert-fulford-pauline-marois-monocultural-dream.

Gasque, W. Ward
    1982   "Jew." *International Standard Bible Encyclopedia*, edited by G. W. Bromiley, 2:1056. Rev. ed. Grand Rapids: Eerdmans.

Gellately, Robert
    2013   *Stalin's Curse: Battling for Communism in War and Cold War.* New York: Knopf.

Geoghegan, Jeffrey C.
    2003   "'Until This Day' and the Preexilic Redaction of the Deuteronomistic History." *Journal of Biblical Literature* 122:201–27.

Gerbrandt, Henry J.
    1970   *Adventure in Faith: The Background in Europe and the Development in Canada of the Bergthaler Mennonite Church of Manitoba*. Altona, MB: Friesen & Sons.

Gill, Dan
    1994   "How They Met: Geology Solves the Long-Standing Mystery of Hezekiah's Tunnelers." *Biblical Archaeology Review* 20/4:20–33, 64.

Goldingay, John
    1975   "The Chronicler as Theologian." *Biblical Theology Bulletin* 5:99–126.

Haran, Menahem
    1999   "The Books of the Chronicles 'of the Kings of Judah' and 'the Kings of Israel': What Sort of Books Were They?" *Vetus Testamentum* 49/2:156–64.

Hess, Richard S.
    2002   "Literacy in Iron Age Israel." In *Windows into Old Testament History: Evidence, Argument, and the Crisis of "Biblical Israel,"* edited by V. P. Long, D. W. Baker, and G. J. Wenham, 82–102. Grand Rapids: Eerdmans.

Hitchens, Christopher
    2007   *God Is Not Great: How Religion Poisons Everything*. New York: Hachette.

Holland, Tom
    2013   *Herodotus: The Histories*. New York: Penguin.

Huizinga, Johan
    1936   "A Definition of the Concept of History." In *Philosophy and History: Essays Presented to Ernst Cassirer*, edited by R. Klibansky and H. J. Paton, 1–10. Oxford: Clarendon.

Hunter, James Davison
    2010   *To Change the World: The Irony, Tragedy, and Possibility of Christianity in the Late Modern World*. Oxford: Oxford University Press.

Japhet, Sara
    1968   "The Supposed Common Authorship of Chronicles and Ezra-Nehemiah Investigated Anew." *Vetus Testamentum* 18:330–71.
    1979   "Conquest and Settlement in Chronicles." *Journal of Biblical Literature* 98:205–18.
    1987   "Interchanges of Hebrew Roots in Parallel Texts in Chronicles." *Hebrew Studies* 28:9–50.
    1989   *The Ideology of the Book of Chronicles and Its Place in Biblical Thought*. Beiträge zur Erforschung des Alten Testaments und des Antiken Judentums 9. Frankfurt: Lang; Freiburg: Herder.
    1993   *I & II Chronicles: A Commentary*. Old Testament Library. Louisville: Westminster John Knox.
    2006   *From the Rivers of Babylon to the Highlands of Judah: Collected Studies on the Restoration Period*. Winona Lake, IN: Eisenbrauns.

Jenni, Ernst, and Claus Westermann, eds.
    1976   *Theologisches Handwörterbuch zum Alten Testament*. 2 vols. Munich: Kaiser; Zurich: Theologischer.

Jeon, Yong Ho
    2013   *Impeccable Solomon? A Study of Solomon's Faults in Chronicles*. Eugene, OR: Pickwick.

Bibliography

Jerome
- 1864 *Hieronymus [Jerome]*, vol. 1. Vol. 22 of *Patrologia Latina*. Edited by J.-P. Migne. Paris. Reprinted, Ridgewood, NJ: Gregg, 1965.
- 1893 *St. Jerome: Letters and Select Works*. Translated by W. H. Fremantle. Vol. 6 of *A Select Library of the Nicene and Post-Nicene Fathers of the Christian Church*. Christian Literature Publishing. http://www.bible-researcher.com/jerome.html#note2.

Johnson, E. Elizabeth
- 1989 *The Function of Apocalyptic and Wisdom Traditions in Romans 9–11*. Society of Biblical Literature Dissertation Series 109. Atlanta: Scholars Press.

Kalimi, Isaac
- 2002 "The View of Jerusalem in the Ethnographical Introduction of Chronicles (1 Chron 1–9)." *Biblica* 83:556–62.
- 2005a *The Reshaping of Ancient Israelite History in Chronicles*. Winona Lake, IN: Eisenbrauns.
- 2005b *An Ancient Israelite Historian: Studies in the Chronicler, His Time, Place and Writing*. Assen: Van Gorcum.

Katzenstein, H. Jacob
- 1973 *The History of Tyre*. Jerusalem: Schocken Institute for Jewish Research of the Jewish Theological Seminary of America.

Keel, Othmar
- 1997 *The Symbolism of the Biblical World: Ancient Near Eastern Iconography and the Book of Psalms*. Winona Lake, IN: Eisenbrauns.

Keneally, Thomas
- 1982 *Schindler's List*. [A novel.] New York: Simon & Schuster.

Klein, Ralph W.
- 1992 "Chronicles, Book of 1–2." In *Anchor Bible Dictionary*, edited by David Noel Freedman, 1:992–1002. New York: Doubleday.
- 1998 *1 Samuel*. Word Biblical Commentary 10. Dallas: Word.
- 2006 *1 Chronicles: A Commentary*. Hermeneia. Minneapolis: Fortress.
- 2012 *2 Chronicles: A Commentary*. Hermeneia. Minneapolis: Fortress.

Knauf, Ernst Axel
- 1992 "Meunim." In *Anchor Bible Dictionary*, edited by David Noel Freedman, 4:801–2. New York: Doubleday.

Knoppers, Gary A.
- 1993 *The Reign of Solomon and the Rise of Jeroboam*. Vol. 1 of *Two Nations under God: The Deuteronomic History of Solomon and the Dual Monarchies*. Harvard Semitic Monographs 52. Atlanta: Scholars Press.
- 1995 "Prayer and Propaganda: The Dedication of Solomon's Temple and the Deuteronomist's Program." *Catholic Biblical Quarterly* 57:229–54.
- 1996 "Ancient Near Eastern Royal Grants and the Davidic Covenant: A Parallel?" *Journal of the American Oriental Society* 116:670–97.
- 1999 "Hierodules, Priests, or Janitors? The Levites in Chronicles and the History of the Israelite Priesthood." *Journal of Biblical Literature* 118:49–72.
- 2004a *1 Chronicles 1–9*. Anchor Bible 12. New York: Doubleday.
- 2004b *1 Chronicles 10–29*. Anchor Bible 12A. New York: Doubleday.

Konkel, August H.
- 1987 *Hezekiah in Biblical Tradition*. Ann Arbor, MI: University Microfilms International.
- 1993 "The Sources of the Hezekiah Story in Isaiah." *Vetus Testamentum* 43:462–82.
- 1997 "gwr." In *New International Dictionary of Old Testament Theology and Exegesis*, edited by W. A. VanGemeren, 1:836–39. Grand Rapids: Zondervan.
- 2006 *1 & 2 Kings*. NIV Application Commentary. Grand Rapids: Zondervan.

Lance, H. Darrell
- 1992 "Stamps, Royal Jar Handle." In *Anchor Bible Dictionary*, edited by David Noel Freedman, 6:184–85. New York: Doubleday.

Levenson, Jonathan D.
- 2001 "How Not to Conduct Jewish-Christian Dialogue." *Commentary* 112/5: 31–37.

Levin, Yigal
- 2003 "Who Was the Chronicler's Audience? A Hint from His Genealogies." *Journal of Biblical Literature* 122:229–45.
- 2004 "From Lists to History: Chronological Aspects of the Chronicler's Genealogies." *Journal of Biblical Literature* 123:601–36.

L'Heureux, Conrad E.
- 1976 "The *yĕlîdê hārāpāʾ*: A Cultic Association of Warriors." *Bulletin of American Schools of Oriental Research* 221:83–85.

Lind, Millard
- 1980 *Yahweh Is a Warrior: The Theology of Warfare in Ancient Israel*. Scottdale, PA: Herald Press.

Lipinski, Edward
- 2014 "Edward Lipinski Responds." *Biblical Archaeology Review* 40/3:8–11.

Lonergan, Bernard
- 1972 *Method in Theology*. New York: Herder & Herder.

Longhurst, John
- 2004 "Faith." *Winnipeg Free Press*, March 6, E-9.

Lyotard, Jean-François
- 1984 *The Postmodern Condition: A Report on Knowledge*. Translated by Geoff Bennington and Brian Massumi. Theory and History of Literature 10. Minneapolis: University of Minnesota Press.

MacMillan, Margaret
- 2013 *The War That Ended Peace: The Road to 1914*. New York: Random House.

Mazar, Amihai
- 1990 *Archaeology of the Land of the Bible: 10,000–586 B.C.E.* Anchor Yale Bible Reference Library. New York: Doubleday.

McCarter, P. Kyle, Jr.
- 1980 *I Samuel*. Anchor Bible 8. New York: Doubleday.
- 1984 *II Samuel*. Anchor Bible 9. New York: Doubleday.

Meyer, Eduard
- 1896 *Die Entstehung des Judentums: Eine historische Untersuchung*. Halle: Niemeyer.

Milgrom, Jacob
- 1976 *Cult and Conscience: The Asham and the Priestly Doctrine of Repentance*. Studies in Judaism in Late Antiquity 18. Leiden: Brill.

1983   *Studies in Cultic Theology and Terminology.* Studies in Judaism in Late Antiquity 36. Leiden: Brill.
1990   *Numbers.* Jewish Publication Society Torah Commentary. Philadelphia: Jewish Publication Society.
1991   *Leviticus 1-16.* Anchor Bible 3. New York: Doubleday.

Millard, Alan
1994   "King Solomon's Shields." In *Scripture and Other Artifacts: Essays on the Bible and Archaeology in Honor of Philip J. King,* edited by Michael Coogan, J. Cheryl Exum, Lawrence E. Stager, and Joseph A. Greene, 286-95. Louisville: Westminster John Knox.

Mitchell, Stephen
1992   *The Book of Job.* New York: Harper.

Mitchell, T. C.
1988   *Biblical Archaeology: Documents from the British Museum.* Cambridge: Cambridge University Press.

Monson, John M.
2000   "The New ʿAin Dara Temple: Closest Solomonic Parallel." *Biblical Archaeology Review* 26/3:20-35.

Moor, Johannes C. de
1987   *An Anthology of Religious Texts from Ugarit.* Religious Texts Translation Series, Nisaba 16. Leiden: Brill.

Moor, Johannes C. de, and Klaas Spronk
1987   *A Cuneiform Anthology of Religious Texts from Ugarit: Autographed Texts and Glossaries.* Semitic Study Series: New Series 6. Leiden: Brill.

Morgan, Timothy C.
2006   "Jabez Author Quits Africa: Disappointments Prompt Early Retirement." *Christianity Today* 50/2 (February): 76.

Mosis, Rudolf
1973   *Untersuchungen zur Theologie des chronistischen Geschichtswerkes.* Freiburger theologische Studien 92. Freiburg: Herder.

Newsome, James D.
1975   "Toward a New Understanding of the Chronicler and His Purposes." *Journal of Biblical Literature* 94/2:201-15.

Niditch, Susan
1993   *War in the Hebrew Bible: A Study in the Ethics of Violence.* New York: Oxford University Press.

Noss, David S., and Blake R. Grangaard
2008   *A History of the World's Religions.* 12th ed. Upper Saddle River, NJ: Pearson Prentice Hall.

Noth, Martin
1981   *The Deuteronomistic History.* Journal for the Study of the Old Testament Supplement Series 15. Sheffield: JSOT Press, 1981.

Parker, Simon
1994   "Siloam Inscription Memorializes Engineering Achievement." *Biblical Archaeology Review* 20/4:36-38.

Person, Raymond F., Jr.
2010   *Deuteronomic History and the Book of Chronicles: Scribal Works in an Oral World.* Society of Biblical Literature Ancient Israel and Its Literature 6. Atlanta: Society of Biblical Literature.

Pritchard, James B.
1961   "A Bronze Age Necropolis at Gibeon." *Biblical Archaeologist* 24/1:19-24.

Rad, Gerhard von
    1930   *Das Geschichtsbild des chronistischen Werkes*. Stuttgart: Kohlhammer.
    1966   "The Levitical Sermon in I and II Chronicles." In *The Problem of the Hexateuch and Other Essays*, 267–80. Edinburgh: Oliver & Boyd.

Rainey, Anson F.
    1970   "Compulsory Labour Gangs in Ancient Israel." *Israel Exploration Journal* 20:191–202.
    1979   "Beer-sheba." In *International Standard Bible Encyclopedia*. Edited by G. W. Bromiley. Rev. ed. 1:448–51. Grand Rapids, Eerdmans.
    1997   "The Chronicler and His Sources: Historical and Geographical." In *The Chronicler as Historian*, edited by M. Patrick Graham, Kenneth G. Hogland, and Steven L. McKenzie, 30–72. JSOTSup 238. Sheffield: Sheffield Academic Press.

Rainey, Anson F., and R. Steven Notley
    2006   *The Sacred Bridge: Carta's Atlas of the Biblical World*. Jerusalem: Carta.

Rendsburg, Gary
    1990   "The Internal Consistency and Historical Reliability of the Biblical Genealogies." *Vetus Testamentum* 40:185–206.

Rosenbaum, Jonathan
    1979   "Hezekiah's Reform and the Deuteronomic Tradition." *Harvard Theological Review* 72:23–43.

Rudolph, Wilhelm
    1955   *Chronikbücher*. Handbuch zum Alten Testament 21. Tübingen: Mohr.

Sanders, James A.
    1965   *The Psalms Scroll of Qumrân Cave 11 (11QPs^a)*. Discoveries in the Judean Desert of Jordan 4. Oxford: Clarendon.

Sawatzky, John
    1996   *One Out of Three: How My Family and I Survived Russian Communism*. Mountain Lake, MN: J. Sawatzky.

Sarna, Nahum M.
    1989   *Genesis*. Jewish Publication Society Torah Commentary. Philadelphia: Jewish Publication Society.
    1991   *Exodus*. Jewish Publication Society Torah Commentary. Philadelphia: Jewish Publication Society.

Schreiner, J., and G. Johannes Botterweck
    1990   "*yālad, yeled, yaldâ, yalĕdût, yālîd, tôlĕdôt*." In *Theological Dictionary of the Old Testament*, edited by G. Johannes Botterweck and Helmer Ringgren, 6:76–81. Grand Rapids: Eerdmans.

Schweitzer, Steven
    2013   "The Genealogies of 1 Chronicles 1–9: Purposes, Forms, and the Utopian Identity of Israel." In *Chronicling the Chronicler*, edited by Paul S. Evans and Tyler F. Williams, 9–27. Winona Lake, IN: Eisenbrauns.

Severy, Merle
    1983   "The World of Luther." *National Geographic* 164/4 (October): 418–63.

Snijders, L. A.
    1997   "*mālēʾ, mĕlōʾ, milluʾâ, milluʾîm, millôʾ*." In *Theological Dictionary of the Old Testament*, edited by G. Johannes Botterweck, Helmer Ringgren, and Heinz-Josef Fabry, 8:297–307. Grand Rapids: Eerdmans.

Spalinger, Anthony
    1992   "Egypt, History of: 3rd Intermediate-Saite Period (Dyn. 21–26)." In *Anchor Bible Dictionary*, edited by David Noel Freedman, 6:353–64. New York: Doubleday.

Sparks, James T.
    2008   *The Chronicler's Genealogies: Towards an Understanding of 1 Chronicles 1-9*. Academia Biblica. Atlanta: Society of Biblical Literature.

Sparks, Kenton L.
    2005   *Ancient Texts for the Study of the Hebrew Bible: A Guide to the Background Literature*. Peabody, MA: Hendrickson.

Stern, Ephraim
    2001   *The Assyrian, Babylonian, and Persian Periods (732-332 B.C.E.)*. Vol. 2 of *Archaeology of the Land of the Bible*. Anchor Yale Bible Reference Library. New York: Doubleday.

Stinespring, William Franklin
    1961   "Eschatology in Chronicles." *Journal of Biblical Literature* 80:209–19.

Talmon, Shemaryahu
    1958   "Divergences in Calendar-Reckoning in Ephraim and Judah." *Vetus Testamentum* 8/1:48–74.
    1976   "Ezra and Nehemiah." In *Interpreter's Dictionary of the Bible: Supplementary Volume*, edited by K. Crim, 317–28. Nashville: Abingdon.

Thiele, Edwin R.
    1983   *The Mysterious Numbers of the Hebrew Kings*. Grand Rapids: Zondervan.

Tigay, Jeffrey H.
    1996   *Deuteronomy*. Jewish Publication Society Torah Commentary. Philadelphia: Jewish Publication Society.

Toorn, Karel van der
    2007   *Scribal Culture and the Making of the Hebrew Bible*. Cambridge, MA: Harvard University Press.

Torrey, Charles C.
    1896   *The Composition and Historical Value of Ezra-Nehemiah*. Beihefte zur Zeitschrift für die alttestamentliche Wissenschaft 2. Giessen: Ricker.

Ussishkin, David
    1976   "The Original Length of the Siloam Tunnel in Jerusalem." *Levant* 8:82–95.
    1992   "Megiddo (Place)." In *Anchor Bible Dictionary*, edited by David Noel Freedman, 4:666–79. New York: Doubleday.
    1997   "Jezreel, Samaria and Megiddo: Royal Centers of Omri and Ahab." In *Congress Volume: Cambridge 1995*, edited by J. A. Emerton, 351–64. Supplements to Vetus Testamentum 46. Leiden: Brill.

Van Dam, Cornelis
    1988   "Urim and Thummim." In *International Standard Bible Encyclopedia*, edited by G. W. Bromiley, 4:957–59. Rev. ed. Grand Rapids: Eerdmans.
    1997   "ʾûrîm, tummîm." In *New International Dictionary of Old Testament Theology and Exegesis*, edited by W. A. VanGemeren, 1:329–31. Grand Rapids: Zondervan.

Van Seters, John
  1997 *In Search of History: Historiography in the Ancient World and the Origins of Biblical History.* Winona Lake, IN: Eisenbrauns.
Vaughn, Andrew G.
  1999 *Theology, History, and Archaeology in the Chronicler's Account of Hezekiah.* Archaeology and Biblical Studies 4. Atlanta: Scholars Press.
Waltke, Bruce K., and M. O'Connor
  1990 *An Introduction to Biblical Hebrew Syntax.* Winona Lake, IN: Eisenbrauns.
Weinfeld, Moshe
  1970 "The Covenant of Grant in the Old Testament and in the Ancient Near East." *Journal of the American Oriental Society* 90:184–203.
Welch, Adam C.
  1939 *The Work of the Chronicler: Its Purpose and Its Date.* London: Oxford University Press.
Wellhausen, Julius
  1885 *Prolegomena to the History of Ancient Israel.* Translated by J. Sutherland Black and A. Menzies. Edinburgh: A&C Black.
Wenham, John W.
  1967 "Large Numbers in the Old Testament." *Tyndale Bulletin* 18:19–53.
Wette, Wilhelm Martin Lebrecht de
  1850 *A Critical and Historical Introduction to the Canonical Scriptures of the Old Testament.* Vol. 2. 2nd ed. Boston: Little & Brown.
Wilkinson, Bruce
  2000 *The Prayer of Jabez: Breaking Through to the Blessed Life.* Sisters, OR: Multnomah.
Willi, Thomas
  1972 *Die Chronik als Auslegung: Untersuchungen zur literarischen Gestaltung der historischen Überlieferung Israels.* Göttingen: Vandenhoeck & Ruprecht.
Williamson, Hugh G. M.
  1976 "The Accession of Solomon in the Books of Chronicles." *Vetus Testamentum* 26:351–61.
  1977a *Israel in the Books of Chronicles.* Cambridge: Cambridge University Press.
  1977b "Eschatology in Chronicles." *Tyndale Bulletin* 28:115–54.
  1979 "The Origin of the Twenty-Four Priestly Courses: A Study of 1 Chronicles xxiii–xxvii." In *Studies in the Historical Books of the Old Testament*, edited by J. A. Emerton, 251–68. Leiden: Brill.
  1981 "'We Are Yours, O David': The Setting and Purpose of 1 Chronicles xii 1–23." In *Remembering All the Way: A Collection of Old Testament Studies*, edited by Bertil Albrektson, 164–76. Old Testament Studies 21. Leiden: Brill.
  1982 *1 and 2 Chronicles.* New Century Bible Commentary. Grand Rapids: Eerdmans.
  1991 "The Temple in the Books of Chronicles." In *Templum Amicitiae: Essays on the Second Temple Presented to Ernst Bammel*, edited by W. Horbury, 15–31. Journal for the Study of the New Testament Supplement Series 48. Sheffield: JSOT Press.

Bibliography

Wise, Michael O., Martin G. Abegg Jr., and Edward M. Cook
    2005   *The Dead Sea Scrolls: A New Translation*. New York: HarperOne.

Wright, John W.
    1990   "Guarding the Gates: 1 Chronicles 26.1–19 and the Roles of Gatekeepers in Chronicles." *Journal for the Study of the Old Testament* 48: 69–81.
    1991   "The Legacy of David in Chronicles: The Narrative Function of 1 Chronicles 23–27." *Journal of Biblical Literature* 110:229–42.
    1997   "The Fight for Peace." In *The Chronicler as Historian*, edited by M. Patrick Graham, Kenneth G. Hogland, and Steven L. McKenzie, 150–77. Journal for the Study of the Old Testament Supplement Series 238. Sheffield: Sheffield Academic Press.

Youngblood, Ronald F.
    1997   "*maśśāʾ*." In *New International Dictionary of Old Testament Theology and Exegesis*, edited by W. A. VanGemeren, 2:1112–13. Grand Rapids: Zondervan.

Younger, K. Lawson, Jr.
    1998   "The Deportations of the Israelites." *Journal of Biblical Literature* 117:201–27.
    2000   "Tiglath-pileser III." In *The Context of Scripture*, edited by W. W. Hallo and K. Lawson Younger Jr., 2:284–86. Leiden: Brill.

Zevit, Ziony
    2001   *The Religions of Ancient Israel: A Synthesis of Parallactic Approaches*. London: Continuum.

Selected Resources

Boda, Mark J. *1–2 Chronicles.* Cornerstone Biblical Commentary 5a. Carol Stream, IL: Tyndale House, 2010. This is a commentary on the New Living Translation, done by a scholar specializing in biblical theology of the postexilic period. It is concise, provides informative exposition with significance for the contemporary reader, and is most helpful for pastoral work.

Braun, Roddy. *1 Chronicles.* Word Biblical Commentary 14. Waco: Word, 1986. This commentary was among the first in a prestigious series of evangelical commentaries. Braun brings attention to the centrality of the temple for the message and theology of Chronicles. It has text and form-critical notes, exegesis, and exposition.

Childs, Brevard S. *Isaiah and the Assyrian Crisis.* Studies in Biblical Theology 2/3. London: SCM, 1967. This is a groundbreaking form-critical study of all the biblical narratives on the Assyrian crisis. Though some of its source-critical conclusions are no longer held as conclusive, it remains a most informative analysis of the methods of biblical composition and is very helpful for understanding the Chronicler's use of biblical sources.

Dillard, Raymond B. *2 Chronicles.* Word Biblical Commentary 15. Waco: Word, 1987. The commentary by Dillard is notable for its translation, which is based on careful text-critical work. The theology of Chronicles is carefully developed, with attention to ideological conformity in the presentation of the rule of each king. This consistency helps explain both the methods and goals of Chronicles.

Evans, Paul S., and Tyler F. Williams, eds. *Chronicling the Chronicler: The Book of Chronicles and Early Second Temple Historiography*. Winona Lake, IN: Eisenbrauns, 2013. This collection of thirteen studies is divided into two main sections. The first section reviews particular topics of history, such as the function of the genealogies and the Chronicler's presentation of several significant kings, including Saul, David, Hezekiah, and Manasseh. The second section deals with several important themes, including the interpretation of legislation, retribution, and the concept of hope.

Graham, M. Patrick, Kenneth G. Hogland, and Steven L. McKenzie, eds. *The Chronicler as Historian*. Journal for the Study of the Old Testament Supplement Series 238. Sheffield: Sheffield Academic, 1996. This is a collection of fourteen essays in recognition of the work of Raymond Dillard. The essays are grouped into studies of history, narrative, and specific historical questions. The topics provide valuable insight into the Chronicler as a historian, his use of sources, and his shaping of information.

Japhet, Sara. *The Ideology of the Book of Chronicles and Its Place in Biblical Thought*. Beiträge zur Erforschung des Alten Testaments und des Antiken Judentums 9. Frankfurt: Lang; Freiburg: Herder, 1989. This pioneering study, originally done in Hebrew, changed the direction of Chronicles studies, distinguishing its ideology from that of other books of the postexilic period. It draws out the distinct themes and perspectives to be found in the Chronicles composition.

———. *I & II Chronicles: A Commentary*. Old Testament Library. Louisville: Westminster John Knox, 1993. This commentary is classic for its innovation in developing the thought of the Chronicler. It is based on the Revised Standard Version, with notes to that version as well as to the Masoretic Text. It is an erudite and detailed study, a reference work for almost any question on Chronicles.

Klein, Ralph W. *1 Chronicles: A Commentary*. Hermeneia. Minneapolis: Fortress, 2006. *2 Chronicles*. 2012. Like the other commentaries of this series, this commentary is something of an encyclopedia in terms of its detail. It is not particularly innovative, but it deals with every question that has been discussed or written on Chronicles. For amount of information, it can replace many books on Chronicles.

Knoppers, Gary N. *1 Chronicles 1–9*. Anchor Bible 12. New York: Doubleday, 2004. *1 Chronicles 10–29*. Anchor Bible 12A. 2004. The detail and creativity of this commentary is unparalleled. All the textual information of the Hebrew and Greek texts is reproduced and evaluated. The translation is lucid and based on a carefully constructed critical text. The source and form-critical analysis is thorough for every section. Knoppers has a thorough grasp of the social and political situation of this period.

Myers, Jacob M. *I Chronicles.* Anchor Bible 12. New York: Doubleday, 1964. *II Chronicles.* Anchor Bible 13. 1965. This commentary is classic for understanding Chronicles studies in the modern period. Creative and informative in its time, it represents the best of Chronicles interpretation, given the knowledge of text and critical conclusions of compositions in that period.

Williamson, Hugh G. M. *1 and 2 Chronicles.* New Century Bible Commentary. Grand Rapids: Eerdmans, 1982. This is still the best commentary of its size for understanding critical issues in Chronicles. The information it contains is greater than its brevity may initially suggest. Williamson was on the leading edge of reforming critical conclusions of the modern period. His insights are original and creative; they can be consulted in minutes, though the significance of their import often takes considerable reflection.

Index of Ancient Sources

OLD TESTAMENT

OT
.......................28, 467, 474

Genesis-Kings
....23

Genesis
....121
1:2 218
1:14-16 287
1:22 85
2–3 273
2:1-2 219
3:5 ....49, 310
3:5-6 85
3:15-18 85
3:16 66
4:17-23 75
4:23-24 ....49, 484
4:24 339
5 49–50
5:28-32 145
6:5 484
6:11 ....49, 339
7:11 49
9:1 ....49, 339
9:5 49
9:6 484
9:6-7 339
9:7 49

10 49
10:1-32 57
10:8-12 51
10:25 51
10:28-29 292
11 49–50
11:10 51
11:10-26 ....50, 52
11:27 51
11:27-32 145
11:31-32 51
12:1-3 ....57, 356
12:4-6 51
12:6 323
12:10-20 174
13:18 323
14:5 193
14:14 193
15:5 466
15:5-6 262
15:18 281
15:19 75
16:15-16 95
17:1-14 57
17:5 466
17:15-21 58
18:1 323
20:1-18 174
21:1-7 58
21:12 58
22 270
22–23 209

22:2 ....209, 270
22:8 270
22:14 ....209, 270
22:17 466
23:6 92
24:8 442
24:41 442
25 49
25:1 58
25:1-4 52
25:5-6 58
25:9 52
25:12 52
25:13-14 92
25:15 97
25:19 52
25:19-26 52
25:22-23 58
25:24-26 58
25:25 52
26:1 93
26:5 51
26:6 93
26:6-11 174
26:17 93
26:26 93
27:41–28:5 59
28:14 165
31:21 54
32:3 53
32:28 137
33:1-4 59

34:2 92
34:25-29 93
35–36 49
35:22 .... 67, 94
35:22-26 .... 55, 90
35:23-26 238–39
36:2 54
36:2-14 52
36:5 54
36:10-13 52
36:11 .... 54, 81
36:12 53
36:14 54
36:15 54
36:18 54
36:20 53
36:20-22 53
36:20-30 52
36:25 54
36:28 53
36:31 53
36:40 54
36:43 54
37:18-36 47
37:22 119
37:26-27 .... 82, 119
38:1-2 82
38:1-11 83
38:3-5 83
38:5 82
38:9-10 83
38:10 68
38:26 83
42:37-38 119
43:1-14 47
43:3-5 82
43:8-10 82
43:8-14 119
44:14-16 82
44:18-34 .... 82, 119
46:8-27 55
46:9 84
46:10 91
46:11 99
46:12 .... 69, 83
46:13 107
46:14 109
46:16 96
46:17 112
46:20 110–11
46:21 108
46:23 .... 109, 1141
46:24-25a 109
46:28 82
47:9 66
47:25–48:22 118
48–49 106
48:5 94
48:5-6 67
48:22 .... 94, 118
49:3-4 .... 67, 94, 118
49:5-7 93
49:8-12 94
49:9-12 119
49:10 119
49:22-26 118
49:27 114
50:20 66
50:23 71

Exodus

1:1 31
1:5 471
3:12 387
6:2-8 175
6:13-26 467
6:14 .... 84, 94
6:14-26 232
6:14-27 134
6:15 91
6:16-25 99
6:17-19 101
6:18 .... 170, 231
6:21 102
6:23 .... 71, 84
6:24 229
6:25 134
12:1 397
12:2-6 391
12:9 432
12:44 73
12:49 73
15 338
15:15 54
16:32-34 277
17:8-16 53
19:9 289
19:18 281
19:22 170
20:1 481
20:1-17 217
21:1 481
21:4-6 73
21:5 370
23:15 391
25:1-7 248
25:7 248
25:9 247
25:40 247
28:36 352
29:38-42 103
30:1-10 .... 103, 370
30:11-16 354
31:1-3 261
31:2 71
31:6 269
32 307
32:4 3878
33:17-23 279
33:19 .... 206, 387
34:1 387
34:5-6 387
34:6 206
35:4-9 248
35:20-29 248
35:30 71
35:30-35 261
35:34 269

Leviticus

1:1 31
1:4 386
2:13 314
4:2-3 386
4:13-14 386
5 165
7:11-15 282
7:30-36 282
9:24 .... 202, 207
14:34 136
16:29-31 281
23:34-36 281
25:24 136
25:39-55 376
26:1 261
26:14-17 443
26:34-35 443
26:43 443
27:30-33 401

Numbers

......................................121
1 107

Index of Ancient Sources

1–10 .... 205, 236	14:30 .... 69, 84	**Deuteronomy**
1:1-19 238	14:38 .... 69, 84	.... 29–30, 121, 465
1:2-3 203	17:10-11 277	1:8 175
1:3 .... 221, 430	18:3 224	1:36 .... 69, 84
1:4 92	18:8-11 402	2:10-11 193
1:5-15 94	18:9-10 404	2:12 53
1:7 70	21:17 278	2:20-21 193
1:16 92	23:7-8 73	3:9 98
1:16-17 70	24:1 270	3:10 96
1:21 97	24:18 53	3:11 191
1:25 97	24:21-22 75	3:13 193
1:29 107	26 107	3:14 81
1:35 97	26:5-6 94	3:20 175
1:37 108	26:6 84	3:23-29 .... 212, 246
1:41 113	26:7 97	4:1-8 280
1:49 204	26:12-14 91	4:7-8 177
1:49-50 221	26:15-17 96	4:43 96
2:3 70	26:18 97	5:1 333
2:3-31 94	26:21 .... 69, 83	5:14 .... 216, 218
2:33 204	26:23-24 107	7:1-6 86
3:2-4 225	26:25 107	8:2 412
3:17-20 99	26:26-27 109	10:8 169
3:18-20 101	26:29 .... 71, 110	10:12-16 288
3:30 170	26:29-34 .... 98, 110	11:29-32 432
3:32 134	26:31 81	12:1-7 216
4:2-15 101	26:32 110	12:2-4 384
4:3 222	26:34 97	12:3 375
4:4-15 169	26:35-37 111	12:5-7 207
4:21-28 101	26:38 108	12:5-14 175
4:23 222	26:38-41 113	12:10 175
4:29-33 101	26:41 108	12:15 401
4:30 222	26:47 113	13:6 334
4:39 222	26:65 .... 69, 84	14:24-26 401
4:43 222	27:1 71	16:1-8 394
4:47 471	27:1-7 223	16:5-6 .... 432, 434
4:49 169	27:1-11 84	16:7 432
5:6 165	27:21 168	16:16 270
5:21 442	31:6 315	16:18–17:13 336
7:6-9 170	31:19-24 215	17:2-7 323
7:12-83 94	32:3 95	17:14-20 432
8:23-26 223	32:12 80	17:18-20 333
8:25-26 224	32:33-42 90	18:1-8 .... 276, 471
9:9-11 .... 392, 394	32:34 95–96	18:9-10 375
10:4 205	32:37-38 95	20:2-4 337
10:9 315	32:39-42 71	20:16-18 93
10:35-36 .... 165, 280	32:41 71	21:15-17 307
12:1 321	34:4 84	21:17 .... 94, 118
13:6 .... 69, 84	35:1-5 96	23:7-8 62
13:30 .... 69, 84	35:33-34 215	25:19 175
14:6 .... 69, 84	36:1 110	27:1-8 432
14:24 .... 69, 84	36:1-12 223	31:6-7 212–13

Joshua–Kings
... 465

Joshua
... 212
1:1 ... 31
1:12-18 ... 90
1:13-15 ... 214
1:1-9 ... 212–13
1:6-9 ... 245
1:7-8 ... 215, 245
1:8 ... 245
1:11 ... 246
1:15 ... 246
1:18 ... 245
3:7-11 ... 54
5–6 ... 315
7:1 ... 68, 83
7:17-18 ... 83
7:18-20 ... 83
7:24 ... 83
7:24-25 ... 69
8:10 ... 203
8:30-35 ... 217
9:3-7 ... 115
10:12 ... 278
11:6-9 ... 188
11:17 ... 98
11:23 ... 214, 222
12:5 ... 81, 96
12:7 ... 222
13:5 ... 98
13:11 ... 96
13:15 ... 95
13:16 ... 95
13:24 ... 95
13:25 ... 95
13:29 ... 95
14:1-5 ... 55
14:6 ... 80
14:6-15 ... 69, 84, 105
14:13-15 ... 54
14:14 ... 80
14:15 ... 214
31:9 ... 277
31:9-13 ... 432
31:10-13 ... 215
33:8-10 ... 169
33:13-17 ... 118
34:7 ... 246

15:3 ... 84
15:6 ... 94
15:9 ... 285
15:11 ... 368
15:13-17 ... 69, 84
15:13-19 ... 73
15:15-16 ... 74
15:16-17 ... 74, 80
15:17 ... 69, 85
15:23 ... 80
15:24 ... 81
15:25 ... 84
15:26 ... 75
15:33 ... 79, 82
15:34 ... 73
15:44 ... 73, 82
15:55 ... 73, 81, 93
15:58 ... 73
15:63 ... 90
16:3 ... 113
17:1 ... 110
17:1-3 ... 110–11
17:2 ... 81
18:1 ... 172
18:10 ... 222
18:14 ... 74
18:17 ... 94
18:22 ... 314
18:22-23 ... 315
18:24 ... 114
19:1 ... 91
19:1-9 ... 92
19:2-6 ... 93
19:35 ... 75
19:41 ... 79
19:49-50 ... 112
19:51 ... 172
20:1-9 ... 106
20:8 ... 334
21 ... 90, 104
21:1-9 ... 104
21:1-18 ... 104
21:5 ... 105
21:5-7 ... 105
21:10-26 ... 105
21:13 ... 106
21:20-42 ... 105
21:21 ... 106
21:27 ... 106
21:32 ... 106
21:36 ... 106
21:38 ... 106
21:39 ... 231
21:43-45 ... 319
21:44 ... 175, 214
22:4 ... 214
22:19 ... 172
22:29 ... 172
23:1 ... 214
23:14 ... 81
24:1 ... 304
24:1-29 ... 217
24:30 ... 112

Judges
1:1 ... 31
1:1-3 ... 91
1:3-20 ... 121–22
1:11-12 ... 74
1:12-13 ... 54, 74, 80
1:12-15 ... 73
1:16 ... 75
1:21 ... 90
3:3 ... 98
3:7 ... 323
3:9 ... 69, 85
3:15 ... 113, 147
4–5 ... 338
4:11 ... 75, 113
4:17 ... 113
4:21 ... 113
5:1-31 ... 106–7
5:8 ... 205
6 ... 209
6:15 ... 188, 205
8:14 ... 305
9:7-15 ... 362
10:3-5 ... 71
13:2 ... 79
17:7-8 ... 101
20:12-16 ... 114

Ruth
4:13-22 ... 186, 464
4:18-22 ... 69, 84
4:19-20 ... 71
4:19-22 ... 70

Samuel–Kings
... 459

Index of Ancient Sources

1 Samuel

..................27, 179, 468
1:1 ....31, 101–2, 462
1:20 102
2:18 171
2:28 171
4:1-11 165
5:1–7:1 165
6:19-20 165
8:2 101
9:1 116
10:1 .... 149, 190
10:5 227
10:27–11:2 190
11:8 203
11:1-11 190
13:5 191
13:13-15 148
13:14 175
13:15 203
13:19-22 159
14:48 93
14:49 117
14:50-51 116
15:2-3 93
15:4 203
15:26-28 148
16:1-13 157
16:1-14 66
16:6 239
16:6-9 70
16:10 70
17:12 239
17:13 .... 70, 239
17:28 239
17:50-51 194
18:7 158
18:20-27 171
19:11-14 171
22:1 167
22:1-2 158
22:2 93
22:3-4 158
22:4 167
22:18 171
22:20 189
22:20-23 241
23:1-13 81
23:6 189
23:9-12 168
23:13 .... 93, 158
23:24-25 73
24:22 167
25:44 171
27:2 166
27:5-7 158
27:8-10 84
27:10 73
28:4-5 158
28:16-19 148
29:4 204
30:1 93
30:7 189
30:26-30 84
30:29 72
31:1-13 145
31:5 146
31:6 146
31:12 146

2 Samuel

..................27, 179, 468
2:1-4 151
2:1–4:12 161
2:8 117
2:8-9 147
2:10 117
2:18 71
2:18-23 237
3:1 151
3:2-5 76
3:3 313
3:6-11 147
3:14-16 171
3:39 156
4:2-3 114
4:4 147
4:5-12 147
4:16 206
5:1 154
5:1-3 159
5:1-10 151
5:2 152
5:3 152
5:4-5 153
5:5 153
5:5-8 154
5:6-10 .... 153, 167
5:11 213
5:11-25 167
5:14-16 .... 76, 168
5:17–6:12 163
6:12 168
6:12-19 168
6:13 171
6:20 171
7 440
7:1 175
7:11 175
7:11-14 32
7:13-15 480
7:14 176
7:16 176
8:1-18 184
8:3 187
8:4 187
8:4-6 187
8:12 93
8:13 361
8:13-14 54
8:17 100
8:18 190
9:1-13 147
9:6 117
9:10-11 117
9:12-13 117
10:1–11:1 184
10:6 .... 81, 191
10:16-17 192
11:1 192
11:1–21:14 193
12:11-12 143
12:24-25 214
12:26 .... 184, 191–92
12:26-27 191
12:27 191
12:27-29 193
12:30-31 .... 184, 192
13:1 76
13:11 81
14:2 72
14:27 313
15:27 100
15:37 240
16:9-10 156
16:15-19 240
16:23 241
17:4 305
17:15 305
17:23 .... 146, 241
17:24-25 70
17:24-29 158
17:25 71

19:13 71	3:5 262	9:18 284–85
20:1-2 158	3:9 .... 262, 264	9:20-21 131
20:23 189	3:15 .... 115, 262	9:24–25 286
21 185	3:16-28 264	9:25 .... 266, 273, 283
21:1 203	4 242258	9:26–10:29 291
21:7 147	4–5 237	10:2 216
21:15-17 193	4:2 99–100	10:7 263
21:15-22 194	4:13 .... 72, 334	10:10 216
21:17 312	4:13-14 121	10:10-12 292
21:18 193	4:19 121	10:23 263
21:18-22 185	4:21 189	10:26 .... 187, 294
23 185	4:26 294	10:26-29 262
23:8 155	4:31 .... 69, 83	10:27 467
23:8-12 155	5:1 268	11 .... 259, 292
23:8-39 .... 152, 154, 200	5:1-12 213	11–12 473–74
23:10-11 155	5:3-5 215	11:1 286
23:13-14 167	5:4 175	11:5-6 143
23:18 156	5:6 .... 187, 213	11:5-7 192
23:24 156	5:13-15 285	11:6 263
23:39 157	5:30 286	11:14 262
24 200	6:1 .... 100, 266, 270	11:14-15 53
24:1 203–4	6:2-18 271	11:14-22 345
24:5 121	6:15 272	11:19 323
24:5-7 204	6:23 272	11:23 262
24:9 .... 108, 314	6:28 272	11:29-33 300
24:10 205	6:31-32 272	11:29-34 119
24:23 270	6:37 282	11:29-39 305
24:25 207	7:1 282	11:33 192
	7:13-14 269	11:38-40 303
1 Kings	7:15 273	11:40 482
.. 22, 27, 313, 468, 473–75	7:16-20 273	11:41-43 292
1–2 483	7:23-24 274	12 24
1–4 156	7:23-26 273	12:1-3 304
1:1 31	7:40-51 275	12:20 304
1:7 241	7:51 266	12:23 300
1:18-21 143	8:1-66 177	12:25 80
2:2-9 245	8:3-4 276	12:25-30 396
2:4 283	8:12 182	12:28 307
2:12 245	8:12-13 278	12:31-32 261
2:19 323	8:22 273	13 295
2:26 471	8:25 283	14:29 250–51
2:26-27 241	8:53 LXX 278	14:30 316
2:28-35 .... 189, 241	8:54 279	15:1-8 312
3–11 258	8:62-64 293	15:3-4 315
3:1 286	8:64 273	15:7 316
3:1-3 .... 259, 295	9:1 .... 266, 282	15:9 316
3:2-3 261	9:2 115	15:11 320
3:3 261	9:10 282	15:13 313
3:3-14 115	9:11-13 284	15:16 322
3:4 .... 169, 172	9:14 .... 216, 293	15:17-22 319
3:4-15 200	9:16 286	15:20 325

Index of Ancient Sources

15:22 114
15:23 475
15:27-29 326
16:8 324
16:17 326
16:18 146
16:23 475
16:29 475
18 334
18:19 323
20:7-9 305
21 335
21:8 305
21:8-11 129
21:25 334
22:3-8 334
22:10-11 99
22:32-33 342
22:43-46 337
22:45 475
22:47 345
22:48-49 337
22:50 345

2 Kings

.. 22, 27, 313, 468, 473-75
1:17 345
2:12 345
3 .... 332, 345
3:1-27 345
3:4 73
3:9 345
3:15 227
3:27 332
8:16-17 345
8:18 .... 343, 347
8:19 .... 343, 480
8:23 474
8:26 347
9:1-10 347
9:21-24 344
9:27-29 344
10:5 305
10:13 323
10:22 433
10:32-33 .... 355, 360
11:14 370
11:18-20 370
12:2-3 351
12:4-12 353
12:6 354

12:9 134
12:13-14 354
12:17 360
12:32-33 397
14:7 361
14:18-22 367
14:23 363
14:23-29 368
15:1 .... 363, 367
15:1-2 368
15:5 368
15:6-8 367
15:13 367
15:17 367
15:23 367
15:27 367
15:29 .... 94, 98, 109
15:30-34 367
15:37 371
16 317
16:5-7 375
16:6 54
16:10-13 376
16:11 99
16:14 273
16:18 423
17:6 98
17:9-11 60
18-19 .... 240, 409-11
18-20 .... 380, 413-14
18:1-3 383
18:3-7 476
18:5 415
18:5-6 .... 388, 404, 426
18:7-8 93
18:8-19:37 476
18:13 408
18:13-16 .... 309, 414
18:14 .... 249, 441
18:17-20:19 475
18:22 .... 396, 435
19:14-15 388
19:37 316
20:1 426
20:1-19 476
20:8-19 412
20:12 426
20:12-19 .... 408, 415
20:16-19 ...... 420, 423, 426
20:18 422
20:20 .... 412, 475

20:20-21 413
21:7 424
21:10-16 424
21:18 425
21:25 474
21:26 425
22:1-23:27 327
22:19 432-33
23:2 432
23:4 134
23:6 .... 382, 429
23:6-20 429
23:16 429
23:19-20 429
23:25 422
23:26-27 .... 420, 425
23:29-30 435
23:30 77
23:31 77
23:33 441
23:34 77
23:36 436
24:2-3 327
24:3 422
24:3-4 425
24:6 .... 77, 442
24:8 77
24:17 77
24:18-25:30 439-40
24:20 440
25:7 77
25:17 273
25:18 134
25:18-21 99
25:23 81
25:25 73
25:26 466
25:27-30 .... 78, 421

1 & 2 Chronicles
(not indexed)

Ezra

.... 26-27, 30-32, 127,
222, 473, 457-61
1:1 31
1:1-2 440
1:3-4 444
1:8 78
2:36-39 132
2:42 .... 133, 229

2:43 131	11:19 229	78:51 50
2:58 131	11:31 114	83:6 95
2:69 249	11:31-35 115	88–89 83
3:1-13 26	12 225	88:6 370
3:2 .... 78, 99	12:12-21 222	89 179–80
3:8 78	12:22 466	89:2-4 175
3:8-9 222	12:25 229	89:3-4 .... 178, 181
3:12-13 21	12:28 133	95:7-11 .... 214, 216–18
3:13 458		96 .... 173–74, 249
4:3 399	**Esther**	96:9-13 173
4:7-24 458	1:1 31	98 174
5:1 25	9:15 25	99:1-5 477
5:1–6:19 458		99:9 478
5:8 25	**Job**	103–4 227
6 171	1:1 53	103:7-8 206
6:3-5 444	1:6-12 204	104 254
6:7 .... 25, 458	2:11 53	104:24-30 .... 178, 219
6:13-15 253	3:19 370	104:29 178
7:1 132	4:1 53	105 174
7:1-5 100	12:12 305	105–6 249
7:14 25	15:1 53	105:1-15 173
8:16 156	22:1 53	105:6 .... 52, 393
8:20 131	26:11 273	105:6-7 174
9:1-3 24	40:7-14 349	105:10 393
10:3 399	42:6 349	105:23 50
10:6-44 461	42:7 53	105:27 50
	42:9 53	106:1 .... 173, 281
Nehemiah		106:22 51
.... 26–27, 30–32, 127,	**Psalms**	106:47-48 173
222, 399, 473, 457–61	.... 22, 228	120–22 246
1:1–7:71 458	2 .... 180, 440	123:1-4 310
3:1 248	2:1-9 32	127:1-5 175
4:1-8 26	2:2 421	128:1-6 175
5:1 25	2:6 289	132 .... 179–80, 246, 279
5:8 25	2:7-12 21	132:1-5 216
5:15 135	8 254	132:5-8 165
7:6-73 461	12 171	132:8-10 280
7:45 229	20:1-4 176	132:10 480
7:73–8:13 461	24:3 .... 209, 270	132:11-12 .... 178, 181
8 30	32:5 445	134:2-3 287
8:1-12 461	36:8-9 287	137:7 73
8:7 333	39:1 227	
8:13–13:31 458	48:1-2 154	**Ecclesiastes**
11:3 131	60 .... 54, 361	7:10 130
11:3-19 130	62:1 227	9:11 144
11:4-19 136	72:1-3 296	38:15 50
11:5-11 132	72:8 296	
11:10-11 100	74:12-17 .... 218, 253	**Isaiah-Malachi**
11:10-14 .... 222, 483	74:13-14 274–75	 22
11:12-16 132	77 227	
11:17-19 133	77:1 227	

Index of Ancient Sources

Isaiah
1:1	367
1:24	339
2:2-4	297
2:3	209, 270
2:6-4:1	372
6:1	371-72
6:1-4	182-83
6:9	372
6:9-10	364
6:10	182-83, 381
6:11-12	372
7:1	371
7:1-6	375
7:1-9	377
7:3	40
7:9	374
7:12	374, 377
7:14	377, 411
7:18-25	377
8:2	368
8:3	433
8:7-8	374
8:8	377, 411
8:10	411
8:21-9:1	38
9:1	376
9:6-7	377
10:5	252
10:5-6	362
10:21	40
11:1	377
11:9	377
19:19	261
26:16-27:1	252
27:1	253
28:16	288
30:29	209
36-39	413
36:2-39:8	475
38:1-8	415
38:1-22	377
38:9-20	415
39:8	426
42:18-19	59
43:1-4	356
43:8-11	56
44:1-2	56
44:1-5	356
44:2	137
45:1	421
48:22	426
51:9-10	218
51:9-11	253
53:5	381
54:1-13	21
55:3	480
55:3-5	36
56:4-7	388
57:21	426
65:1-16	135
65:17-25	416
66:1-2	287

Jeremiah
1:1	108
7:4	181-82, 415
7:12-14	172
7:31	375
19:5	375
22:10	435
22:10-12	77
22:11	441
22:11-17	441
22:15	435
22:18-19	442
22:24	77
24:1	77
25:11-12	443
25:3	435
26:6	172
26:9	172
26:18-19	396
27-28	442
28:4	77
29:10	443
29:18	384
31:31-34	126, 182, 218, 443
31:40	353
32:6-7	433
32:35	375
34	442
34:5	326
36:30	442
37-38	442
40-41	439-40
41:1	73
43-44	466
48:1	95
48:6	95
48:19	95
48:22	95
49:20	53
52	439-40
52:1-11	442
52:24-27	99

Lamentations
	446

Ezekiel
	446
1:1	31
1:1-2	442
1:4-24	247
10:1-22	247
17:14-20	442
17:19-21	443
38	413
40-48	236, 458
40:5	271
43:13	271

Daniel
	340
1:1-2	439
2	447
2:25	25
5:13	25
6:14	25

Hosea
1:1	367
3:4	322
8:5	307
10:5-6	307
15:1	308

Joel
3:19	73
3:19-21	59

Amos
1:1	72, 367, 369, 372
3:9	322
4:1	96
5:1-17	372
6:2	186
8:5	431

Obadiah
10-15	59

17-19 59
18 73

Micah
1:15 73
5:2 283

Habakkuk
1:1-2 .... 21, 26
1:14-17 288
2:7-20 288
2:18-19 21
2:20 288
3:7 321

Zephaniah
3:16 322

Haggai
.... 26, 253, 440, 443
1:1 76
1:1-2 99
2:1-2 99
2:23 458

Zechariah
.... 26, 443
1–6 253
1–8 440
1:1 28
1:3-6 393
1:4 .... 130, 135
1:6 423
1:7–6:15 21
3:1-2 203
3:1–4:14 250
3:8 458
4:6-7 76
4:9 28
4:14 458
6:1 273
7:3 446
7:7 .... 130, 135
7:12 135
8:10 322
9:9-10 296
10:6 82
11:6 322
14:5 .... 367, 369

Malachi
1:2-5 59
2:14-16 26

NEW TESTAMENT

Matthew
.... 26
1 463
1:1 421
1:1-17 123
1:12 .... 124, 463
2:11 293
4:13-17 38
4:17 180
12:41 182–83
13:14-15 365
16:16 447
16:18 149
18:15-20 16
21:12-13 388
23:35 37
24:4-44 37
24:36 125
27:51 273

Mark
.... 26
1:14-15 180
13:26-27 340
15:32 26

Luke
.... 26
2:25-38 124
3:23-38 123
3:27 124
4:42-44 180
10:9 38
11:20 38
11:51 37
21:9 .... 38, 124
21:12 126
21:20 125
22:14-18 37
22:20 181–82

John
.... 26
1:14 289
2:19 182

2:22 182
12:39-42 63
14:6 63
14:27 219
18:36 340
20:19 219

Acts
.... 26
5:38-39 317
7:14 471
8:34 63
20:7 219

Romans
.... 26
1:16-17 34
4:16-17 38
6:1-11 373
6:4-5 328
8:19-21 290
9–11 38
9:1-5 .... 38, 126
9:8 38
9:24 38
9:31 38
10:1-3 38
11:1-6 38
11:11-12 39
11:11-36 38
11:15 39
13:1-7 484

1 Corinthians
9:16 418
11:17-33 373
11:19 447
16:2 219

2 Corinthians
5:17 126
12:7-8 88

Galatians
6:15-16 126

Ephesians
2:19-21 389
2:19-22 .... 38, 289
2:21-22 255
4:11 405

Index of Ancient Sources

4:20-24 265
4:28 265

Philippians
1:1 406
2:6-11 63
2:9-11 438
4:13 264

1 Timothy
3:1-13 406
6:17 264

Hebrews
1:4-5 180
3:7-11 218
4:1 218
4:4-7 218
4:9-10 218
8:7-12 218
8:8-12 180
9:4 277
10:15-18 180
10:16-17 218
10:24-25 255
13:14-16 255

1 Peter
2:2-8 398
2:4-5 .... 289, 389
2:5 407
2:9 .... 289, 407
2:13-17 484

Jude
12 406

Revelation
.... 37
2:4 416
18 124-25
19 342
19:1-8 340
19:11-15 41
21:1-2 .... 253-54, 297

APOCRYPHA
.... 25

1 Esdras
.... 27, 30-31, 457-61

1:1-5:65 458
1:20-23 459
1:23-24 458
1:24 459
2:16-30 458
3:1-5:6 458
4:7-24 458
6:27 458
9 461

1 Maccabees
.... 340

2 Maccabees
.... 340
2:9-12 385

Sirach
48:17-25 413

Tobit
.... 446

Wisdom
.... 446

JOSEPHUS
.... 192
Antiquities
8.231 295
8.249 314
8.277 314
9.153 353
9.277 370
10.6.3 442

QUMRAN (DSS)
.... 25, 28, 42, 190, 471
Community Rule
  1QS 288
  1QS 8.1 288
  1QS 8.5-9 288-89
  1QSa 1.12-19 224
Damascus Document.. 250
  CD 12.23 250
  CD 14.19 250
  CD 19.10 250
Temple Scroll
  11Q19-20 233-34
  11QT 5.13 229
  11QT 35.10 229

War Scroll 340
  1QM 7.3 224
1QSam[a] 206
4Q255-264a 288
4Q327 233
4Q329 233
4Q394 233
5Q11 288
11QPs[a] = 11Q5 173

RABBIS
Babylonian Talmud
Baba Batra 15 457
Berakot 28b 413-14
Sanhedrin 93b 457

Mishnah
.... 25

Other Rabbinic Works
Sifre Num 63 224
Sifre Zut on Num 8:26 ..224

OTHER JEWISH TEXTS
Aramaic source 473
  See also Targums
Letter of Aristeas 468
Masoretic Text 130,
    278, 333, 356, 371,
    414, 426, 443, 458,
    468, 470-71
Nehemiah's Memoirs
  473
Septuagint ...468-69, 471
Targums 111, 192, 297,
    370

ARTIFACTS, INSCRIPTIONS, PAPYRI
Akkadian
  bow cases 188
  texts 293
Amarna tablets 188,
    278, 464
Babylonian
  astronomers 107
Chronicles ...442, 464-65
chariot-throne, figures
  of king's 247
coins 25

Cyrus Cylinder 86–87
Elephantine papyri
.... 122, 210, 466, 473
Hadad depicted on bull
.... 307
Hezekiah Tunnel
   Inscription 410
iconography 165, 307,
                           369, 424
king lists, ANE
.... 50, 55, 462
King of Hatti Inscription
.... 179
Mari 205
Megiddo horse stables
.... 263
Mesha Inscription 96
papyri 179, 187
   See also Elephantine
pottery, "to the king"
.... 420
priestly lineages ... 462–64
Punic inscriptions 431
Rameses III texts 188
royal inscriptions 192
Sennacherib
   inscriptions 414
   murals re Lachish
        .... 369, 414
   Rassam Cylinder 414
temples, ANE 271
Tiglath-Pileser III
   inscription 98
"Uzziah" named 369
Ugarit, tablets of 188,
   193, 205, 293, 370, 464,
                              467–68
Uzziah tomb inscription
.... 370

EARLY CHRISTIAN TEXTS
Diognetus 5.1–16 61
Jerome, Ep. 53.8.... 445–46
Nicene Creed..... 183, 438

GRECO-ROMAN TEXTS
Dionysius of Halicarnassus
Roman Antiquities 1
1.1–8.4 27

Herodotus
.... 470
1.1 27

The Author

August H. Konkel is professor of Old Testament at McMaster Divinity College in Hamilton, Ontario, and president emeritus of Providence University College and Seminary in Otterburne, Manitoba (2001–12). He began work at Providence in 1984 as professor of Old Testament. His publications include work as a translator for the New Living Translation (NLT), a contributor of notes for the *Study Bible* of the NLT in Chronicles, and notes for the *Study Bible* of the English Standard Version of Job. He contributed to lexical and theological articles in the *New International Dictionary of Old Testament Theology and Exegesis* (Zondervan). Konkel has published commentaries on Job in the Cornerstone Biblical Commentary series (Tyndale House) and 1 & 2 Kings in the NIV Application Commentary (Zondervan). His scholarly research includes published articles in the areas of literary and textual criticism of the Old Testament.

Konkel was ordained in what is now known as Mennonite Church Canada in 1972. He served as pastor of the Bethel Bergthaler Mennonite Church in Winkler, Manitoba, from 1971 to 1982. He lives in Paris, Ontario, with his wife, Esther. They have four adult children, who have made their homes in Ontario, England, and Guatemala, plus eight grandchildren.

"This commentary is well-written, clear, and helpful in discussing the main issues of Chronicles and its theology. As someone who cares deeply about this book, I can legitimately affirm Konkel's perspective and his handling of the text. This will be a valuable resource in opening up a neglected biblical book." —Steven Schweitzer, academic dean, Bethany Theological Seminary

"Konkel brings his extensive research and profound understanding of the book of Chronicles to bear in his insightful and relevant commentary on this often neglected book. He not only illumines the book's message to its ancient audience but also reveals Chronicles' important continuing relevance to us in the twenty-first century." —Tremper Longman III, professor of biblical studies, Westmont College

"Konkel is an engaging and insightful guide for navigating the Chronicler's unique account of Israelite history and identity. Ever attentive to the sources utilized by the Chronicler, the original target audience, and the theological nuances of the text, Konkel offers the riches of two oft-neglected biblical books to the contemporary church." —Dan Epp-Tiessen, associate professor of Bible, Canadian Mennonite University, Winnipeg, Canada

"Chronicles has many hermeneutical, historical, and literary issues that we should only interpret with utmost care. In this commentary, Konkel has provided a superb orientation to the specifics of the text and the overall shape of the book that will be useful to leaders in the church. He provides enough information to initiate the serious reader without overwhelming the nonacademic." —Mark J. Boda, professor of Old Testament, McMaster Divinity College; professor, McMaster University

"Konkel's enthusiasm for the writer of the books of Chronicles as theologian and historian makes for a compelling read. Faced with the challenge of writing a commentary on a text that begins with a lengthy genealogy, followed by what has been pejoratively called midrash by critical scholars, Konkel demonstrates that an inspiring interpretation of this inspired text engages all of Scripture in conversation. In Konkel's hands, Chronicles becomes a central canonical voice, a nexus in the biblical metanarrative." —Lynn Jost, professor of Old Testament and preaching, Fresno Pacific Biblical Seminary

www.ingramcontent.com/pod-product-compliance
Lightning Source LLC
Chambersburg PA
CBHW071431300426
44114CB00013B/1392